CLASSICAL TEXTS
EDITORIAL ADVISOR: M. M. Willcock

LUCIAN
A SELECTION

M. D. Macleod

Aris & Phillips — Warminster — England

British Library Cataloguing in Publication Data
Lucian
    Lucian: a Selection. (Classical Texts ISSN 0953-7961)
    I. Title II. Macleod, M. D. (Matthew D.) III. Series
    887.0109

The Greek Text is reproduced with the permission of Oxford University Press

ISBNs   0 85668 415 5   (cloth)
         0 85668 416 3   (limp)

To Tony Camps to mark his recent eightieth birthday

PA
4231
.A58
1991
160495
Dec.1993

Printed and published by Aris & Phillips Ltd., Teddington House, Warminster, Wiltshire   BA12 8PQ

CONTENTS

PREFACE

Lucian's inclusion in this series needs little justification. His wit, liveliness and variety place him alongside Herodotus and Aristophanes as one of the three most entertaining figures of Greek literature. But he is more than a mere entertainer; he is a literary artist who writes with clarity and grace and, despite his lateness and Syrian origin, his Greek reads almost as well and certainly as naturally as that of the masters of Attic Greek prose he strove to emulate, so that he is classical in all but date.

My aim in this selection has been to produce a representative coverage of Lucian's works illustrating his satire, humour, literary artistry and variety and including at least a few works not easily available in English editions or translations of selected works. It has been hard to deny the claims for inclusion of *Nigrinus* and *De Mercede Conductis*[1] with their satire of Roman life, *Juppiter confutatus* and *Juppiter Tragoedus, Icaromenippus, Timon, Charon, Vitarum Auctio, Bis Accusatus, Philopseudeis, Alexander* and *Navigium*, not to mention the hilarious *Dialogues of the Gods* and the three other sets of minor dialogues. I have omitted perhaps Lucian's most influential work, *Verae Historiae*, because it is already well catered for. Sacrifices had to be made to find room for Lucian's major work of literary criticism, *How to write History*, which deserves to be better known than it is; in view, however, of its length and comparative difficulty I have relegated it to last place.

Thanks are due to the Syndics of Oxford University Press for their permission to use the text and a simplified version of the apparatus criticus of the selected works from Vols. 2 and 3 of the Oxford Classical Text (1974, 1976) into which I have introduced a few corrections, all indicated by asterisks.

Matthew D. Macleod,
New Milton, Hampshire, March 1990.

---

[1]   See p. 306 for List of Lucian's Works giving Latin titles and the English equivalents and abbreviations used in this volume.

INTRODUCTION

1. The Life of Lucian and Chronology of his Works

Lucian came from Samosata[1] on the middle Euphrates, the capital of Commagene, an outlying part of the province of Syria, and so on the eastern fringes of the Roman Empire. The native tongue of the inhabitants was Syriac, a dialect of Aramaic, and therefore Lucian jokingly called himself a barbarian: some Greek, however, was spoken here, particularly by the more educated of the population, and, Samosata being the headquarters of a Roman legion, a few must also have known Latin, a language of which Lucian only once[2] admits any knowledge. He must have been born in the reign of Hadrian, perhaps between 120 and 125 A.D. Only a few of his works[3] can be dated with much precision and most of these fall within the reign of Marcus Aurelius, 161–180, whose death he survived but by how long is uncertain. For details of his life we rely mainly on what he himself tells us in three of his works, *Somnium* (*The Dream*), *Bis Accusatus* (*Twice Accused*) and *Apologia*.

In *The Dream* Lucian would have us believe that his parents were too poor to give him a good education and so he was apprenticed to his uncle who was a sculptor. This choice was made, says Lucian, because he was always playing with wax and making life-like wax models when he should have been studying at school and he got many a thrashing from his teachers for it. Early in his apprenticeship, however, he broke a slab of his uncle's marble, and when his uncle beat him, he ran home in tears to mother. That night he claims he had a dream in which two women were fighting over him. One woman was rough, dirty, unkempt and ungrammatical; she was Sculpture. The other was better dressed, easier on the eye, more genteel and very much more grammatical; her name was *Paideia* (Culture or Education) and she carried the day or rather the night and Lucian became hers. It is typical of Lucian that even when being autobiographical he resorts to classical literary models, as he takes the allegorical dream from Xenophon[4] who describes how Heracles has to choose between two females, Virtue and Vice.

For information about his subsequent career we must turn to *Bis Acc.*, another allegory, a dialogue in which the Syrian (Lucian) is arraigned first by Mistress Rhetoric and then by Sir Dialogue. Rhetoric's accusation is as follows: 'When the defendant was a mere boy still talking with a foreign accent and almost wearing a turban in Syrian style, I found him wandering about in Ionia not knowing what to make of himself, so I took him in hand and gave him an

---

1. Cf. *Hist.* 24.
2. *Laps.* 13.
3. The best account of L.'s life and the chronology of his works is Hall, 1–63: see also Jones 6–23, 167–9. (For works of which the title is not given see Bibliography; for abbreviated titles see List of Works.)
4. See p.249.

education. He was an apt and conscientious pupil, and so I promised to marry him, though I had richer suitors, and I brought him a dowry of many fine speeches. After we were married I got him irregularly registered among my own folk and made him a citizen. When he was seized by the wander lust, I trailed after him everywhere and made him famous. We travelled to Greece, Ionia, Italy and even Gaul, where I made him rich. But now he has deserted me for that bearded fellow Dialogue, who is said to be the son of Philosophy.'

The Syrian in his defence says he has deserted Rhetoric because she is no longer respectable as she was in Demosthenes' day, but has cheapened herself and is now no better than a painted hussy. In any case, now he's about forty, it's high time he gave up noisy court cases, letting the gentlemen of the jury rest in peace, stopping accusing tyrants[5] and praising princes,[6] and went to the Academy[7] or the Lyceum[8] and walked around with that excellent fellow Dialogue.

Lucian's description of himself as a conscientious pupil is no idle boast. The range of his quotations and literary allusions[9] confirms that he acquired a good knowledge of the main classical authors, who formed the staple diet of a rhetorical education, in particular Homer, Plato and Demosthenes. He must have practised in the courts for a time, before becoming a fully-fledged sophist, a high class teacher of rhetoric, travelling around giving displays of his rhetorical skill to audiences and charging high fees. We know that he commanded a good income in Gaul, and had, perhaps *en route*, visited the Po valley as well as Rome, in addition to Antioch in Syria, Ionia and Greece.

He is acquitted but then has to face his second accuser, Dialogue, who, c.33, complains: 'The Syrian has stripped me of all my dignity, breaking my wings and bringing me down to the level of the common herd. He has taken away my respectable tragic mask and replaced it with one of comedy and satyric[10] drama. He has locked me up with jest and lampoon and Cynicism and Eupolis[11] and Aristophanes and lastly with Menippus,[12] an old dog he has dug up, one with a loud bark and sharp teeth, all the more formidable because he laughed as he bit.' (Here Lucian is advertising his own originality with his comic dialogues. The passage also suggests that in his dialogues Lucian is deliberately blending many elements, practising what Bompaire well calls 'contamination', something which is a feature of many of Lucian's works and not just of his dialogues.) Dialogue goes on to complain: 'Moreover I'm no longer prose with my feet on the ground, nor yet verse, but a strange mixture like a Centaur.'[13]   (Here

---

5. i.e. 'desisting from the *suasoria*', a typical rhetorical exercise, see p.5.
6. i.e. 'and from the encomium', another rhetorical exercise, see p.5.
7. Plato's school.
8. Aristotle's school, also called Peripatos, on which 'walked around' is a pun.
9. As seems evident from Householder's statistics and the index of vol. 4 of my O.C.T.; for a less complimentary estimate of L.'s educational range see G. Anderson, 'Lucian's Classics; some Shortcuts to Culture', *BICS* 23 (1959), 59–68.
10. A play like Euripides' *Cyclops*, less serious than tragedy but more so than comedy, with chorus of Satyrs, mythical creatures, half horse, half man.
11. A comic poet contemporary with Aristophanes.
12. On Menippus see pp.264–5; see also Index for cynicism, diatribe.
13. Mythical monsters, partly horse, partly man; they were four-legged, whereas Satyrs were two-legged.

Dialogue refers to a feature of Menippus' lost works, the mixture of prose and verse, something which Lucian only used to a limited extent in a few dialogues.) Lucian in his defence says that he has made Dialogue attractive and human, when before he was grim and serious. Needless to say Lucian is acquitted on this charge also and by a unanimous verdict.

Although Lucian says in this passage that at the age of forty he gave up rhetoric for dialogue, he never really stopped being a sophist, travelling around, mainly in Greece and Ionia, giving readings of his work. No doubt he may have done well enough for a time, so that he felt able to write *De Mercede Conductis*, which deplored the hard life of dependent scholars living in rich households, but eventually he seems to have fallen on hard times himself so that he was obliged to indulge in servile compliments to patrons, real or prospective, and finally, perhaps much against the grain, he accepted paid employment in the service of the Emperor in Egypt, as he tells us in *Apologia*. We don't know whether the emperor in question was Marcus or Commodus (180–192); Lucian makes a critic say he 'has one foot in Charon's bark', but on the other hand he still feels young enough to express hopes of promotion to an even higher post. Lucian describes this post[14] as important and well-paid and represents his duties as introducing lawsuits, organising proceedings in court, and then producing a clear, accurate and permanent record of the proceedings.

Fitting Lucian's works within the framework suggested by the autobiographical references is difficult, because few of the seventy or more works generally regarded as genuine can be dated even approximately, and there is little evidence that similarities of subject matter, form or attitude[15] necessarily suggest a similar date.

The earliest datable works are three dialogues composed in 163–4 at Antioch in Syria, when Lucius Verus, Marcus' co-emperor, was there with his mistress Pantheia. *Imagines* is in her praise; *Pro Imaginibus* is Lucian's defence of it, when Pantheia complains that he has been too complimentary, while *De Saltatione* is a tongue-in-cheek *technē*, treatise on an art form, in this case on dancing.

Between the stay at Antioch and attendance at the Olympic Games of 165 should probably be fitted a return to Samosata, uncomfortably close to the fighting in the Parthian War (162–6) to take his father and family with him to Ionia and Greece, and perhaps also to read *The Dream* and a dialogue introduced by it. He tells us in *Alexander* 56 how he had sent his father ahead to the port of Amastris in Paphlagonia on the Black Sea, while he himself visited the oracle established by Alexander, the bogus prophet, at Abonuteichos and according to his own account exposed the prophet as an impostor and bit his hand, but later became reconciled to him and accepted Alexander's offer of a passage on a ship arranged by him. This was, if true, incredibly naive behaviour on the part of the Lucian we know. And so it turned out, for Lucian goes on to

---

14. The post has been variously interpreted as *eisagōgeus, hypomnēmatographos*, or *archistatōr*, see Jones 20–21, Hall 441–2.
15. For a reasoned rejection of this type of approach, used most recently by J. Schwartz, *Biographie de Lucien de Samosate*, (Brussels, 1965), see Hall 44–63.

tell how he was lucky to escape being thrown overboard by the crew on Alexander's instructions.

Lucian was in Greece for the Olympic Games of 165, memorable for the suicide of Peregrinus, to which he refers in *Fugitivi*, a dialogue probably written soon after the Games, and which he describes in *On the Death of Peregrinus*, a work of uncertain date. *Bis Acc.* can also be dated to 165, as it, c.2, refers to the celebration of the Olympic Games and fighting at Babylon in the Parthian War as concurrent, and also suggests an approximate date for Lucian's birth, as he is 'about forty', c.32. *Hermotimus*, a long dialogue about the futility of Stoicism, also has its character, Lycinus, a pseudonym for Lucian, as 'about 40' and mentions a recent visit to Olympia, and so presumably can also be dated to about 165.

Thus we see *Herm.*, Lucian's only truly philosophical dialogue, and *Bis Acc.* which presupposes Lucian's comic dialogue with all its various components as fully developed, to be roughly contemporary. It follows that Lucian's mention of his deserting rhetoric for philosophy does not refer to a 'philosophic period' in an evolving Lucian, unless perhaps only to a very short-lived flirtation with philosophy proper, but rather indicates an adoption of the medium of philosophy, dialogue. Alternatively 'philosophy' could be taken very loosely to include satirical dialogue, as being influenced by Cynicism and Menippus[16] in particular, in view of its vague connection with moral philosophy. Theories about an evolving Lucian can be carried too far, particularly as 'and lastly Menippus' in *Bis Acc.* 33 may only mean 'last in a list' rather than 'last chronologically to be included in the mixture'. All that can be said for certain is that by 163 Lucian was publishing non-satirical dialogues, while by 165 he was giving readings of dialogues of the new type. There is, of course, no telling how long he had been storing these new weapons in his entertainer's armoury.)

How to Write History can be dated to 166, as the Parthian War is all over 'bar the shouting'. *Pro Lapsu* is comparatively late, as Lucian refers to himself as a 'senior citizen'[17] and by now is reduced to greeting a patron in an early morning *salutatio*, and to having to admit to some knowledge of Latin. The preludes *Bacchus* and *Hercules* were delivered in what Lucian calls his 'old age'. *Eunuchus*, a scurrilous dialogue, postdates the foundation of philosophical chairs at Athens in 176; by now Lucian had a young son. The encomiastic biography *Demonax* was probably written after 180 and certainly after 171. The latest firm date however is for *Alex.*, as c.48 shows it postdates the death of Marcus in 180.

A further piece of information about Lucian has recently been discovered[18] in an Arabic version of a commentary by Galen, the doctor and voluminous writer, who refers with approval to the activities of a contemporary, Lūqiyānūs in the Arabic, in exposing the ignorance of pretentious sophists. This Lucian composed a book full of dark sayings making no sense, which he ascribed to Heraclitus and passed on to others. They took it to a famous philosopher who

---

16. On Cynicism, see p. 265 and Index; for Menippus, see pp.124 ff., 264 etc.

17. A *presbutēs*, presumably younger than a *gerōn*.

18. By G. Strohmaier, Übersehenes zur Biographie Lukians, *Philologus* 120 (1976), 117–122; see also M.D. Macleod, Lucian's Activities as a Misalazon, *ibid.* 123 (1979), 326–8.

produced his own interpretation, unaware that it was a forgery. This Lucian also fabricated meaningless expressions which he sent to several grammarians who managed to make 'sense' out of them and explain them. No wonder he was unpopular with other sophists. This may explain why Philostratus writing his *Lives of the Sophists* a generation after Lucian's death makes no mention of him: he regarded Lucian as an anti-sophist, and perhaps he also judged Lucian by his wordly success and found him wanting.

2. The Second Sophistic

The really great days of Greece had ended long ago with the death of Alexander in 323 B.C. and the breakup of his empire, but worse was to follow in the second century B.C., when she lost her independence and became part of the Roman Empire. Moreover in the next century Rome annexed the various Hellenistic kingdoms of the Middle East, wherein Greek language and culture survived under Greek dynasties. In Lucian's time Greece consisted of two provinces, Achaea in the south and Macedonia in the north, with a few cities such as Athens, technically at least, independent allies of Rome. Though Greek literature had long been admired and studied by educated Romans, this did little for the provincials of Greece, though Corinth prospered because of her position and Athens drew some limited benefit from being a 'university' centre for young Romans. No doubt Juvenal's portrait of the 'starveling Greek' owed something to a satirist's exaggerations, but many Greeks found Greece's humble present a depressing contrast with her glorious past.

Things took a turn for the better with the philhellenic emperor Hadrian (A.D. 117–138), who amongst other things gave Athens a new library and completed the temple of Olympian Zeus. By the time of the next two emperors and the Antonine Age, a tremendous awareness of Greece's cultural heritage and enthusiasm for all things connected with classical Greece had manifested itself among educated Greeks. In particular they flocked to lecture-halls to hear sophists declaiming in the best Attic style, spirit and vocabulary on themes based on the famous periods of ancient Greek history, particularly those involving Athens, Sparta and Alexander the Great. The favourite exercise was the *suasoria*, urging a course of action in a historical situation long past. Thus Lucian's contemporary Aelius Aristides produces two *Sicilian Discourses* set during the Sicilian Expedition, one urging reinforcements for Nicias, the other the recall of the expedition. *Suasoriae* of this sort, along with other exercises such as the *controversia*, pleading an imaginary and often unlikely case in a lawsuit, had long been practised both in Greek and Latin, as we learn from the works of the Elder Seneca, but performances of them by sophists became so popular in Lucian's day that the Antonine Age is often thought of as the period of the Second Sophistic (Sophistic = the *technē*, art or craft, of the sophist).

The term Second Sophistic was first used by Philostratus, writing in the early third century A.D., to distinguish its practitioners from the old sophists such as Gorgias or Protagoras, whom Philostratus regarded as treating more philosophical subjects, whereas the Second Sophistic 'used the types of poor and rich men, nobles and tyrants, and specific themes to which history leads the

way'. Though Philostratus says that the Second Sophistic was invented by Demosthenes' enemy Aeschines, it is usually thought of as starting in the first century A.D., reaching its zenith in the Antonine Age and persisting into the third century. Worth particular mention among the sophists discussed by Philostratus is Dio of Prusa (Chrysostom, c.40–115), who had some claim to be regarded as a Cynic philosopher and because of this, together with the range and variety of his works and his occasional use of light dialogue, is something of a proto-Lucian. The great sophists[19] often represented their cities as ambassadors or 'public orators' and amassed great fortunes, none more so than Herodes Atticus, Lucian's older contemporary and a munificent benefactor of Athens.

Graeco-Roman education had long advocated *mimēsis* (imitation) of the best classical authors. Horace had advised poets to 'thumb their Greek exemplars by night and day' and Dio and his contemporary Quintilian drew up lists of Greek authors to be studied. At its best *mimēsis* need not be servile imitation,[20] but emulation, imaginative reuse of the same material, as shown by Quintilian 10.2. *Mimēsis* could take the form of Atticism of vocabulary, (only words used by a few authors such as Thucydides, Plato or Demosthenes would be acceptable to strict grammarians like Pollux or Phrynichus), syntax, and style (e.g. Lucian's *De Syria Dea* and *Astrologia* in imitation of Herodotus), or could be imitation of contents, as Lucian does in *Charon* when he rewrites scenes from Herodotus or in *The Dream* with its adaptation of Xenophon's Choice of Heracles.

Mimēsis could also apply in a wider sense to a general aspiration to the culture[21] of the ancients in all its aspects, history, law, philosophy and the visual arts, and Lucian was an enthusiastic exponent of this wider *mimēsis*. Despite his innovations, particularly in the field of dialogue, Lucian was true to the spirit of the Second Sophistic in aiming at *mimēsis* of the language, literature and above all culture of classical Greece, as shown by Bompaire who had every justification for devoting a monumental book to a study of Lucian's *mimēsis*. Lucian, however, differed from his contemporaries by adding comedy, wit and variety to that *mimēsis*.

3. The Works of Lucian

Lucian's works are immensely varied in form, contents and spirit. This is the result not of chance but of the design of Lucian, who uses his repertoire of amusing material and the tricks of his entertainer's trade in various permutations and combinations and with various additions or adaptations. Though Lucian is mainly admired for his dialogues about half of his genuine works are not dialogues at all. (For titles and abbreviations see List of Works).

NON-DIALOGUE WORKS
Rhetorical Exercises. Most of these are probably early, though the influence of rhetoric and interest in it clearly remained with Lucian throughout his career.

---

19. See G.W. Bowersock, *Greek Sophists in the Roman Empire* (Oxford, 1969).
20. Cf. *Hist.* 15 ff.
21. See Bowie.

Phalaris 1 and *2* are *suasoriae*, while *Tyrannicida* and *Abdicatus* are *controversiae* and *Lis Consonantium* (*Trial of the Consonants*) is a humorous parody of such activities. The encomium is represented by the serious *Patriae Encomium* and the light-hearted *Muscae Encomium* (*Praise of the Fly*), while *Hippias*, describing a bath-house, is an example of the *ecphrasis*, a description, often of a work of art. We find all these elements along with the *psogos*, the exercise in abuse, incorporated within longer works, e.g. in Lucian's strictures on the private lives of Alexander (the bogus prophet) or Peregrinus or personal enemies. The lively *De Syria Dea* and the colourless *Astrologia* should perhaps also be categorised as rhetorical exercises in imitation of the dialect and style of Herodotus.

Preludes. *Bacchus, Hercules, Electrum, De Domo* (*The Hall*), *Dipsades, Herodotus, Harmonides* and *Scytha*, like *Zeuxis*, see p.188, are *prolaliai* (literally 'preliminary chats'), brief, informal pieces, detached from, but serving to introduce longer works (usually dialogues), used by Lucian to describe his literary aims and advertise himself. They also contain samples of his rhetorical expertise in *ecphrasis*, as he describes a painting or a building, or story-telling (*narratio*) or both.

Pamphlets and Letters. *Adversus Indoctum* lampoons an 'ignorant' buyer of books and *Pseudologista* is Lucian's retort to the sophist who had dared to pick him up on a linguistic point) are full of vindictive *psogos* against personal enemies and may be classified as pamphlets. *Prometheus es in Verbis* (lib. 71) also appears to be a pamphlet as it contains Lucian's reply to the man, whether friend or foe, who called Lucian 'a Prometheus in his Works (*logoi*)', but it fulfils much the same function as a *prolalia* as Lucian discusses his literary aims and advertises himself. *Nigrinus* and *Peregrinus* are both letters, the first incorporating an encomiastic dialogue, the other an abusive obituary, while *Epistulae Saturnales* (the later parts of *Saturnalia*, see p.9), are imaginary letters. *De Mercede Conductis* (see p.3), *Rhetorum Praeceptor, Alexander, How to write History, A Slip of the Tongue* (*Laps.*) and *Apology* have addressees and so presumably are letters also, though all very different in contents and purpose. Thus *The Teacher of Rhetoricians* addresses an enemy abusively and contains a parody of a *technē*, while *How to Write History* is a serious *technē*, but contains a comic section of caricatures of bad historians.

Novels. *Verae Historiae 1* and *2*, though full of satire and parody, have the form of a novel, while, according to the most likely theory, *Asinus* (*The Ass*) is an abbreviation of a longer work, itself a lost Lucianic work. We also find many short stories, some possibly invented by Lucian, within other works, e.g. *Toxaris, How to write History*.

Verse. As we might expect from his frequent quotations, parodies and adaptations of epic and dramatic verse Lucian tried his hand at poetry. A number of epigrams are attributed to him, a few with good reason, in the *Palatine* and *Planudean Anthologies*, while *Podagra*, a witty parody of a tragedy with its young 'hero' falling victim to the cruel goddess, Gout, displays skill in the basic dramatic metres and several more recherché ones.

Biography. *Demonax* is a complimentary biography of one of the two contemporary philosophers of whom Lucian approved (*Nigrinus*, see p.10 being the other), describing his life-style and sayings. *Alexander*, though technically a

letter, is a parody of the encomiastic biography, as Lucian gives his version of the life and deceptions of the Sham Prophet.

Diatribes. *Calumnia, De Sacrificiis* (see p.177) and *De Luctu* are examples of the diatribe, the moral chat or informal sermon, as often delivered in a public place, by Cynics etc.

DIALOGUES.

Miniature Dialogues. There are four collections of miniature dialogues, twenty-five *Dialogues of the Gods*, purely comic and lacking all seriousness, see pp.10, 12, fifteen *Dialogues of the Sea-Gods*, most of them also comic, thirty *Dialogues of the Dead*, combining seriousness and humour after the manner of Menippus and other Cynics, and fifteen *Dialogues of the Courtesans*, realistic sketches written in the spirit of Menander and often employing situations with precedents in New Comedy. Other short dialogues are *Zeus Crossexamined*, in which a Cynic floors Zeus with his awkward questions about fate and providence, *Prometheus*, in which Prometheus, being nailed on Caucasus as in *Prometheus Vinctus*, complains about the injustice of it all to Hephaestus and Hermes, *The Judging of the Goddesses, The Assembly of the Gods, The Eunuch* and *A Conversation with Hesiod*, in which the poet is taken to task by Lycinus (Lucian) for claiming to prophesy the future.

Philosophical Dialogues. Only three dialogues at most can be described as philosophical, *Hermotimus* (its inordinate length and negative conclusions perhaps being designed to symbolise the length and futility of a training in Stoicism, as Lycinus subjects the fictitious Stoic to a protracted grilling), *Anacharsis* (a discussion between Solon and the Scythian on Greek gymnastics and athletics and their usefulness, in a Platonic frame reminiscent of the *Euthydemus* and *Lysis*), and *Navigium* (*The Ship*) on human aspirations, cf. Juvenal *Sat.* 10, again set in a Platonic frame).

Though Lucian has been dubbed Eclectic, Sceptic, Epicurean or Cynic by various scholars, his interest in philosophy was superficial, his main concern being to exploit its theories and practitioners for comic or satiric purposes. His rationalism and scorn of human credulity smack somewhat of Scepticism or Epicureanism, particularly in *Juppiter Tragoedus*, where he makes the Epicurean triumph over the Stoic in an argument about divine providence and in the praise[22] of Epicurus at the end of *Alexander*. The spirit and motifs of some of his works owe much to the Cynics and he certainly approved of their outspokenness and self-sufficiency, but not of their shameless conduct, sensationalism and scruffiness. His general attitude to the philosophical schools is well illustrated in cc.34–35 of *Symposium*, a comic and satiric account of a wedding-feast at which imaginary philosophers misbehave disgracefully, so that Lycinus reflects on the uselessness of book-learning and philosophy in promoting good behaviour, which was shown only by the *idiōtai*, the ordinary folk unversed in philosophy; cf. also *Menippus* 21.

Major Comical-Satirical Dialogues. Much of Lucian's best work occurs in a group of full-scale dialogues, each of which includes within its texture several of the ingredients enumerated in *Bis Acc.* 33, jest, lampoon, Cynicism (in general), Eupolis, Aristophanes and Menippus, as Lucian waxing now comic,

---

22. Probably partly due to the fact that the addressee, Celsus, was an Epicurean.

now bitter, now semi-serious, uses the fantastic elements of Old Comedy and/or Menippus, including occasionally a little of the Menippean admixture of verse. In addition to the works discussed elsewhere, and *Bis Accusatus* (pp.1–3), *Vitarum Auctio* and *Piscator* (pp.258–63), *Icaromenippus* and *Menippus* (pp.264–8) and *Fugitivi* (pp.269–71) these are:

Symposium, see p.8, which in addition to being a travesty of the proceedings at Plato's *Symp.* probably also includes elements from a lost work of Menippus also entitled *Symposium*,

Cataplus, in which a Cynic taunts the other dead as they cross the Styx in Charon's boat, in much the same way as Menippus does in *Dialogues of the Dead* 20,

Juppiter Tragoedus, see p.8, so called because initially Zeus is in such a panic over the outcome of the debate about his very existence and powers that he spouts tragic verses, giving the work a Menippean start,

Gallus (The Cock), a discussion between Micyllus a cobbler, (Mr. Small) and his cock who turns out to be Pythagoras reincarnated and from the wealth of his experiences in lives leads Micyllus to the Cynic conclusion that a humble, poor life has its advantages,

Timon,[23] in which Timon, now a recluse and misanthrope after having squandered his original wealth on ungrateful friends, reluctantly accepts a crock of gold from Plutus (Wealth) and gives short shrift to the toadies who reappear,

Charon, in which the ferryman, visiting the world above, is taken by Hermes to a high viewpoint from which they survey the lots of sixth century characters from Herodotus, illustrating the transience of human prosperity,

Saturnalia, written with a Cynic sympathy for the poor, and consisting of (a) a dialogue in which Cronos (Saturn) is asked awkward mythical and theological questions by his priest who sounds like Lucian (b) laws for the Saturnalia announced by the priest (c) letters (1) from the priest to Cronos (2) his reply (3) from Cronos to the rich, with a message from the poor urging them to be more generous or else they'll institute legal proceedings against them for a redistribution of wealth[24] (4) the reply of the rich.

Miscellaneous Dialogues. Mention has already been made of Lucian's use of dialogue for encomium in *Imag.* and *Nigr.*, for *psogos* in *Eun.* and for a *technē* in *Salt.*; there is also *Parasitus*, a mock eulogy of the art of sponging, simultaneously parodying a *technē* and a Platonic dialogue. Another example of Lucian's ingenuity in variation is *Toxaris*, in which the Greek contributes five short stories illustrating Greek friendship and the Scythian five on Scythian friendship, perhaps all fictions by Lucian wearing his novelist's hat. The novelist also appears in *Philopseudeis (The Lovers of Lies)*[25] with Tychiades, a sceptic in Lucian's own image, recalling a discussion on the supernatural and recounting the tall stories told including that of the sorcerer's apprentice. The

---

23. The chief source for Shakespeare's *Timon of Athens* was North's Plutarch. Evidence for S.'s use of L. is very thin; in any case no English translation seems to have been available and despite his 'small Latin and less Greek' would have had to cope with Erasmus' Latin translation or the original.

24. Hardly an ancient 'Communist manifesto', as Baldwin who once suggested it, now realises.

25. Scholars have been strangely reluctant to accept Rothstein's correction of the title from singular to plural.

most unreadable of the dialogues is *Lexiphanes* (*The Word-Flaunter*), wherein a pedant favours Lycinus with a reading of a *Symposium* of his own full of rare, archaic words, till Lycinus gets a doctor[26] to give him an emetic and suggest he models himself on Thucydides and Plato in future.

4. Lucian's Satire

Lucian's satire ranged from general ridicule of human faults and follies to bitter lampoons directed against individuals.

The Cynic themes of the vanity of human wishes and man's mistaken pursuit of wealth and power despite their transience are treated in the *Dialogues of the Dead* and several longer dialogues such *Charon, Cataplus* and *Ship*. The benefits of a simple lifestyle in fortifying oneself against the cruel wind of change in later life, or after death when all men are equal and all luxuries gone, are stressed in dialogues involving Menippus and other Cynics and in *The Cock*. Similarly Lucian makes Nigrinus praise the simple cultured life of Athens as opposed to the pretentious and dissolute luxury of Rome. *Nigrinus* and other works including uncomplimentary references to distinctive features of Roman society, such as *captatio, salutatio* and the *Saturnalia*, should not be regarded as attacking Rome but merely what Rome symbolised, the wealth and power which Lucian's Cynic models denigrate; Lucian's attitude to Rome, at least till adversity forced him to cultivate Roman patrons or employers, was one of studied indifference. He was pro-Greek, rather than anti-Roman, and his enthusiasm for things Greek usually took him back into the past, so that he was more interested in the Persian Wars than in Marcus' Marcomannic campaigns, while his interest in the Parthian Wars was only kindled by their proximity to his homeland and the chance to wax satirical at the expense of the historians they spawned. The Cynic influence is also obvious in the diatribes[27] *On Grief*, ridiculing the way men fear death and regard it as an evil, and *On Sacrifices*, deriding the folly of bartering with the gods for benefits.

Another favourite topic is human credulity, whether about the underworld and afterlife (*Menippus, Dialogues of the Dead, True Stories 2* etc.) or about ghosts and the supernatural (*The Lovers of Lies*) or the tall stories about the gods.[28] At this point it should be noted that Lucian makes comparatively little mention of contemporary religious cults such as those of Sarapis, Mithras and Asclepius, while Christians are only mentioned *en passant* in *Peregrinus* and *Alexander*, although the flourishing of various cults, particularly oriental and Egyptian ones, mysticism and a belief in magic were characteristic features of the second century. Lucian, however, preferred to take his examples of religious credulity from the old stories about the Olympian gods, partly because of his own predilections, partly because of the cultural nostalgia of his audience, partly to avoid giving offence to individual members of his audience, but also

---

26. Baldwin convincingly suggests that the character of Dr Sopolis is modelled on Galen, who was interested in linguistic problems as well as medicine; see p.4.
27. See p.8.
28. See pp.11–12.

because these old myths offered better scope for satire and comedy. And how well he succeeded in the *Dialogues of the Gods*! Credulous acceptance of oracles is also attacked by Lucian, though rather less than the dispensers of such oracles.

Whether writing satirical dialogues in general terms or making venomous attacks on individuals, Lucian was a self-appointed scourge and exposer of charlatans and hypocrites. Thus in *Pisc.* 20 he describes himself as *misalazōn kai misogoēs kai misopseudēs kai misotyphos*, hater of impostors, charlatans, lies and pretentious airs, a description we now know, thanks to the reference from Galen, see pp.4–5, to be true of him in real life and not just of his literary persona, and justifying the pseudonym he gives himself in *Pisc.* 19, *Parrhēsiadēs Alēthiōnos tou Elenxicleous* (Frank Verity Tester). He particularly disliked philosophers who fail to practise what they preach, as in *Symp.* where they misbehave at a feast, *Pisc.* where the present unworthy representatives of the founders of the schools are satirised, and *Fug.*, an attack on degenerate Cynics of the day. Impostors attacked after their deaths were Alexander, the founder of a flourishing oracle by, according to Lucian, dubious devices, and Peregrinus, whom at first Lucian despised for his vanity and folly but probably only decided to attack in writing after an oracle had been founded in his name.

Lucian's satire also dealt with literary and linguistic issues, particularly in *Hist.*, p.198 ff., with its caricatures of 'historians' ignorant of the true nature of historiography. Hyperatticism is also derided in some of these 'historians', in Lexiphanes who practised, and in the Teacher of Rhetoricians who is depicted as recommending, the use of rare old words. Lucian himself is a moderate Atticist, recommending, Thucydides, Plato and Demosthenes as linguistic models to others, but himself allowing *koinē* (Hellenistic vocabulary and syntax) to have a place in his Greek, and indeed occasionally being guilty of some of the worst forms he derides in others. Linguistic purists are also satirised in *Pseudolog.* (Lucian's retort to a sophist who was called *apophras* by Lucian and objected to the word on linguistic grounds) and, if by L., (*The Solecist* a dialogue satirising solecism-hunting).

5. Lucian's Literary Habits

Lucian's best work, whether in dialogue form or not, combines humour to amuse his audience or readers and a display of culture in moderation calculated to enable them to recognise and appreciate his references to the classical period, his quotations, parodies and adaptations of the best classical authors and his use of their style, vocabulary and motifs along with liveliness, variety and novelty.

Humour. Humour is usually easier to enjoy than to analyse and categorise and that of Lucian is no exception.

Lucian makes great play of incongruity for humorous effect, nowhere more than in his portrayal of the traditional Olympian gods as ludicrously human in their behaviour and frailties. He had of course been anticipated in his humorous picture of the gods by two of his favourite authors, Homer, (e.g. in Demodocus' song about Hephaestus' punishment of his wife, Aphrodite and her lover, Ares,

a scene reworked by Lucian for greater comic effect, or in his picture of Zeus' ridiculous insensitivity in listing his mortal girl-friends to Hera when seeking her favours) and Aristophanes, (e.g. in the *Frogs* where Dionysus is cowardly, obtuse and ignorant of the finer points of tragedy). Moreover the attention of Lucian, in his other hat as satirist, had been drawn to this aspect of the gods by a long line of thinkers including Xenophanes, Euripides, Plato, Epicureans such as Philodemus and, if he knew their works, Aristides and other Christian apologists. Zeus comes in for particularly rough treatment particularly in *Dialogues of the Gods*, *JTr.* and *JConf.*, see p.8, for his annoyance with Eros for forcing him to turn into everything under the sun in his lecherous pursuit of mortal women, his panic in case the Epicurean proves that he and the other gods don't exist, his fallibility with his thunderbolts in hitting his own temples and destroying the just and pious with the ungodly. We also have the injured wife, Hera, complaining about Ganymede and all those mortal women, and also about the Ixion affair. Apollo is ridiculed as unable to tell the future and suffering metrical difficulties in composing his oracles and Hermes as complaining about being overworked. See also *Dear. Jud.* for the unedifying conduct of the three goddesses in competing for the Golden Apple. Lucian often adds to the humour by suggesting an environment more suited to New Comedy than to Olympus with Zeus confined to a sickbed when pregnant with Dionysus or *apokoitos*, sleeping out. Another use of the humour of the incongruous is Lucian's selection of oaths, with a Cynic swearing by the spindle of the Destiny he derides, or Menippus' friend swearing by Heracles, when he sees Menippus dressed in Heracles' lionskin.

A major source of humour is the interspersion of caustic comments, from Lucian himself in the non-dialogue works, as Lucian encourages his readers (audience) to join with him in looking at things from an intellectually superior viewpoint. Dialogue is even better for this purpose as Lucian can use Menippus, Diogenes, Cyniscus and other Cynic mouthpieces to indulge in sarcasms and ask awkward questions. Likewise he introduces his pseudonym Lycinus or characters in his own image such as Tychiades or Momus to perform this function, providing a destructive running commentary, or using sophistry or the subtlest of logic to cause embarrassment. Any character can, indeed, be used for this purpose; once Lucian even uses Apollo, whom elsewhere he derides, to make a typically Lucianic comment on the ill-considered mythological arrangement whereby the devoted twin brothers Castor and Polydeuces never spend any time together.

Another form of Lucianic humour is the pun or play on words, depending for its effect on the acumen and literary knowledge of his clientele. Thus in *The Ship*, in a setting reminiscent of Plato's *Republic*, one of the characters is given the good Platonic name, Adeimantus, and then is twitted, c.35, on his cowardice. Again in *DMer.* 2.4 Pamphilus' *hēlikiōtēs* Charmides *gamei ēdē kai sōphronei*, where readers would recognise the allusion to the subject of Plato's *Charmides* and some of them spot the echo of *Charmides* 157 D, when Charmides is praised for surpassing *tōn hēlikiōtōn* in *sōphrosynē*. This type of punning merely follows the precedent of Lucian's beloved Plato, who shows particular interest in the subject in his *Cratylus*.

Another humorous ploy, again dependent on the awareness of the readers, is the use of parody. Thus Homer and oracles are regularly parodied in centos, Parrhesiades, in defending himself in *Pisc.*, several times parodies Socrates' words in Plato's *Apology*, and indeed a whole work, *The Parasite*, is a large scale parody of a Platonic dialogue, while elsewhere the Athenian assembly and its decrees are parodied.

Culture. Lucian often compares the *pepaideumenoi*, the cultured, i.e. his clientele, favourably with the common mob, and throughout his work has them very much in mind. His references to the history,[29] art[30] and above all literature of classical Greece are designed not to show his erudition[31] but to be clear and straightforward enough for his audience to recognise and appreciate. The importance to Lucian of audience response is illustrated by *VH* 1.2, where they are invited to spot and enjoy allusions to 'old poets, prosewriters and philosophers', cf. also *Pisc.* 6. Most of Lucian's allusions, quotations, verbal echoes and adaptations come from a fairly limited range of authors, mainly Homer (*Iliad* and *Odyssey* 1–12), Hesiod, the early books of Herodotus, Plato (particularly *Apology*, *Republic* and, above all, *Phaedrus*), and Demosthenes (*Olynthiacs*, *Philippics* and *De Corona*). His quotations of whole lines from Aristophanes and Menander are rather less frequent but the influence of Aristophanes is obvious in many dialogues and that of Menander in *Dialogues of the Courtesans* from Lucian's reproduction of the spirit, motifs, and vocabulary of both poets.

Variety and liveliness. Lucian's deliberate attempt to give his works variety of form and subject matter should be obvious from the preceding survey of his works. Many of the qualities by which he achieves liveliness are those of the Cynic diatribe.[32] In addition to humour, parody, quotations understandable to his audience, his liveliness is enhanced by occasional uses of everyday or comic vocabulary, proverbs, fable, allegory and rhetorical hyperbole. Above all like the open-air preacher he aims to have a close rapport with his audience. This is why in *Bis Acc.* 33 he mentions Cynicism as one of the ingredients in his new genre.

Novelty. Though in his preludes Lucian claims that his main aims are unity, harmony and Attic grace rather than being praised for the novelty of his dialogues, he takes good care to mention that novelty and is obviously proud of it. Plato could be said to have anticipated Lucian by introducing comic elements into some dialogues, particularly *Euthydemus*, and closer to Lucian's time the 58th *Discourse* of Dio of Prusa and the *Gryllus*[34] attributed to Plutarch are humorous dialogues, but Lucian was the first to realise the full possibilities of comic dialogue as a literary form and to develop it by use of a versatile and inventive mind. Not only does he ingeniously adapt his literary sources, but he adds original touches of his own, something he also shows when he turns to novel writing, see p.7, and to coining anecdotes, see on *Hist.* 1.

---

29. Despite his sensible attitude to history in *Hist.*, his knowledge of Classical Greek history was limited and his references conventional.

30. See p.280.

31. See note 9.

32. Cf. A. Oltramare, *Les Origines de la Distribe romaine* (Lausanne, 1926).

34. On the doubtful attribution see vol. xii of the Loeb of Plutarch's *Moralia*, 489–91.

Contamination (Literary Blend). One of Lucian's characteristics is the way he blends material from a variety of sources into individual works, dialogue or otherwise. Bompaire's use of the term contamination for this process is eminently justified, provided one is not misled by the original application of the term to Plautus and Terence when they used a mere *two* Greek plays to make one Latin comedy; Lucian's literary blend is often of several genres and several sources. Thus *Timon* is a blend of Cynic ideas, Aristophanes *Plutus*, Menander *Dyscolus* and probably at least two other comedies, and similar blends occur in *The Fisherman* and *Menippus*, see pp.259–60 and 264–5, and above all in *How to Write History*, see p. 287 ff.

In *Prom. Es* and *Zeuxis*, see p.280 ff., Lucian talks to his audience about his literary aims in attempting to unite the disparate elements of dialogue and comedy into a beautiful, harmonious whole. In both works he pretends to show little interest in the compliments paid to the novelty of his literary creations, saying in *Prom. Es* he would rather have them applauded for gracefulness, beauty, harmony and symmetry, while in *Zeuxis* he laments the absence of praise for 'fine language composed according to the good old rules, intellectual sharpness and thoughtfulness, Attic grace, co-ordination and overall craftmanship'. As in *Prom. Es* Lucian is at pains to stress the originality of Prometheus as a craftsman and to reject any ideas that he himself is a plagiarist, and in *Zeuxis* he makes much of the compliments paid to the novelty of his dialogues, his disclaimers of interest in these compliments are rather disingenuous. The purpose of these works and other *prolaliai* is to advertise his claims to be regarded *both* as a literary artist *and* a literary innovator.

Repetitiveness and reworking of material. One less admirable habit of Lucian more obvious to us as readers of his collected works than to purchasers or audiences of individual pieces is his tendency to repeat literary allusions (e.g. to the winged chariot and other features of the myth of Plato's *Phaedrus*), quotations (particularly of Homer, e.g. the golden cord of *Iliad* 8.19), motifs (e.g. Zeus turning into many shapes in pursuit of mortal women, Socrates chattering with Nestor and Palamedes in Hades, the reincarnations of Pythagoras, the hypocritical philosophers with grave looks and long beards), and phrases first built up and then repeated, e.g. 'What is one to do, when friend compels?' (see on *Menippus* 1) or the horrible fate of being devoured by sixteen vultures. Sometimes instead of repetition he resorts to adaptation, what G. Anderson calls 'self-imitation', or extending or condensing themes already used. (Some motifs occur both in *VH* 2 in summary form and in more extended form in individual *Dialogues of the Dead* or in *Menippus* and related dialogues, but it is impossible to decide which form came first.) Schwartz[35] tried to date most of Lucian's works via shared motifs, but Lucian probably used and reused earlier material over a long period. Perhaps the best clues to Lucian's methods of reworking material are afforded by comparison of two of the few datable works, *On the Dance* (163 or 164) and *How to Write History* (2–3 years later) showing how Lucian varies the form and structure of a discussion of a *technē* and adapts and reuses many of the motifs and ideas from the earlier work, see pp.287 ff.

---

35. See n. 15.

6. The Influence of Lucian on Posterity[36]

Literature. The popularity of Lucian in Byzantium is shown by the numerous mss. from the tenth century onwards and by imitations such as the *Sale of the Lives* by Theodorus Prodromus, *Timarion* and *Mazaris.* Knowledge of L. had reached Italy by the early fifteenth century and works with a moralising flavour such as *Timon, Charon* and *Dialogues of the Dead* were translated into Latin; fifteenth century imitations included the dialogues *Palinurus* by Vegio and *Virtus Dea* by Boiardo.

Lucian's works became more widely available after the first edition of 1496 and more particularly the first Aldine of 1503, which was probably used by Erasmus and Sir Thomas More for their Latin translations. The tremendous debt of both to Lucian is obvious in Erasmus' *Praise of Folly* and *Colloquies* and in More's *Utopia.* Other sixteenth century writers to know Lucian well were Rabelais and Ulrich von Hutten.

The highly educated Ben Jonson clearly used *Lexiphanes* in the *Poetaster* and *Dialogues of the Dead* in *Volpone.* The influence of Lucian on *Timon of Athens*, is at best probably only indirect; see n. 23. Meanwhile in Spain too Cervantes and Quevedo betrayed Lucian's influence.

Nearer our own times *True Stories* inspired many imitations with Cyrano de Bergerac taking readers to the moon (1656) and the sun (1661), with *Gulliver's Travels* (1726–7) by Dean Swift, perhaps the most Lucianic of satirists, with Raspo narrating the adventures of Baron Münchausen (1785) and Jules Verne with his two fantastic voyages (1864–5); if Verne is the father of modern science fiction, Lucian has a claim to be its great grandfather. The *Dialogues of the Dead* too had their imitators in Fontenelle (1683), Fénelon (1700) and Lord Lyttelton (1760), while Voltaire, acclaimed the 'Lucian of the eighteenth century', primarily for his *Candide* (1759), wrote a dialogue *Lucien, Érasme et Rabelais* also involving Swift. In this country the work of Fielding, who owned nine editions of Lucian, and contemplated translating all Lucian (no doubt to repair the damage done by the 'translators' employed by Dryden for his 1711 Lucian) is full of Lucianic spirit, particularly in *The History of the Adventures of Joseph Andrews* (1742), *The Life of Jonathan Wild the Great* and the incomplete *A Journey from this World to the Next* (1743). In Germany Wieland, the translator of Lucian, produced *Gespräche in Elysium* (1780), *Göttergespräche* (1790–3) and other works with a Lucianic flavour, and his contemporaries Schiller and Goethe, especially in his poem on the Sorcerer's Apprentice, take ideas from Lucian.

In the nineteenth century Sir Walter Scott, though castigated by some for his deficiencies as a Greek scholar, quotes Lucian in several novels and makes him the favourite author of arguably his favourite character, the Antiquary, while W.S. Landor's *Imaginary Conversations* (1824–9) and Andrew Lang's *Letters to dead Authors* (1886) deserve special mention.

---

36. The most useful survey of the vast subject of the Lucianic *Nachleben* is by C. Robinson, *Lucian*, (Duckworth, 1979) 65 ff.

The influence of Lucian on twentieth century writers in less obvious, though a resurrected Lucian would have recognised kindred spirits such as George Orwell and the writers of several television scripts including *Yes Minister* and *Yes Prime Minister*.

Art. Lucian strongly influenced the art of the fifteenth and sixteenth centuries. Thanks mainly to the writings of Alberti, the attention of Italian artists was drawn to Lucian; his description of Apelles' Calumny in *Slander* inspired paintings by Botticelli, Raphael and Mantegna; Aetion's Marriage of Alexander and Roxana was sketched by Raphael from *Herod*. The eloquent Heracles Ogmios in Lucian's *Hercules* was reproduced in sketches by Raphael, Dürer and Holbein. Holbein's associations with Erasmus and More aroused an interest in Lucian, so that the *Dialogues of the Dead* inspired his series of woodcuts, The Dance of Death, a theme often copied by later artists.

7. The Transmission of the Text

We know of only one mention of Lucian by a contemporary, Galen, and his name is absent from Philostratus' *Lives of the Sophists*. Thereafter comparatively few[38] mention him or betray knowledge[39] of him, but he was at least popular enough to have inspired a few imitations[40] which have infiltrated into the Lucianic corpus.

Apart from a fourth century parchment containing a few lines of *Asin*. and a Syriac paraphrase of *Cal.*, our earliest texts of Lucian are Vaticanus graecus 90 (Γ) of the early tenth century, which has survived virtually complete and Harleianus 5694 (E), written for Arethas c. 914, of which about three quarters are now lost. There are five other important tenth or eleventh century mss., all substantial but far from complete. In all we have about 200 mss. containing one or more works of Lucian,[43] but as we might expect with such a heterogeneous corpus of so many works, most of the larger scale mss. are composite, putting together such a collection as they could amass from a variety of sources, so that they vary in quality from work to work.

Of the copious scholia[44] the earliest datable are a few by Basilius, a ninth century Pisidian bishop. Arethas composed many scholia which he added to E and which were transcribed into many other mss. Γ is also rich in scholia added both by the original scribe and by the *diorthōtēs*, Alexander, Bishop of Nicaea up to c. 945.

---

38. Lactantius, Eunapius, Isidore of Pelusium, and, much later, Photius.

39. Alciphron, if later than L., Julian, Libanius and his friend Acacius, and Aristaenetus Epistolographus.

40. E.g. *Sol.*, if not by L., *Amor.* and *Cyn.*; other spuria seem to have infiltrated by error or accident. On spuria see Loeb vol. 8 and OCT vol. 4, xii–xix.

43. See M. Wittek, *Scriptorium*, 1952, 309–23, and *Prolegomena* to Nilén's Teubner. Further details about many mss. are given by Mras, Coenen and Itzkowitz, *Prolegomena to a new Text of Lucian's Vitarum Auctio and Piscator*, (Hildesheim, 1986).

44. See Rabe's Teubner edition of 1906.

Although some details of the complicated manuscript tradition[45] are disputed, the generally accepted view, based on a consideration of the readings and the arrangement of the works in the various mss. is that in more than half of the works we have a single tradition coming to us mainly or entirely[46] via γ, the presumed ancestor of Γ and comprising a collection of all the works available,[47] whereas for the remaining works there was an alternative version of the text, β, the presumed ancestor of B, mainly containing works selected for their popularity.

Establishing what γ read presents comparatively few problems, as, in addition to the outstandingly reliable Γ, there usually are other good witnesses of γ independent of Γ, notably Marc. gr. 434 (Ω) and related mss., and in a few works Laur. C.S. 77 (Φ).

There are, however, greater difficulties with β, because the only consistently trustworthy representatives of the β tradition, Vind. Phil. gr. 123 (B) and Vat. gr. 1324 (U), between them lack a number[48] of the works which seem to have existed in β, and for most of these we have to use a variety of *recentes* which in some works offer a text vitiated by interpolations or infiltrated by contaminations from the γ tradition. Fortunately in some of these works we have some sort of check on the reliability of these *recentes* by the variant readings or corrections added to Γ by its diorthotes, Γ^a, which usually seem to be derived from β, and in a very few of these works[49] despite the absence of B and U, we can be confident that the β tradition has survived well enough.

In works where β is well represented, one has to choose between each variant reading of γ and β on its merits, even if γ seems to be generally superior, as being freer from recognisable errors and interpolations or offering more readings that by the criteria of textual criticism seem preferable. In a few works, however, notably the miniature dialogues, β seems to approach γ in merit. Where, however, the best representatives of β are lost, it seems safer to follow γ, unless there are strong attractions in the alternative reading.

Of the works in this volume *Peregr., Zeux.* and *Hist.* come to us via γ alone, *D. Jud., Pisc., Men.* and *Sacr.* have the alternative β tradition well preserved, whereas *Somn.* and *Deor. Conc.* seem to have existed in β, but its best witnesses are now lost.

---

45. The most important studies are by M. Rothstein, *Quaestiones Lucianeae* (Berlin, 1888), H. Wingels, 'De Ordine Libellorum Lucianeorum', *Philologus* 72 (1913), 125–48 and particularly K. Mras, *Die Ueberlieferung Lucians* (Vienna, 1911), which, though questionable on some theoretical details, was of immense practical value for its evaluation of the merits of the main mss.; see also OCT vol. 1, ix–xxi.

46. Conceivably lib. 1–12 originally existed as a block in β not γ.

47. Presumably L., after delivering works orally, published them individually. Collections of various sizes would have been made, but some works are now lost, e.g. the biography of Sostratus (see *Demonax* 1), the Pseudo-Heraclitean concoctions (see pp.4–5) and, if by L., the *Metamorphoseis* of which *Asinus* is an abbreviation.

48. The evidence for a distinctive *ordo libellorum* which can be reconstructed for B and related mss. suggests there were approximately 34 works derived from β, of which only 21 survive in B or U; in a handful of these 21 works, however, the readings of B and/or U differ very little from those of γ.

49. Notably *VH* 1,2.

Important Manuscripts

HARLEIANUS 5694 (E) written for Arethas, Bishop of Caesarea in Cappadocia, by Baanes c. 914. Corrections, mainly on linguistic or orthographical minutiae, added to text by Arethas (E^a) along with his own marginal scholia. What has survived is the final or penultimate section containing 19 works, all of single tradition, with a text of equal authority with Γ, similar to, but not identical with it. E seems to have started with all the works contained in β, and then added a succession of supplements from parts of γ to complete the corpus.

Chief Mss. derived from γ

VATICANUS GRAECUS 90 (Γ), early tenth century. Contained lib. 1–80, but lib. 41 and 80 now only in 15th century supplement. Corrections and variant readings to many works were added by Γ^a, who tells us in several *subscriptiones* he is Alexander, Bishop of Nicaea; these corrections usually come from the β tradition. Several other correctors include Isidorus Ruthenus (Γ^c), the fifteenth century scribe of the supplement.

LAURENTIANUS C.S. 77 (Φ), with 21 works in the first (tenth century) hand, in all but one a good witness of γ, perhaps inferior to Γ but independent of it and occasionally preserving the true reading; generally superior to Ω.

MARCIANUS 840 (formerly 434) (Ω) contains 43 works in a late tenth or more probably early eleventh century hand and the rest in a fifteenth century supplement. Scholia in two old hands, several correctors, including Ω^b using a β text. Independent of Γ, but rather prone to errors, interpolations and contaminations from β.

Good witnesses of β.

VIND. PHIL. GR. 123 (B), eleventh century. Only central section of 31 works has survived, at first offering a β text, and thereafter works of single tradition. Text and scholia apparently transcribed from E.

VAT. GR. 1324 (U), late tenth or eleventh century. Surviving portion contains 20 works, some of single tradition, others with text derived from β. Close to B where both survive.

Intermittent or less reliable witnesses of β.

LAUR. 57.51 (L) with 29 works in 11th century hand. Usually fairly close to Γ, but in *Dear. Jud.* and some *Dialogi Minores* a good witness of β.

VAT. GR. 87 (A) with complete corpus, 14th century. Offers a heavily interpolated text, sometimes based on β, but elsewhere on γ or much contaminated by γ readings.

PARISINUS GRAECUS 2957 (N) with complete corpus, 15th century. Very occasionally offers good β text, but usually heavily interpolated. Though more often than not based on β, elsewhere offers a γ text or a mixture of both traditions. Rather better than A but often close to it.

VAT. GR. 76 (P), 14th century, with 32 works in a tiny, barely legible hand, generally based on β but with interpolations and frequent contaminations from γ.

VAT. GR. 1323 (Z), 13–14th century, preserves 30 works with first section including *Somn.* based on β; at times close to N.

The Main Editions

J. Lascaris (Florence 1496), the first edition, with a text based on Par. gr. 2954, a good γ ms., and far superior to the First Aldine, (Venice, 1503) and to a profusion of 16th and 17th century editions largely based on it.

Hemsterhuis and Reitz (Amsterdam, 1743–6), 4 vols. with variorum comments, Latin translations and *index verborum*.

I. Lehmann (Leipzig, 1822–31), 9 vols. with variorum comments.

C. Jacobitz   (1) (Leipzig, 1836–41), *editio maior* in 4 vols. with textual notes and excellent indices. J. was a careful editor but relied mainly on a 15th century copy of an indifferent 14th century ms.

(2) (Leipzig, 1851), *editio minor*, 3 vols. in Teubner Series.

I. Bekker (Leipzig, 1853) 2 vols. with some good conjectures.

G. Dindorf (Leipzig, 1850–8), 3 vols. in Tauchnitz Edition.

F. Fritzsche (Rostock, 1860–82), 30 works in 3 vols. with good critical notes.

J. Sommerbrodt (Berlin, 1886–99) 65 works in 3 vols. with textual notes and a compilation of manuscript readings, useful though often inaccurate and haphazard. Unfortunately S. had rejected the pioneering work of T. Siemonsen (Hadersleben 1865–6) and Rothstein in establishing the existence of a bipartite mss. tradition.

N. Nilén (Leipzig, 1906–23) in Teubner Series, 19 works in 2 fascicles with very detailed and accurate apparatus reporting the readings of many mss. preceded by invaluable fascicle of *Prolegomena* listing mss. and their contents and describing main mss. in detail.

A.M. Harmon, K. Kilburn and M.D. Macleod (London and Harvard, 1913–67), 8 vols. in Loeb Series.

M.D. Macleod (Oxford, 1972–87), 4 vols. in Oxford Classical Texts Series.

A Select Bibliography

General Discussion
G. Anderson, *Lucian: Theme and Variation in the Second Sophistic* (*Mnemosyne* Suppl. 41, 1976).

B. Baldwin, *Studies in Lucian* (Toronto, 1973).

J. Bompaire, *Lucien Écrivain: Imitation et Création* (Paris, 1958).

E.L. Bowie, 'Greeks and their Past in the Second Sophistic' *Past and Present* 46, (1970), 3–41.

M. Caster, *Lucien et la Pensée religieuse de son Temps* (Paris, 1937).

M. Croiset, *Essai sur la Vie et les Oeuvres de Lucien* (Paris, 1882).

D.R. Dudley, *A History of Cynicism* (London, 1937).

G.M.A. Grube, *The Greek and Roman Critics* (London, 1965).

J. Hall, *Lucian's Satire* (New York, 1981).

R. Helm, *Lucian und Menipp* (Leipzig, 1906).

F.W. Householder, *Literary Quotation and Allusion in Lucian* (New York, 1941).

C.P. Jones, *Culture and Society in Lucian* (Harvard, 1986).

C. Robinson, *Lucian and his Influence in Europe* (London, 1979).

Translations
Complete Works:

H.W. and F.G. Fowler, 4 vols. (Oxford, 1905).

A.M. Harmon, K. Kilburn, M.D. Macleod, Loeb Classical Library, 8 vols. (London and Harvard, 1913–67).

E. Talbot, 2 vols. (Paris, 1874).

C.M. Wieland (6 vols. in 3, Darmstadt 1971 reprint of Leipzig edition of 1788–9).

Select Works:
L. Casson (New York, 1962).

S.T. Irwin (London, 1894).

K. Mras (Gernsbach, 1954, in Tusculum Series).

B.P. Reardon (New York, 1965).

P. Turner, (Harmondsworth, 1961 in Penguin Classics).

H. Williams (London, 1903, in Bohn Series).

Annotated Editions
Two or More Works:

F.G. Allinson, *Lucian, Selected Writings* (Boston, 1905).

W.E. Heitland, *The Dream, Charon, Fisher, Of Mourning* (Cambridge, 1885).

H.L. Levy, *Lucian: 70 Dialogues* (Oklahoma U.P., 1976).

E.C. Mackie, *Menippus and Timon* (Cambridge, 1904).

J. Schwartz, *Philopseudes et De Morte Peregrini* (Paris, 1951).

J. Zimmermann, *Luciani quae feruntur Podagra et Ocypus* (Leipzig, 1909).

Individual Works:
T. Beaupère, *Lucien: Philosophes à l'Encan* (Paris, 1967).

M. Caster, *Études sur Alexandre ou le Faux Prophète de Lucien* (Paris, 1938).

J. Coenen, *Zeus Tragōdos* (Meisenheim, 1977, including good apparatus and description of mss.).

H. Homeyer, *Lukian: Wie man Geschichte schreiben soll* (Munich, 1965).

G. Husson, *Lucien: Le Navire ou les Souhaits* (Paris, 1970).

C.S. Jerram, *Vera Historia* (Oxford, 1879).

F. Ollier, *Histoire Vraie* (Paris, 1962).

LUCIAN
A SELECTION

ΠΕΡΙ ΤΟΥ ΕΝΥΠΝΙΟΥ
ΗΤΟΙ
ΒΙΟΣ ΛΟΥΚΙΑΝΟΥ

Ἄρτι μὲν ἐπεπαύμην εἰς τὰ διδασκαλεῖα φοιτῶν ἤδη τὴν ἡλικίαν 1
πρόσηβος ὤν, ὁ δὲ πατὴρ ἐσκοπεῖτο μετὰ τῶν φίλων ὅ τι καὶ
διδάξαιτό με. τοῖς πλείστοις οὖν ἔδοξεν παιδεία μὲν καὶ πόνου
πολλοῦ καὶ χρόνου μακροῦ καὶ δαπάνης οὐ μικρᾶς καὶ τύχης
δεῖσθαι λαμπρᾶς, τὰ δ' ἡμέτερα μικρά τε εἶναι καὶ ταχεῖάν
τινα τὴν ἐπικουρίαν ἀπαιτεῖν· εἰ δέ τινα τέχνην τῶν βαναύσων
τούτων ἐκμάθοιμι, τὸ μὲν πρῶτον εὐθὺς ἂν αὐτὸς ἔχειν τὰ
ἀρκοῦντα παρὰ τῆς τέχνης καὶ μηκέτ' οἰκόσιτος εἶναι τηλικοῦτος
ὤν, οὐκ εἰς μακρὰν δὲ καὶ τὸν πατέρα εὐφρανεῖν ἀποφέρων ἀεὶ
τὸ γιγνόμενον.

Δευτέρας οὖν σκέψεως ἀρχὴ προὐτέθη, τίς ἀρίστη τῶν 2
τεχνῶν καὶ ῥᾴστη ἐκμαθεῖν καὶ ἀνδρὶ ἐλευθέρῳ πρέπουσα καὶ
πρόχειρον ἔχουσα τὴν χορηγίαν καὶ διαρκῆ τὸν πόρον. ἄλλου
τοίνυν ἄλλην ἐπαινοῦντος, ὡς ἕκαστος γνώμης ἢ ἐμπειρίας εἶχεν,
ὁ πατὴρ εἰς τὸν θεῖον ἀπιδών—παρῆν γὰρ ὁ πρὸς μητρὸς θεῖος,
ἄριστος ἑρμογλύφος εἶναι δοκῶν [λιθοξόος ἐν τοῖς μάλιστα
εὐδόκιμος]—Οὐ θέμις, εἶπεν, ἄλλην τέχνην ἐπικρατεῖν σοῦ παρόν-
τος, ἀλλὰ τοῦτον ἄγε—δείξας ἐμέ*—δίδασκε παραλαβὼν λίθων
ἐργάτην ἀγαθὸν εἶναι καὶ συναρμοστὴν καὶ ἑρμογλυφέα· δύναται
γὰρ καὶ τοῦτο, φύσεώς γε, ὡς οἶσθα, ἔχων δεξιῶς.

Ἐτεκμαίρετο δὲ ταῖς ἐκ τοῦ κηροῦ παιδιαῖς· ὁπότε γὰρ
ἀφεθείην ὑπὸ τῶν διδασκάλων, ἀποξέων ἂν τὸν κηρὸν ἢ βόας
ἢ ἵππους ἢ καὶ νὴ Δί' ἀνθρώπους ἀνέπλαττον, εἰκότως, ὡς ἐδόκουν
τῷ πατρί· ἐφ' οἷς παρὰ μὲν τῶν διδασκάλων πληγὰς ἐλάμβανον,
τότε δὲ ἔπαινος εἰς τὴν εὐφυΐαν καὶ ταῦτα ἦν, καὶ χρηστὰς εἶχον
ἐπ' ἐμοὶ τὰς ἐλπίδας ὡς ἐν βραχεῖ μαθήσομαι τὴν τέχνην, ἀπ'
ἐκείνης γε τῆς πλαστικῆς.

Ἅμα τε οὖν ἐπιτήδειος ἐδόκει ἡμέρα τέχνης ἐνάρχεσθαι, κἀγὼ 3
παραδεδόμην τῷ θείῳ μὰ τὸν Δί' οὐ σφόδρα τῷ πράγματι ἀχθό-
μενος, ἀλλά μοι καὶ παιδιάν τινα οὐκ ἀτερπῆ ἐδόκει ἔχειν καὶ
πρὸς τοὺς ἡλικιώτας ἐπίδειξιν, εἰ φαινοίμην θεούς τε γλύφων

*add καὶ

THE DREAM

[1] When I had just stopped attending school and was now close to manhood, my father began discussing my further education with his friends. Most of them thought higher education required much hard work, a great deal of time, no small expense and a conspicuous fortune, whereas our circumstances were humble and in need of quick relief; but if I learned one of the artisan crafts, I would from the very start have sufficient income from my craft and no longer need to be fed at home at my age, and very soon I would gladden my father by making regular contributions from my earnings.

[2] A second topic raised for discussion was which of the crafts is best, easiest to learn, suitable for a respectable free man, with necessary materials to hand and bringing in enough income. So when each praised a different craft according to his personal opinion or experience, my father looked at my uncle – for my uncle on my mother's side was present, a man considered an excellent sculptor – and said 'It's wrong for any other craft to prevail in *your* presence.' He then pointed at me and continued '*You* take him and teach him to be a good stone-cutter, mason and sculptor; for he is capable of that, since, as you know, he has natural talent.'

He was judging by my playful efforts with wax. For whenever I was dismissed by my teachers, I'd scrape the wax from my tablets and make models of oxen or horses or even people, and in a life-like manner in my father's opinion. That would bring me beatings from my teachers, but on this occasion praise for my cleverness and they had great hopes of my quickly learning the craft, on the evidence of that skill of mine in modelling.

[3] So no sooner had a day come that seemed suitable for me to start in a craft than I had been handed over to my uncle, and, upon my word, I was not at all displeased but thought it provided me with pleasant sport and a chance to show off to my companions, if I was seen carving gods

καὶ ἀγαλμάτια μικρά τινα κατασκευάζων ἐμαυτῷ τε κἀκείνοις
οἷς προῃρούμην. καὶ τό γε πρῶτον ἐκεῖνο καὶ σύνηθες τοῖς
ἀρχομένοις ἐγίγνετο. ἐγκοπέα γάρ τινά μοι δοὺς ὁ θεῖος ἐκέλευσέ
μοι ἠρέμα καθικέσθαι πλακὸς ἐν μέσῳ κειμένης, ἐπειπὼν τὸ
κοινὸν Ἀρχὴ δέ τοι ἥμισυ παντός. σκληρότερον δὲ κατενεγκόντος
ὑπ' ἀπειρίας κατεάγη μὲν ἡ πλάξ, ὁ δὲ ἀγανακτήσας σκυτάλην
τινὰ πλησίον κειμένην λαβὼν οὐ πράως οὐδὲ προτρεπτικῶς μου
κατήρξατο, ὥστε δάκρυά μοι τὰ προοίμια τῆς τέχνης.

Ἀποδρὰς οὖν ἐκεῖθεν ἐπὶ τὴν οἰκίαν ἀφικνοῦμαι συνεχὲς 4
ἀναλύζων καὶ δακρύων τοὺς ὀφθαλμοὺς ὑπόπλεως, καὶ διηγοῦμαι
τὴν σκυτάλην καὶ τοὺς μώλωπας ἐδείκνυον, καὶ κατηγόρουν
πολλήν τινα ὠμότητα, προσθεὶς ὅτι ὑπὸ φθόνου ταῦτα ἔδρασεν,
μὴ αὐτὸν ὑπερβάλωμαι κατὰ τὴν τέχνην. ἀνακτησαμένης δὲ τῆς
μητρὸς καὶ πολλὰ τῷ ἀδελφῷ λοιδορησαμένης, ἐπεὶ νὺξ ἐπῆλθεν
κατέδαρθον ἔτι ἔνδακρυς καὶ τὴν σκυτάλην ἐννοῶν.

Μέχρι μὲν δὴ τούτων γελάσιμα καὶ μειρακιώδη τὰ εἰρημένα· 5
τὰ μετὰ ταῦτα δὲ οὐκέτι εὐκαταφρόνητα, ὦ ἄνδρες, ἀκούσεσθε,
ἀλλὰ καὶ πάνυ φιληκόων ἀκροατῶν δεόμενα· ἵνα γὰρ καθ'
Ὅμηρον εἴπω,
     θεῖός μοι ἐνύπνιον ἦλθεν ὄνειρος
ἀμβροσίην διὰ νύκτα,
ἐναργὴς οὕτως ὥστε μηδὲν ἀπολείπεσθαι τῆς ἀληθείας. ἔτι
γοῦν καὶ μετὰ τοσοῦτον χρόνον τά τε σχήματά μοι τῶν φανέντων
ἐν τοῖς ὀφθαλμοῖς παραμένει καὶ ἡ φωνὴ τῶν ἀκουσθέντων ἔναυ-
λος· οὕτω σαφῆ πάντα ἦν.

Δύο γυναῖκες λαβόμεναι ταῖν χεροῖν εἷλκόν με πρὸς ἑαυτὴν 6
ἑκατέρα μάλα βιαίως καὶ καρτερῶς· μικροῦ γοῦν με διεσπάσαντο
πρὸς ἀλλήλας φιλοτιμούμεναι· καὶ γὰρ ἄρτι μὲν ἂν ἡ ἑτέρα
ἐπεκράτει καὶ παρὰ μικρὸν ὅλον εἶχέ με, ἄρτι δ' ἂν αὖθις ὑπὸ
τῆς ἑτέρας εἰχόμην. ἐβόων δὲ πρὸς ἀλλήλας ἑκατέρα, ἡ μὲν ὡς
αὑτῆς ὄντα με κεκτῆσθαι βούλοιτο, ἡ δὲ ὡς μάτην τῶν ἀλλο-
τρίων ἀντιποιοῖτο. ἦν δὲ ἡ μὲν ἐργατικὴ καὶ ἀνδρικὴ καὶ αὐχμηρὰ
τὴν κόμην, τὼ χεῖρε τύλων ἀνάπλεως, διεζωσμένη τὴν ἐσθῆτα,
τιτάνου καταγέμουσα, οἷος ἦν ὁ θεῖος ὁπότε ξέοι τοὺς λίθους·
ἡ ἑτέρα δὲ μάλα εὐπρόσωπος καὶ τὸ σχῆμα εὐπρεπὴς καὶ κόσμιος
τὴν ἀναβολήν.

Τέλος δ' οὖν ἐφιᾶσί μοι δικάζειν ὁποτέρᾳ βουλοίμην συνεῖναι

and making little statuettes for myself and others of my choice. Then the first thing that usually happens to beginners happened to me. For my uncle gave me a chisel and told me to give a gentle tap to a slab that lay to hand, adding the proverbial' "Well begun is half done.' But in my inexperience I struck too hard and the slab broke, whereupon my uncle lost his temper and grabbed a stick that lay near and performed an initiation ceremony on me that was neither gentle nor encouraging, so that my first steps in the craft brought me tears.

[4] So I ran off from there and arrived home sobbing without stop with my eyes full of tears and told them about the stick and kept showing my weals and accusing my uncle of great cruelty, adding that he had acted out of jealousy for fear that I would surpass him in his own craft. After my mother had consoled me and said many hard things about her brother, I fell asleep after nightfall still tearful and thinking of the stick.

[5] So far my story has dealt with amusing juvenile matters. But what you will hear next, gentlemen, is nothing trivial but requires serious attention from my audience. For, to quote Homer,

'A god-sent dream there came to me, a vision as I slept,
On through the immortal night,'

a dream so vivid it seemed absolutely real. Indeed even after so long the shapes of what I saw remain with my eyes and the sound of what I heard still rings in my ears. So clear was it all.

[6] Two women caught hold of me by the hands and each tried to drag me to her with great violence and strength; indeed they almost tore me apart in their eager competition with each other. For now one would be winning and have almost all of me in her clutches, and then in turn I'd be in the power of the other one. They kept shouting to each other, the one saying 'He's mine; I want possession of him,' and the other 'It won't do any good; you can't claim what isn't yours.' One was a working woman of masculine appearance, with filthy hair and calluses all over her hands, with her clothes tucked up, covered in dust, just like my uncle when he was chipping at his marble, while the other had a lovely face and an attractive figure and was neatly dressed. In the end, however, they left it up to me to decide which of them I wanted to live with.

αὐτῶν. προτέρα δὲ ἡ σκληρὰ ἐκείνη καὶ ἀνδρώδης ἔλεξεν·

Ἐγώ, φίλε παῖ, Ἑρμογλυφικὴ τέχνη εἰμί, ἣν χθὲς ἤρξω 7
μανθάνειν, οἰκεία τέ σοι καὶ συγγενὴς μητρόθεν. ὅ τε γὰρ
πάππος σου—εἰποῦσα τοὔνομα τοῦ μητροπάτορος—λιθοξόος ἦν
καὶ τὼ θείω ἀμφοτέρω καὶ μάλα εὐδοκιμεῖτον δι᾽ ἡμᾶς. εἰ δ᾽
ἐθέλεις λήρων μὲν καὶ φληνάφων τῶν παρὰ ταύτης ἀπέχεσθαι—
δείξασα τὴν ἑτέραν—ἕπεσθαι δὲ καὶ συνοικεῖν ἐμοί, πρῶτα μὲν
θρέψῃ γεννικῶς καὶ τοὺς ὤμους ἕξεις καρτερούς, φθόνου δὲ
παντὸς ἀλλότριος ἔσῃ· καὶ οὔποτε ἄπει ἐπὶ τὴν ἀλλοδαπήν, τὴν
πατρίδα καὶ τοὺς οἰκείους καταλιπών, οὐδὲ ἐπὶ λόγοις ἐπαινέσονταί σε πάντες.

Μὴ μυσαχθῇς δὲ τοῦ σώματος τὸ εὐτελὲς μηδὲ τῆς ἐσθῆτος τὸ 8
πιναρόν· ἀπὸ γὰρ τοιούτων ὁρμώμενος καὶ Φειδίας ἐκεῖνος ἔδειξε
τὸν Δία καὶ Πολύκλειτος τὴν Ἥραν εἰργάσατο καὶ Μύρων
ἐπῃνέθη καὶ Πραξιτέλης ἐθαυμάσθη. προσκυνοῦνται γοῦν οὗτοι
μετὰ τῶν θεῶν. εἰ δὴ τούτων εἷς γένοιο, πῶς μὲν οὐ κλεινὸς αὐτὸς
παρὰ πᾶσιν ἀνθρώποις γένοιο, ζηλωτὸν δὲ καὶ τὸν πατέρα
ἀποδείξεις, περίβλεπτον δὲ ἀποφανεῖς καὶ τὴν πατρίδα;

Ταῦτα καὶ ἔτι τούτων πλείονα, διαπταίουσα καὶ βαρβαρίζουσα
πάμπολλα, εἶπεν ἡ Τέχνη, μάλα δὴ σπουδῇ συνείρουσα καὶ
πείθειν με πειρωμένη, ἀλλ᾽ οὐκέτι μέμνημαι· τὰ πλεῖστα γὰρ
ἤδη μου τὴν μνήμην διέφυγεν.

Ἐπεὶ δ᾽ οὖν ἐπαύσατο, ἄρχεται ἡ ἑτέρα ὧδέ πως· 9

Ἐγὼ δέ, ὦ τέκνον, Παιδεία εἰμὶ ἤδη συνήθης σοι καὶ γνωρίμη,
εἰ καὶ μηδέπω εἰς τέλος μου πεπείρασαι. ἡλίκα μὲν οὖν τὰ
ἀγαθὰ ποριῇ λιθοξόος γενόμενος, αὕτη προείρηκεν· οὐδὲν γὰρ
ὅτι μὴ ἐργάτης ἔσῃ τῷ σώματι πονῶν κἂν τούτῳ τὴν ἅπασαν
ἐλπίδα τοῦ βίου τεθειμένος, ἀφανὴς μὲν αὐτὸς ὤν, ὀλίγα καὶ
ἀγεννῆ λαμβάνων, ταπεινὸς τὴν γνώμην, εὐτελὴς δὲ τὴν πρόοδον,
οὔτε φίλοις ἐπιδικάσιμος οὔτε ἐχθροῖς φοβερὸς οὔτε τοῖς πολίταις
ζηλωτός, ἀλλ᾽ αὐτὸ μόνον ἐργάτης καὶ τῶν ἐκ τοῦ πολλοῦ δήμου
εἷς, ἀεὶ τὸν προὔχοντα ὑποπτήσσων καὶ τὸν λέγειν δυνάμενον
θεραπεύων, λαγὼ βίον ζῶν καὶ τοῦ κρείττονος ἕρμαιον ὤν· εἰ
δὲ καὶ Φειδίας ἢ Πολύκλειτος γένοιο καὶ πολλὰ θαυμαστὰ ἐξεργάσαιο, τὴν μὲν τέχνην ἅπαντες ἐπαινέσονται, οὐκ ἔστι δὲ
ὅστις τῶν ἰδόντων, εἰ νοῦν ἔχοι, εὔξαιτ᾽ ἂν σοὶ ὅμοιος γενέσθαι·
οἷος γὰρ ἂν ᾖς, βάναυσος καὶ χειρῶναξ καὶ ἀποχειροβίωτος
νομισθήσῃ.

[7] The first to speak was the rough, masculine one, saying 'I, dear boy, am Sculpture, the craft you started learning yesterday, one of your own kind and related to you on your mother's side, for your grandfather' (at this point she mentioned the name of my mother's father) 'was a sculptor, as are both your uncles and thanks to us they enjoy an excellent reputation. But if you are prepared to keep clear of *her* nonsense and rubbish' – now she pointed to the other woman – 'and to follow *me* and live with *me*, you'll be fed like a lord, have sturdy shoulders and never know envy; you'll never have to go abroad, leaving country and family, but you'll still be praised by everyone and not just for your words.

[8] 'And don't be revolted by the coarseness of my bodily appearance or the squalor of my clothes. For starting from equally humble beginnings the great Phidias revealed his Zeus to the world, Polyclitus fashioned his Hera, Myron won acclaim and Praxiteles admiration. Indeed they are worshipped along with the gods they sculpted. Should you become one of their company, wouldn't you too be famed amongst mankind, making your father the envy of all and your native city celebrated?'

This and still more was what the Craft said, with much stuttering and bad grammar, stringing her words together very fast in her efforts to persuade me, but I no longer remember too well, for most of her words have now escaped my memory.

[9] But when she stopped, the other began after this fashion: 'I, child, am Education and already familiar and well known to you, even if you haven't yet full experience of me. What benefits you'll gain by becoming a stone-mason, she has already told you. For you'll be nothing but a workman, toiling with your body, with all your hopes of livelihood vested in that, insignificant as a person, earning a meagre and mean income, with a lowly mentality, cutting a cheap figure in public, one whose support isn't sought by friends, causing enemies no fear and fellow citizens no envy, but purely and simply a workman and one of the common mob, cringing before the distinguished, courting the articulate, living a dog's life at the mercy of your superiors. Even if you should turn out a Phidias or a Polyclitus and complete many wonderful works, though everyone will praise your craftsmanship, nobody who sees you, if he had any sense, would want to be like you. For regardless of your qualities you'll be considered a working class artisan who lives by manual labour.

Ἢν δ' ἐμοὶ πείθῃ, πρῶτον μέν σοι πολλὰ ἐπιδείξω παλαιῶν 10
ἀνδρῶν ἔργα καὶ πράξεις θαυμαστὰς καὶ λόγους αὐτῶν ἀπαγγελῶ,
καὶ πάντων ὡς εἰπεῖν ἔμπειρον ἀποφανῶ, καὶ τὴν ψυχήν, ὅπερ
σου κυριώτατόν ἐστι, κατακοσμήσω πολλοῖς καὶ ἀγαθοῖς κοσμή-
μασι—σωφροσύνῃ, δικαιοσύνῃ, εὐσεβείᾳ, πραότητι, ἐπιεικείᾳ,
συνέσει, καρτερίᾳ, τῷ τῶν καλῶν ἔρωτι, τῇ πρὸς τὰ σεμνότατα
ὁρμῇ· ταῦτα γάρ ἐστιν ὁ τῆς ψυχῆς ἀκήρατος ὡς ἀληθῶς κόσμος.
λήσει δέ σε οὔτε παλαιὸν οὐδὲν οὔτε νῦν γενέσθαι δέον, ἀλλὰ καὶ
τὰ μέλλοντα προόψει μετ' ἐμοῦ, καὶ ὅλως ἅπαντα ὁπόσα ἐστί,
τά τε θεῖα τά τ' ἀνθρώπινα, οὐκ εἰς μακράν σε διδάξομαι.

Καὶ ὁ νῦν πένης ὁ τοῦ δεῖνος, ὁ βουλευσάμενός τι περὶ ἀγεννοῦς 11
οὕτω τέχνης, μετ' ὀλίγον ἅπασι ζηλωτὸς καὶ ἐπίφθονος ἔσῃ,
τιμώμενος καὶ ἐπαινούμενος καὶ ἐπὶ τοῖς ἀρίστοις εὐδοκιμῶν καὶ
ὑπὸ τῶν γένει καὶ πλούτῳ προὐχόντων ἀποβλεπόμενος, ἐσθῆτα
μὲν τοιαύτην ἀμπεχόμενος—δείξασα τὴν ἑαυτῆς· πάνυ δὲ
λαμπρὰν ἐφόρει—ἀρχῆς δὲ καὶ προεδρίας ἀξιούμενος. κἄν που
ἀποδημῇς, οὐδ' ἐπὶ τῆς ἀλλοδαπῆς ἀγνὼς οὐδ' ἀφανὴς ἔσῃ· τοι-
αὐτά σοι περιθήσω τὰ γνωρίσματα ὥστε τῶν ὁρώντων ἕκαστος
τὸν πλησίον κινήσας δείξει σε τῷ δακτύλῳ, Οὗτος ἐκεῖνος, λέγων.
ἂν δέ τι σπουδῆς ἄξιον ἢ τοὺς φίλους ἢ καὶ τὴν πόλιν ὅλην κατα- 12
λαμβάνῃ, εἰς σὲ πάντες ἀποβλέψονται· κἄν πού τι λέγων τύχῃς,
κεχηνότες οἱ πολλοὶ ἀκούσονται, θαυμάζοντες καὶ εὐδαιμονίζοντές
σε τῆς δυνάμεως τῶν λόγων καὶ τὸν πατέρα τῆς εὐποτμίας. ὃ δὲ
λέγουσιν, ὡς ἄρα καὶ ἀθάνατοι γίγνονταί τινες ἐξ ἀνθρώπων,
τοῦτό σοι περιποιήσω· καὶ γὰρ ἢν αὐτὸς ἐκ τοῦ βίου ἀπέλθῃς,
οὔποτε παύσῃ συνὼν τοῖς πεπαιδευμένοις καὶ προσομιλῶν τοῖς
ἀρίστοις. ὁρᾷς τὸν Δημοσθένην ἐκεῖνον, τίνος υἱὸν ὄντα ἐγὼ
ἡλίκον ἐποίησα. ὁρᾷς τὸν Αἰσχίνην, ὡς τυμπανιστρίας υἱὸς ἦν,
ἀλλ' ὅμως αὐτὸν δι' ἐμὲ Φίλιππος ἐθεράπευεν. ὁ δὲ Σωκράτης
καὶ αὐτὸς ὑπὸ τῇ Ἑρμογλυφικῇ ταύτῃ τραφείς, ἐπειδὴ τάχιστα
συνῆκεν τοῦ κρείττονος καὶ δραπετεύσας παρ' αὐτῆς ηὐτομόλησεν
ὡς ἐμέ, ἀκούεις ὡς παρὰ πάντων ᾄδεται.

Ἀφεὶς δὲ αὖ τοὺς τηλικούτους καὶ τοιούτους ἄνδρας καὶ πράξεις 13
λαμπρὰς καὶ λόγους σεμνοὺς καὶ σχῆμα εὐπρεπὲς καὶ τιμὴν
καὶ δόξαν καὶ ἔπαινον καὶ προεδρίας καὶ δύναμιν καὶ ἀρχὰς
καὶ τὸ ἐπὶ λόγοις εὐδοκιμεῖν καὶ τὸ ἐπὶ συνέσει εὐδαιμονίζεσθαι,
χιτώνιόν τι πιναρὸν ἐνδύσῃ καὶ σχῆμα δουλοπρεπὲς ἀναλήψῃ

[10] 'But if you listen to me, I'll show you many works of men of old, and tell you of their wonderful deeds and words, making you expert in almost everything, and I'll embellish your soul, your most vital part, with many fine graces – self-control, justice, piety, gentleness, decency, intelligence, fortitude, love of beauty and an impulse towards the sublime. For these are the things which bring truly perfect beauty to the soul. Nothing will be hidden to you either from the distant past or of what needs to be done for the present, but with my help you'll foresee the future; in short I'll soon teach you about everything under the sun, whether relating to the gods or to men.

[11] 'And you, who at present are the impoverished son of a nobody and have been giving thought to so ignoble a craft, will before long be admired and envied by all, honoured, praised and esteemed for what's best, the focus of attention from men of outstanding birth or wealth, wearing clothes as fine as *these*' – here she showed me the clothes she wore which were quite magnificent – 'and given posts of authority and the best seats everywhere. And if you travel from home, you'll be recognised and acclaimed even on foreign soil; for I'll give you such marks of distinction that everyone who sees you will nudge his neighbour, point to you and say "Look, there's the great man."

[12] 'And if any serious problem overtakes your friends or your whole city, everyone will look to you. Whenever and wherever you speak well, the majority of men will listen to you in open-mouthed admiration, thinking you lucky to be so eloquent and your father fortunate to be blessed with such a son. They say that some become immortal from human beginnings; well, I'll do that for you. For even when you leave this life, you'll never stop being with men of culture and talking to the best of men. You can see what sort of a father the great Demosthenes had, and how great I made him. You can see how Aeschines was the son of a woman who played the tambourine but how in spite of that he was courted by Philip thanks to *me*. The great Socrates too was brought up under Sculpture here, but you've heard how his praises have been sung by all, once he gained understanding of what's better and ran away from her and came over to *my* ranks.

[13] 'You *may* reject men of such greatness and quality, glorious deeds, august discourses, magnificent appearance, honour, glory, praise, privileged positions, power, offices, a reputation for eloquence and admiration for intelligence; but that'll mean wearing a filthy slip, looking like a slave and handling crowbars, gravers, chipping tools and chisels,

καὶ μοχλία καὶ γλυφεῖα καὶ κοπέας καὶ κολαπτῆρας ἐν ταῖν
χεροῖν ἕξεις κάτω νενευκὼς εἰς τὸ ἔργον, χαμαιπετὴς καὶ
χαμαίζηλος καὶ πάντα τρόπον ταπεινός, ἀνακύπτων δὲ οὐδέποτε
οὐδὲ ἀνδρῶδες οὐδὲ ἐλεύθερον οὐδὲν ἐπινοῶν, ἀλλὰ τὰ μὲν ἔργα
ὅπως εὔρυθμα καὶ εὐσχήμονα ἔσται σοι προνοῶν, ὅπως δὲ αὐτὸς
εὔρυθμός τε καὶ κόσμιος ἔσῃ, ἥκιστα πεφροντικώς, ἀλλ᾽ ἀτιμό-
τερον ποιῶν σεαυτὸν λίθων.

Ταῦτα ἔτι λεγούσης αὐτῆς οὐ περιμείνας ἐγὼ τὸ τέλος τῶν 14
λόγων ἀναστὰς ἀπεφηνάμην, καὶ τὴν ἄμορφον ἐκείνην καὶ
ἐργατικὴν ἀπολιπὼν μετέβαινον πρὸς τὴν Παιδείαν μάλα γε-
γηθώς, καὶ μάλιστα ἐπεί μοι καὶ εἰς νοῦν ἦλθεν ἡ σκυτάλη καὶ
ὅτι πληγὰς εὐθὺς οὐκ ὀλίγας ἀρχομένῳ μοι χθὲς ἐνετρίψατο.
ἡ δὲ ἀπολειφθεῖσα τὸ μὲν πρῶτον ἠγανάκτει καὶ τὼ χεῖρε συν-
εκρότει καὶ τοὺς ὀδόντας συνέπριε· τέλος δέ, ὥσπερ τὴν Νιόβην
ἀκούομεν, ἐπεπήγει καὶ εἰς λίθον μετεβέβλητο. εἰ δὲ παράδοξα
ἔπαθεν, μὴ ἀπιστήσητε· θαυματοποιοὶ γὰρ οἱ ὄνειροι.

Ἡ ἑτέρα δὲ πρός με ἀπιδοῦσα, Τοιγαροῦν ἀμείψομαί σε, ἔφη, 15
τῆσδε τῆς δικαιοσύνης, ὅτι καλῶς τὴν δίκην ἐδίκασας, καὶ ἐλθὲ
ἤδη, ἐπίβηθι τούτου τοῦ ὀχήματος—δείξασά τι ὄχημα ὑποπτέρων
ἵππων τινῶν τῷ Πηγάσῳ ἐοικότων—ὅπως ἴδῃς *οἷα καὶ ἡλίκα
μὴ ἀκολουθήσας ἐμοὶ ἀγνοήσειν ἔμελλες.

Ἐπεὶ δὲ ἀνῆλθον, ἡ μὲν ἤλαυνε καὶ ὑφηνιόχει, ἀρθεὶς δὲ εἰς
ὕψος ἐγὼ ἐπεσκόπουν ἀπὸ τῆς ἕω ἀρξάμενος ἄχρι πρὸς τὰ
ἑσπέρια πόλεις καὶ ἔθνη καὶ δήμους, καθάπερ ὁ Τριπτόλεμος
ἀποσπείρων τι εἰς τὴν γῆν. οὐκέτι μέντοι μέμνημαι ὅ τι τὸ
σπειρόμενον ἐκεῖνο ἦν, πλὴν τοῦτο μόνον ὅτι κάτωθεν ἀφορῶντες
ἄνθρωποι ἐπήνουν καὶ μετ᾽ εὐφημίας καθ᾽ οὓς γενοίμην τῇ
πτήσει παρέπεμπον. δείξασα δέ μοι τὰ τοσαῦτα κἀμὲ τοῖς 16
ἐπαινοῦσιν ἐκείνοις ἐπανήγαγεν αὖθις, οὐκέτι τὴν αὐτὴν ἐσθῆτα
ἐκείνην ἐνδεδυκότα ἣν εἶχον ἀφιπτάμενος, ἀλλ᾽ ἐμοὶ ἐδόκουν
εὐπάρυφός τις ἐπανήκειν. καταλαβοῦσα οὖν καὶ τὸν πατέρα
ἑστῶτα καὶ περιμένοντα ἐδείκνυεν αὐτῷ ἐκείνην τὴν ἐσθῆτα
κἀμέ, οἷος ἥκοιμι, καί τι καὶ ὑπέμνησεν οἷα μικροῦ δεῖν περὶ
ἐμοῦ ἐβουλεύσαντο.

Ταῦτα μέμνημαι ἰδὼν ἀντίπαις ἔτι ὤν, ἐμοὶ δοκεῖν ἐκταρα-
χθεὶς πρὸς τὸν τῶν πληγῶν φόβον.

bent down over your work, a groundling in body and mind, and humble in every way, never looking up, with never a single manly or noble idea in your head; but for all your care for your work being well proportioned and shapely, you'll pay very little attention to ensuring your own life is harmonious and orderly, but make yourself of less account than the stones you work.'

[14] That was what she had to say, but I didn't wait for her to finish, for I got up and gave my decision by going away from that ugly, workaday creature and crossing over to Education with great joy, particularly when I thought of the stick and how the previous day at the very outset of my efforts it had inflicted so many blows on me. On being deserted by me Sculpture was angry at first, wringing her hands and gnashing her teeth, but in the end, just like Niobe in the story, she stiffened up and turned to stone. What happened to her *was* surprising, but you musn't doubt my word, for dreams can work miracles.

[15] Then Education looked straight at me and said 'Well I'll reward you for your justice in coming to the right decision. Come now, step on this chariot' – she showed me a chariot drawn by winged horses like Pegasus – 'so that you can see what fine and great things you'd have missed by not following me.'

After I climbed in, she drove off with the reins in her hands; I was carried up high into the skies and started looking from the east and going all the way round to the west, seeing cities, nations and peoples, and dropping seeds down on the earth like Triptolemus, though I no longer remember what sort of seeds they were, but only that men looked up from below praising me and all those I was over in my flight sent me on my way with blessings.

[16] After she had shown all this to me and me to those who had been praising me, she brought me back home, no longer wearing the same clothes as when I flew away, but I saw myself returning dressed like an aristocrat. Well, she found my father standing waiting and showed him those clothes of mine and what a fine figure I now cut, and also gave him a gentle reminder of the decision they had almost taken about me.

This is the vision I remember having when I was still little more than a boy, the result, I suppose, of my panic from the fright the thrashing had given me.

Μεταξὺ δὲ λέγοντος, Ἡράκλεις, ἔφη τις, ὡς μακρὸν τὸ ἐν- 17
ύπνιον καὶ δικανικόν.

Εἶτ᾽ ἄλλος ὑπέκρουσε, Χειμερινὸς ὄνειρος, ὅτε μήκισταί εἰσιν
αἱ νύκτες, ἢ τάχα που τριέσπερος, ὥσπερ ὁ Ἡρακλῆς* καὶ αὐτός
ἐστι. τί δ᾽ οὖν ἐπῆλθεν αὐτῷ ληρῆσαι ταῦτα πρὸς ἡμᾶς καὶ
μνησθῆναι παιδικῆς νυκτὸς καὶ ὀνείρων παλαιῶν καὶ γεγηρα-
κότων; ἕωλος γὰρ ἡ ψυχρολογία. μὴ ὀνείρων τινὰς ὑποκριτὰς
ἡμᾶς ὑπείληφεν;

Οὔκ, ὦγαθέ· οὐδὲ γὰρ ὁ Ξενοφῶν ποτε διηγούμενος τὸ ἐνύπνιον,
ὡς ἐδόκει αὐτῷ καίεσθαι ἡ πατρῴα οἰκία καὶ τὰ ἄλλα—ἴστε
γάρ—οὐχ ὑπόκρισιν τὴν ὄψιν οὐδ᾽ ὡς φλυαρεῖν ἐγνωκὼς αὐτὰ
διεξῄει, καὶ ταῦτα ἐν πολέμῳ καὶ ἀπογνώσει πραγμάτων, περιεστώτων πολεμίων, ἀλλά τι καὶ χρήσιμον εἶχεν ἡ διήγησις.

Καὶ τοίνυν κἀγὼ τοῦτον <τὸν> ὄνειρον ὑμῖν διηγησάμην 18
ἐκείνου ἕνεκα, ὅπως οἱ νέοι πρὸς τὰ βελτίω τρέπωνται καὶ παιδείας ἔχωνται, καὶ μάλιστα εἴ τις αὐτῶν ὑπὸ πενίας ἐθελοκακεῖ
καὶ πρὸς τὴν ἥττω ἀποκλίνει, φύσιν οὐκ ἀγεννῆ διαφθείρων.
ἐπιρρωσθήσεται εὖ οἶδ᾽ ὅτι κἀκεῖνος ἀκούσας τοῦ μύθου, ἱκανὸν
ἑαυτῷ παράδειγμα ἐμὲ προστησάμενος, ἐννοῶν οἷος μὲν ὢν πρὸς
τὰ κάλλιστα ὥρμησα καὶ παιδείας ἐπεθύμησα, μηδὲν ἀποδει-
λιάσας πρὸς τὴν πενίαν τὴν τότε, οἷος δὲ πρὸς ὑμᾶς ἐπανελήλυθα,
εἰ καὶ μηδὲν ἄλλο, οὐδενὸς γοῦν τῶν λιθογλύφων ἀδοξότερος.

[17] But while I've been speaking, someone has been saying 'By Heracles, what a long-winded dream! It's as tedious as what you hear in the court-room!' And now someone else has interrupted to say 'It's a dream for wintertime, when nights are longest, or perhaps a three night job, just like Heracles. Why did it come into his head to tell us this rubbish and recall a night from his boyhood and antique dreams from the distant past? What hackneyed dreary stuff! Does he take us for interpreters of dreams?'

Certainly not, my good fellow. For when Xenophon described his dream, telling how he saw his father's house burning and everything else – you know the passage – he didn't narrate his vision to have it interpreted or give the details because he had decided to engage in idle chatter, particularly as it was wartime and a desperate situation with enemies all around. No, what he had to tell served a useful purpose.

[18] Well, I also had a purpose in describing this dream to you. It is so that young men may turn to the better alternative and hold fast to Education, especially if any of them is faint-hearted through poverty and deviates to the worse path, wasting the fine gifts given him by nature. He'll be encouraged, I'm sure, by hearing my story and taking me as a good example for himself, if he considers what I was like when I set out in pursuit of all that's best and set my heart on Education, without flinching in the face of my poverty of the time, and what I'm like now on my return to you; for, if nothing else, at least I'm as distinguished as any sculptor.

ΘΕΩΝ ΚΡΙΣΙΣ

ΖΕΥΣ

Ἑρμῆ, λαβὼν τουτὶ τὸ μῆλον ἄπιθι εἰς τὴν Φρυγίαν παρὰ τὸν 1
Πριάμου παῖδα τὸν βουκόλον—νέμει δὲ τῆς Ἴδης ἐν τῷ Γαργάρῳ
—καὶ λέγε πρὸς αὐτόν ὅτι Σέ, ὦ Πάρι, κελεύει ὁ Ζεύς, ἐπειδὴ
καλός τε αὐτὸς εἶ καὶ σοφὸς τὰ ἐρωτικά, δικάσαι ταῖς θεαῖς,
ἥτις αὐτῶν ἡ καλλίστη ἐστίν· τοῦ δὲ ἀγῶνος τὸ ἆθλον ἡ νικῶσα
λαβέτω τὸ μῆλον.

Ὥρα δὲ ἤδη καὶ ὑμῖν αὐταῖς ἀπιέναι παρὰ τὸν δικαστήν· ἐγὼ
γὰρ ἀπωθοῦμαι τὴν δίαιταν ἐπ᾽ ἴσης τε ὑμᾶς ἀγαπῶν, καὶ εἴ γε
οἷόν τε ἦν, ἡδέως ἂν ἁπάσας νενικηκυίας ἰδών. ἄλλως τε καὶ
ἀνάγκη, μιᾷ τὸ καλλιστεῖον ἀποδόντα πάντως ἀπεχθάνεσθαι ταῖς
πλείοσιν. διὰ ταῦτα αὐτὸς μὲν οὐκ ἐπιτήδειος ὑμῖν δικαστής, ὁ δὲ
νεανίας οὗτος ὁ Φρὺξ ἐφ᾽ ὃν ἄπιτε βασιλικὸς μέν ἐστι καὶ
Γανυμήδους τουτουὶ συγγενής, τὰ ἄλλα δὲ ἀφελὴς καὶ ὄρειος,
κοὐκ ἄν τις αὐτὸν ἀπαξιώσαι τοιαύτης θέας.

ΑΦΡΟΔΙΤΗ

Ἐγὼ μέν, ὦ Ζεῦ, εἰ καὶ τὸν Μῶμον αὐτὸν ἐπιστήσειας ἡμῖν 2
δικαστήν, θαρροῦσα βαδιοῦμαι πρὸς τὴν ἐπίδειξιν· τί γὰρ ἂν
καὶ μωμήσαιτό μου; χρὴ δὲ καὶ ταύταις ἀρέσκειν τὸν ἄνθρωπον.

ΗΡΑ

Οὐδ᾽ ἡμεῖς, ὦ Ἀφροδίτη, δεδίαμεν οὐδ᾽ ἂν ὁ Ἄρης ὁ σὸς ἐπι-
τραπῇ τὴν δίαιταν· ἀλλὰ δεχόμεθα καὶ τοῦτον, ὅστις ἂν ᾖ, τὸν
Πάριν.

ΖΕΥΣ

Ἦ καὶ σοὶ ταῦτα, ὦ θύγατερ, συνδοκεῖ; τί φῄς; ἀποστρέφῃ
καὶ ἐρυθριᾷς; ἔστι μὲν ἴδιον τὸ αἰδεῖσθαι τά γε τοιαῦτα ὑμῶν τῶν
παρθένων· ἐπινεύεις δ᾽ ὅμως. ἄπιτε οὖν καὶ ὅπως μὴ χαλεπήνητε
τῷ δικαστῇ αἱ νενικημέναι μηδὲ κακὸν ἐντρίψησθε τῷ νεανίσκῳ·
οὐ γὰρ οἷόν τε ἐπ᾽ ἴσης πάσας εἶναι καλάς.

THE JUDGING OF THE GODDESSES

ZEUS

[1] Hermes, take this apple and be off with you to Priam's son, the cowherd, in Phrygia – he's pasturing his herd on Gargaron on Mt. Ida – and say to him 'Paris, Zeus commands you, being good-looking yourself and clever about sex, to judge for the goddesses and decide which of them is the most beautiful. The prize for the competition is the apple and the winner is to take it.

(*To the three goddesses*) Now it's time for you yourselves to be off to your judge; for *I* refuse to adjudicate, because I love you all equally, and, if it were possible, I'd gladly have seen you *all* victorious. Besides, after awarding the prize for beauty to one of you, the judge must inevitably be unpopular with the other two. So I myself am not a proper judge for you, but this young Phrygian, to whom you are going, is a prince and related to Ganymede here, and apart from all that he is unsophisticated and countrified and nobody would think him undeserving of such a feast for the eyes.

APHRODITE

[2] Personally, Zeus, even if you should appoint Momus himself as our judge, *I* shall present myself for inspection with complete confidence. For what feature of *mine* could he criticise? But the human must be acceptable to these ladies as well.

HERA

We're not afraid either, Aphrodite, even if your Ares is entrusted with the arbitration. No, we accept this fellow, whoever he is, this Paris.

ZEUS

(*To Athene*) And what about *you*, daughter? Are *you* satisfied? What do *you* have to say about it? What, turning away and blushing? It's only natural for you unmarried girls to be shy about such things, but all the same I see you nod your consent. So be off with you and don't the two of you that are beaten be angry with the judge or inflict any harm on the lad. You can't all be equally beautiful.

ΕΡΜΗΣ

Προΐωμεν εὐθὺ τῆς Φρυγίας, ἐγὼ μὲν ἡγούμενος, ὑμεῖς δὲ μὴ 3
βραδέως ἀκολουθεῖτέ μοι καὶ θαρρεῖτε. οἶδα ἐγὼ τὸν Πάριν.
νεανίας ἐστὶ καλὸς καὶ τἆλλα ἐρωτικὸς καὶ τὰ τοιαῦτα κρίνειν
ἱκανώτατος. οὐκ ἂν ἐκεῖνος δικάσειεν κακῶς.

ΑΦΡΟΔΙΤΗ

Τοῦτο μὲν ἅπαν ἀγαθὸν καὶ πρὸς ἐμοῦ λέγεις, τὸ δίκαιον εἶναι
τὸν δικαστήν· πότερα δὲ ἄγαμός ἐστιν οὗτος ἢ καὶ γυνή τις
αὐτῷ σύνεστιν;

ΕΡΜΗΣ

Οὐ παντελῶς ἄγαμος, ὦ Ἀφροδίτη.

ΑΦΡΟΔΙΤΗ

Πῶς λέγεις;

ΕΡΜΗΣ

Δοκεῖ τις αὐτῷ συνοικεῖν Ἰδαία γυνή, ἱκανὴ μέν, ἄγροικος δὲ
καὶ δεινῶς ὄρειος, ἀλλ᾽ οὐ σφόδρα προσέχειν αὐτῇ ἔοικε. τίνος
δ᾽ οὖν ἕνεκα ταῦτα ἐρωτᾷς;

ΑΦΡΟΔΙΤΗ

Ἄλλως ἠρόμην.

ΑΘΗΝΑ

Παραπρεσβεύεις, ὦ οὗτος, ἰδίᾳ πάλαι ταύτῃ κοινολογούμενος. 4

ΕΡΜΗΣ

Οὐδέν, ὦ Ἀθηνᾶ, δεινὸν οὐδὲ καθ᾽ ὑμῶν, ἀλλ᾽ ἤρετό με εἰ
ἄγαμος ὁ Πάρις ἐστίν.

ΑΘΗΝΑ

Ὡς δὴ τί τοῦτο πολυπραγμονοῦσα;

ΕΡΜΗΣ

Οὐκ οἶδα· φησὶ δ᾽ οὖν ὅτι ἄλλως ἐπελθόν, οὐκ ἐξεπίτηδες
ἤρετο.

ΑΘΗΝΑ

Τί οὖν; ἄγαμός ἐστιν;

HERMES

[3] Let's make straight for Phrygia with me leading and you follow me without dawdling and don't be nervous. I know Paris. He's a good-looking young man and besides he's passionate and ideally suited to judging such matters. *He* couldn't get his verdict wrong.

APHRODITE

What you say is all to the good and in my favour, that our judge is fair. But is he a bachelor or does he have a wife living with him?

HERMES

He's not entirely a bachelor.

APHRODITE

How do you mean?

HERMES

It appears he has a woman of Ida living with him, adequate enough but rustic and terribly countrified, but he doesn't seem to pay a great deal of attention to her. But why do you ask?

APHRODITE

It was just an idle question.

ATHENA

[4] (*To Hermes*) It's official misconduct, my lad, to have a long private conversation with *her* (*pointing to Aphrodite*).

HERMES

It was nothing terrible, Athena, or directed against you. She merely asked me if Paris is a bachelor.

ATHENA

Why did she poke her nose into that?

HERMES

I don't know. In any case she says the question just came into her head for no particular reason.

ATHENA

Well then? Is he a bachelor?

ΕΡΜΗΣ

Οὐ δοκεῖ.

ΑΘΗΝΑ

Τί δέ; τῶν πολεμικῶν ἐστιν αὐτῷ ἐπιθυμία καὶ φιλόδοξός τις, ἢ τὸ πᾶν βουκόλος;

ΕΡΜΗΣ

Τὸ μὲν ἀληθὲς οὐκ ἔχω λέγειν, εἰκάζειν δὲ χρὴ νέον ὄντα καὶ τούτων ὀρέγεσθαι τυχεῖν καὶ βούλεσθαι ἂν πρῶτον αὐτὸν εἶναι κατὰ τὰς μάχας.

ΑΦΡΟΔΙΤΗ

Ὁρᾷς; οὐδὲν ἐγὼ μέμφομαι οὐδὲ προσεγκαλῶ σοι τὸ πρὸς ταύτην ἰδίᾳ λαλεῖν· μεμψιμοίρων γὰρ καὶ οὐκ Ἀφροδίτης τὰ τοιαῦτα.

ΕΡΜΗΣ

Καὶ αὕτη σχεδὸν τὰ αὐτά με ἤρετο· διὸ μὴ χαλεπῶς ἔχε μηδ' οἴου μειονεκτεῖν, εἴ τι καὶ ταύτῃ κατὰ τὸ ἁπλοῦν ἀπεκρινάμην. ἀλλὰ μεταξὺ λόγων ἤδη πολὺ προϊόντες ἀπεσπάσαμεν τῶν ἀστέρων καὶ σχεδόν γε κατὰ τὴν Φρυγίαν ἐσμέν. ἐγὼ δὲ καὶ τὴν Ἴδην ὁρῶ καὶ τὸ Γάργαρον ὅλον ἀκριβῶς, εἰ δὲ μὴ ἐξαπατῶμαι, καὶ αὐτὸν ὑμῶν τὸν δικαστὴν τὸν Πάριν. 5

ΗΡΑ

Ποῦ δέ ἐστιν; οὐ γὰρ κἀμοὶ φαίνεται.

ΕΡΜΗΣ

Ταύτῃ, ὦ Ἥρα, πρὸς τὰ λαιὰ περισκόπει, μὴ πρὸς ἄκρῳ τῷ ὄρει, παρὰ δὲ τὴν πλευράν, οὗ τὸ ἄντρον, ἔνθα καὶ τὴν ἀγέλην ὁρᾷς.

ΗΡΑ

Ἀλλ' οὐχ ὁρῶ τὴν ἀγέλην.

ΕΡΜΗΣ

Τί φής; οὐχ ὁρᾷς βοΐδια κατὰ τὸν ἐμὸν οὑτωσὶ δάκτυλον ἐκ μέσων τῶν πετρῶν προερχόμενα καί τινα τοῦ σκοπέλου καταθέοντα καλαύροπα ἔχοντα καὶ ἀνείργοντα μὴ πρόσω διασκίδνασθαι τὴν ἀγέλην;

HERMES

Apparently not.

ATHENA

Well, tell me, is he keen on war and eager for glory or is he one hundred per cent herdsman?

HERMES

I can't say for certain, but I must imagine that being young he does have aspirations in that direction and wants to distinguish himself in battle.

APHRODITE

(*To Hermes*) Do you see? I don't criticise *you* or accuse *you* of having a private conversation with *her* (*pointing to Athena*). These are the ways of fault-finders and not of Aphrodite.

HERMES

(*To Aphrodite*) She asked me almost the same question you did. So don't be angry or think you're being hard done by, if I've given her a straightforward answer just as I've done to you.

[5] But while we've been talking, we've already come a long way and left the stars behind and are almost at Phrygia. I can see Ida and all of Gargaron clearly and, if I'm not mistaken, your judge himself, Paris.

HERA

Where is he? I can't see him.

HERMES

Look over there, Hera, to your left, not on the top of the mountain but on its side, where the cave is, where you can see the herd as well.

HERA

But I don't see the herd.

HERMES

What's that you say? Don't you see the tiny little cows – follow my finger, that's right – coming out of the middle of the rocks and someone running down from the cliff holding a crook and stopping the herd from scattering far and wide?

HPA

Ὁρῶ νῦν, εἴ γε ἐκεῖνός ἐστιν.

ΕΡΜΗΣ

Ἀλλὰ ἐκεῖνος. ἐπειδὴ δὲ πλησίον ἤδη ἐσμέν, ἐπὶ τῆς γῆς, εἰ δοκεῖ, καταστάντες βαδίζωμεν, ἵνα μὴ διαταράξωμεν αὐτὸν ἄνωθεν ἐξ ἀφανοῦς καθιπτάμενοι.

HPA

Εὖ λέγεις, καὶ οὕτω ποιῶμεν. ἐπεὶ δὲ καταβεβήκαμεν, ὥρα σοί, ὦ Ἀφροδίτη, προϊέναι καὶ ἡγεῖσθαι ἡμῖν τῆς ὁδοῦ· σὺ γὰρ ὡς τὸ εἰκὸς ἔμπειρος εἶ τοῦ χωρίου πολλάκις, ὡς λόγος, κατελθοῦσα πρὸς Ἀγχίσην.

ΑΦΡΟΔΙΤΗ

Οὐ σφόδρα, ὦ Ἥρα, τούτοις ἄχθομαι τοῖς σκώμμασιν.

ΕΡΜΗΣ

Ἀλλ᾽ οὖν ἐγὼ ὑμῖν ἡγήσομαι· καὶ γὰρ αὐτὸς ἐνδιέτριψα τῇ 6 Ἴδῃ, ὁπότε ὁ Ζεὺς ἤρα τοῦ μειρακίου τοῦ Φρυγός, καὶ πολλάκις δεῦρο ἦλθον ὑπ᾽ ἐκείνου καταπεμφθεὶς ἐς ἐπισκοπὴν τοῦ παιδός. καὶ ὁπότε γε ἤδη ἐν τῷ ἀετῷ ἦν, συμπαριπτάμην αὐτῷ καὶ συνεκούφιζον τὸν καλόν, καὶ εἴ γε μέμνημαι, ἀπὸ ταυτησὶ τῆς πέτρας αὐτὸν ἀνήρπασεν. ὁ μὲν γὰρ ἔτυχε τότε συρίζων πρὸς τὸ ποίμνιον, καταπτάμενος δὲ ὄπιθεν αὐτοῦ ὁ Ζεὺς κούφως μάλα τοῖς ὄνυξι περιβαλὼν καὶ τῷ στόματι τὴν ἐπὶ τῇ κεφαλῇ τιάραν δακὼν ἀνέφερε τὸν παῖδα τεταραγμένον καὶ τῷ τραχήλῳ ἀπεστραμμένῳ εἰς αὐτὸν ἀποβλέποντα. τότε οὖν ἐγὼ τὴν σύριγγα λαβών, ἀποβεβλήκει γὰρ αὐτὴν ὑπὸ τοῦ δέους—ἀλλὰ γὰρ ὁ διαιτητὴς οὑτοσὶ πλησίον, ὥστε προσείπωμεν αὐτόν. Χαῖρε, ὦ 7 βουκόλε.

ΠΑΡΙΣ

Νὴ καὶ σύ γε, ὦ νεανίσκε. τίς δὲ ὢν δεῦρο ἀφῖξαι πρὸς ἡμᾶς; ἢ τίνας ταύτας ἄγεις τὰς γυναῖκας; οὐ γὰρ ἐπιτήδειαι ὀρεοπολεῖν, οὕτως γε οὖσαι καλαί.

HERA

I see now, if that's him.

HERMES

Yes, it is. But now that we're near, let's put our feet on the ground, if you don't mind, and walk on, so that we don't frighten him by flying down suddenly from above.

HERA

Quite right. Let's do so. And now we're down, it's time for you, Aphrodite, to go ahead and lead the way. For you probably knew the area well, since, by all accounts, you often came down to visit Anchises.

APHRODITE

These jibes of yours, Hera, don't upset me all that much.

HERMES

[6] Well, *I'll* lead the way. For I spent some time on Ida myself, when Zeus was in love with the Phrygian lad, and I often came here, when I was sent down by him to keep an eye on the boy. And when Zeus had now become the eagle, I flew alongside him and helped him to carry the beautiful creature and, if I remember right, this is the rock from which he snatched him up into the sky. For he was giving his herd a tune on his pipe at the time, but Zeus flew down behind him, caught him ever so gently in his talons and, biting into the turban on his head with his beak, carried the boy off up. He was scared stiff and kept straining his neck to stare at the eagle. So then I picked his pipe up, for he had dropped it in his fright – but here is the umpire close at hand, so let's talk to him. Good day, herdsman.

PARIS

[7] And the same to you, young fellow. But who are you that have come to visit us? And who are these women you have with you? For they're much too beautiful to be wandering the mountains.

ΕΡΜΗΣ

Ἀλλ' οὐ γυναῖκές εἰσιν, Ἥραν δέ, ὦ Πάρι, καὶ Ἀθηνᾶν καὶ
Ἀφροδίτην ὁρᾷς· κἀμὲ τὸν Ἑρμῆν ἀπέστειλεν ὁ Ζεύς—ἀλλὰ τί
τρέμεις καὶ ὠχριᾷς; μὴ δέδιθι· χαλεπὸν γὰρ οὐδέν. κελεύει δέ σε
δικαστὴν γενέσθαι τοῦ κάλλους αὐτῶν· Ἐπεὶ γάρ, φησί, καλός τε
αὐτὸς εἶ καὶ σοφὸς τὰ ἐρωτικά, σοὶ τὴν γνῶσιν ἐπιτρέπω. τοῦ
δὲ ἀγῶνος τὸ ἆθλον εἴσῃ ἀναγνοὺς τὸ μῆλον.

ΠΑΡΙΣ

Φέρ' ἴδω τί καὶ βούλεται. Ἡ καλή, φησίν, λαβέτω. πῶς
ἂν οὖν, ὦ δέσποτα Ἑρμῆ, δυνηθείην ἐγὼ θνητὸς αὐτὸς καὶ
ἄγροικος ὢν δικαστὴς γενέσθαι παραδόξου θέας καὶ μείζονος ἢ
κατὰ βουκόλον; τὰ γὰρ τοιαῦτα κρίνειν τῶν ἁβρῶν μᾶλλον καὶ
ἀστικῶν· τὸ δὲ ἐμόν, αἶγα μὲν αἰγὸς ὁποτέρα ἡ καλλίων καὶ
δάμαλιν ἄλλης δαμάλεως, τάχ' ἂν δικάσαιμι κατὰ τὴν τέχνην·
αὗται δὲ πᾶσαί τε ὁμοίως καλαὶ καὶ οὐκ οἶδ' ὅπως ἄν τις ἀπὸ   8
τῆς ἑτέρας ἐπὶ τὴν ἑτέραν μεταγάγοι τὴν ὄψιν ἀποσπάσας· οὐ
γὰρ ἐθέλει ἀφίστασθαι ῥᾳδίως, ἀλλ' ἔνθα ἂν ἀπερείσῃ τὸ πρῶτον,
τούτου ἔχεται καὶ τὸ παρὸν ἐπαινεῖ· κἂν ἐπ' ἄλλο μεταβῇ,
κἀκεῖνο καλὸν ὁρᾷ καὶ παραμένει, καὶ ὑπὸ τῶν πλησίον κατα-
λάμπεται. καὶ ὅλως περικέχυταί μοι τὸ κάλλος αὐτῶν καὶ ὅλον
περιείληφέ με καὶ ἄχθομαι, ὅτι μὴ καὶ αὐτὸς ὥσπερ ὁ Ἄργος ὅλῳ
βλέπειν δύναμαι τῷ σώματι. δοκῶ δὲ καλῶς ἂν δικάσαι πάσαις
ἀποδοὺς τὸ μῆλον. καὶ γὰρ αὖ καὶ τόδε, ταύτην μὲν εἶναι συμ-
βέβηκεν τοῦ Διὸς ἀδελφὴν καὶ γυναῖκα, ταύτας δὲ θυγατέρας·
πῶς οὖν οὐ χαλεπὴ καὶ οὕτως ἡ κρίσις;

ΕΡΜΗΣ

Οὐκ οἶδα· πλὴν οὐχ οἷόν τε ἀναδῦναι πρὸς τοῦ Διὸς κεκελευσμένον.

ΠΑΡΙΣ

Ἐν τοῦτο, ὦ Ἑρμῆ, πεῖσον αὐτάς, μὴ χαλεπῶς ἔχειν μοι τὰς   9
δύο τὰς νενικημένας, ἀλλὰ μόνων τῶν ὀφθαλμῶν ἡγεῖσθαι τὴν δι-
αμαρτίαν.

ΕΡΜΗΣ

Οὕτω φασὶ ποιήσειν· ὥρα δέ σοι ἤδη περαίνειν τὴν κρίσιν.

HERMES

They're not women, Paris, but it's Hera you see and Athena and Aphrodite. And I'm Hermes sent by Zeus – but why are you trembling and going pale? Don't be afraid. It's nothing very difficult. His orders are for you to judge their beauty. 'Since you' he says 'are beautiful yourself and clever about sex, I entrust you with the decision. You'll know the prize for the competition after you've read the apple.'

PARIS

Come then, let me see what it wants. LET HER THAT IS FAIR TAKE ME, it says. Well, Lord Hermes, how could I, a humble mortal and simple country fellow, pass judgment on an unbelievable spectacle too important for a mere herdsman? Such matters are rather for fine city gentlemen to judge. *My* skills perhaps enable me to decide which is the better goat or calf.

[8] But all these ladies are equally beautiful and I don't know how anyone could tear his eyes away from one of them and transfer it to another. For they won't easily leave, but wherever they first fix their gaze, there they glue themselves and praise what's before them; and if they move on elsewhere, they see that's beautiful too and stay there, dazzled by what's close at hand. And I'm completely swamped and enthralled by their beauty and am only sorry that I don't have eyes everywhere in my body like Argus. I think I could make a good decision by awarding the apple to all of them. And, another thing, this lady turns out to be Zeus' sister and wife, and these two his daughters. Doesn't that make the decision extra difficult?

HERMES

I don't know; but I *do* know it's impossible for you to back out, when you've had your orders from Zeus.

PARIS

[9] One thing, Hermes. You must persuade the two losers not to be angry with me, but to think it's only my eyes that are at fault.

HERMES

They promise to do that. But now it's time for you to get on with the judging.

ΠΑΡΙΣ

Πειρασόμεθα· τί γὰρ ἂν*πάθοι τις; ἐκεῖνο δὲ πρότερον
εἰδέναι βούλομαι, πότερ᾽ ἐξαρκέσει σκοπεῖν αὐτὰς ὡς ἔχουσιν,
ἢ καὶ ἀποδῦσαι δεήσει πρὸς τὸ ἀκριβὲς τῆς ἐξετάσεως;

ΕΡΜΗΣ

Τοῦτο μὲν σὸν ἂν εἴη τοῦ δικαστοῦ, καὶ πρόσταττε ὅπῃ καὶ
θέλεις.

ΠΑΡΙΣ

Ὅπῃ καὶ θέλω; γυμνὰς ἰδεῖν βούλομαι.

ΕΡΜΗΣ

Ἀπόδυτε, ὦ αὗται· σὺ δ᾽ ἐπισκόπει· ἐγὼ δὲ ἀπεστράφην.

ΑΦΡΟΔΙΤΗ

Καλῶς, ὦ Πάρι· καὶ πρώτη γε ἀποδύσομαι, ὅπως μάθῃς 10
ὅτι μὴ μόνον ἔχω τὰς ὠλένας λευκὰς μηδὲ τῷ βοῶπις εἶναι μέγα
φρονῶ, ἐπ᾽ ἴσης δέ εἰμι πᾶσα καὶ ὁμοίως καλή.

ΑΘΗΝΑ

Μὴ πρότερον ἀποδύσῃς αὐτήν, ὦ Πάρι, πρὶν ἂν τὸν κεστὸν
ἀπόθηται— φαρμακὶς γάρ ἐστιν—μή σε καταγοητεύσῃ δι᾽ αὐτοῦ.
καίτοι γε ἐχρῆν μηδὲ οὕτω κεκαλλωπισμένην παρεῖναι μηδὲ
τοσαῦτα ἐντετριμμένην χρώματα καθάπερ ὡς ἀληθῶς ἑταίραν
τινά, ἀλλὰ γυμνὸν τὸ κάλλος ἐπιδεικνύειν.

ΠΑΡΙΣ

Εὖ λέγουσι τὸ περὶ τοῦ κεστοῦ, καὶ ἀπόθου.

ΑΦΡΟΔΙΤΗ

Τί οὖν οὐχὶ καὶ σύ, ὦ Ἀθηνᾶ, τὴν κόρυν ἀφελοῦσα ψιλὴν τὴν
κεφαλὴν ἐπιδεικνύεις, ἀλλ᾽ ἐπισείεις τὸν λόφον καὶ τὸν δικαστὴν
φοβεῖς; ἢ δέδιας μή σοι ἐλέγχηται τὸ γλαυκὸν τῶν ὀμμάτων
ἄνευ τοῦ φοβεροῦ βλεπόμενον;

ΑΘΗΝΑ

Ἰδού σοι ἡ κόρυς αὕτη ἀφῄρηται.

*add καὶ

PARIS

I'll try. What else can a chap do? But there's something I'd like to know first. Will it be enough to inspect them as they are or shall I have to strip them for a minute examination?

HERMES

That would be up to *you* as judge. *You* must tell them what *you* want.

PARIS

What do I want? I want to see them in the nude.

HERMES

Off with your clothes, ladies. *You* inspect them, Paris. *I'm* not looking.

APHRODITE

[10] Well done, Paris. I'll undress first, so that you can find out that *I* have more than white arms (*pointing at Hera*) and more to be proud of than just big eyes like an ox but am equally beautiful all over.

ATHENA

No, Paris, don't undress *her* (*pointing to Aphrodite*) until she puts her girdle away – she's got magic powers and I'm afraid she'll use it to put a spell on you. And in any case she shouldn't have appeared in all that make-up and paint, just like a call girl; she ought to be showing her beauty unadorned.

PARIS

(*To Aphrodite*) They're right about the girdle; put it aside.

APHRODITE

Why don't you take your helmet off, Athena, and let us see your bare head instead of shaking your crest and frightening the judge? Are you afraid the colour of your eyes won't come up to scratch when seen away from the frightening helmet?

ATHENA

Look, there it is; I've taken it off.

ΑΦΡΟΔΙΤΗ

Ἰδοὺ καί σοι ὁ κεστός. ἀλλὰ ἀποδυσώμεθα.

ΠΑΡΙΣ

Ὦ Ζεῦ τεράστιε, τῆς θέας, τοῦ κάλλους, τῆς ἡδονῆς. οἷα μὲν 11
ἡ παρθένος, ὡς δὲ βασιλικὸν αὕτη καὶ σεμνὸν ἀπολάμπει καὶ
ἀληθῶς ἄξιον τοῦ Διός, ἥδε δὲ ὁρᾷ ἡδύ τι καὶ γλαφυρόν, καὶ
προσαγωγὸν ἐμειδίασεν—ἀλλ' ἤδη μὲν ἅλις ἔχω τῆς εὐδαιμονίας·
εἰ δοκεῖ δέ, καὶ ἰδίᾳ καθ' ἑκάστην ἐπιδεῖν βούλομαι, ὡς νῦν γε
ἀμφίβολός εἰμι καὶ οὐκ οἶδα πρὸς ὅ τι ἀποβλέψω, πάντῃ τὰς
ὄψεις περισπώμενος.

ΘΕΑΙ

Οὕτω ποιῶμεν.

ΠΑΡΙΣ

Ἄπιτε οὖν αἱ δύο· σὺ δέ, ὦ Ἥρα, περίμενε.

ΗΡΑ

Περιμενῶ, κἀπειδάν με ἀκριβῶς ἴδῃς, ὥρα σοι καὶ τἄλλα ἤδη
σκοπεῖν εἰ καλά σοι, τὰ δῶρα τῆς νίκης τῆς ἐμῆς. ἢν γάρ με,
ὦ Πάρι, δικάσῃς εἶναι καλήν, ἁπάσης ἔσῃ τῆς Ἀσίας δεσπότης.

ΠΑΡΙΣ

Οὐκ ἐπὶ δώροις μὲν τὰ ἡμέτερα. πλὴν ἄπιθι· πεπράξεται γὰρ 12
ἅπερ ἂν δοκῇ. σὺ δὲ πρόσιθι ἡ Ἀθηνᾶ.

ΑΘΗΝΑ

Παρέστηκά σοι, κᾆτα ἤν με, ὦ Πάρι, δικάσῃς καλήν, οὔποτε
ἥττων ἄπει ἐκ μάχης, ἀλλ' ἀεὶ κρατῶν· πολεμιστὴν γάρ σε καὶ
νικηφόρον ἀπεργάσομαι.

ΠΑΡΙΣ

Οὐδέν, ὦ Ἀθηνᾶ, δεῖ μοι πολέμου καὶ μάχης· εἰρήνη γάρ, ὡς
ὁρᾷς, τὰ νῦν ἐπέχει τήν τε Φρυγίαν καὶ Λυδίαν καὶ ἀπολέμητος
ἡμῖν ἡ τοῦ πατρὸς ἀρχή. θάρρει δέ· οὐ μειονεκτήσεις γάρ, κᾶν μὴ
ἐπι οωροις δικάζωμεν. ἀλλ' ἔνδυθι ἤδη καὶ ἐπίθου τὴν κόρυν·
ἱκανῶς γὰρ εἶδον. τὴν Ἀφροδίτην παρεῖναι καιρός.

APHRODITE

And see, there's my girdle. But let's undress.

PARIS

[11] (*Aside*) Zeus, Lord of Miracles, what a sight! What beauty! How delightful! How attractive are this one's (*pointing to Athena*) maidenly charms, and what a dazzling royal majesty this one has (*pointing to Hera*), truly worthy of Zeus' wife! And the look in this one's eyes (*pointing to Aphrodite*) is sweet and charming and her smile so alluring. But now I'm having too much of a good thing. (*To the goddesses*) If you don't mind, ladies, I want to inspect you in private one by one, for at present I can't make up my mind, and don't know what to look at, as I twist my eyes in every direction.

GODDESSES

Let's do as he says.

PARIS

Then *you* and *you* go away, but *you*, Hera, stay.

HERA

I'll stay, and when you inspect me closely, that's also a good time to consider whether the other things I have to offer aren't beautiful too – I mean the presents that go with my victory. For if you give *me* the verdict for beauty, Paris, you'll be lord of all Asia.

PARIS

[12] *My* decisions don't depend on bribery. But off with you, Hera; for things will be as *I* decide. Now, Athena, *you* come here.

ATHENA

Here I am at your side, and, Paris, if you give *me* the verdict for beauty, you'll never leave a battle defeated, but always victorious. For I'll make you into a warrior and a conquering hero.

PARIS

I don't have any need for war or fighting, Athena. For at present, as you can see, there's peace throughout Phrygia and Lydia and there are no wars in my father's kingdom. But don't worry. I won't discriminate against you, even if my verdict can't be bought. But get dressed now and put on your helmet. I've seen enough. It's now time for Aphrodite to come to me.

ΑΦΡΟΔΙΤΗ

Αὕτη σοι ἐγὼ πλησίον, καὶ σκόπει καθ᾽ ἓν ἀκριβῶς μηδὲν 13
παρατρέχων, ἀλλ᾽ ἐνδιατρίβων ἑκάστῳ τῶν μελῶν. εἰ δ᾽ ἐθέλεις,
ὦ καλέ, καὶ τάδε μου ἄκουσον. ἐγὼ γὰρ πάλαι ὁρῶσά σε νέον
ὄντα καὶ καλὸν ὁποῖον οὐκ οἶδα εἴ τινα ἕτερον ἡ Φρυγία τρέφει,
μακαρίζω μὲν τοῦ κάλλους, αἰτιῶμαι δὲ τὸ μὴ ἀπολιπόντα τοὺς
σκοπέλους καὶ ταυτασὶ τὰς πέτρας κατ᾽ ἄστυ ζῆν, ἀλλὰ δια-
φθείρειν τὸ κάλλος ἐν ἐρημίᾳ. τί μὲν γὰρ ἂν σὺ ἀπολαύσειας τῶν
ὁρῶν; τί δ᾽ ἂν ἀπόναιντο τοῦ σοῦ κάλλους αἱ βόες; ἔπρεπεν δὲ
ἤδη σοι καὶ γεγαμηκέναι, μὴ μέντοι ἄγροικόν τινα καὶ χωρῖτιν,
οἷαι κατὰ τὴν Ἴδην αἱ γυναῖκες, ἀλλά τινα ἐκ τῆς Ἑλλάδος, ἢ
Ἀργόθεν ἢ ἐκ Κορίνθου ἢ Λάκαιναν οἵαπερ ἡ Ἑλένη ἐστίν, νέα
καὶ καλὴ καὶ κατ᾽ οὐδὲν ἐλάττων ἐμοῦ, καὶ τὸ δὴ μέγιστον,
ἐρωτική· ἐκείνη γὰρ εἰ καὶ μόνον θεάσαιτό σε, εὖ οἶδα ἐγὼ ὡς
ἅπαντα ἀπολιποῦσα καὶ παρασχοῦσα ἑαυτὴν ἔκδοτον ἕψεται καὶ
συνοικήσει. πάντως δὲ καὶ σὺ ἀκήκοάς τι περὶ αὐτῆς.

ΠΑΡΙΣ

Οὐδέν, ὦ Ἀφροδίτη· νῦν δὲ ἡδέως ἂν ἀκούσαιμί σου τὰ πάντα
διηγουμένης.

ΑΦΡΟΔΙΤΗ

Αὕτη θυγάτηρ μέν ἐστι Λήδας ἐκείνης τῆς καλῆς ἐφ᾽ ἣν ὁ 14
Ζεὺς κατέπτη κύκνος γενόμενος.

ΠΑΡΙΣ

Ποία δὲ τὴν ὄψιν ἐστί;

ΑΦΡΟΔΙΤΗ

Λευκὴ μέν, οἵαν εἰκὸς ἐκ κύκνου γεγενημένην, ἁπαλὴ δέ, ὡς ἐν
ᾠῷ τραφεῖσα, γυμνὰς τὰ πολλὰ καὶ παλαιστική, καὶ οὕτω δή τι
περισπούδαστος ὥστε καὶ πόλεμον ἀμφ᾽ αὐτῇ γενέσθαι, τοῦ
Θησέως ἄωρον ἔτι ἁρπάσαντος· οὐ μὴν ἀλλ᾽ ἐπειδήπερ εἰς ἀκμὴν
κατέστη, πάντες οἱ ἄριστοι τῶν Ἀχαιῶν ἐπὶ τὴν μνηστείαν
ἀπήντησαν, προεκρίθη δὲ Μενέλαος τοῦ Πελοπιδῶν γένους. εἰ
δὴ θέλοις, ἐγώ σοι καταπράξομαι τὸν γάμον.

APHRODITE

[13] Here I am close to you. Inspect me closely in every detail, without hurrying over anything but giving plenty of time to every part of me. And, my handsome fellow, please listen to this. I saw long ago that you are as good-looking a young chap as any, I shouldn't wonder, to be found in all Phrygia and I congratulate you on these good looks, but I think you're wrong not to have left these cliffs and rocks and gone to live in the city, instead of wasting your good looks on the desert air. For what enjoyment can you get from the mountains, and how can your good looks help your cattle? You ought to be married by now, and not to some local peasant girl of the sort you get on Ida here, but someone from Greece, from Argos or Corinth or Sparta, like Helen, who is young and beautiful and not one whit inferior to myself, and, what's most important, amorous. If she should just clap eyes on you, I know she'd leave everything and put herself completely at your disposal, following you and living with you. You must certainly have heard about *her*.

PARIS

Not a word, Aphrodite, so please tell me all about her at once.

APHRODITE

[14] She's the daughter of Leda, the well-known beauty, who had Zeus flying down after her, after turning himself into a swan.

PARIS

What does she look like?

APHRODITE

She has a white skin as you might expect from the daughter of a swan, and is soft and delicate, being born from an egg; she's fond of exercising in the nude and wrestling, and is so sought after that there's even been a war fought over her; Theseus carried her off when she was still a child. But when she reached her prime, all the leading nobles of Greece met to try for her hand, and Menelaus, a descendant of Pelops, was judged the winner. If you like, I'll arrange for you to marry her.

ΠΑΡΙΣ

Πῶς φής; τὸν τῆς γεγαμημένης;

ΑΦΡΟΔΙΤΗ

Νέος εἶ σὺ καὶ ἄγροικος, ἐγὼ δὲ οἶδα ὡς χρὴ τὰ τοιαῦτα δρᾶν.

ΠΑΡΙΣ

Πῶς; ἐθέλω γὰρ καὶ αὐτὸς εἰδέναι.

ΑΦΡΟΔΙΤΗ

Σὺ μὲν ἀποδημήσεις ὡς ἐπὶ θέαν τῆς Ἑλλάδος, κἀπειδὰν 15
ἀφίκῃ εἰς τὴν Λακεδαίμονα, ὄψεταί σε ἡ Ἑλένη. τοὐντεῦθεν δὲ
ἐμὸν ἂν εἴη τὸ ἔργον, ὅπως ἐρασθήσεταί σου καὶ ἀκολουθήσει.

ΠΑΡΙΣ

Τοῦτ᾽ αὐτὸ ἄπιστον εἶναί μοι δοκεῖ, τὸ ἀπολιποῦσαν τὸν ἄνδρα
ἐθελῆσαι βαρβάρῳ καὶ ξένῳ συνεκπλεῦσαι.

ΑΦΡΟΔΙΤΗ

Θάρρει τούτου γε ἕνεκα. παῖδε γάρ μοι ἐστὸν δύο καλώ,
Ἵμερος καὶ Ἔρως· τούτω σοι παραδώσω ἡγεμόνε τῆς ὁδοῦ
γενησομένω· καὶ ὁ μὲν Ἔρως ὅλος παρελθὼν εἰς αὐτὴν ἀναγκάσει
τὴν γυναῖκα ἐρᾶν, ὁ δ᾽ Ἵμερος αὐτῷ σοι περιχυθεὶς τοῦθ᾽ ὅπερ ἐστίν,
ἱμερτόν τε θήσει καὶ ἐράσμιον. καὶ αὐτὴ δὲ συμπαροῦσα δεήσομαι
καὶ τῶν Χαρίτων συνακολουθεῖν καὶ οὕτως ἅπαντες αὐτὴν ἀνα-
πείσομεν.

ΠΑΡΙΣ

Ὅπως μὲν ταῦτα χωρήσει, ἄδηλον, ὦ Ἀφροδίτη· πλὴν ἐρῶ
γε ἤδη τῆς Ἑλένης καὶ οὐκ οἶδ᾽ ὅπως καὶ ὁρᾶν αὐτὴν οἴομαι καὶ
πλέω εὐθὺ τῆς Ἑλλάδος καὶ τῇ Σπάρτῃ ἐπιδημῶ καὶ ἐπάνειμι
ἔχων τὴν γυναῖκα—καὶ ἄχθομαι ὅτι μὴ ἤδη πάντα ταῦτα ποιῶ.

ΑΦΡΟΔΙΤΗ

Μὴ πρότερον ἐρασθῇς, ὦ Πάρι, πρὶν ἐμὲ τὴν προμνήστριαν καὶ 16
νυμφαγωγὸν ἀμείψασθαι τῇ κρίσει· πρέποι γὰρ ἂν κἀμὲ νικηφόρον ὑμῖν συμπαρεῖναι καὶ ἑορτάζειν ἅμα καὶ τοὺς γάμους καὶ
τὰ ἐπινίκια. πάντα γὰρ ἔνεστί σοι—τὸν ἔρωτα, τὸ κάλλος, τὸν
γάμον—τουτουὶ τοῦ μήλου πρίασθαι.

PARIS

How do you mean? Marriage to a married woman?

APHRODITE

You're young and countrified, but I know how to conduct such matters.

PARIS

How? I'd like to know too.

APHRODITE

[15] You'll go travelling, making out you're on a sightseeing tour of Greece, and when you reach Sparta, Helen will see you. What happens after that will be up to me; I'll see that she falls in love with you and follows you.

PARIS

It seems quite incredible to me that she should desert her husband and want to sail away with a foreigner she doesn't know from Adam.

APHRODITE

Don't worry about that. I have two handsome page-boys, Desire and Love. I'll give you them to guide you on your way. Love will pass into her with all his powers and compel her to fall in love, while Desire will wrap himself around you and make you what he is himself, desirable and lovely. And I shall lend my own presence and ask the Graces to come along too and we'll all combine to win her over.

PARIS

I can't tell how all this will turn out, Aphrodite, but I *do* know I'm in love with Helen already. Somehow I think I can see her before my eyes and myself sailing straight to Greece and visiting Sparta and returning here with her; indeed I'm sorry I'm not doing it all already.

APHRODITE

[16] Stop, Paris. Don't fall in love before you've paid for my services as match-maker and bridesmaid by giving me the verdict. It would be most appropriate for me to accompany you with a victory of my own behind me and to celebrate your wedding and my victory at the same time. For with this apple (*she fingers the apple*) you can buy everything – love, beauty, marriage.

ΠΑΡΙΣ

Δέδοικα μή μου ἀμελήσῃς μετὰ τὴν κρίσιν.

ΑΦΡΟΔΙΤΗ

Βούλει οὖν ἐπομόσωμαι;

ΠΑΡΙΣ

Μηδαμῶς, ἀλλ᾽ ὑπόσχου πάλιν.

ΑΦΡΟΔΙΤΗ

Ὑπισχνοῦμαι δή σοι τὴν Ἑλένην παραδώσειν γυναῖκα, καὶ ἀκολουθήσειν γέ σοι αὐτὴν καὶ ἀφίξεσθαι παρ᾽ ὑμᾶς εἰς τὴν Ἴλιον· καὶ αὐτὴ παρέσομαι καὶ συμπράξω τὰ πάντα.

ΠΑΡΙΣ

Καὶ τὸν Ἔρωτα καὶ τὸν Ἵμερον καὶ τὰς Χάριτας ἄξεις;

ΑΦΡΟΔΙΤΗ

Θάρρει, καὶ τὸν Πόθον καὶ τὸν Ὑμέναιον ἔτι πρὸς τούτοις παραλήψομαι.

ΠΑΡΙΣ

Οὐκοῦν ἐπὶ τούτοις δίδωμι τὸ μῆλον· ἐπὶ τούτοις λάμβανε.

PARIS

I'm afraid you'll forget about me after I've given my verdict.

APHRODITE

Well, do you want me to take an oath?

PARIS

No, just repeat your promise.

APHRODITE

I hereby promise that I will indeed hand over Helen to you to be your wife and that she will follow you and go to Troy with you. And I myself will accompany you and help to arrange everything.

PARIS

And you'll bring Love, Desire and the Graces?

APHRODITE

Don't worry; I'll also bring Yearning and Wedlock for good measure.

PARIS

Then on these conditions I give you the apple; take it on these conditions.

ΘΕΩΝ ΕΚΚΛΗΣΙΑ

ΖΕΥΣ

Μηκέτι τονθορύζετε, ὦ θεοί, μηδὲ κατὰ γωνίας συστρεφό- **1**
μενοι πρὸς οὓς ἀλλήλοις κοινολογεῖσθε, ἀγανακτοῦντες εἰ πολλοὶ
ἀνάξιοι μετέχουσιν ἡμῖν τοῦ συμποσίου, ἀλλ' ἐπείπερ ἀποδέ-
δοται περὶ τούτων ἐκκλησία, λεγέτω ἕκαστος ἐς τὸ φανερὸν τὰ
δοκοῦντά οἱ καὶ κατηγορείτω. σὺ δὲ κήρυττε, ὦ Ἑρμῆ, τὸ κήρυγμα τὸ ἐκ τοῦ νόμου.

ΕΡΜΗΣ

Ἄκουε, σίγα. τίς ἀγορεύειν βούλεται τῶν τελείων θεῶν οἷς
ἔξεστιν; ἡ δὲ σκέψις περὶ τῶν μετοίκων καὶ ξένων.

ΜΩΜΟΣ

Ἐγὼ ὁ Μῶμος, ὦ Ζεῦ, εἴ μοι ἐπιτρέψειας εἰπεῖν.

ΖΕΥΣ

Τὸ κήρυγμα ἤδη ἐφίησιν· ὥστε οὐδὲν ἐμοῦ δεήσει.

ΜΩΜΟΣ

Φημὶ τοίνυν δεινὰ ποιεῖν ἐνίους ἡμῶν, οἷς οὐκ ἀπόχρη θεοὺς **2**
ἐξ ἀνθρώπων αὐτοὺς γεγενῆσθαι, ἀλλ', εἰ μὴ καὶ τοὺς ἀκολού-
θους καὶ θεράποντας αὐτῶν ἰσοτίμους ἡμῖν ἀποφανοῦσιν, οὐδὲν
μέγα οὐδὲ νεανικὸν οἴονται εἰργάσθαι. ἀξιῶ δέ, ὦ Ζεῦ, μετὰ
παρρησίας μοι δοῦναι εἰπεῖν· οὐδὲ γὰρ ἂν ἄλλως δυναίμην,
ἀλλὰ πάντες με ἴσασιν ὡς ἐλεύθερός εἰμι τὴν γλῶτταν καὶ οὐδὲν
ἂν κατασιωπήσαιμι τῶν οὐ καλῶς γιγνομένων· διελέγχω γὰρ
ἅπαντα καὶ λέγω τὰ δοκοῦντά μοι ἐς τὸ φανερὸν οὔτε δεδιώς τινα
οὔτε ὑπ' αἰδοῦς ἐπικαλύπτων τὴν γνώμην· ὥστε καὶ ἐπαχθὴς
δοκῶ τοῖς πολλοῖς καὶ συκοφαντικὸς τὴν φύσιν, δημόσιός τις
κατήγορος ὑπ' αὐτῶν ἐπονομαζόμενος. πλὴν ἀλλ' ἐπείπερ ἔξεστιν
καὶ κεκήρυκται καὶ σύ, ὦ Ζεῦ, δίδως μετ' ἐξουσίας εἰπεῖν, οὐδὲν
ὑποστειλάμενος ἐρῶ.

Πολλοὶ γάρ, φημί, οὐκ ἀγαπῶντες ὅτι αὐτοὶ μετέχουσι τῶν **3**

THE ASSEMBLY OF THE GODS

ZEUS

[1] Stop muttering, you gods, and collecting in corners for whispered discussions with each other, angry that our parties are shared by many unworthy of the privilege. No, since a session of the assembly has been allotted to this issue, let each express his opinion publicly and make his accusations. You, Hermes, make the statutory proclamation.

HERMES

Oyez! Silence! Who wants to speak from among the qualified gods? We're discussing resident aliens and foreigners.

MOMUS

I, Momus, want to speak, if, Zeus, you'll allow me.

ZEUS

The proclamation already allows you; so there's no need for my permission.

MOMUS

[2] Then I allege shocking conduct by some of us, who aren't satisfied with having changed from men to gods themselves, but don't think they have accomplished anything heroic or mettlesome, unless they also get their attendants and lackeys to enjoy equal honours with ourselves. Please, Zeus, allow me to speak frankly, for I can't do anything else; indeed everybody knows that I'm free of tongue and can't keep quiet about anything improper. For I probe into everything and speak my mind openly without concealing my opinion through fear of anyone or embarrassment. So most people think me offensive and of a libellous nature and call me a sort of public prosecutor. However, since I am authorised by the proclamation, and you, Zeus, allow me to speak freely, I shall do so without any reserve.

[3] Many, I say, are not content that they themselves share the same

αὐτῶν ἡμῖν ξυνεδρίων καὶ εὐωχοῦνται ἐπ' ἴσης, καὶ ταῦτα θνητοὶ
ἐξ ἡμισείας ὄντες, ἔτι καὶ τοὺς ὑπηρέτας καὶ θιασώτας τοὺς
αὐτῶν ἀνήγαγον ἐς τὸν οὐρανὸν καὶ παρενέγραψαν, καὶ νῦν ἐπ'
ἴσης διανομάς τε νέμονται καὶ θυσιῶν μετέχουσιν, οὐδὲ καταβα-
λόντες ἡμῖν τὸ μετοίκιον.

ΖΕΥΣ

Μηδὲν αἰνιγματῶδες, ὦ Μῶμε, ἀλλὰ σαφῶς καὶ διαρρήδην
λέγε, προστιθεὶς καὶ τοὔνομα, νῦν γὰρ ἐς τὸ μέσον ἀπέρριπταί
σοι ὁ λόγος, ὡς πολλοὺς εἰκάζειν καὶ ἐφαρμόζειν ἄλλοτε ἄλλον
τοῖς λεγομένοις. χρὴ δὲ παρρησιαστὴν ὄντα μηδὲν ὀκνεῖν λέγειν.

ΜΩΜΟΣ

Εὖ γε, ὦ Ζεῦ, ὅτι καὶ παροτρύνεις με πρὸς τὴν παρρησίαν· **4**
ποιεῖς γὰρ τοῦτο βασιλικὸν ὡς ἀληθῶς καὶ μεγαλόφρον, ὥστε
ἐρῶ καὶ τοὔνομα. ὁ γάρ τοι γενναιότατος οὗτος Διόνυσος ἡμιάν-
θρωπος ὤν, οὐδὲ Ἕλλην μητρόθεν ἀλλὰ Συροφοίνικός τινος
ἐμπόρου τοῦ Κάδμου θυγατριδοῦς, ἐπείπερ ἠξιώθη τῆς ἀθανα-
σίας, οἷος μὲν αὐτός ἐστιν οὐ λέγω, οὔτε τὴν μίτραν οὔτε τὴν μέθην
οὔτε τὸ βάδισμα· πάντες γάρ, οἶμαι, ὁρᾶτε ὡς θῆλυς καὶ γυναικεῖος τὴν φύσιν, ἡμιμανής, ἀκράτου ἔωθεν ἀποπνέων· ὁ δὲ
καὶ ὅλην φατρίαν ἐσεποίησεν ἡμῖν καὶ τὸν χορὸν ἐπαγόμενος
πάρεστι καὶ θεοὺς ἀπέφηνε τὸν Πᾶνα καὶ τὸν Σιληνὸν καὶ Σα-
τύρους, ἀγροίκους τινὰς καὶ αἰπόλους τοὺς πολλούς, σκιρτητικοὺς
ἀνθρώπους καὶ τὰς μορφὰς ἀλλοκότους· ὧν ὁ μὲν κέρατα ἔχων
καὶ ὅσον ἐξ ἡμισείας ἐς τὸ κάτω αἰγὶ ἐοικὼς καὶ γένειον βαθὺ
καθειμένος ὀλίγον τράγου διαφέρων ἐστίν, ὁ δὲ φαλακρὸς γέρων,
σιμὸς τὴν ῥῖνα, ἐπὶ ὄνου τὰ πολλὰ ὀχούμενος, Λυδὸς οὗτος, οἱ
δὲ Σάτυροι ὀξεῖς τὰ ὦτα, καὶ αὐτοὶ φαλακροί, κεράσται, οἷα τοῖς
ἄρτι γεννηθεῖσιν ἐρίφοις τὰ κέρατα ὑποφύεται, Φρύγες τινὲς
ὄντες· ἔχουσι δὲ καὶ οὐρὰς ἅπαντες. ὁρᾶτε οἵους ἡμῖν θεοὺς ποιεῖ
ὁ γεννάδας;

Εἶτα θαυμάζομεν εἰ καταφρονοῦσιν ἡμῶν οἱ ἄνθρωποι ὁρῶν- **5**
τες οὕτω γελοίους θεοὺς καὶ τεραστίους; ἐῶ γὰρ λέγειν ὅτι καὶ
δύο γυναῖκας ἀνήγαγεν, τὴν μὲν ἐρωμένην οὖσαν αὐτοῦ, τὴν
Ἀριάδνην, ἧς καὶ τὸν στέφανον ἐγκατέλεξε τῷ τῶν ἄστρων

council-chambers as we do and feast with us on equal terms, even though they are half-mortal, but have also brought their servants and worshippers up to heaven and foisted them on us, and now they have equal enjoyment of any handouts that come along and share our sacrifices, without even having paid us their dues as resident aliens.

ZEUS

No riddles, Momus, but speak clearly and explicitly, adding the name of the accused party. For now that you've spoken out publicly, many of us are indulging in guesswork and applying your words now to one, now to another. Being one for frankness you must have no hesitation in speaking.

MOMUS

[4] Well done, Zeus. I'm glad you encourage me to be frank. You're behaving like a true king with a noble spirit and so I'll name the name. It's this most noble fellow here, Dionysus, who is half human and not even a Greek on his mother's side, but the grandson of a Syro-Phoenician trader, one Cadmus; seeing that he has been voted immortality, I won't say what he is like himself or mention his turban or his drunkenness or his way of walking. For I think you can all see how effeminate and womanish he is by nature, half crazy and reeking of strong drink from first thing in the morning. And he has foisted a whole clan on us and is in our midst with his troop of dancers and has made gods of Pan, Silenus and his Satyrs, most of them peasants and goatherds, skittish humans with outlandish shapes. The first of them has horns, a bottom half like a goat and a long beard, so that he scarcely differs from a goat, the second is a bald old fellow with a flat nose, usually riding on a donkey – he comes from Lydia; while the Satyrs have pointed ears and are also bald, and they have horns like the ones which grow on newborn kids – they come from Phrygia. What's more they all have tails. Do you see the sort of gods the noble Dionysus is bringing us?

[5] So, can we be surprised that humans despise us when they see such ridiculous, misshapen gods? I won't mention that he has fetched up two women as well, one of them, Ariadne, his lady love, even adding her

χορῷ, τὴν δὲ Ἰκαρίου τοῦ γεωργοῦ θυγατέρα. καὶ ὃ πάντων γε-
λοιότατον, ὦ θεοί, καὶ τὸν κύνα τῆς Ἠριγόνης, καὶ τοῦτον ἀνήγαγεν, ὡς μὴ ἀνιῷτο ἡ παῖς εἰ μὴ ἕξει ἐν τῷ οὐρανῷ τὸ ξύνηθες
ἐκεῖνο καὶ ὅπερ ἠγάπα κυνίδιον. ταῦτα οὐχ ὕβρις ὑμῖν δοκεῖ καὶ
παροινία καὶ γέλως; ἀκούσατε δ' οὖν καὶ ἄλλους.

ΖΕΥΣ

Μηδέν, ὦ Μῶμε, εἴπῃς μήτε περὶ Ἀσκληπιοῦ μήτε περὶ Ἡρα- 6
κλέους· ὁρῶ γὰρ οἷ φέρῃ τῷ λόγῳ. οὗτοι γάρ, ὁ μὲν αὐτῶν ἰᾶται
καὶ ἀνίστησιν ἐκ τῶν νόσων καὶ ἔστιν "πολλῶν ἀντάξιος ἄλλων,"
ὁ δὲ Ἡρακλῆς υἱὸς ὢν ἐμὸς οὐκ ὀλίγων πόνων ἐπρίατο τὴν ἀθανα-
σίαν· ὥστε μὴ κατηγόρει αὐτῶν.

ΜΩΜΟΣ

Σιωπήσομαι, ὦ Ζεῦ, διὰ σέ, πολλὰ εἰπεῖν ἔχων. καίτοι εἰ
μηδὲν ἄλλο, ἔτι τὰ σημεῖα ἔχουσι τοῦ πυρός. εἰ δὲ ἐξῆν καὶ πρὸς
αὐτὸν σὲ τῇ παρρησίᾳ χρῆσθαι, πολλὰ ἂν εἶχον εἰπεῖν.

ΖΕΥΣ

Καὶ μὴν πρὸς ἐμὲ ἔξεστιν μάλιστα. μῶν οὖν κἀμὲ ξενίας
διώκεις;

ΜΩΜΟΣ

Ἐν Κρήτῃ μὲν οὐ μόνον τοῦτο ἀκοῦσαι ἔστιν, ἀλλὰ καὶ ἄλλο
τι περὶ σοῦ λέγουσιν καὶ τάφον ἐπιδεικνύουσιν· ἐγὼ δὲ οὔτε ἐκείνοις πείθομαι οὔτε Ἀχαιῶν Αἰγιεῦσιν ὑποβολιμαῖόν σε εἶναι
φάσκουσιν. ἃ δὲ μάλιστα ἐλεγχθῆναι δεῖν ἡγοῦμαι, ταῦτα ἐρῶ.
Τὴν γάρ τοι ἀρχὴν τῶν τοιούτων παρανομημάτων καὶ τὴν αἰ- 7
τίαν τοῦ νοθευθῆναι ἡμῶν τὸ ξυνέδριον σύ, ὦ Ζεῦ, παρέσχες
θνηταῖς ἐπιμιγνύμενος καὶ κατιὼν παρ' αὐτὰς ἐν ἄλλοτε ἄλλῳ
σχήματι, ὥστε ἡμᾶς δεδιέναι μή σε καταθύσῃ τις ξυλλαβών,
ὁπόταν ταῦρος ᾖς, ἢ τῶν χρυσοχόων τις κατεργάσηται χρυσὸν
ὄντα, καὶ ἀντὶ Διὸς ἢ ὅρμος ἢ ψέλιον ἢ ἐλλόβιον ἡμῖν γένῃ.
πλὴν ἀλλὰ ἐμπέπληκάς γε τὸν οὐρανὸν τῶν ἡμιθέων τούτων· οὐ
γὰρ ἂν ἄλλως εἴποιμι. καὶ τὸ πρᾶγμα γελοιότατόν ἐστιν, ὁπόταν τις ἄφνω ἀκούσῃ ὅτι ὁ Ἡρακλῆς μὲν θεὸς ἀπεδείχθη, ὁ δὲ

tiara to the ranks of the stars, and the other, the daughter of Icarius, the farmer; and, what's most ridiculous of all, he's even brought Erigone's dog as well up here, so that the child won't be upset at not having with her in heaven her usual companion, her darling little puppy. Don't you find all this insulting and drunken behaviour quite ridiculous? And let me tell you about some others.

ZEUS

[6] Not a word, Momus, about Asclepius or Heracles. For I can see where your argument is carrying you. As for them, one is a doctor and cures folk of their illnesses, one 'whose worth is as the worth of many', while the other, my son Heracles, has purchased immortality by his many labours. So don't accuse *them*.

MOMUS

I'll be quiet for *your* sake, Zeus, though there's a lot I *could* say. However, if nothing else, I *will* just mention that they still keep the marks of the fire. But if I were allowed to direct my frankness against yourself, I could say a great deal.

ZEUS

On the contrary you may be frank about *me* most of all. Surely you're not prosecuting *me* too as being an alien?

MOMUS

Well, in Crete that's not the only thing which can be heard but they say something else about you and point out your tomb, though I don't believe them or the folk of Aegium in Achaea when they say you are a changeling, but I *will* mention the things that in my opinion are most deserving of criticism. [7] It was *you*, Zeus, who started off such illegalities and caused our conclave to be filled with bastards when you associated with mortal women and went down to earth after them from time to time in various forms, causing us to fear that you'd be seized and sacrificed when a bull, or that a goldsmith might get to work on you and finish you off when you were gold, changing you from Zeus into a necklace or bracelet or earring. In any case you've filled heaven with these half-gods – I've *got* to put it like that – and the whole thing is most ridiculous when one suddenly hears that Heracles has been deified,

Εὐρυσθεύς, ὃς ἐπέταττεν αὐτῷ, τέθνηκεν, καὶ πλησίον Ἡρακλέους νεὼς οἰκέτου ὄντος καὶ Εὐρυσθέως τάφος τοῦ δεσπότου
αὐτοῦ. καὶ πάλιν ἐν Θήβαις Διόνυσος μὲν θεός, οἱ δ' ἀνεψιοὶ αὐτοῦ
ὁ Πενθεὺς καὶ ὁ Ἀκταίων καὶ ὁ Λέαρχος ἀνθρώπων ἁπάντων
κακοδαιμονέστατοι.

Ἀφ' οὗ δὲ ἅπαξ σύ, ὦ Ζεῦ, ἀνέῳξας τοῖς τοιούτοις τὰς θύρας 8
καὶ ἐπὶ τὰς θνητὰς ἐτράπου, ἅπαντες μεμίμηνταί σε, καὶ οὐχ οἱ
ἄρρενες μόνον, ἀλλ', ὅπερ αἴσχιστον, καὶ αἱ θήλειαι θεοί. τίς
γὰρ οὐκ οἶδεν τὸν Ἀγχίσην καὶ τὸν Τιθωνὸν καὶ τὸν Ἐνδυμίωνα
καὶ τὸν Ἰασίωνα καὶ τοὺς ἄλλους; ὥστε ταῦτα μὲν ἐάσειν μοι
δοκῶ· μακρὸν γὰρ ἂν τὸ διελέγχειν γένοιτο.

ΖΕΥΣ

Μηδὲν περὶ τοῦ Γανυμήδους, ὦ Μῶμε, εἴπῃς· χαλεπανῶ γὰρ
εἰ λυπήσεις τὸ μειράκιον ὀνειδίσας ἐς τὸ γένος.

ΜΩΜΟΣ

Οὐκοῦν μηδὲ περὶ τοῦ ἀετοῦ εἴπω, ὅτι καὶ οὗτος ἐν τῷ οὐρανῷ
ἐστιν, ἐπὶ τοῦ βασιλείου σκήπτρου καθεζόμενος καὶ μονονουχὶ
ἐπὶ κεφαλήν σοι νεοττεύων, θεὸς εἶναι δοκῶν; ἢ καὶ τοῦτον 9
τοῦ Γανυμήδους ἕνεκα ἐάσομεν;

Ἀλλ' ὁ Ἄττης γε, ὦ Ζεῦ, καὶ ὁ Κορύβας καὶ ὁ Σαβάζιος,
πόθεν ἡμῖν ἐπεισεκυκλήθησαν οὗτοι, ἢ ὁ Μίθρης ἐκεῖνος, ὁ
Μῆδος, ὁ τὸν κάνδυν καὶ τὴν τιάραν, οὐδὲ ἑλληνίζων τῇ φωνῇ,
ὥστε οὐδ' ἢν προπίῃ τις ξυνίησι; τοιγαροῦν οἱ Σκύθαι ταῦτα
ὁρῶντες, οἱ Γέται αὐτῶν, μακρὰ ἡμῖν χαίρειν εἰπόντες αὐτοὶ
ἀπαθανατίζουσι καὶ θεοὺς χειροτονοῦσιν οὓς ἂν ἐθελήσωσι,
τὸν αὐτὸν τρόπον ὅνπερ καὶ Ζάμολξις δοῦλος ὢν παρενεγράφη
οὐκ οἶδ' ὅπως διαλαθών.

Καίτοι πάντα ταῦτα, ὦ θεοί, μέτρια. σὺ δέ, ὦ κυνοπρόσωπε 10
καὶ σινδόσιν ἐσταλμένε Αἰγύπτιε, τίς εἶ, βέλτιστε, ἢ πῶς ἀξιοῖς
θεὸς εἶναι ὑλακτῶν; τί δὲ βουλόμενος καὶ ὁ ποικίλος οὗτος ταῦρος
ὁ Μεμφίτης προσκυνεῖται καὶ χρᾷ καὶ προφήτας ἔχει; αἰσχύ-
νομαι γὰρ ἴβιδας καὶ πιθήκους εἰπεῖν* καὶ ἄλλα πολλῷ γελοιότερα οὐκ οἶδ' ὅπως ἐξ Αἰγύπτου παραβυσθέντα ἐς τὸν οὐρανόν, ἃ ὑμεῖς, ὦ θεοί, πῶς ἀνέχεσθε ὁρῶντες ἐπ' ἴσης ἢ καὶ

* add καὶ τράγους

whereas his taskmaster Eurystheus is dead and near each other are a temple of Heracles, who was a servant, and a tomb of Eurystheus, his lord and master, and again in Thebes Dionysus is a god, while his cousins, Pentheus, Actaeon and Learchus, were the most unfortunate of men.

[8] Once you, Zeus, opened our portals to such fellows and turned to mortal women, all have copied you, and not just the males, but, shame of shame, the female divinities as well. For who doesn't know about Anchises, Tithonus, Endymion, Iasion and all the others? So I think I'll pass over that subject, for detailed criticism would take a long time.

ZEUS

Momus, I won't have any mention of Ganymede, for I'll be angry if you upset the lad by sneers about his parentage.

MOMUS

Then I musn't mention the eagle either; for it's in heaven too, perched on your royal sceptre, almost nesting on your head, so that *it's* taken for a god. Or shall we say nothing about *it* either for Ganymede's sake?

[9] But what about Attis and Corybas and Sabazius? Where did *they* come from to be trundled into our midst? Or Mithras over there, the Mede with the caftan and headdress, who can't so much as talk Greek, so that he doesn't even understand toasts in his honour? So when this is seen by the Scythians, or at least the Getans amongst them, they tell us to go to blazes and make immortals of their own, voting to make gods of their own choice, just as Zamolxis, though a slave, was fraudulently enrolled, slipping in somehow or other.

[10] However, gods, all these things I've mentioned are within bounds, but, you dog-faced Egyptian swathed in linens, who are *you*, my excellent fellow? How do *you* claim to be a god, *you* with your barking? And what's the meaning of this spotted bull from Memphis being worshipped, giving oracles and having prophets? For I'm ashamed to mention the ibises, apes, goats and other creatures much more ludicrous, which have somehow been stuffed into heaven from Egypt. How, gods, can you bear to see them being worshipped equally or even more than

μᾶλλον ὑμῶν προσκυνούμενα; ἢ σύ, ὦ Ζεῦ, πῶς φέρεις ἐπειδὰν
κριοῦ κέρατα φύσωσί σοι;

ΖΕΥΣ

Αἰσχρὰ ὡς ἀληθῶς ταῦτα φὴς τὰ περὶ τῶν Αἰγυπτίων· ὅμως **11**
δ' οὖν, ὦ Μῶμε, τὰ πολλὰ αὐτῶν αἰνίγματά ἐστιν, καὶ οὐ πάνυ
χρὴ καταγελᾶν ἀμύητον ὄντα.

ΜΩΜΟΣ

Πάνυ γοῦν μυστηρίων, ὦ Ζεῦ, δεῖ ἡμῖν, ὡς εἰδέναι θεοὺς μὲν
τοὺς θεούς, κυνοκεφάλους δὲ τοὺς κυνοκεφάλους.

ΖΕΥΣ

Ἔα, φημί, τὰ περὶ Αἰγυπτίων· ἄλλοτε γὰρ περὶ τούτων
ἐπισκεψόμεθα ἐπὶ σχολῆς. σὺ δὲ τοὺς ἄλλους λέγε.

ΜΩΜΟΣ

Τὸν Τροφώνιον, ὦ Ζεῦ, καὶ ὃ μάλιστά με ἀποπνίγει, τὸν Ἀμφί- **12**
λοχον, ὃς ἐναγοῦς ἀνθρώπου καὶ μητραλῴου υἱὸς ὢν μαντεύεται
ὁ γενναῖος ἐν Κιλικίᾳ, ψευδόμενος τὰ πολλὰ καὶ γοητεύων τοῖν
δυοῖν ὀβολοῖν ἕνεκα. τοιγαροῦν οὐκέτι σύ, ὦ Ἄπολλον, εὐδο-
κιμεῖς, ἀλλὰ ἤδη πᾶς λίθος καὶ πᾶς βωμὸς χρησμῳδεῖ, ὃς ἂν
ἐλαίῳ περιχυθῇ καὶ στεφάνους ἔχῃ καὶ γόητος ἀνδρὸς εὐπο-
ρήσῃ, οἷοι πολλοί εἰσιν. ἤδη καὶ ὁ Πολυδάμαντος τοῦ ἀθλητοῦ
ἀνδριὰς ἰᾶται τοὺς πυρέττοντας ἐν Ὀλυμπίᾳ καὶ ὁ Θεαγέ-
νους ἐν Θάσῳ, καὶ Ἕκτορι θύουσιν ἐν Ἰλίῳ καὶ Πρωτεσιλάῳ
καταντικρὺ ἐν Χερρονήσῳ. ἀφ' οὗ δ' οὖν τοσοῦτοι γεγόναμεν,
ἐπιδέδωκε μᾶλλον ἡ ἐπιορκία καὶ ἱεροσυλία, καὶ ὅλως καταπε-
φρονήκασιν ἡμῶν—εὖ ποιοῦντες.

Καὶ ταῦτα μὲν περὶ τῶν νόθων καὶ παρεγγράπτων. ἐγὼ δὲ **13**
καὶ ξένα ὀνόματα πολλὰ ἤδη ἀκούων οὔτε ὄντων τινῶν παρ'
ἡμῖν οὔτε συστῆναι ὅλως δυναμένων, πάνυ, ὦ Ζεῦ, καὶ ἐπὶ τούτοις γελῶ. ἢ ποῦ γάρ ἐστιν ἡ πολυθρύλητος ἀρετὴ καὶ φύσις
καὶ εἱμαρμένη καὶ τύχη, ἀνυπόστατα καὶ κενὰ πραγμάτων ὀνόματα ὑπὸ βλακῶν ἀνθρώπων τῶν φιλοσόφων ἐπινοηθέντα; καὶ
ὅμως αὐτοσχέδια ὄντα οὕτω τοὺς ἀνοήτους πέπεικεν, ὥστε οὐδεὶς
ἡμῖν οὐδὲ θύειν βούλεται, εἰδὼς ὅτι, κἂν μυρίας ἑκατόμβας παρα-

yourselves? Or how can *you* endure it, Zeus, when they make you grow a ram's horns?

ZEUS

[11]   These details you mention about the Egyptians are truly disgraceful. Nevertheless, Momus, most of them have a hidden meaning and shouldn't at all be mocked by anyone who is uninitiated.

MOMUS

Some need we have of mysteries, Zeus, to know that gods are gods and dogheads dogheads!

ZEUS

Stop this talk about Egyptians, I tell you. We'll consider the question another time when we're not busy. Name the other offenders.

MOMUS

[12]   There's Trophonius, Zeus, and what particularly makes me choke with rage, Amphilochus, who, though the son of a blood-guilty matricide, gives oracles, noble fellow, in Cilicia, lying and cheating for the most part to earn his two coppers. That's why you're no longer respected, Apollo, but now oracles are spouted by every stone and altar that's drenched in oil, wears garlands and has an impostor available, and there are lots of them! Now even the statues of Polydamas, the athlete, cures fevers at Olympia, as does that of Theagenes on Thasos, and they sacrifice to Hector in Troy and to Protesilaus on the Chersonnese opposite. Indeed ever since we've become so numerous, perjury and sacrilege have been on the increase and men have become utterly contemptuous of us – and quite right too!

[13]   So much for the bastards and fraudulently registered ones. But now I also hear a great many outlandish names of creatures not found amongst us and completely incapable of existence, and that, Zeus, gives me great amusement. For where is to be found Virtue, that's on everyone's tongue, or Nature or Destiny or Chance, mere immaterial names devoid of all substance, invented by fools of philosophers. But nevertheless, though improvised concoctions, they have gained such credence with fools that nobody will even sacrifice to us any more. They

στήσῃ, ὅμως τὴν τύχην πράξουσαν τὰ μεμοιραμένα καὶ ἃ ἐξ ἀρχῆς ἑκάστῳ ἐπεκλώσθη. ἡδέως ἂν οὖν ἐροίμην σε, ὦ Ζεῦ, εἴ που εἶδες ἢ ἀρετὴν ἢ φύσιν ἢ εἱμαρμένην; ὅτι μὲν γὰρ ἀεὶ καὶ σὺ ἀκούεις ἐν ταῖς τῶν φιλοσόφων διατριβαῖς, οἶδα, εἰ μὴ καὶ κωφός τις εἶ, ὡς βοώντων αὐτῶν μὴ ἐπαΐειν.

Πολλὰ ἔτι ἔχων εἰπεῖν καταπαύσω τὸν λόγον· ὁρῶ γοῦν πολλοὺς ἀχθομένους μοι λέγοντι καὶ συρίττοντας, ἐκείνους μάλιστα ὧν καθήψατο ἡ παρρησία τῶν λόγων. πέρας γοῦν, εἰ **14** ἐθέλεις, ὦ Ζεῦ, ψήφισμά τι περὶ τούτων ἀναγνώσομαι ἤδη ξυγγεγραμμένον.

ΖΕΥΣ

'Ανάγνωθι· οὐ πάντα γὰρ ἀλόγως ἠτιάσω. καὶ δεῖ τὰ πολλὰ αὐτῶν ἐπισχεῖν, ὡς μὴ ἐπὶ πλεῖον ἂν γίγνηται.

ΜΩΜΟΣ

Ψήφισμα ἀγαθῇ τύχῃ. 'Εκκλησίας ἐννόμου ἀγομένης ἑβδόμῃ ἱσταμένου ὁ Ζεὺς ἐπρυτάνευε καὶ προήδρευε Ποσειδῶν, ἐπεστάτει 'Απόλλων, ἐγραμμάτευε Μῶμος Νυκτὸς καὶ ὁ Ὕπνος τὴν γνώμην εἶπεν.

'Επειδὴ πολλοὶ τῶν ξένων, οὐ μόνον Ἕλληνες ἀλλὰ καὶ βάρβαροι, οὐδαμῶς ἄξιοι ὄντες κοινωνεῖν ἡμῖν τῆς πολιτείας, παρεγγραφέντες οὐκ οἶδα ὅπως καὶ θεοὶ δόξαντες ἐμπεπλήκασι μὲν τὸν οὐρανὸν ὡς μεστὸν εἶναι τὸ συμπόσιον ὄχλου ταραχώδους πολυγλώσσων τινῶν καὶ ξυγκλύδων ἀνθρώπων, ἐπιλέλοιπε δὲ ἡ ἀμβροσία καὶ τὸ νέκταρ, ὥστε μνᾶς ἤδη τὴν κοτύλην εἶναι διὰ τὸ πλῆθος τῶν πινόντων,* οἱ δὲ ὑπὸ αὐθαδείας παρωσάμενοι τοὺς παλαιούς τε καὶ ἀληθεῖς θεοὺς προεδρίας ἠξιώκασιν αὐτοὺς παρὰ πάντα τὰ πάτρια καὶ ἐν τῇ γῇ προτιμᾶσθαι θέλουσι, δ ἐδόχθω* τῇ βουλῇ καὶ τῷ δήμῳ ξυλλεγῆναι μὲν ἐκκλησίαν ἐν **15** τῷ 'Ολύμπῳ περὶ τροπὰς χειμερινάς, ἑλέσθαι δὲ ἐπιγνώμονας τελείους θεοὺς ἑπτά, τρεῖς μὲν ἐκ τῆς παλαιᾶς βουλῆς τῆς ἐπὶ Κρόνου, τέτταρας δὲ ἐκ τῶν δώδεκα, καὶ ἐν αὐτοῖς τὸν Δία· τούτους δὲ τοὺς ἐπιγνώμονας αὐτοὺς μὲν καθέζεσθαι ὀμόσαντας τὸν νόμιμον ὅρκον τὴν Στύγα, τὸν Ἑρμῆν δὲ κηρύξαντα ξυναγαγεῖν ἅπαντας ὅσοι ἀξιοῦσι ξυντελεῖν ἐς τὸ ξυνέδριον, τοὺς δὲ

know that, even if they offer countless hecatombs, it will be Chance that will accomplish what has been fated and spun out for each man from the beginning. So I'd like to ask you, Zeus, if you've ever seen Virtue or Nature or Destiny; for I know that you too continually hear their names at the philosophers' discussions – unless you're deaf, so that you don't hear them as they shout.

Though there's a lot more I *could* say, I'll end my speech; I can see many are annoyed at what I say and hissing, particularly those censured by my frank words. [14] So, to end, Zeus, I'll read out a resolution that I've already composed.

ZEUS

Read it, for your complaints have not been entirely unjustified and we must check most of these abuses to stop them getting any worse.

MOMUS

May this resolution be blessed with good luck. At a regular meeting of the assembly on the seventh of the month Zeus was in charge, Posidon supervised, Apollo was chairman, Momus, the son of Night, acted as clerk and Sleep proposed the motion.

'Whereas many outsiders, not only Greeks but foreigners as well, quite unworthy of sharing our citizen privileges, fraudulently enrolled somehow and passing off as gods, have filled the heavens, so that our feasting chamber is crowded with a disorderly mob of fellows of many different languages and races, and whereas there is a shortage of ambrosia and nectar, so that a half pint now costs a fortune owing to the great number of drinkers, and whereas they have wilfully thrust aside the real gods and claimed the front seats for themselves, contrary to all the traditions of our forefathers and want to have preferential honour on earth, [15] let it be the resolve of the Council and the People that an assembly be convened on Olympus about the time of the Winter Solstice, that a Commission be chosen of seven fully qualified Gods, three to be from the old Council of Cronos' time and four including Zeus to be from the Twelve Gods, that these Commissioners before going into session should take the customary oath and swear by the Styx, that Hermes should act as herald and summon all who claim to be members of our conclave, that they should come bringing sworn witnesses and documentary evidence of

ἥκειν μάρτυρας ἐπαγομένους ἐνωμότους καὶ ἀποδείξεις τοῦ
γένους. τοὐντεῦθεν δὲ οἱ μὲν παρίτωσαν καθ᾽ ἕνα, οἱ δὲ ἐπι-
γνώμονες ἐξετάζοντες ἢ θεοὺς εἶναι ἀποφανοῦνται ἢ κατα-
πέμψουσιν ἐπὶ τὰ σφέτερα ἠρία καὶ τὰς θήκας τὰς προγονικάς.
ἢν δέ τις ἁλῷ τῶν ἀδοκίμων καὶ ἅπαξ ὑπὸ τῶν ἐπιγνωμόνων ἐκ-
κριθέντων ἐπιβαίνων τοῦ οὐρανοῦ, ἐς τὸν Τάρταρον ἐμπεσεῖν
τοῦτον.

Ἐργάζεσθαι δὲ τὰ αὐτοῦ ἕκαστον, καὶ μήτε τὴν Ἀθηνᾶν ἰᾶ- **16**
σθαι μήτε τὸν Ἀσκληπιὸν χρησμῳδεῖν μήτε τὸν Ἀπόλλω τοσαῦτα μόνον ποιεῖν, ἀλλὰ ἕν τι ἐπιλεξάμενον μάντιν ἢ κιθαρῳ-
δὸν ἢ ἰατρὸν εἶναι. τοῖς δὲ φιλοσόφοις προειπεῖν μὴ ἀναπλάτ- **17**
τειν κενὰ ὀνόματα μηδὲ ληρεῖν περὶ ὧν οὐκ ἴσασιν. ὁπόσοι δὲ **18**
ἤδη ναῶν ἢ θυσιῶν ἠξιώθησαν, ἐκείνων μὲν καθαιρεθῆναι τὰ
ἀγάλματα, ἐντεθῆναι δὲ ἢ Διὸς ἢ Ἥρας ἢ Ἀπόλλωνος ἢ τῶν
ἄλλων τινός, ἐκείνοις δὲ τάφον χῶσαι τὴν πόλιν καὶ στήλην
ἐπιστῆσαι ἀντὶ βωμοῦ. ἢν δέ τις παρακούσῃ τοῦ κηρύγματος
καὶ μὴ ἐθελήσῃ ἐπὶ τοὺς ἐπιγνώμονας ἐλθεῖν, ἐρήμην αὐτοῦ
καταδιαιτησάτωσαν.

ΖΕΥΣ

Τοῦτο μὲν ὑμῖν τὸ ψήφισμα δικαιότατον, ὦ Μῶμε· καὶ ὅτῳ **19**
δοκεῖ, ἀνατεινάτω τὴν χεῖρα· μᾶλλον δέ, οὕτω γιγνέσθω, πλείους
γὰρ οἶδ᾽ ὅτι ἔσονται οἱ μὴ χειροτονήσοντες. ἀλλὰ νῦν μὲν ἄπιτε·
ὁπόταν δὲ κηρύξῃ ὁ Ἑρμῆς, ἥκετε κομίζοντες ἕκαστος ἐναργῆ
τὰ γνωρίσματα καὶ σαφεῖς τὰς ἀποδείξεις, πατρὸς ὄνομα καὶ
μητρός, καὶ ὅθεν καὶ ὅπως θεὸς ἐγένετο, καὶ φυλὴν καὶ φράτορας.
ὡς ὅστις ἂν μὴ ταῦτα παράσχηται, οὐδὲν μελήσει τοῖς ἐπιγνώ-
μοσιν εἰ νεών τις μέγαν ἐν τῇ γῇ*καὶ οἱ ἄνθρωποι θεὸν αὐτὸν
εἶναι νομίζουσιν.

* add ἔχει

their parentage, that thereafter they should come forward individually to be examined by the Commissioners who will either pronounce them to be gods or send them back down to their tombs and ancestral graves, and that if anyone, who is disqualified and has been rejected once and for all by the verdict of the Commissioners, be caught setting foot in heaven, he should be cast into Tartarus, [16] and that each should practise his own trade, that Athena should not cure the sick or Asclepius give oracles or Apollo perform so many functions singlehanded but should choose one single profession and be *either* prophet *or* lyre player *or* doctor, [17] and that the philosophers be forbidden to invent empty names or talk nonsense about things of which they are completely ignorant, [18] and that those who have already been accorded temples or sacrificial privileges should have their images destroyed to be replaced by those of Zeus or Hera or Apollo or one of the others, and their cities should raise tombs in their honour and erect gravestones in place of their altars, and that anyone disregarding this proclamation and refusing to appear before the Commissioners should be condemned by them *in absentia*.

ZEUS

[19] Here you all have an extremely fair proposal, Momus. Hands up all who approve! Or rather, motion carried, since I know that the majority will vote against it. But disperse for the time being and when Hermes makes the proclamation each of you come, bringing clear evidence of identity and sure proofs of parentage, name of father and mother, origin and manner of deification and name of tribe and clan. For if anyone fails to provide this evidence, it won't matter a bit to the Commissioners that he has a large temple on earth and men think him a god.

ΑΝΑΒΙΟΥΝΤΕΣ Η ΑΛΙΕΥΣ

ΣΩΚΡΑΤΗΣ

Βάλλε βάλλε τὸν κατάρατον ἀφθόνοις τοῖς λίθοις· ἐπίβαλλε τῶν 1
βώλων· προσεπίβαλλε καὶ τῶν ὀστράκων· παῖε τοῖς ξύλοις τὸν
ἀλιτήριον· ὅρα μὴ διαφύγῃ· καὶ σὺ βάλλε, ὦ Πλάτων· καὶ σύ, ὦ
Χρύσιππε, καὶ σὺ δέ, καὶ πάντες ἅμα συνασπίσωμεν ἐπ' αὐτόν,

ὡς πήρη πήρηφιν ἀρήγῃ, βάκτρα δὲ βάκτροις,

κοινὸς γὰρ πολέμιος, καὶ οὐκ ἔστιν ἡμῶν ὅντινα οὐχ ὕβρικεν.
σὺ δέ, ὦ Διόγενες, εἴ ποτε καὶ ἄλλοτε, χρῶ τῷ ξύλῳ· μηδὲ
ἀνῆτε· διδότω τὴν ἀξίαν βλάσφημος ὤν. τί τοῦτο; κεκμήκατε, ὦ
Ἐπίκουρε καὶ Ἀρίστιππε; καὶ μὴν οὐκ ἐχρῆν.

ἀνέρες ἔστε, σοφοί, μνήσασθε δὲ θούριδος ὀργῆς.

Ἀριστότελες, ἐπισπούδασον· ἔτι θᾶττον. εὖ ἔχει· ἑάλωκεν τὸ 2
θηρίον. εἰλήφαμέν σε, ὦ μιαρέ. εἴσῃ γοῦν αὐτίκα οὕστινας
ἡμᾶς ὄντας ἐκακηγόρεις. τῷ τρόπῳ δέ τις αὐτὸν καὶ μετέλθῃ;
ποικίλον γάρ τινα θάνατον ἐπινοῶμεν κατ' αὐτοῦ πᾶσιν ἡμῖν
ἐξαρκέσαι δυνάμενον· καθ' ἕκαστον γοῦν ἑπτάκις δίκαιός ἐστιν
ἀπολωλέναι.

ΦΙΛΟΣΟΦΟΣ
Ἐμοὶ μὲν ἀνεσκολοπίσθαι δοκεῖ αὐτόν.

ΑΛΛΟΣ
Νὴ Δία, μαστιγωθέντα γε πρότερον.

ΑΛΛΟΣ
Πολὺ πρότερον τοὺς ὀφθαλμοὺς ἐκκεκολάφθω.

ΑΛΛΟΣ
Τὴν γλῶτταν αὐτὴν ἔτι πολὺ πρότερον ἀποτετμήσθω.

THE FISHERMAN

SOCRATES

[1] Pelt, pelt the villain with lots of stones. Pelt him with clods too. Pelt him with potsherds as well. Hit the scoundrel with your sticks. See he doesn't escape. *You* join in as well, Plato, – and *you*, Chrysippus, – and *you* too, and let us all attack him with a united front,

'That to pouch my pouch give aid, and staff to staff.'

For he's the enemy of us all and has affronted everyone of us. *You*, Diogenes, if ever you've used your stick, use it *now*. Don't stop, any of you. Let him be properly punished for his wicked tongue. What's this? Tired, Epicurus and Aristippus? That's quite wrong,

'Quit ye like men, ye sages; mindful be of doughty wrath'.

[2] Hurry up, Aristotle! Faster still! That's good; the beast is caught. We've got you, you blackguard. You'll soon know what sort of men we are that you've been maligning. But just how is one to punish him? Let's plan some elaborate death for him, one that can satisfy us all. He deserves to die seven times over for each one of us.

PHILOSOPHER A

I'd like him crucified.

PHILOSOPHER B

Yes indeed, but whipped first.

PHILOSOPHER C

Long before that he should have his eyes gouged out.

PHILOSOPHER D

And long before that again, he must have that tongue of his cut out.

THE FISHERMAN

ΣΩΚΡΑΤΗΣ

Σοὶ δὲ τί, Ἐμπεδόκλεις, δοκεῖ;

ΕΜΠΕΔΟΚΛΗΣ

Εἰς τοὺς κρατῆρας ἐμπεσεῖν αὐτόν, ὡς μάθῃ μὴ λοιδορεῖσθαι
τοῖς κρείττοσιν.

ΠΛΑΤΩΝ

Καὶ μὴν ἄριστον ἦν καθάπερ τινὰ Πενθέα ἢ Ὀρφέα

λακιστὸν ἐν πέτραισιν εὑρέσθαι μόρον,

ἵνα ἂν καὶ τὸ μέρος αὐτοῦ ἕκαστος ἔχων ἀπηλλάττετο.

ΠΑΡΡΗΣΙΑΔΗΣ

Μηδαμῶς· ἀλλὰ πρὸς Ἱκεσίου φείσασθέ μου.   3

ΣΩΚΡΑΤΗΣ

Ἄραρεν· οὐκ ἂν ἀφεθείης ἔτι. ὁρᾷς δὲ δὴ καὶ τὸν Ὅμηρον ἃ
φησιν,

ὡς οὐκ ἔστι λέουσι καὶ ἀνδράσιν ὅρκια πιστά.

ΠΑΡΡΗΣΙΑΔΗΣ

Καὶ μὴν καθ᾽ Ὅμηρον ὑμᾶς καὶ αὐτὸς ἱκετεύσω· αἰδέσεσθε γὰρ
ἴσως τὰ ἔπη καὶ οὐ παρόψεσθε ῥαψῳδήσαντά με·

ζωγρεῖτ᾽ οὐ κακὸν ἄνδρα καὶ ἄξια δέχθε ἄποινα,
χαλκόν τε χρυσόν τε, τὰ δὴ φιλέουσι σοφοί περ.

ΣΩΚΡΑΤΗΣ

Ἀλλ᾽ οὐδὲ ἡμεῖς ἀπορήσομεν πρὸς σὲ Ὁμηρικῆς ἀντιλογίας.
ἄκουε δή·

μὴ δή μοι φύξιν γε, κακηγόρε, βάλλεο θυμῷ
χρυσόν περ λέξας, ἐπεὶ ἵκεο χεῖρας ἐς ἁμάς.

ΠΑΡΡΗΣΙΑΔΗΣ

Οἴμοι τῶν κακῶν. ὁ μὲν Ὅμηρος ἡμῖν ἄπρακτος, ἡ μεγίστη
ἐλπίς. ἐπὶ τὸν Εὐριπίδην δή μοι καταφευκτέον· τάχα γὰρ
ἐκεῖνος σώσειέ με.

μὴ κτεῖνε· τὸν ἱκέτην γὰρ οὐ θέμις κτανεῖν.

SOCRATES
And what's *your* opinion, Empedocles?

EMPEDOCLES
He should be thrown into my crater, to teach him not to revile his betters.

PLATO
However it would be best that he, like a Pentheus or Orpheus,
'Be torn apart 'mid rocks and find his doom',
so that each of us should go away with a part of him.

FRANK
[3] No; in the name of the God of Suppliants, spare me.

SOCRATES
It's all settled. You can't be released now. You know quite well what Homer says
'For 'twixt men and lions no trusted pledges be.'

FRANK
But I too can quote Homer to beg for your mercy. For perhaps you'll respect his poetry and won't ignore me if I put together some epic verse
'Oh take me live; not vile am I; get ransom meet,
Get bronze and gold, that even sages wise do love.'

SOCRATES
But we in turn will find a Homeric argument to counter yours; just listen to this.
'Escape consider not, I say, thou foul of tongue,
Though offering gold, for now you're in my power.'

FRANK
Alas, how terrible! Homer, who was my best hope, is no good to me. Now I must take refuge with Euripides; perhaps he will save me.
'Oh slay me not; to slay your suppliant is wrong.'

ΠΛΑΤΩΝ

Τί δέ; οὐχὶ κἀκεῖνα Εὐριπίδου ἐστίν,

οὐ δεινὰ πάσχειν δεινὰ τοὺς εἰργασμένους;

ΠΑΡΡΗΣΙΑΔΗΣ

Νῦν οὖν ἕκατι ῥημάτων κτενεῖτέ με;

ΠΛΑΤΩΝ

Νὴ Δία· φησὶ γοῦν ἐκεῖνος αὐτός,

ἀχαλίνων στομάτων
ἀνόμου τ' ἀφροσύνας
τὸ τέλος δυστυχία.

ΠΑΡΡΗΣΙΑΔΗΣ

Οὐκοῦν ἐπεὶ δέδοκται πάντως ἀποκτιννύναι καὶ οὐδεμία μηχανὴ 4
τὸ διαφυγεῖν με, φέρε τοῦτο γοῦν εἴπατέ μοι, τίνες ὄντες ἢ τί
πεπονθότες ἀνήκεστον πρὸς ἡμῶν ἀμείλικτα ὀργίζεσθε καὶ ἐπὶ
θανάτῳ συνειλήφατε;

ΠΛΑΤΩΝ

Ἅτινα μὲν εἴργασαι ἡμᾶς τὰ δεινά, σεαυτὸν ἐρώτα, ὦ κάκιστε,
καὶ τοὺς καλοὺς ἐκείνους σου λόγους ἐν οἷς φιλοσοφίαν τε αὐτὴν
κακῶς ἡγόρευες καὶ εἰς ἡμᾶς ὕβριζες, ὥσπερ ἐξ ἀγορᾶς ἀποκηρύττων σοφοὺς ἄνδρας, καὶ τὸ μέγιστον, ἐλευθέρους· ἐφ' οἷς
ἀγανακτήσαντες ἀνεληλύθαμεν ἐπὶ σὲ παραιτησάμενοι πρὸς
ὀλίγον τὸν Ἀϊδωνέα, Χρύσιππος οὑτοσὶ καὶ Ἐπίκουρος καὶ
ὁ Πλάτων ἐγὼ καὶ Ἀριστοτέλης ἐκεῖνος καὶ ὁ σιωπῶν οὗτος
Πυθαγόρας καὶ Διογένης καὶ ἅπαντες ὁπόσους διέσυρες ἐν τοῖς
λόγοις.

ΠΑΡΡΗΣΙΑΔΗΣ

Ἀνέπνευσα· οὐ γὰρ ἀποκτενεῖτέ με, εἰ μάθητε ὁποῖος ἐγὼ 5
περὶ ὑμᾶς ἐγενόμην· ὥστε ἀπορρίψατε τοὺς λίθους, μᾶλλον δὲ
φυλάττετε. χρήσεσθε γὰρ αὐτοῖς κατὰ τῶν ἀξίων.

ΠΛΑΤΩΝ

Ληρεῖς. σὲ δὲ χρὴ τήμερον ἀπολωλέναι, καὶ ἤδη γε

λάϊνον ἔσσο χιτῶνα κακῶν ἕνεχ' ὅσσα ἔοργας.

PLATO

Indeed? Doesn't Euripides also say?
'Who dire deeds do, should suffer penance dire.'

FRANK

'So now you'll slay me, all because of words?'

PLATO

Yes indeed. Euripides himself says
'Of tongues unbridled
And folly lawless
The end is misery.'

FRANK

[4] Then since you're absolutely resolved on execution and there's no
way I can escape, please tell me one thing. Who are you and what
irreparable harm have you suffered at my hands that you show such
implacable anger, arresting me and wanting to kill me?

PLATO

What terrible things have you done to us? Just ask yourself, you utter
villain, and ask those fine dialogues of yours in which you were rude to
Philosophy herself and insulting to us, putting up for sale like slaves in
the market men who are wise and, greatest enormity of all, free. That's
why we got angry, begged Hades to let us away for a little and have come
up here to get you, we being Chrysippus here, Epicurus, Plato – that's me
– Aristotle over there, Pythagoras (the silent one here), Diogenes and all
the others you slated in your dialogues.

FRANK

[5] That's a relief, for you won't kill me, if you realise how I've
behaved to you. So throw away your stones – or better still, keep them;
you can use them against those that deserve them.

PLATO

Rubbish. It's *you* must die and to-day. This instant you must
'A shirt of stone put on for all the wrongs you've done.'

ΠΑΡΡΗΣΙΑΔΗΣ

Καὶ μήν, ὦ ἄριστοι, ὃν ἐχρῆν μόνον ἐξ ἁπάντων ἐπαινεῖν οἰκεῖόν τε ὑμῖν ὄντα καὶ εὔνουν καὶ ὁμογνώμονα καί, εἰ μὴ φορτικὸν εἰπεῖν, κηδεμόνα τῶν ἐπιτηδευμάτων εὖ ἴστε ἀποκτενοῦντες, ἢν ἐμὲ ἀποκτείνητε τοσαῦτα ὑπὲρ ὑμῶν πεπονηκότα. ὁρᾶτε γοῦν μὴ κατὰ τοὺς πολλοὺς τῶν νῦν φιλοσόφων αὐτοὶ ποιεῖτε, ἀχάριστοι καὶ ὀργίλοι καὶ ἀγνώμονες φαινόμενοι πρὸς ἄνδρα εὐεργέτην.

ΠΛΑΤΩΝ

Ὦ τῆς ἀναισχυντίας. καὶ χάριν σοι τῆς κακηγορίας προσοφείλομεν; οὕτως ἀνδραπόδοις ὡς ἀληθῶς οἴει διαλέγεσθαι; ἢ καὶ εὐεργεσίαν καταλογιῇ πρὸς ἡμᾶς ἐπὶ τῇ τοσαύτῃ ὕβρει καὶ παροινίᾳ τῶν λόγων;

ΠΑΡΡΗΣΙΑΔΗΣ

Ποῦ γὰρ ἐγὼ ὑμᾶς ἢ πότε ὕβρικα, ὃς ἀεὶ φιλοσοφίαν τε θαυ- 6 μάζων διατετέλεκα καὶ ὑμᾶς αὐτοὺς ὑπερεπαινῶν καὶ τοῖς λόγοις οἷς καταλελοίπατε ὁμιλῶν; αὐτὰ γοῦν ἅ φημι ταῦτα, πόθεν ἄλλοθεν ἢ παρ' ὑμῶν παραλαβὼν καὶ κατὰ τὴν μέλιτταν ἀπανθισάμενος ἐπιδείκνυμαι τοῖς ἀνθρώποις; οἱ δὲ ἐπαινοῦσι καὶ γνωρίζουσιν ἕκαστος τὸ ἄνθος ὅθεν καὶ παρ' ὅτου καὶ ὅπως ἀνελεξάμην, καὶ λόγῳ μὲν ἐμὲ ζηλοῦσι τῆς ἀνθολογίας, τὸ δὲ ἀληθὲς ὑμᾶς καὶ τὸν λειμῶνα τὸν ὑμέτερον, οἳ τοιαῦτα ἐξηνθήκατε ποικίλα καὶ πολυειδῆ τὰς βαφάς, εἴ τις ἀναλέξασθαί γε αὐτὰ ἐπίσταιτο καὶ ἀναπλέξαι καὶ ἁρμόσαι, ὡς μὴ ἀπᾴδειν θάτερον θατέρου. ἔσθ' ὅστις οὖν ταῦτα εὖ πεπονθὼς παρ' ὑμῶν κακῶς ἂν εἰπεῖν ἐπιχειρήσειεν εὐεργέτας ἄνδρας, ἀφ' ὧν εἶναί τις ἔδοξεν; ἐκτὸς εἰ μὴ κατὰ τὸν Θάμυριν ἢ τὸν Εὔρυτον εἴη τὴν φύσιν ὡς ταῖς Μούσαις ἀντᾴδειν, παρ' ὧν εἰλήφει τὴν ᾠδήν, ἢ τῷ Ἀπόλλωνι ἐριδαίνειν ἐναντία τοξεύων, καὶ ταῦτα δοτῆρι ὄντι τῆς τοξικῆς.

ΦΙΛΟΣΟΦΟΣ

Τοῦτο μέν, ὦ γενναῖε, κατὰ τοὺς ῥήτορας εἴρηταί σοι· 7 ἐναντιώτατον γοῦν ἐστι τῷ πράγματι καὶ χαλεπωτέραν σου ἐπιδείκνυσι τὴν τόλμαν, εἴ γε τῇ ἀδικίᾳ καὶ ἀχαριστίᾳ πρόσεστιν, ὃς παρ' ἡμῶν τὰ τοξεύματα, ὡς φής, λαβὼν καθ' ἡμῶν ἐτόξευσες, ἕνα τοῦτον ὑποθέμενος τὸν σκοπόν, ἅπαντας ἡμᾶς ἀγορεύειν κακῶς· τοιαῦτα παρὰ σοῦ ἀπειλήφαμεν ἀνθ' ὧν σοι τὸν

FRANK

But, good sirs, you should know that you'll be killing the only man in the world you should applaud for being friendly to you, well-disposed and like -minded, and, if it's not illbred to say so, a protector of your way of life – assuming you execute me after I've toiled so hard on your behalf. Just be sure that you yourselves aren't acting like the philosophers of today and proving yourselves ungrateful, bad-tempered and insensitive towards a benefactor.

PLATO

What bare-faced cheek! *We* should be grateful to *you* for maligning *us*, should we? Do you really think you can talk to *us* as though we were slaves? Will you claim credit from *us* as our benefactor for such insults and wild, drunken words?

FRANK

[6] Where or when have I ever insulted you? Why, I've ever been a constant admirer of philosophy, loud in my praises of yourselves and a close companion of the writings you've left behind you. And as for these very works of mine, where else did I get them but from you, culling your flowers like the bee and putting them on display for men? They one and all applaud, recognising where, from whom and how I've picked the flower, and though they seem to be admiring me for my flower-picking, in truth their admiration is for you and your meadow, you who've produced such a variety of blossoms of so many colours for anyone with the knowledge to pick them, make them into garlands and fit them together so that they are in harmony with each other. So is there anyone who, after receiving such benefits from you, would try to revile the benefactors who have given him his reputation, unless of course he's naturally like Thamyris or Eurytus, so as to sing in competition with the Muses who had given him song or to compete with Apollo in rivalry of bow, though owing to him the gift of archery.

PHILOSOPHER

[7] You're talking like the rhetoricians, my good sir; your argument is in complete contradiction of the facts and shows up your effrontery as even more intolerable, involving not only injustice but ingratitude as well, since you got your arrows from us, as you admit, and then fired them against us, your sole aim being to disparage all of us. That's the recompense we've had from you for throwing open that meadow of ours

λειμῶνα ἐκεῖνον ἀναπετάσαντες οὐκ ἐκωλύομεν δρέπεσθαι καὶ
τὸ προκόλπιον ἐμπλησάμενον ἀπελθεῖν· ὥστε διά γε τοῦτο μάλιστα
δίκαιος ἂν εἴης ἀποθανεῖν.

ΠΑΡΡΗΣΙΑΔΗΣ

Ὁρᾶτε; πρὸς ὀργὴν ἀκούετε καὶ οὐδὲν τῶν δικαίων προσίεσθε. 8
καίτοι οὐκ ἂν ᾠήθην ποτὲ ὡς ὀργὴ Πλάτωνος ἢ Χρυσίππου ἢ
Ἀριστοτέλους ἢ τῶν ἄλλων ὑμῶν καθίκοιτο ἄν, ἀλλά μοι
ἐδοκεῖτε μόνοι δὴ πόρρω εἶναι τοῦ τοιούτου. πλὴν ἀλλὰ μὴ
ἄκριτόν γε, ὦ θαυμάσιοι, μηδὲ πρὸ δίκης ἀποκτείνητέ με. ὑμέτερον γοῦν καὶ τοῦτο ἦν, μὴ βίᾳ μηδὲ κατὰ τὸ ἰσχυρότερον
πολιτεύεσθαι, δίκῃ δὲ τὰ διάφορα διαλύεσθαι διδόντας λόγον καὶ
δεχομένους ἐν τῷ μέρει. ὥστε δικαστὴν ἑλόμενοι κατηγορήσατε
μὲν ὑμεῖς ἢ ἅμα πάντες ἢ ὅντινα ἂν χειροτονήσητε ὑπὲρ ἁπάντων,
ἐγὼ δὲ ἀπολογήσομαι πρὸς τὰ ἐγκλήματα. κᾆτα ἢν μέν τι
ἀδικῶν φαίνωμαι καὶ τοῦτο περὶ ἐμοῦ γνῷ τὸ δικαστήριον,
ὑφέξω δηλαδὴ τὴν ἀξίαν· ὑμεῖς δὲ βίαιον οὐδὲν τολμήσετε· ἢν δὲ
τὰς εὐθύνας ὑποσχὼν καθαρὸς ὑμῖν καὶ ἀνεπίληπτος εὑρίσκωμαι,
ἀφήσουσί με οἱ δικασταί, ὑμεῖς δὲ ἐς τοὺς ἐξαπατήσαντας ὑμᾶς
καὶ παροξύναντας καθ' ἡμῶν τὴν ὀργὴν τρέψατε.

ΠΛΑΤΩΝ

Τοῦτο ἐκεῖνο· εἰς πεδίον τὸν ἵππον, ὡς παρακρουσάμενος τοὺς 9
δικαστὰς ἀπέλθῃς. φασὶ γοῦν ῥήτορά σε καὶ δικανικόν τινα
εἶναι καὶ πανοῦργον ἐν τοῖς λόγοις. τίνα δὲ καὶ δικαστὴν ἐθέλεις
γενέσθαι, ὅντινα μὴ σὺ δωροδοκήσας, οἷα πολλὰ ποιεῖτε, ἄδικα
πείσεις ὑπὲρ σοῦ ψηφίσασθαι;

ΠΑΡΡΗΣΙΑΔΗΣ

Θαρρεῖτε τούτου γε ἕνεκα· οὐδένα τοιοῦτον διαιτητὴν ὕποπτον
ἢ ἀμφίβολον ἀξιώσαιμ' ἂν γενέσθαι καὶ ὅστις ἀποδώσεταί μοι
τὴν ψῆφον. ὁρᾶτε γοῦν, τὴν Φιλοσοφίαν αὐτὴν μεθ' ὑμῶν
ποιοῦμαι δικάστριαν ἔγωγε.

ΠΛΑΤΩΝ

Καὶ τίς ἂν κατηγορήσειεν, εἴ γε ἡμεῖς δικάσομεν;

ΠΑΡΡΗΣΙΑΔΗΣ

Οἱ αὐτοὶ κατηγορεῖτε καὶ δικάζετε· οὐδὲν οὐδὲ τοῦτο δέδια.

to you and allowing you to pick our flowers and go away with your arms full of them. So for *that* most of all you deserve to die.

FRANK

[8] Do you see? You listen in anger and reject every just argument. And I'd never have thought that anger would affect Plato or Chrysippus or Aristotle or the rest of you; you seemed to me to be far removed from that sort of thing. But one thing, excellencies, don't execute me untried or before hearing my case; at any rate it used to be your style not to use violence or *force majeure* in your civic dealings, but to resolve your differences in court, affording and listening to explanations in turn. So choose a judge and prosecute me, either all of you at once or through anyone you elect to represent you all, and I shall defend myself against the charges. Then, if I'm shown to be guilty of any wrongdoing and that's the court's decision about me, I shall of course pay the proper penalty and you won't have to venture any show of force; but if, once I've submitted my accounts, I am found to be guiltless in your opinion and blameless, the jury will acquit me, and you must vent your wrath against those who have deceived you and incited you against me.

PLATO

[9] Just as I thought; it's 'horses on to the plain', so that you may trick the jury and escape. They say you're an orator and courtroom expert and cunning in the use of words. But whom do you want for judge, apart from someone you'll be able to bribe, as your type often do, and persuade to cast an unjust vote in your favour?

FRANK

Have no fears on that score; I wouldn't accept any untrustworthy or dubious arbitrator of that sort or one who'd sell me his vote. See, my choice for judge is Philosophy herself and with you all to accompany her.

PLATO

And who can prosecute, if we're on the jury?

FRANK

You be prosecutors and jurors as well; I have no fears even of that. I

τοσοῦτον ὑπερφέρω τοῖς δικαίοις καὶ ἐκ περιουσίας ἀπολογή-
σεσθαι ὑπολαμβάνω.

ΠΛΑΤΩΝ*

Τί ποιῶμεν, ὦ Πυθαγόρα καὶ Σώκρατες; ἔοικε γὰρ ἀνὴρ οὐκ   10
ἄλογα προκαλεῖσθαι δικάζεσθαι ἀξιῶν.

ΣΩΚΡΑΤΗΣ

Τί δὲ ἄλλο ἢ βαδίζωμεν ἐπὶ τὸ δικαστήριον καὶ τὴν Φιλοσοφίαν
παραλαβόντες ἀκούσωμεν ὅ τι καὶ ἀπολογήσεται; τὸ πρὸ δίκης
γὰρ οὐχ ἡμέτερον, ἀλλὰ δεινῶς ἰδιωτικόν, ὀργίλων τινῶν
ἀνθρώπων καὶ τὸ δίκαιον ἐν τῇ χειρὶ τιθεμένων. παρέξομεν γοῦν
ἀφορμὰς τοῖς κακηγορεῖν ἐθέλουσιν καταλεύσαντες ἄνδρα μηδὲ
ἀπολογησάμενον ὑπὲρ ἑαυτοῦ, καὶ ταῦτα δικαιοσύνῃ χαίρειν
αὐτοὶ λέγοντες. ἢ τί ἂν εἴποιμεν Ἀνύτου καὶ Μελήτου πέρι, τῶν
ἐμοῦ κατηγορησάντων, ἢ τῶν τότε δικαστῶν, εἰ οὗτος τεθνήξεται
μηδὲ τὸ παράπαν ὕδατος μεταλαβών;

ΠΛΑΤΩΝ*

Ἄριστα παραινεῖς, ὦ Σώκρατες· ὥστε ἀπίωμεν ἐπὶ τὴν
Φιλοσοφίαν. ἡ δὲ δικασάτω, καὶ ἡμεῖς ἀγαπήσομεν οἷς ἂν
ἐκείνη διαγνῷ.

ΠΑΡΡΗΣΙΑΔΗΣ

Εὖ γε, ὦ σοφώτατοι, ἀμείνω ταῦτα καὶ νομιμώτερα. τοὺς   11
μέντοι λίθους φυλάττετε, ὡς ἔφην· δεήσει γὰρ αὐτῶν μικρὸν
ὕστερον ἐν τῷ δικαστηρίῳ.

Ποῦ δὲ τὴν Φιλοσοφίαν εὕροι τις ἄν; οὐ γὰρ οἶδα ἔνθα οἰκεῖ·
καίτοι πάνυ πολὺν ἐπλανήθην χρόνον ἀναζητῶν τὴν οἰκίαν, ὡς
συγγενοίμην αὐτῇ. εἶτα ἐντυγχάνων ἄν τισι τριβώνια περι-
βεβλημένοις καὶ πώγωνας βαθεῖς καθειμένοις παρ’ αὐτῆς
ἐκείνης ἥκειν φάσκουσιν, οἰόμενος εἰδέναι αὐτοὺς ἀνηρώτων· οἱ
δὲ πολὺ μᾶλλον ἐμοῦ ἀγνοοῦντες ἢ οὐδὲν ὅλως ἀπεκρίνοντό μοι,
ὡς μὴ ἐλέγχοιντο οὐκ εἰδότες, ἢ ἄλλην θύραν ἀντ’ ἄλλης ἐπεδεί-
κνυον. οὐδέπω γοῦν καὶ τήμερον ἐξευρεῖν δεδύνημαι τὴν οἰκίαν.

Πολλάκις δὲ ἢ αὐτὸς εἰκάσας ἢ ξεναγήσαντός τινος ἧκον   12
ἂν ἐπί τινας θύρας βεβαίως ἐλπίσας τότε γοῦν εὑρηκέναι, τεκμαι-
ρόμενος τῷ πλήθει τῶν εἰσιόντων τε καὶ ἐξιόντων, ἁπάντων
σκυθρωπῶν καὶ τὰ σχήματα εὐσταλῶν καὶ φροντιστικῶν τὴν

have such superiority of justice on my side and think I'll have more than enough to use in my defence.

PLATO

[10] What are we to do, Pythagoras and Socrates? The fellow seems to be reasonable in challenging us and asking for a trial.

SOCRATES

What else should we do but go to the courtroom, taking Philosophy with us and listening to his defence? To reach a verdict before a trial is not our style, but dreadfully amateurish and typical of hot-tempered fellows who take the law into their own hands. We'll certainly provide ammunition for those who want to disparage us, if we stone to death a man who hasn't even spoken in his own defence, especially as we ourselves claim to rejoice in justice. What can we say about Anytus and Meletus, my accusers, or the jurors on that occasion, if this man is executed without even being allowed any time to speak in his defence?

PLATO

Excellent advice, Socrates; so let's go and fetch Philosophy. Let *her* decide the case and we'll be content with any verdict she gives.

FRANK

[11] Bravo, learned gentlemen; that's a better and more regular procedure. But keep your stones, as I said before; they'll be needed in court a little later.

But where can one find Philosophy? *I* don't know where she lives. And yet I've wandered about for ever so long looking for her house, so that I could keep company with her. Then I kept meeting some men with tattered cloaks and long beards who claimed they'd just come from her and I would question them, thinking they knew the answer. But they were much more ignorant than I was and either gave me no answer at all, so as not to have their ignorance shown up, or else kept showing me one door after another. So up to this day I've been unable to locate her house. [12] Often either from personal guesswork or from another's guidance I would arrive at particular doors, firmly expecting that this time I'd found the place, basing my convictions on the numbers of people going in and out, all of them grim-faced, respectably dressed and of studious

πρόσοψιν· μετὰ τούτων οὖν συμπαραβυσθεὶς καὶ αὐτὸς εἰσῆλθον
ἄν. εἶτα ἑώρων γύναιόν τι οὐχ ἁπλοϊκόν, εἰ καὶ ὅτι μάλιστα εἰς
τὸ ἀφελὲς καὶ ἀκόσμητον ἑαυτὴν ἐπερρύθμιζεν, ἀλλὰ κατεφάνη μοι
αὐτίκα οὐδὲ τὸ ἄφετον δοκοῦν τῆς κόμης ἀκαλλώπιστον ἐῶσα
οὐδὲ τοῦ ἱματίου τὴν ἀναβολὴν ἀνεπιτηδεύτως περιστέλλουσα·
πρόδηλος δὲ ἦν κοσμουμένη αὐτοῖς καὶ πρὸς εὐπρέπειαν τῷ
ἀθεραπεύτῳ δοκοῦντι προσχρωμένη. ὑπεφαίνετο δέ τι καὶ
ψιμύθιον καὶ φῦκος, καὶ τὰ ῥήματα πάνυ ἑταιρικά, καὶ ἐπαινου-
μένη ὑπὸ τῶν ἐραστῶν εἰς κάλλος ἔχαιρε, καὶ εἰ δοίη τις προχείρως
ἐδέχετο, καὶ τοὺς πλουσιωτέρους ἂν παρακαθισαμένη πλησίον
τοὺς πένητας τῶν ἐραστῶν οὐδὲ προσέβλεπεν. πολλάκις δὲ καὶ
γυμνωθείσης αὐτῆς κατὰ τὸ ἀκούσιον ἑώρων περιδέραια χρύσεα
τῶν κλοιῶν παχύτερα. ταῦτα ἰδὼν ἐπὶ πόδας ἂν εὐθὺς ἀνέστρεφον,
οἰκτείρας δηλαδὴ τοὺς κακοδαίμονας ἐκείνους ἑλκομένους πρὸς
αὐτῆς οὐ τῆς ῥινὸς ἀλλὰ τοῦ πώγονος καὶ κατὰ τὸν Ἰξίονα
εἰδώλῳ ἀντὶ τῆς Ἥρας συνόντας.

ΠΛΑΤΩΝ

Τοῦτο μὲν ὀρθῶς ἔλεξας· οὐ γὰρ πρόδηλος οὐδὲ πᾶσι γνώριμος 13
ἡ θύρα. πλὴν ἀλλ' οὐδὲν δεήσει βαδίζειν ἐπὶ τὴν οἰκίαν· ἐνταῦθα
γὰρ ἐν Κεραμεικῷ ὑπομενοῦμεν αὐτήν. ἡ δὲ ἤδη που ἀφίξεται
ἐπανιοῦσα ἐξ Ἀκαδημίας, ὡς περιπατήσειε καὶ ἐν τῇ Ποικίλῃ·
τοῦτο γὰρ ὁσημέραι ποιεῖν ἔθος αὐτῇ· μᾶλλον δὲ ἤδη πρόσεισιν.
ὁρᾷς τὴν κόσμιον τὴν ἀπὸ τοῦ σχήματος, τὴν προσηνῆ τὸ
βλέμμα, τὴν ἐπὶ συννοίας ἠρέμα βαδίζουσαν;

ΠΑΡΡΗΣΙΑΔΗΣ

Πολλὰς ὁμοίας ὁρῶ τό γε σχῆμα καὶ τὸ βάδισμα καὶ τὴν
ἀναβολήν. καίτοι μία πάντως ἤ γε ἀληθὴς Φιλοσοφία καὶ ἐν
αὐταῖς.

ΠΛΑΤΩΝ

Εὖ λέγεις. ἀλλὰ δηλώσει ἥτις ἐστὶ φθεγξαμένη μόνον.

ΦΙΛΟΣΟΦΙΑ

Παπαῖ· τί Πλάτων καὶ Χρύσιππος ἄνω καὶ Ἀριστοτέλης καὶ 14
οἱ λοιποὶ ἅπαντες, αὐτὰ δὴ τὰ κεφάλαιά μου τῶν μαθημάτων;
τί αὖθις εἰς τὸν βίον; ἆρά τι ὑμᾶς ἐλύπει τῶν κάτω; ὀργιζομέ-

appearance. So I would push myself into their midst and go in too. Then I'd see a poor female specimen who was anything but unaffected though trying her utmost to make herself appear natural and unadorned, but I could see at once that in the apparent disorder of her hair she hadn't neglected the beautician's art and that the loose folds of her mantle didn't lack careful arrangement. It was quite clear that she used these devices to make herself attractive and her apparent lack of make-up as a further aid to beauty. There were also some traces of powder and paint on her face, she talked just like a prostitute, she enjoyed being praised for her beauty by her lovers, she readily accepted gifts from anyone, and would seat her wealthier suitors beside her, but wouldn't so much as look at the poorer ones. Often when she accidentally bared her flesh, I could see golden necklaces thicker than shackles. When I saw all this, I would immediately return home, sorry of course for those poor creatures being dragged by her, not by the proverbial nose but by their beards, and like Ixion keeping company with a phantom instead of the real Hera.

PLATO

[13] You're quite correct; for her door isn't obvious or known to everyone. However there'll be no need to go to her house; we'll wait for her here in the Potters' Quarter; I'm sure she'll come any minute on her way back from the Academy, to take a walk in the Painted Porch as well, for that's her daily habit. Indeed she's coming now. Do you see the respectably dressed lady with the pleasant look, the one walking slowly deep in thought?

FRANK

I see many women alike in appearance, gait and style of dress but surely only one of them is the genuine Philosophy.

PLATO

True enough, but she'll reveal her identity the moment she speaks.

PHILOSOPHY

[14] Good heavens! What are *you* doing up here, Plato, Chrysippus, Aristotle and the rest of you, you leading lights of my studies? Why have you returned to life? Did something down below distress you? You certainly seem angry. And who is this fellow you've seized and are taking off? Is he a thief or a murderer or guilty of sacrilege?

νοις γοῦν ἐοίκατε. καὶ τίνα τοῦτον συλλαβόντες ἄγετε; ἦ που λωποδύτης τις ἢ ἀνδροφόνος ἢ ἱερόσυλός ἐστιν;

ΠΛΑΤΩΝ

Νὴ Δία, ὦ Φιλοσοφία, πάντων γε ἱεροσύλων ἀσεβέστατος, ὃς τὴν ἱερωτάτην σὲ κακῶς ἀγορεύειν ἐπεχείρησεν καὶ ἡμᾶς ἅπαντας, ὁπόσοι τι παρὰ σοῦ μαθόντες τοῖς μεθ᾽ ἡμᾶς καταλελοίπαμεν.

ΦΙΛΟΣΟΦΙΑ

Εἶτα ἠγανακτήσατε λοιδορησαμένου τινός, καὶ ταῦτα εἰδότες ἐμέ, οἷα πρὸς τῆς Κωμῳδίας ἀκούουσα ἐν Διονυσίοις ὅμως φίλην τε αὐτὴν ἥγημαι καὶ οὔτε ἐδικασάμην οὔτε ᾐτιασάμην προσελθοῦσα, ἐφίημι δὲ παίζειν τὰ εἰκότα καὶ τὰ συνήθη τῇ ἑορτῇ; οἶδα γὰρ ὡς οὐκ ἄν τι ὑπὸ σκώμματος χεῖρον γένοιτο, ἀλλὰ τοὐναντίον ὅπερ ἂν ᾖ καλόν, ὥσπερ τὸ χρυσίον ἀποσμώμενον τοῖς κόμμασιν, λαμπρότερον ἀποστίλβει καὶ φανερώτερον γίγνεται. ὑμεῖς δὲ οὐκ οἶδα ὅπως ὀργίλοι καὶ ἀγανακτικοὶ γεγόνατε. τί δ᾽ οὖν αὐτὸν ἄγχετε;

ΑΝΑΒΙΟΥΝΤΕΣ

Μίαν ἡμέραν ταύτην παραιτησάμενοι ἥκομεν ἐπ᾽ αὐτὸν ὡς ὑπόσχῃ τὴν ἀξίαν ὧν δέδρακεν. φῆμαι γὰρ ἡμῖν διήγγελλον οἷα ἔλεγεν ἐς τὰ πλήθη καθ᾽ ἡμῶν.

ΦΙΛΟΣΟΦΙΑ

Εἶτα πρὸ δίκης οὐδὲ ἀπολογησάμενον ἀποκτενεῖτε; δῆλος 15 γοῦν ἐστιν εἰπεῖν τι θέλων.

ΑΝΑΒΙΟΥΝΤΕΣ

Οὔκ, ἀλλ᾽ ἐπὶ σὲ τὸ πᾶν ἀνεβαλόμεθα, καὶ σοὶ ὅτι ἂν δοκῇ, τοῦτο ποιήσει τέλος τῆς δίκης.

ΦΙΛΟΣΟΦΙΑ

Τί φῇς σύ;

ΠΑΡΡΗΣΙΑΔΗΣ

Τοῦτο αὐτό, ὦ δέσποινα Φιλοσοφία, ἥπερ καὶ μόνη τἀληθὲς ἐξευρεῖν δύναιο· μόλις γοῦν εὑρόμην πολλὰ ἱκετεύσας τὸ σοὶ φυλαχθῆναι τὴν δίκην.

ΑΝΑΒΙΟΥΝΤΕΣ

Νῦν, ὦ κατάρατε, δέσποιναν αὐτὴν καλεῖς; πρῴην* δὲ τὸ

* read πρῴην

PHILOSOPHER

Yes indeed, Philosophy, the most impious of all sacrilegious creatures. Why, he has attempted to disparage the most sacred one of all, your own self, and all of us who have learned anything from you and passed it on to later generations!

PHILOSOPHY

So you got angry when ridiculed? Though you know what names I've been called by Comedy at the Dionysia and how nevertheless I've treated her as a friend, never taking her to court or accosting her with accusations, but allowing her to indulge in such fun as is appropriate and habitual at her festival? For I know that nothing can be harmed by jests but on the contrary anything beautiful shines more brilliantly and becomes brighter, just like gold that gains lustre from being stamped and coined. But somehow you've become hot-tempered and irascible. Anyhow why *are* you throttling him?

PHILOSOPHERS RETURNED TO LIFE

We've gained leave of absence for to-day and have come after him to make him pay the proper penalty for what he's done. For reports kept telling us what sort of things he would say against us in public.

PHILOSOPHY

[15] So you're going to kill him before trying him and without even letting him speak in his defence? He certainly makes it clear he has something he wants to say.

PHILOSOPHERS

No, we pass the whole matter over to you and whatever you decide will bring the trial to a close.

PHILOSOPHY

What do you have to say, sir?

FRANK

The very same as them, Philosophy, my Mistress and the only one who can discover the truth. Indeed, only with great difficulty and after many requests, have I managed to get the case reserved for you.

PHILOSOPHERS

So now, you scoundrel, you call her *your* mistress? Yet only the other

ἀτιμότατον Φιλοσοφίαν ἀπέφαινες ἐν τοσούτῳ θεάτρῳ ἀποκηρύττων κατὰ μέρη δύ᾽ ὀβολῶν ἕκαστον εἶδος αὐτῆς τῶν λόγων.

ΦΙΛΟΣΟΦΙΑ

Ὁρᾶτε μὴ οὐ Φιλοσοφίαν οὗτός γε ἀλλὰ γόητας ἄνδρας ἐπὶ τῷ ἡμετέρῳ ὀνόματι πολλὰ καὶ μιαρὰ πράττοντας ἠγόρευεν κακῶς.

ΠΑΡΡΗΣΙΑΔΗΣ

Εἴσῃ αὐτίκα, ἢν ἐθέλῃς ἀπολογουμένου ἀκούειν μόνον.

ΦΙΛΟΣΟΦΙΑ

Ἀπίωμεν εἰς Ἄρειον πάγον, μᾶλλον δὲ εἰς τὴν ἀκρόπολιν αὐτήν, ὡς ἂν ἐκ περιωπῆς ἅμα καταφανείη πάντα τὰ ἐν τῇ πόλει. ὑμεῖς 16 δέ, ὦ φίλαι, ἐν τῇ Ποικίλῃ τέως περιπατήσατε· ἤξω γὰρ ὑμῖν ἐκδικάσασα τὴν δίκην.

ΠΑΡΡΗΣΙΑΔΗΣ

Τίνες δέ εἰσιν, ὦ Φιλοσοφία; πάνυ γάρ*μοι κόσμιαι καὶ αὗται δοκοῦσιν.

ΦΙΛΟΣΟΦΙΑ

Ἀρετὴ μὲν ἡ ἀνδρώδης αὕτη, Σωφροσύνη δὲ ἐκείνη καὶ Δικαιοσύνη παρ᾽ αὐτήν. ἡ προηγουμένη δὲ Παιδεία, ἡ ἀμυδρὰ δὲ καὶ ἀσαφὴς τὸ χρῶμα ἡ Ἀλήθειά ἐστιν.

ΠΑΡΡΗΣΙΑΔΗΣ

Οὐχ ὁρῶ ἥντινα καὶ λέγεις.

ΦΙΛΟΣΟΦΙΑ

Τὴν ἀκαλλώπιστον ἐκείνην οὐχ ὁρᾷς, τὴν γυμνήν, τὴν ὑποφεύγουσαν ἀεὶ καὶ διολισθάνουσαν;

ΠΑΡΡΗΣΙΑΔΗΣ

Ὁρῶ νῦν μόλις. ἀλλὰ τί οὐχὶ καὶ ταύτας ἄγεις, ὡς πλῆρες γένοιτο καὶ ἐντελὲς τὸ συνέδριον; τὴν Ἀλήθειαν δέ γε καὶ συνήγορον ἀναβιβάσασθαι πρὸς τὴν δίκην βούλομαι.

ΦΙΛΟΣΟΦΙΑ

Νὴ Δία, ἀκολουθήσατε καὶ ὑμεῖς· οὐ βαρὺ γὰρ μίαν δικάσαι δίκην, καὶ ταῦτα περὶ τῶν ἡμετέρων ἐσομένην.

* read γὰρ κόσμιαι

day you depicted Philosophy as something absolutely despicable before a huge audience by offering for sale for a couple of coppers at a time each form of her theories.

PHILOSOPHY
Take care; his harsh words may have been directed not against Philosophy but against impostors perpetrating many villainies in our name.

FRANK
You'll soon find out, if only you agree to listen to my defence speech.

PHILOSOPHY
[16] Let's be off to the Areopagus, or better to the Acropolis itself, so that everything in Athens can be seen simultaneously from a viewpoint. But you, (*she turns to her five companions*) dear ladies, have a walk around for the meantime in the Porch. For I'll join you once I've decided the case.

FRANK
Who are they, Philosophy? They too seem to me very respectable.

PHILOSOPHY
This one here with the manly appearance is Virtue; over there is Temperance and beyond her is Justice. The one leading them is Culture and the indeterminate one with the faint colouring is Truth.

FRANK
I can't see the one you mean.

PHILOSOPHY
Don't you see the unadorned one over there, the naked one who is ever hanging back and trying to slip away?

FRANK
Now I can see her, but only just. But why don't you take these ladies along as well so that your conclave can be full and complete? In fact I want to call Truth too into court as counsel for my defence.

PHILOSOPHY
Yes indeed; you ladies follow too; for it's no hardship to decide a single case, particularly one that will concern our interests.

ΑΛΗΘΕΙΑ

Ἄπιτε ὑμεῖς· ἐγὼ γὰρ οὐδὲν δέομαι ἀκούειν ἃ πάλαι οἶδα   17
ὁποῖά ἐστιν.

ΦΙΛΟΣΟΦΙΑ

Ἀλλ' ἡμῖν, ὦ Ἀλήθεια, ἐν δέοντι συνδικάζοις ἂν καὶ κατα-
μηνύοις ἕκαστα.

ΑΛΗΘΕΙΑ

Οὐκοῦν ἐπάγωμαι καὶ τὼ θεραπαινιδίω τούτω συνοικοτάτω
μοι ὄντε;

ΦΙΛΟΣΟΦΙΑ

Καὶ μάλα ὁπόσας ἂν ἐθέλῃς.

ΑΛΗΘΕΙΑ

Ἔπεσθον, ὦ Ἐλευθερία καὶ Παρρησία, μεθ' ἡμῶν, ὡς τὸν
δείλαιον τουτονὶ ἀνθρωπίσκον ἐραστὴν ἡμέτερον ὄντα καὶ κιν-
δυνεύοντα ἐπὶ μηδεμιᾷ προφάσει δικαίᾳ σῶσαι δυνηθῶμεν. σὺ
δέ, ὦ Ἔλεγχε, αὐτοῦ περίμεινον.

ΠΑΡΡΗΣΙΑΔΗΣ

Μηδαμῶς, ὦ δέσποινα· ἡκέτω δὲ καὶ οὗτος, εἰ καί τις ἄλλος·
οὐ γὰρ τοῖς τυχοῦσι θηρίοις προσπολεμῆσαι δεήσει με ἀλαζόσιν
ἀνθρώποις καὶ δυσελέγκτοις, ἀεί τινας ἀποφυγὰς εὑρισκομένοις,
ὥστε ἀναγκαῖος ὁ Ἔλεγχος.

ΕΛΕΓΧΟΣ

Ἀναγκαιότατος μὲν οὖν· ἄμεινον δέ, εἰ καὶ τὴν Ἀπόδειξιν
παραλάβοις.

ΑΛΗΘΕΙΑ

Ἔπεσθε πάντες, ἐπείπερ ἀναγκαῖοι δοκεῖτε πρὸς τὴν δίκην.

ΑΝΑΒΙΟΥΝΤΕΣ

Ὁρᾷς; προσεταιρίζεται καθ' ἡμῶν, ὦ Φιλοσοφία, τὴν Ἀλή-   18
θειαν.

ΦΙΛΟΣΟΦΙΑ

Εἶτα δέδιτε, ὦ Πλάτων καὶ Χρύσιππε καὶ Ἀριστότελες, μή τι
ψεύσηται ὑπὲρ αὐτοῦ Ἀλήθεια οὖσα;

TRUTH

[17] The rest of you go; *I've* no need to hear things I've known about for a long time.

PHILOSOPHY

But, Truth, please help us in our time of need by joining in the judging and informing us about everything.

TRUTH

Then may I bring along as well these two maids of mine, who are my very close associates?

PHILOSOPHY

Certainly; bring as many as you like.

TRUTH

You come along with us, Freedom and Frankness, so that we can save this poor, unfortunate human who is in love with us and in danger for no just cause. But you, Examination, stay here.

FRANK

No, no, Mistress; let him of all people come too. For it's no ordinary beasts I'll have to fight but charlatans who are hard to catch out, always finding some means of escape, so that Examination is necessary.

EXAMINATION

Yes, I am absolutely necessary; but it'd be better if you took Proof along as well.

TRUTH

Follow me, all of you, since you seem to be needed for the trial.

PHILOSOPHERS

[18] Do you see, Philosophy? He wants Truth's collusion in attacking us.

PHILOSOPHY

So are you afraid, Plato, Chrysippus and Aristotle, of Truth telling any lies on his behalf?

ΑΝΑΒΙΟΥΝΤΕΣ

Οὐ τοῦτο, ἀλλὰ δεινῶς πανοῦργός ἐστιν καὶ κολακικός· ὥστε παραπείσει αὐτήν.

ΦΙΛΟΣΟΦΙΑ

Θαρρεῖτε· οὐδὲν μὴ γένηται ἄδικον, Δικαιοσύνης ταύτης συμ- 19
παρούσης. ἀνίωμεν οὖν. ἀλλὰ εἰπέ μοι σύ, τί σοι τοὔνομα;

ΠΑΡΡΗΣΙΑΔΗΣ

Ἐμοί; Παρρησιάδης Ἀληθίωνος τοῦ Ἐλεγξικλέους.

ΦΙΛΟΣΟΦΙΑ

Πατρὶς δέ;

ΠΑΡΡΗΣΙΑΔΗΣ

Σύρος, ὦ Φιλοσοφία, τῶν Ἐπευφρατιδίων. ἀλλὰ τί τοῦτο;
καὶ γὰρ τούτων τινὰς οἶδα τῶν ἀντιδίκων μου οὐχ ἧττον ἐμοῦ
βαρβάρους τὸ γένος· ὁ τρόπος δὲ καὶ ἡ παιδεία οὐ κατὰ Σολέας
ἢ Κυπρίους ἢ Βαβυλωνίους ἢ Σταγειρίτας. καίτοι πρός γε σὲ
οὐδὲν ἂν ἔλαττον γένοιτο οὐδ᾽ εἰ τὴν φωνὴν βάρβαρος εἴη τις,
εἴπερ ἡ γνώμη ὀρθὴ καὶ δικαία φαίνοιτο οὖσα.

ΦΙΛΟΣΟΦΙΑ

Εὖ λέγεις· ἄλλως γοῦν ἠρόμην. ἡ τέχνη δέ σοι τίς; ἄξιον γὰρ 20
ἐπίστασθαι τοῦτό γε.

ΠΑΡΡΗΣΙΑΔΗΣ

Μισαλαζών εἰμι καὶ μισογόης καὶ μισοψευδὴς καὶ μισότυφος
καὶ μισῶ πᾶν τὸ τοιουτῶδες εἶδος τῶν μιαρῶν ἀνθρώπων· πάνυ
δὲ πολλοί εἰσιν, ὡς οἶσθα.

ΦΙΛΟΣΟΦΙΑ

Ἡράκλεις, πολυμισῆ τινα μέτει τὴν τέχνην.

ΠΑΡΡΗΣΙΑΔΗΣ

Εὖ λέγεις· ὁρᾷς γοῦν ὁπόσοις ἀπεχθάνομαι καὶ ὡς κινδυνεύω
δι᾽ αὐτήν.
Οὐ μὴν ἀλλὰ καὶ τὴν ἐναντίαν αὐτῇ πάνυ ἀκριβῶς οἶδα, λέγω
δὲ τὴν ἀπὸ τοῦ φιλο τὴν ἀρχὴν ἔχουσαν· φιλαλήθης γὰρ καὶ
φιλόκαλος καὶ φιλαπλοϊκὸς καὶ ὅσα τῷ φιλεῖσθαι συγγενῆ. πλὴν
ἀλλ᾽ ὀλίγοι πάνυ ταύτης ἄξιοι τῆς τέχνης, οἱ δὲ ὑπὸ τῇ ἐναντίᾳ
ταττόμενοι καὶ τῷ μίσει οἰκειότεροι πεντακισμύριοι. κινδυνεύω

PHILOSOPHERS

No, but he's awfully unscrupulous and skilled at flattery; so he'll talk
her over.

PHILOSOPHY

[19] Don't worry; nothing unjust can possibly occur while Justice is
here with us. So let's go up to the court. (*They start climbing to the
Acropolis*). But *you* , sir, tell me your name.

FRANK

My name? It's Frank, the son of Truthful, son of Examiner the
Famous.

PHILOSOPHY

And your Country?

FRANK

I'm a Syrian, Philosophy, born on the banks of the Euphrates. But
what's this? I know that some of my opponents in the case are just as
much foreigners as myself; but their habits and culture are untypical of
men of Soli, Cyprus, Babylon or Stagira. Yet that wouldn't stand against
anyone in your eyes, even if he spoke like a foreigner, provided his
thoughts were clearly upright and just.

PHILOSOPHY

[20] Well said. It was an idle question of mine. But what's your
trade? That's worth knowing.

FRANK

I am an impostor-hater, charlatan-hater, liar-hater, affectation-hater and
hate all villains of that sort; they're very numerous, as you know.

PHILOSOPHY

By Heracles, there's great scope for hating in the trade you ply.

FRANK

Very true. You can see how many enemies I have and what dangers I
run because of it.
  However I also have a close knowledge of the diametrically opposite
trade, the one that begins with 'lover'; for I'm a lover of truth, lover of
beauty, lover of sincerity, and of everything else naturally lovable.
However very few are fit subjects for the lover's trade, while those that
are liable to the opposite one and come within the hateful category number

τοιγαροῦν τὴν μὲν ὑπ᾽ ἀργίας ἀπομαθεῖν ἤδη, τὴν δὲ πάνυ
ἠκριβωκέναι.

ΦΙΛΟΣΟΦΙΑ

Καὶ μὴν οὐκ ἐχρῆν· τοῦ γὰρ αὐτοῦ καὶ τάδε, φασί, καὶ τάδε·
ὥστε μὴ διαίρει τὼ τέχνα· μία γὰρ ἐστὸν δύ᾽ εἶναι δοκοῦσα.

ΠΑΡΡΗΣΙΑΔΗΣ

Ἄμεινον σὺ οἶσθα ταῦτα, ὦ Φιλοσοφία. τὸ μέντοι ἐμὸν τοιοῦτόν
ἐστιν, οἷον τοὺς μὲν πονηροὺς μισεῖν, ἐπαινεῖν δὲ τοὺς χρηστοὺς
καὶ φιλεῖν.

ΦΙΛΟΣΟΦΙΑ

Ἄγε δή, πάρεσμεν γὰρ ἔνθα ἐχρῆν, ἐνταῦθά που ἐν τῷ προνάῳ　21
τῆς Πολιάδος δικάσωμεν. ἡ Ἱέρεια διάθες ἡμῖν τὰ βάθρα, ἡμεῖς
δὲ ἐν τοσούτῳ προσκυνήσωμεν τὴν θεόν.

ΠΑΡΡΗΣΙΑΔΗΣ

Ὦ Πολιάς, ἐλθέ μοι κατὰ τῶν ἀλαζόνων σύμμαχος ἀναμνη-
σθεῖσα ὁπόσα ἐπιορκούντων ὁσημέραι ἀκούεις αὐτῶν· καὶ ἃ
πράττουσι δὲ μόνη ὁρᾷς ἅτε δὴ ἐπὶ σκοπῆς οἰκοῦσα. νῦν
καιρὸς ἀμύνασθαι αὐτούς. ἐμὲ δὲ ἤν που κρατούμενον ἴδῃς καὶ
πλείους ὦσιν αἱ μέλαιναι, σὺ προσθεῖσα τὴν σεαυτῆς σῷζέ με.

ΦΙΛΟΣΟΦΙΑ

Εἶέν· ἡμεῖς μὲν ὑμῖν καὶ δὴ καθήμεθα ἕτοιμοι ἀκούειν τῶν　22
λόγων, ὑμεῖς δὲ προελόμενοί τινα ἐξ ἁπάντων, ὅστις ἄριστα
κατηγορήσειν δοκῇ, συνείρετε τὴν κατηγορίαν καὶ διελέγχετε·
οὐ γὰρ οἷόν τε πάντας ἅμα λέγειν. σὺ δέ, ὦ Παρρησιάδη, ἀπο-
λογήσῃ τὸ μετὰ τοῦτο.

ΠΛΑΤΩΝ

Τίς οὖν ὁ ἐπιτηδειότατος ἐξ ἡμῶν ἂν γένοιτο πρὸς τὴν δίκην;

ΑΝΑΒΙΟΥΝΤΕΣ

Σύ, ὦ Πλάτων. ἥ τε γὰρ μεγαλόνοια θαυμαστὴ καὶ ἡ καλλι-
φωνία δεινῶς Ἀττικὴ καὶ τὸ κεχαρισμένον καὶ πειθοῦς μεστὸν
ἥ τε σύνεσις καὶ τὸ ἀκριβὲς καὶ τὸ ἐπαγωγὸν ἐν καιρῷ τῶν ἀποδείξεων, πάντα ταῦτά σοι ἀθρόα πρόσεστι· ὥστε τὴν προηγορίαν
δέχου καὶ ὑπὲρ ἁπάντων εἰπὲ τὰ εἰκότα. νῦν ἀναμνήσθητι πάντων
ἐκείνων καὶ συμφόρει εἰς τὸ αὐτό, εἴ τί σοι πρὸς Γοργίαν ἢ Πῶλον

countless thousands. So I am already in danger of forgetting the one trade through lack of use, but of becoming a past master in the other one.

PHILOSOPHY

But that's not as it should be. For according to the proverb the same man should practise both this and that; so don't separate your two trades; for they are but one, though they seem two.

FRANK

You are the better judge of that, Philosophy; but my case is such that I hate villains but praise and love good men.

PHILOSOPHY

[21] Come now, as we've reached the required place, let's hold the trial in the antechamber of Athene, Protectress of Our City. Priestess, you put out the benches for us, and in the meanwhile let us pay our respects to the goddess.

FRANK

Lady Protectress, come to my aid, I beg you, against the charlatans, remembering all the false oaths you hear them swearing every day. And what's more you're the only one who sees their doings, dwelling as you do on a watch-tower. Now is the time to punish them, and, if you see me losing my case and the black pebbles in the majority, add your own vote and save me.

PHILOSOPHY

[22] Well then, we're at your service, gentlemen, and seated ready to hear your speeches, and you must choose the one of your number, who you think will be the best prosecutor, piece together your speech for the prosecution and show up the accused; for it's not possible for all to speak at once. And after that you, Frank, will make your defence.

PLATO

Well, who of us would be the best qualified to take on the case?

PHILOSOPHERS

You, Plato, for wonderful magnificence of thought, marvellously Attic elegance of speech, charm, abundance of persuasiveness, intellect, precision and well-timed attractiveness in expounding arguments are all combined in you. So accept the spokesmanship and say the right things for all of us. Remember now all these qualities and combine into the same speech anything you've said against Gorgias, Polus, Prodicus or Hippias.

ἢ Πρόδικον ἢ Ἱππίαν εἴρηται· δεινότερος οὗτός ἐστιν. ἐπίπαττε
οὖν καὶ τῆς εἰρωνείας καὶ τὰ κομψὰ ἐκεῖνα καὶ συνεχῆ ἐρώτα, κἂν
σοι δοκῇ, κἀκεῖνό που παράβυσον, ὡς ὁ μέγας ἐν οὐρανῷ Ζεὺς
πτηνὸν ἅρμα ἐλαύνων ἀγανακτήσειεν ἄν, εἰ μὴ οὗτος ὑπόσχοι τὴν
δίκην.

ΠΛΑΤΩΝ

Μηδαμῶς, ἀλλά τινα τῶν σφοδροτέρων προχειρισώμεθα, 23
Διογένη τοῦτον ἢ Ἀντισθένη ἢ Κράτητα ἢ καὶ σέ, ὦ Χρύσιππε·
οὐ γὰρ δὴ κάλλους ἐν τῷ παρόντι καὶ δεινότητος συγγραφικῆς
ὁ καιρός, ἀλλά τινος ἐλεγκτικῆς καὶ δικανικῆς παρασκευῆς· ῥήτωρ
δὲ ὁ Παρρησιάδης ἐστίν.

ΔΙΟΓΕΝΗΣ

Ἀλλ' ἐγὼ αὐτοῦ κατηγορήσω· οὐδὲ γὰρ πάνυ μακρῶν οἶμαι
τῶν λόγων δεήσεσθαι. καὶ ἄλλως ὑπὲρ ἅπαντας ὕβρισμαι δύ'
ὀβολῶν πρῴην ἀποκεκηρυγμένος.

ΠΛΑΤΩΝ

Ὁ Διογένης, ὦ Φιλοσοφία, τὸν λόγον ἐρεῖ τὸν ὑπὲρ ἁπάντων.
μέμνησο δέ, ὦ γενναῖε, μὴ τὰ σεαυτοῦ μόνον πρεσβεύειν ἐν τῇ
κατηγορίᾳ, τὰ κοινὰ δὲ ὁρᾶν· εἰ γάρ τι καὶ πρὸς ἀλλήλους δια-
φερόμεθα ἐν τοῖς δόγμασι, σὺ δὲ τοῦτο μὲν μὴ ἐξέταζε, μηδὲ
ὅστις ἐστὶν ὁ ἀληθέστερος νῦν λέγε, ὅλως δὲ ὑπὲρ Φιλοσοφίας
αὐτῆς ἀγανάκτει περιυβρισμένης καὶ κακῶς ἀκουούσης ἐν τοῖς
Παρρησιάδου λόγοις, καὶ τὰς προαιρέσεις ἀφείς, ἐν αἷς διαλ-
λάττομεν, ὃ κοινὸν ἅπαντες ἔχομεν, τοῦτο ὑπερμάχει. ὅρα·
σὲ μόνον προεστησάμεθα καὶ ἐν σοὶ τὰ πάντα ἡμῶν νῦν κιν-
δυνεύεται, ἢ σεμνότατα δόξαι ἢ τοιαῦτα πιστευθῆναι οἷα οὗτος
ἀπέφηνε.

ΔΙΟΓΕΗΝΣ

Θαρρεῖτε, οὐδὲν ἐλλείψομεν· ὑπὲρ ἁπάντων ἐρῶ. κἂν ἡ 24
Φιλοσοφία δὲ πρὸς τοὺς λόγους ἐπικλασθεῖσα—φύσει γὰρ
ἥμερος καὶ πρᾶός ἐστιν—ἀφεῖναι διαβουλεύηται αὐτόν, ἀλλ' οὐ τὰ
ἐμὰ ἐνδεήσει· δείξω γὰρ αὐτῷ ὅτι μὴ μάτην ξυλοφοροῦμεν.

ΦΙΛΟΣΟΦΙΑ

Τοῦτο μὲν μηδαμῶς, ἀλλὰ τῷ λόγῳ μᾶλλον· ἄμεινον γὰρ ἤπερ
τῷ ξύλῳ. μὴ μέλλε δ' οὖν. ἤδη γὰρ ἐγκέχυται τὸ ὕδωρ καὶ πρὸς
σὲ τὸ δικαστήριον ἀποβλέπει.

This opponent is even cleverer than they were. So sprinkle on some irony as well and ask those polished, continuous questions and, if you please, also push in somewhere that 'mighty Zeus driving his winged chariot in heaven' would be angry if this fellow didn't pay the penalty.

PLATO

[23] Oh no, let us appoint someone more forceful, Diogenes here or Antisthenes or Crates or even you, Chrysippus; for the present occasion doesn't call for beauty and skill as a writer, but equipment for showing the opponent up and arguing in court; Frank is a trained orator.

DIOGENES

Well, I'll prosecute him; for I don't think I'll need to speak at any great length; besides I've been insulted more than the others, when sold off the other day for a mere two coppers.

PLATO

Diogenes will speak for us all, Philosophy; but you, my noble friend, (*turning to Diogenes*) must remember not to give pride of place just to your own grievances in your prosecution, but to maintain a common viewpoint. For even if we disagree somewhat with each other in our beliefs, you musn't go into that or tell us for the moment which of us gets closer to the truth, but vent our general anger on behalf of Philosophy herself, since she has been terribly insulted and maligned in Frank's dialogues and you must put aside our doctrinal differences and fight our common cause. Note this; we've made *you* our sole champion and *all* our schools are in danger and it depends on *you* whether they are to be held in the highest esteem or whether *his* portrayal of them is to be believed.

DIOGENES

[24] Have no fear, we shall be well served. I shall speak for all of us. Even if Philosophy relents in the face of his speeches, she being naturally gentle and kind, and decides to acquit him, *my* efforts, however, won't be found wanting. *I'll* show him it's not for nothing we carry sticks.

PHILOSOPHY

None of that please; I'd prefer you to use words; that's better than using your stick. Anyhow don't dawdle; the time allotted to your speech has already started, and the jury's eyes are on you.

THE FISHERMAN

ΠΑΡΡΗΣΙΑΔΗΣ

Οἱ λοιποὶ καθιζέτωσαν, ὦ Φιλοσοφία, καὶ ψηφοφορείτωσαν μεθ᾽ ὑμῶν, Διογένης δὲ κατηγορείτω μόνος.

ΦΙΛΟΣΟΦΙΑ

Οὐ δέδιας οὖν μή σου καταψηφίσωνται;

ΠΑΡΡΗΣΙΑΔΗΣ

Οὐδαμῶς· πλείοσι γοῦν κρατῆσαι βούλομαι.

ΦΙΛΟΣΟΦΙΑ

Γενναῖά σου ταῦτα· καθίσατε δ᾽ οὖν. σὺ δέ, ὦ Διόγενες, λέγε.

ΔΙΟΓΕΝΗΣ

Οἷοι μὲν ἡμεῖς ἄνδρες ἐγενόμεθα παρὰ τὸν βίον, ὦ Φιλοσοφία, 25
πάνυ ἀκριβῶς οἶσθα καὶ οὐδὲν δεῖ λόγων· ἵνα γὰρ τὸ κατ᾽ ἐμὲ
σιωπήσω, ἀλλὰ Πυθαγόραν τοῦτον καὶ Πλάτωνα καὶ Ἀριστοτέλη καὶ Χρύσιππον καὶ τοὺς ἄλλους τίς οὐκ οἶδεν ὅσα εἰς τὸν
βίον καλὰ εἰσεκομίσαντο; ἃ δὲ τοιούτους ὄντας ἡμᾶς ὁ τρισκατ-
άρατος οὑτοσὶ Παρρησιάδης ὕβρικεν ἤδη ἐρῶ.

Ῥήτωρ γάρ τις, ὥς φασιν, ὤν, ἀπολιπὼν τὰ δικαστήρια καὶ
τὰς ἐν ἐκείνοις εὐδοκιμήσεις, ὁπόσον ἢ δεινότητος ἢ ἀκμῆς ἐπε-
πόριστο ἐν τοῖς λόγοις, τοῦτο πᾶν ἐφ᾽ ἡμᾶς συσκευασάμενος οὐ
παύεται μὲν ἀγορεύων κακῶς γόητας καὶ ἀπατεῶνας ἀποκαλῶν,
τὰ πλήθη δὲ ἀναπείθων καταγελᾶν ἡμῶν καὶ καταφρονεῖν ὡς τὸ
μηδὲν ὄντων· μᾶλλον δὲ καὶ μισεῖσθαι πρὸς τῶν πολλῶν ἤδη
πεποίηκεν αὐτούς τε ἡμᾶς καὶ σὲ τὴν Φιλοσοφίαν, φληνάφους καὶ
λήρους ἀποκαλῶν τὰ σὰ καὶ τὰ σπουδαιότατα ὧν ἡμᾶς ἐπαίδευσας
ἐπὶ χλεύῃ διεξιών, ὥστε αὐτὸν μὲν κροτεῖσθαι καὶ ἐπαινεῖσθαι
πρὸς τῶν θεατῶν, ἡμᾶς δὲ ὑβρίζεσθαι. φύσει γάρ τι τοιοῦτόν ἐστιν
ὁ πολὺς λεώς, χαίρουσι τοῖς ἀποσκώπτουσιν καὶ λοιδορουμένοις,
καὶ μάλισθ᾽ ὅταν τὰ σεμνότατα εἶναι δοκοῦντα διασύρηται,
ὥσπερ ἀμέλει καὶ πάλαι ἔχαιρον Ἀριστοφάνει καὶ Εὐπόλιδι
Σωκράτη τουτονὶ ἐπὶ χλεύῃ παράγουσιν ἐπὶ τὴν σκηνὴν καὶ
κωμῳδοῦσιν ἀλλοκότους τινὰς περὶ αὐτοῦ κωμῳδίας.

Καίτοι ἐκεῖνοι μὲν καθ᾽ ἑνὸς ἀνδρὸς ἐτόλμων τὰ τοιαῦτα,
καὶ ἐν Διονύσου ἐφειμένον αὐτὸ ἔδρων, καὶ τὸ σκῶμμα ἐδόκει
μέρος τι τῆς ἑορτῆς, καὶ

FRANK

Let the rest be seated and vote along with you and your companions, Philosophy, and let Diogenes prosecute on his own.

PHILOSOPHY

Then you're not afraid they'll condemn you?

FRANK

Certainly not; I want to win with a bigger majority.

PHILOSOPHY

Bravo, Frank. Sit down, gentlemen, and you, Diogenes, start your speech.

DIOGENES

[25]   What sort of men we were throughout our lives, you, Philosophy, know very well and I don't need to tell you. I won't say anything about myself, but everyone knows about Pythagoras here, and Plato and Aristotle and Chrysippus and the others and the benefits they've conferred on human life; that's what we're like, but now let me tell you how we've been abused by this scoundrel, curse him, curse him, curse him.

He was a barrister of sorts, they say, but has abandoned the courts and his kudos there and concentrated all his rhetorical power and skill against us and never stops abusing us, branding us as impostors and cheats and persuading the masses to laugh at us and despise us as worthless. What's more, he has now made both you, Philosophy, and ourselves to be hated by the populace, calling your activities nonsense and rubbish and giving a satirical version of the finest and most serious of the things you've taught us, so that he is clapped and applauded by his audience, and we are insulted by them. For this is what the general public is like: they delight in purveyors of derision and insults, particularly when the most respected of things are ridiculed, just as, of course, they enjoyed having Aristophanes and Eupolis put Socrates here on the stage and compose outrageous comedies about him.

However *they* ventured to make such attacks merely on *one* individual and did so in the permissiveness of Dionysus' theatre, and the mockery was considered part of the festival and

ὁ θεὸς ἴσως ἔχαιρε φιλόγελώς τις ὤν.

ὁ δὲ τοὺς ἀρίστους συγκαλῶν, ἐκ πολλοῦ φροντίσας καὶ παρα- 26
σκευασάμενος καὶ βλασφημίας τινὰς εἰς παχὺ βιβλίον ἐγγράψας,
μεγάλῃ τῇ φωνῇ ἀγορεύει κακῶς Πλάτωνα, Πυθαγόραν,
Ἀριστοτέλη τοῦτον, Χρύσιππον ἐκεῖνον, ἐμὲ καὶ ὅλως ἅπαντας
οὔτε ἑορτῆς ἐφιείσης οὔτε ἰδίᾳ τι πρὸς ἡμῶν παθών· εἶχε γὰρ
ἄν τινα συγγνώμην αὐτῷ τὸ πρᾶγμα, εἰ ἀμυνόμενος ἀλλὰ μὴ
ἄρχων αὐτὸς ἔδρα.

Καὶ τὸ πάντων δεινότατον, ὅτι τοιαῦτα ποιῶν καὶ ὑπὸ τὸ σὸν
ὄνομα, ὦ Φιλοσοφία, ὑποδύεται καὶ ὑπελθὼν τὸν Διάλογον
ἡμέτερον οἰκέτην ὄντα, τούτῳ συναγωνιστῇ καὶ ὑποκριτῇ χρῆται
καθ' ἡμῶν, ἔτι καὶ Μένιππον ἀναπείσας ἑταῖρον ἡμῶν ἄνδρα
συγκωμῳδεῖν αὐτῷ τὰ πολλά, ὃς μόνος οὐ πάρεστιν οὐδὲ κατη-
γορεῖ μεθ' ἡμῶν, προδοὺς τὸ κοινόν.

Ἀνθ' ὧν ἁπάντων ἄξιόν ἐστιν ὑποσχεῖν αὐτὸν τὴν δίκην. ἢ τί 27
γὰρ ἂν εἰπεῖν ἔχοι τὰ σεμνότατα διασύρας ἐπὶ τοσούτων μαρτύ-
ρων; χρήσιμον γοῦν καὶ πρὸς ἐκείνους τὸ τοιοῦτον, εἰ θεάσαιντο
αὐτὸν κολασθέντα, ὡς μηδὲ ἄλλος τις ἔτι καταφρονοίη Φιλο-
σοφίας· ἐπεὶ τό γε τὴν ἡσυχίαν ἄγειν καὶ ὑβριζόμενον ἀνέχεσθαι
οὐ μετριότητος, ἀλλὰ ἀνανδρίας καὶ εὐηθείας εἰκότως ἂν νομί-
ζοιτο. τὰ μὲν γὰρ τελευταῖα τίνι φορητά; ὃς καθάπερ τὰ ἀνδρά-
ποδα παραγαγὼν ἡμᾶς ἐπὶ τὸ πωλητήριον καὶ κήρυκα ἐπιστήσας
ἀπημπόλησεν, ὥς φασιν, τοὺς μὲν ἐπὶ πολλῷ, ἐνίους δὲ μνᾶς
Ἀττικῆς, ἐμὲ δὲ ὁ παμπονηρότατος οὗτος δύ' ὀβολῶν· οἱ παρόντες
δὲ ἐγέλων.

Ἀνθ' ὧν αὐτοί τε ἀνεληλύθαμεν ἀγανακτήσαντες καὶ σὲ ἀξι-
οῦμεν τιμωρήσειν ἡμῖν τὰ ἔσχατα ὑβρισμένοις.

ΑΝΑΒΙΟΥΝΤΕΣ

Εὖ γε, ὦ Διόγενες, ὑπὲρ ἁπάντων καλῶς ὁπόσα ἐχρῆν ἅπαντα 28
εἴρηκας.

ΦΙΛΟΣΟΦΙΑ

Παύσασθε ἐπαινοῦντες· ἔγχει τῷ ἀπολογουμένῳ. σὺ δὲ ὁ
Παρρησιάδης λέγε ἤδη ἐν τῷ μέρει· σοὶ γὰρ τὸ ὕδωρ ῥεῖ νῦν.
μὴ μέλλε οὖν.

ΠΑΡΡΗΣΙΑΔΗΣ

Οὐ πάντα μου, ὦ Φιλοσοφία, κατηγόρησε Διογένης, ἀλλὰ τὰ 29

'Perhaps the god rejoiced because he likes a laugh',

[26] whereas *this fellow* assembles the cream of society and after long deliberations and preparations and filling a thick book with his libels bellows out insults against Plato, Pythagoras, Aristotle here, Chrysippus over there, myself, and absolutely everyone of us, without the licence of any festival or having suffered any private injury at our hands. For his behaviour could have some excuse, if he was getting his own back, but in fact he is the one who started it.

What's most outrageous of all is that while behaving like that he takes shelter under your name, Philosophy, and has got round our servant Dialogue, using him against us to serve in his act, and furthermore has persuaded our companion, Menippus, to co-operate with him in most of his comic efforts, Menippus who is the only absentee and the only one to fail to join us in our prosecution and to have betrayed our common cause. [27] Frank deserves to be punished for all this. What could he say for himself after ridiculing before so many witnesses all that's most respected? In any case it would be a useful lesson to them too, if they saw him punished so as to stop anyone else in future despising Philosophy. For keeping quiet and putting up with being abused isn't a sign of moderation but could well be thought to show cowardice and feeblemindedness. For who could tolerate his most recent activities? Why, he brought us forth like slaves to the market, put an auctioneer in charge of us and sold us off, they say, some for a high price, others for a mere fiver and me, curse him for an utter villain, for tuppence.

That's why we're angry and have come up to earth. We beg you to avenge us, for we've been abused to the limit.

PHILOSOPHERS

[28] Bravo, Diogenes; you've spoken well for us all and said everything that had to be said.

PHILOSOPHY

Stop praising him. Fill the water-clock for the defendant's speech. Your allotted time has started, Frank; so get on with it.

FRANK

[29] Diogenes hasn't included in his speech *all* the charges against me,

πλείω καὶ ὅσα ἦν χαλεπώτερα οὐκ οἶδα ὅ τι παθὼν παρέλιπεν. ἐγὼ δὲ τοσούτου δέω ἔξαρνος γενέσθαι ὡς οὐκ εἶπον αὐτά, ἢ ἀπολογίαν τινὰ μεμελετηκὼς ἀφῖχθαι, ὥστε καὶ εἴ τινα ἢ αὐτὸς ἀπεσιώπησεν ἢ ἐγὼ μὴ πρότερον ἔφθην εἰρηκώς, νῦν προσθήσειν μοι δοκῶ. οὕτως γὰρ ἂν μάθοις οὕστινας ἀπεκήρυττον καὶ κακῶς ἠγόρευον ἀλαζόνας καὶ γόητας ἀποκαλῶν. καί μοι μόνον τοῦτο παραφυλάττετε, εἰ ἀληθῆ περὶ αὐτῶν ἐρῶ. εἰ δέ τι βλάσφημον ἢ τραχὺ φαίνοιτο ἔχων ὁ λόγος, οὐ τὸν διελέγχοντα ἐμέ, ἀλλ᾽ ἐκείνους ἂν οἶμαι δικαιότερον αἰτιάσεσθε, τοιαῦτα ποιοῦντας.

Ἐγὼ γὰρ ἐπειδὴ τάχιστα συνεῖδον ὁπόσα τοῖς ῥητορεύουσιν ἀναγκαῖον τὰ δυσχερῆ προσεῖναι, ἀπάτην καὶ ψεῦδος καὶ θρασύτητα καὶ βοὴν καὶ ὠθισμοὺς καὶ μυρία ἄλλα, ταῦτα μέν, ὥσπερ εἰκὸς ἦν, ἀπέφυγον, ἐπὶ δὲ τὰ σά, ὦ Φιλοσοφία, καλὰ ὁρμήσας ἠξίουν ὁπόσον ἔτι μοι λοιπὸν τοῦ βίου καθάπερ ἐκ ζάλης καὶ κλύδωνος εἰς εὔδιόν τινα λιμένα ἐσπλεύσας ὑπὸ σοὶ σκεπόμενος καταβιῶναι.

Κἀπειδὴ μόνον παρέκυψα εἰς τὰ ὑμέτερα, σὲ μέν, ὥσπερ 30 ἀναγκαῖον ἦν, καὶ τούσδε ἅπαντας ἐθαύμαζον ἀρίστου βίου νομοθέτας ὄντας καὶ τοῖς ἐπ᾽ αὐτὸν ἐπειγομένοις χεῖρα ὀρέγοντας, τὰ κάλλιστα καὶ συμφορώτατα παραινοῦντας, εἴ τις μὴ παραβαίνοι αὐτὰ μηδὲ διολισθάνοι, ἀλλ᾽ ἀτενὲς ἀποβλέπων εἰς τοὺς κανόνας οὓς προτεθείκατε, πρὸς τούτους ῥυθμίζοι καὶ ἀπευθύνοι τὸν ἑαυτοῦ βίον, ὅπερ νὴ Δία καὶ τῶν καθ᾽ ὑμᾶς αὐτοὺς ὀλίγοι ποιοῦσιν.

Ὁρῶν δὲ πολλοὺς οὐκ ἔρωτι φιλοσοφίας ἐχομένους ἀλλὰ 31 δόξης μόνον τῆς ἀπὸ τοῦ πράγματος ἐφιεμένους, καὶ τὰ μὲν πρόχειρα ταῦτα καὶ δημόσια καὶ ὁπόσα παντὶ μιμήσασθαι ῥᾴδιον εὖ μάλα ἐοικότας ἀγαθοῖς ἀνδράσι, τὸ γένειον λέγω καὶ τὸ βάδισμα καὶ τὴν ἀναβολήν, ἐπὶ δὲ τοῦ βίου καὶ τῶν πραγμάτων ἀντιφθεγγομένους τῷ σχήματι καὶ τὰ ἐναντία ὑμῖν ἐπιτηδεύοντας καὶ διαφθείροντας τὸ ἀξίωμα τῆς ὑποσχέσεως, ἠγανάκτουν, καὶ τὸ πρᾶγμα ὅμοιον ἐδόκει μοι καθάπερ ἂν εἴ τις ὑποκριτὴς τραγῳδίας μαλθακὸς αὐτὸς ὢν καὶ γυναικίας Ἀχιλλέα ἢ Θησέα ἢ καὶ τὸν Ἡρακλέα ὑποκρίνοιτο αὐτὸν μήτε βαδίζων μήτε βοῶν ἡρωϊκόν, ἀλλὰ θρυπτόμενος ὑπὸ τηλικούτῳ προσωπείῳ, ὃν οὐδ᾽ ἂν ἡ Ἑλένη ποτὲ ἢ Πολυξένη ἀνάσχοιτο πέρα τοῦ μέτρου αὐταῖς προσεοικότα, οὐχ ὅπως ὁ Ἡρακλῆς ὁ Καλλίνικος,

Philosophy, but for some reason has omitted most of them and indeed the more serious ones. But I am so far from denying that I said these things or from coming here with a defence speech prepared that I propose now to add things he has left unmentioned or I haven't already said in the past. Thus you'll discover who it was I was auctioning off and reviling, dubbing them impostors and charlatans. The only point I want you to look out for is whether what I say about them is true. But if my words should clearly be defamatory or harsh, I think you'll act more justly in blaming not me, who am showing them up, but them for acting like that.

For once I realised the many disagreeable but unavoidable aspects of a barrister's life, the deceit, the lies, the effrontery, the shouting, the jostling, to mention but a few of them, naturally I fled from all that, and set out in search of the admirable things you, Philosophy, had to offer and decided to live the rest of my life under your shelter by sailing as it were from stormy angry waves into a peaceful haven.

[30] After a single peep into your domain, I started inevitably to admire you and all these men as being legislators for the ideal life, stretching out a hand to those eager for it and recommending the most honourable and expedient measures, provided one didn't contravene them or backslide but, keeping one's eyes intently fixed on the rules you've propounded, ordered and regulated one's life by them – and, by heaven, that's something few even of your own disciples do!

[31] When I saw many possessed not by a love of philosophy but merely eager for the kudos conferred thereby, and very closely resembling virtuous men in particulars easily achievable, commonplace and simple for anyone to imitate, I mean the beard, the gait and style of dressing, but in their life and activities contradicting their appearance, pursuing objects different from yours and destroying the good name of their profession, it made me angry and the situation seemed to me to be like having a tragic actor, though personally an effeminate weakling, playing Achilles or Theseus or even Heracles himself, though he couldn't walk or talk like a hero, but merely minced along under such a magnificent mask, one whom even Helen or Polyxena wouldn't tolerate resembling themselves too closely, much less Heracles, the conquering hero! No, I think he'd very

ἀλλά μοι δοκεῖ τάχιστα ἂν ἐπιτρῖψαι τῷ ῥοπάλῳ παίων τοιοῦτον
αὐτόν τε καὶ τὸ προσωπεῖον, οὕτως ἀτίμως κατατεθηλυμμένος
πρὸς αὐτοῦ.

Τοιαῦτα καὶ αὐτὸς ὑμᾶς πάσχοντας ὑπ᾽ ἐκείνων ὁρῶν οὐκ　32
ἤνεγκα τὴν αἰσχύνην τῆς ὑποκρίσεως, εἰ πίθηκοι ὄντες ἐτόλμησαν
ἡρώων προσωπεῖα περιθέσθαι ἢ τὸν ἐν Κύμῃ ὄνον μιμήσασθαι, ὃς
λεοντῆν περιβαλόμενος ἠξίου λέων αὐτὸς εἶναι, πρὸς ἀγνοοῦντας
τοὺς Κυμαίους ὀγκώμενος μάλα τραχὺ καὶ καταπληκτικόν, ἄχρι
δή τις αὐτὸν ξένος καὶ λέοντα ἰδὼν καὶ ὄνον πολλάκις ἤλεγξε
καὶ ἀπεδίωξε παίων τοῖς ξύλοις.

Ὃ δὲ μάλιστά μοι δεινόν, ὦ Φιλοσοφία, κατεφαίνετο, τοῦτο
ἦν· οἱ γὰρ ἄνθρωποι εἴ τινα τούτων ἑώρων πονηρὸν ἢ ἄσχημον
ἢ ἀσελγές τι ἐπιτηδεύοντα, οὐκ ἔστιν ὅστις οὐ Φιλοσοφίαν
αὐτὴν ᾐτιᾶτο καὶ τὸν Χρύσιππον εὐθὺς ἢ Πλάτωνα ἢ Πυθαγόραν
ἢ ὅτου ἐπώνυμον αὐτὸν ὁ διαμαρτάνων ἐκεῖνος ἐποιεῖτο καὶ οὗ
τοὺς λόγους ἐμιμεῖτο· καὶ ἀπὸ τοῦ κακῶς βιοῦντος πονηρὰ περὶ
ὑμῶν εἴκαζον τῶν πρὸ πολλοῦ τεθνηκότων· οὐ γὰρ παρὰ ζῶντας
ὑμᾶς ἡ ἐξέτασις αὐτοῦ ἐγίνετο, ἀλλ᾽ ὑμεῖς μὲν ἐκποδών, ἐκεῖνον
δὲ ἑώρων σαφῶς ἅπαντες δεινὰ καὶ ἄσεμνα ἐπιτηδεύοντα, ὥστε
ἐρήμην ἡλίσκεσθε μετ᾽ αὐτοῦ καὶ ἐπὶ τὴν ὁμοίαν διαβολὴν συγ-
κατεσπᾶσθε.

Ταῦτα οὐκ ἤνεγκα ὁρῶν ἔγωγε, ἀλλ᾽ ἤλεγχον αὐτοὺς καὶ　33
διέκρινον ἀφ᾽ ὑμῶν· ὑμεῖς δέ, τιμᾶν ἐπὶ τούτοις δέον, εἰς δικαστή-
ριόν με ἄγετε. οὐκοῦν ἤν τινα καὶ τῶν μεμυημένων ἰδὼν ἐξαγο-
ρεύοντα ταῖν θεαῖν τὰ ἀπόρρητα καὶ ἐξορχούμενον ἀγανακτήσω
καὶ διελέγξω, ἐμὲ τὸν ἀσεβοῦντα ἡγήσεσθε εἶναι; ἀλλ᾽ οὐ δίκαιον.
ἐπεὶ καὶ οἱ ἀγωνοθέται μαστιγοῦν εἰώθασιν, ἤν τις ὑποκριτὴς
Ἀθηνᾶν ἢ Ποσειδῶνα ἢ τὸν Δία ὑποδεδυκὼς μὴ καλῶς ὑποκρίνηται
μηδὲ κατ᾽ ἀξίαν τῶν θεῶν, καὶ οὐ δή που ὀργίζονται αὐτοῖς
ἐκεῖνοι, διότι τὸν περικείμενον αὐτῶν τὰ προσωπεῖα καὶ τὸ
σχῆμα ἐνδεδυκότα ἐπέτρεψαν παίειν τοῖς μαστιγοφόροις, ἀλλὰ
καὶ ἤδοιντ᾽ ἄν, οἶμαι, μᾶλλον*μαστιγουμένων· οἰκέτην μὲν γάρ
τινα ἢ ἄγγελον μὴ δεξιῶς ὑποκρίνασθαι μικρὸν τὸ πταῖσμα, τὸν
Δία δὲ ἢ τὸν Ἡρακλέα μὴ κατ᾽ ἀξίαν ἐπιδείξασθαι τοῖς θεαταῖς,
ἀποτρόπαιον ὡς αἰσχρόν.

Καὶ γὰρ αὖ καὶ τόδε πάντων ἀτοπώτατόν ἐστιν, ὅτι τοὺς μὲν　34
λόγους ὑμῶν πάνυ ἀκριβοῦσιν οἱ πολλοὶ αὐτῶν, καθάπερ δὲ ἐπὶ

---

* read ἤδοιντ᾽ ἂν μᾶλλον

quickly use his club to smash up a creature like that and his mask as well, after being so disgracefully unmanned by him.

[32] When I could see for myself that you were suffering so terribly at their hands, I couldn't endure the disgraceful play-acting of apes with the effrontery to put on the masks of heroes or copy the donkey at Cyme who put on a lionskin and passed himself off as a lion, roaring most savagely and fearsomely at the ignorant folk of Cyme, till a visitor who'd often seen a real lion and a donkey showed him up and drove him off by beating him with sticks.

But what seemed most dreadful to me, Philosophy, was this: if folk saw any of these men engaging in evil, unseemly or indecent practices, without exception they would immediately blame Philosophy herself and Chrysippus or Plato or Pythagoras or the particular philosopher after whom that delinquent named himself and whose theories he took as his model, and so the wicked life of the individual would lead them to ugly imaginings about you who are long dead; for when *he* was examined you weren't alive for comparisons to be made; no, *you* were out of the way, but everyone could clearly see *his* dreadful and disgraceful behaviour, and so you were condemned in absentia along with him and dragged down with him to share the same disgrace.

[33] When I saw this, I couldn't put up with it, but started exposing them and differentiating them from you. But *you*, instead of honouring me for that as you ought, bring me to court. So, if I see any of the initiates divulging the mysteries of the Two Goddesses and mimicking the secret dances, and get angry and show him up, will you think me to be the impious one? No, that's unjust. For the officials at the competitions are in the habit of whipping any actor in the role of Athene, Posidon or Zeus who plays the part badly, letting the gods down, and then of course the gods aren't angry with the officials for allowing the men with the whips to belay the wearer of their masks and costumes; indeed the gods would be pleased if they were whipped even more; for though playing a servant or messenger incompetently is a trifling peccadillo, failure to do justice to Zeus or Heracles before one's audience is abominably disgraceful.

[34] Moreover the most ridiculous thing of all is that, though most of these philosophers have a close knowledge of every detail of your words,

τοῦτο μόνον ἀναγινώσκοντες αὐτοὺς καὶ μελετῶντες, ὡς τἀναντία ἐπιτηδεύοιεν, οὕτως βιοῦσιν. πάντα μὲν γὰρ ὅσα φασὶν
οἷον χρημάτων καταφρονεῖν καὶ δόξης καὶ μόνον τὸ καλὸν ἀγαθὸν
οἴεσθαι καὶ ἀόργητον εἶναι καὶ μὴν τῶν λαμπρῶν τούτων ὑπερορᾶν
καὶ ἐξ ἰσοτιμίας αὐτοῖς διαλέγεσθαι, καλά, ὦ θεοί, καὶ σοφὰ
καὶ θαυμάσια λίαν ὡς ἀληθῶς. οἱ δὲ καὶ αὐτὰ ταῦτα ἐπὶ μισθῷ
διδάσκουσιν καὶ τοὺς πλουσίους τεθήπασιν καὶ πρὸς τὸ ἀργύριον
κεχήνασιν, ὀργιλώτεροι μὲν τῶν κυνιδίων ὄντες, δειλότεροι δὲ
τῶν λαγωῶν, κολακικώτεροι δὲ τῶν πιθήκων, ἀσελγέστεροι
δὲ τῶν ὄνων, ἁρπακτικώτεροι δὲ τῶν γαλῶν, φιλονικότεροι
δὲ τῶν ἀλεκτρυόνων. τοιγαροῦν γέλωτα ὀφλισκάνουσιν ὠθιζό-
μενοι ἐπ᾽ αὐτὰ καὶ περὶ τὰς τῶν πλουσίων πυλῶνας ἀλλήλους
παραγκωνιζόμενοι καὶ δεῖπνα πολυάνθρωπα δειπνοῦντες καὶ ἐν
αὐτοῖς τούτοις ἐπαινοῦντες φορτικῶς καὶ πέρα τοῦ καλῶς
ἔχοντος ἐμφορούμεονι* καὶ μεμψίμοιροι φαινόμενοι καὶ ἐπὶ τῆς
κύλικος ἀτερπῆ καὶ ἀπῳδὰ φιλοσοφοῦντες καὶ τὸν ἄκρατον οὐ
φέροντες· οἱ ἰδιῶται δὲ ὁπόσοι πάρεισιν, γελῶσι δηλαδὴ καὶ κατα-
πτύουσιν φιλοσοφίας, εἰ τοιαῦτα καθάρματα ἐκτρέφει.

Τὸ δὲ πάντων αἴσχιστον, ὅτι μηδενὸς δεῖσθαι λέγων ἕκαστος   35
αὐτῶν, ἀλλὰ μόνον πλούσιον εἶναι τὸν σοφὸν κεκραγὼς μικρὸν
ὕστερον προσελθὼν αἰτεῖ καὶ ἀγανακτεῖ μὴ λαβών, ὅμοιον ὡς εἰ
τις ἐν βασιλικῷ σχήματι ὀρθὴν τιάραν ἔχων καὶ διάδημα καὶ τὰ
ἄλλα ὅσα βασιλείας γνωρίσματα μεταίτης ὢν φαίνοιτο καὶ τῶν
ὑποδεεστέρων δεόμενος.

Ὅταν μὲν οὖν λαβεῖν αὐτοὺς δέῃ, πολὺς ὁ περὶ τοῦ κοινωνικὸν
εἶναι δεῖν λόγος καὶ ὡς ἀδιάφορον ὁ πλοῦτος καί, Τί γὰρ τὸ
χρυσίον ἢ τἀργύριον, οὐδὲν τῶν ἐν τοῖς αἰγιαλοῖς ψήφων διαφέρον;
ὅταν δέ τις ἐπικουρίας δεόμενος ἑταῖρος ἐκ παλαιοῦ καὶ φίλος ἀπὸ
πολλῶν ὀλίγα αἰτῇ προσελθών, σιωπὴ καὶ ἀπορία καὶ ἀμαθία καὶ
παλινῳδία τῶν δογμάτων πρὸς τὸ ἐναντίον· οἱ δὲ πολλοὶ περὶ
φιλίας ἐκεῖνοι λόγοι καὶ ἡ ἀρετὴ καὶ τὸ καλὸν οὐκ οἶδα ὅποι
ποτὲ οἴχεται ταῦτα ἀποπτάμενα πάντα, πτερόεντα ὡς ἀληθῶς
ἔπη, μάτην ὁσημέραι πρὸς αὐτῶν ἐν ταῖς διατριβαῖς σκια-
μαχούμενα. μέχρι γὰρ τούτου φίλος ἕκαστος αὐτῶν, εἰς ὅσον ἂν   36
μὴ ἀργύριον ἢ χρυσίον ᾖ προκείμενον ἐν τῷ μέσῳ· ἢν δέ τις
ὀβολὸν ἐπιδείξηται μόνον, λέλυται μὲν ἡ εἰρήνη, ἄσπονδα δὲ
κἀκήρυκτα πάντα, καὶ τὰ βιβλία ἐξαλήλιπται καὶ ἡ ἀρετὴ

* read ἐμφορούμενοι

yet they live as though they read them and study them for the sole purpose of acting in contradiction to them. For all that they preach, such as despising money and fame and considering honour the only good, being free from passion and despising these big-wigs and conversing with them as equals, all these things, good heavens, are admirable and wise and truly wonderful beyond measure. But they take payment for teaching these very things, gaze on the rich with awe and on silver with open-mouthed greed: they are more hot-tempered than curs, more cowardly than hares, more fawning than monkeys, more lecherous than jackasses, more rapacious than cats, and more contentious than cocks. So they come in for ridicule as they jostle after what they preach against, elbow past each other round the portals of the rich, attend crowded dinners, and at them utter vulgar compliments, stuff themselves beyond all decency, show a faultfinding disposition, spoil the pleasure and atmosphere by philosophising over their cups, and are unable to carry the strong drink. But all the ordinary people present, laugh at them of course and show their contempt for philosophy for nurturing such filthy objects.

[35] But what's most shameful of all is that each of them, saying he needs nothing, and bawling out that the only rich man is the sage, comes up to you to ask for something and is annoyed if he doesn't get it, just as if someone dressed like a king, wearing a tiara upright and a royal head-band round it and all the other distinguishing marks of royalty, were to make it obvious he was a beggar and needed the help of his inferiors.

What's more, when they need to get something, there's much talk about the necessity for sharing, about wealth being 'something indifferent' and words like 'What's gold or silver? Nothing better than the pebbles on the beaches.' But when some long-standing friend and companion in need of help comes and asks for a little of what they have in plenty, there's silence and embarrassment and ignorance and complete recantation and reversal of all their doctrines. Those numerous discourses about friendship, along with their 'virtue' and 'the beautiful' have all flown away and disappeared, I know not where, real 'winged words', meaningless products of the verbal shadow-boxing in their daily discussions. [36] For each of them is a friend only as long as there is no gold or silver coming between them. But if anyone gives them a mere glimpse of a farthing, the peace is shattered, there's 'war to the death', everything in their books is wiped out and virtue has taken flight.

πέφευγεν. οἷόν τι καὶ οἱ κύνες πάσχουσιν ἐπειδάν τις ὀστοῦν εἰς μέσους αὐτοὺς ἐμβάλῃ· ἀναπηδήσαντες δάκνουσιν ἀλλήλους καὶ τὸν προαρπάσαντα τὸ ὀστοῦν ὑλακτοῦσιν.

Λέγεται δὲ καὶ βασιλεύς τις Αἰγύπτιος πιθήκους ποτὲ πυρριχίζειν διδάξαι καὶ τὰ θηρία—μιμηλότατα δέ ἐστι τῶν ἀνθρωπίνων—ἐκμαθεῖν τάχιστα καὶ ὀρχεῖσθαι ἁλουργίδας ἀμπεχόμενα καὶ προσωπεῖα περικείμενα, καὶ μέχρι γε πολλοῦ εὐδοκιμεῖν τὴν θέαν, ἄχρι δὴ θεατής τις ἀστεῖος κάρυα ὑπὸ κόλπον ἔχων ἀφῆκεν εἰς τὸ μέσον· οἱ δὲ πίθηκοι ἰδόντες καὶ ἐκλαθόμενοι τῆς ὀρχήσεως, τοῦθ᾽ ὅπερ ἦσαν, πίθηκοι ἐγένοντο ἀντὶ πυρριχιστῶν καὶ συνέτριβον τὰ προσωπεῖα καὶ τὴν ἐσθῆτα κατερρήγνυον καὶ ἐμάχοντο περὶ τῆς ὀπώρας πρὸς ἀλλήλους, τὸ δὲ σύνταγμα τῆς πυρρίχης διελέλυτο καὶ κατεγελᾶτο ὑπὸ τοῦ θεάτρου.

Τοιαῦτα καὶ οὗτοι ποιοῦσιν, καὶ ἔγωγε τοὺς τοιούτους 37 κακῶς ἠγόρευον καὶ οὔποτε παύσομαι διελέγχων καὶ κωμῳδῶν, περὶ ὑμῶν δὲ ἢ τῶν ὑμῖν παραπλησίων—εἰσὶ γάρ, εἰσί τινες ὡς ἀληθῶς φιλοσοφίαν ζηλοῦντες καὶ τοῖς ὑμετέροις νόμοις ἐμμένοντες—μὴ οὕτως μανείην ἔγωγε ὡς βλάσφημον εἰπεῖν τι ἢ σκαιόν. ἢ τί γὰρ εἰπεῖν ἔχοιμι; τί γὰρ ὑμῖν τοιοῦτον βεβίωται; τοὺς δὲ ἀλαζόνας ἐκείνους καὶ θεοῖς ἐχθροὺς ἄξιον οἶμαι μισεῖν. ἢ σὺ γάρ, ὦ Πυθαγόρα καὶ Πλάτων καὶ Χρύσιππε καὶ Ἀριστότελες, τί φατε προσήκειν ὑμῖν τοὺς τοιούτους ἢ οἰκεῖόν τί καὶ συγγενὲς ἐπιδείκνυσθαι τῷ βίῳ; νὴ Δι᾽ Ἡρακλῆς, φασίν, καὶ πίθηκος. ἢ διότι πώγωνας ἔχουσι καὶ φιλοσοφεῖν φάσκουσι καὶ σκυθρωποί εἰσι, διὰ τοῦτο χρὴ ὑμῖν εἰκάζειν αὐτούς; ἀλλὰ ἤνεγκα ἄν, εἰ πιθανοὶ γοῦν ἦσαν καὶ ἐπὶ τῆς ὑποκρίσεως αὐτῆς· νῦν δὲ θᾶττον ἂν γὺψ ἀηδόνα μιμήσαιτο ἢ οὗτοι φιλοσόφους.

Εἴρηκα τὰ ὑπὲρ ἐμαυτοῦ ὁπόσα εἶχον. σὺ δέ, ὦ Ἀλήθεια, μαρτύρει πρὸς αὐτοὺς εἰ ἀληθῆ ἐστιν.

ΦΙΛΟΣΟΦΙΑ

Μετάστηθι, ὦ Παρρησιάδη· ἔτι πορρωτέρω. τί ποιῶμεν 38 ἡμεῖς; πῶς ὑμῖν εἰρηκέναι ἀνὴρ ἔδοξεν;

ΑΛΗΘΕΙΑ

Ἐγὼ μέν, ὦ Φιλοσοφία, μεταξὺ λέγοντος αὐτοῦ κατὰ τῆς γῆς δῦναι ηὐχόμην· οὕτως ἀληθῆ πάντα εἶπεν. ἐγνώριζον γοῦν

It's like what happens to dogs when a bone is thrown into their midst; they leap up biting one another and barking at the first one to get hold of the bone.

It's said that once upon a time a king of Egypt taught monkeys to dance the war-dance and that the creatures, being extremely adept at imitating anything human, learned very quickly and danced wearing cloaks of purple and masks; the show was well received till a wag in the audience, who had nuts in his pocket, threw them into their midst, and the monkeys, seeing the nuts and forgetting about their dancing, became what they always had been, monkeys instead of performers of war-dances, smashed their masks, tore their costumes to shreds and fought with each other for the nuts, but the dance formation was reduced to a shambles to the derisive laughter of the spectators.

[37] These philosophers behave just like those monkeys. It was men like that I vilified and indeed I shall never stop exposing them and ridiculing them, but where you or those like you are concerned – for there are some, I admit it, who show a true zeal for philosophy and abide by your rules – I hope I won't be so demented as to say anything scurrilous or unpleasant. What *could* I say? What behaviour like that has there been in *your* lives? But those charlatans and impious creatures deserve to be hated in my opinion. For, Pythagoras, Plato, Chrysippus and Aristotle, what connection can you say such men have with *you*? What evidence do they give in their lives of being your kith and kin? Good heavens, they are as different as Heracles and the proverbial monkey in the lionskin: Just because they have beards, claim to be philosophers and scowl, does that mean we should think of them like you? However I could have stomached it, if they had been convincing in their acting; but as it is, a vulture could sooner imitate a nightingale than they philosophers.

I've said all I could in my own defence. Now it's up to you, Truth, to testify whether it's the truth.

PHILOSOPHY

[38] Stand away, Frank; a little further, please. What are we to do? What's your opinion of his speech?

TRUTH

Personally, Philosophy, I wanted to sink beneath the ground while he was speaking; so true was everything he said. As I listened, I could

ἀκούουσα ἕκαστον τῶν ποιούντων αὐτὰ καὶ ἐφήρμοζον μεταξὺ
τοῖς λεγομένοις, τοῦτο μὲν εἰς τόνδε, τοῦτο δὲ ὁ δεῖνα ποιεῖ· καὶ
ὅλως ἔδειξε τοὺς ἄνδρας ἐναργῶς καθάπερ ἐπί τινος γραφῆς τὰ
πάντα προσεοικότας, οὐ τὰ σώματα μόνον ἀλλὰ καὶ τὰς ψυχὰς
αὐτὰς εἰς τὸ ἀκριβέστατον ἀπεικάσας.

ΦΙΛΟΣΟΦΙΑ

Κἀγὼ πάνυ ἠρυθρίασα, ὦ Ἀλήθεια· ὑμεῖς δὲ τί φατε;*

ΑΝΑΒΙΟΥΝΤΕΣ

Τί δὲ ἄλλο ἢ ἀφεῖσθαι αὐτὸν τοῦ ἐγκλήματος καὶ φίλον ἡμῖν
καὶ εὐεργέτην ἀναγεγράφθαι; τὸ γοῦν τῶν Ἰλιέων ἀτεχνῶς
πεπόνθαμεν· τραγῳδόν τινα τοῦτον ἐφ᾽ ἡμᾶς κεκινήκαμεν
ᾀσόμενον τὰς Φρυγῶν συμφοράς. ᾀδέτω δ᾽ οὖν καὶ τοὺς θεοῖς
ἐχθροὺς ἐκτραγῳδείτω.

ΔΙΟΓΕΝΗΣ

Καὶ αὐτός, ὦ Φιλοσοφία, πάνυ ἐπαινῶ τὸν ἄνδρα καὶ ἀνα-
τίθεμαι τὰ κατηγορούμενα καὶ φίλον ποιοῦμαι αὐτὸν γενναῖον
ὄντα.

ΦΙΛΟΣΟΦΙΑ

Εὖ ἔχει· πρόσιθι Παρρησιάδη· ἀφίεμέν σε τῆς αἰτίας, καὶ 3
ἁπάσαις κρατεῖς, καὶ τὸ λοιπὸν ἴσθι ἡμέτερος ὤν.

ΠΑΡΡΗΣΙΑΔΗΣ

Προσεκύνησα τήν γε πρώτην· μᾶλλον δέ, τραγικώτερον αὐτὸ
ποιήσειν μοι δοκῶ· σεμνότερον γάρ·

ὦ μέγα σεμνὴ Νίκη, τὸν ἐμὸν
βίοτον κατέχοις
καὶ μὴ λήγοις στεφανοῦσα.

ΑΡΕΤΗ

Οὐκοῦν δευτέρου κρατῆρος ἤδη καταρχώμεθα· προσκαλῶμεν
κἀκείνους, ὡς δίκην ὑπόσχωσιν ἀνθ᾽ ὧν εἰς ἡμᾶς ὑβρίζουσιν·
κατηγορήσει δὲ Παρρησιάδης ἑκάστου.

identify each of the men acting like that and all the while could associate individuals with what he said, saying 'This refers to A, and that's what B does.' In short he has produced a vivid picture of the fellows, making them as true to life in every respect as any painting, depicting quite perfectly not only their persons but their very souls as well.

PHILOSOPHY

I was thoroughly ashamed too, Truth. (*Turning to the Philosophers*) But what do *you* say?

PHILOSOPHERS

What else but that he has been acquitted of the charge and officially recorded as our friend and benefactor? We've experienced just what happened to the Trojans; in him we've brought upon ourselves a tragic actor to sing of the disasters of the Phrygians. However let him sing on and expose the accursed scoundrels by his performance.

DIOGENES

I too, Philosophy, thoroughly applaud the man, retract my accusations and consider him a friend, for he's a grand fellow.

PHILOSOPHY

[39] That's good. Come here, Frank; we acquit you of the charge. You win by a unanimous verdict and should consider yourself one of us from now on.

FRANK

First I pay my homage to the goddess; or rather I think I'll do so in more theatrical fashion; that's more reverent.

'O Victory, goddess right reverend,
Me through my life may you attend,
And victor's wreathes me ever send.'

VIRTUE

Then let us now initiate the second part of the proceedings; let's summon those villains to be tried for their outrages against us. Frank will prosecute each individually.

ΦΙΛΟΣΟΦΙΑ

Ὀρθῶς, ὦ Ἀρετή, ἔλεξας. ὥστε σύ, παῖ Συλλογισμέ, κατα-
κύψας εἰς τὸ ἄστυ προσκήρυττε τοὺς φιλοσόφους.

ΣΥΛΛΟΓΙΣΜΟΣ

Ἄκουε, σίγα· τοὺς φιλοσόφους ἥκειν εἰς ἀκρόπολιν ἀπολογη- 40
σομένους ἐπὶ τῆς Ἀρετῆς καὶ Φιλοσοφίας καὶ Δίκης.

ΠΑΡΡΗΣΙΑΔΗΣ

Ὁρᾷς; ὀλίγοι ἀνίασι γνωρίσαντες τὸ κήρυγμα, καὶ ἄλλως
δεδίασι τὴν Δίκην· οἱ πολλοὶ δὲ αὐτῶν οὐδὲ σχολὴν ἄγουσιν ἀμφὶ
τοὺς πλουσίους ἔχοντες. εἰ δὲ βούλει πάντας ἥκειν, κατὰ τάδε, ὦ
Συλλογισμέ, κήρυττε—

ΦΙΛΟΣΟΦΙΑ

Μηδαμῶς, ἀλλὰ σύ, ὦ Παρρησιάδη, προσκάλει καθ᾽ ὅ τι σοι
δοκεῖ.

ΠΑΡΡΗΣΙΑΔΗΣ

Οὐδὲν τόδε χαλεπόν. Ἄκουε, σίγα. ὅσοι φιλόσοφοι εἶναι 41
λέγουσιν καὶ ὅσοι προσήκειν αὐτοῖς οἴονται τοῦ ὀνόματος, ἥκειν
εἰς ἀκρόπολιν ἐπὶ τὴν διανομήν. δύο μναῖ ἑκάστῳ δοθήσονται καὶ
σησαμαῖος πλακοῦς· ὃς δ᾽ ἂν πώγωνα βαθὺν ἐπιδείξηται, καὶ
παλάθην ἰσχάδων οὗτός γε προσεπιλήψεται. κομίζειν δὲ ἕκαστον
σωφροσύνην μὲν ἢ δικαιοσύνην ἢ ἐγκράτειαν μηδαμῶς· οὐκ
ἀναγκαῖα γὰρ ταῦτά γε, ἢν μὴ παρῇ· πέντε δὲ συλλογισμοὺς ἐξ
ἅπαντος· οὐ γὰρ θέμις ἄνευ τούτων εἶναι σοφόν.

κεῖται δ᾽ ἐν μέσσοισι δύο χρυσοῖο τάλαντα,
τῷ δόμεν, ὃς μετὰ πᾶσιν ἐριζέμεν ἔξοχος εἴη.

ΦΙΛΟΣΟΦΙΑ

Βαβαί, ὅσοι· πλήρης μὲν ἡ ἄνοδος ὠθιζομένων ἐπὶ τὰς δύο 42
μνᾶς, ὡς ἤκουσαν μόνον· παρὰ δὲ τὸ Πελασγικὸν ἄλλοι καὶ κατὰ
τὸ Ἀσκληπιεῖον ἕτεροι καὶ παρὰ τὸν Ἄρειον ⟨πάγον⟩ ἔτι πλείους,
ἔνιοι δὲ καὶ κατὰ τὸν Τάλω τάφον, οἱ δὲ καὶ πρὸς τὸ Ἀνάκειον
προσθέμενοι κλίμακας ἀνέρπουσι βομβηδὸν νὴ Δία καὶ βοτρυδὸν
ἑσμοῦ δίκην, ἵνα καὶ καθ᾽ Ὅμηρον εἴπω· ἀλλὰ κἀκεῖθεν εὖ μάλα
πολλοὶ κἀντεῦθεν

μυρίοι, ὅσσα τε φύλλα καὶ ἄνθεα γίνεται ὥρῃ.

PHILOSOPHY

Well spoken, Virtue; so you, Syllogism, my child, pop down into town and proclaim a summons to the philosophers.

SYLLOGISM

[40] Oyez. Silence. The philosophers to be at the Acropolis to make their defence before Virtue, Philosophy and Justice.

FRANK

Do you see? Few have heeded the proclamation and come up; besides they fear Justice, and most of them are busy concentrating on the rich. If you want them all to come, this is how, Syllogism, you must make your proclamation –

PHILOSOPHY

No, Frank; *you* summons them in any way *you* want.

FRANK

[41] That's no problem. Oyez, silence. All that say they are philosophers and think they have any connection with the name to report to the acropolis for their handout. Each will be given two minas and a sesame cake and anyone who can show a long beard will also receive a basket of dried figs. There's no need at all for each to bring temperance, justice or self-control; they're not essential, if not available; but they should particularly bring five syllogisms; for it's ordained that without these no man is wise,

'And talents twain of gold 'midst all do rest
To give to him who argufies the best.'

PHILOSOPHY

[42] Gracious, what a lot of them! The road up is crowded with them all pushing and shoving to get their two minas, once they heard about them. Others are coming by the Pelasgicum, others by the Precinct of Asclepius, still more via the Areopagus, and some over the Tomb of Talos; and some have put ladders against the Temple of the Dioscuri and, good heavens, are coming buzzing up and, to quote Homer, 'in clusters' like a swarm of bees. Indeed ever so many are coming up from this side and from that 'In thousands like the leaves and flowers that grow in

μεστὴ δὲ ἡ ἀκρόπολις ἐν βραχεῖ "κλαγγηδὸν προκαθιζόντων" καὶ πανταχοῦ πήρα κολακεία πώγων ἀναισχυντία βακτηρία λιχνεία συλλογισμὸς φιλαργυρία· οἱ ὀλίγοι δέ, ὁπόσοι πρὸς τὸ πρῶτον κήρυγμα ἐκεῖνο ἀνήεσαν, ἀφανεῖς καὶ ἄσημοι, ἀναμιχθέντες τῷ πλήθει τῶν ἄλλων, καὶ λελήθασιν ἐν τῇ ὁμοιότητι τῶν ἄλλων σχημάτων.

ΠΑΡΡΗΣΙΑΔΗΣ

Τοῦτο γοῦν τὸ δεινότατόν ἐστιν, ὦ Φιλοσοφία, καὶ ὅ τις ἂν μέμψαιτο μάλιστά σου, τὸ μηδὲν ἐπιβαλεῖν γνώρισμα καὶ σημεῖον αὐτοῖς· πιθανώτεροι γὰρ οἱ γόητες οὗτοι πολλάκις τῶν ἀληθῶς φιλοσοφούντων.

ΦΙΛΟΣΟΦΙΑ

Ἔσται τοῦτο μετ' ὀλίγον, ἀλλὰ δεχώμεθα ἤδη αὐτούς.

ΠΛΑΤΩΝΙΚΟΣ

Ἡμᾶς πρώτους χρὴ τοὺς Πλατωνικοὺς λαβεῖν.   43

ΠΥΘΑΓΟΡΙΚΟΣ

Οὔκ, ἀλλὰ τοὺς Πυθαγορικοὺς ἡμᾶς· πρότερος γὰρ ὁ Πυθαγόρας ἦν.

ΣΤΩΙΚΟΣ

Ληρεῖτε· ἀμείνους ἡμεῖς οἱ ἀπὸ τῆς Στοᾶς.

ΠΕΡΙΠΑΤΗΤΙΚΟΣ

Οὐ μὲν οὖν, ἀλλ' ἔν γε τοῖς χρήμασι πρῶτοι ἡμεῖς εἴημεν οἱ ἐκ τοῦ Περιπάτου.

ΕΠΙΚΟΥΡΕΙΟΣ

Ἡμῖν τοῖς Ἐπικουρείοις τοὺς πλακοῦντας δότε καὶ τὰς παλάθας· περὶ δὲ τῶν μνῶν περιμενοῦμεν, κἂν ὑστάτους δέῃ λαβεῖν.

ΑΚΑΔΗΜΑΙΚΟΣ

Ποῦ τὰ δύο τάλαντα; δείξομεν γὰρ οἱ Ἀκαδημαϊκοὶ ὅσον τῶν ἄλλων ἐσμὲν ἐριστικώτεροι.

ΣΤΩΙΚΟΣ

Οὐχ ἡμῶν γε τῶν Στωϊκῶν παρόντων.

spring', and in no time at all the acropolis has filled with them 'as noisily they perch' and everywhere are pouches and flattery, beards and shamelessness, staffs and gluttony, syllogisms and avarice, but the few who came up in answer to that first summons, cannot be seen or distinguished, but have been swallowed up by the hordes of others and can't be made out where all appearances are so similar.

FRANK

That, Philosophy, is the most shocking feature of all and the thing for which you could most be criticised; you haven't given them any distinguishing marks; for those charlatans are often more convincing than the real philosophers.

PHILOSOPHY

That'll be done soon, but for the moment let's welcome them.

PLATONIST

[43] *Us* first; you must let *us* Platonists be first.

PYTHAGOREAN

No, it should be *us* Pythagoreans; for Pythagoras was earlier.

STOIC

Nonsense! *We* from the Porch are superior.

PERIPATETIC

No, in money matters *we* from the Lyceum would be first.

EPICUREAN

Give *us* Epicureans the cakes and the figs; the money we'll wait for, even if we have to be last to get it.

ACADEMIC

Where are the two talents? We Academics will demonstrate how much better than everyone else *we* are at arguing.

STOIC

Not while *we* Stoics are present.

ΦΙΛΟΣΟΦΙΑ

Παύσασθε φιλονικοῦντες· ὑμεῖς δὲ οἱ Κυνικοὶ μὴ παίετε ἀλλή- **44** λους τοῖς ξύλοις· ἐπ' ἄλλα γὰρ ἴστε κεκλημένοι. καὶ νῦν ἔγωγε ἡ Φιλοσοφία καὶ Ἀρετὴ αὕτη καὶ Ἀλήθεια δικάσομεν οἵτινες οἱ ὀρθῶς φιλοσοφοῦντές εἰσιν. εἶτα ὅσοι μὲν ἂν εὑρεθῶσι κατὰ τὰ ἡμῖν δοκοῦντα βιοῦντες, εὐδαιμονήσουσιν ἄριστοι κεκριμένοι· τοὺς γόητας δὲ καὶ οὐδὲν ἡμῖν προσήκοντας κακοὺς κακῶς ἐπιτρίψομεν, ὡς μὴ ἀντιποιῶνται τῶν ὑπὲρ αὐτοὺς ἀλαζόνες ὄντες. τί τοῦτο; φεύγετε; νὴ Δία, κατὰ τῶν γε κρημνῶν οἱ πολλοὶ ἁλλόμενοι. κενὴ δ' οὖν ἡ ἀκρόπολις, πλὴν ὀλίγων τούτων ὁπόσοι μεμενήκασιν οὐ φοβηθέντες τὴν κρίσιν. οἱ ὑπηρέται **45** ἀνέλεσθε τὴν πήραν, ἣν ὁ Κυνικὸς ἀπέρριψεν ἐν τῇ τροπῇ. φέρ' ἴδω τί καὶ ἔχει· ἦ που θέρμους ἢ βιβλίον ἢ ἄρτους τῶν αὐτο-πυριτῶν;

ΥΠΗΡΕΤΗΣ

Οὔκ, ἀλλὰ χρυσίον τουτὶ καὶ μύρον καὶ μαχαίριον κουρικὸν καὶ κάτοπτρον καὶ κύβους.

ΦΙΛΟΣΟΦΙΑ

Εὖ γε, ὦ γενναῖε. τοιαῦτα ἦν σοι τὰ ἐφόδια τῆς ἀσκήσεως καὶ μετὰ τούτων ἠξίους λοιδορεῖσθαι πᾶσιν καὶ τοὺς ἄλλους παιδα-γωγεῖν;

ΠΑΡΡΗΣΙΑΔΗΣ

Τοιοῦτοι μὲν οὖν ὑμῖν οὗτοι. χρὴ δὲ ὑμᾶς σκοπεῖν ὄντινα τρόπον ἀγνοούμενα ταῦτα πεπαύσεται καὶ διαγνώσονται οἱ ἐντυγχάνοντες, οἵτινες οἱ ἀγαθοὶ αὐτῶν εἰσι καὶ οἵτινες αὖ πάλιν οἱ τοῦ ἑτέρου βίου.

ΦΙΛΟΣΟΦΙΑ

Σύ, ὦ Ἀλήθεια, ἐξεύρισκε· ὑπὲρ σοῦ γοῦν τὸ τοιοῦτο γένοιτ' ἄν, ὡς μὴ ἐπικρατῇ σου τὸ Ψεῦδος μηδὲ ὑπὸ τῇ Ἀγνοίᾳ λαν-θάνωσιν οἱ φαῦλοι τῶν ἀνδρῶν σε τοὺς χρηστοὺς μεμιμημένοι.

ΑΛΗΘΕΙΑ

Ἐπ' αὐτῷ, εἰ δοκεῖ, Παρρησιάδῃ ποιησόμεθα τὸ τοιοῦτο, **46** ἐπεὶ χρηστὸς ὦπται καὶ εὔνους ἡμῖν καὶ σέ, ὦ Φιλοσοφία, μάλιστα θαυμάζων, παραλαβόντα μεθ' ἑαυτοῦ τὸν Ἔλεγχον ἅπασι τοῖς φάσκουσι φιλοσοφεῖν ἐντυγχάνειν. εἶθ' ὃν μὲν ἂν εὕρῃ γνήσιον

PHILOSOPHY

[44] Stop squabbling. You Cynics stop thumping each other with your sticks; that's not why you've been invited. Now I, Philosophy, and Virtue here and Truth will judge who are the proper philosophers. Then those found living by our precepts will be adjudged best and will prosper, but the impostors who have nothing in common with us we shall bring to a nasty end, nasty creatures that they are, to stop their fraudulent claims to things too high for them. What's this? Running away, are you? Yes, by heavens, and most of them are jumping over the cliffs. Anyhow the Acropolis is empty apart from those few who have stayed on because they don't fear the trial. [45] Servants, pick up the pouch which the Cynic has thrown away in his flight. Come, let me see its contents. Is it lupines or a book or some wholemeal bread?

SERVANT

No, there's gold here, perfume, a razor, a mirror and dice.

PHILOSOPHY

Well done, you noble fellow! So that's the sort of equipment you had for your hard life? Were those the things with which you felt entitled to abuse all and to supervise everybody else?

FRANK

Well, now you can see what these fellows are like. But we must consider how to stop ignorance of these matters and how to enable those who meet them to determine which of these men are virtuous and which lead the other sort of life.

PHILOSOPHY

You, Truth, devise a solution; for that would benefit you and prevent Falsehood prevailing over you and villains using the protection of Ignorance to remain undetected by you when they imitate virtuous men.

TRUTH

[46] We'll leave that to Frank himself, if you agree, for he has shown himself to be virtuous and sympathetic to us and, Philosophy, a particular admirer of yours; he must take Examination with him and talk to all who claim to be philosophers. Then anyone he finds to be a genuine child of

ὡς ἀληθῶς φιλοσοφίας, στεφανωσάτω θαλλοῦ στεφάνῳ καὶ εἰς
τὸ Πρυτανεῖον καλεσάτω, ἢν δέ τινι—οἷοι πολλοί εἰσι—κατ-
αράτῳ ἀνδρὶ ὑποκριτῇ φιλοσοφίας ἐντύχῃ, τὸ τριβώνιον περι-
σπάσας ἀποκειράτω τὸν πώγωνα ἐν χρῷ πάνυ τραγοκουρικῇ
μαχαίρᾳ καὶ ἐπὶ τοῦ μετώπου στίγματα ἐπιβαλέτω ἢ ἐγκαυσάτω
κατὰ τὸ μεσόφρυον· ὁ δὲ τύπος τοῦ καυτῆρος ἔστω ἀλώπηξ ἢ
πίθηκος.

ΦΙΛΟΣΟΦΙΑ

Εὖ γε, ὦ Ἀλήθεια, φῄς· ὁ δὲ ἔλεγχος, Παρρησιάδη, τοιόσδε
ἔστω, οἷος ὁ τῶν ἀετῶν πρὸς τὸν ἥλιον εἶναι λέγεται, οὐ μὰ
Δί' ὥστε κἀκείνους ἀντιβλέπειν τῷ φωτὶ καὶ πρὸς ἐκεῖνο δοκι-
μάζεσθαι, ἀλλὰ προθεὶς χρυσίον καὶ δόξαν καὶ ἡδονὴν ὃν μὲν
ἂν αὐτῶν ἴδῃς ὑπερορῶντα καὶ μηδαμῶς ἑλκόμενον πρὸς τὴν
ὄψιν, οὗτος ἔστω ὁ τῷ θαλλῷ στεφόμενος, ὃν δ' ἂν ἀτενὲς ἀποβλέποντα καὶ τὴν χεῖρα ὀρέγοντα ἐπὶ τὸ χρυσίον, ἀπάγειν ἐπὶ τὸ
καυτήριον τοῦτον ἀποκείρας πρότερον τὸν πώγωνα ὡς ἔδοξεν.

ΠΑΡΡΗΣΙΑΔΗΣ

Ἔσται ταῦτα, ὦ Φιλοσοφία, καὶ ὄψει αὐτίκα μάλα τοὺς πολ· 47
λοὺς αὐτῶν ἀλωπεκίας ἢ πιθηκοφόρους, ὀλίγους δὲ καὶ ἐστεφανω-
μένους· εἰ βούλεσθε μέντοι, κἀνταῦθα ὑμῖν ἀνάξω τινὰς ἤδη
αὐτῶν.

ΦΙΛΟΣΟΦΙΑ

Πῶς λέγεις; ἀνάξεις τοὺς φυγόντας;

ΠΑΡΡΗΣΙΑΔΗΣ

Καὶ μάλα, ἤνπερ ἡ ἱερειά μοι ἐθελήσῃ πρὸς ὀλίγον χρῆσαι τὴν
ὁρμιὰν ἐκείνην καὶ τὸ ἄγκιστρον, ὅπερ ὁ ἁλιεὺς ἀνέθηκεν ὁ ἐκ
Πειραιῶς.

ΙΕΡΕΙΑ

Ἰδοὺ δὴ λαβέ, καὶ τὸν κάλαμόν γε ἅμα, ὡς πάντα ἔχῃς.

ΠΑΡΡΗΣΙΑΔΗΣ

Οὐκοῦν, ὦ ἱέρεια, καὶ ἰσχάδας μοί τινας δὸς ἀνύσασα καὶ
ὀλίγον τοῦ χρυσίου.

philosophy, he must crown with an olive wreath and invite to free meals in the Magistrates' Hall. But when he meets any foul scoundrel acting the philosopher, as he often will, let him strip off his ragged cloak, crop off his beard close to the skin with goat-shears and tattoo his forehead or brand him between the eyebrows and let the mark made by the branding-iron be that of a fox or monkey.

PHILOSOPHY

Well said, Truth. But, Frank, the test must be like the one they say eagles have when facing the sun, though of course they won't have to stare into the light or be approved in that way, but you must put gold and fame and pleasure before them, and anyone you see to be contemptuous of these things and unattracted by the sight of them, is the one to be wreathed with the olive, whereas him you see staring hard at the gold and reaching out for it, you are to take off for branding, after first cutting off his beard, as we agreed.

FRANK

[47] That'll be done, Philosophy, and very soon you'll see most of them bearing the brand of the fox or the monkey, and only a few with wreathes. However, if you like, I'll fetch some of them up here to you at once.

PHILOSOPHY

How do you mean? Fetch up the fugitives?

FRANK

Certainly, if the priestess will be kind enough to lend me for a short time that line and hook given by the fisherman from Piraeus in payment of his vow.

PRIESTESS

There you are, take the rod at the same time, so that you have everything.

FRANK

Then, priestess, give me some figs as well, quickly please, and a little gold.

ΙΕΡΕΙΑ

Λάμβανε.

ΦΙΛΟΣΟΦΙΑ

Τί πράττειν ἀνὴρ διανοεῖται; δελεάσας τὸ ἄγκιστρον ἰσχάδι καὶ τῷ χρυσίῳ καθίσας ἐπὶ τὸ ἄκρον τοῦ τειχίου καθῆκεν εἰς τὴν πόλιν. τί ταῦτα, ὦ Παρρησιάδη, ποιεῖς; ἦ που τοὺς λίθους ἁλιεύσειν διέγνωκας ἐκ τοῦ Πελασγικοῦ;

ΠΑΡΡΗΣΙΑΔΗΣ

Σιώπησον, ὦ Φιλοσοφία, καὶ τὴν ἄγραν περίμενε· σὺ δέ, ὦ Πόσειδον ἀγρεῦ καὶ Ἀμφιτρίτη φίλη, πολλοὺς ἡμῖν ἀνάπεμπε τῶν ἰχθύων. ἀλλ' ὁρῶ τινα λάβρακα εὐμεγέθη, μᾶλλον δὲ χρύσοφρυν· 48 οὔκ, ἀλλὰ γαλεός ἐστιν. πρόσεισι γοῦν τῷ ἀγκίστρῳ κεχηνώς· ὀσφρᾶται τοῦ χρυσίου· πλησίον ἤδη ἐστίν· ἔψαυσεν· εἴληπται· ἀνασπάσωμεν. καὶ σύ, ὦ Ἔλεγχε, ἀνάσπα· Ἔλεγχε, συνεπιλαβοῦ τῆς ὁρμιᾶς.

ΕΛΕΓΧΟΣ

Ἄνω ἐστί. φέρ' ἴδω τίς εἶ, ὦ βέλτιστε ἰχθύων; κύων οὗτός γε. Ἡράκλεις τῶν ὀδόντων. τί τοῦτο, ὦ γεννιαότατε; εἴληψαι λιχνεύων περὶ τὰς πέτρας, ἔνθα λήσειν ἤλπισας ὑποδεδυκώς; ἀλλὰ νῦν ἔσῃ φανερὸς ἅπασιν ἐκ τῶν βραγχίων ἀπηρτημένος. ἐξέλωμεν τὸ ἄγκιστρον καὶ τὸ δέλεαρ. μὰ Δί' ἔπιεν. τουτὶ κενόν σοι τὸ ἄγκιστρον· ἡ δ' ἰσχὰς ἤδη προσέσχηται καὶ τὸ χρυσίον ἐν τῇ κοιλίᾳ.

ΠΑΡΡΗΣΙΑΔΗΣ

Ἐξεμεσάτω νὴ Δία, ὡς καὶ ἐπ' ἄλλους δελεάσωμεν. εὖ ἔχει· τί φῄς, ὦ Διόγενες; οἶσθα τοῦτον ὅστις ἐστίν, ἢ προσήκει τί σοι ἀνήρ;

ΔΙΟΓΕΝΗΣ

Οὐδαμῶς.

ΠΑΡΡΗΣΙΑΔΗΣ

Τί οὖν; πόσου ἄξιον αὐτὸν χρὴ φάναι; ἐγὼ μὲν γὰρ δύ' ὀβολῶν πρώην* αὐτὸν ἐτιμησάμην.

PRIESTESS

There you are.

PHILOSOPHY

What's the fellow up to? He has baited his hook with a fig and the gold, and cast it down to the city from a seat he has taken on the parapet. Why are you doing that, Frank? Have you decided to fish up the stones from the Pelasgicum?

FRANK

[48] Shush, Philosophy, and wait for my catch. And you, Posidon, Friend of Fishermen, and beloved Amphitrite, please send us up lots of fish. But I see a large bass or rather a gilthead. No, he's a cat-fish; at any rate he's approaching the hook open-mouthed. He can scent the gold. He's near it now. He has touched it. He's caught! Let's pull him up. Help to pull him up, Examination. Examination, help to hold the line.

EXAMINATION

He's up now. Come, let me see who you are, you prize specimen. He's a dogfish; Heracles, what teeth! What's this, my noble creature? Have you been caught guzzling round the rocks, where you expected to lie low and escape notice? But now you'll be strung up by your gills in full view of all. Let's remove the hook and the bait. Ye gods, he has swallowed it! See, there's the hook bare; the fig and the gold are already lodged in his belly.

FRANK

Good heavens, let's have him disgorge them for us to use as bait for others. That's good. Tell me, Diogenes, do you know who this fellow is? Has he any connection with you?

DIOGENES

Certainly not.

FRANK

Well, how much should we say he's worth? I priced him at tuppence the other day.

ΔΙΟΓΕΝΗΣ

Πολὺ λέγεις· ἄβρωτός τε γάρ ἐστιν καὶ εἰδεχθὴς καὶ σκληρὸς καὶ ἄτιμος· ἄφες αὐτὸν ἐπὶ κεφαλὴν κατὰ τῆς πέτρας· σὺ δὲ ἄλλον ἀνάσπασον καθεὶς τὸ ἄγκιστρον. ἐκεῖνο μέντοι ὅρα, ὦ Παρρησιάδη, μὴ καμπτόμενός σοι ὁ κάλαμος ἀποκλασθῇ.

ΠΑΡΡΗΣΙΑΔΗΣ

Θάρρει, ὦ Διόγενες· κοῦφοί εἰσι καὶ τῶν ἀφύων ἐλαφρότεροι.

ΔΙΟΓΕΝΗΣ

Νὴ Δί', ἀφυέστατοί γε· ἀνάσπα δὲ ὅμως.

ΠΑΡΡΗΣΙΑΔΗΣ

Ἰδού τις ἄλλος ὑπόπλατυς ὥσπερ ἡμίτομος ἰχθὺς πρόσεισιν, 49 ψῆττά τις, κεχηνὼς εἰς τὸ ἄγκιστρον· κατέπιεν, ἔχεται, ἀνεσπάσθω. τίς ἐστιν;

ΕΛΕΓΧΟΣ

Ὁ Πλατωνικὸς εἶναι λέγων.

ΠΑΡΡΗΣΙΑΔΗΣ

Καὶ σύ, ὦ κατάρατε, ἥκεις ἐπὶ τὸ χρυσίον; τί φῄς, ὦ Πλάτων; τί ποιῶμεν αὐτόν;

ΠΛΑΤΩΝ

Ἀπὸ τῆς αὐτῆς πέτρας καὶ οὗτος· ἐπ' ἄλλον καθείσθω.   50

ΠΑΡΡΗΣΙΑΔΗΣ

Καὶ μὴν ὁρῶ τινα πάγκαλον προσιόντα, ὡς ἂν ἐν βυθῷ δόξειεν, ποικίλον τὴν χρόαν, ταινίας τινὰς ἐπὶ τοῦ νώτου ἐπιχρύσους ἔχοντα. ὁρᾷς, ὦ Ἔλεγχε;

ΕΛΕΓΧΟΣ

Ὁ τὸν Ἀριστοτέλη προσποιούμενος οὗτός ἐστιν. ἦλθεν, εἶτα πάλιν ἄπεισιν. περισκοπεῖ ἀκριβῶς, αὖθις ἐπανῆλθεν, ἔχανεν, εἴληπται, ἀνιμήσθω.

ΑΡΙΣΤΟΤΕΛΗΣ

Μὴ ἀνέρῃ με, ὦ Παρρησιάδη, περὶ αὐτοῦ· ἀγνοῶ γὰρ ὅστις ἐστίν.

DIOGENES

That was dear, for he's inedible, ugly, hard and worthless. Throw him headlong over the rock. Let down your hook and pull up another one; only watch out, Frank, in case your rod bends and breaks.

FRANK

Have no fear, Diogenes; they're lighter than minnows.

DIOGENES

Good God yes; their intelligence is *minuscule* enough; pull them up nevertheless.

FRANK

[49] Look, there's another one; he has the look of a plate on him; he's like one of those flat fish that's been cut in two, a sort of turbot; he's coming close to the hook with open mouth; he has gobbled it down, he's caught, pull him up. Who is he?

EXAMINATION

The one who says he's a Platonist.

FRANK

So you've come for the gold as well, you scoundrel? What's your opinion, Plato? What are we to do with him?

PLATO

[50] Over the same rock with him too! Cast your line down for another one.

FRANK

Look, I can see an absolute beauty coming; as far as I can judge with him so far down, he's multi-coloured, with golden stripes on his back. Do you see him, Examination?

EXAMINATION

He's the one who claims to be an Aristotle. He's come, now he's going away again; he's having a careful look round; he's come back; his mouth is wide open; he's caught; up with him.

ARISTOTLE

Don't ask *me* about him, Frank; I don't know who he is.

ΠΑΡΡΗΣΙΑΔΗΣ

Οὐκοῦν καὶ οὗτος, ὦ Ἀριστότελες, κατὰ τῶν πετρῶν. ἀλλ' 51
ἢν ἰδού, πολλούς που τοὺς ἰχθῦς ὁρῶ κατὰ ταὐτὸν ὁμόχροας,
ἀκανθώδεις καὶ τὴν ἐπιφάνειαν ἐκτετραχυσμένους, ἐχίνων δυσ-
ληπτοτέρους. ἢ που σαγήνης ἐπ' αὐτοὺς δεήσει;

ΦΙΛΟΣΟΦΙΑ

Ἀλλ' οὐ πάρεστιν. ἱκανὸν εἰ κἂν ἕνα τινὰ ἐκ τῆς ἀγέλης ἀνα-
σπάσαιμεν. ἥξει δὲ ἐπὶ τὸ ἄγκιστρον δηλαδὴ ὃς ἂν αὐτῶν θρασύ-
τατος ᾖ.

ΕΛΕΓΧΟΣ

Κάθες, εἰ δοκεῖ, σιδηρώσας γε πρότερον ἐπὶ πολὺ τῆς ὁρμιᾶς,
ὡς μὴ ἀποπρίσῃ τοῖς ὀδοῦσι καταπιὼν τὸ χρυσίον.

ΠΑΡΡΗΣΙΑΔΗΣ

Καθῆκα. καὶ σὺ δέ, ὦ Πόσειδον, ταχεῖαν ἐπιτέλει τὴν ἄγραν.
βαβαί, μάχονται περὶ τοῦ δελέατος, καὶ οἱ μὲν συνάμα πολλοὶ
περιτρώγουσι τὴν ἰσχάδα, οἱ δὲ προσφύντες ἔχονται τοῦ χρυσίου.
εὖ ἔχει· περιεπάρη τις μάλα καρτερός. φέρ' ἴδω τίνος ἐπώνυμον
σεαυτὸν εἶναι λέγεις; καίτοι γελοῖός εἰμι ἀναγκάζων ἰχθὺν
λαλεῖν· ἄφωνοι γὰρ οὗτοί γε. ἀλλὰ σύ, ὦ Ἔλεγχε, εἰπὲ ὅντινα
ἔχει διδάσκαλον αὐτοῦ.

ΕΛΕΓΧΟΣ

Χρύσιππον τουτονί.

ΠΑΡΡΗΣΙΑΔΗΣ

Μανθάνω· διότι χρυσίον προσῆν, οἶμαι, τῷ ὀνόματι. σὺ δ'
οὖν, Χρύσιππε, πρὸς τῆς Ἀθηνᾶς εἰπέ, οἶσθα τοὺς ἄνδρας ἢ
τοιαῦτα παρῄνεις αὐτοῖς ποιεῖν;

ΧΡΥΣΙΠΠΟΣ

Νὴ Δί', ὑβριστικὰ ἐρωτᾷς, ὦ Παρρησιάδη, προσήκειν τι ἡμῖν
ὑπολαμβάνων τοιούτους ὄντας.

ΠΑΡΡΗΣΙΑΔΗΣ

Εὖ γε, ὦ Χρύσιππε, γενναῖος εἶ. οὗτος δὲ καὶ αὐτὸς ἐπὶ
κεφαλὴν μετὰ τῶν ἄλλων, ἐπεὶ καὶ ἀκανθώδης ἐστί, καὶ δέος μὴ
διαπαρῇ τις τὸν λαιμὸν ἐσθίων.

FRANK

[51] Then, Aristotle, he must go down over the rocks too. But look, I see lots of fish, all the same colour, prickly and rough-skinned, harder to handle than sea-urchins. Will we need a net for them?

PHILOSOPHY

We haven't got one. It'll be enough to pull up one from the shoal. The boldest one of them will no doubt come to the hook.

EXAMINATION

Let your line down, please, but first reinforce most of it with iron, so that he doesn't gnaw through it with his teeth, once he's swallowed the gold.

FRANK

Down it goes. Please, Posidon, make my catch a quick one. Gracious, they're fighting over the bait, and lots of them all together are nibbling round the fig, and others clinging close to the gold. Good; there's a really strong one hooked. Well, let me see whose name *you* give yourself. But I'm being ridiculous in trying to make a fish talk; for they're dumb. But you, Examination, tell me whom he has for master.

EXAMINATION

Chrysippus here.

FRANK

I understand; he was attracted by the gold in the name. But in Athena's name, Chrysippus, tell me, do *you* know the fellows? Was it on *your* advice they act like this?

CHRYSIPPUS

By Zeus, Frank, you insult me by your questions, if you think *they* have any connection with *us*.

FRANK

Well said, Chrysippus; you're a splendid fellow. This creature too must be thrown down head first with the others, for he's prickly and anyone eating him is in danger of having his throat spiked.

ΦΙΛΟΣΟΦΙΑ

Ἅλις, ὦ Παρρησιάδη, τῆς ἄγρας, μὴ καί τίς σοι, οἷοι πολλοί   52
εἰσιν, οἴχηται ἀποσπάσας τὸ χρυσίον καὶ τὸ ἄγκιστρον, εἶτά σε
ἀποτῖσαι τῇ ἱερείᾳ δεήσῃ. ὥστε ἡμεῖς μὲν ἀπίωμεν περι-
πατήσουσαι· καιρὸς δὲ καὶ ὑμᾶς ἀπιέναι ὅθεν ἥκετε, μὴ καὶ
ὑπερήμεροι γένησθε τῆς προθεσμίας. σφὼ δέ, σὺ καὶ ὁ Ἔλεγχος,
ὦ Παρρησιάδη, ἐν κύκλῳ ἐπὶ πάντας αὐτοὺς ἰόντες ἢ στεφανοῦτε
ἢ ἐγκαίετε, ὡς ἔφην.

ΠΑΡΡΗΣΙΑΔΗΣ

Ἔσται ταῦτα, ὦ Φιλοσοφία. χαίρετε, ὦ βέλτιστοι ἀνδρῶν.
ἡμεῖς δὲ κατίωμεν, ὦ Ἔλεγχε, καὶ τελῶμεν τὰ παρηγγελμένα.

ΕΛΕΓΧΟΣ

Ποῖ δὲ καὶ πρῶτον ἀπιέναι δεήσει; μῶν εἰς τὴν Ἀκαδημίαν ἢ
εἰς τὴν Στοάν; ⟨ἢ⟩ ἀπὸ τοῦ Λυκείου ποιησώμεθα τὴν ἀρχήν;

ΠΑΡΡΗΣΙΑΔΗΣ

Οὐδὲν διοίσει τοῦτο. πλὴν οἶδά γε ὡς ἔνθα ἂν ἀπέλθωμεν,
ὀλίγων μὲν τῶν στεφάνων, πολλῶν δὲ τῶν καυτηρίων δεησόμεθα.

PHILOSOPHY

[52] That's quite enough fishing, Frank, in case one of them, as many are capable of doing, goes off dragging your gold and hook with him, and then you have to pay the priestess for them. So let's go off for a stroll and (*to the dead philosophers*) it's time for you to be off to where you came from, in case you overstay your leave. But the pair of you, Frank and Examination, go round in search of them all and wreathe them or brand them as per my instructions.

FRANK

That will be done, Philosophy. (*To the dead philosophers*). Good-bye, best of men. Let's go down, Examination, and complete our commission.

EXAMINATION

Where must we go first? The Academy or the Porch? Or are we to start with the Lyceum?

FRANK

It won't make any difference. However, I *do* know that wherever we go, we'll need few wreaths but lots of branding-irons.

ΜΕΝΙΠΠΟΣ Η ΝΕΚΥΟΜΑΝΤΕΙΑ

ΜΕΝΙΠΠΟΣ

Ὦ χαῖρε μέλαθρον πρόπυλά θ’ ἑστίας ἐμῆς,   1
ὡς ἄσμενός σ’ ἐσεῖδον ἐς φάος μολών.

ΦΙΛΟΣ

Οὐ Μένιππος οὗτός ἐστιν ὁ κύων; οὐ μὲν οὖν ἄλλος τις, εἰ
μὴ ἐγὼ παραβλέπω· Μένιππος ὅλος. τί οὖν αὐτῷ βούλεται τὸ
ἀλλόκοτον τοῦ σχήματος, πῖλος καὶ λύρα καὶ λεοντῆ; πλὴν ἀλλὰ
προσιτέον γε αὐτῷ. χαῖρε, ὦ Μένιππε· καὶ πόθεν ἡμῖν ἀφῖξαι;
πολὺς γὰρ χρόνος οὐ πέφηνας ἐν τῇ πόλει.

ΜΕΝΙΠΠΟΣ

Ἥκω νεκρῶν κευθμῶνα καὶ σκότου πύλας
λιπών, ἵν’ Ἅιδης χωρὶς ᾦκισται θεῶν.

ΦΙΛΟΣ

Ἡράκλεις, ἐλελήθει Μένιππος ἡμᾶς ἀποθανών, κᾆτα ἐξ
ὑπαρχῆς ἀναβεβίωκεν;

ΜΕΝΙΠΠΟΣ

Οὔκ, ἀλλ’ ἔτ’ ἔμπνουν Ἅιδης μ’ ἐδέξατο.

ΦΙΛΟΣ

Τίς δὴ ἡ αἰτία σοι τῆς καινῆς*παραδόξου ταύτης ἀποδημίας;

ΜΕΝΙΠΠΟΣ

Νεότης μ’ ἐπῆρε καὶ θράσος τοῦ νοῦ πλέον.

ΦΙΛΟΣ

Παῦσαι, μακάριε, τραγῳδῶν καὶ λέγε οὑτωσί πως ἁπλῶς καταβὰς ἀπὸ τῶν ἰαμβείων, τίς ἡ στολή; τί σοι τῆς κάτω πορείας
ἐδέησεν; ἄλλως γὰρ οὐχ ἡδεῖά τις οὐδὲ ἀσπάσιος ἡ ὁδός.

ΜΕΝΙΠΠΟΣ

Ὦ φιλότης, χρειώ με κατήγαγεν εἰς Ἀίδαο
ψυχῇ χρησόμενον Θηβαίου Τειρεσίαο.

*add καὶ

MENIPPUS OR CONSULTING THE ORACLE IN HADES

MENIPPUS

[1] Greetings ye halls and portals of mine hearth and home.
Welcome your sight to me now that I'm back in light.

FRIEND

(*To himself*) Isn't that Menippus, the Dog? Indeed it is, unless my eyes deceive me. It's Menippus from head to toe. Then what's the meaning of his strange attire? The cap? The lyre? The lionskin? However I must go up to him. (*To Menippus*) Good day, Menippus. Tell us where you've come from, for it's a long time since you've been seen in the city.

MENIPPUS

I come from dead men's den and gates of dark,
Leaving the place where Hades dwells from other gods remote.

FRIEND

By Heracles, was Menippus dead without our knowing it and has he been restored to life all over again?

MENIPPUS

Not so; I still did live when I to Hades went.

FRIEND

What was your reason for such an unusual and surprising journey?

MENIPPUS

'Twas youth to blame and recklessness bereft of sense.

FRIEND

Stop spouting from plays, my good chap, get down from your tragic lines and tell me in plain language like mine why you're dressed like that. Why did you need to travel down under? It isn't usually a pleasant or welcome journey.

MENIPPUS

Dear friend, dire need made me to Hades' House descend,
And ghost of Theban Tiresias consult.

ΦΙΛΟΣ

Οὗτος, ἀλλ᾽ ἦ παραπαίεις; οὐ γὰρ ἂν οὕτως ἐμμέτρως ἐρραψῴδεις πρὸς ἄνδρας φίλους.

ΜΕΝΙΠΠΟΣ

Μὴ θαυμάσῃς, ὦ ἑταῖρε· νεωστὶ γὰρ Εὐριπίδῃ καὶ Ὁμήρῳ συγγενόμενος οὐκ οἶδ᾽ ὅπως ἀνεπλήσθην τῶν ἐπῶν καὶ αὐτόματά μοι τὰ μέτρα ἐπὶ τὸ στόμα ἔρχεται. ἀτὰρ εἰπέ μοι, πῶς τὰ ὑπὲρ   2
γῆς ἔχει καὶ τί ποιοῦσιν οἱ ἐν τῇ πόλει;

ΦΙΛΟΣ

Καινὸν οὐδέν, ἀλλ᾽ οἷα καὶ πρὸ τοῦ ἁρπάζουσιν, ἐπιορκοῦσιν, τοκογλυφοῦσιν, ὀβολοστατοῦσιν.

ΜΕΝΙΠΠΟΣ

Ἄθλιοι καὶ κακοδαίμονες· οὐ γὰρ ἴσασιν οἷα ἔναγχος κεκύρωται παρὰ τοῖς κάτω καὶ οἷα κεχειροτόνηται τὰ ψηφίσματα κατὰ τῶν πλουσίων, ἃ μὰ τὸν Κέρβερον οὐδεμία μηχανὴ τὸ διαφυγεῖν αὐτούς.

ΦΙΛΟΣ

Τί φῄς; δέδοκταί τι νεώτερον τοῖς κάτω περὶ τῶν ἐνθάδε;

ΜΕΝΙΠΠΟΣ

Νὴ Δία, καὶ πολλά γε· ἀλλ᾽ οὐ θέμις ἐκφέρειν αὐτὰ πρὸς ἅπαντας οὐδὲ ἐξαγορεύειν τὰ ἀπόρρητα, μὴ καί τις ἡμᾶς γράψηται γραφὴν ἀσεβείας ἐπὶ τοῦ Ῥαδαμάνθυος.

ΦΙΛΟΣ

Μηδαμῶς, ὦ Μένιππε, πρὸς τοῦ Διός, μὴ φθονέσῃς φίλῳ ἀνδρὶ τῶν λόγων. πρὸς γὰρ εἰδότα σιωπᾶν ἐρεῖς, τά τ᾽ ἄλλα καὶ πρὸς μεμνημένον.

ΜΕΝΙΠΠΟΣ

Χαλεπὸν μὲν ἐπιτάττεις τὸ ἐπίταγμα καὶ οὐ πάντῃ εὐσεβές· πλὴν ἀλλὰ σοῦ γε ἕνεκα τολμητέον. ἔδοξε δὴ τοὺς πλουσίους τούτους καὶ πολυχρημάτους καὶ τὸ χρυσίον κατάκλειστον ὥσπερ τὴν Δανάην φυλάττοντας—

ΦΙΛΟΣ

Μὴ πρότερον εἴπῃς, ὠγαθέ, τὰ δεδογμένα πρὶν ἐκεῖνα διελθεῖν

FRIEND

Are you mad, fellow? Otherwise you'd not string together epic lines to friends in that way.

MENIPPUS

No need for surprise, my dear chap. I've just been keeping company with Euripides and Homer and have somehow become infected with their poetry, and their metres come into my mouth of their own accord. [2] But tell me, how are things up on earth? What are the city folks doing?

FRIEND

Nothing unusual, but just like they did before, stealing, perjuring themselves, lending money, and calculating their interest to the nearest farthing.

MENNIPUS

The poor unfortunates! They don't know about the recent enactments down below and the decrees passed against the rich, ones which, by Cerberus, there's no way they can escape.

FRIEND

How do you mean? Have those below decided on any radical changes for those up here?

MENIPPUS

Yes, by Zeus, lots of them. But it's wrong to noise them abroad to all and sundry or to reveal what's strictly secret, and I'm afraid of someone prosecuting me for impiety before Rhadamanthys.

FRIEND

Please, Menippus, please don't grudge a friend the information; for you'll be telling one who knows how to hold his tongue and what's more is an initiate.

MENIPPUS

What you're asking me to do isn't easy and is hardly pious, but for your sake I must take the risk. It was in fact decided that these rich men, these men of great wealth who keep their gold locked up like Danae –

FRIEND

Don't inform me of the decisions, my good chap, before explaining

ἃ μάλιστα ἂν ἡδέως ἀκούσαιμί σου, τίς ἡ ἐπίνοιά σου τῆς
καθόδου ἐγένετο, τίς δ' ὁ τῆς πορείας ἡγεμών, εἶθ' ἐξῆς ἅ τε
εἶδες ἅ τε ἤκουσας παρ' αὐτοῖς· εἰκὸς γὰρ δὴ φιλόκαλον ὄντα
σε μηδὲν τῶν ἀξίων θέας ἢ ἀκοῆς παραλιπεῖν.

ΜΕΝΙΠΠΟΣ

Ὑπουργητέον καὶ ταῦτά σοι· τί γὰρ ἂν καὶ πάθοι τις, ὁπότε 3
φίλος ἀνὴρ βιάζοιτο; καὶ δὴ πρῶτά σοι δίειμι τὰ περὶ τῆς γνώμης
τῆς ἐμῆς, ὅθεν ὡρμήθην πρὸς τὴν κατάβασιν. ἐγὼ γάρ, ἄχρι
μὲν ἐν παισὶν ἦν, ἀκούων Ὁμήρου καὶ Ἡσιόδου πολέμους καὶ
στάσεις διηγουμένων οὐ μόνον τῶν ἡμιθέων, ἀλλὰ καὶ αὐτῶν ἤδη
τῶν θεῶν, ἔτι δὲ μοιχείας αὐτῶν καὶ βίας καὶ ἁρπαγὰς καὶ δίκας
καὶ πατέρων ἐξελάσεις καὶ ἀδελφῶν γάμους, πάντα ταῦτα ἐνόμιζον
εἶναι καλὰ καὶ οὐ παρέργως ἐκινούμην πρὸς αὐτά. ἐπεὶ δὲ εἰς
ἄνδρας τελεῖν ἠρξάμην, πάλιν αὖ ἐνταῦθα ἤκουον τῶν νόμων
τἀναντία τοῖς ποιηταῖς κελευόντων, μήτε μοιχεύειν μήτε στα-
σιάζειν μήτε ἁρπάζειν. ἐν μεγάλῃ οὖν καθειστήκειν ἀμφιβολίᾳ,
οὐκ εἰδὼς ὅ τι χρησαίμην ἐμαυτῷ· οὔτε γὰρ τοὺς θεοὺς ἄν ποτε
μοιχεῦσαι καὶ στασιάσαι πρὸς ἀλλήλους ἡγούμην εἰ μὴ ὡς περὶ
καλῶν τούτων ἐγίγνωσκον, οὔτ' ἂν τοὺς νομοθέτας τἀναντία
παραινεῖν εἰ μὴ λυσιτελεῖν ὑπελάμβανον.

Ἐπεὶ δὲ διηπόρουν, ἔδοξέ μοι ἐλθόντα παρὰ τοὺς καλουμένους 4
τούτους φιλοσόφους ἐγχειρίσαι τε ἐμαυτὸν καὶ δεηθῆναι αὐτῶν
χρῆσθαί μοι ὅ τι βούλοιντο καί τινα ὁδὸν ἁπλῆν καὶ βέβαιον ὑπο-
δεῖξαι τοῦ βίου. ταῦτα μὲν δὴ φρονῶν προσῄειν αὐτοῖς, ἐλελή-
θειν δ' ἐμαυτὸν εἰς αὐτό, φασί, τὸ πῦρ ἐκ τοῦ καπνοῦ βιαζόμενος.
παρὰ γὰρ δὴ τούτοις μάλιστα εὕρισκον ἐπισκοπῶν τὴν ἄγνοιαν καὶ
τὴν ἀπορίαν πλείονα, ὥστε μοι τάχιστα χρυσοῦν ἀπέδειξαν οὗτοι
τὸν τῶν ἰδιωτῶν τοῦτον βίον.

Ἀμέλει ὁ μὲν αὐτῶν παρῄει τὸ πᾶν ἥδεσθαι καὶ μόνον τοῦτο
ἐκ παντὸς μετιέναι· τοῦτο γὰρ εἶναι τὸ εὔδαιμον. ὁ δέ τις ἔμπαλιν,
πονεῖν τὰ πάντα καὶ μοχθεῖν καὶ τὸ σῶμα καταναγκάζειν
ῥυπῶντα καὶ αὐχμῶντα καὶ πᾶσι δυσαρεστοῦντα καὶ λοιδορού-
μενον, συνεχὲς ἐπιρραψῳδῶν τὰ πάνδημα ἐκεῖνα τοῦ Ἡσιόδου
περὶ τῆς ἀρετῆς ἔπη καὶ τὸν ἱδρῶτα καὶ τὴν ἐπὶ τὸ ἄκρον
ἀνάβασιν. ἄλλος καταφρονεῖν χρημάτων παρεκελεύετο καὶ ἀδιάφορον οἴεσθαι τὴν κτῆσιν αὐτῶν· ὁ δέ τις ἔμπαλιν ἀγαθὸν εἶναι

what I'd particularly like you to tell me. What was your purpose in going down there, who was your guide for the journey, and following that what did you see and hear among the dead? For being a man of taste you can be expected to include everything that was worth seeing or hearing.

MENIPPUS

[3] I must oblige you once more; for what is one to do when friend compels? Well, first I'll tell you about the thoughts I had which impelled me to make the descent. For, as long as I was a lad and heard Homer and Hesiod describing wars and quarrels not only between the demigods but even the gods themselves and moreover how they indulged in adultery, violent conduct, abduction and litigation, how sons drove out fathers, and brothers and sisters married, I personally considered all these things admirable and was uncommonly attracted to them. But when first I reached manhood's estate, then on the contrary I heard the laws prescribing the opposite of the poets, forbidding adultery, quarrelling and theft. So I was in a terrible quandary, not knowing what to do with myself. For I didn't think the gods would ever have committed adultery or quarrelled with each other, unless they considered such behaviour admirable, nor would the lawmakers have recommended the opposite, unless they thought it beneficial.

[4] In my bewilderment, I decided to go to those so-called philosophers, put myself in their hands and ask them to do anything they wanted with me and show me a simple and reliable course of life. I approached them with these objects in mind, but didn't realise I was forcing myself from the proverbial frying-pan into the fire. For on examination I found the ignorance and bewilderment to be greater among them than elsewhere so that these philosophers very quickly convinced me that the golden life was that of the average man.

Indeed one of them would recommend devoting oneself entirely to pleasure and seeking that above all, happiness consisting in that. Another conversely recommended a life of complete toil, tribulation and mortification of the flesh, remaining filthy and unkempt, making oneself unpleasant and abusive to all, continually spouting those banal verses of Hesiod about virtue and going on about sweat and the ascent to the summit. Another would bid us despise money and consider possessing it something indifferent; yet another contradicted him, believing wealth was

καὶ τὸν πλοῦτον ἀπεφαίνετο. περὶ μὲν γὰρ τοῦ κόσμου τί χρὴ
καὶ λέγειν; ὅς γε ἰδέας καὶ ἀσώματα καὶ ἀτόμους καὶ κενὰ
καὶ τοιοῦτόν τινα ὄχλον ὀνομάτων ὁσημέραι παρ' αὐτῶν ἀκούων
ἐναντίων. καὶ τὸ πάντων ἀτοπώτατον, ὅτι περὶ τῶν ἐναντιωτάτων
ἕκαστος αὐτῶν λέγων σφόδρα νικῶντας καὶ πιθανοὺς λόγους
ἐπορίζετο, ὥστε μήτε τῷ θερμὸν τὸ αὐτὸ πρᾶγμα λέγοντι μήτε
τῷ ψυχρὸν ἀντιλέγειν ἔχειν, καὶ ταῦτ' εἰδότα σαφῶς ὡς οὐκ ἄν
ποτε θερμὸν εἴη τι καὶ ψυχρὸν ἐν ταὐτῷ χρόνῳ. ἀτεχνῶς οὖν
ἔπασχον τοῖς νυστάζουσιν τούτοις ὅμοιον, ἄρτι μὲν ἐπινεύων,
ἄρτι δὲ ἀνανεύων ἔμπαλιν.

Πολλῷ δὲ τούτων ἐκεῖνο ἀλογώτερον· τοὺς γὰρ αὐτοὺς τούτους 5
εὕρισκον ἐπιτηρῶν ἐναντιώτατα τοῖς αὐτῶν λόγοις ἐπιτηδεύοντας.
τοὺς γοῦν καταφρονεῖν παραινοῦντας χρημάτων ἑώρων ἀπρὶξ
ἐχομένους αὐτῶν καὶ περὶ τόκων διαφερομένους καὶ ἐπὶ μισθῷ
παιδεύοντας καὶ πάντα ἕνεκα τούτων ὑπομένοντας, τούς τε τὴν
δόξαν ἀποβαλλομένους αὐτῆς ταύτης χάριν τὰ πάντα καὶ πράττοντας καὶ λέγοντας, ἡδονῆς τε αὖ σχεδὸν ἅπαντας κατηγοροῦντας,
ἰδίᾳ δὲ μόνῃ ταύτῃ προσηρτημένους.

Σφαλεὶς οὖν καὶ ταύτης τῆς ἐλπίδος ἔτι μᾶλλον ἐδυσχέραινον, 6
ἠρέμα παραμυθούμενος ἐμαυτὸν ὅτι μετὰ πολλῶν καὶ σοφῶν καὶ
σφόδρα ἐπὶ συνέσει διαβεβοημένων ἀνόητός τέ εἰμι καὶ τἀληθὲς
ἔτι ἀγνοῶν περιέρχομαι. καί μοί ποτε διαγρυπνοῦντι τούτων
ἕνεκα ἔδοξεν εἰς Βαβυλῶνα ἐλθόντα δεηθῆναί τινος τῶν μάγων
τῶν Ζωροάστρου μαθητῶν καὶ διαδόχων· ἤκουον δ' αὐτοὺς
ἐπῳδαῖς τε καὶ τελεταῖς τισιν ἀνοίγειν τοῦ Ἅιδου τὰς πύλας
καὶ κατάγειν ὃν ἂν βούλωνται ἀσφαλῶς καὶ ὀπίσω αὖθις ἀνα-
πέμπειν. ἄριστον οὖν ἡγούμην εἶναι παρά τινος τούτων δια-
πραξάμενον τὴν κατάβασιν ἐλθόντα παρὰ Τειρεσίαν τὸν Βοιώτιον
μαθεῖν παρ' αὐτοῦ ἅτε μάντεως καὶ σοφοῦ, τίς ἐστιν ὁ ἄριστος
βίος καὶ ὃν ἄν τις ἕλοιτο εὖ φρονῶν.

Καὶ δὴ ἀναπηδήσας ὡς εἶχον τάχους ἔτεινον εὐθὺ Βαβυλῶνος·
ἐλθὼν δὲ συγγίγνομαί τινι τῶν Χαλδαίων σοφῷ ἀνδρὶ καὶ
θεσπεσίῳ τὴν τέχνην, πολιῷ μὲν τὴν κόμην, γένειον δὲ μάλα
σεμνὸν καθειμένῳ, τοὔνομα δὲ ἦν αὐτῷ Μιθροβαρζάνης. δεηθεὶς
δὲ καὶ καθικετεύσας μόγις ἐπέτυχον παρ' αὐτοῦ, ἐφ' ὅτῳ
βούλοιτο μισθῷ, καθηγήσασθαί μοι τῆς ὁδοῦ. παραλαβὼν δέ με 7
ὁ ἀνὴρ πρῶτα μὲν ἡμέρας ἐννέα καὶ εἴκοσιν ἅμα τῇ σελήνῃ

good. For why need I say anything about cosmologies? For I was sickened every day by hearing them talking about forms, things incorporeal, atoms and voids and a whole lot of names like that. The strangest thing of all was that, in urging the most diametrically opposed views, each of them would provide absolutely convincing and persuasive arguments so that when one man said something was hot and another said the same thing was cold, I couldn't contradict either of them, even though I knew perfectly well that a thing couldn't be hot and cold at the same time, so that I was literally in the same state as people who nod off, for now I would drop my head in assent and then raise it again in dissent.

[5] But here's something much more absurd. On observation I found these same people practising the very opposite of what they preached. I saw those who advocated despising money clinging to it tooth and nail, quarrelling about interest, charging for teaching and enduring anything and everything for money, and those who would have us reject fame doing and saying everything for just that, and again pretty well all of them speaking out against pleasure, but in private clinging to it alone.

[6] Disappointed therefore in this hope too, I was still more despondent, but quietly consoled myself with the thought that among many wise men greatly renowned for their intelligence I was a fool going around still ignorant of the truth. One night when I couldn't sleep for all this, I resolved to go to Babylon, and beg help from one of the Magi, the disciples and successors of Zoroaster; I heard that by incantations and rituals they open the gates of Hades to send anyone they want safely down there and bring him back again. So I thought it best to negotiate for my descent with one of them and go to Tiresias, the Boeotian, and learn from him, being a seer and sage, which is the best life and the one a sensible man would choose.

Well, I leapt up with all the speed I could muster and made straight for Babylon. When I arrived, I consulted one of the Chaldaeans, a wise man of wondrous skill, who had white hair and a very impressive beard; his name was Mithrobarzanes. By my appeals and prayers I gained his grudging consent to conduct me on my journey down naming his price. [7] The man took me, and first, for nine and twenty days starting with the

ἀρξάμενος ἔλουε καταγαγὼν ἔωθεν ἐπὶ τὸν Εὐφράτην πρὸς
ἀνίσχοντα τὸν ἥλιον, ῥῆσίν τινα μακρὰν ἐπιλέγων ἧς οὐ σφόδρα
κατήκουον· ὥσπερ γὰρ οἱ φαῦλοι τῶν ἐν τοῖς ἀγῶσι κηρύκων
ἐπίτροχόν τι καὶ ἀσαφὲς ἐφθέγγετο. πλὴν ἀλλ’ ἐῴκει γέ τινας
ἁγίους ἐπικαλεῖσθαι δαίμονας. μετὰ δ’ οὖν τὴν ἐπῳδὴν τρὶς ἄν
μου πρὸς τὸ πρόσωπον ἀποπτύσας, ἐπανῄει πάλιν οὐδένα τῶν
ἀπαντώντων προσβλέπων. καὶ σιτία μὲν ἦν ἡμῖν τὰ ἀκρόδρυα,
ποτὸν δὲ γάλα καὶ μελίκρατον καὶ τὸ τοῦ Χοάσπου ὕδωρ, εὐνὴ δὲ
ὑπαίθριος ἐπὶ τῆς πόας.

Ἐπεὶ δ’ ἅλις εἶχε τῆς προδιαιτήσεως, περὶ μέσας νύκτας ἐπὶ
τὸν Τίγρητα ποταμὸν ἀγαγὼν ἐκάθηρέν τέ με καὶ ἀπέμαξε καὶ
περιήγνισεν δᾳδὶ καὶ σκίλλῃ καὶ ἄλλοις πλείοσιν, ἅμα καὶ τὴν
ἐπῳδὴν ἐκείνην ὑποτονθορύσας. εἶτά με ὅλον καταμαγεύσας καὶ
περιελθών, ἵνα μὴ βλαπτοίμην ὑπὸ τῶν φασμάτων, ἐπανάγει εἰς
τὴν οἰκίαν, ὡς εἶχον, ἀναποδίζοντα, καὶ τὸ λοιπὸν ἀμφὶ πλοῦν
εἴχομεν. αὐτὸς μὲν οὖν μαγικήν τινα ἐνέδυ στολὴν τὰ πολλὰ 8
ἐοικυῖαν τῇ Μηδικῇ, ἐμὲ δὲ τουτοισὶ φέρων ἐνεσκεύασε, τῷ πίλῳ
καὶ τῇ λεοντῇ καὶ προσέτι τῇ λύρᾳ, καὶ παρεκελεύσατο, ἤν τις
ἔρηταί με τοὔνομα, Μένιππον μὴ λέγειν, Ἡρακλέα δὲ ἢ Ὀδυσσέα
ἢ Ὀρφέα.

ΦΙΛΟΣ

Ὡς δὴ τί τοῦτο, ὦ Μένιππε; οὐ γὰρ συνίημι τὴν αἰτίαν οὔτε
τοῦ σχήματος οὔτε τῶν ὀνομάτων.

ΜΕΝΙΠΠΟΣ

Καὶ μὴν πρόδηλόν γε τοῦτο καὶ οὐ παντελῶς ἀπόρρητον· ἐπεὶ
γὰρ οὗτοι πρὸ ἡμῶν ζῶντες εἰς Ἅιδου κατεληλύθεσαν, ἡγεῖτο, εἴ
με ἀπεικάσειεν αὐτοῖς, ῥᾳδίως ἂν τὴν τοῦ Αἰακοῦ φρουρὰν δια-
λαθεῖν καὶ ἀκωλύτως ἂν παρελθεῖν ἅτε συνηθέστερον, τραγικῶς
μάλα παραπεμπόμενον ὑπὸ τοῦ σχήματος.

Ἤδη δ’ οὖν ὑπέφαινεν ἡμέρα, καὶ κατελθόντες ἐπὶ τὸν ποταμὸν 9
περὶ ἀναγωγὴν ἐγιγνόμεθα. παρεσκεύαστο δὲ αὐτῷ καὶ σκάφος
καὶ ἱερεῖα καὶ μελίκρατον καὶ ἄλλα ὅσα πρὸς τὴν τελετὴν χρή-
σιμα. ἐμβαλόμενοι οὖν ἅπαντα τὰ παρεσκευασμένα οὕτω δὴ

καὶ αὐτοὶ
βαίνομεν ἀχνύμενοι, θαλερὸν κατὰ δάκρυ χέοντες.

new moon, he would lead me down to the Euphrates at dawn and wash me facing the rising sun, delivering a long speech I couldn't hear very well. For like inferior heralds at the games his delivery was rapid and indistinct; he seemed however to be invoking certain sacred spirits. Anyhow after the incantation he would spit thrice in my face and then return without looking at anyone who met us. Our food was nuts, our drink milk, honey and the water of the Choaspes, and we slept in the open on the grass.

When he had had enough of the preparatory regimen, he brought me to the river Tigris about midnight, purified, cleansed and sanctified me with a torch and a squill and many other things, all the while murmuring that incantation of his. Then after he had worked his magic on me all over and walked all round me to stop my being harmed by the ghosts, he brought me back to the house, just as I was, making me walk backwards, and thereafter we concentrated on the voyage. [8] He himself put on the robe of a Magos, largely resembling that worn by the Medes, while for me he brought the things you see, the cap, the lionskin and the lyre as well, and fitted me out with them, instructing me, if anyone asked my name, not to say Menippus, but Heracles, Odysseus or Orpheus.

FRIEND

Why was that, Menippus? I don't understand the reason for the costume or the names.

MENIPPUS

But it's obvious and hardly a secret. Since they had preceded us in descending live to Hades, he thought, if he made me resemble them, I would easily elude Aeacus' watch and pass by unhindered as being a more familiar sight, sped along thanks to my costume, just like a character from tragedy.

[9] Well, day was now beginning to show, and we had gone down to the river and were putting out from the shore. He had laid on a boat, sacrificial victims, mead and everything else needed for the ritual. So we put everything prepared on board and then

'ourselves as well
Embarked with heavy hearts, letting great tears down fall'.

Καὶ μέχρι μέν τινος ὑπεφερόμεθα ἐν τῷ ποταμῷ, εἶτα δὲ
εἰσεπλεύσαμεν εἰς τὸ ἕλος καὶ τὴν λίμνην εἰς ἣν ὁ Εὐφράτης
ἀφανίζεται. περαιωθέντες δὲ καὶ ταύτην ἀφικνούμεθα εἴς τι
χωρίον ἔρημον καὶ ὑλῶδες καὶ ἀνήλιον, εἰς ὃ καὶ δὴ ἀποβάντες—
ἡγεῖτο δὲ ὁ Μιθροβαρζάνης—βόθρον τε ὠρυξάμεθα καὶ τὰ μῆλα
κατεσφάξαμεν καὶ τὸ αἷμα περὶ αὐτὸν ἐσπείσαμεν. ὁ δὲ μάγος ἐν
τοσούτῳ δᾷδα καιομένην ἔχων οὐκέτ' ἠρεμαίᾳ τῇ φωνῇ, παμμέγεθες δέ, ὡς οἷός τε ἦν ἀνακραγών, δαίμονάς τε ὁμοῦ πάντας
ἐπεβοᾶτο καὶ Ποινὰς καὶ Ἐρινύας

    καὶ νυχίαν Ἑκάτην καὶ ἐπαινὴν Περσεφόνειαν,

παραμιγνὺς ἅμα καὶ βαρβαρικά τινα καὶ ἄσημα ὀνόματα καὶ
πολυσύλλαβα.

Εὐθὺς οὖν ἅπαντα ἐκεῖνα ἐσαλεύετο καὶ ὑπὸ τῆς ἐπῳδῆς
τοὔδαφος ἀνερρήγνυτο καὶ ὑλακὴ τοῦ Κερβέρου πόρρωθεν ἠκούετο   10
καὶ τὸ πρᾶγμα ὑπερκατηφὲς ἦν καὶ σκυθρωπόν.

    ἔδδεισεν δ' ὑπένερθεν ἄναξ ἐνέρων Ἀϊδωνεύς—

κατεφαίνετο γὰρ ἤδη τὰ πλεῖστα, καὶ ἡ λίμνη καὶ ὁ Πυριφλεγέθων
καὶ τοῦ Πλούτωνος τὰ βασίλεια. κατελθόντες δ' ὅμως διὰ τοῦ
χάσματος τὸν μὲν Ῥαδάμανθυν εὕρομεν τεθνεῶτα μικροῦ δεῖν ὑπὸ
τοῦ φόβου· ὁ δὲ Κέρβερος ὑλάκτησε μέν τι καὶ παρεκίνησε, ταχὺ
δέ μου κρούσαντος τὴν λύραν παραχρῆμα ἐκηλήθη ὑπὸ τοῦ μέλους.
ἐπεὶ δὲ πρὸς τὴν λίμνην ἀφικόμεθα, μικροῦ μὲν οὐδὲ ἐπεραιώθη-
μεν· ἦν γὰρ πλῆρες ἤδη τὸ πορθμεῖον καὶ οἰμωγῆς ἀνάπλεων,
τραυματίαι δὲ πάντες ἐπέπλεον, ὁ μὲν τὸ σκέλος, ὁ δὲ τὴν
κεφαλήν, ὁ δὲ ἄλλο τι συντετριμμένος, ὡς ἐμοὶ δοκεῖν, ἔκ τινος
πολέμου παρόντες.

Ὅμως δ' οὖν ὁ βέλτιστος Χάρων ὡς εἶδε τὴν λεοντῆν, οἰηθείς
με τὸν Ἡρακλέα εἶναι, εἰσεδέξατο καὶ διεπόρθμευσέν τε ἄσμενος
καὶ ἀποβᾶσι διεσήμηνε τὴν ἀτραπόν. ἐπεὶ δὲ ἦμεν ἐν τῷ σκότῳ,   11
προῄει μὲν ὁ Μιθροβαρζάνης, εἱπόμην δὲ ἐγὼ κατόπιν ἐχόμενος
αὐτοῦ, ἕως πρὸς λειμῶνα μέγιστον ἀφικνούμεθα τῷ ἀσφοδέλῳ
κατάφυτον, ἔνθα δὴ περιεπέτοντο ἡμᾶς τετριγυῖαι τῶν νεκρῶν
αἱ σκιαί. κατ' ὀλίγον δὲ προϊόντες παραγινόμεθα πρὸς τὸ τοῦ
Μίνω δικαστήριον· ἐτύγχανε δὲ ὁ μὲν ἐπὶ θρόνου τινὸς ὑψηλοῦ
καθήμενος, παρεστήκεσαν δὲ αὐτῷ Ποιναὶ καὶ Ἐρινύες καὶ
Ἀλάστορες. ἑτέρωθεν δὲ προσήγοντο πολλοί τινες ἐφεξῆς, ἁλύσει

For a time we slipped downstream, but then we sailed into the marsh into which the Euphrates disappears. After crossing this lake, we reached a deserted, heavily wooded, sunless spot, where we disembarked with Mithrobarzanes in the lead, dug a pit, sacrificed the sheep, and scattered the blood by way of libation round the pit. Meanwhile the Magos was holding a burning torch and in a voice no longer quiet raised an enormous cry with all the power he could muster and invoked all the deities at once, Torments and Furies

'And Night Queen Hecate and grim Persephone',
at the same time adding in outlandish, unintelligible, polysyllabic names.
[10] Immediately all these regions shook, the ground was rent asunder by the incantation, the barking of Cerberus was heard in the distance, and all was shrouded in gloom and assumed a lowering look

'And down below Aidoneus, Lord of Ghosts, did fear';
for now most things were visible – the lake, Pyriphlegethon and Pluto's palace. But nevertheless we descended through the gaping hole and found Rhadamanthys almost dead with fear. Cerberus barked a little and stirred, but I quickly strummed my lyre and he was immediately soothed by the music. When we reached the lake, we almost failed even to get across. For the boat was already crowded and filled with groans, as all on board were wounded, some injured in the leg, others in the head or elsewhere, having come, I suppose, from some war.

However when Charon, bless him, saw the lionskin, he thought I was Heracles, admitted us aboard, gladly ferried us over and showed us the path when we had disembarked. [11] Since we were in the dark, Mithrobarzanes led the way and I followed behind clinging tight to him, till we reached a vast meadow overgrown with asphodel, and the shades of the dead flitted around us screeching. We progressed gradually till we arrived at Minos' courtroom; he was sitting on a high throne with Torments, Furies and Avengers standing on one side of him; on the other

μακρᾷ δεδεμένοι· ἐλέγοντο δὲ εἶναι τελῶναι καὶ μοιχοὶ καὶ πορνοβοσκοὶ καὶ κόλακες καὶ συκοφάνται καὶ τοιοῦτος ὅμιλος τῶν πάντα κυκώντων ἐν τῷ βίῳ. χωρὶς δὲ οἵ τε πλούσιοι καὶ τοκογλύφοι προσῇεσαν ὠχροὶ καὶ προγάστορες καὶ ποδαγροί, κλοιὸν ἕκαστος αὐτῶν καὶ κόρακα διτάλαντον ἐπικείμενος. ἐφεστῶτες οὖν ἡμεῖς ἑωρῶμέν τε τὰ γιγνόμενα καὶ ἠκούομεν τῶν ἀπολογουμένων· κατηγόρουν δὲ αὐτῶν καινοί τινες καὶ παράδοξοι ῥήτορες.

ΦΙΛΟΣ

Τίνες οὗτοι, πρὸς Διός; μὴ γὰρ ὀκνήσῃς καὶ τοῦτο εἰπεῖν.

ΜΕΝΙΠΠΟΣ

Οἶσθά που ταυτασὶ τὰς πρὸς τὸν ἥλιον ἀποτελουμένας σκιὰς ἀπὸ τῶν σωμάτων;

ΦΙΛΟΣ

Πάνυ μὲν οὖν.

ΜΕΝΙΠΠΟΣ

Αὗται τοίνυν, ἐπειδὰν ἀποθάνωμεν, κατηγοροῦσί τε καὶ καταμαρτυροῦσι καὶ διελέγχουσι τὰ πεπραγμένα ἡμῖν παρὰ τὸν βίον, καὶ σφόδρα τινὲς ἀξιόπιστοι δοκοῦσιν ἅτε ἀεὶ συνοῦσαι καὶ μηδέποτε ἀφιστάμεναι τῶν σωμάτων.

Ὁ δ' οὖν Μίνως ἐπιμελῶς ἐξετάζων ἀπέπεμπεν ἕκαστον εἰς τὸν 12
τῶν ἀσεβῶν χῶρον δίκην ὑφέξοντα κατ' ἀξίαν τῶν τετολμημένων, καὶ μάλιστα ἐκείνων ἥπτετο τῶν ἐπὶ πλούτοις τε καὶ ἀρχαῖς τετυφωμένων καὶ μονονουχὶ καὶ προσκυνεῖσθαι περιμενόντων, τήν τε ὀλιγοχρόνιον ἀλαζονείαν αὐτῶν καὶ τὴν ὑπεροψίαν μυσαττόμενος, καὶ ὅτι μὴ ἐμέμνηντο θνητοί τε ὄντες αὐτοὶ καὶ θνητῶν ἀγαθῶν τετυχηκότες. οἱ δὲ ἀποδυσάμενοι τὰ λαμπρὰ ἐκεῖνα πάντα, πλούτους λέγω καὶ γένη καὶ δυναστείας, γυμνοὶ κάτω νενευκότες παρειστήκεσαν ὥσπερ τινὰ ὄνειρον ἀναπεμπαζόμενοι τὴν παρ' ἡμῖν εὐδαιμονίαν· ὥστ' ἔγωγε ταῦτα ὁρῶν ὑπερέχαιρον καὶ εἴ τινα γνωρίσαιμι αὐτῶν, προσιὼν ἂν ἡσυχῇ πως ὑπεμίμνησκον οἷος ἦν παρὰ τὸν βίον καὶ ἡλίκον ἐφύσα τότε, ἡνίκα πολλοὶ μὲν ἕωθεν ἐπὶ τῶν πυλώνων παρεστήκεσαν τὴν πρόοδον αὐτοῦ περιμένοντες ὠθούμενοί τε καὶ ἀποκλειόμενοι πρὸς τῶν οἰκετῶν· ὁ δὲ μόλις ἄν ποτε ἀνατείλας αὐτοῖς πορφυροῦς τις ἢ περίχρυσος

side great numbers were being led up, one after the other, bound by a long chain; they were said to be tax-collectors, adulterers, pimps, toadies, informers and a vast throng of people like that who bring upheaval to every aspect of life. Approaching separately were the rich and usurers, pale, pot-bellied and gout-ridden, each of them wearing a neck-iron and a 'crow' weighing a hundredweight. So we stood watching the proceedings and listening to the defendants giving their explanations, but their accusers were quite unusual, unexpected speakers.

FRIEND

Good heavens, who were they? Don't be afraid to add that information.

MENIPPUS

Do you know the shadows made by our bodies in the sun?

FRIEND

Of course.

MENIPPUS

Well, when we're dead, they accuse us and inform against us, exposing everything done by us in our lives, and they are thought exceedingly reliable witnesses, since they always accompany us and never leave our bodies.

[12] To continue, Minos would carefully examine each individual and send him to the place for the impious, to be punished as he deserved for his misdeeds and he was particularly hard on those who prided themselves on their wealth and offices and who had expected men almost to fall down and worship them, for he was disgusted by their ephemeral effrontery and pride and the fact that they had forgotten that they were mortal themselves and the benefits they enjoyed were mortal too. They had stripped off all their former glories, I mean their wealth, ancestry and powerful positions, and were standing naked with their heads down, pondering over their prosperity in life, as though it were some dream. So I was very pleased when I saw this and if I recognised any of them, I'd go up to him and quietly remind him what he was like in life and how proud he had been then, with many men standing before his portals from dawn onwards waiting for him to emerge and being pushed about and kept out by his servants, and the man himself eventually condescending to shine forth upon them like the rising sun, clad in purple, or covered in

ἢ διαποίκιλος εὐδαίμονας ᾤετο καὶ μακαρίους ἀποφαίνειν τοὺς
προσειπόντας, ἢν τὸ στῆθος ἢ τὴν δεξιὰν προτείνων δοίη κατα-
φιλεῖν. ἐκεῖνοι μὲν οὖν ἠνιῶντο ἀκούοντες.

Τῷ δὲ Μίνῳ μία τις καὶ πρὸς χάριν ἐδικάσθη· τὸν γάρ τοι 13
Σικελιώτην Διονύσιον πολλά γε καὶ δεινὰ καὶ ἀνόσια ὑπό τε
Δίωνος κατηγορηθέντα καὶ ὑπὸ τῆς σκιᾶς καταμιτυρηθέντα
παρελθὼν Ἀρίστιππος ὁ Κυρηναῖος—ἄγουσι δ' αὐτὸν ἐν τιμῇ
καὶ δύναται μέγιστον ἐν τοῖς κάτω—μικροῦ δεῖν τῇ Χιμαίρᾳ
προσδεθέντα παρέλυσε τῆς καταδίκης λέγων πολλοῖς αὐτὸν τῶν
πεπαιδευμένων πρὸς ἀργύριον γενέσθαι δεξιόν.

Ἀποστάντες δὲ ὅμως τοῦ δικαστηρίου πρὸς τὸ κολαστήριον 14
ἀφικνούμεθα. ἔνθα δή, ὦ φιλότης, πολλὰ καὶ ἐλεεινὰ ἦν καὶ ἀκοῦσαι καὶ ἰδεῖν· μαστίγων τε γὰρ ὁμοῦ ψόφος ἠκούετο καὶ οἰμω-
γὴ τῶν ἐπὶ τοῦ πυρὸς ὀπτωμένων καὶ στρέβλαι καὶ κύφωνες καὶ
τροχοί, καὶ ἡ Χίμαιρα ἐσπάραττεν καὶ ὁ Κέρβερος ἐδάρδαπτεν.
ἐκολάζοντό τε ἅμα πάντες, βασιλεῖς, δοῦλοι, σατράπαι, πένητες,
πλούσιοι, πτωχοί, καὶ μετέμελε πᾶσι τῶν τετολμημένων. ἐνίους
δὲ αὐτῶν καὶ ἐγνωρίσαμέν γε ἰδόντες, ὁπόσοι ἦσαν τῶν ἔναγχος
τετελευτηκότων· οἱ δὲ ἐνεκαλύπτοντό τε καὶ ἀπεστρέφοντο, εἰ δὲ
καὶ προσβλέποιεν, μάλα δουλοπρεπές τι καὶ κολακευτικόν, καὶ
ταῦτα πῶς οἴει βαρεῖς ὄντες καὶ ὑπερόπται παρὰ τὸν βίον; τοῖς
μέντοι πένησιν ἡμιτέλεια τῶν κακῶν ἐδίδοτο, καὶ διαπαυόμε-
νοι πάλιν ἐκολάζοντο. καὶ μὴν κἀκεῖνα εἶδον τὰ μυθώδη, τὸν
Ἰξίονα καὶ τὸν Σίσυφον καὶ τὸν Φρύγα Τάνταλον, χαλεπῶς γε
ἔχοντα, καὶ τὸν γηγενῆ Τιτυόν, Ἡράκλεις ὅσος· ἔκειτο γοῦν
τόπον ἐπέχων ἀγροῦ.

Διελθόντες δὲ καὶ τούτους εἰς τὸ πεδίον εἰσβάλλομεν τὸ 15
Ἀχερούσιον, εὑρίσκομέν τε αὐτόθι τοὺς ἡμιθέους τε καὶ τὰς
ἡρωίνας καὶ τὸν ἄλλον ὅμιλον τῶν νεκρῶν κατὰ ἔθνη καὶ κατὰ
φῦλα διαιτωμένους, τοὺς μὲν παλαιούς τινας καὶ εὐρωτιῶντας
καὶ ὥς φησιν Ὅμηρος, ἀμενηνούς, τοὺς δ' ἔτι νεαλεῖς καὶ συν-
εστηκότας, καὶ μάλιστα τοὺς Αἰγυπτίους αὐτῶν διὰ τὸ πολυ-
αρκὲς τῆς ταριχείας. τὸ μέντοι διαγιγνώσκειν ἕκαστον οὐ πάνυ
τι ἦν ῥᾴδιον· ἅπαντες γὰρ ἀτεχνῶς ἀλλήλοις γίγνονται ὅμοιοι
τῶν ὀστέων γεγυμνωμένων. πλὴν ἀλλὰ μόλις γε διὰ πολλοῦ
ἀναθεωροῦντες αὐτοὺς ἐγιγνώσκομεν. ἔκειντο δ' ἐπάλληλοι
καὶ ἀμαυροὶ καὶ ἄσημοι καὶ οὐδὲν ἔτι τῶν παρ' ἡμῖν καλῶν

gold or resplendent in many colours and thinking he conferred happiness and bliss on those who had said 'Good morning' to him, if he offered them his breast or right hand to kiss. So it upset them to hear me.

[13] Minos showed favouritism in one of his decisions. For when Dionysius of Sicily had been accused of many terrible and impious deeds by Dio and his own shadow had testified against him, Aristippus of Cyrene stepped forward, Aristippus who is held in honour and has very great influence among those below, and when Dionysius was almost by now chained to the Chimaera, he saved him from condemnation by saying that many cultured men had found him helpful with money.

[14] However we left the court and arrived at the punishment area, where I assure you, my friend, many piteous things could be heard and seen. For at the same time could be heard the sound of lashes and the agonised cries of those roasting on the fire and there were racks and pillories and wheels, and the Chimaera was tearing her victims apart and Cerberus devouring them. All were being punished together, kings, slaves, satraps, poor men, rich men, beggars, and all were regretting their crimes. We actually recognised some of them when we saw them, all these being among the recently dead. But others covered their faces and turned away, or, if they did look at us, did so in servile and fawning fashion, although you can hardly imagine how overbearing and proud they had been in life. The poor, however, were only being given half as much pain to suffer and were being allowed a respite before their punishments restarted. I also saw the sights famed in stories, Ixion, Sisyphus, Phrygian Tantalus in sore distress, and the earth-born Tityus; by Heracles, how huge he was, lying there covering the area of a field!

[15] After making our way through them too, we entered the Acherusian Plain, and found there the demi-gods and heroines and the general crowd of the dead, arranged by tribes and nations, some of them old and mouldy and, to quote Homer, 'strengthless', others still fresh and firm, particularly the Egyptians amongst them, because of the durability of their embalmment. However distinguishing individuals was not at all easy, for quite simply they all become similar to each other, once their bones have been laid bare. However long examination enabled us with difficulty to recognise them; they were lying on top of each other, faint and indistinct and no longer keeping any of the attractive features they had

φυλάττοντες. ἀμέλει πολλῶν ἐν ταὐτῷ σκελετῶν κειμένων καὶ πάντων ὁμοίως φοβερόν τι καὶ διάκενον δεδορκότων καὶ γυμνοὺς τοὺς ὀδόντας προφαινόντων, ἠπόρουν πρὸς ἐμαυτὸν ᾧτινι διακρίναιμι τὸν Θερσίτην ἀπὸ τοῦ καλοῦ Νιρέως ἢ τὸν μεταίτην Ἶρον ἀπὸ τοῦ Φαιάκων βασιλέως ἢ Πυρρίαν τὸν μάγειρον ἀπὸ τοῦ Ἀγαμέμνονος. οὐδὲν γὰρ ἔτι τῶν παλαιῶν γνωρισμάτων αὐτοῖς παρέμενεν, ἀλλ᾽ ὅμοια τὰ ὀστᾶ ἦν, ἄδηλα καὶ ἀνεπίγραφα καὶ ὑπ᾽ οὐδενὸς ἔτι διακρίνεσθαι δυνάμενα.

Τοιγάρτοι ἐκεῖνα ὁρῶντί μοι ἐδόκει ὁ τῶν ἀνθρώπων βίος 16 πομπῇ τινι μακρᾷ προσεοικέναι, χορηγεῖν δὲ καὶ διατάττειν ἕκαστα ἡ Τύχη, διάφορα καὶ ποικίλα τοῖς πομπεύουσι τὰ σχήματα προσάπτουσα· τὸν μὲν γὰρ λαβοῦσα, εἰ τύχοι, βασιλικῶς διεσκεύασεν, τιάραν τε ἐπιθεῖσα καὶ δορυφόρους παραδοῦσα καὶ τὴν κεφαλὴν στέψασα τῷ διαδήματι, τῷ δὲ οἰκέτου σχῆμα περιέθηκεν· τὸν δέ τινα καλὸν εἶναι ἐκόσμησεν, τὸν δὲ ἄμορφον καὶ γελοῖον παρεσκεύασεν· παντοδαπὴν γάρ, οἶμαι, δεῖ γενέσθαι τὴν θέαν. πολλάκις δὲ καὶ διὰ μέσης τῆς πομπῆς μετέβαλε τὰ ἐνίων σχήματα οὐκ ἐῶσα εἰς τέλος διαπομπεῦσαι ὡς ἐτάχθησαν, ἀλλὰ μεταμφιέσασα τὸν μὲν Κροῖσον ἠνάγκασε τὴν τοῦ οἰκέτου καὶ αἰχμαλώτου σκευὴν ἀναλαβεῖν, τὸν δὲ Μαιάνδριον τέως ἐν τοῖς οἰκέταις πομπεύοντα τὴν τοῦ Πολυκράτους τυραννίδα μετενέδυσε. καὶ μέχρι μέν τινος εἴασε χρῆσθαι τῷ σχήματι· ἐπειδὰν δὲ ὁ τῆς πομπῆς καιρὸς παρέλθῃ, τηνικαῦτα ἕκαστος ἀποδοὺς τὴν σκευὴν καὶ ἀποδυσάμενος τὸ σχῆμα μετὰ τοῦ σώματος ἐγένετο οἷόσπερ ἦν πρὸ τοῦ γενέσθαι, μηδὲν τοῦ πλησίον διαφέρων. ἔνιοι δὲ ὑπ᾽ ἀγνωμοσύνης, ἐπειδὰν ἀπαιτῇ τὸν κόσμον ἐπιστᾶσα ἡ Τύχη, ἄχθονταί τε καὶ ἀγανακτοῦσιν ὥσπερ οἰκείων τινῶν στερισκόμενοι καὶ οὐχ ἃ πρὸς ὀλίγον ἐχρήσαντο ἀποδιδόντες.

Οἶμαι δὲ καὶ τῶν ἐπὶ τῆς σκηνῆς πολλάκις ἑωρακέναι σε τοὺς τραγικοὺς τούτους ὑποκριτὰς πρὸς τὰς χρείας τῶν δραμάτων ἄρτι μὲν Κρέοντας, ἐνίοτε δὲ Πριάμους γιγνομένους ἢ Ἀγαμέμνονας, καὶ ὁ αὐτός, εἰ τύχοι, μικρὸν ἔμπροσθεν μάλα σεμνῶς τὸ τοῦ Κέκροπος ἢ Ἐρεχθέως σχῆμα μιμησάμενος μετ᾽ ὀλίγον οἰκέτης προῆλθεν ὑπὸ τοῦ ποιητοῦ κεκελευσμένος. ἤδη δὲ πέρας ἔχοντος τοῦ δράματος ἀποδυσάμενος ἕκαστος αὐτῶν τὴν χρυσόπαστον ἐκείνην ἐσθῆτα καὶ τὸ προσωπεῖον ἀποθέμενος καὶ καταβὰς ἀπὸ τῶν ἐμβατῶν πένης καὶ ταπεινὸς περίεισιν, οὐκέτ᾽

in life. Indeed with many skeletons lying together and all presenting a similarly frightening, empty gaze and bare teeth, I puzzled with myself how I could distinguish Thersites from the handsome Nireus or the beggar Irus from the King of the Phaeacians or Pyrrhias the cook from Agamemnon. For none of their old distinguishing marks remained, but their bones were all alike, indistinct, unlabelled and no longer recognisable by anyone.

[16] Therefore when I saw this, it seemed to me that human life is like a long pageant, with everything provided and organised by Chance, as she fits the processors in varied, motley costumes. For she took one man and perhaps dressed him like a king, giving him a tiara to wear and bodyguards to escort him and crowning his head with the royal diadem, while another she graced with good looks, and another she made ridiculously ugly; for, I suppose, the spectacle must be full of variety. Often in the middle of the pageant she changed some people's costumes, not allowing them to retain the original allocations to the end, but assigned different costumes, forcing Croesus to take over the dress of the slave and captive, while she gave Maeandrius, who till now had been processing among the slaves, a new costume and the tyranny of Polycrates, and for a time allowed him to enjoy his costume. But when the time for the procession is over, then each man gives back his costume, strips off his apparel along with his body and becomes as he was before his birth, no different from his neighbour. But some, when Chance comes to them and asks for her trappings back, are annoyed and angry, as though being deprived of their own property, rather than returning what they'd borrowed for a short period.

I suppose you've often seen what happens with actors on the stage when those who play tragic roles serve the needs of the plays and become now a Creon, now a Priam or an Agamemnon and the same man, who perhaps shortly before had played the role of Cecrops or Erechtheus with great authority, after a little while comes on stage as a servant on the poet's orders. But when now the play is ended, each of them takes off that gold-spangled robe, discards his mask, steps down from those tragic boots and goes about as a poor, humble fellow, and is no longer called

Ἀγαμέμνων ὁ Ἀτρέως οὐδὲ Κρέων ὁ Μενοικέως, ἀλλὰ Πῶλος
Χαρικλέους Σουνιεὺς ὀνομαζόμενος ἢ Σάτυρος Θεογείτονος
Μαραθώνιος. τοιαῦτα καὶ τὰ τῶν ἀνθρώπων πράγματά ἐστιν,
ὡς τότε μοι ὁρῶντι ἔδοξεν.

ΦΙΛΟΣ

Εἰπὲ δέ μοι, ὦ Μένιππε, οἱ δὲ τοὺς πολυτελεῖς τούτους καὶ 17
ὑψηλοὺς τάφους ἔχοντες ὑπὲρ γῆς καὶ στήλας καὶ εἰκόνας καὶ
ἐπιγράμματα οὐδὲν τιμιώτεροι παρ' αὐτοῖς εἰσι τῶν ἰδιωτῶν
νεκρῶν;

ΜΕΝΙΠΠΟΣ

Ληρεῖς, ὦ οὗτος· εἰ γοῦν ἐθεάσω τὸν Μαύσωλον αὐτόν—
λέγω δὲ τὸν Κᾶρα, τὸν ἐκ τοῦ τάφου περιβόητον—εὖ οἶδα ὅτι
οὐκ ἂν ἐπαύσω γελῶν, οὕτω ταπεινὸς ἔρριπτο ἐν παραβύστῳ που
λανθάνων ἐν τῷ λοιπῷ δήμῳ τῶν νεκρῶν, ἐμοὶ δοκεῖν, τοσοῦτον ἀπολαύων τοῦ μνήματος, παρ' ὅσον ἐβαρύνετο τηλικοῦτον
ἄχθος ἐπικείμενος· ἐπειδὰν γάρ, ὦ ἑταῖρε, ὁ Αἰακὸς ἀπομετρήσῃ
ἑκάστῳ τὸν τόπον—δίδωσι δὲ τὸ μέγιστον οὐ πλέον ποδός—
ἀνάγκη ἀγαπῶντα κατακεῖσθαι πρὸς τὸ μέτρον συνεσταλμένον.
πολλῷ δ' ἂν οἶμαι μᾶλλον ἐγέλασας, εἰ ἐθεάσω τοὺς παρ' ἡμῖν
βασιλέας καὶ σατράπας πτωχεύοντας παρ' αὐτοῖς καὶ ἤτοι
ταριχοπωλοῦντας ὑπ' ἀπορίας ἢ τὰ πρῶτα διδάσκοντας γράμματα καὶ ὑπὸ τοῦ τυχόντος ὑβριζομένους καὶ κατὰ κόρρης παιο-
μένους ὥσπερ τῶν ἀνδραπόδων τὰ ἀτιμότατα. Φίλιππον γοῦν
τὸν Μακεδόνα ἐγὼ θεασάμενος οὐδὲ κρατεῖν ἐμαυτοῦ δυνατὸς ἦν·
ἐδείχθη δέ μοι ἐν γωνίᾳ τινὶ μισθοῦ ἀκούμενος τὰ σαθρὰ τῶν
ὑποδημάτων. πολλοὺς δὲ καὶ ἄλλους ἦν ἰδεῖν ἐν ταῖς τριόδοις
μεταιτοῦντας, Ξέρξας λέγω καὶ Δαρείους καὶ Πολυκράτας.

ΦΙΛΟΣ

Ἄτοπα διηγῇ τὰ περὶ τῶν βασιλέων καὶ μικροῦ δεῖν ἄπιστα. 18
τί δὲ ὁ Σωκράτης ἔπραττεν καὶ Διογένης καὶ εἴ τις ἄλλος τῶν
σοφῶν;

ΜΕΝΙΠΠΟΣ

Ὁ μὲν Σωκράτης κἀκεῖ περίεισιν διελέγχων πάντας· σύνεστι
δ' αὐτῷ Παλαμήδης καὶ Ὀδυσσεὺς καὶ Νέστωρ καὶ εἴ τις ἄλλος
λάλος νεκρός. ἔτι μέντοι ἐπεφύσητο αὐτῷ καὶ διῳδήκει ἐκ τῆς

Agamemnon, son of Atreus, or Creon, son of Menoeceus but Polus of
Sunium, son of Charicles, or Satyrus of Marathon, son of Theogiton.
That's what the affairs of mankind are like too, as I realised then as I
watched.

FRIEND

[17] But tell me, Menippus, are the men who have those expensive,
lofty tombs on the earth and those gravestones, statues and inscriptions
any more honoured down there than the ordinary dead?

MENIPPUS

Nonsense, man. If you'd seen Mausolus himself – the Carian, I
mean, him who was famous for his tomb – I know you'd never have
stopped laughing, such was his degradation as he lay where he had been
thrown in some corner, unnoticed among the other dead commoners; in
my opinion the only benefit he got from his monument was the weight he
had to bear with all that heavy burden on top of him! For, my friend,
when Aeacus measures out each men's place for him, giving at most no
more than a foot, he must be content to lie there, tucked up to the proper
dimensions; and I think you'd have laughed a great deal more, if you'd
seen those who had been kings and satraps among us reduced to beggary
amongst them and either selling fish out of poverty or teaching elementary
reading and being insulted by any Tom, Dick or Harry and having their
ears boxed like the meanest slave. At any rate when I saw Philip of
Macedon, I couldn't control myself; he was pointed out to me stitching
rotten sandals in a corner for payment. Many others also could be seen
begging at the street corners, I mean the likes of Xerxes, Darius and
Polycrates.

FRIEND

[18] What you recount about the kings is surprising and barely
credible. But how about Socrates, Diogenes and the other sages?

MENIPPUS

Socrates goes round grilling everyone with his questions there too, and
for company he has Palamedes, Odysseus, Nestor and all the other dead
chatterboxes, but his legs were still puffed and swollen from drinking the

φαρμακοποσίας τὰ σκέλη. ὁ δὲ βέλτιστος Διογένης παροικεῖ μὲν Σαρδαναπάλλῳ τῷ Ἀσσυρίῳ καὶ Μίδᾳ τῷ Φρυγὶ καὶ ἄλλοις τισὶ τῶν πολυτελῶν· ἀκούων δὲ οἰμωζόντων αὐτῶν καὶ τὴν παλαιὰν τύχην ἀναμετρουμένων γελᾷ τε καὶ τέρπεται, καὶ τὰ πολλὰ ὕπτιος κατακείμενος ᾄδει μάλα τραχείᾳ καὶ ἀπηνεῖ τῇ φωνῇ τὰς οἰμωγὰς αὐτῶν ἐπικαλύπτων, ὥστε ἀνιᾶσθαι τοὺς ἄνδρας καὶ διασκέπτεσθαι μετοικεῖν οὐ φέροντας τὸν Διογένη.

ΦΙΛΟΣ

Ταυτὶ μὲν ἱκανῶς· τί δὲ τὸ ψήφισμα ἦν, ὅπερ ἐν ἀρχῇ ἔλεγες 19 κεκυρῶσθαι κατὰ τῶν πλουσίων;

ΜΕΝΙΠΠΟΣ

Εὖ γε ὑπέμνησας· οὐ γὰρ οἶδ᾽ ὅπως περὶ τούτου λέγειν προθέμενος πάμπολυ ἀπεπλανήθην τοῦ λόγου.

Διατρίβοντος γάρ μου παρ᾽ αὐτοῖς προὔθεσαν οἱ πρυτάνεις ἐκκλησίαν περὶ τῶν κοινῇ συμφερόντων· ὁρῶν οὖν πολλοὺς συνθέοντας ἀναμίξας ἐμαυτὸν τοῖς νεκροῖς εὐθὺς εἷς καὶ αὐτὸς ἦν τῶν ἐκκλησιαστῶν. διῳκήθη μὲν οὖν καὶ ἄλλα, τελευταῖον δὲ τὸ περὶ τῶν πλουσίων· ἐπεὶ γὰρ αὐτῶν κατηγόρητο πολλὰ καὶ δεινά, βίαι καὶ ἀλαζονεῖαι καὶ ὑπεροψίαι καὶ ἀδικίαι, τέλος ἀναστάς τις τῶν δημαγωγῶν ἀνέγνω ψήφισμα τοιοῦτον.

ΨΗΦΙΣΜΑ

Ἐπειδὴ πολλὰ καὶ παράνομα οἱ πλούσιοι δρῶσι παρὰ τὸν 20 βίον ἁρπάζοντες καὶ βιαζόμενοι καὶ πάντα τρόπον τῶν πενήτων καταφρονοῦντες, δεδόχθαι τῇ βουλῇ καὶ τῷ δήμῳ, ἐπειδὰν ἀποθάνωσι, τὰ μὲν σώματα αὐτῶν κολάζεσθαι καθάπερ καὶ τὰ τῶν ἄλλων πονηρῶν, τὰς δὲ ψυχὰς ἀναπεμφθείσας ἄνω εἰς τὸν βίον καταδύεσθαι εἰς τοὺς ὄνους, ἄχρις ἂν ἐν τῷ τοιούτῳ διαγάγωσι μυριάδας ἐτῶν πέντε καὶ εἴκοσιν, ὄνοι ἐξ ὄνων γιγνόμενοι καὶ ἀχθοφοροῦντες καὶ ὑπὸ τῶν πενήτων ἐλαυνόμενοι, τοὐντεῦθεν δὲ λοιπὸν ἐξεῖναι αὐτοῖς ἀποθανεῖν.

Εἶπε τὴν γνώμην Κρανίων Σκελετίωνος Νεκυσιεὺς φυλῆς Ἀλιβαντίδος.

Τούτου ἀναγνωσθέντος τοῦ ψηφίσματος ἐπεψήφισαν μὲν αἱ

poison; but Diogenes, bless him, has taken up residence with Sardana-
pallus, the Assyrian, Midas of Phrygia and some other millionaires, and
when he hears them groaning and recalling the extent of their former
prosperity, he laughs with joy and spends most of his time lying on his
back, singing in a most rough and unpleasant voice loud enough to drown
their moans so that the fellows are annoyed and consider moving
elsewhere, because they can't put up with Diogenes.

FRIEND

[19] You've told me enough of that; but what was the decree which
you originally told me had been passed against the rich?

MENIPPUS

I'm glad you reminded me; for I'd intended to tell you about it, but
somehow wandered a long way off the subject.

During my time with them the presidents announced a meeting of the
assembly to deal with matters of common interest. So when I saw large
numbers all rushing along, I joined in with the dead and at once I too was
a member of the assembly. Well, the other business had been settled, but
the final issue concerned the rich. After they'd been accused of many
terrible crimes involving violence, imposture, pride and injustice, finally
one of the demagogues rose to his feet and read out the following
resolution:

RESOLUTION

[20] 'Whereas the rich during their lifetime perpetrate many unlawful
deeds of pillaging, violence and manifold abuse of the poor, be it hereby
resolved by the Council and the People that when they die, their bodies be
punished like those of other villains, but their souls be sent back to life
and demoted to enter donkeys, till in that state they pass 250,000 years,
being born as donkey after donkey, carrying heavy loads and driven by
the poor, and only then finally should they be allowed to die. Motion
proposed by Scullion, son of Skeleton, of the Morgueville Deme and the
Dedman Tribe.

After this motion had been read out, the magistrates put it to the vote,

ἀρχαί, ἐπεχειροτόνησε δὲ τὸ πλῆθος καὶ ἐβριμήσατο ἡ Βριμὼ καὶ ὑλάκτησεν ὁ Κέρβερος· οὕτω γὰρ ἐντελῆ γίγνεται καὶ κύρια τὰ ἐγνωσμένα.

Ταῦτα μὲν δή σοι τὰ ἐν τῇ ἐκκλησίᾳ. ἐγὼ δέ, οὗπερ ἀφίγμην 21 ἕνεκα, τῷ Τειρεσίᾳ προσελθὼν ἱκέτευον αὐτὸν τὰ πάντα διηγησάμενος εἰπεῖν πρός με ποῖόν τινα ἡγεῖται τὸν ἄριστον βίον. ὁ δὲ γελάσας—ἔστι δὲ τυφλόν τι γερόντιον καὶ ὠχρὸν καὶ λεπτόφωνον—Ὦ τέκνον, φησί, τὴν μὲν αἰτίαν οἶδά σοι τῆς ἀπορίας ὅτι παρὰ τῶν σοφῶν ἐγένετο οὐ ταὐτὰ γιγνωσκόντων ἑαυτοῖς· ἀτὰρ οὐ θέμις λέγειν πρὸς σέ· ἀπείρηται γὰρ ὑπὸ τοῦ Ῥαδαμάνθυος.

Μηδαμῶς, ἔφην, ὦ πατέριον, ἀλλ' εἰπὲ καὶ μὴ περιίδῃς με σοῦ τυφλότερον περιιόντα ἐν τῷ βίῳ.

Ὁ δὲ δή με ἀπαγαγὼν καὶ πολὺ τῶν ἄλλων ἀποσπάσας ἠρέμα προσκύψας πρὸς τὸ οὖς φησίν, Ὁ τῶν ἰδιωτῶν ἄριστος βίος καὶ σωφρονέστερος. παυσάμενος τοῦ μετεωρολογεῖν καὶ τέλη καὶ ἀρχὰς ἐπισκοπεῖν καὶ καταπτύσας τῶν σοφῶν τούτων συλλογισμῶν καὶ τὰ τοιαῦτα λῆρον ἡγησάμενος τοῦτο μόνον ἐξ ἅπαντος θηράσῃ, ὅπως τὸ παρὸν εὖ θέμενος παραδράμῃς γελῶν τὰ πολλὰ καὶ περὶ μηδὲν ἐσπουδακώς.

ὣς εἰπὼν πάλιν ὦρτο κατ' ἀσφοδελὸν λειμῶνα.

Ἐγὼ δέ—καὶ γὰρ ἤδη ὀψὲ ἦν—Ἄγε δή, ὦ Μιθροβαρζάνη, 22 φημί, τί διαμέλλομεν καὶ οὐκ ἄπιμεν αὖθις εἰς τὸν βίον;

Ὁ δὲ πρὸς ταῦτα, Θάρρει, φησίν, ὦ Μένιππε· ταχεῖαν γάρ σοι καὶ ἀπράγμονα ὑποδείξω ἀτραπόν.

Καὶ δὴ ἀγαγών με πρός τι χωρίον τοῦ ἄλλου ζοφερώτερον δείξας τῇ χειρὶ πόρρωθεν ἀμαυρὸν καὶ λεπτὸν ὥσπερ διὰ κλειθρίας φῶς εἰσρέον, Ἐκεῖνο, ἔφη, ἐστὶν τὸ ἱερὸν τὸ Τροφωνίου, κἀκεῖθεν κατίασιν οἱ ἀπὸ Βοιωτίας. ταύτην οὖν ἄνιθι καὶ εὐθὺς ἔσῃ ἐπὶ τῆς Ἑλλάδος.

Ἡσθεὶς δὴ τοῖς εἰρημένοις ἐγὼ καὶ τὸν μάγον ἀσπασάμενος χαλεπῶς μάλα διὰ τοῦ στομίου ἀνερπύσας οὐκ οἶδ' ὅπως ἐν Λεβαδείᾳ γίγνομαι.

the commoners voted their approval, Brimo roared and Cerberus barked; for that's how decisions are ratified and validated.

[21] Well, there you have the proceedings in the assembly, but I, in pursuit of my purpose in going, went up to Tiresias and begged him to explain everything and tell me which sort of life he thought the best. But he laughed – he's a blind old creature, pale and thin-voiced – and said 'My child, I know the reason for your bewilderment; it has arisen from the sages differing from one another in their beliefs. But I'm not permitted to answer your question, for it's forbidden by Rhadamanthys.' 'Oh no, dear father,' said I 'please tell me, and don't allow me to go around in life blinder than you are yourself.'

Then he led me off, taking me far away from the others, stooped slightly and whispered into my ear 'The life of the ordinary man is best and the wiser choice. So stop studying the heavens and investigating first beginnings and final ends, spit in the teeth of those learned syllogisms and, thinking all such matters rubbish, make it your one and only pursuit to arrange the present well and pass on laughing for the most part and taking nothing seriously.'

'Thus he spake and sped again o'er mead of asphodel.'

[22] But, it now being late, I said 'Come now, Mithrobarzanes, why do we delay? Why don't we depart again to life?' In answer to this he said 'Never fear, Menippus; I'll show you a quick, easy path.'

Lo and behold he led me to a spot darker than elsewhere and pointed to a feeble, slender light in the distance seeping in as through a keyhole and said 'That's the shrine of Trophonius, and it's from there that people from Boeotia come down. So go up by that route and you'll be in Greece immediately.'

I was delighted by his words and after saying goodbye to the Magus crept up through the tiny hole with great difficulty and somehow have found myself in Lebadeia.

ΠΕΡΙ ΤΗΣ ΠΕΡΕΓΡΙΝΟΥ ΤΕΛΕΥΤΗΣ

Λουκιανὸς Κρονίῳ εὖ πράττειν.

Ὁ κακοδαίμων Περεγρῖνος, ἢ ὡς αὐτὸς ἔχαιρεν ὀνομάζων **1**
ἑαυτόν, Πρωτεύς, αὐτὸ δὴ ἐκεῖνο τὸ τοῦ Ὁμηρικοῦ Πρωτέως
ἔπαθεν· ἅπαντα γὰρ δόξης ἕνεκα γενόμενος καὶ μυρίας τροπὰς
τραπόμενος, τὰ τελευταῖα ταῦτα καὶ πῦρ ἐγένετο· τοσούτῳ ἄρα
τῷ ἔρωτι τῆς δόξης εἴχετο. καὶ νῦν ἐκεῖνος ἀπηνθράκωταί σοι
ὁ βέλτιστος κατὰ τὸν Ἐμπεδοκλέα, παρ' ὅσον ὁ μὲν κἂν διαλα-
θεῖν ἐπειράθη ἐμβαλὼν ἑαυτὸν εἰς τοὺς κρατῆρας, ὁ δὲ γεννάδας
οὗτος, τὴν πολυανθρωποτάτην τῶν Ἑλληνικῶν πανηγύρεων τη-
ρήσας, πυρὰν ὅτι μεγίστην νήσας ἐνεπήδησεν ἐπὶ τοσούτων μαρτύ-
ρων, καὶ λόγους τινὰς ὑπὲρ τούτου εἰπὼν πρὸς τοὺς Ἕλληνας οὐ
πρὸ πολλῶν ἡμερῶν τοῦ τολμήματος.

Πολλὰ τοίνυν δοκῶ μοι ὁρᾶν σε γελῶντα ἐπὶ τῇ κορύζῃ τοῦ **2**
γέροντος, μᾶλλον δὲ καὶ ἀκούω βοῶντος οἷά σε εἰκὸς βοᾶν, Ὦ
τῆς ἀβελτερίας, ὦ τῆς δοξοκοπίας, ὦ τῶν ἄλλων ἃ λέγειν
εἰώθαμεν περὶ αὐτῶν. σὺ μὲν οὖν πόρρω ταῦτα καὶ μακρῷ
ἀσφαλέστερον, ἐγὼ δὲ παρὰ τὸ πῦρ αὐτὸ καὶ ἔτι πρότερον ἐν πολλῷ
πλήθει τῶν ἀκροατῶν εἶπον αὐτά, ἐνίων μὲν ἀχθομένων, ὅσοι
ἐθαύμαζον τὴν ἀπόνοιαν τοῦ γέροντος· ἦσαν δέ τινες οἳ καὶ
αὐτοὶ ἐγέλων ἐπ' αὐτῷ. ἀλλ' ὀλίγου δεῖν ὑπὸ τῶν Κυνικῶν ἐγώ σοι
διεσπάσθην ὥσπερ ὁ Ἀκταίων ὑπὸ τῶν κυνῶν ἢ ὁ ἀνεψιὸς
αὐτοῦ ὁ Πενθεὺς ὑπὸ τῶν Μαινάδων.

Ἡ δὲ πᾶσα τοῦ πράγματος διασκευὴ τοιάδε ἦν. τὸν μὲν ποιη- **3**
τὴν οἶσθα οἷός τε ἦν καὶ ἡλίκα ἐτραγῴδει παρ' ὅλον τὸν βίον, ὑπὲρ
τὸν Σοφοκλέα καὶ τὸν Αἰσχύλον. ἐγὼ δὲ ἐπεὶ τάχιστα εἰς τὴν
Ἦλιν ἀφικόμην, διὰ τοῦ γυμνασίου ἀλύων ἐπήκουον ἅμα Κυνι-
κοῦ τινος μεγάλῃ καὶ τραχείᾳ τῇ φωνῇ τὰ συνήθη ταῦτα καὶ ἐκ
τριόδου τὴν ἀρετὴν ἐπιβοωμένου καὶ ἅπασιν ἀπαξαπλῶς λοιδο-
ρουμένου. εἶτα κατέληξεν αὐτῷ ἡ βοὴ ἐς τὸν Πρωτέα, καὶ ὡς ἂν
οἷός τε ὦ πειράσομαί σοι αὐτὰ ἐκεῖνα ἀπομνημονεῦσαι ὡς ἐλέγετο. σὺ δὲ γνωριεῖς δηλαδή, πολλάκις αὐτοῖς παραστὰς βοῶσιν.

ON THE DEATH OF PEREGRINUS

Lucian sends his greetings to Cronius.

[1] The wretched Peregrinus, or Proteus as he liked to call himself, had the very same thing happen to him as Homer's Proteus. For after trying all manner of changes and countless transformations in search of fame, in the end he too turned into fire; such was the passion for fame gripping him. Now your excellent fellow has been burnt to cinders just like Empedocles, except that *he* tried to be unobserved when he hurled himself into the volcano, whereas this noble specimen waited for the most heavily attended of the Greek festivals, heaped up an enormous pyre and leapt on to it before all those witnesses, after having addressed some words on the subject to the Greeks a few days before the daring deed.

[2] So I imagine you're having a hearty laugh at the stupidity of the old fellow, or rather I can hear you shouting out the appropriate comments 'Oh what folly, oh what presumptuousness, oh ...' adding everything else that we usually say about such behaviour! *You* can talk like that at a distance and in far greater safety, but *I* did so at the actual conflagration and on an earlier occasion as well where vast numbers could hear me, annoying a number of them, who admired the old creature's madness, though there were some who laughed at him as I did. But I can tell you I was almost torn to pieces by the Cynics as Actaeon was by his dogs or his cousin Pentheus by the Maenads.

[3] The whole affair was stage-managed like this. Of course you know what the dramatist was like and how he played to the gallery all through his life, outdoing both Sophocles and Aeschylus. The first thing I did on reaching Elis was to stroll through the gymnasium, where I could hear a Cynic bawling out in a loud, raucous voice, making the usual vulgar appeals for virtue, and utterly abusing all and sundry. Then he concluded his harangue with the topic of Proteus and I shall try to recall the actual words for you, just as they were spoken. I'm sure they'll be familiar to you, as you've often stood near while they've been yelling.

Πρωτέα γάρ τις, ἔφη, κενόδοξον τολμᾷ λέγειν, ὦ γῆ καὶ **4**
ἥλιε καὶ ποταμοὶ καὶ θάλαττα καὶ πατρῷε Ἡράκλεις, Πρωτέα
τὸν ἐν Συρίᾳ δεθέντα, τὸν τῇ πατρίδι ἀνέντα πεντακισχίλια τάλαντα, τὸν ἀπὸ τῆς Ῥωμαίων πόλεως ἐκβληθέντα, τὸν τοῦ Ἡλίου
ἐπισημότερον, τὸν αὐτῷ ἀνταγωνίσασθαι τῷ Ὀλυμπίῳ δυνάμενον;
ἀλλ' ὅτι διὰ πυρὸς ἐξάγειν τοῦ βίου διέγνωκεν ἑαυτόν, εἰς κενο-
δοξίαν τινὲς τοῦτο ἀναφέρουσιν; οὐ γὰρ Ἡρακλῆς οὕτως; οὐ
γὰρ Ἀσκληπιὸς καὶ Διόνυσος κεραυνῷ; οὐ γὰρ τὰ τελευταῖα
Ἐμπεδοκλῆς εἰς τοὺς κρατῆρας;

Ὡς δὲ ταῦτα εἶπεν ὁ Θεαγένης — τοῦτο γὰρ ὁ κεκραγὼς **5**
ἐκεῖνος ἐκαλεῖτο — ἠρόμην τινὰ τῶν παρεστώτων, Τί βούλεται
τὸ περὶ τοῦ πυρός, ἢ τί Ἡρακλῆς καὶ Ἐμπεδοκλῆς πρὸς τὸν
Πρωτέα;

Ὁ δέ, Οὐκ εἰς μακράν, ἔφη, καύσει ἑαυτὸν ὁ Πρωτεὺς
Ὀλυμπίασιν.

Πῶς, ἔφην, ἢ τίνος ἕνεκα;

Εἶτα ὁ μὲν ἐπειρᾶτο λέγειν, ἐβόα δὲ ὁ Κυνικός, ὥστε ἀμήχανον ἦν ἄλλου ἀκούειν. ἐπήκουον οὖν τὰ λοιπὰ ἐπαντλοῦντος
αὐτοῦ καὶ θαυμαστάς τινας ὑπερβολὰς διεξιόντος κατὰ τοῦ Πρω-
τέως· τὸν μὲν γὰρ Σινωπέα ἢ τὸν διδάσκαλον αὐτοῦ Ἀντισθένη
οὐδὲ παραβάλλειν ἠξίου αὐτῷ, ἀλλ' οὐδὲ τὸν Σωκράτη αὐτόν,
ἐκάλει δὲ τὸν Δία ἐπὶ τὴν ἅμιλλαν. εἶτα μέντοι ἔδοξεν αὐτῷ ἴσους
πως φυλάξαι αὐτούς, καὶ οὕτω κατέπαυε τὸν λόγον· Δύο γὰρ **6**
ταῦτα, ἔφη, ὁ βίος ἄριστα δημιουργήματα ἐθεάσατο, τὸν Δία
τὸν Ὀλύμπιον καὶ Πρωτέα· πλάσται δὲ καὶ τεχνῖται, τοῦ μὲν
Φειδίας, τοῦ δὲ ἡ φύσις. ἀλλὰ νῦν ἐξ ἀνθρώπων εἰς θεοὺς τὸ
ἄγαλμα τοῦτο οἰχήσεται, ὀχούμενον ἐπὶ τοῦ πυρός, ὀρφανοὺς
ἡμᾶς καταλιπόν.

Ταῦτα ξὺν πολλῷ ἱδρῶτι διεξελθὼν ἐδάκρυε μάλα γελοίως
καὶ τὰς τρίχας ἐτίλλετο, ὑποφειδόμενος μὴ πάνυ ἕλκειν· καὶ τέλος
ἀπῆγον αὐτὸν λύζοντα μεταξὺ τῶν Κυνικῶν τινες παραμυθούμενοι.

Μετὰ δὲ τοῦτον ἄλλος εὐθὺς ἀναβαίνει, οὐ περιμείνας διαλυ- **7**
θῆναι τὸ πλῆθος ἀλλὰ ἐπ' αἰθομένοις τοῖς προτέροις ἱερείοις
ἐπέχει τῶν σπονδῶν. καὶ τὸ μὲν πρῶτον ἐπὶ πολὺ ἐγέλα καὶ δῆλος

[4] 'Does anyone dare 'he said' to call Proteus conceited, I ask in the name of the Earth, the Sun, the Rivers, the Sea and Heracles, god of our fathers, Proteus who was imprisoned in Syria, who renounced five thousand talents in favour of his native city, Proteus who was expelled from the city of Rome, who is more resplendent than the Sun, and can rival Olympian Zeus himself? Do some people attribute his decision to remove himself from life via fire to empty conceit? Didn't Heracles do the same? Weren't Asclepius and Dionysus sent on their way by the lightning? And finally didn't Empedocles jump into the volcano?'

[5] After this speech by Theagenes, for that was the name of the loud-mouthed one, I asked one of the bystanders 'What's the meaning of all this about fire and what have Heracles and Empedocles got to do with Proteus?'

'Very soon' he said 'Proteus will cremate himself at Olympia.' 'How and why?' said I. Then he tried to tell me, but the Cynic started shouting so loud that it was impossible to hear anyone else. So I listened to him pouring out the rest of his stuff and indulging in amazing exaggerations about Proteus, saying he couldn't even compare the man of Sinope or his teacher Antisthenes with him, or even Socrates himself, and calling on Zeus to challenge him. But then he decided to keep them more or less equal, and went on to finish his discourse like this: [6] 'These are the two finest masterpieces life has seen, I mean the Olympian Zeus and Proteus. The one piece of skilful sculpture we owe to Pheidias, the other to Nature. But now this glorious image will disappear from men and join the gods, wafted on fire, leaving us forlorn.'

After completing this discourse and sweating profusely in the process, he started to weep in utterly ridiculous fashion and to tear at his hair, though he took care not to tear too hard! Finally he was led off sobbing by some of the Cynics who tried to console him.

[7] Another man followed him immediately on to the rostrum, without waiting for the crowd to disperse and poured a libation on the previous sacrificial offering 'while 'twas yet a-burning'. At first he laughed loud and long, obviously doing so from the 'bottom o' his heart', and then

ἦν νειόθεν αὐτὸ δρῶν· εἶτα ἤρξατο ὧδέ πως· Ἐπεὶ ὁ κατάρατος
Θεαγένης τέλος τῶν μιαρωτάτων αὐτοῦ* λόγων τὰ Ἡρακλείτου
δάκρυα ἐποιήσατο, ἐγὼ κατὰ τὸ ἐναντίον ἀπὸ τοῦ Δημοκρίτου
γέλωτος ἄρξομαι.

Καὶ αὖθις ἐγέλα ἐπὶ πολύ, ὥστε καὶ ἡμῶν τοὺς πολλοὺς ἐπὶ
τὸ ὅμοιον ἐπεσπάσατο.

Εἶτα ἐπιστρέψας ἑαυτόν, Ἢ τί γὰρ ἄλλο, ἔφη, ὦ ἄνδρες, **8**
χρὴ ποιεῖν ἀκούοντας μὲν οὕτω γελοίων ῥήσεων, ὁρῶντας δὲ
ἄνδρας γέροντας δοξαρίου καταπτύστου ἕνεκα μονονουχὶ κυβι-
στῶντας ἐν τῷ μέσῳ; ὡς δὲ εἰδείητε οἷόν τι τὸ ἄγαλμά ἐστι τὸ
καυθησόμενον, ἀκούσατέ μου ἐξ ἀρχῆς παραφυλάξαντος τὴν γνώμην αὐτοῦ καὶ τὸν βίον ἐπιτηρήσαντος· ἔνια δὲ παρὰ τῶν πολιτῶν
αὐτοῦ ἐπυνθανόμην καὶ οἷς ἀνάγκη ἦν ἀκριβῶς εἰδέναι αὐτόν.

Τὸ γὰρ τῆς φύσεως τοῦτο πλάσμα καὶ δημιούργημα, ὁ τοῦ   **9**
Πολυκλείτου κανών, [ἔπειτα] ἐπεὶ εἰς ἄνδρας τελεῖν ἤρξατο, ἐν
Ἀρμενίᾳ μοιχεύων ἁλοὺς μάλα πολλὰς πληγὰς ἔλαβεν καὶ τέλος
κατὰ τοῦ τέγους ἁλόμενος διέφυγεν, ῥαφανῖδι τὴν πυγὴν
βεβυσμένος. εἶτα μειράκιόν τι ὡραῖον διαφθείρας τρισχιλίων
ἐξωνήσατο παρὰ τῶν γονέων τοῦ παιδός, πενήτων ὄντων, μὴ
ἐπὶ τὸν ἁρμοστὴν ἀπαχθῆναι τῆς Ἀσίας.

Ταῦτα καὶ τὰ τοιαῦτα ἐάσειν μοι δοκῶ· πηλὸς γὰρ ἔτι ἄπλα- **10**
στος ἦν καὶ οὐδέπω ἐντελὲς ἄγαλμα ἡμῖν δεδημιούργητο. ἃ δὲ
τὸν πατέρα ἔδρασεν καὶ πάνυ ἀκοῦσαι ἄξιον· καίτοι πάντες ἴστε,
καὶ ἀκηκόατε ὡς ἀπέπνιξε τὸν γέροντα, οὐκ ἀνασχόμενος αὐτὸν
ὑπὲρ ἑξήκοντα ἔτη ἤδη γηρῶντα. εἶτα ἐπειδὴ τὸ πρᾶγμα διεβε-
βόητο, φυγὴν ἑαυτοῦ καταδικάσας ἐπλανᾶτο ἄλλοτε ἄλλην ἀμείβων.

Ὅτεπερ καὶ τὴν θαυμαστὴν σοφίαν τῶν Χριστιανῶν ἐξέμαθεν, **11**
περὶ τὴν Παλαιστίνην τοῖς ἱερεῦσιν καὶ γραμματεῦσιν αὐτῶν ξυγ-
γενόμενος. καὶ τί γάρ; ἐν βραχεῖ παῖδας αὐτοὺς ἀπέφηνε, προφή-
της καὶ θιασάρχης καὶ ξυναγωγεὺς καὶ πάντα μόνος αὐτὸς ὤν,
καὶ τῶν βίβλων τὰς μὲν ἐξηγεῖτο καὶ διεσάφει, πολλὰς δὲ αὐτὸς
καὶ συνέγραφεν, καὶ ὡς θεὸν αὐτῶν ἐκεῖνοι ᾐδοῦντο καὶ νομοθέτῃ
ἐχρῶντο καὶ προστάτην ἐπεγράφοντο, μετὰ γοῦν ἐκεῖνον <ὃν>
ἔτι σέβουσι, τὸν ἄνθρωπον τὸν ἐν τῇ Παλαιστίνῃ ἀνασκολοπισθέν-
τα, ὅτι καινὴν ταύτην τελετὴν εἰσῆγεν ἐπὶ τὸν βίον.

began like this: 'Since the accursed Theagenes has ended his villainous speech with the tears of Heraclitus, I'll do the opposite and start with the laughter of Democritus.'

He then started to laugh once more so heartily that he made most of us do the same.

[8] Then, changing his mood, he said 'Well, gentlemen, what else should we do when we hear such ridiculous speeches and see old men practically performing acrobatics all for some cheap notoriety? So that you can know what this veritable idol about to burn is like, you should listen to me, for from the very start I've studied his thoughts and observed his career, and I've also been told a thing or two by his fellow citizens and people who couldn't help knowing him well.

[9] 'For this masterpiece sculpted by Nature, this embodiment of Polyclitan perfection, on reaching manhood's estate, was caught committing adultery in Armenia and given a good thrashing, but in the end escaped by jumping off the roof with a radish stuffed up his behind. Then he seduced a beautiful boy but paid his impoverished parents three thousand drachmas to avoid being brought up for trial before the governor of Asia.

[10] 'These and similar matters I think I shall pass over. For the clay was still unmoulded and our idol had not yet been sculpted to perfection. But what he did to his father is well worth hearing, though you all know and have heard how he strangled the old man, unable to tolerate his being over sixty. Then when the matter had become notorious, he condemned himself to exile and wandered from land to land.

[11] 'At that time he gained a full knowledge of the amazing doctrines of the Christians after studying under their priests and scribes in Palestine. And what happened next? Before long he had made them all look like children; he had become prophet, cult-leader, convener of meetings and everything else single-handed; he interpreted and explained some of their books, writing many himself as well. They revered him as a god of theirs, regarded him as a lawgiver and nominated him as their patron and second only to him whom they still revere, the human fellow who was crucified in Palestine for introducing this novel cult to the world.

Τότε δὴ καὶ συλληφθεὶς ἐπὶ τούτῳ ὁ Πρωτεὺς ἐνέπεσεν εἰς τὸ 12
δεσμωτήριον, ὅπερ καὶ αὐτὸ οὐ μικρὸν αὐτῷ ἀξίωμα περιεποίη-
σεν πρὸς τὸν ἑξῆς βίον καὶ τὴν τερατείαν καὶ δοξοκοπίαν ὧν ἐρῶν
ἐτύγχανεν. ἐπεὶ δ' οὖν ἐδέδετο, οἱ Χριστιανοὶ συμφορὰν ποιούμενοι
τὸ πρᾶγμα πάντα ἐκίνουν ἐξαρπάσαι πειρώμενοι αὐτόν. εἶτ', ἐπεὶ
τοῦτο ἦν ἀδύνατον, ἥ γε ἄλλη θεραπεία πᾶσα οὐ παρέργως ἀλλὰ
ξὺν σπουδῇ ἐγίγνετο· καὶ ἕωθεν μὲν εὐθὺς ἦν ὁρᾶν παρὰ τῷ δεσμωτηρίῳ περιμένοντα γραΐδια χήρας τινὰς καὶ παιδία ὀρφανά, οἱ
δὲ ἐν τέλει αὐτῶν καὶ συνεκάθευδον ἔνδον μετ' αὐτοῦ διαφθεί-
ραντες τοὺς δεσμοφύλακας. εἶτα δεῖπνα ποικίλα εἰσεκομίζετο
καὶ λόγοι ἱεροὶ αὐτῶν ἐλέγοντο, καὶ ὁ βέλτιστος Περεγρῖνος —
ἔτι γὰρ τοῦτο ἐκαλεῖτο — καινὸς Σωκράτης ὑπ' αὐτῶν ὠνομά-
ζετο.

Καὶ μὴν κἀκ τῶν ἐν Ἀσίᾳ πόλεων ἔστιν ὧν ἧκόν τινες, τῶν 13
Χριστιανῶν στελλόντων ἀπὸ τοῦ κοινοῦ, βοηθήσοντες καὶ συνα-
γορεύσοντες καὶ παραμυθησόμενοι τὸν ἄνδρα. ἀμήχανον δέ τι
τὸ τάχος ἐπιδείκνυνται, ἐπειδάν τι τοιοῦτον γένηται δημόσιον·
ἐν βραχεῖ γὰρ ἀφειδοῦσι πάντων. καὶ δὴ καὶ τῷ Περεγρίνῳ
πολλὰ τότε ἧκεν χρήματα παρ' αὐτῶν ἐπὶ προφάσει τῶν δεσμῶν,
καὶ πρόσοδον οὐ μικρὰν ταύτην ἐποιήσατο. πεπείκασι γὰρ αὐτοὺς
οἱ κακοδαίμονες τὸ μὲν ὅλον ἀθάνατοι ἔσεσθαι καὶ βιώσεσθαι τὸν
ἀεὶ χρόνον, παρ' ὃ καὶ καταφρονοῦσιν τοῦ θανάτου καὶ ἑκόντες
αὐτοὺς ἐπιδιδόασιν οἱ πολλοί. ἔπειτα δὲ ὁ νομοθέτης ὁ πρῶτος
ἔπεισεν αὐτοὺς ὡς ἀδελφοὶ πάντες εἶεν ἀλλήλων, ἐπειδὰν ἅπαξ
παραβάντες θεοὺς μὲν τοὺς Ἑλληνικοὺς ἀπαρνήσωνται, τὸν δὲ
ἀνεσκολοπισμένον ἐκεῖνον σοφιστὴν αὐτὸν προσκυνῶσιν καὶ κατὰ
τοὺς ἐκείνου νόμους βιῶσιν. καταφρονοῦσιν οὖν ἁπάντων ἐξ ἴσης
καὶ κοινὰ ἡγοῦνται, ἄνευ τινὸς ἀκριβοῦς πίστεως τὰ τοιαῦτα
παραδεξάμενοι. ἢν τοίνυν παρέλθῃ τις εἰς αὐτοὺς γόης καὶ
τεχνίτης ἄνθρωπος καὶ πράγμασι χρῆσθαι δυνάμενος, αὐτίκα
μάλα πλούσιος ἐν βραχεῖ ἐγένετο ἰδιώταις ἀνθρώποις
ἐγχανών.

Πλὴν ἀλλ' ὁ Περεγρῖνος ἀφείθη ὑπὸ τοῦ τότε τῆς Συρίας 14

[12] 'Eventually Proteus was arrested for all this and thrown into prison, something which gained him a great reputation beneficial to his subsequent career with all its miracle-mongering and craving for notoriety. Well, after he was put into prison, the Christians treated it as a disaster and went to all lengths in their efforts to get him out. But when this proved impossible, every other attention was paid him and in no uncertain manner; from dawn onwards one could see poor old widows and orphaned children waiting near the prison, while their officials actually slept inside with him, after bribing the jailors. Then elaborate dinners were brought in and their sacred scriptures recited, and the excellent Peregrinus, for that was still his name, was called 'the New Socrates' by them.

[13] 'Some people also came from the cities in Asia, sent by the Christians from their collective funds, to help the man, plead his cause and comfort him. They show incredible speed whenever any communal action is undertaken. For they promptly lavish their all. So too Pereginus found much money coming to him from them 'because he was in prison' and he gained a considerable income thereby. For the poor creatures have convinced themselves that they will be completely immortal and have eternal life and so they despise death and most of them gladly give themselves up. Moreover their first lawgiver persuaded them that they are all brothers one of another, once they have stepped out of line by denying the Greek gods, worshipping that crucified sophist himself and living by *his* laws. So they despise all material things alike and regard them as common property, accepting such beliefs without any certain proof. So if anyone comes amongst them who is an impostor and a clever twister able to make the most of situations, he can smirk at the simple creatures and enrich himself in no time at all.

[14] 'Peregrinus, however, was released by the governor of Syria, a

ἄρχοντος, ἀνδρὸς φιλοσοφίᾳ χαίροντος, ὃς συνεὶς τὴν ἀπόνοιαν
αὐτοῦ καὶ ὅτι δέξαιτ' ἂν ἀποθανεῖν ὡς δόξαν ἐπὶ τούτῳ ἀπολίποι,
ἀφῆκεν αὐτὸν οὐδὲ τῆς κολάσεως ὑπολαβὼν ἄξιον. ὁ δὲ εἰς τὴν
οἰκείαν ἐπανελθὼν καταλαμβάνει τὸ περὶ τοῦ πατρῴου φόνου
ἔτι φλεγμαῖνον καὶ πολλοὺς τοὺς ἐπανατεινομένους τὴν κατηγορίαν. διήρπαστο δὲ τὰ πλεῖστα τῶν κτημάτων παρὰ τὴν ἀποδη-
μίαν αὐτοῦ καὶ μόνοι ὑπελείποντο οἱ ἀγροὶ ὅσον εἰς πεντεκαίδεκα
τάλαντα. ἦν γὰρ ἡ πᾶσα οὐσία τριάκοντά που ταλάντων ἀξία ἣν
ὁ γέρων κατέλιπεν, οὐχ ὥσπερ ὁ παγγέλοιος Θεαγένης ἔλεγεν
πεντακισχιλίων· τοσούτου γὰρ οὐδὲ ἡ πᾶσα τῶν Παριανῶν πόλις
πέντε σὺν αὐτῇ τὰς γειτνιώσας παραλαβοῦσα πραθείη ἂν αὐτοῖς
ἀνθρώποις καὶ βοσκήμασιν καὶ τῇ λοιπῇ παρασκευῇ.

'Αλλ' ἔτι γε ἡ κατηγορία καὶ τὸ ἔγκλημα θερμὸν ἦν, καὶ ἐῴ- 15
κει οὐκ εἰς μακρὰν ἐπαναστήσεσθαί τις αὐτῷ, καὶ μάλιστα ὁ δῆμος αὐτὸς ἠγανάκτει, χρηστόν, ὡς ἔφασαν οἱ ἰδόντες, γέροντα
πενθοῦντες οὕτως ἀσεβῶς ἀπολωλότα. ὁ δὲ σοφὸς οὗτος Πρωτεὺς
πρὸς ἅπαντα ταῦτα σκέψασθε οἷόν τι ἐξεῦρεν καὶ ὅπως τὸν κίν-
δυνον διέφυγεν. παρελθὼν γὰρ εἰς τὴν ἐκκλησίαν τῶν Παριανῶν
— ἐκόμα δὲ ἤδη καὶ τρίβωνα πιναρὸν ἠμπείχετο καὶ πήραν παρήρ-
τητο καὶ τὸ ξύλον ἐν τῇ χειρὶ ἦν, καὶ ὅλως μάλα τραγικῶς ἐσκεύ-
αστο — τοιοῦτος οὖν ἐπιφανεὶς αὐτοῖς ἀφεῖναι ἔφη τὴν οὐσίαν ἣν
ὁ μακαρίτης πατὴρ αὐτῷ κατέλιπεν δημοσίαν εἶναι πᾶσαν. τοῦτο
ὡς ἤκουσεν ὁ δῆμος, πένητες ἄνθρωποι καὶ πρὸς διανομὰς κεχηνότες, ἀνέκραγον εὐθὺς ἕνα φιλόσοφον, ἕνα φιλόπατριν, ἕνα Διο-
γένους καὶ Κράτητος ζηλωτήν. οἱ δὲ ἐχθροὶ ἐπεφίμωντο, κἂν
εἴ τις ἐπιχειρήσειεν μεμνῆσθαι τοῦ φόνου, λίθοις εὐθὺς ἐβάλλετο.

'Εξήει οὖν τὸ δεύτερον πλανησόμενος, ἱκανὰ ἐφόδια τοὺς Χρι- 16
στιανοὺς ἔχων, ὑφ' ὧν δορυφορούμενος ἐν ἅπασιν ἀφθόνοις ἦν.
καὶ χρόνον μέν τινα οὕτως ἐβόσκετο· εἶτα παρανομήσας τι καὶ
ἐς ἐκείνους — ὤφθη γάρ τι, ὡς οἶμαι, ἐσθίων τῶν ἀπορρήτων
αὐτοῖς — οὐκέτι προσιεμένων αὐτὸν ἀπορούμενος ἐκ παλινῳδίας
ἀπαιτεῖν ᾤετο δεῖν παρὰ τῆς πόλεως τὰ κτήματα, καὶ γραμματεῖ-
ον ἐπιδοὺς ἠξίου ταῦτα κομίσασθαι κελεύσαντος βασιλέως. εἶτα
τῆς πόλεως ἀντιπρεσβευσαμένης οὐδὲν ἐπράχθη, ἀλλ' ἐμμένειν
ἐκελεύσθη οἷς ἅπαξ διέγνω μηδενὸς καταναγκάσαντος.

man fond of philosophy, who realised he was mad and would accept death for the sake of the resultant glory and so released him, not even thinking him worth punishing. He returned to his home country to find things still in a ferment over his father's murder and many threatening to accuse him. Most of his possessions had been looted during his absence and all that remained was farmland worth about fifteen talents, for the property left by his aged father had in all been worth perhaps thirty talents, and not five thousand as that utterly ridiculous Theagenes kept saying. For that amount wouldn't be fetched by the entire city of Parium and its five neighbouring cities with it, though sold along with all its inhabitants, livestock, goods and chattels.'

[15] 'But accusations and complaints against him were still flying fast and it seemed likely someone would press charges against him before long. The whole populace was absolutely incensed against him, as they mourned a fine old gentleman (for so he was described by those who knew him by sight) who had been so impiously killed. But just consider what an ingenious plan our clever Proteus devised to counter all this and how he escaped from danger! He attended the assembly of the people of Parium, now with hair grown long, wearing a filthy, tattered cloak, with a pouch hanging by his side and the staff in his hand, in short got up just like a figure out of a tragedy. Well, that was what he looked like when he manifested himself and told them he renounced in their favour the entire estate bequeathed to him by his dear departed father, and that it now belonged to the people. When the people heard this, as they were impoverished fellows and open-mouthed in their hopes of largesse, they immediately acclaimed him as the one true philosopher, the one true patriot, the one true disciple of Diogenes and Crates, whereas his enemies were gagged and anyone who tried to mention the murder was immediately stoned.

[16] 'So he left on his wanderings for the second time, adequately financed for his journeying by the Christians, through whose support he was absolutely in clover. He battened on them for some time, but then he committed some offence against them too, being seen, I imagine, eating something forbidden to them, and being in trouble when they no longer welcomed him, he thought he should recant and ask his property back from the city and so filed a petition claiming the restitution of the property by the emperor's command. But the city sent a delegation to oppose him and he lost his plea and was ordered to abide by the decision he had originally made under no compulsion.

Τρίτη ἐπὶ τούτοις ἀποδημία εἰς Αἴγυπτον παρὰ τὸν Ἀγαθό- 17
βουλον, ἵναπερ τὴν θαυμαστὴν ἄσκησιν διηικεῖτο, ξυρόμενος μὲν
τῆς κεφαλῆς τὸ ἥμισυ, χριόμενος δὲ πηλῷ τὸ πρόσωπον, ἐν πολλῷ
δὲ τῶν περιεστώτων δήμῳ ἀναφλῶν τὸ αἰδοῖον καὶ τὸ ἀδιάφορον
δὴ τοῦτο* καλούμενον ἐπιδεικνύμενος, εἶτα παίων καὶ παιόμενος
νάρθηκι εἰς τὰς πυγὰς καὶ ἄλλα πολλὰ νεανικώτερα θαυματοποιῶν.

Ἐκεῖθεν δὲ οὕτω παρεσκευασμένος ἐπὶ Ἰταλίας ἔπλευσεν καὶ 18
ἀποβὰς τῆς νεὼς εὐθὺς ἐλοιδορεῖτο πᾶσι, καὶ μάλιστα τῷ βασιλεῖ,
πραότατον αὐτὸν καὶ ἡμερώτατον εἰδώς, ὥστε ἀσφαλῶς ἐτόλμα·
ἐκείνῳ γάρ, ὡς εἰκός, ὀλίγον ἔμελεν τῶν βλασφημιῶν καὶ οὐκ
ἠξίου τὸν φιλοσοφίαν ὑποδυόμενόν τινα κολάζειν ἐπὶ ῥήμασι
καὶ μάλιστα τέχνην τινὰ τὸ λοιδορεῖσθαι πεποιημένον. τούτῳ
δὲ καὶ ἀπὸ τούτων τὰ τῆς δόξης ηὐξάνετο, παρὰ γοῦν τοῖς ἰδιώταις, καὶ περίβλεπτος ἦν ἐπὶ τῇ ἀπονοίᾳ, μέχρι δὴ ὁ τὴν πόλιν
ἐπιτετραμμένος ἀνὴρ σοφὸς ἀπέπεμψεν αὐτὸν ἀμέτρως ἐντρυφῶν-
τα τῷ πράγματι, εἰπὼν μὴ δεῖσθαι τὴν πόλιν τοιούτου φιλοσόφου.
πλὴν ἀλλὰ καὶ τοῦτο κλεινὸν αὐτοῦ καὶ διὰ στόματος ἦν ἅπασιν,
ὁ φιλόσοφος διὰ τὴν παρρησίαν καὶ τὴν ἄγαν ἐλευθερίαν ἐξελα-
σθείς, καὶ προσήλαυνε κατὰ τοῦτο τῷ Μουσωνίῳ καὶ Δίωνι καὶ
Ἐπικτήτῳ καὶ εἴ τις ἄλλος ἐν περιστάσει τοιαύτῃ ἐγένετο.

Οὕτω δὴ ἐπὶ τὴν Ἑλλάδα ἐλθὼν ἄρτι μὲν Ἠλείοις ἐλοιδορεῖ- 19
το, ἄρτι δὲ τοὺς Ἕλληνας ἔπειθεν ἀντάρασθαι ὅπλα Ῥωμαίοις,
ἄρτι δὲ ἄνδρα παιδείᾳ καὶ ἀξιώματι προὔχοντα, διότι καὶ ἐν τοῖς
ἄλλοις εὖ ἐποίησεν τὴν Ἑλλάδα καὶ ὕδωρ ἐπήγαγεν τῇ Ὀλυμπίᾳ
καὶ ἔπαυσε δίψει ἀπολλυμένους τοὺς πανηγυριστάς, κακῶς
ἠγόρευεν ὡς καταθηλύναντα τοὺς Ἕλληνας, δέον τοὺς θεατὰς
τῶν Ὀλυμπίων διακαρτερεῖν διψῶντας καὶ νὴ Δία γε καὶ ἀποθνή-
σκειν πολλοὺς αὐτῶν ὑπὸ σφοδρῶν τῶν νόσων, αἳ τέως διὰ τὸ
ξηρὸν τοῦ χωρίου ἐν πολλῷ τῷ πλήθει ἐπεπόλαζον. καὶ ταῦτα
ἔλεγεν πίνων τοῦ αὐτοῦ ὕδατος.

Ὡς δὲ μικροῦ κατέλευσαν αὐτὸν ἐπιδραμόντες ἅπαντες, τότε 20
μὲν ἐπὶ τὸν Δία καταφυγὼν ὁ γενναῖος εὕρετο μὴ ἀποθανεῖν, ἐς
δὲ τὴν ἑξῆς Ὀλυμπιάδα λόγον τινὰ διὰ τεττάρων ἐτῶν συνθεὶς
τῶν διὰ μέσου ἐξήνεγκε πρὸς τοὺς Ἕλληνας, ἔπαινον ὑπὲρ τοῦ
τὸ ὕδωρ ἐπαγαγόντος καὶ ἀπολογίαν ὑπὲρ τῆς τότε φυγῆς.

[17] 'After this he left home for a third time and went to visit Agathobulus in Egypt where he subjected himself to that wonderful regimen, shaving half his head, rubbing mud on his face, masturbating in the middle of a large crowd and making an exhibition of his object of so-called indifference, and then beating others and being beaten himself with a stalk of fennel and performing many other feats of miraculous exuberance.

[18] 'After preparing in this way he set sail from Egypt to Italy, and the moment he disembarked started abusing everyone and particularly the emperor, knowing he was exceedingly kindly and gentle, so that his effrontery involved no danger. For the emperor, as one might expect, paid little attention to his profanities and felt no need to punish for mere words one who used philosophy as a guise and in particular had made abusiveness into a profession. But even this added to his reputation, at least among the ignorant, and his madness made him a celebrity till the urban prefect, a man of wisdom, expelled him for his inordinate pride in the matter, saying that Rome didn't need a philosopher like that. This incident however made him a notability on everyone's lips as the philosopher who had been banished for his outspokenness and excessive independence and in this respect he came close to Musonius, Dio and Epictetus and any others who encountered similar circumstances.

[19] 'So it was that he came to Greece and was now abusing the people of Elis, now urging the Greeks to take up arms against the Romans, and now berating a man of outstanding culture and reputation for his general benefactions to Greece, and in particular for bringing water to Olympia, and stopping the visitors to the festival from dying of thirst, on the grounds that he had made the Greeks soft, whereas spectators at the Olympic games ought to endure thirst with fortitude – yes, upon my word, and die in large numbers from the violent infections, which till then were rife among the vast crowds because the place was so dry! And though he spoke like that he drank that same water!

[20] 'This led to a general onrush against him and he was almost stoned to death. On that occasion our noble fellow escaped being killed by taking refuge with Zeus, but over the intervening four years composed a speech for the next Olympic games and delivered it to the Greeks, praising the man who had brought the water there and defending his flight on the previous occasion.

Ἤδη δὲ ἀμελούμενος ὑφ' ἁπάντων καὶ μηκέθ' ὁμοίως περίβλεπτος ὤν — ἕωλα γὰρ ἦν ἅπαντα καὶ οὐδὲν ἔτι καινουργεῖν
ἐδύνατο ἐφ' ὅτῳ ἐκπλήξειε τοὺς ἐντυγχάνοντας καὶ θαυμάζειν καὶ
πρὸς αὐτὸν ἀποβλέπειν ποιήσει, οὗπερ ἐξ ἀρχῆς δριμύν τινα ἔρωτα
ἐρῶν ἐτύγχανεν — τὸ τελευταῖον τοῦτο τόλμημα ἐβουλεύσατο
περὶ τῆς πυρᾶς, καὶ διέδωκε λόγον ἐς τοὺς Ἕλληνας εὐθὺς
ἀπὸ Ὀλυμπίων τῶν ἔμπροσθεν ὡς ἐς τοὐπιὸν καύσων ἑαυτόν. καὶ
νῦν αὐτὰ ταῦτα θαυματοποιεῖ, ὥς φασι, βόθρον ὀρύττων καὶ ξύλα
συγκομίζων καὶ δεινήν τινα τὴν καρτερίαν ὑπισχνούμενος.

Ἐχρῆν δέ, οἶμαι, μάλιστα μὲν περιμένειν τὸν θάνατον καὶ μὴ **21**
δραπετεύειν ἐκ τοῦ βίου· εἰ δὲ καὶ πάντως διέγνωστό οἱ ἀπαλ-
λάττεσθαι, μὴ πυρὶ μηδὲ τοῖς ἀπὸ τῆς τραγῳδίας τούτοις χρῆσθαι,
ἀλλ' ἕτερόν τινα θανάτου τρόπον, μυρίων ὄντων, ἑλόμενον ἀπελ-
θεῖν. εἰ δὲ καὶ τὸ πῦρ ὡς Ἡράκλειόν τι ἀσπάζεται, τί δή ποτε
οὐχὶ κατὰ σιγὴν ἑλόμενος ὄρος εὔδενδρον ἐν ἐκείνῳ ἑαυτὸν ἐνέ-
πρησεν μόνος, ἕνα τινὰ οἷον Θεαγένη τοῦτον Φιλοκτήτην παραλα-
βών; ὁ δὲ ἐν Ὀλυμπίᾳ τῆς πανηγύρεως πληθούσης μόνον οὐκ
ἐπὶ σκηνῆς ὀπτήσει ἑαυτόν, οὐκ ἀνάξιος ὤν, μὰ τὸν Ἡρακλέα,
εἴ γε χρὴ καὶ τοὺς πατραλοίας καὶ τοὺς ἀθέους δίκας διδόναι τῶν
τολμημάτων. καὶ κατὰ τοῦτο πάνυ ὀψὲ δρᾶν αὐτὸ ἔοικεν, ὃν
ἐχρῆν πάλαι ἐς τὸν τοῦ Φαλάριδος ταῦρον ἐμπεσόντα τὴν ἀξίαν
ἀποτετικέναι, ἀλλὰ μὴ ἅπαξ χανόντα πρὸς τὴν φλόγα ἐν ἀκαρεῖ
τενθᾶναι. καὶ γὰρ αὖ καὶ τόδε οἱ πολλοί μοι λέγουσιν, ὡς οὐδεὶς
ὀξύτερος ἄλλος θανάτου τρόπος τοῦ διὰ πυρός· ἀνοῖξαι γὰρ δεῖν
μόνον τὸ στόμα καὶ αὐτίκα τεθνάναι.

Τὸ μέντοι θέαμα ἐπινοεῖται, οἶμαι, ὡς σεμνόν, ἐν ἱερῷ χωρίῳ **22**
καιόμενος ἄνθρωπος, ἔνθα μηδὲ θάπτειν ὅσιον τοὺς ἄλλους ἀπο-
θνῄσκοντας. ἀκούετε δέ, οἶμαι, ὡς καὶ πάλαι θέλων τις ἔνδοξος
γενέσθαι, ἐπεὶ κατ' ἄλλον τρόπον οὐκ εἶχεν ἐπιτυχεῖν τούτου,
ἐνέπρησε τῆς Ἐφεσίας Ἀρτέμιδος τὸν νεών. τοιοῦτόν τι καὶ
αὐτὸς ἐπινοεῖ, τοσοῦτος ἔρως τῆς δόξης ἐντέτηκεν αὐτῷ.

Καίτοι φησὶν ὅτι ὑπὲρ τῶν ἀνθρώπων αὐτὸ δρᾷ, ὡς διδάξειεν **23**
αὐτοὺς θανάτου καταφρονεῖν καὶ ἐγκαρτερεῖν τοῖς δεινοῖς. ἐγὼ
δὲ ἡδέως ἂν ἐροίμην οὐκ ἐκεῖνον ἀλλ' ὑμᾶς, εἰ καὶ τοὺς κακούργους

'But when now he was being neglected by all and no longer such a celebrity, since all his stunts were old hat and he couldn't produce any further novelties to elicit the astonishment and admiration of people meeting him or to make him the cynosure of all eyes, the thing he'd passionately desired from the start, he planned this final piece of dare-devilry with the pyre and immediately after the previous Olympic Games spread word among the Greeks that he'd cremate himself at the next Olympics and now he's working on the actual miracle, they tell me, digging a pit, collecting wood and promising a wonderful display of fortitude.

[21] 'In my opinion it would have been best to wait for death and not to be a fugitive from life, but, if he was absolutely determined to get away, he shouldn't have used fire or these ploys from tragedy but should have departed by choosing some other type of death, and there are hundreds available! But if he is keen on fire as something Herculean, why didn't he quietly choose some wooded mountain and cremate himself there on his own, taking along someone like Theagenes here, to be his Philoctetes? Instead he's going to roast himself at Olympia during the crowded festival almost as though on a stage and, by Heracles, just what he deserves, if it's right for parricides and ungodly villains to be punished for their audacious deeds! And if that is so, it all seems very belated, for he ought long ago to have been thrown into Phalaris' bull and paid the penalty he deserves rather than die an instant death 'by mouthing once for all' the flames. Also I'm told by many that there's no swifter method of death than by fire, for one need only open one's mouth and die instantly!

[22] 'However I think he visualises the spectacle as something awe-inspiring, to have a man being cremated on hallowed ground, where even to bury others who die is sacrilege. I'm sure you've heard of the man who had long wanted to become famous, and, finding it impossible to win fame any other way, set fire to the temple of Artemis at Ephesus. That's the sort of thing *he* has in mind, such is his deep-seated passion for glory!

[23] 'However he says he's acting thus for the good of mankind, to teach them to despise death and face dangers with fortitude, though I'd like to ask not him but you whether you'd like criminals to become his

βούλοισθε ἂν μαθητὰς αὐτοῦ γενέσθαι τῆς καρτερίας ταύτης καὶ καταφρονεῖν θανάτου καὶ καύσεως καὶ τῶν τοιούτων δειμάτων. ἀλλ' οὐκ ἂν εὖ οἶδ' ὅτι βουληθείητε. πῶς οὖν ὁ Πρωτεὺς τοῦτο διακρινεῖ καὶ τοὺς μὲν χρηστοὺς ὠφελήσει, τοὺς δὲ πονηροὺς οὐ φιλοκινδυνοτέρους καὶ τολμηροτέρους ἀποφανεῖ;

Καίτοι δυνατὸν ἔστω ἐς τοῦτο μόνους ἀπαντήσεσθαι τοὺς πρὸς **24** τὸ ὠφέλιμον ὀψομένους τὸ πρᾶγμα. ὑμᾶς δ' οὖν αὖθις ἐρήσομαι, δέξαισθ' ἂν ὑμῶν τοὺς παῖδας ζηλωτὰς τοῦ τοιούτου γενέσθαι; οὐκ ἂν εἴποιτε. καὶ τί τοῦτο ἠρόμην, ὅπου μηδ' αὐτῶν τις τῶν μαθητῶν αὐτοῦ ζηλώσειεν ἄν; τὸν γοῦν Θεαγένη τοῦτο μάλιστα αἰτιάσαιτο ἄν τις, ὅτι τἆλλα ζηλῶν τἀνδρὸς οὐχ ἕπεται τῷ διδα- σκάλῳ καὶ συνοδεύει παρὰ τὸν Ἡρακλέα, ὥς φησιν, ἀπιόντι. δυνάμενος ἐν βραχεῖ πανευδαίμων γενέσθαι συνεμπεσὼν ἐπὶ κεφαλὴν ἐς τὸ πῦρ.

Οὐ γὰρ ἐν πήρᾳ καὶ βάκτρῳ καὶ τρίβωνι ὁ ζῆλος, ἀλλὰ ταῦτα μὲν ἀσφαλῆ καὶ ῥᾴδια καὶ παντὸς ἂν εἴη, τὸ τέλος δὲ καὶ τὸ κε- φάλαιον χρὴ ζηλοῦν καὶ πυρὰν συνθέντα κορμῶν συκίνων ὡς ἔνι μάλιστα χλωρῶν ἐναποπνιγῆναι τῷ καπνῷ· τὸ πῦρ γὰρ αὐτὸ οὐ μόνον Ἡρακλέους καὶ Ἀσκληπιοῦ, ἀλλὰ καὶ τῶν ἱεροσύλων καὶ ἀνδροφόνων, οὓς ὁρᾶν ἔστιν ἐκ καταδίκης αὐτὸ πάσχοντας. ὥστε ἄμεινον τὸ διὰ τοῦ καπνοῦ· ἴδιον γὰρ καὶ ὑμῶν ἂν μόνων γένοιτο.

Ἄλλως τε ὁ μὲν Ἡρακλῆς, εἴπερ ἄρα καὶ ἐτόλμησέν τι τοι- **25** οῦτο, ὑπὸ νόσου αὐτὸ ἔδρασεν, ὑπὸ τοῦ Κενταυρείου αἵματος, ὥς φησιν ἡ τραγῳδία, κατεσθιόμενος· οὗτος δὲ τίνος αἰτίας ἕνεκεν ἐμβάλλει φέρων ἑαυτὸν εἰς τὸ πῦρ; νὴ Δί', ὅπως τὴν καρτερίαν ἐπιδείξηται καθάπερ οἱ Βραχμᾶνες· ἐκείνοις γὰρ αὐτὸν ἠξίου Θεαγένης εἰκάζειν, ὥσπερ οὐκ ἐνὸν καὶ ἐν Ἰνδοῖς εἶναί τινας μωροὺς καὶ κενοδόξους ἀνθρώπους. ὅμως δ' οὖν κἂν ἐκείνους μιμείσθω· ἐκεῖνοι γὰρ οὐκ ἐμπηδῶσιν ἐς τὸ πῦρ, ὡς Ὀνησίκριτος ὁ Ἀλεξάνδρου κυβερνήτης ἰδὼν Κάλανον καόμενόν φησιν, ἀλλ' ἐπειδὰν νήσωσι, πλησίον παραστάντες ἀκίνητοι ἀνέχονται παρο- πτώμενοι, εἶτ' ἐπιβάντες κατὰ σχῆμα καίονται, οὐδ' ὅσον ὀλίγον ἐντρέψαντες τῆς κατακλίσεως.

Οὗτος δὲ τί μέγα εἰ ἐμπεσὼν τενθήξεται* συναρπασθεὶς ὑπὸ

* read τεθνήξεται

disciples, learning this fortitude from him and how to despise death and burning and terrors like that. No, I'm sure you'd not like that! How then will Proteus be able to make this distinction and benefit the righteous without making the villains bolder and keener for danger?

[24] 'However let us assume it possible for only those to be present at this spectacle who will put what they see to beneficial use. Well, I'll ask you another question. Would you agree to have your sons become disciples of anyone like him? And why do I ask, when not even one disciple of his would follow his example? Indeed the greatest fault one can find with Theagenes is that, though he emulates everything else about the fellow, he doesn't follow his teacher's lead and accompany him on what he calls 'his departure to Heracles', though he could obtain absolute bliss in an instant by jumping headlong into the fire along with him!

'For emulation doesn't depend on pouch or staff or threadbare cloak; all these are safe and easy and open to anyone. No, he ought to emulate him in his final, culminating act, putting together a pyre of fig trunks as green as possible so that he suffocates in the smoke. For fire itself isn't associated only with Heracles and Asclepius, but also with temple-robbers and murderers, whom one can see sentenced to endure it. So death from smoke is superior. That would be unique and peculiar to yourselves!

[25] 'Besides, even if Heracles did venture to do something similar, he did so because of his affliction when he was being eaten away by the Centaur's blood, as we are told in the tragedy. But what reason does Peregrinus have for throwing himself into the flames? "So that" you suggest "he puts his fortitude on display like the Brahmins." Theagenes, I suppose, thought fit to liken him to them, as if it wasn't possible to find fools and publicity seekers in India too! However I wish he'd imitate them properly; for according to Onesicritus, Alexander's pilot, who saw Calanus cremate himself, they don't jump into the flames but once they've heaped up the pyre, they stand motionless beside it, putting up with being singed, and later ascend the pyre and submit to burning with decorum and without moving at all from where they lie.

'But how will it be a great achievement for this fellow to jump in, be

τοῦ πυρός; οὐκ ἀπ' ἐλπίδος μὴ ἀναπηδήσασθαι αὐτὸν καὶ ἡμί-
φλεκτον, εἰ μή, ὅπερ φασί, μηχανήσεται βαθεῖαν γενέσθαι καὶ
ἐν βόθρῳ τὴν πυράν. εἰσὶ δ' οἳ καὶ μεταβαλέσθαι φασὶν αὐτὸν 26
καί τινα ὀνείρατα διηγεῖσθαι, ὡς τοῦ Διὸς οὐκ ἐῶντος μιαίνειν
ἱερὸν χωρίον. ἀλλὰ θαρρείτω τούτου γε ἕνεκα· ἐγὼ γὰρ διομο-
σαίμην ἂν ἦ μὴν μηδένα τῶν θεῶν ἀγανακτήσειν, εἰ Περεγρῖνος
κακῶς ἀποθάνοι. οὐ μὴν οὐδὲ ῥάδιον αὐτῷ ἔτ' ἀναδῦναι· οἱ γὰρ
συνόντες κύνες παρορμῶσιν καὶ συνωθοῦσιν ἐς τὸ πῦρ καὶ ὑπεκ-
κάουσι τὴν γνώμην, οὐκ ἐῶντες ἀποδειλιᾶν· ὧν εἰ δύο συγκατα-
σπάσας ἐμπέσοι ἐς τὴν πυράν, τοῦτο μόνον χάριεν ἐργάσαιτο.

Ἤκουον δὲ ὡς οὐδὲ Πρωτεὺς ἔτι καλεῖσθαι ἀξιοῖ, ἀλλὰ Φοί- 27
νικα μετωνόμασεν ἑαυτόν, ὅτι καὶ φοῖνιξ, τὸ Ἰνδικὸν ὄρνεον, ἐπι-
βαίνειν πυρᾶς λέγεται πορρωτάτω γήρως προβεβηκώς. ἀλλὰ καὶ
λογοποιεῖ καὶ χρησμούς τινας διέξεισιν παλαιοὺς δή, ὡς χρεὼν
εἴη δαίμονα νυκτοφύλακα γενέσθαι αὐτόν, καὶ δῆλός ἐστι βωμῶν
ἤδη ἐπιθυμῶν καὶ χρυσοῦς ἀναστήσεσθαι ἐλπίζων.

Καὶ μὰ Δία οὐδὲν ἀπεικὸς ἐν πολλοῖς τοῖς ἀνοήτοις εὑρεθή- 28
σεσθαί τινας τοὺς καὶ τεταρταίων ἀπηλλάχθαι δι' αὐτοῦ φήσον-
τας καὶ νύκτωρ ἐντετυχηκέναι τῷ δαίμονι τῷ νυκτοφύλακι. οἱ
κατάρατοι δὲ οὗτοι μαθηταὶ αὐτοῦ καὶ χρηστήριον, οἶμαι, καὶ
ἄδυτον ἐπὶ τῇ πυρᾷ μηχανήσονται, διότι καὶ Πρωτεὺς ἐκεῖνος
ὁ Διός, ὁ προπάτωρ τοῦ ὀνόματος, μαντικὸς ἦν. μαρτύρομαι δὲ ἦ
μὴν καὶ ἱερέας αὐτοῦ ἀποδειχθήσεσθαι μαστίγων ἢ καυτηρίων
ἤ τινος τοιαύτης τερατουργίας, ἢ καὶ νὴ Δία τελετήν τινα ἐπ'
αὐτῷ συστήσεσθαι νυκτέριον καὶ δᾳδουχίαν ἐπὶ τῇ πυρᾷ.

Θεαγένης δὲ ἔναγχος, ὥς μοί τις τῶν ἑταίρων ἀπήγγειλεν, 29
καὶ Σίβυλλαν ἔφη προειρηκέναι περὶ τούτων· καὶ τὰ ἔπη γὰρ
ἀπεμνημόνευεν·

Ἀλλ' ὁπόταν Πρωτεὺς Κυνικῶν ὄχ' ἄριστος ἁπάντων
Ζηνὸς ἐριγδούπου τέμενος κάτα πῦρ ἀνακαύσας
ἐς φλόγα πηδήσας ἔλθῃ ἐς μακρὸν Ὄλυμπον,
δὴ τότε πάντας ὁμῶς, οἳ ἀρούρης καρπὸν ἔδουσιν,
νυκτιπόλον τιμᾶν κέλομαι ἥρωα μέγιστον
σύνθρονον Ἡφαίστῳ καὶ Ἡρακλῆϊ ἄνακτι.

consumed by flames and die? Anyway it's not inconceivable that he jumps out again, though half-scorched, unless he arranges, as they say he will, for the pyre to be a tall one and set in a pit. [26] Some say he has changed his plans and is recounting various dreams, claiming Zeus won't allow him to pollute holy ground. But he shouldn't fear on that account. For I can swear on oath that none of the gods will be angry, if Peregrinus should come to a nasty end. Moreover it's difficult for him to get out of it now; for his fellow 'Dogs' are urging him on, pushing him into the fire and keeping his resolve burning, and they won't allow him to chicken out of it. If only he'd take a couple of them with him when he jumps into the fire, that would be the one act of grace he could accomplish!

[27] 'I heard that he no longer wants to be called Proteus but has changed his name to Phoenix, because the Indian bird, the phoenix, is said to climb on to a pyre when far advanced in old age. Moreover he fabricates rumours and recites prophecies, purporting them to be old and to say that it was ordained for him to become a guardian spirit of the night, and he obviously has his heart set on altars and hopes to have his statue erected in gold.

[28] 'In heaven's name, it's not unlikely that among numerous fools some should be found to say they've been cured of quartan fevers through him and that they've had nocturnal encounters with the guardian spirit of the night, and these damned disciples of his will engineer an oracle, I suppose, or a shrine dedicated to him at the pyre, because the well-known Proteus, the son of Zeus, the progenitor of the name, had second sight. And I can assure you on oath that priests of his will be appointed to preside over scourges or branding-irons or some such hocus-pocus, or, by gad, some nocturnal mystery festival be inaugurated in his honour involving a torch-light procession at the pyre.

[29] 'Theagenes, as reported to me by one of his companions, recently said that the Sibyl had made a prophecy on these matters; for he remembered her verses:

> But when Proteus, 'mid Cynics all of highest worth,
> In sanctuary of thundering Zeus a fire doth light,
> And leap into the flames and reach Olympus high,
> 'Tis then that all alike who eat the fruits of earth
> I bid honour the hero great who walks by night,
> Whose seat to Fire-god and Lord Heracles is nigh.

Ταῦτα μὲν Θεαγένης Σιβύλλης ἀκηκοέναι φησίν. ἐγὼ δὲ Βάκι- 30
δος αὐτῷ χρησμὸν ὑπὲρ τούτων ἐρῶ· φησὶν δὲ ὁ Βάκις οὕτω,
σφόδρα εὖ ἐπειπών,

'Αλλ' ὁπόταν Κυνικὸς πολυώνυμος ἐς φλόγα πολλὴν
πηδήσῃ δόξης ὑπ' ἐρινύι θυμὸν ὀρινθείς,
δὴ τότε τοὺς ἄλλους κυναλώπεκας, οἳ οἱ ἕπονται,
μιμεῖσθαι χρὴ πότμον ἀποιχομένοιο λύκοιο.
ὃς δέ κε δειλὸς ἐὼν φεύγῃ μένος 'Ηφαίστοιο,
λάεσσιν βαλέειν τοῦτον τάχα πάντας 'Αχαιούς,
ὡς μὴ ψυχρὸς ἐὼν θερμηγορέειν ἐπιχειρῇ
χρυσῷ σαξάμενος πήρην μάλα πολλὰ δανείζων,
ἐν καλαῖς Πάτραισιν ἔχων τρὶς πέντε τάλαντα.

τί ὑμῖν δοκεῖ, ἄνδρες; ἆρα φαυλότερος χρησμολόγος ὁ Βάκις τῆς
Σιβύλλης εἶναι; ὥστε ὥρα τοῖς θαυμαστοῖς τούτοις ὁμιληταῖς τοῦ
Πρωτέως περισκοπεῖν ἔνθα ἑαυτοὺς ἐξαερώσουσιν· τοῦτο γὰρ
τὴν καῦσιν καλοῦσιν.

Ταῦτ' εἰπόντος ἀνεβόησαν οἱ περιεστῶτες ἅπαντες, "Ηδη καιέ- 31
σθωσαν ἄξιοι τοῦ πυρός.

Καὶ ὁ μὲν κατέβη γελῶν, Νέστορα δ' οὐκ ἔλαθεν ἰαχή, τὸν Θεαγένη, ἀλλ' ὡς ἤκουσεν τῆς βοῆς, ἧκεν εὐθὺς καὶ ἀναβὰς ἐκεκρά-
γει καὶ μυρία κακὰ διεξῄει περὶ τοῦ καταβεβηκότος· οὐ γὰρ οἶδα
ὅστις ἐκεῖνος ὁ βέλτιστος ἐκαλεῖτο. ἐγὼ δὲ ἀφεὶς αὐτὸν διαρρη-
γνύμενον ἀπῄειν ὀψόμενος τοὺς ἀθλητάς· ἤδη γὰρ 'Ελλανοδί-
και ἐλέγοντο εἶναι ἐν τῷ Πλεθρίῳ.

Ταῦτα μέν σοι τὰ ἐν "Ηλιδι. ἐπεὶ δὲ ἐς τὴν 'Ολυμπίαν ἀφικόμε- 32
θα, μεστὸς ἦν ὁ ὀπισθόδομος τῶν κατηγορούντων Πρωτέως ἢ
ἐπαινούντων τὴν προαίρεσιν αὐτοῦ, ὥστε καὶ εἰς χεῖρας αὐτῶν
ἦλθον οἱ πολλοί, ἄχρι δὴ παρελθὼν αὐτὸς ὁ Πρωτεὺς μυρίῳ τῷ
πλήθει παραπεμπόμενος κατόπιν τοῦ τῶν κηρύκων ἀγῶνος λόγους
τινὰς διεξῆλθεν περὶ ἑαυτοῦ, τὸν βίον τε ὡς ἐβίω καὶ τοὺς κινδύ-
νους οὓς ἐκινδύνευσεν διηγούμενος καὶ ὅσα πράγματα φιλοσοφίας
ἕνεκα ὑπέμεινεν. τὰ μὲν οὖν εἰρημένα πολλὰ ἦν, ἐγὼ δὲ ὀλίγων
ἤκουσα ὑπὸ πλήθους τῶν περιεστώτων, εἶτα φοβηθεὶς μὴ συντρι-
βείην ἐν τοσαύτῃ τύρβῃ, ἐπεὶ καὶ πολλοὺς τοῦτο πάσχοντας

[30] 'That's what Theagenes claims he heard the Sibyl say. But I'll supply him with a prophecy of Bacis on the subject. This is what Bacis says, and a capital pronouncement it is!

But when doth leap the Cynic called by many a name
Into great fire with frenzied heart in quest of fame,
'Tis then the other foxy dogs who him revere
Must emulate the doom of wolf that's gone from here.
But whoso craven is and flees Hephaestus' flame
That wight Achaeans all must stone without delay,
So that the frigid one hot words may not essay,
He that hath stuffed his purse with gold from usury,
He that in Patras fair hath talents five times three.

What do *you* think, gentlemen? Surely not that Bacis is an inferior oracle-monger to the Sibyl? And so it's high time for those wonderful disciples of Proteus to look round for a place in which to 'aerate' themselves; for that's what they call burning.'

[31] When he had finished talking, all the bystanders shouted 'Let them burn this instant; they deserve the flames.'

The speaker stepped down with a laugh, 'But Nestor failed not to note their cries' or rather it was Theagenes, for when he heard the shouting, he came at once, climbed on the rostrum and started bawling and telling slanderous tales about the last speaker – I don't know the name of that capital fellow. Anyway I left Theagenes bursting his lungs and went off to see the athletes, for the umpires were already said to be in the Plethrium.

[32] There you have what happened in Elis. But when we reached Olympia, the rear porch of the temple was crowded with people either criticising Proteus or applauding his purpose, so that most of them had actually come to blows. But finally, after the contest for heralds was over, Proteus himself came forward escorted by a vast entourage and delivered a speech about himself, describing the life he'd led, the dangers he'd faced and all the troubles he'd endured for the sake of philosophy. So he had a lot to say, but I only heard a little of it because there was a large crowd of bystanders and I became afraid of being crushed in all the turmoil, as I could see that happening to many people, and I went off

ἑώρων, ἀπῆλθον μακρὰ χαίρειν φράσας θανατῶντι σοφιστῇ τὸν
ἐπιτάφιον ἑαυτοῦ πρὸ τελευτῆς διεξιόντι.

Πλὴν τό γε τοσοῦτον ἐπήκουσα· ἔφη γὰρ βούλεσθαι χρυσῷ 33
βίῳ χρυσῆν κορώνην ἐπιθεῖναι· χρῆναι γὰρ τὸν Ἡρακλείως βε-
βιωκότα Ἡρακλείως ἀποθανεῖν καὶ ἀναμιχθῆναι τῷ αἰθέρι.
Καὶ ὠφελῆσαι, ἔφη, βούλομαι τοὺς ἀνθρώπους δείξας αὐτοῖς ὃν
χρὴ τρόπον θανάτου καταφρονεῖν· πάντας οὖν δεῖ μοι τοὺς ἀνθρώπους Φιλοκτήτας γενέσθαι.

Οἱ μὲν οὖν ἀνοητότεροι τῶν ἀνθρώπων ἐδάκρυον καὶ ἐβόων,
Σῴζου τοῖς Ἕλλησιν, οἱ δὲ ἀνδρωδέστεροι ἐκεκράγεσαν, Τέλει
τὰ δεδογμένα, ὑφ' ὧν ὁ πρεσβύτης οὐ μετρίως ἐθορυβήθη ἐλπίζων πάντας ἕξεσθαι αὐτοῦ καὶ μὴ προήσεσθαι τῷ πυρί, ἀλλὰ
ἄκοντα δὴ καθέξειν ἐν τῷ βίῳ. τὸ δέ, Τέλει τὰ δεδογμένα, πάνυ
ἀδόκητον αὐτῷ προσπεσὸν ὠχριᾶν ἔτι μᾶλλον ἐποίησεν, καίτοι
ἤδη νεκρικῶς τὴν χροιὰν ἔχοντι, καὶ νὴ Δία καὶ ὑποτρέμειν,
ὥστε κατέπαυσε τὸν λόγον.

Ἐγὼ δέ, εἰκάζεις, οἶμαι, πῶς ἐγέλων· οὐδὲ γὰρ ἐλεεῖν ἄξιον 34
ἦν οὕτω δυσέρωτα τῆς δόξης ἄνθρωπον ὑπὲρ ἅπαντας ὅσοι τῇ
αὐτῇ Ποινῇ ἐλαύνονται. παρεπέμπετο δὲ ὅμως ὑπὸ πολλῶν καὶ
ἐνεφορεῖτο τῆς δόξης ἀποβλέπων ἐς τὸ πλῆθος τῶν θαυμαζόντων,
οὐκ εἰδὼς ὁ ἄθλιος ὅτι καὶ τοῖς ἐπὶ τὸν σταυρὸν ἀπαγομένοις ἢ
ὑπὸ τοῦ δημίου ἐχομένοις πολλῷ πλείους ἕπονται.

Καὶ δὴ τὰ μὲν Ὀλύμπια τέλος εἶχεν, κάλλιστα Ὀλυμπίων 35
γενόμενα ὧν ἐγὼ εἶδον, τετράκις ἤδη ὁρῶν. ἐγὼ δέ — οὐ γὰρ
ἦν εὐπορῆσαι ὀχήματος ἅμα πολλῶν ἐξιόντων — ἄκων ὑπελειπό-
μην. ὁ δὲ ἀεὶ ἀναβαλλόμενος νύκτα τὸ τελευταῖον προειρήκει
ἐπιδείξασθαι τὴν καῦσιν· καί με τῶν ἑταίρων τινὸς παραλαβόντος
περὶ μέσας νύκτας ἐξαναστὰς ἀπῄειν εὐθὺ τῆς Ἀρπίνης, ἔνθα
ἦν ἡ πυρά. στάδιοι πάντες οὗτοι*εἴκοσιν ἀπὸ τῆς Ὀλυμπίας κατὰ
τὸν ἱππόδρομον ἀπιόντων πρὸς ἕω. καὶ ἐπεὶ τάχιστα ἀφικόμεθα,
καταλαμβάνομεν πυρὰν νενησμένην ἐν βόθρῳ ὅσον ἐς ὀργυιὰν
τὸ βάθος. δᾷδες ἦσαν τὰ πολλὰ καὶ παρεβέβυστο τῶν φρυγάνων,
ὡς ἀναφθείη τάχιστα.

Καὶ ἐπειδὴ ἡ σελήνη ἀνέτελλεν — ἔδει γὰρ κἀκείνην θεάσα- 36
σθαι τὸ κάλλιστον τοῦτο ἔργον — πρόεισιν ἐκεῖνος ἐσκευασμένος

heartily cursing the sophist with the death wish who was delivering a funeral oration on himself *before* he was dead.

[33] This much however I *did* hear: he said he wanted on a golden life 'a seal of gold to put'; for he who had lived like Heracles must die like Heracles and blend into the upper air. 'For' he continued 'I too want to benefit mankind by showing them how to scorn death; so all men must play the Philoctetes to me.'

Well the stupider folk started to weep and call out 'Save yourself for the Greeks', but the stouter hearts among them kept shouting 'Carry out your intentions', upsetting the old fellow inordinately, for he had hoped they'd all cling to him, and not abandon him to the fire, but keep him alive 'against his will'. But the 'Carry out your intentions' came as a complete surprise to him and made him paler still, though he already looked like death, and upon my word made his knees knock so that he stopped talking.

[34] I think you can imagine how I laughed. For it wouldn't have been right to pity the fellow so much more wretchedly in love with glory than all others hounded by the same scourge. However he was escorted by a large crowd and had his fill of glory as he gazed at the host of admirers, unaware, poor creature, that those being led off to crucifixion or in the hands of the executioner have a far greater following!

[35] And now the games were at an end, the finest Olympic games I've seen in my four visits. But I had to remain there against my will, as there was a shortage of transport with many people leaving all at once. But he kept putting things off, though finally he had announced that he would stage the cremation one particular night. I got up about midnight and, accepting an invitation from one of my companions, made straight for Harpina where the pyre was. This is about two and a half miles in all from Olympia for people leaving by the hippodrome and going east. When we got there, we found the pyre had been heaped up in a ditch about six feet deep. The pyre consisted mainly of torchwood billets and was packed with brushwood to ensure instant ignition.

[36] When the moon was rising – for she too had to see this splendid deed – the great man came forward dressed in his invariable fashion, accompanied by the Cynic bigwigs and in particular the noble fellow from

ἐς τὸν ἀεὶ τρόπον καὶ ξὺν αὐτῷ τὰ τέλη τῶν κυνῶν, καὶ μάλιστα
ὁ γεννάδας ὁ ἐκ Πατρῶν, δᾷδα ἔχων, οὐ φαῦλος δευτεραγωνιστής·
ἐδᾳδοφόρει δὲ καὶ ὁ Πρωτεύς. καὶ προσελθόντες ἄλλος ἀλλαχόθεν
ἀνῆψαν τὸ πῦρ μέγιστον ἅτε ἀπὸ δᾴδων καὶ φρυγάνων. ὁ δέ —
καί μοι πάνυ ἤδη πρόσεχε τὸν νοῦν — ἀποθέμενος τὴν πήραν καὶ
τὸ τριβώνιον καὶ τὸ Ἡράκλειον ἐκεῖνο ῥόπαλον, ἔστη ἐν ὀθόνῃ
ῥυπώσῃ ἀκριβῶς. εἶτα ᾔτει λιβανωτόν, ὡς ἐπιβάλοι ἐπὶ τὸ πῦρ,
καὶ ἀναδόντος τινὸς ἐπέβαλέν τε καὶ εἶπεν ἐς τὴν μεσημβρίαν
ἀποβλέπων — καὶ γὰρ καὶ τοῦτ' αὐτὸ πρὸς τὴν τραγῳδίαν ἦν,
ἡ μεσημβρία — Δαίμονες μητρῷοι καὶ πατρῷοι, δέξασθαί με
εὐμενεῖς. ταῦτα εἰπὼν ἐπήδησεν ἐς τὸ πῦρ. οὐ μὴν ἑωρᾶτό γε,
ἀλλὰ περιεσχέθη ὑπὸ τῆς φλογὸς πολλῆς ἠρμένης.

Αὖθις ὁρῶ γελῶντά σε, ὦ καλὲ Κρόνιε, τὴν καταστροφὴν τοῦ **37**
δράματος. ἐγὼ δὲ τοὺς μητρῴους μὲν δαίμονας ἐπιβοώμενον μὰ
τὸν Δί' οὐ σφόδρα ᾐτιώμην· ὅτε δὲ καὶ τοὺς πατρῴους ἐπεκαλέ-
σατο, ἀναμνησθεὶς τῶν περὶ τοῦ φόνου εἰρημένων οὐδὲ κατέχειν
ἠδυνάμην τὸν γέλωτα. οἱ Κυνικοὶ δὲ περιστάντες τὴν πυρὰν οὐκ
ἐδάκρυον μέν, σιωπῇ δὲ ἐνεδείκνυντο λύπην τινὰ εἰς τὸ πῦρ ὁρῶντες, ἄχρι δὴ ἀποπνιγεὶς ἐπ' αὐτοῖς, Ἀπίωμεν, φημί, ὦ μάταιοι·
οὐ γὰρ ἡδὺ τὸ θέαμα ὠπτημένον γέροντα ὁρᾶν κνίσης ἀναπιμπλα-
μένους πονηρᾶς. ἢ περιμένετε ἔστ' ἂν γραφεύς τις ἐπελθὼν ἀπει-
κάσῃ ὑμᾶς οἵους τοὺς ἐν τῷ δεσμωτηρίῳ ἑταίρους τῷ Σωκράτει
παραγράφουσιν;

Ἐκεῖνοι μὲν οὖν ἠγανάκτουν καὶ ἐλοιδοροῦντό μοι, ἔνιοι δὲ καὶ
ἐπὶ τὰς βακτηρίας ᾖξαν. εἶτα, ἐπειδὴ ἠπείλησα ξυναρπάσας τινὰς
ἐμβαλεῖν εἰς τὸ πῦρ, ὡς ἂν ἕποιντο τῷ διδασκάλῳ, ἐπαύσαντο καὶ
εἰρήνην ἦγον.

Ἐγὼ δὲ ἐπανιὼν ποικίλα, ὦ ἑταῖρε, πρὸς ἐμαυτὸν ἐνενόουν, **38**
τὸ φιλόδοξον οἷον τί ἐστιν ἀναλογιζόμενος, ὡς μόνος οὗτος ὁ ἔρως
ἄφυκτος καὶ τοῖς πάνυ θαυμαστοῖς εἶναι δοκοῦσιν, οὐχ ὅπως ἐκείνῳ
τἀνδρὶ καὶ τἄλλα ἐμπλήκτως καὶ ἀπονενοημένως βεβιωκότι καὶ
οὐκ ἀναξίως τοῦ πυρός. εἶτα ἐνετύγχανον πολλοῖς ἀπιοῦσιν ὡς **39**
θεάσαιντο καὶ αὐτοί· ᾤοντο γὰρ ἔτι καταλήψεσθαι ζῶντα αὐτόν.
καὶ γὰρ καὶ τόδε τῇ προτεραίᾳ διεδέδοτο ὡς πρὸς ἀνίσχοντα τὸν
ἥλιον ἀσπασάμενος, ὥσπερ ἀμέλει καὶ τοὺς Βραχμᾶνάς φασιν

Patras who was holding a torch and showing himself no mean player of the secondary role. Proteus too was holding a torch. They came and kindled the fire from all sides into a mighty flame thanks to the torches and brushwood. But he – please pay particular attention at this point – discarded his pouch, tattered cloak and that Heracles club of his and stood there in utterly filthy underclothes. Then he asked for frankincense to throw on the fire and on being given some threw it on and gazing to the south – for here with the south we had one more theatrical touch – he said 'Spirits of my mother and father, receive me with favour.' After these words, he leapt into the fire, but couldn't be seen as he was engulfed by the mighty flames that rose.

[37] I can see you laughing once more, my good Cronios, at the finale of the drama. I personally didn't blame him too much, I assure you, for invoking his mother's gods, but when he called upon those of his father, my memories of what I'd been told about the murder made it impossible for me to check my laughter. But the Cynics round the pyre instead of weeping gave a silent display of grief of sorts as they gazed into the fire, till I boiled over with rage at them and said 'Let's be off, fools. It's not a pleasant spectacle to see an old man roasted and to be contaminated by the foul reek. Or are you waiting for some painter to come along and portray you in the way they do Socrates' companions with him in the prison?'

That made them angry and abusive towards me and some even reached for their sticks, but after I'd threatened to grab some of them and throw them into the flames, so that they could follow their mentor, they stopped and kept quiet.

[38] But on my way back, my friend, a variety of thoughts passed through my mind as I reflected on the nature of love of glory and how this is the only passion that is irresistible even to those considered absolutely wonderful and not just to that fellow whose life had been wild and desperate and deserved to end in burning. [39] Then I met many people on their way out to share in the spectacle, thinking they'd find him still alive. For another message had circulated the day before to the effect that he would greet the sun at dawn, as indeed they say the Brahmans do, and then mount the pyre. I managed to turn back most of them by telling them

ποιεῖν, ἐπιβήσεται τῆς πυρᾶς. ἀπέστρεφον δ' οὖν τοὺς πολλοὺς
αὐτῶν λέγων ἤδη τετελέσθαι τὸ ἔργον, οἷς μὴ καὶ τοῦτ' αὐτὸ
περισπούδαστον ἦν, κἂν αὐτὸν ἰδεῖν τὸν τόπον καί τι λείψανον
καταλαμβάνειν τοῦ πυρός.

Ἔνθα δή, ὦ ἑταῖρε, μυρία πράγματα εἶχον ἅπασιν διηγούμενος
καὶ ἀνακρίνουσιν καὶ ἀκριβῶς ἐκπυνθανομένοις. εἰ μὲν οὖν ἴδοι-
μί τινα χαρίεντα, ψιλὰ ἂν ὥσπερ σοὶ τὰ πραχθέντα διηγούμην,
πρὸς δὲ τοὺς βλᾶκας καὶ πρὸς τὴν ἀκρόασιν κεχηνότας ἐτρα-
γῴδουν τι παρ' ἐμαυτοῦ, ὡς ἐπειδὴ ἀνήφθη μὲν ἡ πυρά, ἐνέβαλεν
δὲ φέρων ἑαυτὸν ὁ Πρωτεύς, σεισμοῦ πρότερον μεγάλου γενομένου σὺν μυκηθμῷ τῆς γῆς, γὺψ ἀναπτάμενος ἐκ μέσης τῆς
φλογὸς οἴχοιτο ἐς τὸν οὐρανὸν ἀνθρωπιστὶ μεγάλῃ τῇ φωνῇ λέγων

Ἔλιπον γᾶν, βαίνω δ' ἐς Ὄλυμπον.

ἐκεῖνοι μὲν οὖν ἐτεθήπεσαν καὶ προσεκύνουν ὑποφρίττοντες καὶ
ἀνέκρινόν με πότερον πρὸς ἔω ἢ πρὸς δυσμὰς ἐνεχθείη ὁ γύψ·
ἐγὼ δὲ τὸ ἐπελθὸν ἀπεκρινάμην αὐτοῖς.

Ἀπελθὼν δὲ ἐς τὴν πανήγυριν ἐπέστην τινὶ πολιῷ ἀνδρὶ καὶ **40**
νὴ τὸν Δί' ἀξιοπίστῳ τὸ πρόσωπον ἐπὶ τῷ πώγωνι καὶ τῇ λοιπῇ
σεμνότητι, τά τε ἄλλα διηγουμένῳ περὶ τοῦ Πρωτέως καὶ ὡς
μετὰ τὸ καυθῆναι θεάσαιτο αὐτὸν ἐν λευκῇ ἐσθῆτι μικρὸν ἔμπροσθεν, καὶ νῦν ἀπολίποι περιπατοῦντα φαιδρὸν ἐν τῇ ἑπταφώνῳ
στοᾷ κοτίνῳ τε ἐστεμμένον. εἶτ' ἐπὶ πᾶσι προσέθηκε τὸν γῦπα,
διομνύμενος ἦ μὴν αὐτὸς ἑωρακέναι ἀναπτάμενον ἐκ τῆς πυρᾶς,
ὃν ἐγὼ μικρὸν ἔμπροσθεν ἀφῆκα πέτεσθαι καταγελῶντα τῶν
ἀνοήτων καὶ βλακικῶν τὸν τρόπον.

Ἐννόει τὸ λοιπὸν οἷα εἰκὸς ἐπ' αὐτῷ γενήσεσθαι, ποίας μὲν **41**
οὐ μελίττας ἐπιστήσεσθαι ἐπὶ τὸν τόπον, τίνας δὲ τέττιγας οὐκ
ἐπάσεσθαι, τίνας δὲ κορώνας οὐκ ἐπιπτήσεσθαι καθάπερ ἐπὶ τὸν
Ἡσιόδου τάφον, καὶ τὰ τοιαῦτα. εἰκόνας μὲν γὰρ παρά τε Ἠλείων
αὐτῶν παρά τε τῶν ἄλλων Ἑλλήνων, οἷς καὶ ἐπεσταλκέναι
ἔλεγεν, αὐτίκα μάλα οἶδα πολλὰς ἀναστησομένας, φασὶ δὲ
πάσαις σχεδὸν ταῖς ἐνδόξοις πόλεσιν ἐπιστολὰς διαπέμψαι αὐτόν,
διαθήκας τινὰς καὶ παραινέσεις καὶ νόμους· καί τινας ἐπὶ

the deed was already done, those that is who weren't absolutely set on seeing the actual spot and finding some relic left by the fire.

At this point I was put to endless trouble describing things to everybody in answer to their questions and detailed enquiries. Whenever I saw anyone intelligent, I would relate the bald facts to them as I am doing to you, but for the morons who listened open-mouthed I would add some theatrical touches of my own, how once the fire had blazed up and Proteus had thrown himself on it, first there had been a mighty earthquake and rumbling of the ground, and then a vulture had flown up into the heavens from the midst of the flames crying out in a loud human voice 'Earth I have left, to Olympus I go.' They were amazed and made gestures of reverence, trembling and asking whether the vulture had flown to the east or the west, and I answered the first thing that came into my head.

[40] On leaving there for the festival I came across a grey-haired old man whose looks certainly inspired confidence thanks to his long beard and general dignity. He was discoursing on the topic of Proteus, describing in particular how after his cremation he had seen him a little while ago clad in white and how he had now left him walking about in the Porch of the Seven Voices, garlanded in wild olive. Then on top of all he added the vulture, swearing on oath that he had seen it with his own eyes flying up from the pyre, the vulture I had released into flight a little earlier to have a laugh at the expense of people with stupid, foolish natures.

[41] Just imagine what's likely to happen with Proteus in the future, all the bees that will settle on the place, all the cicadas that will sing there, all the crows that will fly to it as to Hesiod's burial place, and so forth! For I know that many statues will instantly be raised in Peregrinus' honour by the Eleans themselves and by the rest of the Greeks to whom he claimed to have sent missives; they say he has sent nearly every well-known city missives containing his testamentary wishes, advice and laws.

τούτῳ πρεσβευτὰς τῶν ἑταίρων ἐχειροτόνησεν, νεκραγγέλους καὶ νερτεροδρόμους προσαγορεύσας.

Τοῦτο τέλος τοῦ κακοδαίμονος Πρωτέως ἐγένετο, ἀνδρός, **42** ὡς βραχεῖ λόγῳ περιλαβεῖν, πρὸς ἀλήθειαν μὲν οὐδεπώποτε ἀποβλέψαντος, ἐπὶ δόξῃ δὲ καὶ τῷ παρὰ τῶν πολλῶν ἐπαίνῳ ἅπαντα εἰπόντος αἰεὶ καὶ πράξαντος, ὡς καὶ ἐς πῦρ ἁλέσθαι, ὅτε μηδὲ ἀπολαύειν τῶν ἐπαίνων ἔμελλεν ἀναίσθητος αὐτῶν γενόμενος.

Ἐν ἔτι σοι προσδιηγησάμενος παύσομαι, ὡς ἔχῃς ἐπὶ πολὺ **43** γελᾶν. ἐκεῖνα μὲν γὰρ πάλαι οἶσθα, εὐθὺς ἀκούσας μου ὅτε ἥκων ἀπὸ Συρίας διηγούμην ὡς ἀπὸ Τρῳάδος συμπλεύσαιμι αὐτῷ καὶ τήν τε ἄλλην τὴν ἐν τῷ πλῷ τρυφὴν καὶ τὸ μειράκιον τὸ ὡραῖον ὃ ἔπεισε κυνίζειν ὡς ἔχοι τινὰ καὶ αὐτὸς Ἀλκιβιάδην, καὶ ὡς, ἐπεὶ ταραχθείημεν τῆς νυκτὸς ἐν μέσῳ τῷ Αἰγαίῳ γνόφου καταβάντος καὶ κῦμα παμμέγεθες ἐγείραντος, ἐκώκυε μετὰ τῶν γυναικῶν ὁ θαυμαστὸς καὶ θανάτου κρείττων εἶναι δοκῶν. ἀλλὰ **44** μικρὸν πρὸ τῆς τελευτῆς, πρὸ ἐννέα σχεδόν που ἡμερῶν, πλεῖον, οἶμαι, τοῦ ἱκανοῦ ἐμφαγὼν ἤμεσέν τε τῆς νυκτὸς καὶ ἑάλω πυρετῷ μάλα σφοδρῷ. ταῦτα δέ μοι Ἀλέξανδρος ὁ ἰατρὸς διηγήσατο μετακληθεὶς ὡς ἐπισκοπήσειεν αὐτόν. ἔφη οὖν καταλαβεῖν αὐτὸν χαμαὶ κυλιόμενον καὶ τὸν φλογμὸν οὐ φέροντα καὶ ψυχρὸν αἰτοῦντα πάνυ ἐρωτικῶς, ἑαυτὸν δὲ μὴ δοῦναι. καίτοι εἰπεῖν ἔφη πρὸς αὐτὸν ὡς εἰ πάντως θανάτου δέοιτο, ἥκειν αὐτὸν ἐπὶ τὰς θύρας αὐτόματον, ὥστε καλῶς ἔχειν ἕπεσθαι μηδὲν τοῦ πυρὸς δεόμενον· τὸν δ' αὖ φάναι, Ἀλλ' οὐχ ὁμοίως ἔνδοξος ὁ τρόπος γένοιτ' ἄν, πᾶσιν κοινὸς ὤν.

Ταῦτα μὲν Ἀλέξανδρος. ἐγὼ δὲ οὐδ' αὐτὸς πρὸ πολλῶν ἡμερῶν **45** εἶδον αὐτὸν ἐγκεχρισμένον, ὡς ἀποδακρύσειε τῷ δριμεῖ φαρμάκῳ. ὁρᾷς; οὐ πάνυ τοὺς ἀμβλυωποῦντας ὁ Αἰακὸς παραδέχεται. ὅμοιον ὡς εἴ τις ἐπὶ σταυρὸν ἀναβήσεσθαι μέλλων τὸ ἐν τῷ δακτύλῳ πρόσπταισμα θεραπεύοι. τί σοι δοκεῖ ὁ Δημόκριτος, εἰ ταῦτα εἶδε; κατ' ἀξίαν γελάσαι ἂν ἐπὶ τῷ ἀνδρί; καίτοι πόθεν εἶχεν ἐκεῖνος τοσοῦτον γέλωτα; σὺ δ' οὖν, ὦ φιλότης, γέλα καὶ αὐτός, καὶ μάλιστα ὁπόταν τῶν ἄλλων ἀκούῃς θαυμαζόντων αὐτόν.

He has also appointed some of his companions as his envoys for this purpose, calling them 'messengers from the dead' and 'couriers from the grave'.

[42] Such was the end of the wretched Proteus, a man who, to put it briefly, never fixed his gaze on the truth, but ever said and did everything to win glory and praise from the public, so that he even leapt into fire, though he had no chance of enjoying the resultant applause, being no longer able to hear it!

[43] Before I stop I'll tell you one thing more, so that you can have a good laugh. You've long known the earlier details, having heard them from me immediately after my arrival from Syria, when I described my voyage with him from Alexandria in the Troad, his luxurious life-style en voyage and the handsome lad he'd persuaded to become another Cynic, so that he too could have an Alcibiades, and how when we were panic-stricken in mid-Aegean one night after a storm had come down and raised up tremendous waves, he started wailing with the women, this wonderful man considered superior to death!

[44] Indeed shortly before his death, about nine days or so, having, I suppose, eaten more than he needed, he vomited during the night and was seized by a violent fever. I was told this by Alexander the doctor who had been sent for to look after him. He said he found him rolling on the ground, unable to bear the fever and begging most passionately for cold water, though Alexander didn't give it to him. However he said he told him that, if death was absolutely essential to him, it had come to his doors of its own accord, so that it would be an excellent thing to follow where she led without needing the fire, but he said Proteus' reply was 'But that kind of death would be less glorious; it's shared by all.'

[45] That's what Alexander said and I personally not many days ago saw him smeared with a pungent ointment to make him weep and clear his eyes. Do you see my point? No doubt Aeacus absolutely refuses to admit those with weak sight! It's as if someone about to be crucified were to treat the sore on his toe. What do you think would have been Democritus' reaction if he'd seen this? Wouldn't he have laughed at the fellow with good reason? Yet where could he have found laughter enough? In any case, my friend, you should have a laugh of your own, particularly when you hear everyone else expressing their admiration for Peregrinus.

ΠΕΡΙ ΘΥΣΙΩΝ

Ἃ μὲν γὰρ ἐν ταῖς θυσίαις οἱ μάταιοι πράττουσι καὶ ταῖς 1
ἑορταῖς καὶ προσόδοις τῶν θεῶν καὶ ἃ αἰτοῦσι καὶ ἃ εὔχονται
καὶ ἃ γινώσκουσι περὶ αὐτῶν, οὐκ οἶδα εἴ τις οὕτως κατηφής
ἐστι καὶ λελυπημένος ὅστις οὐ γελάσεται τὴν ἀβελτερίαν ἐπι-
βλέψας τῶν δρωμένων. καὶ πολύ γε, οἶμαι, πρότερον τοῦ γελᾶν
πρὸς ἑαυτὸν ἐξετάσει πότερον εὐσεβεῖς αὐτοὺς χρὴ καλεῖν ἢ
τοὐναντίον θεοῖς ἐχθροὺς καὶ κακοδαίμονας, οἵ γε οὕτω ταπει-
νὸν καὶ ἀγεννὲς τὸ θεῖον ὑπειλήφασιν ὥστε εἶναι ἀνθρώπων ἐν-
δεὲς καὶ κολακευόμενον ἥδεσθαι καὶ ἀγανακτεῖν ἀμελούμενον.

Τὰ γοῦν Αἰτωλικὰ πάθη καὶ τὰς τῶν Καλυδωνίων συμφορὰς
καὶ τοὺς τοσούτους φόνους καὶ τὴν Μελεάγρου διάλυσιν, πάντα
ταῦτα ἔργα φασὶν εἶναι τῆς Ἀρτέμιδος μεμψιμοιρούσης ὅτι
μὴ παρελήφθη πρὸς τὴν θυσίαν ὑπὸ τοῦ Οἰνέως· οὕτως ἄρα
βαθέως καθίκετο αὐτῆς ἡ τῶν ἱερῶν διαμαρτία. καί μοι δοκῶ
ὁρᾶν αὐτὴν ἐν τῷ οὐρανῷ τότε μόνην τῶν ἄλλων θεῶν εἰς Οἰνέως
πεπορευμένων, δεινὰ ποιοῦσαν καὶ σχετλιάζουσαν οἵας ἑορτῆς
ἀπολειφθήσεται.

Τοὺς δ' αὖ Αἰθίοπας καὶ μακαρίους καὶ τρισευδαίμονας εἴποι 2
τις ἄν, εἴ γε ἀπομνημονεύοι τὴν χάριν αὐτοῖς ὁ Ζεὺς ἣν [ἐν ἀρχῇ
τῆς Ὁμήρου ποιήσεως] πρὸς αὐτὸν ἐπεδείξαντο δώδεκα ἑξῆς
ἡμέρας ἑστιάσαντες, καὶ ταῦτα ἐπαγόμενον καὶ τοὺς ἄλλους
θεούς. οὕτως οὐδέν, ὡς ἔοικεν, ἀμισθὶ ποιοῦσιν ὧν ποιοῦσιν,
ἀλλὰ πωλοῦσιν τοῖς ἀνθρώποις τἀγαθά, καὶ ἔνεστι πρίασθαι παρ'
αὐτῶν τὸ μὲν ὑγιαίνειν, εἰ τύχοι, βοϊδίου, τὸ δὲ πλουτεῖν βοῶν
τεττάρων, τὸ δὲ βασιλεύειν ἑκατόμβης, τὸ δὲ σῶον ἐπανελ-
θεῖν ἐξ Ἰλίου ἐς Πύλον ταύρων ἐννέα, καὶ τὸ ἐκ τῆς Αὐλίδος
εἰς Ἴλιον διαπλεῦσαι παρθένου βασιλικῆς. ἡ μὲν γὰρ Ἑκάβη τὸ
μὴ ἁλῶναι τὴν πόλιν τότε ἐπρίατο παρὰ τῆς Ἀθηνᾶς βοῶν
δώδεκα καὶ πέπλου. εἰκάζειν δὲ χρὴ πολλὰ εἶναι ἀλεκτρυόνος
καὶ στεφάνου καὶ λιβανωτοῦ μόνου παρ' αὐτοῖς ὤνια.

Ταῦτά γε, οἶμαι, καὶ ὁ Χρύσης ἐπιστάμενος ἅτε ἱερεὺς ὢν 3
καὶ γέρων καὶ τὰ θεῖα σοφός, ἐπειδὴ ἄπρακτος ἀπῄει παρὰ τοῦ
Ἀγαμέμνονος, ὡς ἂν καὶ προδανείσας τῷ Ἀπόλλωνι τὴν χάριν

ON SACRIFICES

[1] When considering the behaviour of poor fools at their sacrifices, festivals and processions in honour of the gods, the objects of their prayers, their vows and their beliefs about the gods, I don't know if anyone is so doleful and grief-stricken that he won't laugh at the stupidity of what goes on, and I think a much more immediate reaction than laughing will be to wonder whether these men should be called pious or on the contrary sacrilegious wretches in thinking the gods so abject and ignoble as to have any need of men to enjoy being flattered and to be angry when neglected.

At any rate people say the sufferings of the Aetolians, the disasters of the Calydonians, all those killings and the dissolution of Meleager are all the work of Artemis resentful because she wasn't invited to the sacrifice by Oeneus; so deeply, it seems, did she feel about the loss of the sacrificial victims, and I think I can see her on her own in heaven on the occasion when the other gods had gone to the palace of Oeneus, and grumbling and complaining about the fine feast she would miss.

[2] The Ethiopians, on the other hand, one could call fortunate and thrice-blessed, if Zeus should be duly grateful to them for the kindness they showed him in feasting him for twelve days running, and, what's more, when he brought along the other gods as well. So true is it apparently that they do nothing without payment, but *sell* their benefits to mankind, and it's possible to buy from them good health perhaps for a paltry ox, wealth for four oxen, a kingdom for a hecatomb, a safe return from Troy to Pylos for nine bulls and a voyage from Aulis to Troy at the cost of a princess. For at that time Hecuba paid Athena twelve oxen and a robe to save Troy from capture, and one may conjecture that with them many things may be purchased for a cock or a wreath or a mere grain of frankincense.

[3] Chryses too was aware of this, I imagine, since he was a priest, and aged and expert in the ways of the gods. When he left Agamemnon unsuccessful, he remonstrated with Apollo as though the god owed him a

δικαιολογεῖται καὶ ἀπαιτεῖ τὴν ἀμοιβὴν καὶ μόνον οὐκ ὀνειδίζει λέγων, "'Ὦ βέλτιστε Ἄπολλον, ἐγὼ μέν σου τὸν νεὼν τέως ἀστεφάνωτον ὄντα πολλάκις ἐστεφάνωσα, καὶ τοσαῦτά σοι μηρία ταύρων τε καὶ αἰγῶν ἔκαυσα ἐπὶ τῶν βωμῶν, σὺ δὲ ἀμελεῖς μου τοιαῦτα πεπονθότος καὶ παρ' οὐδὲν τίθεσαι τὸν εὐεργέτην;"

Τοιγαροῦν οὕτω κατεδυσώπησεν αὐτὸν ἐκ τῶν λόγων, ὥστε ἁρπασάμενος τὰ τόξα καὶ ἐπὶ τοῦ ναυστάθμου καθίσας ἑαυτὸν κατετόξευσε τῷ λοιμῷ τοὺς Ἀχαιοὺς αὐταῖς ἡμιόνοις καὶ κυσίν. ἐπεὶ δὲ ἅπαξ τοῦ Ἀπόλλωνος ἐμνήσθην, βούλομαι καὶ τὰ 4 ἄλλα εἰπεῖν, ἃ περὶ αὐτοῦ οἱ σοφοὶ τῶν ἀνθρώπων λέγουσιν, οὐχ ὅσα περὶ τοὺς ἔρωτας ἐδυστύχησεν οὐδὲ τοῦ Ὑακίνθου τὸν φόνον οὐδὲ τῆς Δάφνης τὴν ὑπεροψίαν, ἀλλ' ὅτι καὶ καταδικασθεὶς ἐπὶ τῷ τῶν Κυκλώπων θανάτῳ καὶ ἐξοστρακισθεὶς διὰ τοῦτο ἐκ τοῦ οὐρανοῦ, ἐπέμφθη εἰς τὴν γῆν ἀνθρωπίνῃ χρησόμενος τῇ τύχῃ· ὅτε δὴ καὶ ἐθήτευσεν ἐν Θετταλίᾳ παρὰ Ἀδμήτῳ καὶ ἐν Φρυγίᾳ παρὰ Λαομέδοντι, παρὰ τούτῳ μέν γε οὐ μόνος ἀλλὰ μετὰ τοῦ Ποσειδῶνος, ἀμφότεροι πλινθεύοντες ὑπ' ἀπορίας καὶ ἐργαζόμενοι ἐς τὸ τεῖχος· καὶ οὐδὲ ἐντελῆ τὸν μισθὸν ἐκομίσαντο παρὰ τοῦ Φρυγός, ἀλλὰ προσῶφλεν αὐτοῖς πλέον ἢ τριάκοντα, φασί, δραχμὰς Τρωϊκάς.

Ἢ γὰρ οὐ ταῦτα σεμνολογοῦσιν οἱ ποιηταὶ περὶ τῶν θεῶν καὶ 5 πολὺ τούτων μιαρώτερα περί τε Ἡφαίστου καὶ Προμηθέως καὶ Κρόνου καὶ Ῥέας καὶ σχεδὸν ὅλης τῆς τοῦ Διὸς οἰκίας; καὶ ταῦτα παρακαλέσαντες τὰς Μούσας συνῳδοὺς ἐν ἀρχῇ τῶν ἐπῶν, ὑφ' ὧν δὴ ἔνθεοι γενόμενοι, ὡς τὸ εἰκός, ᾄδουσιν ὡς ὁ μὲν Κρόνος ἐπειδὴ τάχιστα ἐξέτεμε τὸν πατέρα τὸν Οὐρανόν, ἐβασίλευσέν τε ἐν αὐτῷ καὶ τὰ τέκνα κατήσθιεν ὥσπερ ὁ Ἀργεῖος Θυέστης ὕστερον· ὁ δὲ Ζεὺς κλαπεὶς ὑπὸ τῆς Ῥέας ὑποβαλομένης τὸν λίθον ἐς τὴν Κρήτην ἐκτεθεὶς ὑπὸ αἰγὸς ἀνετράφη καθάπερ ὁ Τήλεφος ὑπὸ ἐλάφου καὶ ὁ Πέρσης Κῦρος ὁ πρότερος ὑπὸ τῆς κυνός, εἶτ' ἐξελάσας τὸν πατέρα καὶ εἰς τὸ δεσμωτήριον καταβαλὼν αὐτὸς ἔσχε τὴν ἀρχήν· ἔγημεν δὲ πολλὰς μὲν καὶ ἄλλας, ὑστάτην δὲ τὴν ἀδελφὴν κατὰ τοὺς Περσῶν καὶ Ἀσσυρίων νόμους· ἐρωτικὸς δὲ ὢν καὶ ἐς τὰ ἀφροδίσια κεχυμένος ῥᾳδίως ἐνέπλησε παίδων τὸν οὐρανόν, τοὺς μὲν ἐξ ὁμοτίμων ποιησάμενος, ἐνίους δὲ καὶ νόθους ἐκ τοῦ θνητοῦ καὶ ἐπιγείου γένους, ἄρτι μὲν ὁ γεννάδας γενόμενος χρυσός, ἄρτι δὲ ταῦρος

favour, demanded recompense and went close to telling him off, saying, 'Most worthy Apollo, though I have often garlanded your temple when it had no garlands and burned you all those thigh-pieces of bulls and goats on your altars, do you nevertheless neglect me in my sufferings and have no regard for your benefactor?'

Consequently he so shamed Apollo with his words that he seized his bow and arrows, settled himself where the ships were beached and shot the Achaeans down with pestilence, yes, and their mules and dogs too.

[4] And now I've mentioned Apollo, I want to tell you the other things the sages of mankind say about him; I don't mean all his misfortunes in love or how he killed Hyacinthus or was scorned by Daphne, but how he was tried and condemned for killing the Cyclopes and ostracised from heaven for that, and sent to earth to experience the human lot. At that time he became a serf to Admetus in Thessaly and to Laomedon in Phrygia. He wasn't alone in serving Laomedon but had the company of Poseidon, both of them being forced by poverty to make bricks and work them into the wall. Moreover they weren't paid in full by the Phrygian, but people say he owed them more than thirty Trojan drachmas extra.

[5] For aren't the poets serious in saying these things about the gods in general and much viler things than these about Hephaestus, Prometheus, Cronus, Rhea and almost the entire household of Zeus? Furthermore at the start of their poems they call on the Muses to share in their song, and then, inspired no doubt by them, they sing how Cronus immediately on castrating his father Uranus became king in his place and started eating his own children like Thyestes of Argos and how Zeus was stolen away by Rhea when she substituted the stone, and how he was exposed in Crete and brought up by a nanny-goat as Telephus was by a doe and the Persian Cyrus the Elder by the bitch, and how Zeus drove out his father, cast him into prison and took over the power for himself. He took many wives including finally his own sister, as is customary with the Persians and Assyrians. Being amorous and wholly committed to the pursuit of love, he had no trouble in filling heaven with children, producing some from his equals in station, and others as bastards from mortal women on earth, for the noble fellow turned now into gold, and now into a bull or swan or eagle, and in fact proved more changeable even

ἢ κύκνος ἢ ἀετός, καὶ ὅλως ποικιλώτερος αὐτοῦ Πρωτέως· μόνην δὲ τὴν Ἀθηνᾶν ἔφυσεν ἐκ τῆς ἑαυτοῦ κεφαλῆς ὑπ' αὐτὸν ἀτεχνῶς τὸν ἐγκέφαλον συλλαβών· τὸν μὲν γὰρ Διόνυσον ἡμιτελῆ, φασίν, ἐκ τῆς μητρὸς ἔτι καιομένης ἁρπάσας ἐν τῷ μηρῷ φέρων κατώρυξε κᾆτα ἐξέτεμεν τῆς ὠδῖνος ἐνστάσης.

Ὅμοια δὲ τούτοις καὶ περὶ τῆς Ἥρας ᾄδουσιν, ἄνευ τῆς πρὸς 6 τὸν ἄνδρα ὁμιλίας ὑπηνέμιον αὐτὴν παῖδα γεννῆσαι τὸν Ἥφαιστον, οὐ μάλα εὐτυχῆ τοῦτον, ἀλλὰ βάναυσον καὶ χαλκέα καὶ πυρίτην, ἐν καπνῷ τὸ πᾶν βιοῦντα καὶ σπινθήρων ἀνάπλεων οἷα δὴ καμινευτήν, καὶ οὐδὲ ἄρτιον τὼ πόδε· χωλευθῆναι γὰρ αὐτὸν ἀπὸ τοῦ πτώματος, ὁπότε ἐρρίφη ὑπὸ τοῦ Διὸς ἐξ οὐρανοῦ, καὶ εἴ γε μὴ οἱ Λήμνιοι καλῶς ποιοῦντες ἔτι φερόμενον αὐτὸν ὑπεδέξαντο, κἂν ἐτεθνήκει ἂν ἡμῖν ὁ Ἥφαιστος ὥσπερ ὁ Ἀστυάναξ ἀπὸ τοῦ πύργου καταπεσών.

Καίτοι τὰ μὲν Ἡφαίστου μέτρια· τὸν δὲ Προμηθέα τίς οὐκ οἶδεν οἷα ἔπαθεν, διότι καθ' ὑπερβολὴν φιλάνθρωπος ἦν; καὶ γὰρ αὖ καὶ τοῦτον ἐς τὴν Σκυθίαν ἀγαγὼν ὁ Ζεὺς ἀνεσταύρωσεν ἐπὶ τοῦ Καυκάσου, τὸν ἀετὸν αὐτῷ παρακαταστήσας τὸ ἧπαρ ὁσημέραι κολάψοντα. οὗτος μὲν οὖν ἐξετέλεσε τὴν καταδίκην. ἡ 7 Ῥέα δέ—χρὴ γὰρ ἴσως καὶ ταῦτα εἰπεῖν—πῶς οὐκ ἀσχημονεῖ καὶ δεινὰ ποιεῖ, γραῦς μὲν ἤδη καὶ ἔξωρος οὖσα καὶ τοσούτων μήτηρ θεῶν, παιδεραστοῦσα δὲ ἔτι καὶ ζηλοτυποῦσα καὶ τὸν Ἄττιν ἐπὶ τῶν λεόντων περιφέρουσα, καὶ ταῦτα μηκέτι χρήσιμον εἶναι δυνάμενον; ὥστε πῶς ἂν ἔτι μέμφοιτό τις ἢ τῇ Ἀφροδίτῃ ὅτι μοιχεύεται, ἢ τὴν Σελήνην πρὸς τὸν Ἐνδυμίωνα κατιοῦσαν πολλάκις ἐκ μέσης τῆς ὁδοῦ;

Φέρε δὲ ἤδη τούτων ἀφέμενοι τῶν λόγων εἰς αὐτὸν ἀνέλθωμεν 8 τὸν οὐρανὸν ποιητικῶς ἀναπτάμενοι κατὰ τὴν αὐτὴν Ὁμήρῳ καὶ Ἡσιόδῳ ὁδὸν καὶ θεασώμεθα ὅπως διακεκόσμηται τὰ ἄνω. καὶ ὅτι μὲν χαλκοῦς ἐστιν τὰ ἔξω, καὶ πρὸ ἡμῶν τοῦ Ὁμήρου λέγοντος ἠκούσαμεν· ὑπερβάντι δὲ καὶ ἀνακύψαντι μικρὸν ἐς τὸ ἄνω καὶ ἀτεχνῶς ἐπὶ τοῦ νώτου γενομένῳ φῶς τε λαμπρότερον φαίνεται καὶ ἥλιος καθαρώτερος καὶ ἄστρα διαυγέστερα καὶ χρυσοῦν τὸ δάπεδον καὶ τὸ πᾶν ἡμέρα. εἰσιόντι δὲ πρῶτα μὲν οἰκοῦσιν αἱ Ὧραι· πυλωροῦσι γάρ· ἔπειτα ἡ Ἶρις καὶ ὁ Ἑρμῆς ὄντες ὑπηρέται καὶ ἀγγελιαφόροι τοῦ Διός, ἑξῆς δὲ τοῦ Ἡφαίστου τὸ χαλκεῖον ἀνάμεστον ἁπάσης τέχνης, μετὰ δὲ αἱ τῶν θεῶν

than Proteus; but Athene was unique, for he produced her out of his own head, after literally conceiving her in his brain; for Dionysus, they say, was already half-formed, when he snatched him out of his mother while she was still on fire, carried him buried deep in his thigh, and then cut him out when the pangs of labour started.

[6] They have similar songs to sing about Hera too, how without intercourse with a man she produced her son Hephaestus from the wind, no very fortunate child him, but a mere tradesman, a smith working with fire, spending all his life in smoke and grimy with soot from working at his forge, and not even sound on his feet, for he was lamed by his fall, when he was thrown out of heaven by Zeus, and if the Lemnians, bless them, hadn't caught him while still falling, we'd have had Hephaestus killed like Astyanax when he was thrown from the tower.

However Hephaestus' lot was tolerable compared with that of Prometheus; everyone knows what happened to *him* for being too friendly to mankind: for he was another victim of Zeus, who took him to Scythia and crucified him on Caucasus, stationing an eagle alongside him to peck away at his liver every day. [7] However Prometheus has completed his sentence, but what of Rhea, for perhaps I should mention this too? Isn't her behaviour shameful and disgraceful, for, although already old and long past her prime and the mother of so many gods, she still goes cradle-snatching, shows jealousy and carries Attis around with her on her lions, even though he can no longer be any good to her? After that how could one blame Aphrodite for committing adultery or Selene for her frequent descents from her orbit to visit Endymion?

[8] Come now, let us leave this topic and ascend to heaven on the wings of poetry by the same route as Homer and Hesiod and observe how things up there are ordered. That heaven is bronze on the outside we've heard from Homer who said so long ago. But if you climb up and peep a little way over the top and actually get on the back of heaven, the light seems brighter, the sun clearer and the stars more radiant, the ground is golden and everywhere is bright daylight. On entering you find first the home of the Hours, for they are the door-keepers; then you have Iris and Hermes, for they are servants and messengers of Zeus, and next comes Hephaestus' smithy full of the evidence of his trade, and after that the

οἰκίαι καὶ τοῦ Διὸς τὰ βασίλεια, ταῦτα πάντα περικαλλῆ τοῦ
Ἡφαίστου κατασκευάσαντος. "οἱ δὲ θεοὶ πὰρ Ζηνὶ καθήμενοι"— 9
πρέπει γάρ, οἶμαι, ἄνω ὄντα μεγαληγορεῖν—ἀποσκοποῦσιν ἐς
τὴν γῆν καὶ πάντῃ περιβλέπουσιν ἐπικύπτοντες εἴ ποθεν ὄψονται
πῦρ ἀναπτόμενον ἢ ἀναφερομένην κνῖσαν "ἑλισσομένην περὶ
καπνῷ". κἂν μὲν θύῃ τις, εὐωχοῦνται πάντες ἐπικεχηνότες
τῷ καπνῷ καὶ τὸ αἷμα πίνοντες τοῖς βωμοῖς προσχεόμενον
ὥσπερ αἱ μυῖαι· ἢν δὲ οἰκοσιτῶσιν, νέκταρ καὶ ἀμβροσία τὸ
δεῖπνον. πάλαι μὲν οὖν καὶ ἄνθρωποι συνειστιῶντο καὶ συνέπινον
αὐτοῖς, ὁ Ἰξίων καὶ ὁ Τάνταλος· ἐπεὶ δὲ ἦσαν ὑβρισταὶ καὶ
λάλοι, ἐκεῖνοι μὲν ἔτι νῦν κολάζονται, ἄβατος δὲ τῷ θνητῷ γένει
καὶ ἀπόρρητος ὁ οὐρανός.

Τοιοῦτος ὁ βίος τῶν θεῶν. τοιγαροῦν καὶ οἱ ἄνθρωποι συνῳδὰ 10
τούτοις καὶ ἀκόλουθα περὶ τὰς θρησκείας ἐπιτηδεύουσιν. καὶ
πρῶτον μὲν ὕλας ἀπετέμοντο καὶ ὄρη ἀνέθεσαν καὶ ὄρνεα καθιέρω-
σαν καὶ φυτὰ ἐπεφήμισαν ἑκάστῳ θεῷ. μετὰ δὲ νειμάμενοι κατὰ
ἔθνη σέβουσι καὶ πολίτας αὐτῶν ἀποφαίνουσιν, ὁ μὲν Δελφὸς
τὸν Ἀπόλλω καὶ ὁ Δήλιος, ὁ δὲ Ἀθηναῖος τὴν Ἀθηνᾶν—μαρτυρεῖ-
ται γοῦν τὴν οἰκειότητα τῷ ὀνόματι—καὶ τὴν Ἥραν ὁ Ἀργεῖος
καὶ ὁ Μυγδόνιος τὴν Ῥέαν καὶ τὴν Ἀφροδίτην ὁ Πάφιος. οἱ δ᾽
αὖ Κρῆτες οὐ γενέσθαι παρ᾽ αὐτοῖς οὐδὲ τραφῆναι μόνον τὸν
Δία λέγουσιν, ἀλλὰ καὶ τάφον αὐτοῦ δεικνύουσιν· καὶ ἡμεῖς
ἄρα τοσοῦτον ἠπατήμεθα χρόνον οἰόμενοι τὸν Δία βρονταν τε
καὶ ὕειν καὶ τὰ ἄλλα πάντα ἐπιτελεῖν, ὁ δὲ ἐλελήθει πάλαι τε-
θνεὼς παρὰ Κρησὶ τεθαμμένος.

Ἔπειτα δὲ ναοὺς ἐγείραντες ἵνα αὐτοῖς μὴ ἄοικοι μηδὲ ἀν- 11
έστιοι δῆθεν ὦσιν, εἰκόνας αὐτοῖς ἀπεικάζουσιν παρακαλέσαντες
ἢ Πραξιτέλην ἢ Πολύκλειτον ἢ Φειδίαν, οἱ δὲ οὐκ οἶδ᾽ ὅπου
ἰδόντες ἀναπλάττουσι γενειήτην μὲν τὸν Δία, παῖδα δὲ ἐς ἀεὶ τὸν
Ἀπόλλωνα καὶ τὸν Ἑρμῆν ὑπηνήτην καὶ τὸν Ποσειδῶνα κυανο-
χαίτην καὶ γλαυκῶπιν τὴν Ἀθηνᾶν. ὅμως δ᾽ οὖν οἱ παριόντες
ἐς τὸν νεὼν οὔτε τὸν ἐξ Ἰνδῶν ἐλέφαντα ἔτι οἴονται ὁρᾶν οὔτε
τὸ ἐκ τῆς Θρᾴκης μεταλλευθὲν χρυσίον ἀλλ᾽ αὐτὸν τὸν Κρόνου
καὶ Ῥέας, ἐς τὴν γῆν ὑπὸ Φειδίου μετῳκισμένον καὶ τὴν
Πισαίων ἐρημίαν ἐπισκοπεῖν κεκελευσμένον καὶ ἀγαπῶντα εἰ
διὰ πέντε ὅλων ἐτῶν θύσει τις αὐτῷ πάρεργον Ὀλυμπίων.

Θέμενοι δὲ βωμοὺς καὶ προρρήσεις καὶ περιρραντήρια προσ- 12

houses of the gods and the palace of Zeus, all of outstanding beauty, being the handiwork of Hephaestus.

[9] 'And the gods, by side of Zeus ensconced, – for majestic language is appropriate, I think, since I'm up above – fix their gaze on the earth and look round in every direction in the hope of seeing somewhere fire being lighted or the savour of sacrifice rising 'a-twirling round the smoke'. If anyone sacrifices, they all have a feast, open-mouthed, eager for the smoke, and drinking the blood poured by the altars, behaving like flies. But if they eat at home, they have nectar and ambrosia for dinner. In olden times, moreover, men would feast and drink with them – I refer to Ixion and Tantalus – but because they behaved outrageously and talked too much, they are still being punished to this day, and heaven is out of bounds and forbidden to all mortals.

[10] That's how the gods live. As a result men in their worship follow practices in harmony and keeping with all that. At first they cut off woods, sanctified mountains, consecrated birds and dedicated plants to each deity, and afterwards they shared the gods out between their various peoples, worshipping them and making them their own fellow-citizens, the Delphians and Delians taking Apollo, the Athenians Athene, using her name to prove the relationship, the Argives Hera, the Mygdonians Rhea and the Paphians Aphrodite. Furthermore the Cretans not only claim Zeus was born and brought up amongst them but even show you his burial place, and we, it appears, have been deluded all this time in thinking he thunders and rains and performs all the other functions, whereas all the time unknown to us he died and was buried in Crete long ago.

[11] Then they raised temples so as not to have them without hearth or home, and make idols in their image, sending for a Praxiteles or Polyclitus or Phidias, who must have seen the gods somewhere, for they fashion Zeus with a beard, Apollo as having everlasting youth, Hermes with the first down on his cheek, Poseidon with sea-blue hair and Athene with grey eyes. Yet people entering the temples no longer think they see ivory from India or gold mined from Thrace but the son of Cronus and Rhea in person, transferred to a home on earth by Phidias, told to watch the deserted regions of Pisa, and content to have men sacrificing to him once every five years, as a minor concomitant of the Olympic Games.

[12] Once they have instituted altars, proclamations and lustral areas,

ἄγουσι τὰς θυσίας, βοῦν μὲν ἀροτῆρα ὁ γεωργός, ἄρνα δὲ ὁ ποιμὴν καὶ αἶγα ὁ αἰπόλος, ὁ δέ τις λιβανωτὸν ἢ πόπανον, ὁ δὲ πένης ἱλάσατο τὸν θεὸν κύσας μόνον τὴν ἑαυτοῦ δεξιάν. ἀλλ᾽ οἵ γε θύοντες—ἐπ᾽ ἐκείνους γὰρ ἐπάνειμι—στεφανώσαντες τὸ ζῷον καὶ πολύ γε πρότερον ἐξετάσαντες εἰ ἐντελὲς εἴη, ἵνα μηδὲ τῶν ἀχρήστων τι κατασφάττωσιν, προσάγουσι τῷ βωμῷ καὶ φονεύουσιν ἐν ὀφθαλμοῖς τοῦ θεοῦ γοερόν τι μυκώμενον καὶ ὡς τὸ εἰκὸς εὐφημοῦν καὶ ἡμίφωνον ἤδη τῇ θυσίᾳ ἐπαυλοῦν. τίς οὐκ ἂν εἰκάσειεν ἥδεσθαι ταῦτα ὁρῶντας τοὺς θεούς; καὶ τὸ μὲν **13** πρόγραμμά φησι μὴ παριέναι εἰς τὸ εἴσω τῶν περιρραντηρίων ὅστις μὴ καθαρός ἐστιν τὰς χεῖρας· ὁ δὲ ἱερεὺς αὐτὸς ἕστηκεν ᾑμαγμένος καὶ ὥσπερ ὁ Κύκλωψ ἐκεῖνος ἀνατέμνων καὶ τὰ ἔγκατα ἐξαιρῶν καὶ καρδιουλκῶν καὶ τὸ αἷμα τῷ βωμῷ περιχέων καὶ τί γὰρ οὐκ εὐσεβὲς ἐπιτελῶν; ἐπὶ πᾶσι δὲ πῦρ ἀνακαύσας ἐπέθηκεν αὐτῇ δορᾷ τὴν αἶγα καὶ αὐτοῖς ἐρίοις τὸ πρόβατον· ἡ δὲ κνῖσα θεσπέσιος καὶ ἱεροπρεπὴς χωρεῖ ἄνω καὶ ἐς αὐτὸν τὸν οὐρανὸν ἠρέμα διασκίδναται.

Ὁ μέν γε Σκύθης πάσας τὰς θυσίας ἀφεὶς καὶ ἡγησάμενος ταπεινὰς αὐτοὺς τοὺς ἀνθρώπους τῇ Ἀρτέμιδι παρίστησιν καὶ οὕτως ποιῶν ἀρέσκει τὴν θεόν.

Ταῦτα μὲν δὴ ἴσως μέτρια καὶ τὰ ἀπὸ Ἀσσυρίων γιγνόμενα καὶ **14** τὰ ἀπὸ Λυδῶν ἢ Φρυγῶν, ἢν δ᾽ ἐς τὴν Αἴγυπτον ἔλθῃς, τότε δὴ τότε ὄψει πολλὰ τὰ σεμνὰ καὶ ὡς ἀληθῶς ἄξια τοῦ οὐρανοῦ, κριοπρόσωπον μὲν τὸν Δία, κυνοπρόσωπον δὲ τὸν βέλτιστον Ἑρμῆν καὶ τὸν Πᾶνα ὅλον τράγον καὶ ἶβίν τινα καὶ κροκόδειλον ἕτερον καὶ πίθηκον.

εἰ δ᾽ ἐθέλεις καὶ ταῦτα δαήμεναι, ὄφρ᾽ ἐῢ εἰδῇς,

ἀκούσῃ πολλῶν σοφιστῶν καὶ γραμματέων καὶ προφητῶν ἐξυρημένων διηγουμένων—πρότερον δέ, φησὶν ὁ λόγος, θύρας δ᾽ ἐπίθεσθε βέβηλοι—ὡς ἄρα ὑπὸ τὸν πόλεμον καὶ τῶν γιγάντων τὴν ἐπανάστασιν οἱ θεοὶ φοβηθέντες ἧκον ἐς τὴν Αἴγυπτον ὡς δὴ ἐνταῦθα λησόμενοι τοὺς πολεμίους· εἶθ᾽ ὁ μὲν αὐτῶν ὑπέδυ τράγον, ὁ δὲ κριὸν ὑπὸ τοῦ δέους, ὁ δὲ θηρίον ἢ ὄρνεον· διὸ δὴ εἰσέτι καὶ νῦν φυλάττεσθαι τὰς τότε μορφὰς τοῖς θεοῖς. ταῦτα γὰρ ἀμέλει ἐν τοῖς ἀδύτοις ἀπόκειται γραφέντα πλεῖον ἢ πρὸ ἐτῶν μυρίων.

they bring their sacrifices, the farmer an ox from the plough, the shepherd a lamb, the goatherd a goat, someone else frankincense or a sacrificial cake, whereas the poor man ever appeases the god by merely kissing his own right hand. But sacrificers – for I shall revert to them – after garlanding the victim and having examined it much earlier to see it's unblemished, in case they sacrifice something useless, bring it to the altar and slaughter it before the eyes of the god, while it lows piteously, producing in all probability sounds of good omen and already using muted tones to harmonise with the sacrifice. Who wouldn't surmise that the gods enjoy seeing all this?

[13] Though the official notice forbids anyone with unclean hands from entering the lustral area, the priest himself stands covered in blood and, like that Cyclops, cutting up the victim, plucking out the entrails, pulling out the heart and performing every conceivable pious rite. To cap it all he kindles a fire on which he puts the goat, skin and all, and the sheep still in its fleece; but the savour rises up sanctified and hallowed and gently spreads to heaven itself.

The Scythians, however, reject all sacrifices of beasts, thinking them paltry; they actually offer human sacrifices to Artemis and by so doing please the goddess.

[14] Perhaps one can stomach all that and also the practices of the Assyrians, Lydians or Phrygians, but if you go to Egypt, then's the time you'll really see much that's hallowed and really worthy of heaven, Zeus with the face of a ram, Hermes, bless him, with a dog's face, Pan a goat all over, and other gods in the ibis, crocodile and ape.

'But if thou fain would learn of this to know it well',
you'll hear many sages, scribes and shaven prophets expounding it all; but first, as the saying has it, 'Shut your doors, ye uninitiate'. They tell how during the war and the revolt of the Giants the gods were panic stricken and came to Egypt, hoping there to escape detection from their foes. It was then that through fear one of them took the appearance of a goat, another of a ram, and another that of a beast or a bird. That's why, according to them, the shapes of that time are retained for the gods till this day. All this of course was written down more than 10,000 years ago and is preserved in their sanctuaries.

Αἱ δὲ θυσίαι καὶ παρ' ἐκείνοις αἱ αὐταί, πλὴν ὅτι πενθοῦσι τὸ 15
ἱερεῖον καὶ κόπτονται περιστάντες ἤδη πεφονευμένον. οἱ δὲ
καὶ θάπτουσι μόνον ἀποσφάξαντες. ὁ μὲν γὰρ Ἄπις, ὁ μέγιστος
αὐτοῖς θεός, ἐὰν ἀποθάνῃ, τίς οὕτω περὶ πολλοῦ ποιεῖται τὴν
κόμην ὅστις οὐκ ἀπεξύρησεν καὶ ψιλὸν ἐπὶ τῆς κεφαλῆς τὸ πένθος
ἐπεδείξατο, κἂν τὸν Νίσου ἔχῃ πλόκαμον τὸν πορφυροῦν; ἔστι δὲ
ὁ Ἄπις ἐξ ἀγέλης θεός, ἐπὶ τῷ προτέρῳ χειροτονούμενος ὡς
πολὺ καλλίων καὶ σεμνότερος τῶν ἰδιωτῶν βοῶν.

Ταῦτα οὕτω γιγνόμενα καὶ ὑπὸ τῶν πολλῶν πιστευόμενα
δεῖσθαί μοι δοκεῖ τοῦ μὲν ἐπιτιμήσοντος οὐδενός, Ἡρακλείτου
δέ τινος ἢ Δημοκρίτου, τοῦ μὲν γελασομένου τὴν ἄγνοιαν αὐτῶν,
τοῦ δὲ τὴν ἄνοιαν ὀδυρουμένου.

[15] Sacrifices take the same form among the Egyptians as with us, except that they mourn the victim, standing round it once it's been slaughtered and beating their breasts. But some Egyptians actually bury the victim, after merely cutting its throat. For if Apis, their greatest god, is killed, who values his own hair so highly that he doesn't shave it off and make a show of his naked grief on the top of his head, even if he has the purple lock of Nisus? But Apis is a god chosen from the common herd to replace the previous Apis, as being far more handsome and venerable than the ordinary cattle.

These practices and general beliefs don't seem to me to need anyone to criticise them, but rather a Heraclitus or a Democritus, one to laugh at people's ignorance, the other to lament their folly.

ΖΕΥΞΙΣ Η ΑΝΤΙΟΧΟΣ

Ἔναγχος ἐγὼ μὲν ὑμῖν δείξας τὸν λόγον ἀπήειν οἴκαδε, προσιόν- **1**
τες δέ μοι τῶν ἀκηκοότων πολλοί (κωλύει γὰρ οὐδέν, οἶμαι, καὶ
τὰ τοιαῦτα πρὸς φίλους ἤδη ὄντας ὑμᾶς λέγειν)—προσιόντες οὖν
ἐδεξιοῦντο καὶ θαυμάζουσιν ἐῴκεσαν. ἐπὶ πολὺ γοῦν παρομαρτοῦν-
τες ἄλλος ἄλλοθεν ἐβόων καὶ ἐπῄνουν ἄχρι τοῦ καὶ ἐρυθριᾶν με,
μὴ ἄρα πάμπολυ τῆς ἀξίας τῶν ἐπαίνων ἀπολειποίμην. τὸ δ᾽ οὖν
κεφάλαιον αὐτοῖς τοῦτο ἦν, καὶ πάντες ἓν καὶ τὸ αὐτὸ ἐπεσημαί-
νοντο, τὴν γνώμην τῶν συγγραμμάτων ξένην οὖσαν καὶ πολὺν
ἐν αὐτῇ τὸν νεωτερισμόν. μᾶλλον δὲ αὐτὰ εἰπεῖν ἄμεινον ἅπερ
ἐκεῖνοι ἀπεφθέγγοντο· " Ὦ τῆς καινότητος." " Ἡράκλεις, τῆς
παραδοξολογίας." "Εὐμήχανος ἄνθρωπος." "Οὐδὲν ἄν τις εἴποι
τῆς ἐπινοίας νεαρώτερον." οἱ μὲν τοιαῦτα πολλὰ ἔλεγον, ὡς ἐκε-
κίνηντο δηλαδὴ ὑπὸ τῆς ἀκροάσεως. ἢ τίνα γὰρ αἰτίαν εἶχον
ψεύδεσθαι καὶ κολακεύειν τὰ τοιαῦτα ξένον ἄνθρωπον, οὐ πάνυ
πολλῆς αὐτοῖς φροντίδος ἄξιον τὰ ἄλλα;

Πλὴν ἐμέ γε (εἰρήσεται γάρ) οὐ μετρίως ἠνία ὁ ἔπαινος αὐτῶν, **2**
καὶ ἐπειδή ποτε ἀπελθόντων κατ᾽ ἐμαυτὸν ἐγενόμην ἐκεῖνα
ἐνενόουν· οὐκοῦν τοῦτο μόνον χάριεν τοῖς λόγοις ἔνεστιν, ὅτι μὴ
συνήθη μηδὲ κατὰ τὸ κοινὸν βαδίζει τοῖς ἄλλοις, ὀνομάτων δὲ
ἄρα καλῶν ἐν αὐτοῖς καὶ πρὸς τὸν ἀρχαῖον κανόνα συγκειμένων
ἢ νοῦ ὀξέος ἢ περινοίας τινὸς ἢ χάριτος Ἀττικῆς ἢ ἁρμονίας ἢ
τέχνης τῆς ἐφ᾽ ἅπασι, τούτων δὲ πόρρω ἴσως τοὐμόν. οὐ γὰρ ἄν,
παρέντες αὐτὰ ἐκεῖνα, ἐπῄνουν μόνον τὸ καινὸν τῆς προαιρέσεως
καὶ ξενίζον. ἐγὼ δὲ ὁ μάταιος ᾤμην, ὁπότε ἀναπηδῶντες ἐπαι-
νοῖεν, τάχα μέν τι καὶ αὐτῷ τούτῳ προάγεσθαι αὐτούς· ἀληθὲς
γὰρ εἶναι τὸ τοῦ Ὁμήρου, καὶ τὴν νέαν ᾠδὴν κεχαρισμένην ὑπάρ-
χειν τοῖς ἀκούουσιν· οὐ μὴν τοσοῦτόν γε οὔτε ὅλον τῇ καινότητι
νέμειν ἠξίουν, ἀλλὰ τὴν μὲν ὥσπερ ἐν προσθήκης μοίρᾳ συνεπι-
κοσμεῖν καὶ πρὸς τὸν ἔπαινον συντελεῖν καὶ αὐτήν, τὰ δὲ τῷ
ὄντι ἐπαινούμενα καὶ ὑπὸ τῶν ἀκουόντων εὐφημούμενα ἐκεῖνα εἶναι. ὥστε οὐ μετρίως ἐπήρμην καὶ ἐκινδύνευον πιστεύειν αὐτοῖς

ZEUXIS or ANTIOCHUS

[1] The other day I was starting off for home after putting on one of my literary shows for you, when many of my audience came up to me – for I don't think anything stops me telling you this now that we're friends. Well, they came up to me to greet me, apparently full of admiration. At any rate they escorted me a long way shouting out their praises from all sides till I actually blushed for fear that I might fall a long way short of deserving these compliments. They made one main point and all praised one and the same thing, the unusual thought behind my compositions and the great innovations they contained; or rather it would be better to tell you their actual expressions, 'Oh, what novelty!', 'By Heracles, what unexpected things he says!' 'How ingenious the fellow is!' 'His freshness of thought is beyond all telling!' They said many things like that, for they had clearly been excited by what they'd heard. For what reason could they have for lies and such flattery of a stranger and someone otherwise deserving little consideration by them?

[2] For my part, however, – for I *will* say it – I was extremely vexed by their praises and when they'd finally gone and I was on my own, this was what I thought to myself: 'So the only attractive thing about my discourses is that they're unusual and avoid the beaten tracks, but when it comes to fine language composed according to the good old rules, intellectual sharpness and thoughtfulness, Attic grace, co-ordination or overall craftsmanship, my work is far removed from any of these! Otherwise they wouldn't pass over these particular features and praise only the novelty and strangeness of my undertaking, whereas I, poor fool, thought that when they leapt up in applause, they were perhaps attracted by these particular features, what Homer said being true and it's the new song that finds favour with an audience. I didn't think I should attribute so much or indeed all of my popularity to my novelty, but that that was by way of an adjunct helping to embellish my work and to elicit the compliments, but that the qualities really being praised and lauded by my audience were those I've mentioned.'

So I had been elated beyond all bounds and in danger of believing

ἕνα καὶ μόνον ἐν τοῖς Ἕλλησιν λέγουσι καὶ τὰ τοιαῦτα. τὸ δὲ κατὰ
τὴν παροιμίαν ἄνθρακες ἡμῶν ὁ θησαυρὸς ἦσαν, καὶ ὀλίγου δέω
θαυματοποιοῦ τινος ἔπαινον ἐπαινεῖσθαι πρὸς αὐτῶν.

Ἐθέλω γοῦν ὑμῖν καὶ τὸ τοῦ γραφέως διηγήσασθαι. ὁ Ζεῦ- 3
ξις ἐκεῖνος ἄριστος γραφέων γενόμενος τὰ δημώδη καὶ τὰ κοινὰ
ταῦτα οὐκ ἔγραφεν, ἢ ὅσα πάνυ ὀλίγα, ἥρωας ἢ θεοὺς ἢ πολέμους,
ἀεὶ δὲ καινοποιεῖν ἐπειρᾶτο καί τι ἀλλόκοτον ἂν καὶ ξένον ἐπινο-
ήσας ἐπ᾽ ἐκείνῳ τὴν ἀκρίβειαν τῆς τέχνης ἐπεδείκνυτο. ἐν δὲ τοῖς
ἄλλοις τολμήμασι καὶ θήλειαν Ἱπποκένταυρον ὁ Ζεῦξις αὐτὸς
ἐποίησεν, ἀνατρέφουσάν γε προσέτι παιδίῳ Ἱπποκεντaύρῳ δι-
δύμῳ κομιδῇ νηπίῳ. τῆς εἰκόνος ταύτης ἀντίγραφός ἐστι νῦν
Ἀθήνησι πρὸς αὐτὴν ἐκείνην ἀκριβεῖ τῇ στάθμῃ μετενηνεγμέ-
νη. τὸ ἀρχέτυπον δὲ αὐτὸ Σύλλας ὁ Ῥωμαίων στρατηγὸς ἐλέγετο
μετὰ τῶν ἄλλων εἰς Ἰταλίαν πεπομφέναι, εἶτα περὶ Μαλέαν οἶμαι καταδύσης τῆς ὁλκάδος ἀπολέσθαι ἅπαντα καὶ τὴν γραφήν.
πλὴν ἀλλὰ τήν γε εἰκόνα τῆς εἰκόνος εἶδον, καὶ αὐτὸς ὑμῖν ὡς ἂν
οἷός τε ὦ δείξω τῷ λόγῳ, οὐ μὰ τὸν Δία γραφικός τις ὤν, ἀλλὰ
πάνυ μέμνημαι οὐ πρὸ πολλοῦ ἰδὼν ἔν τινος τῶν γραφέων Ἀθήνησι. καὶ τὸ ὑπερθαυμάσαι τότε τὴν τέχνην τάχ᾽ ἄν μοι καὶ νῦν
πρὸς τὸ σαφέστερον δηλῶσαι συναγωνίσαιτο.

Ἐπὶ χλόης εὐθαλοῦς ἡ Κένταυρος αὕτη πεποίηται ὅλη μὲν τῇ 4
ἵππῳ χαμαὶ κειμένη, καὶ ἀποτέτανται εἰς τοὐπίσω οἱ πόδες·
τὸ δὲ γυναικεῖον ὅσον αὐτῆς ἠρέμα ἐπεγήγερται καὶ ἐπ᾽ ἀγκῶνός
ἐστιν, οἱ δὲ πόδες οἱ ἔμπροσθεν οὐκέτι καὶ οὗτοι ἀποτάδην, οἷον
ἐπὶ πλευρὰν κειμένης, ἀλλ᾽ ὁ μὲν ὀκλάζοντι ἔοικεν ὁ καμπύλος
ὑπεσταλμένη τῇ ὁπλῇ, ὁ δὲ ἔμπαλιν ἐπανίσταται καὶ τοῦ ἐδάφους
ἀντιλαμβάνεται, οἷοί εἰσιν ἵπποι πειρώμενοι ἀναπηδᾶν. τοῖν
νεογνοῖν δὲ τὸ μὲν ἄνω ἔχει αὐτὴ ἐν ταῖς ἀγκάλαις καὶ τρέφει
ἀνθρωπικῶς ἐπέχουσα τὸν γυναικεῖον μαστόν, τὸ δ᾽ ἕτερον ἐκ
τῆς ἵππου θηλάζει ἐς τὸν πωλικὸν τρόπον. ἄνω δὲ τῆς εἰκόνος
οἷον ἀπό τινος σκοπῆς Ἱπποκένταυρός τις, ἀνὴρ ἐκείνης δηλαδὴ
τῆς τὰ βρέφη ἀμφοτέρωθεν τιθηνουμένης, ἐπικύπτει γελῶν οὐχ
ὅλος φαινόμενος, ἀλλ᾽ ἐς μέσον τὸν ἵππον, λέοντος σκύμνον ἀνέ-
χων τῇ δεξιᾷ καὶ ὑπὲρ ἑαυτὸν αἰωρῶν, ὡς δεδίξαιτο σὺν παιδιᾷ
τὰ βρέφη.

them when they called me unique among the Greeks and paid me compliments like that. But in fact, to quote the proverb, our treasures have turned out to be dross and the compliments I'm paid by them are pretty much those accorded a conjurer.

[3] I want to tell you the story of the painter. The great Zeuxis, after establishing himself as the best of painters, would never portray the common and ordinary subjects, like heroes or gods or wars at all or at least wouldn't do so very often, but always would try to innovate and, after thinking up some strange, unusual subject, would use it to display his consummate skill. Among his other bold ventures Zeuxis actually portrayed a mare Centaur, with her moreover suckling a pair of tiny Centaur foals. A copy of this painting, reproduced from the original with perfect accuracy, exists in Athens to-day, but the actual original was said to have been sent to Italy by Sulla with his other booty, and then everything including the painting was lost when the freighter sank, off Malea, I suppose. However I've seen the copy of this painting and shall do my best to describe it for you in words, though heaven knows I'm no artist, but I well remember having seen it not long ago in a painter's house in Athens and the immense admiration for the painter's skill I showed at the time may perhaps help me in my efforts to depict it more vividly.

[4] The Centaur is on lush grass. She is depicted with all the horse part lying on the ground and her feet stretched out backwards. Her human part is slightly raised and she is on her elbows, but her front feet aren't stretched out as to be expected with one lying on her side, but one foot is bent with the hoof tucked up under it and seems to be squatting down, whereas the other one is standing up and firmly fixed on the ground, as horses do when they try to spring up. One of her foals she is holding aloft in her own arms and feeding in human fashion, giving it her woman's breast, while the other one she is suckling from her horse part in equine manner. At the top of the painting, as though on some observation point, is another Centaur, obviously the mate of the female suckling the infants from both areas, bending down and laughing, not completely visible, but only to a point halfway down the horse, holding a lion cub up in his right hoof, suspending it above himself to frighten the babies in fun.

Τὰ μὲν οὖν ἄλλα τῆς γραφῆς, ἐφ' ὅσα τοῖς ἰδιώταις ἡμῖν οὐ   5
πάντῃ ἐμφανῆ ὄντα τὴν ὅλην ἔχει ὅμως δύναμιν τῆς τέχνης—
οἷον τὸ ἀποτεῖναι τὰς γραμμὰς ἐς τὸ εὐθύτατον καὶ τῶν χρωμάτων
ἀκριβῆ τὴν κρᾶσιν καὶ εὔκαιρον τὴν ἐπιβολὴν ποιήσασθαι καὶ
σκιάσαι ἐς δέον καὶ τοῦ μεγέθους τὸν λόγον καὶ τὴν τῶν μερῶν
πρὸς τὸ ὅλον ἰσότητα καὶ ἁρμονίαν—γραφέων παῖδες ἐπαινούντων,
οἷς ἔργον εἰδέναι τὰ τοιαῦτα. ἐγὼ δὲ τοῦ Ζεύξιδος ἐκεῖνο μάλιστα
ἐπῄνεσα, ὅτι ἐν μιᾷ καὶ τῇ αὐτῇ ὑποθέσει ποικίλως τὸ περιττὸν
ἐπεδείξατο τῆς τέχνης, τὸν μὲν ἄνδρα ποιήσας πάντῃ φοβερὸν
καὶ κομιδῇ ἄγριον, σοβαρὸν τῇ χαίτῃ, λάσιον τὰ πολλὰ οὐ κατὰ
τὸν ἵππον αὐτοῦ μόνον, ἀλλὰ καὶ κατὰ στέρνον τοῦ ἀνθρώπου
καὶ ὤμους ἐπὶ πλεῖστον, τὸ *βλέμμα, καίτοι γελῶντος, θηριῶδες
ὅλον ὄρειόν τι καὶ ἀνήμερον.

Τοιοῦτον μὲν ἐκεῖνον. ⟨τὴν⟩ θήλειαν δὲ ἵππου γε τῆς καλλίστης,   6
οἷαι μάλιστα αἱ Θετταλαί εἰσιν, ἀδμῆτες ἔτι καὶ ἄβατοι, τὸ δὲ
ἄνω ἡμίτομον γυναικὸς πάγκαλον ἔξω τῶν ὤτων· ἐκεῖνα δὲ
μόνα σατυρώδη ἐστὶν αὐτῇ. καὶ ἡ μίξις δὲ καὶ ἁρμογὴ τῶν σωμάτων, καθ' ὃ συνάπτεται καὶ συνδεῖται τῷ γυναικείῳ τὸ ἱππικόν,
ἠρέμα καὶ οὐκ ἀθρόως μεταβαίνουσα καὶ ἐκ προσαγωγῆς τρεπο-
μένη λανθάνει τὴν ὄψιν ἐκ θατέρου εἰς τὸ ἕτερον ὑπαγομένη.
τῶν νεογνῶν δὲ τὸ ἐν τῷ νηπίῳ ὅμως ἄγριον καὶ ἐν τῷ ἁπαλῷ
ἤδη φοβερόν, καὶ τοῦτο θαυμαστὸν οἷον ἔδοξέ μοι, καὶ ὅτι παιδι-
κῶς μάλα πρὸς τὸν σκύμνον τοῦ λέοντος ἀναβλέπουσιν, μεταξὺ
τῆς θηλῆς ἑκάτερος ἐπειλημμένοι ἐν χρῷ τῇ μητρὶ προσιστά-
μενοι.

Ταῦτα δ' οὖν ἐπιδειξάμενος ὁ Ζεῦξις αὐτὸς μὲν ᾤετο ἐκπλή-   7
ξειν τοὺς ὁρῶντας ἐπὶ τῇ τέχνῃ, οἱ δὲ αὐτίκα μὲν ἐβόων—ἢ τί
γὰρ ἂν ἐποίουν καλλίστῳ θεάματι ἐντυγχάνοντες; ἐπῄνουν δὲ
μάλιστα πάντες ἅπερ κἀμὲ πρῴην ἐκεῖνοι, τῆς ἐπινοίας τὸ ξένον
καὶ τὴν γνώμην τῆς γραφῆς νέαν καὶ τοῖς ἔμπροσθεν † ἥττον ἔτι †
οὖσαν· ὥστε ὁ Ζεῦξις συνεὶς ὅτι αὐτοὺς ἀσχολεῖ ἡ ὑπόθεσις καινὴ
οὖσα καὶ ἀπάγει τῆς τέχνης, ὡς ἐν παρέργῳ τίθεσθαι τὴν ἀκρίβειαν τῶν πραγμάτων, Ἄγε δή, ἔφη, ὦ Μικίων, πρὸς τὸν μαθη-
τήν, περίβαλε ἤδη τὴν εἰκόνα καὶ ἀράμενοι ἀποκομίζετε οἴκαδε.

*add ⟨δὲ⟩

[5]   As for the other features of the painting, those only partly perceptible to amateurs like myself, but yet embodying the full force of his craftsmanship, for example the perfect straightness of his lines, the accurate blending and happy application of colours, appropriate use of shadows, due regard for proportions, proper balance and harmony between the parts and the whole, let these be praised by the sons of painters, whose business it is to know about such things, but the thing about Zeuxis which I particularly admired was the variety of ways he demonstrated extraordinary craftmanship in one and the same subject. He made the male completely frightening and absolutely fierce, with a proud mane, hairy almost all over and not just in his equine part but over most of his human chest and shoulders, and though he was laughing, with a look in his eye that was altogether that of a wild beast from the mountains.

[6]   That's how he portrayed the male, while to the female he gave the bottom half of a splendidly beautiful mare, particularly resembling Thessalian fillies when still virgin and unmounted, while her upper woman's half was completely beautiful apart from the ears, which alone were those of a Satyr. The blending and joining of the two bodies, where the equine part is linked and united with the woman part, changing gradually with a slow, gentle transition, cheats the eye as the one section merges into the other. The wildness of the foals, though incorporated in babies, and their already frightening appearance at a tender age seemed absolutely wonderful. The way that the foals, though still infants, emanated savagery and were already fearsome at a tender age seemed absolutely marvellous to me, not to mention how they looked up at the lion cub, just like babies, while each kept tight hold of their mother's breast and clung close to her.

[7]   Anyhow after displaying this picture, Zeuxis personally believed he would astound the viewers with his expertise and they did in fact shout their immediate approval. What else could they do on encountering so marvellous a sight? However all particularly praised him for the same things as they did me the other day, I mean the unusual concept and the innovatory and unprecedented idea behind the painting. Consequently Zeuxis realised that their attention was being monopolised and diverted from his technical skill by the novelty of the subject, so that they attached only minor importance to the accuracy of the contents. So he said to his pupil: 'Come now, Micio, cover up the painting and all of you take it

οὗτοι γὰρ ἡμῶν τὸν πηλὸν τῆς τέχνης ἐπαινοῦσι, τῶν δὲ αὖ φώτων
εἰ καλῶς ἔχει καὶ κατὰ τὴν τέχνην, οὐ πολὺν ποιοῦνται λόγον,
ἀλλὰ παρευδοκιμεῖ τὴν ἀκρίβειαν τῶν ἔργων ‹ἡ› τῆς ὑποθέσεως
καινοτομία.

'Ο μὲν γὰρ Ζεῦξις οὕτως, ὀργιλώτερον ἴσως. 'Αντίοχος δὲ ὁ   8
σωτὴρ ἐπικληθεὶς καὶ οὗτος ὅμοιόν τι παθεῖν λέγεται ἐν τῇ πρὸς
Γαλάτας μάχῃ. εἰ βούλεσθε, διηγήσομαι καὶ τοῦτο, ὁποῖον ἐγένετο. εἰδὼς γὰρ ἀλκίμους ὄντας καὶ πλήθει παμπόλλους ὁρῶν
καὶ τὴν φάλαγγα καρτερῶς συναραρυῖαν καὶ ἐπὶ μετώπου μὲν
προασπίζοντας τοὺς χαλκοθώρηκας αὐτῶν, ἐς βάθος δὲ ἐπὶ τεττάρων καὶ εἴκοσι τεταγμένους ὁπλίτας, ἐπὶ κέρως δὲ ἑκατέρωθεν
τὴν ἵππον δισμυρίαν οὖσαν, ἐκ δὲ τοῦ μέσου τὰ ἅρματα ἐκπηδήσε-
σθαι μέλλοντα δρεπανηφόρα ὀγδοήκοντα καὶ συνωρίδας ἐπ' αὐτοῖς
δὶς τοσαύτας, ταῦτα ὁρῶν πάνυ πονηρὰς εἶχε τὰς ἐλπίδας, ὡς
ἀμάχων ὄντων ἐκείνων αὐτοῖς. ἐκεῖνος γὰρ δι' ὀλίγου τῆς στρατιᾶς ἐκείνης παρασκευασθείσης οὐ μεγαλωστὶ οὐδὲ κατ' ἀξίαν τοῦ
πολέμου ἀφίκετο κομιδῇ ὀλίγους ἄγων, καὶ τούτων πελταστικὸν
τὸ πολὺ καὶ ψιλικόν· οἱ γυμνῆτες δὲ ὑπὲρ ἥμισυ τῆς στρατιᾶς
ἦσαν. ὥστε ἐδόκει αὐτῷ ἤδη σπένδεσθαι καί τινα εὐπρεπῆ
διάλυσιν εὑρίσκεσθαι τοῦ πολέμου.

'Αλλὰ Θεοδότας ὁ 'Ρόδιος, ἀνὴρ γενναῖος καὶ τακτικῶν ἔμπει-   9
ρος, οὐκ εἴα παρὼν ἀθυμεῖν. καὶ ἦσαν γὰρ ἑκκαίδεκα ἐλέφαντες
τῷ 'Αντιόχῳ. τούτους ἐκέλευσεν ὁ Θεοδότας τέως μὲν ἔχειν ὡς
οἷόν τε κατακρύψαντα, ὡς μὴ κατάδηλοι εἶεν ὑπερφαινόμενοι
τοῦ στρατοῦ, ἐπειδὰν δὲ σημήνῃ ὁ σαλπιγκτὴς καὶ δέῃ συμπλέ-
κεσθαι καὶ εἰς χεῖρας ἰέναι καὶ ἡ ἵππος ἡ τῶν πολεμίων ἐπελαύ-
νηται καὶ τὰ ἅρματα οἱ Γαλάται ἀνοίξαντες τὴν φάλαγγα καὶ δια-
στήσαντες ἐπαφῶσι, τότε ἀνὰ τέτταρας μὲν τῶν ἐλεφάντων
ἀπαντᾶν ἐφ' ἑκατέροις τοῖς ἱππεῦσιν, τοὺς ὀκτὼ δὲ ἀντεπαφεῖναι
τοῖς ἁρματηλάταις καὶ συνωριασταῖς. εἰ γὰρ τοῦτο γένοιτο,
φοβηθήσονται αὐτῶν, ἔφη, οἱ ἵπποι καὶ ἐς τοὺς Γαλάτας αὖθις
ἐμπεσοῦνται φεύγοντες. καὶ οὕτως ἐγένετο. οὐ γὰρ πρότερον   10
ἰδόντες ἐλέφαντας οὔτε αὐτοὶ Γαλάται οὔτε οἱ ἵπποι αὐτῶν οὕτω
πρὸς τὸ παράδοξον τῆς ὄψεως ἐταράχθησαν, ὥστε πόρρω ἔτι

home. For they praise the mere raw material of my works but pay scant attention to the quality and expertise of my light effects; instead the novelty of my subject outshines the precision achieved in my works.'

[8] That's what Zeuxis said, perhaps with a touch of anger. But Antiochus, the one called the Saviour, is also said to have had a similar experience in his battle with the Galatians. With your permission, I'll add an account of what happened then. Knowing them to be doughty fighters and seeing their enormous numbers, their strong, compact phalanx with a protective front line of warriors in bronze body-armour and their hoplites arrayed twenty-four deep, 20,000 cavalry on both wings, eighty scythed chariots ready to burst forward from the centre and twice as many ordinary two-horsed chariots as well, he felt he had very poor prospects, considering his force no match for the enemy. For his army had been hurriedly organised on a small scale quite inadequate for the needs of the war, and he had arrived with a tiny force, and most of it peltasts and light troops; indeed more than half of them had no protective armour, so that he thought of making an immediate truce and obtaining creditable terms for ending the war.

[9] But Theodotas of Rhodes, a spirited man skilled in military tactics, was there and told him not to be despondent. For Antiochus had sixteen elephants. Theodotas instructed him to keep these hidden as best he could for the meantime, so that they wouldn't be seen towering over the army, but when the trumpeter gave the signal, and they had to engage and come to close quarters, and the enemy cavalry rode against them and the Galatians opened up their phalanx, and made gaps in it to release their chariots against them, then they must confront the enemy cavalry with four elephants on each of the flanks and unleash the other eight against the drivers of the scythed and two-horse chariots. For he told him that, if this was done, their horses would take fright, turn to flight and rush back against the Galatians. [10] And that's what happened! For neither the Galatians nor their horses had seen elephants before and they were thrown

τῶν θηρίων ὄντων ἐπεὶ μόνον τετριγότων ἤκουσαν καὶ τοὺς ὀδόντας εἶδον ἀποστίλβοντας ἐπισημότερον ὡς ἂν ἐκ μέλανος τοῦ παντὸς σώματος καὶ τὰς προνομαίας ὡς ἐς ἁρπαγὴν ὑπεραιωρουμέ-
νας, πρὶν ἢ τόξευμα ἐξικνεῖσθαι, ἐκκλίναντες σὺν οὐδενὶ κόσμῳ
ἔφευγον, οἱ μὲν πεζοὶ περιπειρόμενοι ὑπ᾽ ἀλλήλων τοῖς δορατί-
οις καὶ συμπατούμενοι ὑπὸ τῶν ἱππέων ὡς εἶχον ἐμπεσόντων ἐπ᾽
αὑτούς, τὰ ἅρματα δέ, ἀναστρέψαντα καὶ ταῦτα ἔμπαλιν εἰς τοὺς
οἰκείους, οὐκ ἀναιμωτὶ διεφέρετο ἐν αὐτοῖς, ἀλλὰ τὸ τοῦ Ὁμήρου,
"δίφροι δ᾽ ἀνεκυμβαλίαζον." οἱ ἵπποι δ᾽ ἐπείπερ ἅπαξ τῆς ἐς
τὸ εὐθὺ ὁδοῦ ἀπετρέποντο οὐκ ἀνασχόμενοι τῶν ἐλεφάντων, τοὺς
ἐπιβάτας ἀποβαλόντες "κείν᾽ ὄχεα κροτάλιζον" τέμνοντες νὴ
Δία καὶ διαιροῦντες τοῖς δρεπάνοις εἴ τινας τῶν φίλων καταλά-
βοιεν. πολλοὶ δὲ ὡς ἐν ταράχῳ τοσούτῳ κατελαμβάνοντο. εἵπον-
το δὲ καὶ οἱ ἐλέφαντες συμπατοῦντες καὶ ἀναρριπτοῦντες ⟨ταῖς⟩
προνομαίαις ἐς ὕψος καὶ συναρπάζοντες καὶ τοῖς ὀδοῦσι περιπεί-
ροντες, καὶ τέλος οὗτοι κατὰ κράτος παραδιδόασι τῷ Ἀντιόχῳ
τὴν νίκην.

Οἱ Γαλάται δὲ οἱ μὲν ἐτεθνήκεσαν, πολλοῦ τοῦ φόνου γενομένου,   **11**
οἱ δὲ ζῶντες ἐλαμβάνοντο, πλὴν πάνυ ὀλίγοι ὁπόσοι ἔφθασαν εἰς
τὰ ὄρη ἀναφυγόντες, οἱ Μακεδόνες δὲ ὅσοι σὺν Ἀντιόχῳ ἦσαν,
ἐπαιώνιζον καὶ προσιόντες ἄλλος ἀλλαχόθεν ἀνέδουν τὸν βασιλέα
καλλίνικον ἀναβοῶντες. ὁ δὲ καὶ δακρύσας, ὥς φασιν, Αἰσχυνώ-
μεθα, ἔφη, ὦ στρατιῶται, οἷς γε ἡ σωτηρία ἐν ἑκκαίδεκα τούτοις
θηρίοις ἐγένετο· ὡς εἰ μὴ τὸ καινὸν τοῦ θεάματος ἐξέπληξε τοὺς
πολεμίους, τί ἂν ἡμεῖς ἦμεν πρὸς αὐτούς; ἔπι* τε ⟨τῷ⟩ τροπαίῳ
κελεύει ἄλλο μηδέν, ἐλέφαντα δὲ μόνον ἐγκολάψαι.

Ὥρα τοίνυν με σκοπεῖν μὴ καὶ τοὐμὸν ὅμοιον ᾖ Ἀντιόχῳ,   **12**
ἐλέφαντές γέ τινες καὶ ξένα μορμολύκεια πρὸς τοὺς ὁρῶντας καὶ
θαυματοποιία ἄλλως· ἐκεῖνα γοῦν ἐπαινοῦσι πάντες. οἷς δὲ ἐγὼ
ἐπεποίθειν, οὐ πάνυ ταῦτα ἐν λόγῳ παρ᾽ αὐτοῖς ἐστιν, ἀλλ᾽ ὅτι
μὲν θήλεια Ἱπποκένταυρος γεγραμμένη, τοῦτο μόνον ἐκπλήττον-
ται καί, ὥσπερ ἐστί, καινὸν καὶ τεράστιον δοκεῖ αὐτοῖς. τὰ
δὲ ἄλλα μάτην ἄρα τῷ Ζεύξιδι πεποίηται; ἀλλ᾽ οὐ μάτην—
γραφικοὶ γὰρ ὑμεῖς καὶ μετὰ τέχνης ἕκαστα ὁρᾶτε. εἴη μόνον
ἄξια τοῦ θεάτρου δεικνύειν.

* read ἐπί

into such a panic by the strange sight that, while the beasts were still at some distance, upon merely hearing their trumpeting and seeing their tusks gleaming the more brightly, as coming from completely black bodies, and their trunks hovering in mid-air as though to carry them off, before an arrow reached them, they turned and fled in complete disarray; the infantrymen were being impaled with one another's spears and trampled underfoot by the cavalry riding straight at them, while the chariots too turned back into their own troops and dispersed among them 'not without a-shedding of blood', but, to quote Homer, 'The chariots did a-rattling tumble o'er,' and once their horses had swerved from their straight course unable to face the elephants, they threw their drivers out and 'Their empty chairs did send a-clattering on' in very truth cutting and carving up with their scythes any of their own side they met, and there were plenty of these in all that turmoil. Moreover the elephants pursued them, trampling them down, or tossing them high in the air with their trunks or snatching them up or goring them with their tusks and finally these elephants by their mighty efforts ensured victory for Antiochus.

[11] The Galatians lost many dead, and the rest of them were taken prisoner apart from a very few who were quick enough to escape to the mountains. The Macedonians accompanying Antiochus raised victory hymns, came up to their king from all sides and garlanded his head, loudly acclaiming him as a glorious victor. But, they tell us, he shed tears and said: 'Let us feel ashamed, soldiers, for our safety has depended on these sixteen beasts. For if the enemy hadn't been astounded by the unfamiliarity of what they saw, how could we have compared with them?' And he instructed them to put nothing on the trophy apart from a carving of an elephant.

[12] So the occasion demands I consider whether my resources aren't like those of Antiochus, consisting of a few elephants and hobgoblins strange to the eye and a mere piece of conjuring. For that's what they all praise. But the things on which I relied are of no account at all with them, and the only thing that amazes them is that I've painted a female Centaur, which they think novel and extraordinary, as indeed it is. But the rest of Zeuxis' efforts have been wasted – no, not wasted, for you are artistic and see everything with experts' eyes. I only hope that what I put on show is worthy of my audience.

ΠΩΣ ΔΕΙ ΙΣΤΟΡΙΑΝ ΣΥΓΓΡΑΦΕΙΝ

Ἀβδηρίταις φασὶ Λυσιμάχου ἤδη βασιλεύοντος ἐμπεσεῖν τι **1**
νόσημα, ὦ καλὲ Φίλων, τοιοῦτο· πυρέττειν μὲν γὰρ τὰ πρῶτα
πανδημεὶ ἅπαντας ἀπὸ τῆς πρώτης εὐθὺς ἐρρωμένως καὶ λι-
παρεῖ τῷ πυρετῷ, περὶ δὲ τὴν ἑβδόμην τοῖς μὲν αἷμα πολὺ ἐκ
ῥινῶν ῥυέν, τοῖς δ' ἱδρὼς ἐπιγενόμενος, πολὺς καὶ οὗτος, ἔλυσεν
τὸν πυρετόν. ἐς γελοῖον δέ τι πάθος περιίστη τὰς γνώμας αὐτῶν·
ἅπαντες γὰρ ἐς τραγῳδίαν παρεκίνουν καὶ ἰαμβεῖα ἐφθέγγοντο
καὶ μέγα ἐβόων· μάλιστα δὲ τὴν Εὐριπίδου Ἀνδρομέδαν ἐμο-
νῴδουν καὶ τὴν τοῦ Περσέως ῥῆσιν ἐν μέλει διεξῄεσαν, καὶ
μεστὴ ἦν ἡ πόλις ὠχρῶν ἁπάντων καὶ λεπτῶν τῶν ἑβδομαίων
ἐκείνων τραγῳδῶν,

    σὺ δ' ὦ θεῶν τύραννε κἀνθρώπων Ἔρως,

καὶ τὰ ἄλλα μεγάλῃ τῇ φωνῇ ἀναβοώντων καὶ τοῦτο ἐπὶ πολύ,
ἄχρι δὴ χειμὼν καὶ κρύος δὲ μέγα γενόμενον ἔπαυσε ληροῦντας
αὐτούς. αἰτίαν δέ μοι δοκεῖ τοῦ τοιούτου παρασχεῖν Ἀρχέλαος
ὁ τραγῳδός, εὐδοκιμῶν τότε, μεσοῦντος θέρους ἐν πολλῷ τῷ
φλογμῷ τραγῳδήσας αὐτοῖς τὴν Ἀνδρομέδαν, ὡς πυρέξαι τε
ἀπὸ τοῦ θεάτρου τοὺς πολλοὺς καὶ ἀναστάντας ὕστερον ἐς
τὴν τραγῳδίαν παρολισθαίνειν, ἐπὶ πολὺ ἐμφιλοχωρούσης τῆς
Ἀνδρομέδας τῇ μνήμῃ αὐτῶν καὶ τοῦ Περσέως ἔτι σὺν τῇ
Μεδούσῃ τὴν ἑκάστου γνώμην περιπετομένου.

Ὡς οὖν ἕν, φασίν, ἑνὶ παραβαλεῖν, τὸ Ἀβδηριτικὸν ἐκεῖνο **2**
πάθος καὶ νῦν τοὺς πολλοὺς τῶν πεπαιδευμένων περιελήλυθεν,
οὐχ ὥστε τραγῳδεῖν—ἔλαττον γὰρ ἂν τοῦτο παρέπαιον ἀλλοτρίοις
ἰαμβείοις, οὐ φαύλοις, κατεσχημένοι. ἀλλ' ἀφ' οὗ δὴ τὰ ἐν ποσὶ
ταῦτα κεκίνηται—ὁ πόλεμος ὁ πρὸς τοὺς βαρβάρους καὶ τὸ ἐν Ἀρμενίᾳ τραῦμα καὶ αἱ συνεχεῖς νῖκαι—οὐδεὶς ὅστις οὐχ ἱστορίαν
συγγράφει· μᾶλλον δὲ Θουκυδίδαι καὶ Ἡρόδοτοι καὶ Ξενο-
φῶντες ἡμῖν ἅπαντες, καί, ὡς ἔοικεν, ἀληθὲς ἄρ' ἦν ἐκεῖνο τό
"Πόλεμος ἁπάντων πατήρ," εἴ γε καὶ συγγραφέας τοσούτους
ἀνέφυσεν ὑπὸ μιᾷ τῇ ὁρμῇ.

HOW TO WRITE HISTORY

[1] They say that in the reign of Lysimachus the folk of Abdera were stricken by a plague that was something like this, my good Philo. In the early stages all the population had a violent and persistent fever right from the very beginning, but about the seventh day it was dispelled, in some cases by a copious flow of blood from the nostrils, in others by perspiration, that also copious, but it affected their minds in a ridiculous way; for all had a mad hankering for tragedy, delivering blank verse at the top of their voices. In particular they would chant solos from Euripides' *Andromeda*, singing the whole of Perseus' long speech and the city was full of all those pale, thin seventh-day patients ranting,

'And you, o Eros, lord of gods and men'

and loudly declaiming the other bits, and over a long period too, till the coming of winter and a heavy frost put an end to their nonsense! All this was caused, I think, by Archelaus, the tragic actor then at the height of his fame, whose performance of the *Andromeda* for them in scorching heat in mid-summer had resulted in most of them leaving the theatre with a fever and later, after leaving their sickbeds, having a relapse by turning to tragedy, with Andromeda long haunting their memories and Perseus with his Medusa hovering around in everyone's thoughts.

[2] So, to compare one thing with another, as the saying goes, that affliction of the Abderites is with us now too, besetting most educated people, not by making them spout tragedy – for they'd be less crazy, if possessed by others' verses not lacking in merit. No, right from the outset of the present excitement, I mean the war against the barbarians, the disaster in Armenia and the succession of victories, everyone is writing history, or rather we find everybody has become a Thucydides or a Herodotus or a Xenophon, and apparently the old saying 'War is the Father of all things' has been proved true, judging by the numbers of historians it has produced at one go.

Ταῦτα τοίνυν, ὦ φιλότης, ὁρῶντα καὶ ἀκούοντά με τὸ τοῦ 3
Σινωπέως ἐκεῖνο εἰσῆλθεν· ὁπότε γὰρ ὁ Φίλιππος ἐλέγετο ἤδη
ἐπελαύνειν, οἱ Κορίνθιοι πάντες ἐταράττοντο καὶ ἐν ἔργῳ ἦσαν,
ὁ μὲν ὅπλα ἐπισκευάζων, ὁ δὲ λίθους παραφέρων, ὁ δὲ ὑποικο-
δομῶν τοῦ τείχους, ὁ δὲ ἔπαλξιν ὑποστηρίζων, ὁ δὲ ἄλλος ἄλλο τι
τῶν χρησίμων ὑπουργῶν. ὁ δὴ Διογένης ὁρῶν ταῦτα, ἐπεὶ μηδὲν
εἶχεν ὅ τι καὶ πράττοι—οὐδεὶς γὰρ αὐτῷ ἐς οὐδὲν ἐχρῆτο—δια-
ζωσάμενος τὸ τριβώνιον σπουδῇ μάλα καὶ αὐτὸς ἐκύλιε τὸν πίθον,
ἐν ᾧ ἐτύγχανεν οἰκῶν, ἄνω καὶ κάτω τοῦ Κρανείου. καί τινος
τῶν συνήθων ἐρομένου, Τί ταῦτα ποιεῖς, ὦ Διόγενες; Κυλίω,
ἔφη, κἀγὼ τὸν πίθον, ὡς μὴ μόνος ἀργεῖν δοκοίην ἐν τοσούτοις
ἐργαζομένοις.

Καὐτὸς οὖν, ὦ Φίλων, ὡς μὴ μόνος ἄφωνος εἴην ἐν οὕτω 4
πολυφώνῳ τῷ καιρῷ μηδ᾽ ὥσπερ κωμικὸν δορυφόρημα κεχηνὼς
σιωπῇ παραφεροίμην, καλῶς ἔχειν ὑπέλαβον ὡς δυνατόν μοι
κυλῖσαι τὸν πίθον, οὐχ <ὡς> ἱστορίαν συγγράφειν οὐδὲ πράξεις
αὐτὰς διεξιέναι—οὐχ οὕτως μεγαλότολμος ἐγώ, μηδὲ τοῦτο
δείσῃς περὶ ἐμοῦ. οἶδα γὰρ ἡλίκος ὁ κίνδυνος, εἰ κατὰ τῶν
πετρῶν κυλίοι τις, καὶ μάλιστα οἷον τοὐμὸν τοῦτο πιθάκνιον
οὐδὲ πάνυ καρτερῶς κεκεραμευμένον. δεήσει γὰρ αὐτίκα μάλα
πρὸς μικρόν τι λιθίδιον προσπταίσαντα συλλέγειν τὰ ὄστρακα.

Τί οὖν ἔγνωσταί μοι καὶ πῶς ἀσφαλῶς μεθέξω τοῦ πολέμου,
αὐτὸς ἔξω βέλους ἑστώς, ἐγώ σοι φράσω. "τούτου μὲν καπνοῦ
καὶ κύματος" καὶ φροντίδων, ὅσαι τῷ συγγραφεῖ ἔνεισιν, ἀνέξω
ἐμαυτὸν εὖ ποιῶν. παραίνεσιν δέ τινα μικρὰν καὶ ὑποθήκας
ταύτας ὀλίγας ὑποθήσομαι τοῖς συγγράφουσιν, ὡς κοινωνήσαιμι
αὐτοῖς τῆς οἰκοδομίας, εἰ καὶ μὴ τῆς ἐπιγραφῆς, ἄκρῳ γε τῷ
δακτύλῳ τοῦ πηλοῦ προσαψάμενος.

Καίτοι οὐδὲ παραινέσεως οἱ πολλοὶ δεῖν οἴονται σφίσιν ἐπὶ τὸ 5
πρᾶγμα, οὐ μᾶλλον ἢ τέχνης τινὸς ἐπὶ τὸ βαδίζειν ἢ βλέπειν
ἢ ἐσθίειν, ἀλλὰ πάνυ ῥᾷστον καὶ πρόχειρον καὶ ἅπαντος εἶναι
ἱστορίαν συγγράψαι, ἤν τις ἑρμηνεῦσαι τὸ ἐπελθὸν δύναται. τὸ
δὲ οἶσθά που καὶ αὐτός, ὦ ἑταῖρε, ὡς οὐ τῶν εὐμεταχειρίστων
οὐδὲ ῥαθύμως συντεθῆναι δυναμένων τοῦτ᾽ ἐστίν, ἀλλ᾽, εἴ τι ἐν
λόγοις καὶ ἄλλο, πολλῆς τῆς φροντίδος δεόμενον, ἤν τις, ὡς ὁ

[3] Well, friend, when I see and hear all this, I am reminded of the story about the man from Sinope. For when Philip was already said to be marching against them, the Corinthians were all in panic-stricken activity, preparing their arms, fetching stones, repairing the walls or reinforcing the battlements, with each man in his own way trying to do something useful. Now when Diogenes saw this and had nothing to do, since nobody could find any use for him, he tucked up his tattered cloak and started most energetically to roll the cask which served as his home up and down Cornel Hill. When one of his companions asked him 'Why are you doing that, Diogenes?', he answered 'I am joining in by rolling my cask, so as not to be thought the only idler among so many busy workers.'

[4] So, my dear Philo, so as not to be the only one without a voice at so vociferous a time, nor wander around open-mouthed but silent like an extra in a comedy, I thought it a good idea to roll my cask as best I could, though stopping short of writing history or describing actual events – I'm not as foolhardy as that, don't fear that of me. For I know the great danger of rolling the thing down over the rocks, particularly when it's a poor earthen crock like mine and none too strongly made by the potter. For within a moment I'd dash it against a tiny stone and have to gather up the pieces.

So I'll tell you what I've decided and how I'll take part in the war in safety, staying out of the firing line. I'll keep myself
        'Away from all yon smoke and surge'
and the cares that beset the historian, for that's the best policy. I shall, however, offer a little advice and a few pieces of guidance to historians, so that I can share in the building process with them, even if I don't have my name on the inscription, only having dipped the tip of my finger in the clay.

[5] However most of them don't even imagine they need any advice for their task any more than they need a treatise on the art of walking or seeing or eating, but think historiography absolutely simple and straightforward and within anyone's power, provided he can express his ideas. But, in fact, as I'm sure you know for yourself, my friend, it's not a thing that can be undertaken lightly or easily composed, but it of all prose forms requires a great deal of thought, if, to quote Thucydides, one is to compose 'a possession for ever'.

Θουκυδίδης φησίν, ἐς ἀεὶ κτῆμα συντιθείη. οἶδα μὲν οὖν οὐ πάνυ πολλοὺς αὐτῶν ἐπιστρέψων, ἐνίοις δὲ καὶ πάνυ ἐπαχθὴς δόξων, καὶ μάλιστα ὁπόσοις ἀποτετέλεσται ἤδη καὶ ἐν τῷ κοινῷ δέδεικται ἱστορία· εἰ δὲ καὶ ἐπήνηται ὑπὸ τῶν τότε ἀκροασαμένων, μανία καὶ ἐλπίσαι ὡς οἱ τοιοῦτοι μεταποιήσουσιν ἢ μεταγράψουσίν τι τῶν ἅπαξ κεκυρωμένων καὶ ὥσπερ ἐς τὰς βασιλείους αὐλὰς ἀποκειμένων. ὅμως δὲ οὐ χεῖρον καὶ πρὸς αὐτοὺς ἐκείνους εἰρῆσθαι, ἵν᾿, εἴ ποτε πόλεμος ἄλλος συσταίη, ἢ Κελτοῖς πρὸς Γέτας ἢ Ἰνδοῖς πρὸς Βακτρίους (οὐ γὰρ πρὸς ἡμᾶς γε τολμήσειεν ἄν τις, ἀπάντων ἤδη κεχειρωμένων) ἔχωσιν ἄμεινον συντιθέναι τὸν κανόνα τοῦτον προσάγοντες, ἤνπερ γε δόξῃ αὐτοῖς ὀρθὸς εἶναι· εἰ δὲ μή, αὐτοὶ μὲν καὶ τότε τῷ αὐτῷ πήχει ὥσπερ καὶ νῦν μετρούντων τὸ πρᾶγμα. ὁ ἰατρὸς δὲ οὐ πάνυ ἀνιάσεται, ἢν πάντες Ἀβδηρῖται ἑκόντες Ἀνδρομέδαν τραγῳδῶσι.

Διττοῦ δὲ ὄντος τοῦ τῆς συμβουλῆς ἔργου, τὰ μὲν γὰρ αἱρεῖσθαι, τὰ δὲ φεύγειν διδάσκει, φέρε πρῶτα εἴπωμεν ἄτινα φευκτέον τῷ ἱστορίαν συγγράφοντι καὶ ὧν μάλιστα καθαρευτέον, ἔπειτα οἷς χρώμενος οὐκ ἂν ἁμάρτοι τῆς ὀρθῆς καὶ ἐπ᾿ εὐθὺ ἀγούσης, ἀρχήν τε οἵαν αὐτῷ ἀρκτέον καὶ τάξιν ἥντινα τοῖς ἔργοις ἐφαρμοστέον καὶ μέτρον ἑκάστου καὶ ἃ σιωπητέον καὶ οἷς ἐνδιατριπτέον καὶ ὅσα παραδραμεῖν ἄμεινον καὶ ὅπως ἑρμηνεῦσαι αὐτὰ καὶ συναρμόσαι. **6**

Ταῦτα μὲν καὶ τὰ τοιαῦτα ὕστερον, νῦν δὲ τὰς κακίας ἤδη εἴπωμεν, ὁπόσαι τοῖς φαύλως συγγράφουσιν παρακολουθοῦσιν. ἃ μὲν οὖν κοινὰ πάντων λόγων ἐστὶν ἁμαρτήματα ἔν τε φωνῇ καὶ ἁρμονίᾳ καὶ διανοίᾳ καὶ τῇ ἄλλῃ ἀτεχνίᾳ, μακρόν τε ἂν εἴη ἐπελθεῖν καὶ τῆς παρούσης ὑποθέσεως οὐκ ἴδιον. κοινὰ γάρ, ὡς ἔφην, ἀπάντων λόγων ἐστὶν ἁμαρτήματα [ἔν τε φωνῇ καὶ ἁρμονίᾳ], ἃ δ᾿ ἐν ἱστορίᾳ διαμαρτάνουσι, τὰ τοιαῦτα ἂν εὕροις ἐπιτηρῶν, οἷα κἀμοὶ πολλάκις ἀκροωμένῳ ἔδοξεν, καὶ μάλιστα ἢν ἅπασιν αὐτοῖς ἀναπετάσῃς τὰ ὦτα. οὐκ ἄκαιρον δὲ μεταξὺ καὶ ἀπομνημονεῦσαι ἔνια παραδείγματος ἕνεκα τῶν ἤδη οὕτως συγγεγραμμένων. **7**

Καὶ πρῶτόν γε ἐκεῖνο ἡλίκον ἁμαρτάνουσιν ἐπισκοπήσω-

I know I'll convert very few of them to my way of thinking and may even offend some, particularly those whose history has already been completed and put on public display. And if it has also been praised by its original audiences, it would be mad even to hope that such men will change or rewrite anything of what has already received its official form and, as it were, been deposited in the palace archives. However it won't do any harm to address them too, so that if another war should break out – between Celts and Getans or Indians and Bactrians, for nobody would dare to challenge *us*, now that we've beaten all comers – they may be able to compose better by applying these rules, provided they approve of them. Otherwise let them go on using the same rough and ready measurements as at present. Doctor Lucian will shed no tears if they all choose to be like the folk of Abdera and go on spouting the *Andromeda*.

[6] Since advice has a dual function, instructing us to choose some courses and avoid others, come, let me first tell you what things the writer of history must avoid and what faults above all he must keep out of his system, and next what means to use so as not to lose the proper, straight path, how to start his work, the order to impose upon his facts, the proper proportions for each subject, what to pass over in silence, what to dwell on at length, matters to be treated cursorily and how to express things and put them together.

These and related matters will be treated later, but for the present let us discuss the vices besetting indifferent historians. Discussion of the faults found in all branches of prose alike, faults of diction, of word order, of thought or of general lack of craftsmanship, would be time-consuming and inappropriate to my present purpose. [7] For there are, as I said, faults shared by all branches of prose, but the particular mistakes men make in writing history you may find to be just such as I in my frequent listening to historians' readings have thought them to be – if you are observant and in particular if you listen out for all of them. And it won't be out of place in the course of my remarks to mention by way of example some of the things that have been offered as history.

This is their first fault and let us consider its enormity. Most of them

μεν· ἀμελήσαντες γὰρ οἱ πολλοὶ αὐτῶν τοῦ ἱστορεῖν τὰ γεγενημένα τοῖς ἐπαίνοις ἀρχόντων καὶ στρατηγῶν ἐνδιατρίβουσιν,
τοὺς μὲν οἰκείους ἐς ὕψος φέροντες, τοὺς πολεμίους δὲ πέρα
τοῦ μετρίου καταρρίπτοντες, ἀγνοοῦντες ὡς οὐ στενῷ τῷ ἰσθμῷ
διώρισται καὶ διατετείχισται ἡ ἱστορία πρὸς τὸ ἐγκώμιον,
ἀλλά τι μέγα τεῖχος ἐν μέσῳ ἐστὶν αὐτῶν καὶ τὸ τῶν μουσικῶν
δὴ τοῦτο, δὶς διὰ πασῶν ἐστι πρὸς ἄλληλα—εἴ γε τῷ μὲν ἐγκω-
μιάζοντι μόνου ἑνὸς μέλει, ὁπωσοῦν ἐπαινέσαι καὶ εὐφρᾶναι
τὸν ἐπαινούμενον, καὶ <εἰ> ψευσαμένῳ ὑπάρχει τυχεῖν τοῦ τέλους,
ὀλίγον ἂν φροντίσειεν. ἡ δὲ οὐκ ἄν τι ψεῦδος ἐμπεσὸν ἡ ἱστορία
οὐδὲ ἀκαριαῖον ἀνάσχοιτο, οὐ μᾶλλον ἢ τὴν ἀρτηρίαν ἰατρῶν
παῖδές φασι τὴν τραχεῖαν παραδέξασθαι ἄν τι ἐς αὐτὴν καταποθέν.

Ἔτι ἀγνοεῖν ἐοίκασιν οἱ τοιοῦτοι ὡς ποιητικῆς μὲν καὶ ποιη- 8
μάτων ἄλλαι ὑποσχέσεις καὶ κανόνες ἴδιοι, ἱστορίας δὲ ἄλλοι.
ἐκεῖ μὲν γὰρ ἀκρατὴς ἡ ἐλευθερία καὶ νόμος εἷς—τὸ δόξαν τῷ
ποιητῇ. ἔνθεος γὰρ καὶ κάτοχος ἐκ Μουσῶν, κἂν ἵππων ὑποπτέρων ἅρμα ζεύξασθαι ἐθέλῃ, κἂν ἐφ' ὕδατος ἄλλους ἢ ἐπ' ἀνθε-
ρίκων ἄκρων θευσομένους ἀναβιβάσηται, φθόνος οὐδείς· οὐδὲ
ὁπόταν ὁ Ζεὺς αὐτῶν ἀπὸ μιᾶς σειρᾶς ἀνασπάσας αἰωρῇ ὁμοῦ
γῆν καὶ θάλατταν, δεδίασι μὴ ἀπορραγείσης ἐκείνης συντριβῇ
τὰ πάντα κατενεχθέντα. ἀλλὰ κἂν Ἀγαμέμνονα ἐπαινέσαι
θέλωσιν, οὐδεὶς ὁ κωλύσων Διὶ μὲν αὐτὸν ὅμοιον εἶναι τὴν
κεφαλὴν καὶ τὰ ὄμματα, τὸ στέρνον δὲ τῷ ἀδελφῷ αὐτοῦ τῷ
Ποσειδῶνι, τὴν δὲ ζώνην τῷ Ἄρει, καὶ ὅλως σύνθετον ἐκ πάντων
θεῶν γενέσθαι δεῖ τὸν Ἀτρέως καὶ Ἀερόπης· οὐ γὰρ ἱκανὸς ὁ
Ζεὺς οὐδὲ ὁ Ποσειδῶν οὐδὲ ὁ Ἄρης μόνος ἕκαστος ἀναπλη-
ρῶσαι τὸ κάλλος αὐτοῦ. ἡ ἱστορία δὲ ἤν τινα κολακείαν τοιαύτην
προσλάβῃ, τί ἄλλο ἢ πεζή τις ποιητικὴ γίγνεται, τῆς μεγαλοφω-
νίας μὲν ἐκείνης ἐστερημένη, τὴν λοιπὴν δὲ τερατείαν γυμνὴν
τῶν μέτρων καὶ δι' αὐτὸ ἐπισημοτέραν ἐκφαίνουσα; μέγα τοίνυν
—μᾶλλον δὲ ὑπέρμεγα τοῦτο κακόν—εἰ μὴ εἰδείη τις χωρίζειν
τὰ ἱστορίας καὶ τὰ ποιητικῆς, ἀλλ' ἐπεισάγοι τῇ ἱστορίᾳ τὰ τῆς
ἑτέρας κομμώματα—τὸν μῦθον καὶ τὸ ἐγκώμιον καὶ τὰς ἐν τούτοις
ὑπερβολάς, ὥσπερ ἂν εἴ τις ἀθλητὴν τῶν καρτερῶν τούτων καὶ
κομιδῇ πρινίνων ἁλουργέσι περιβάλοι καὶ τῷ ἄλλῳ κόσμῳ τῷ

pay no regard to the recording of the actual facts but linger long over eulogies of rulers and generals, exalting their own ones to the skies and depreciating immoderately those of the enemy, unaware that it's no narrow isthmus that separates and bars history off from encomium, but there's a mighty wall between the two of them and, to use the musicians' phrase, they are two complete octaves apart – if at least the encomiast's sole concern is to praise in any way he can and to delight the object of his praise, and he won't worry much if he has to lie to gain his end; whereas history can't tolerate the intrusion of any falsehood, however slight, any more than the medical profession say the windpipe would anything swallowed into it.

[8] Furthermore men like this don't seem to know that poetry and poems differ from history in what they profess to do and in the particular rules regulating *them*. *They* have uncontrolled liberty and but one law – the will of the poet. *He* is divinely inspired and possessed by the Muses and whether he chooses to harness a team of winged steeds or to produce others to run on water or the heads of corn, nobody grudges *him* that. Nor when *their* Zeus draws up earth and sea together on a single cord and suspends them in midair, are *they* afraid the cord will break and everything be dashed down and shattered. No, if *they* want to praise Agamemnon, nobody will stop him resembling Zeus in head and eyes, Zeus' brother Poseidon in his chest and Ares in his belt; in short the son of Atreus and Aerope just has to be compounded from all the gods, for neither Zeus nor Poseidon nor Ares on his own could do full justice to his handsome appearance! But if history adds in flattery like that, isn't it becoming a sort of prose poetry, lacking the magnificent sound of poetry, but otherwise revealing the implausibility of its tall stories in non-metrical form and so all the more clearly? It's a great failing or rather an immense one, if one can't differentiate between the historical and the poetical, but introduces into history the cosmetics of poetry, I mean fiction and encomium and the exaggerations they entail; it's like someone dressing up a muscular athlete as sturdy as an oaktree in the purples and all the other

ἑταιρικῷ καὶ φῦκιον ἐντρίβοι καὶ ψιμύθιον τῷ προσώπῳ. Ἡρά
κλεις ὡς καταγέλαστον αὐτὸν ἀπεργάσαιτο αἰσχύνας τῷ κόσμῳ
ἐκείνῳ.

Καὶ <οὐ> τοῦτό φημι, ὡς οὐχὶ καὶ ἐπαινετέον ἐν ἱστορίᾳ 9
ἐνίοτε. ἀλλ' ἐν καιρῷ τῷ προσήκοντι ἐπαινετέον καὶ μέτρον
ἐπακτέον τῷ πράγματι, τὸ μὴ ἐπαχθὲς τοῖς ὕστερον ἀναγνωσο
μένοις αὐτά, καὶ ὅλως πρὸς τὰ ἔπειτα κανονιστέον τὰ τοιαῦτα,
ἅπερ μικρὸν ὕστερον ἐπιδείξομεν.

Ὅσοι δὲ οἴονται καλῶς διαιρεῖν εἰς δύο τὴν ἱστορίαν, εἰς τὸ
τερπνὸν καὶ χρήσιμον, καὶ διὰ τοῦτο εἰσποιοῦσι καὶ τὸ ἐγκώμιον
ἐς αὐτὴν ὡς τερπνὸν καὶ εὐφραῖνον τοὺς ἐντυγχάνοντας, ὁρᾷς
ὅσον τἀληθοῦς ἡμαρτήκασι; πρῶτον μὲν κιβδήλῳ τῇ διαιρέσει
χρώμενοι· ἓν γὰρ ἔργον ἱστορίας καὶ τέλος, τὸ χρήσιμον, ὅπερ
ἐκ τοῦ ἀληθοῦς μόνου συνάγεται. τὸ τερπνὸν δὲ ἄμεινον μὲν εἰ
καὶ αὐτὸ παρακολουθήσειεν, ὥσπερ καὶ κάλλος ἀθλητῇ· εἰ δὲ
μή, οὐδὲν κωλύσει ἀφ' Ἡρακλέους γενέσθαι Νικόστρατον τὸν Ἰσι
δότου, γεννάδαν ὄντα καὶ τῶν ἀνταγωνιστῶν ἑκατέρων ἀλκιμώ
τερον, εἰ αὐτὸς μὲν αἴσχιστος ὀφθῆναι εἴη τὴν ὄψιν, Ἀλκαῖος
δὲ ὁ καλὸς ὁ Μιλήσιος ἀνταγωνίζοιτο αὐτῷ, καὶ ἐρώμενος, ὥς
φασι, τοῦ Νικοστράτου ὤν. καὶ τοίνυν ἡ ἱστορία, εἰ μὲν ἄλλως τὸ
τερπνὸν παρεμπορεύσαιτο, πολλοὺς ἂν τοὺς ἐραστὰς ἐπισπάσαιτο,
ἄχρι δ' ἂν καὶ μόνον ἔχῃ τὸ ἴδιον ἐντελές—λέγω δὲ τὴν τῆς
ἀληθείας δήλωσιν—ὀλίγον τοῦ κάλλους φροντιεῖ.

Ἔτι κἀκεῖνο εἰπεῖν ἄξιον ὅτι οὐδὲ τερπνὸν ἐν αὐτῇ τὸ κομιδῇ 10
μυθῶδες καὶ τὸ τῶν ἐπαίνων μάλιστα πρόσαντες παρ' ἑκάτερον
τοῖς ἀκούουσιν, ἢν μὴ τὸν συρφετὸν καὶ τὸν πολὺν δῆμον ἐπινοῇς,
ἀλλὰ τοὺς δικαστικῶς καὶ νὴ Δία συκοφαντικῶς προσέτι γε
ἀκροασομένους, οὓς οὐκ ἄν τι λάθοι παραδραμόν, ὀξύτερον μὲν τοῦ
Ἄργου ὁρῶντας καὶ πανταχόθεν τοῦ σώματος, ἀργυραμοιβι
κῶς δὲ τῶν λεγομένων ἕκαστα ἐξετάζοντας, ὡς τὰ μὲν παρακε
κομμένα εὐθὺς ἀπορρίπτειν, παραδέχεσθαι δὲ τὰ δόκιμα καὶ
ἔννομα καὶ ἀκριβῆ τὸν τύπον, πρὸς οὓς ἀποβλέποντα χρὴ συγ
γράφειν, τῶν δὲ ἄλλων ὀλίγον φροντίζειν, κἂν διαρραγῶσιν
ἐπαινοῦντες. ἢν δὲ ἀμελήσας ἐκείνων ἡδύνῃς πέρα τοῦ με
τρίου τὴν ἱστορίαν μύθοις καὶ ἐπαίνοις καὶ τῇ ἄλλῃ θωπείᾳ, τά

finery of prostitutes and rubbing rouge and powder all over his face. By Heracles how ridiculous he would make him, defiling him with all that finery! [9] I'm not denying that sometimes praise is appropriate in history, but it must be exercised in due season and kept within the due limits that won't offend later readers and such praises must be regulated by consideration of the future, as we shall show a little later.

As for those who think they're right to divide history into two parts, the pleasurable and the useful, and therefore introduce encomium into it as being pleasurable and delighting the readers, can't you see how wide of the truth they are? In the first place their division is a fallacious one; for there is but a single function and end of history and that is the useful, which is produced only from the truth. Indeed the pleasurable improves history, should it be an extra accompaniment, just as good looks improve an athlete; but in its absence nothing will prevent Heracles being succeeded by Nicostratus, the son of Isidotus, a noble fellow and doughtier than any of his opponents, even if his personal appearance be absolutely hideous and his opponent be Alcaeus, the handsome Milesian and loved, they say, by Nicostratos himself. Should History, then, provide the pleasurable as a side-product, she may attract a great number of lovers, but as long as she keeps her sole particular feature intact, I mean the revelation of the truth, she will show scant concern for her good looks.

[10] Another point worth mentioning is that complete fiction isn't even a pleasurable element in history and eulogising, whichever side it favours, is completely repugnant to listeners, if you don't have the mob and common populace in mind but those who will listen in a judicial or indeed even in a faultfinding spirit, men who wouldn't fail to notice any detail skimped, men with sharper sight than Argus and from every part of their body, scrutinising every word spoken like money-changers, so as immediately to reject what's counterfeit, but accept what's genuine and legal and bears the precise stamp. These are the men to look to when writing history, paying little attention to all others, even if they burst themselves apart with their praises, but if you disregard them and sugar your history beyond all reasonable measure with fictions and eulogies and

χιστ' ἂν ὁμοίαν αὐτὴν ἐξεργάσαιο τῷ ἐν Λυδίᾳ Ἡρακλεῖ. ἑωρακέναι γάρ σέ που εἰκὸς γεγραμμένον, τῇ Ὀμφάλῃ δουλεύοντα,
πάνυ ἀλλόκοτον σκευὴν ἐσκευασμένον, ἐκείνην μὲν τὸν λέοντα
αὐτοῦ περιβεβλημένην καὶ τὸ ξύλον ἐν τῇ χειρὶ ἔχουσαν, ὡς
Ἡρακλέα δῆθεν οὖσαν, αὐτὸν δὲ ἐν κροκωτῷ καὶ πορφυρίδι
ἔρια ξαίνοντα καὶ παιόμενον ὑπὸ τῆς Ὀμφάλης τῷ σανδαλίῳ.
καὶ τὸ θέαμα αἴσχιστον, ἀφεστῶσα ἡ ἐσθὴς τοῦ σώματος καὶ μὴ
προσιζάνουσα καὶ τοῦ θεοῦ τὸ ἀνδρῶδες ἀσχημόνως καταθη-
λυνόμενον.

Καὶ οἱ μὲν πολλοὶ ἴσως καὶ ταῦτά σου ἐπαινέσονται, οἱ ὀλίγοι 11
δὲ ἐκεῖνοι ὧν σὺ καταφρονεῖς μάλα ἡδὺ καὶ ἐς κόρον γελάσον-
ται, ὁρῶντες τὸ ἀσύμφυλον καὶ ἀνάρμοστον καὶ δυσκόλλητον
τοῦ πράγματος. ἑκάστου γὰρ δὴ ἴδιόν τι καλόν ἐστιν· εἰ δὲ τοῦτο
ἐναλλάξειας, ἀκαλλὲς τὸ αὐτὸ παρὰ τὴν χρῆσιν γίγνεται. ἐῶ
λέγειν ὅτι οἱ ἔπαινοι ἑνὶ μὲν ἴσως τερπνοί, τῷ ἐπαινουμένῳ, τοῖς
δὲ ἄλλοις ἐπαχθεῖς, καὶ μάλιστα ἢν ὑπερφυεῖς τὰς ὑπερβολὰς
ἔχωσιν, οἵους αὐτοὺς οἱ πολλοὶ ἀπεργάζονται, τὴν εὔνοιαν τὴν
παρὰ τῶν ἐπαινουμένων θηρώμενοι καὶ ἐνδιατρίβοντες ἄχρι τοῦ
πᾶσι προφανῆ τὴν κολακείαν ἐξεργάσασθαι. οὐδὲ γὰρ κατὰ τέχνην
αὐτὸ δρᾶν ἴσασιν οὐδ' ἐπισκιάζουσι τὴν θωπείαν, ἀλλ' ἐμπεσόν-
τες ἀθρόα πάντα καὶ ἀπίθανα καὶ γυμνὰ διεξίασιν. ὥστ' οὐδὲ 12
τυγχάνουσιν οὗ μάλιστα ἐφίενται· οἱ γὰρ ἐπαινούμενοι πρὸς αὐτῶν
μισοῦσι μᾶλλον καὶ ἀποστρέφονται ὡς κόλακας, εὖ ποιοῦντες,
καὶ μάλιστα ἢν ἀνδρώδεις τὰς γνώμας ὦσιν. <

> Ἀλεξάν-
δρου καὶ Πώρου, καὶ ἀναγνόντος αὐτῷ τοῦτο μάλιστα τὸ
χωρίον τῆς γραφῆς—ᾤετο γὰρ χαριεῖσθαι τὰ μέγιστα τῷ
βασιλεῖ ἐπιψευδόμενος ἀριστείας τινὰς αὐτῷ καὶ ἀναπλάττων ἔργα
μείζω τῆς ἀληθείας—λαβὼν τὸ βιβλίον—πλέοντες δὲ ἐτύγχανον
ἐν τῷ ποταμῷ τῷ Ὑδάσπῃ—ἔρριψεν ἐπὶ κεφαλὴν ἐς τὸ ὕδωρ
ἐπειπών, Καὶ σὲ δὲ οὕτως ἐχρῆν, ὦ Ἀριστόβουλε, τοιαῦτα
ὑπὲρ ἐμοῦ μονομαχοῦντα καὶ ἐλέφαντας ἑνὶ ἀκοντίῳ φονεύοντα.
καὶ ἔμελλέ γε οὕτως ἀγανακτήσειν ὁ Ἀλέξανδρος, ὅς γε οὐδὲ
τὴν τοῦ ἀρχιτέκτονος τόλμαν ἠνέσχετο, ὑποσχομένου τὸν
Ἄθων εἰκόνα ποιήσειν αὐτοῦ καὶ μετακοσμήσειν τὸ ὄρος ἐς

general flattery, you'd very soon make it resemble Heracles in Lydia; for you've probably seen paintings of him as Omphale's slave, dressed in the most absurd fashion, with her wearing *his* lion's skin and carrying *his* club, pretending to be Heracles, and him dressed in saffron and purple, carding wool and being beaten by Omphale with her slipper, and, most shocking of sights, with his clothing loose and hanging off his body and the masculinity of the god reduced to an unsightly femininity!

[11] Perhaps the majority will praise you even for this, but the select few whom you despise will enjoy a good laugh, when they see what an incongruous and inharmonious patchwork it all is. For each thing has its own particular beauty; but should you alter that, it loses its beauty through being misused. I won't mention the fact that though expressions of praise may please one individual, the person praised, they annoy everyone else, particularly if containing monstrous exaggerations, as most historians make them do, as they court the goodwill of those praised and linger over the topic till they make their flattery quite obvious to everyone. For they don't know how to praise with the proper skills, but, failing to veil their flattery, jump in headlong to indulge in a mass of blatantly improbable statements. [12] So they fail even to achieve what they most desire; for those praised by them quite rightly hate them the more and spurn them as flatterers, especially if they have the spirit of real men! (Take Alexander's reaction to Aristobulus' account of the single combat) between him and Porus. When Aristobulus had read out to him this particular part of his work, thinking he would gratify his king by falsely attributing heroic deeds to him and inventing exploits too great to be true, Alexander took the book – at the time they were sailing on the River Hydaspes – and threw it straight into the water, adding the words 'I ought to do the same with you too, Aristobulus, for fighting such single combats on my behalf and killing elephants for me with a single spear.' 'It wasn't surprising that Alexander should be so angry, when he couldn't tolerate the audacity of the architect who promised to make Mount Athos into a statue of his king and to remodel the mountain to look like him. No, he immediately

ὁμοιότητα τοῦ βασιλέως, ἀλλὰ κόλακα εὐθὺς ἐπιγνοὺς τὸν ἄνθρωπον οὐκέτ᾽ οὐδ᾽ ἐς τὰ ἄλλα ὁμοίως ἐχρῆτο.

Ποῦ τοίνυν τὸ τερπνὸν ἐν τούτοις, ἐκτὸς εἰ μή τις κομιδῇ ἀνό- 13 ητος εἴη ὡς χαίρειν τὰ τοιαῦτα ἐπαινούμενος ὧν παρὰ πόδας οἱ ἔλεγχοι; ὥσπερ οἱ ἄμορφοι τῶν ἀνθρώπων, καὶ μάλιστά γε τὰ γύναια τοῖς γραφεῦσι παρακελευόμενα ὡς καλλίστας αὐτὰς γράφειν. οἴονται γὰρ ἄμεινον ἕξειν τὴν ὄψιν, ἢν ὁ γραφεὺς αὐταῖς ἐρύθημά τε πλεῖον ἐπανθίσῃ καὶ τὸ λευκὸν ἐγκαταμίξῃ πολὺ τῷ φαρμάκῳ.

Τοιοῦτοι πολλοὶ τῶν συγγραφόντων [οἱ πολλοί] εἰσι τὸ τήμερον καὶ τὸ ἴδιον καὶ τὸ χρειῶδες ὅ τι ἂν ἐκ τῆς ἱστορίας ἐλπίσωσι θεραπεύοντες· οὓς μισεῖσθαι καλῶς εἶχεν, ἐς μὲν τὸ παρὸν κόλακας προδήλους καὶ ἀτέχνους ὄντας, ἐς τοὐπιὸν δὲ ὕποπτον ταῖς ὑπερβολαῖς τὴν ὅλην πραγματείαν ἀποφαίνοντας. εἰ δέ τις πάντως τὸ τερπνὸν ἡγεῖται καταμεμῖχθαι δεῖν τῇ ἱστορίᾳ, ἄλλα σὺν ἀληθείᾳ τερπνά ἐστιν ἐν τοῖς ἄλλοις κάλλεσι τοῦ λόγου, ὧν ἀμελήσαντες οἱ πολλοὶ τὰ μηδὲν προσήκοντα ἐπεισκυκλοῦσιν.

Ἐγὼ δ᾽ οὖν καὶ διηγήσομαι ὁπόσα μέμνημαι ἔναγχος ἐν Ἰω- 14 νίᾳ συγγραφέων τινῶν, καὶ νὴ Δία ἐν Ἀχαΐᾳ πρώην ἀκούσας τὸν αὐτὸν τοῦτον πόλεμον διηγουμένων. καὶ πρὸς Χαρίτων μηδεὶς ἀπιστήσῃ τοῖς λεχθησομένοις· ὅτι γὰρ ἀληθῆ ἐστιν κἂν ἐπωμοσάμην, εἰ ἀστεῖον ἦν ὅρκον ἐντιθέναι συγγράμματι. εἷς μέν τις αὐτῶν ἀπὸ Μουσῶν εὐθὺς ἤρξατο παρακαλῶν τὰς θεὰς συνεφάψασθαι τοῦ συγγράμματος. ὁρᾷς ὡς ἐμμελὴς ἡ ἀρχὴ καὶ περὶ πόδα τῇ ἱστορίᾳ καὶ τῷ τοιούτῳ εἴδει τῶν λόγων πρέπουσα; εἶτα μικρὸν ὑποβὰς Ἀχιλλεῖ μὲν τὸν ἡμέτερον ἄρχοντα εἴκαζε, Θερσίτῃ δὲ τὸν τῶν Περσῶν βασιλέα, οὐκ εἰδὼς ὅτι ὁ Ἀχιλλεὺς ἀμείνων ἦν αὐτῷ, εἰ Ἕκτορα μᾶλλον ἢ Θερσίτην καθήρει, καὶ εἰ πρόσθε μὲν ἔφευγεν ἐσθλός τις, 'ἐδίωκε δέ μιν μέγ᾽ ἀμείνων'. εἶτ᾽ ἐπῆγεν ὑπὲρ αὐτοῦ τι ἐγκώμιον, καὶ ὡς ἄξιος εἴη συγγράψαι τὰς πράξεις οὕτω λαμπρὰς οὔσας. ἤδη δὲ κατιὼν ἐπῄνει καὶ τὴν πατρίδα τὴν Μίλητον, προστιθεὶς ὡς ἄμεινον ποιοῖ τοῦτο τοῦ Ὁμήρου μηδὲν μνησθέντος τῆς πατρίδος. εἶτ᾽ ἐπὶ τέλει τοῦ φροιμίου ὑπισχνεῖτο διαρρήδην καὶ σαφῶς, ἐπὶ μεῖζον μὲν αἴρειν

spotted the fellow was a flatterer and stopped employing him as he had done before.

[13] What pleasure, then, is there in this sort of thing, unless one should be so completely stupid as to enjoy receiving such praises, though they can instantly be disproved? That's like ugly people, and females in particular who urge painters to make them as beautiful as possible, thinking their appearance will be improved if the painter gives them an extra rosy bloom and mixes a great deal of white into his pigment.

Many historians act like that, assiduously seeking short-term ends, personal objectives and any advantages they hope to gain from their history. Such men ought to be reviled, at the present time for being transparent flatterers and for their lack of craftsmanship, and by future generations for making all historical activity suspect by their exaggerations. But if anyone thinks the pleasurable an absolutely essential ingredient in history, there are among the various literary embellishments some features which are pleasurable without offending the truth, but most of those fellows neglect these and introduce inappropriate material into their scenario.

[14] Now I'm going to tell you what I remember from personal experience. I listened to various historians recently in Ionia, yes, by gad, and others only the other day in Achaea, describing this same war, and in the name of the Graces, let nobody disbelieve what I am going to tell you! Indeed I'd have vouched for my truthfulness on oath, if it were good form to add an affidavit to a prose work! One of them started right away with the Muses, appealing to the goddesses to help him in his work. Can you see how well his exordium strikes the right note, and fits history and how appropriate it is to this type of literature? Then a little later he likened our leader to Achilles and the Persian king to Thersites, unaware that Achilles was improved by killing a Hector rather than a Thersites, and having a valiant warrior fleeing before him 'pursued by one still mightier far.' Then he introduced an encomium in praise of himself, claiming to be a worthy historian for such glorious deeds. Then he went on to praise his native city of Miletus, adding that in so doing he was superior to Homer who made no mention of his native place. Then at the end of his proem he promised in clear, unmistakable terms to magnify our achievements

τὰ ἡμέτερα, τοὺς βαρβάρους δὲ καταπολεμήσειν καὶ αὐτός, ὡς
ἂν δύνηται. καὶ ἤρξατό γε τῆς ἱστορίας οὕτως, αἴτια ἅμα τῆς τοῦ
πολέμου ἀρχῆς διεξιών· "Ὁ γὰρ μιαρώτατος καὶ κάκιστα ἀπο-
λούμενος Οὐολόγεσος ἤρξατο πολεμεῖν δι᾽ αἰτίαν τοιάνδε."

Οὗτος μὲν τοιαῦτα. ἕτερος δὲ Θουκυδίδου ζηλωτὴς ἄκρος, **15**
οἷος εὖ μάλα τῷ ἀρχετύπῳ εἰκασμένος, καὶ τὴν ἀρχὴν ὡς ἐκεῖνος σὺν τῷ ἑαυτοῦ ὀνόματι ἤρξατο, χαριεστάτην ἀρχῶν ἁπασῶν
καὶ θύμου τοῦ Ἀττικοῦ ἀποπνέουσαν. ὅρα γάρ· "Κρεπέρηος
Καλπουρνιανὸς Πομπηϊουπολίτης συνέγραψε τὸν πόλεμον τὸν
Παρθυαίων καὶ Ῥωμαίων, ὡς ἐπολέμησαν πρὸς ἀλλήλους, ἀρξάμενος εὐθὺς συνισταμένου." ὥστε μετά γε τοιαύτην ἀρχὴν τί
ἄν σοι τὰ λοιπὰ λέγοιμι—ὁποῖα ἐν Ἀρμενίᾳ ἐδημηγόρησεν τὸν
Κερκυραῖον αὐτὸν ῥήτορα παραστησάμενος, ἢ οἷον Νισιβηνοῖς
λοιμὸν τοῖς μὴ τὰ Ῥωμαίων αἱρουμένοις ἐπήγαγεν παρὰ Θουκυδίδου χρησάμενος ὅλον ἄρδην πλὴν μόνου τοῦ Πελασγικοῦ καὶ
τῶν τειχῶν τῶν μακρῶν, ἐν οἷς οἱ τότε λοιμώξαντες ᾤκησαν; τὰ
δ᾽ ἄλλα καὶ ἀπὸ Αἰθιοπίας ἤρξατο, ὥστε καὶ ἐς Αἴγυπτον κατέβη
καὶ ἐς τὴν βασιλέως [τὴν] γῆν τὴν πολλήν, καὶ ἐν ἐκείνη γε ἔμει-
νεν εὖ ποιῶν. ἐγὼ γοῦν θάπτοντα ἔτι αὐτὸν καταλιπὼν τοὺς
ἀθλίους Ἀθηναίους ἐν Νισίβι ἀπῆλθον ἀκριβῶς εἰδὼς καὶ
ὅσα ἀπελθόντος ἐρεῖν ἔμελλεν. καὶ γὰρ αὖ καὶ τοῦτο ἐπιεικῶς
πολὺ νῦν ἐστιν, τὸ οἴεσθαι τοῦτ᾽ εἶναι τοῖς Θουκυδίδου ἐοικότα
λέγειν, εἰ ὀλίγον ἐντρέψας τὰ αὐτοῦ ἐκείνου λέγοι τις.† μικρὰ
κακειαοως καὶ αὐτὸς ἂν φαίης οὐ δι᾽ αὐτὴν† ‹ν›ἢ Δία κά-
κεῖνο ὀλίγου δεῖν παρέλιπον· ὁ γὰρ αὐτὸς οὗτος συγγραφεὺς
πολλὰ καὶ τῶν ὅπλων καὶ τῶν μηχανημάτων ὡς Ῥωμαῖοι αὐτὰ
ὀνομάζουσιν οὕτως ἀνέγραψεν, καὶ τάφρον ὡς ἐκεῖνοι καὶ γέ-
φυραν καὶ τὰ τοιαῦτα. καί μοι ἐννόησον ἡλίκον τὸ ἀξίωμα τῆς
ἱστορίας καὶ ὡς Θουκυδίδῃ πρέπον, μεταξὺ τῶν Ἀττικῶν ὀνομάτων τὰ Ἰταλιωτικὰ ταῦτα ἐγκεῖσθαι, ὥσπερ τὴν πορφύραν
ἐπικοσμοῦντα καὶ ἐμπρέποντα καὶ πάντως συνᾴδοντα.

Ἄλλος δέ τις αὐτῶν ὑπόμνημα τῶν γεγονότων γυμνὸν συνα- **16**
γαγὼν ἐν γραφῇ κομιδῇ πεζὸν καὶ χαμαιπετές, οἷον καὶ στρα-
τιώτης ἄν τις τὰ καθ᾽ ἡμέραν ὑπογραφόμενος συνέθηκεν ἢ
τέκτων ἢ κάπηλός τις συμπερινοστῶν τῇ στρατιᾷ. πλὴν ἀλλὰ

and to do his best to reduce the barbarians to defeat by adding his own contribution. This is how he began his history, at the same time adding the reasons for the start of the war: 'That foulest of villains, that accursed scoundrel Vologesus, began the war for the following reason.'

[15] That was how *he* did it. But another, a consummate imitator of Thucydides, modelling himself very carefully on his exemplar, even began his proem like Thucydides with his own name, producing the most elegant of all proems and one with as Attic an aroma as thyme! Just look at this: 'Crepereius Calpurnianus, the Pompeiopolitan, wrote the history of the war between the Parthians and the Romans, and how they fought against each other, beginning from the moment it broke out.' So after such a start need I tell you about the rest of it – the kind of public address he produced in Armenia by putting the Corcyrean envoy unchanged on the rostrum, or the sort of plague he visited on the folk of Nisibis for not choosing the Roman side, borrowing it lock, stock and barrel from Thucydides, except only the Pelasgicum and the Long Walls, in which those then suffering from the plague had made their homes? But consider its other details; *it* too started in Ethiopia, so that *it* too passed down into Egypt and most of the territories of the Great King, where I'm glad to say it stayed! In any case I left him still burying his unfortunate Athenians in Nisibis, since I knew exactly what he was going to say after my departure. For it's a pretty common occurrence these days for someone to think he's talking like Thucydides if he uses Thucydides' own words with a few changes. (However perhaps you'd call that a small fault, as it saved us from having to hear the fellow's *own* words!) But, in heaven's name, I almost forgot to tell you that this same historian referred to many weapons and military engines by their Roman names, using Latin terms for ditch, bridge and the like. Just consider how well it upholds the prestige of history and the Thucydidean spirit to have in amongst your true Attic words these Italianate ones inserted, as though they added beauty, like the purple on a garment, matching it well and looking just right.

[16] Another of them compiled a bare record of events, making it completely lowbrow and down-to-earth, just as a soldier writing up his diary would have composed or an artisan or a tradesman trailing round with the army. However this amateur was less unsatisfactory than the

μετριώτερός γε ὁ ἰδιώτης οὗτος ἦν, αὐτὸς μὲν αὐτίκα δῆλος
ὢν οἷος ἦν, ἄλλῳ δέ τινι χαρίεντι καὶ δυνησομένῳ ἱστορίαν
μεταχειρίσασθαι προπεπονηκώς. τοῦτο μόνον ἠτιασάμην αὐτοῦ,
ὅτι οὕτως ἐπέγραψε τὰ βιβλία τραγικώτερον ἢ κατὰ <τὴν>
τῶν συγγραμμάτων τύχην—"Καλλιμόρφου ἰατροῦ τῆς τῶν
κοντοφόρων ἕκτης ἱστοριῶν Παρθικῶν," καὶ ὑπεγέγραπτο
ἑκάστῃ ὁ ἀριθμός. καὶ νὴ Δία καὶ τὸ προοίμιον ὑπέρψυχρον
ἐποίησεν οὕτως συναγαγών· οἰκεῖον εἶναι ἰατρῷ ἱστορίαν
συγγράφειν, εἴ γε ὁ Ἀσκληπιὸς μὲν Ἀπόλλωνος υἱός, Ἀπόλλων
δὲ Μουσηγέτης καὶ πάσης παιδείας ἄρχων· καὶ ὅτι ἀρξάμενος
ἐν τῇ Ἰάδι γράφειν οὐκ οἶδα ὅ τι δόξαν αὐτίκα μάλα ἐπὶ τὴν κοινὴν
μετῆλθεν, ἰητρικὴν μὲν λέγων καὶ πείρην καὶ ὁκόσα καὶ νοῦσοι,
τὰ δ' ἄλλα ὁμοδίαιτα τοῖς πολλοῖς καὶ τὰ πλεῖστα οἷα ἐκ τριόδου.

Εἰ δέ με δεῖ καὶ σοφοῦ ἀνδρὸς μνησθῆναι, τὸ μὲν ὄνομα ἐν **17**
ἀφανεῖ κείσθω, τὴν γνώμην δὲ ἐρῶ καὶ τὰ πρῴην ἐν Κορίνθῳ
συγγράμματα, κρείττω πάσης ἐλπίδος. ἐν ἀρχῇ μὲν γὰρ εὐθὺς
ἐν τῇ πρώτῃ τοῦ προοιμίου περιόδῳ συνηρώτησε τοὺς ἀναγινώ-
σκοντας λόγον πάνσοφον δεῖξαι σπεύδων, ὡς μόνῳ ἂν τῷ σοφῷ
πρέποι ἱστορίαν συγγράφειν. εἶτα μετὰ μικρὸν ἄλλος συλλογι-
σμός, εἶτα ἄλλος· καὶ ὅλως ἐν ἅπαντι σχήματι συνηρώτητο
αὐτῷ τὸ προοίμιον. τὸ τῆς κολακείας ἐς κόρον, καὶ τὰ ἐγκώμια
φορτικὰ καὶ κομιδῇ βωμολοχικά, οὐκ ἀσυλλόγιστα μέντοι, ἀλλὰ
συνηρωτημένα καὶ συνηγμένα κἀκεῖνα. καὶ μὴν κἀκεῖνο φορτικὸν ἔδοξέν μοι καὶ ἥκιστα φιλοσόφῳ ἀνδρὶ καὶ πώγωνι πολιῷ καὶ βαθεῖ πρέπον, τὸ ἐν τῷ προοιμίῳ εἰπεῖν, ὡς ἐξαίρετον
τοῦτο ἕξει ὁ ἡμέτερος ἄρχων, οὗ γε τὰς πράξεις καὶ φιλόσοφοι
ἤδη συγγράφειν ἀξιοῦσιν. τὸ γὰρ τοιοῦτο, εἴπερ ἄρα, ἡμῖν <κάλ-
λιον ἦν> καταλιπεῖν λογίζεσθαι ἢ αὐτὸν εἰπεῖν.

Καὶ μὴν οὐδ' ἐκείνου ὅσιον ἀμνημονῆσαι, ὃς τοιάνδε ἀρχὴν **18**
ἤρξατο· "Ἔρχομαι ἐρέων περὶ Ῥωμαίων καὶ Περσέων," καὶ
μικρὸν ὕστερον· "ἔδεε γὰρ Πέρσῃσι γενέσθαι κακῶς," καὶ
πάλιν· "ἦν Ὀσρόης, τὸν οἱ Ἕλληνες Ὀξυρόην ὀνυμέουσιν,"
καὶ ἄλλα πολλὰ τοιαῦτα. ὁρᾷς; ὅμοιος οὗτος ἐκείνῳ παρ' ὅσον
ὁ μὲν Θουκυδίδῃ, οὗτος δὲ Ἡροδότῳ εὖ μάλα ἐῴκει.

others; he made it quite clear from the start what he was, and had merely done the groundwork for someone else with the polish and ability to undertake the writing of history. The only fault I found with him was that he headed his books with titles of greater magnificence than his writings deserved such as 'By Callimorphus, Surgeon of the Sixth Company of Pikemen, Parthian Histories' followed by the number of each book. And, ye gods, he made his preface far too insipid by concluding 'It's appropriate for a doctor to write history, as Asclepius is the son of Apollo and Apollo is the leader of the Muses and in charge of all culture.' Furthermore, after starting writing in Ionic, he took it into his head for some reason to switch into everyday speech; thus, though he had used the Ionic forms for 'medicine', 'attempt', 'as many as' and 'illnesses', otherwise his language resembled that of ordinary folk, or indeed usually that of the gutter.

[17] But, if I may add a mention of a philosopher, his name must remain a secret, but I shall tell you about his thoughts and his recent writings in Corinth, which surpassed all expectations! For right at the start in the first sentence of his preface he subjected his readers to dialectic as he strove to prove the highly intellectual thesis that only the philosopher was the proper person to write history! This was followed by another syllogism and then by a third one. In short his preface consisted of dialectical arguments of every shape and form. He used flattery *ad nauseam* and encomia that were crude and absolutely vulgar, but these too included philosophical arguments full of dialectic and deductions. Another thing that struck me as ill-bred and quite inappropriate for a philosopher and a long white beard was saying in his preface that it would be a special privilege for our general that now even philosophers consent to record his exploits in history. If he had to use this sort of idea at all, it would have been far better to leave it to occur to us than to express it himself!

[18] Again it would be quite wrong to omit mention of the fellow who began like this: 'I do come to tell of Romans and Persians' and a little later said 'For 'twas decreed of fate that ill should the Persians fare,' and again ' 'Twas Osroes whom the Greeks do Oxyroes call' and many other things like that. Do you see? He's similar to the other fellow, only he was a carbon copy of Thucydides and this fellow of Herodotus.

Ἄλλος τις ἀοίδιμος ἐπὶ λόγων δυνάμει Θουκυδίδῃ καὶ αὐτὸς **19**
ὅμοιος ἢ ὀλίγῳ ἀμείνων αὐτοῦ, πάσας πόλεις καὶ πάντα ὄρη καὶ
πεδία καὶ ποταμοὺς ἑρμηνεύσας πρὸς τὸ σαφέστατον καὶ ἰσχυ-
ρότατον, ὡς ᾤετο. τὸ δὲ ἐς ἐχθρῶν κεφαλὰς ὁ ἀλεξίκακος τρέψειε·
τοσαύτη ψυχρότης ἐνῆν ὑπὲρ τὴν Κασπιακὴν χιόνα καὶ τὸν κρύ-
σταλλον τὸν Κελτικόν. ἡ γοῦν ἀσπὶς ἡ τοῦ αὐτοκράτορος ὅλῳ
βιβλίῳ μόγις ἐξηρμηνεύθη αὐτῷ, καὶ Γοργὼν ἐπὶ τοῦ ὀμφαλοῦ
καὶ οἱ ὀφθαλμοὶ αὐτῆς ἐκ κυανοῦ καὶ λευκοῦ καὶ μέλανος καὶ
ζώνη ἰριοειδὴς καὶ δράκοντες ἑλικηδὸν καὶ βοστρυχηδόν. ἡ μὲν
γὰρ Οὐολογέσου ἀναξυρὶς ἢ ὁ χαλινὸς τοῦ ἵππου, Ἡράκλεις,
ὅσαι μυριάδες ἐπῶν ἕκαστον τούτων, καὶ οἷα ἦν ἡ Ὀσρόου κόμη,
διανέοντος τὸν Τίγρητα, καὶ ἐς οἷον ἄντρον κατέφυγε, κιττοῦ καὶ
μυρρίνης καὶ δάφνης ἐς ταὐτὸ συμπεφυκότων καὶ σύσκιον ἀκριβῶς ποιούντων αὐτό. σκόπει ὡς ἀναγκαῖα τῇ ἱστορίᾳ ταῦτα,
καὶ ὧν ἄνευ οὐκ <ἂν> ᾔδειμέν τι τῶν ἐκεῖ πραχθέντων.

Ὑπὸ γὰρ ἀσθενείας τῆς ἐν τοῖς χρησίμοις ἢ ἀγνοίας τῶν **20**
λεκτέων ἐπὶ τὰς τοιαύτας τῶν χωρίων καὶ ἄντρων ἐκφράσεις
τρέπονται, καὶ ὁπόταν ἐς πολλὰ καὶ μεγάλα πράγματα ἐμπέσω-
σιν ἐοίκασιν οἰκέτῃ νεοπλούτῳ ἄρτι κληρονομήσαντι τοῦ δεσπότου, ὃς οὔτε τὴν ἐσθῆτα οἶδεν ὡς χρὴ περιβαλέσθαι οὔτε δει-
πνῆσαι κατὰ νόμον, ἀλλ' ἐμπηδήσας, πολλάκις ὀρνίθων καὶ
συείων καὶ λαγῶων προκειμένων, ὑπερεμπίμπλαται ἔτνους τινὸς
ἢ ταρίχους ἔστ' ἂν διαρραγῇ ἐσθίων. οὗτος δ' οὖν ὃν προεῖπον
καὶ τραύματα συνέγραψεν πάνυ ἀπίθανα καὶ θανάτους ἀλλοκότους, ὡς εἰς δάκτυλον τοῦ ποδὸς τὸν μέγαν τρωθείς τις αὐτίκα
ἐτελεύτησε, καὶ ὡς ἐμβοήσαντος μόνον Πρίσκου τοῦ στρατηγοῦ
ἑπτὰ καὶ εἴκοσι τῶν πολεμίων ἐξέθανον. ἔτι δὲ καὶ ἐν τῷ τῶν
νεκρῶν ἀριθμῷ τοῦτο μὲν καὶ παρὰ τὰ γεγραμμένα ἐν ταῖς τῶν
ἀρχόντων ἐπιστολαῖς ἐψεύσατο· ἐπὶ γὰρ Εὐρώπῳ τῶν μὲν πολεμίων ἀποθανεῖν μυριάδας ἑπτὰ καὶ τριάκοντα καὶ ἓξ πρὸς δια-
κοσίοις, Ῥωμαίων δὲ μόνους <δύο> καὶ τραυματίας γενέσθαι
ἐννέα. ταῦτα οὐκ οἶδα εἴ τις ἂν εὖ φρονῶν ἀνάσχοιτο.

Καὶ μὴν κἀκεῖνο λεκτέον οὐ μικρὸν ὄν· ὑπὸ γὰρ τοῦ κομιδῇ **21**
Ἀττικὸς εἶναι καὶ ἀποκεκαθάρθαι τὴν φωνὴν ἐς τὸ ἀκριβέστατον ἠξίωσεν οὗτος καὶ τὰ ὀνόματα μεταποιῆσαι τὰ Ῥωμαίων

[19] There's another man, one celebrated for his command of words, who too is another Thucydides, or indeed a slight improvement on him, one who has described every city, every mountain, plain and river with the utmost clarity and power – in his own opinion at least! But may all of that be diverted on to our enemies' heads by the divine protector; for *his* works were so frigid that they outdid the Caspian snows and the ice of Galatia. He only just managed to describe our emperor's shield in a whole book, what with the Gorgon on its boss, her eyes of blue and white and black, her girdle with all the colours of the rainbow, and the serpents entwined around her in clusters. And then there were Vologesus' trousers or the bridle of his horse; god give me strength to tell you how many thousands of words they all needed, yes and there was his description of Osroes' hair as he swam the Tigris and of the cave where he took refuge, with the ivy and myrtle and laurel growing together and making it completely dark! Just think how essential to history all that is! Without it we'd have known nothing of events in that region!

[20] For through their weakness in useful departments and ignorance of the right things to say they turn to such descriptions of places and caves and, when they embark on important major topics, they are like a *nouveau-riche* servant who has just inherited his master's property, and doesn't know how to dress or the correct procedure for dining, but, perhaps when delicacies like fowls and pork and hare are on the menu, gorges himself on soup or salt fish till he's at bursting point. The man I have just mentioned also recorded quite incredible wounds and extraordinary deaths – how someone was wounded in the big toe and died immediately and how a mere shout from the general Priscus killed twentyseven of the enemy. Furthermore in recording the number of dead he contradicted the commanders' despatches and gave false figures, saying that at Europus enemy dead numbered 70, 236 while the Romans suffered only two dead and nine wounded. I don't know if anyone in his right mind could put up with that!

[21] Now there is something else of importance I must say. This fellow, being an out-and-out Atticist and having purified his style to absolute perfection, actually presumed to change the names of the Romans, rewriting them in Greek, so that he called Saturninus Cronios,

καὶ μεταγράψαι ἐς τὸ Ἑλληνικόν, ὡς Κρόνιον μὲν Σατουρνῖνον λέγειν, Φρόντιν δὲ τὸν Φρόντωνα, Τιτάνιον δὲ τὸν Τιτιανὸν καὶ ἄλλα πολλῷ γελοιότερα. ἔτι ὁ αὐτὸς οὗτος περὶ τῆς Σεουηριανοῦ τελευτῆς ἔγραψεν ὡς οἱ μὲν ἄλλοι πάντες ἐξηπάτηνται οἰόμενοι ξίφει τεθνάναι αὐτόν, ἀποθάνοι δὲ ἀνὴρ σιτίων ἀποσχόμενος· τοῦτον γὰρ αὐτῷ ἀλυπότατον δόξαι τὸν θάνατον, οὐκ εἰδὼς ὅτι τὸ μὲν πάθος ἐκείνῳ πᾶν τριῶν οἶμαι ἡμερῶν ἐγένετο, ἀπόσιτοι δὲ καὶ ἐς ἑβδόμην διαρκοῦσιν οἱ πολλοί—ἐκτὸς εἰ μὴ τοῦθ' ὑπολάβοι τις, ὡς Ὀσρόης τις εἰστήκει περιμένων, ἔστ' ἂν Σεουηριανὸς λιμῷ ἀπόληται, καὶ διὰ τοῦτο οὐκ ἐπῆγε διὰ τῆς ἑβδόμης.

Τοὺς δὲ καὶ ποιητικοῖς ὀνόμασιν, ὦ καλὲ Φίλων, ἐν ἱστορίᾳ **22** χρωμένους, ποῦ δ' ἄν τις θείη, τοὺς λέγοντας, "ἐλέλιξε μὲν ἡ μηχανή, τὸ τεῖχος δὲ πεσὸν μεγάλως ἐδούπησε," καὶ πάλιν ἐν ἑτέρῳ μέρει τῆς καλῆς ἱστορίας, "Ἔδεσσα μὲν δὴ οὕτω τοῖς ὅπλοις περιεσμαραγεῖτο καὶ ὄτοβος ἦν καὶ κόναβος ἄπαντα ἐκεῖνα" καὶ "ὁ στρατηγὸς ἐμερμήριζεν ᾧ τρόπῳ μάλιστα προσαγάγοι πρὸς τὸ τεῖχος." εἶτα μεταξὺ οὕτως εὐτελῆ ὀνόματα καὶ δημοτικὰ καὶ πτωχικὰ πολλὰ παρενεβέβυστο—τό "ἐπέστειλεν ὁ στρατοπεδάρχης τῷ κυρίῳ," καὶ "οἱ στρατιῶται ἠγόραζον τὰ ἐγχρήζοντα" καὶ "ἤδη λελουμένοι περὶ αὑτοὺς* ἐγίγνοντο" καὶ τὰ τοιαῦτα· ὥστε τὸ πρᾶγμα ἐοικὸς εἶναι τραγῳδῷ τὸν ἕτερον μὲν πόδα ἐπ' ἐμβάτου ὑψηλοῦ ἐπιβεβηκότι, θατέρῳ δὲ σάνδαλον ὑποδεδεμένῳ.

Καὶ μὴν καὶ ἄλλους ἴδοις ἂν τὰ μὲν προοίμια λαμπρὰ καὶ **23** τραγικὰ καὶ εἰς ὑπερβολὴν μακρὰ συγγράφοντας, ὡς ἐλπίσαι θαυμαστὰ ἡλίκα τὰ μετὰ ταῦτα πάντως ἀκούσεσθαι, τὸ σῶμα δὲ αὐτὸ τῆς ἱστορίας μικρόν τι καὶ ἀγεννὲς ἐπαγαγόντας ὡς καὶ τοῦτο ἐοικέναι παιδίῳ, εἴ που Ἔρωτα εἶδες παίζοντα, προσωπεῖον Ἡρακλέους πάμμεγα ἢ Τιτᾶνος περικείμενον. εὐθὺς γοῦν οἱ ἀκούσαντες ἐπιφθέγγονται αὐτοῖς τό "Ὤδινεν ὄρος."

Χρὴ δὲ οἶμαι μὴ οὕτως, ἀλλ' ὅμοια τὰ πάντα καὶ ὁμόχροα εἶναι καὶ συνᾷδον τῇ κεφαλῇ τὸ ἄλλο σῶμα, ὡς μὴ χρυσοῦν μὲν τὸ κράνος εἴη, θώραξ δὲ πάνυ γελοῖος ἐκ ῥακῶν ποθὲν ἢ ἐκ δερμάτων σαπρῶν συγκεκαττυμένος καὶ ἡ ἀσπὶς οἰσυΐνη καὶ

Fronto Phrontis and Titianus Titanios and produced other far more ludicrous names. Moreover in his description of the death of Severianus, this same fellow wrote that everyone else is wrong in thinking he died by the sword and that he starved himself to death, because that seemed to Severianus the least painful death. The historian didn't know that what happened to Severianus took place within, I believe, three days at most, whereas most people who starve themselves last out till the seventh day – unless one imagines Osroes stood around waiting for Severianus to die of starvation and therefore withheld his attack throughout the week.

[22] But where, my good Philo, would one rank those who use poetic words in history, those who say 'the siege-engine did quake and the wall fall down with a mighty clangor', and again in another section of his history 'Edessa was so begirt with the hubbub of weaponry and all was hurly-burly and bobilation' and 'the general did bethink himself how best to attack the wall'? Then in amongst this were stuffed many vulgar, plebeian and slangy words like 'the boss of the camp sent a despatch to the guvnor', and 'the soldiers were buying the needful' or 'they had washed and were looking after number one' and expressions like that. So the thing is like a tragic actor with one foot propped up on an elevated buskin, but wearing a loose comic slipper on the other.

[23] You'll see others again composing prefaces that are brilliant, grandiloquent and excessively long so that we expect what we hear next will certainly be a miracle of magnitude, but what they add as the actual body of their history is so puny and stunted that it resembles a tiny child, just like Cupid, if you've ever seen him at play, wearing the enormous mask of a Heracles or a Titan. The immediate response of the audience is to heckle them, calling out 'The mountain was in travail'.

I don't consider that the right way. Instead everything ought to present a uniform and homogeneous appearance with the rest of the body corresponding to the head, so that you don't have the equivalent of a helmet of gold going with an absolutely ridiculous breastplate stitched together from rags or rotting leather, and a shield made of twigs and

χοιρίνη περὶ ταῖς κνήμαις. ἴδοις γὰρ ἂν ἀφθόνους τοιούτους
συγγραφέας, τοῦ ʽΡοδίων κολοσσοῦ τὴν κεφαλὴν νανώδει σώματι
ἐπιτιθέντας· ἄλλους αὖ ἔμπαλιν ἀκέφαλα τὰ σώματα εἰσάγοντας,
ἀπροοιμίαστα καὶ εὐθὺς ἐπὶ τῶν πραγμάτων, οἳ καὶ προσεταιρί-
ζονται τὸν Ξενοφῶντα οὕτως ἀρξάμενον, "Δαρείου καὶ Παρυ-
σάτιδος παῖδες γίγνονται δύο," καὶ ἄλλους τῶν παλαιῶν, οὐκ
εἰδότες ὡς δυνάμει τινὰ προοίμιά ἐστι λεληθότα τοὺς πολλούς,
ὡς ἐν ἄλλοις δείξομεν.

Καίτοι ταῦτα πάντα φορητὰ ἔτι, ὅσα ἢ ἑρμηνείας ἢ τῆς ἄλλης **24**
διατάξεως ἁμαρτήματά ἐστιν· τὸ δὲ καὶ παρὰ τοὺς τόπους
αὐτοὺς ψεύδεσθαι οὐ παρασάγγας μόνον ἀλλὰ καὶ σταθμοὺς
ὅλους, τίνι τῶν καλῶν ἔοικεν; εἷς γοῦν οὕτω ῥαθύμως συνήγαγε
τὰ πράγματα, οὔτε Σύρῳ τινὶ ἐντυχὼν οὔτε τὸ λεγόμενον δὴ
τοῦτο τῶν ἐπὶ κουρείῳ τὰ τοιαῦτα μυθολογούντων ἀκούσας, ὥστε
περὶ Εὐρώπου λέγων οὕτως ἔφη, " Ἡ δὲ Εὔρωπος κεῖται μὲν
ἐν τῇ Μεσοποταμίᾳ σταθμοὺς δύο τοῦ Εὐφράτου ἀπέχουσα,
ἀπῴκισαν δὲ αὐτὴν ʼΕδεσσαῖοι." καὶ οὐδὲ τοῦτο ἀπέχρησεν
αὐτῷ, ἀλλὰ καὶ τὴν ἐμὴν πατρίδα τὰ Σαμόσατα ὁ αὐτὸς ἐν τῷ
αὐτῷ βιβλίῳ ἀράμενος ὁ γενναῖος αὐτῇ ἀκροπόλει καὶ τείχεσιν
μετέθηκεν ἐς τὴν Μεσοποταμίαν, ὡς περιρρεῖσθαι αὐτὴν ὑπʼ
ἀμφοτέρων τῶν· ποταμῶν, ἑκατέρωθεν ἐν χρῷ παραμειβομένων
καὶ μονονουχὶ τοῦ τείχους ψαυόντων. τὸ δὲ καὶ γελοῖον εἴ σοι
νῦν, ὦ Φίλων, ἀπολογοίμην ὡς οὐ Παρθυαίων οὐδὲ Μεσοπο-
ταμίτης σοι ἐγώ, οἵ με φέρων ὁ θαυμαστὸς συγγραφεὺς
ἀπῴκισε.

Νὴ Δία κἀκεῖνο κομιδῇ πιθανὸν περὶ τοῦ Σεουηριανοῦ ὁ αὐτὸς **25**
οὗτος εἶπεν ἐπομοσάμενος, ἦ μὴν ἀκοῦσαί τινος τῶν ἐξ αὐτοῦ
τοῦ ἔργου διαφυγόντων· οὔτε γὰρ ξίφει ἐθελῆσαι αὐτὸν ἀποθανεῖν
οὔτε φαρμάκου πιεῖν οὔτε βρόχον ἅψασθαι ἀλλά τινα θάνατον
ἐπινοῆσαι τραγικὸν καὶ τῇ τόλμῃ ξενίζοντα· τυχεῖν μὲν γὰρ
αὐτὸν ἔχοντα παμμεγέθη ἐκπώματα ὑαλᾶ τῆς καλλίστης ὑάλου,
ἐπεὶ δὲ πάντως ἀποθανεῖν ἔγνωστο, κατάξαντα τὸν μέγιστον
τῶν σκύφων ἑνὶ τῶν θραυμάτων χρήσασθαι εἰς τὴν σφαγὴν ἐντε-
μόντα τῇ ὑάλῳ τὸν λαιμόν. οὕτως οὐ ξιφίδιον, οὐ λογχάριον
εὗρεν ὡς ἀνδρεῖός γε αὐτῷ καὶ ἡρωϊκὸς ὁ θάνατος γένοιτο. εἶτʼ **26**

greaves of pig-skin. You can see an abundance of historians like that, adding the head of the Colossus of Rhodes to the body of a dwarf, though others do the opposite, introducing headless bodies, jumping *in medias res* without any preface, men who claim camaraderie with Xenophon who started his work like this: 'Darius and Parysatis had two sons' and with others of the ancients; they are unaware that there do exist, though undetected by most people, some virtual prologues, as I shall demonstrate later.

[24] However all these faults of style or general arrangement are still tolerable, but to make errors that offend against actual geography and get places wrong not simply by a few parasangs but by whole days' journeys, what merit can we find in that? One man was so careless in gathering his facts that, though he'd never met a single Syrian or even, to quote the saying, heard such tittle-tattle in a barber's shop, this was what he said about Europus: 'Europus lies in Mesopotamia, two days' journey distant from the Euphrates, and it was founded by colonists from Edessa.' And even this didn't satisfy him, but this splendid fellow picked up my native city of Samosata and transported it, acropolis, walls and all, into Mesopotamia so that it is flanked by the waters of both the rivers passing close to it on both sides and almost touching the city walls. It would be quite ridiculous for me now to have to plead my case before you, my dear friend, and prove that I don't come from Parthia or Mesopotamia, the lands to which this admirable historian removed me.

[25] Upon my word, there's another quite incredible thing this same fellow told us about Severianus, for he swore upon oath he'd heard from one of the survivors of the actual events that he hadn't wanted to die by the sword or to drink poison or to hang himself but he thought up a theatrical death for himself and an extraordinarily bold one. It so happened he had some enormous goblets made of the finest crystal. Now once he was absolutely determined upon death, he shattered the largest of the glasses and used one of the splinters to commit suicide by cutting his throat with the crystal. So it wasn't by mere dagger or lance that he contrived a courageous and heroic death for himself.

ἐπειδὴ Θουκυδίδης ἐπιτάφιόν τινα εἶπεν τοῖς πρώτοις τοῦ πολέμου ἐκείνου νεκροῖς, καὶ αὐτὸς ἡγήσατο χρῆναι ἐπειπεῖν τῷ
Σεουηριανῷ. ἄπασι γὰρ αὐτοῖς πρὸς τὸν οὐδὲν αἴτιον τῶν ἐν
Ἀρμενίᾳ κακῶν τὸν Θουκυδίδην ἡ ἅμιλλα. θάψας οὖν τὸν
Σεουηριανὸν μεγαλοπρεπῶς ἀναβιβάζεται ἐπὶ τὸν τάφον Ἀφρά-
νιόν τινα Σίλωνα ἑκατόνταρχον ἀνταγωνιστὴν Περικλέους ὃς
τοιαῦτα καὶ τοσαῦτα ἐπερρητόρευσεν αὐτῷ ὥστε με νὴ τὰς
Χάριτας πολλὰ πάνυ δακρῦσαι ὑπὸ τοῦ γέλωτος καὶ μάλιστα
ὁπότε ῥήτωρ ὁ Ἀφράνιος ἐπὶ τέλει τοῦ λόγου δακρύων ἅμα
σὺν οἰμωγῇ περιπαθεῖ ἐμέμνητο τῶν πολυτελῶν ἐκείνων δεί-
πνων καὶ προπόσεων, εἶτα ἐπέθηκεν Αἰάντειόν τινα τὴν κορω-
νίδα· σπασάμενος γὰρ τὸ ξίφος, εὐγενῶς πάνυ καὶ ὡς Ἀφράνιον*
εἰκὸς ἦν, πάντων ὁρώντων ἀπέσφαξεν ἑαυτὸν ἐπὶ τῷ τάφῳ—οὐκ
ἀνάξιος ὢν μὰ τὸν Ἐννάλιον πρὸ πολλοῦ ἀποθανεῖν εἰ τοιαῦτα ἐρρητόρευεν. καὶ τοῦτο ἔφη ἰδόντας τοὺς παρόντας ἅπαντας
θαυμάσαι καὶ ὑπερεπαινέσαι τὸν Ἀφράνιον. ἐγὼ δὲ καὶ τὰ
ἄλλα μὲν αὐτοῦ κατεγίγνωσκον μονονουχὶ ζωμῶν καὶ λοπάδων
μεμνημένου καὶ ἐπιδακρύοντος τῇ τῶν πλακούντων μνήμῃ, τοῦτο
δὲ μάλιστα ᾐτιασάμην, ὅτι μὴ τὸν συγγραφέα καὶ διδάσκαλον τοῦ δράματος προαποσφάξας ἀπέθανεν.

Πολλοὺς δὲ καὶ ἄλλους ὁμοίως τούτοις ἔχων σοι, ὦ ἑταῖρε, **27**
καταριθμήσασθαι, ὀλίγων ὅμως ἐπιμνησθεὶς ἐπὶ τὴν ἑτέραν
ὑπόσχεσιν ἤδη μετελεύσομαι, τὴν συμβουλὴν ὅπως ἂν ἄμεινον
συγγράφοι τις. εἰσὶ γάρ τινες, οἳ τὰ μεγάλα μὲν τῶν πεπραγμέ-
νων καὶ ἀξιομνημόνευτα παραλείπουσιν ἢ παραθέουσιν, ὑπὸ δὲ
ἰδιωτείας καὶ ἀπειροκαλίας καὶ ἀγνοίας τῶν λεκτέων ἢ σιωπη-
τέων τὰ μικρότατα πάνυ λιπαρῶς καὶ φιλοπόνως ἑρμηνεύουσιν
ἐμβραδύνοντες, ὥσπερ ἂν εἴ τις τοῦ Διὸς τοῦ ἐν Ὀλυμπίᾳ τὸ
μὲν ὅλον κάλλος τοσοῦτο καὶ τοιοῦτο ὂν μὴ βλέποι μηδὲ ἐπαινοῖ
μηδὲ τοῖς οὐκ εἰδόσιν ἐξηγοῖτο, τοῦ ὑποποδίου δὲ τό τε εὐθυερ-
γὲς καὶ τὸ εὔξεστον θαυμάζοι καὶ τῆς κρηπῖδος τὸ εὔρυθμον,
καὶ ταῦτα πάνυ μετὰ πολλῆς φροντίδος διεξιών.

Ἐγὼ γοῦν ἤκουσά τινος τὴν μὲν ἐπ' Εὐρώπῳ μάχην ἐν οὐδ' **28**
ὅλοις ἑπτὰ ἔπεσι παραδραμόντος, εἴκοσι δὲ μέτρα ἢ ἔτι πλείω
ὕδατος ἀναλωκότος ἐς ψυχρὰν καὶ οὐδὲν ἡμῖν προσήκουσαν διή-

* read Ἀφρόνιον

[26] Next, since Thucydides delivered a funeral oration over the first casualties of that war of his, he too thought he just had to do the same for Severianus. For they all compete with Thucydides, though he can't be held responsible in any way for all that went wrong in Armenia! So after giving Severianus a magnificent burial, he made Afranius Silo, a centurion, mount the funeral mound for his rostrum in competition with Pericles and produced over Severianus so extraordinary and so long an oration that, I swear it by the Graces, I wept many tears of laughter, especially when, at the end of his speech, the eloquent Afranius, weeping and with emotional lamentation, recalled those magnificent banquets and toasts and ended it all in the same way as Ajax, for he drew his sword, and, in a noble manner worthy of an Aphronius, before all eyes cut his own throat over the grave – though, I swear by the God of War, he had deserved to die a lot earlier for being so bad an orator. The historian told us that, on seeing this, all present felt admiration and expressed the utmost praise for Afranius. I personally condemned him in general for being close to recording soup and fish dishes and for shedding tears over the memory of those cakes, but what in particular I held against him was that before his own suicide he hadn't killed the writer who produced this piece of theatricality!

[27] Though I could continue in similar fashion and enumerate many other bad historians for you, my friend, I'll just mention a few, before passing on to my other promise, that of advice how to write history better. There are some who omit or treat cursorily those events that are important and noteworthy, but, through amateurism, lack of taste and ignorance of what to say and what to pass over in silence, linger over descriptions of quite unimportant things most earnestly and laboriously. That's just as if one were to be blind to the overall beauty of the statue of Zeus at Olympia despite its magnificent scale and supreme quality, and to say nothing in its praise or describe it to those who don't know it, and instead go into raptures over the precise workmanship and fine finish of the footstool and the excellent proportions of the base, and, what's more, describe all these with the utmost care.

[28] I listened to one man who sped through the battle at Europus in less than seven complete lines but had already expended twenty or even more measures of the water-clock on a dull account of no concern to us, telling how a Moorish trooper called Mausacas, when forced by thirst to

γησιν ὡς Μαυρός τις ἱππεὺς Μαυσάκας τοὔνομα ὑπὸ δίψους
πλανώμενος ἀνὰ τὰ ὄρη καταλάβοι Σύρους τινὰς τῶν ἀγροίκων
ἄριστον παρατιθεμένους καὶ τὰ μὲν πρῶτα ἐκεῖνοι φοβηθεῖεν
αὐτόν, εἶτα μέντοι μαθόντες ὡς τῶν φίλων εἴη κατεδέξαντο
καὶ εἱστίασαν· καὶ γάρ τινα τυχεῖν αὐτῶν ἀποδεδημηκότα καὶ
αὐτὸν ἐς <τὴν> τῶν Μαύρων, ἀδελφοῦ αὐτῷ ἐν τῇ γῇ στρατευ-
ομένου. μῦθοι τὸ μετὰ τοῦτο μακροὶ καὶ διηγήσεις ὡς θηράσειεν
αὐτὸς ἐν τῇ Μαυρουσίᾳ καὶ ὡς ἴδοι τοὺς ἐλέφαντας πολλοὺς
ἐν τῷ αὐτῷ συννεμομένους καὶ ὡς ὑπὸ λέοντος ὀλίγου δεῖν κατα-
βρωθείη καὶ ἡλίκους ἰχθῦς ἐπρίατο ἐν Καισαρείᾳ. καὶ ὁ θαυμαστὸς συγγραφεὺς ἀφεὶς τὰς ἐν Εὐρώπῳ γιγνομένας σφαγὰς
τοσαύτας καὶ ἐπελάσεις καὶ σπονδὰς ἀναγκαίας καὶ φυλακὰς
καὶ ἀντιφυλακὰς καὶ ἄχρι βαθείας ἑσπέρας ἐφειστήκει ὁρῶν
Μαλχίωνα τὸν Σύρον ἐν Καισαρείᾳ σκάρους παμμεγέθεις ἀξίους
ὠνούμενον. εἰ δὲ μὴ νὺξ κατέλαβεν, τάχ' ἂν καὶ συνεδείπνει
μετ' αὐτοῦ ἤδη [δὲ] τῶν σκάρων ἐσκευασμένων. ἅπερ εἰ μὴ ἐνε-
γέγραπτο ἐπιμελῶς τῇ ἱστορίᾳ, μεγάλα ἂν ἡμεῖς ἠγνοηκότες
ἦμεν, καὶ ἡ ζημία Ῥωμαίοις ἀφόρητος εἰ Μαυσάκας ὁ Μαῦρος
διψῶν μὴ εὗρεν πιεῖν ἀλλ' ἄδειπνος ἐπανῆλθεν ἐπὶ τὸ στρατόπε-
δον. καίτοι πόσα ἄλλα μακρῷ ἀναγκαιότερα ἑκὼν ἐγὼ νῦν παρί-
ημι. ὡς καὶ αὐλητρὶς ἧκεν ἐκ τῆς πλησίον κώμης αὐτοῖς καὶ ὡς
δῶρα ἀλλήλοις ἀντέδοσαν, ὁ Μαῦρος μὲν τῷ Μαλχίωνι λόγχην,
ὁ δὲ τῷ Μαυσάκᾳ πόρπην, καὶ ἄλλα πολλὰ τοιαῦτα τῆς ἐπ' Εὐρώπῳ μάχης αὐτὰ δὴ τὰ κεφάλαια. τοιγάρτοι εἰκότως ἄν τις
εἴποι τοὺς τοιούτους τὸ μὲν ῥόδον αὐτὸ μὴ βλέπειν, τὰς ἀκάνθας
δὲ αὐτοῦ τὰς παρὰ τὴν ῥίζαν ἀκριβῶς ἐπισκοπεῖν.

Ἄλλος, ὦ Φίλων, μάλα καὶ οὗτος γελοῖος, οὐδὲ τὸν ἕτερον **29**
πόδα ἐκ Κορίνθου πώποτε προβεβηκὼς οὐδ' ἄχρι Κεγχρειῶν
ἀποδημήσας, οὔτι γε Συρίαν ἢ Ἀρμενίαν ἰδών, ὧδε ἤρξατο—
μέμνημαι γάρ— " Ὦτα ὀφθαλμῶν ἀπιστότερα. γράφω τοίνυν ἃ
εἶδον, οὐχ ἃ ἤκουσα." καὶ οὕτως ἀκριβῶς ἅπαντα ἑωράκει ὥστε
τοὺς δράκοντας ἔφη τῶν Παρθυαίων —σημεῖον δὲ πλήθους τοῦτο
αὐτοῖς· χιλίους γὰρ οἶμαι ὁ δράκων ἄγει— ζῶντας δράκοντας
παμμεγέθεις εἶναι γεννωμένους ἐν τῇ Περσίδι μικρὸν ὑπὲρ
τὴν Ἰβηρίαν, τούτους δὲ τέως μὲν ἐπὶ κοντῶν μεγάλων ἐκδε-

wander up in the mountains, came upon some Syrian peasants laying out their lunch. At first they were frightened of him but then they discovered he belonged to their side and they welcomed him and fed him; for one of them had actually visited Mauritania when his brother had served in the army there. Then followed long stories and accounts of how he himself had been hunting in Mauritania, had seen many elephants grazing together and had almost been eaten up by a lion, and what big fish he had bought in Caesarea. Our marvellous historian dispensed with all the carnage at Europus, the cavalry attacks, the enforced truce, the pickets and the counter-pickets and stood around till late evening, watching Malchion, the Syrian, buying wrasses cheap in Caesarea. And if he hadn't been overtaken by nightfall, perhaps he'd have had the fish already cooked and been dining with him. If all this hadn't been carefully recorded in his history, we'd have stayed ignorant of important matters and the Romans would have suffered an intolerable loss, if Mausacas the Moor hadn't found a drink when thirsty, but had returned to camp unfed! But how many far more important details I'm now deliberately omitting! How a music girl came to them from the nearby village, and how they exchanged gifts, the Moor giving Malchion a spear and he giving Mausacas a brooch, and many other such details absolutely essential to the battle of Europus! So one could well say that men like that are blind to the rose itself, but inspect the thorns by its root in minute detail.

[29] There's another man, my dear Philo, also quite ridiculous, who had never taken a step outside Corinth or gone as far afield as Cenchreae, much less seen Syria or Armenia, but began as follows, I remember it well: 'Ears are less trustworthy than eyes, and so I write what I've seen, not what I've heard.' And he'd observed everything with such accuracy that he said that the serpents of the Parthians, (which in fact are standards with numerical significance, with, I believe each 'serpent' at the head of a thousand men), are real live serpents of enormous size that breed in Persia in the area beyond Iberia and that they are temporarily attached to huge

δεμένους ὑψηλοὺς αἰωρεῖσθαι καὶ πόρρωθεν ἐπελαυνόντων δέος
ἐμποιεῖν, ἐν αὐτῷ δὲ τῷ ἔργῳ ἐπειδὰν ὁμοῦ ὦσι λύσαντες
αὐτοὺς ἐπαφιᾶσι τοῖς πολεμίοις· ἀμέλει πολλοὺς τῶν ἡμετέρων οὕτω καταποθῆναι καὶ ἄλλους περισπειραθέντων αὐτοῖς
ἀποπνιγῆναι καὶ συγκλασθῆναι· ταῦτα δὲ ἐφεστὼς ὁρᾶν αὐτός,
ἐν ἀσφαλεῖ μέντοι ἀπὸ δένδρου ὑψηλοῦ ποιούμενος τὴν σκοπήν.
καὶ εὖ γε ἐποίησε μὴ ὁμόσε χωρήσας τοῖς θηρίοις, ἐπεὶ οὐκ ἂν
ἡμεῖς οὕτω θαυμαστὸν συγγραφέα νῦν εἴχομεν καὶ ἀπὸ χειρὸς
αὐτὸν μεγάλα καὶ λαμπρὰ ἐν τῷ πολέμῳ τούτῳ ἐργασάμενον·
καὶ γὰρ ἐκινδύνευσε πολλὰ καὶ ἐτρώθη περὶ Σοῦραν, ἀπὸ τοῦ
Κρανείου δῆλον ὅτι βαδίζων ἐπὶ τὴν Λέρναν. καὶ ταῦτα Κοριν-
θίων ἀκουόντων ἀνεγίνωσκεν τῶν ἀκριβῶς εἰδότων ὅτι μηδὲ κατὰ
τοίχου γεγραμμένον πόλεμον ἑωράκει. ἀλλὰ οὐδὲ ὅπλα ἐκεῖνός γε ᾔδει οὐδὲ μηχανήματα οἷά ἐστιν οὐδὲ τάξεων ἢ καταλοχι-
σμῶν ὀνόματα. πάνυ γοῦν ἔμελεν αὐτῷ πλαγίαν μὲν τὴν ⟨ὀρθίαν⟩
φάλαγγα, ἐπὶ κέρως δὲ λέγειν τὸ ἐπὶ μετώπου ἄγειν.

Εἷς δέ τις βέλτιστος ἅπαντα ἐξ ἀρχῆς ἐς τέλος τὰ πεπραγμένα **30**
ὅσα ἐν Ἀρμενίᾳ, ὅσα ἐν Συρίᾳ, ὅσα ἐν Μεσοποταμίᾳ, τὰ ἐπὶ
τῷ Τίγρητι, τὰ ἐν Μηδίᾳ, πεντακοσίοις οὐδ' ὅλοις ἔπεσι περι-
λαβὼν συνέτριψε καὶ τοῦτο ποιήσας ἱστορίαν συγγεγραφέναι
φησίν· τὴν μέντοι ἐπιγραφὴν ὀλίγου δεῖν μακροτέραν τοῦ βιβλίου
ἐπέγραψεν, " Ἀντιοχιανοῦ τοῦ Ἀπόλλωνος ἱερονίκου"—δό-
λιχον γάρ που οἶμαι ἐν παισὶν νενίκηκεν—"τῶν ἐν Ἀρμενίᾳ
καὶ Μεσοποταμίᾳ καὶ ἐν Μηδίᾳ νῦν Ῥωμαίοις πραχθέντων
ἀφήγησις."

Ἤδη δ' ἐγώ τινος καὶ τὰ μέλλοντα συγγεγραφότος ἤκουσα, **31**
καὶ τὴν λῆψιν τὴν Οὐολογέσου καὶ τὴν Ὀσρόου σφαγήν—ὡς
παραβληθήσεται τῷ λέοντι, καὶ ἐπὶ πᾶσι τὸν τριπόθητον ἡμῖν
θρίαμβον. οὕτω μαντικῶς ἅμα ἔχων ἔσπευδεν ἤδη πρὸς τὸ τέλος
τῆς γραφῆς. ἀλλὰ καὶ πόλιν ἤδη ἐν τῇ Μεσοποταμίᾳ ᾤκισε
μεγέθει τε μεγίστην καὶ ⟨κάλλει⟩ καλλίστην. ἔτι μέντοι ἐπι-
σκοπεῖ καὶ διαβουλεύεται εἴτε Νίκαιαν αὐτὴν ἀπὸ τῆς νίκης χρὴ
ὀνομάζεσθαι εἴτε Ὁμόνοιαν εἴτε Εἰρηνίαν. καὶ τοῦτο μὲν ἔτι
ἄκριτον καὶ ἀνώνυμος ἡμῖν ἡ καλὴ πόλις ἐκείνη λήρου πολλοῦ
καὶ κορύζης συγγραφικῆς γέμουσα. τὰ δ' ἐν Ἰνδοῖς πραχθησό-

poles and suspended high in the air causing fear in the enemy when the Persians are advancing from a distance, but during the actual battle, when the Persians are at close quarters, they release them and set them on the enemy. Of course by this means many of our men were swallowed up and others choked within the serpents' coils and crushed to pieces! He claimed to have been an eye-witness of all this, but carrying out his observation from safety up a tall tree. I'm glad he didn't engage the creatures at close quarters or we'd now be without a wonderful historian who has performed mighty and glorious deeds of his own in this war without too much trouble! For he faced many dangers and was wounded at Sura, when on his way, no doubt, from Cornel Hill to Lerna! What's more, he read all this out to an audience of Corinthians who knew perfectly well he'd never seen warfare even on a fresco. Indeed he didn't even know what weapons or siege-engines are like or the meaning of the terms company or section. He certainly took good care to call a line a column, and to talk about marching in column instead of marching in line.

[30] One capital fellow has included everything from beginning to end, all the happenings in Armenia, Syria, Mesopotamia, by the Tigris and in Media, but squeezed it all into less than five hundred lines and after doing that claims to have written history! However the title he gave it was almost longer than the book itself: 'By Antiochianus, Apollo's Victor at his Sacred Games' – I presume he has won a long distance race in the boys' section – 'a Narration of the recent Achievements of the Romans in Armenia and in Mesopotamia and in Media.'

[31] I've already listened to a man who has written a history of future events, the capture of Vologesus, the killing of Osroes and how he will be locked up with the lion, and, to crown everything, our eagerly awaited triumph. He was now speeding to the end of his work in this prophetic vein, but had already founded a city in Mesopotamia 'in extent most extensive and in beauty most beautiful.' However he is still contemplating and pondering whether it ought to be called Victoria after the victory or Concord or Peaceville. This problem is still unresolved and we haven't as yet got a name for that beautiful city so full of utter nonsense and historiographical drivel. He has also promised already to

μενα ὑπέσχετο ἤδη γράψειν καὶ τὸν περίπλουν τῆς ἔξω θαλάσ-
σης—καὶ οὐχ ὑπόσχεσις ταῦτα μόνον, ἀλλὰ καὶ τὸ προοίμιον
τῆς Ἰνδικῆς ἤδη συντέτακται, καὶ τὸ τρίτον τάγμα καὶ οἱ
Κελτοὶ καὶ Μαύρων μοῖρα ὀλίγη σὺν Κασσίῳ πάντες οὗτοι
ἐπεραιώθησαν τὸν Ἰνδὸν ποταμόν. ὅ τι δὲ πράξουσιν ἢ πῶς
δέξονται τὴν τῶν ἐλεφάντων ἐπέλασιν, οὐκ εἰς μακρὰν ἡμῖν
⟨ὁ⟩ θαυμαστὸς συγγραφεὺς ἀπὸ Μουζίριδος ἢ ἀπ’ Ὀξυδρακῶν
ἐπιστελεῖ.

Τοιαῦτα πολλὰ ὑπὸ ἀπαιδευσίας ληροῦσι, τὰ μὲν ἀξιόρατα **32**
οὔτε ὁρῶντες οὔτ’ εἰ βλέποιεν κατ’ ἀξίαν εἰπεῖν δυνάμενοι,
*ἐπινοῦντες δὲ καὶ ἀναπλάττοντες ὅ τι κεν ἐπ’ ἀκαιρίμαν γλῶσσαν,
φασίν, ἔλθῃ, καὶ ἐπὶ τῷ ἀριθμῷ τῶν βιβλίων ἔτι σεμνυνόμενοι
καὶ μάλιστα ἐπὶ ταῖς ἐπιγραφαῖς· καὶ γὰρ αὖ καὶ αὗται παγ-
γέλοιοι· "τοῦ δεῖνος Παρθικῶν νικῶν τοσάδε". καὶ αὖ· "Παρθί-
δος πρῶτον, δεύτερον", ὡς Ἀτθίδος δῆλον ὅτι. ἄλλος ἀστειό-
τερον παρὰ πολύ—ἀνέγνων γάρ—"Δημητρίου Σαγαλασσέως
Παρθονικικά ⟨   ⟩ οὐδ’ ὡς ἐν
γέλωτι ποιήσασθαι καὶ ἐπισκῶψαι τὰς ἱστορίας οὕτω καλὰς
οὔσας, ἀλλὰ τοῦ χρησίμου ἕνεκα. ὡς ὅστις ἂν ταῦτα καὶ τὰ τοιαῦτα φεύγῃ πολὺ μέρος ἤδη ἐς τὸ ὀρθῶς συγγράφειν οὗτος
προείληφεν, μᾶλλον δὲ ὀλίγων ἔτι προσδεῖται, εἴ γε ἀληθὲς
ἐκεῖνό φησιν ἡ διαλεκτικὴ ὡς τῶν ἀμέσων ἡ θατέρου ἄρσις
τὸ ἕτερον πάντως ἀντεισάγει.

Καὶ δὴ τὸ χωρίον σοι, φαίη τις ἄν, ἀκριβῶς ἀνακεκάθαρται **33**
καὶ αἵ τε ἄκανθαι ὁπόσαι ἦσαν καὶ βάτοι ἐκκεκομμέναι εἰσί, τὰ δὲ
τῶν ἄλλων ἐρείπια ἤδη ἐκπεφόρηται, καὶ εἴ τι τραχύ, ἤδη καὶ
τοῦτο λεῖόν ἐστιν, ὥστε οἰκοδόμει τι ἤδη καὶ αὐτὸς ὡς δείξῃς
οὐκ ἀνατρέψαι μόνον τὸ τῶν ἄλλων γεννάδας ὢν ἀλλά τι καὶ
αὐτὸς ἐπινοῆσαι δεξιὸν καὶ ὃ οὐδεὶς ἄν, ἀλλ’ ⟨οὐδ’⟩ ὁ Μῶμος,
μωμήσασθαι δύναιτο.

Φημὶ τοίνυν τὸν ἄριστα ἱστορίαν συγγράφοντα δύο μὲν ταῦτα **34**
κορυφαιότατα οἴκοθεν ἔχοντα ἥκειν, σύνεσίν τε πολιτικὴν καὶ
δύναμιν ἑρμηνευτικήν, τὴν μὲν ἀδίδακτόν τι τῆς φύσεως δῶρον,
ἡ δύναμις δὲ πολλῇ τῇ ἀσκήσει καὶ συνεχεῖ τῷ πόνῳ καὶ ζήλῳ
τῶν ἀρχαίων προσγεγενημένη ἔστω. ταῦτα μὲν οὖν ἄτεχνα

* read ἐπινοοῦντες

write of future events in India and of the circumnavigation of the outer sea. These aren't mere promises, but the preface of his *Indica* has already been composed and the third legion, the Celts and a small contingent of Moors have already crossed the River Indus with Cassius. What they'll achieve and how they'll cope with the onslaught of the elephants we'll soon be told by this wonderful historian in a dispatch from Muziris or the Oxydracae.

[32] Such is the rubbish they produce in great quantities, because they don't know any better. They fail to see what's noteworthy or to find adequate words for it even if they should see it; but they invent and fabricate whatever, to quote the proverb, 'comes to the tip of an unfortunate tongue' and also take pride in the number of their books and particularly in their titles. For these too are absolutely ridiculous, 'So-and-so's Parthian Victories in so many Books' and again 'Parthis Book 1', 'Parthis Book 2', obviously modelling the name on Atthis. Another did things far more elegantly; for I've read his work, and he called it 'By Demetrius of Sagalassus, Parthonikika [?in so many Books. I've no personal quarrel with these men, nor am I out to afford pleasure by?] subjecting such fine historians to ridicule and mockery but merely trying to do something useful. For whoever avoids these and similar faults, has already gone a long way towards being a proper historian, or rather there are only a few extra things he still needs, if what logic maintains is true and, when things are diametrically opposed, the destruction of the one inevitably leads to its replacement by the other.

[33] 'There now,' someone might say 'all the ground has been carefully cleared by you, all the thorns and brambles rooted out, other people's debris now removed and any rough patches smoothed over, so now you must build something yourself to show you have prowess not only at overturning other people's work but also at devising something skilful which no one, not even Momus, could criticise.'

[34] I say then that the two qualities of supreme importance that the best historian should have from the outset are political understanding and the power to communicate, one of them an untaught gift of nature, whereas the other should be one added by much practising, continuous hard work and emulation of the ancients. These prerequisites, then, are

καὶ οὐδὲν ἐμοῦ συμβούλου δεόμενα· οὐ γὰρ συνετοὺς καὶ ὀξεῖς ἀποφαίνειν τοὺς μὴ παρὰ τῆς φύσεως τοιούτους φησὶ τοῦτο ἡμῖν τὸ βιβλίον. ἐπεὶ πολλοῦ, μᾶλλον δὲ τοῦ παντὸς ‹ἂν› ἦν ἄξιον, εἰ μεταπλάσαι καὶ μετακοσμῆσαι τὰ τηλικαῦτα ἐδύνατο ἢ ἐκ μολύβδου χρυσὸν ἀποφῆναι ἢ ἄργυρον ἐκ κασσιτέρου ἢ ἀπὸ Κόνωνος Τίτορμον ἢ ἀπὸ Λεωτροφίδου Μίλωνα [ἢ] ἐξεργάσασθαι.

Ἀλλὰ ποῦ τὸ τῆς τέχνης καὶ τὸ τῆς συμβουλῆς χρήσιμον; **35** οὐκ ἐς ποίησιν τῶν προσόντων, ἀλλ' ἐς χρῆσιν αὐτῶν τὴν προσή-κουσαν. οἷόν τι ἀμέλει καὶ Ἴκκος καὶ Ἡρόδικος καὶ Θέων καὶ εἴ τις ἄλλος γυμναστὴς ὑπόσχοιντο ἄν σοι, οὐ τὸν Περδίκκαν παραλαβόντες—εἰ δὴ οὗτός ἐστιν ὁ τῆς μητρυιᾶς ἐρασθεὶς καὶ διὰ ταῦτα κατεσκληκώς, ἀλλὰ μὴ Ἀντίοχος ὁ τοῦ Σελεύκου Στρατονίκης ἐκείνης—ἀποφαίνειν Ὀλυμπιονίκην καὶ Θεαγένει τῷ Θασίῳ ἢ Πολυδάμαντι τῷ Σκοτουσσαίῳ ἀντίπαλον, ἀλλὰ δοθεῖσαν ὑπόθεσιν εὐφυᾶ πρὸς ὑποδοχὴν τῆς γυμναστικῆς παρὰ πολὺ ἀμείνω ἀποφαίνειν μετὰ τῆς τέχνης. ὥστε ἀπέστω καὶ ἡμῶν τὸ ἐπίφθονον τοῦτο τῆς ὑποσχέσεως εἰ τέχνην φαμὲν ἐφ' οὕτω μεγάλῳ καὶ χαλεπῷ τῷ πράγματι εὑρηκέναι· οὐ γὰρ ὁντινοῦν παραλαβόντες ἀποφαίνειν συγγραφέα φαμέν, ἀλλὰ τῷ φύσει συνετῷ καὶ ἄριστα πρὸς λόγους ἠσκημένῳ ὑποδεί-ξειν ὁδούς τινας ὀρθάς (εἰ δὴ τοιαῦται φαίνονται) αἷς χρώμενος θᾶττον ἂν καὶ εὐμαρέστερον τελέσειεν ἄχρι καὶ πρὸς τὸν σκοπόν.

καίτοι οὐ γὰρ ἂν φαίης ἀπροσδεῆ τὸν συνετὸν εἶναι τῆς τέχνης **36** καὶ διδασκαλίας ὧν ἀγνοεῖ· ἐπεὶ κἂν ἐκιθάριζε μὴ μαθὼν καὶ ηὔλει καὶ πάντα ἂν ἠπίστατο. νῦν δὲ μὴ μαθὼν οὐκ ἄν τι αὐτῶν χειρουργήσειεν, ὑποδείξαντος δέ τινος ῥᾷστά τε ἂν μάθοι καὶ εὖ μεταχειρίσαιτο ἐφ' αὑτοῦ.

Καὶ τοίνυν καὶ ἡμῖν τοιοῦτός τις [ἐστὶν] ὁ μαθητὴς νῦν παρα- **37** δεδόσθω, συνεῖναί τε καὶ εἰπεῖν οὐκ ἀγεννής, ἀλλ' ὀξὺ δεδορκώς, οἷος καὶ πράγμασι χρήσασθαι ἂν εἰ ἐπιτραπείη, καὶ γνώμην στρα-τιωτικὴν ἀλλὰ μετὰ τῆς πολιτικῆς καὶ ἐμπειρίαν στρατηγικὴν ἔχειν, καὶ νὴ Δία καὶ ἐν στρατοπέδῳ γεγονώς ποτε καὶ γυμνα-ζομένους ἢ ταττομένους στρατιώτας ἑωρακὼς καὶ ὅπλα εἰδὼς καὶ μηχανήματα ἔνια καὶ τί ἐπὶ κέρως καὶ τί ἐπὶ μετώπου, πῶς οἱ λόχοι, πῶς οἱ ἱππεῖς καὶ πόθεν καὶ τί ἐξελαύνειν ἢ πε-

not specialized skills and there's no need for me to give advice about them; for this book of ours doesn't claim to make men of intelligence and acumen out of those not so by nature; for it would be worth a lot, or indeed the whole world, if it could effect such great changes and transformations, or make gold out of lead or silver out of tin or a Titormos out of a Conon or a Milo out of a Leotrophides.

[35] But wherein lies the usefulness of technical advice? Not for the creation of attributes but for the proper use of existing ones. For example you can be sure that Iccus or Herodicos or Theon or any other trainer wouldn't promise to take a Perdiccas – always assuming it's he who fell in love with his stepmother and pined away, rather than Antiochus, the son of Seleucus, out of love for the famous Stratonice – and make him into an Olympic victor and a match for Theagenes of Thasos or Polydamas of Scotussa, but, if given good natural material to receive his training, he'd guarantee to improve it greatly with the help of specialised skill. So please don't think we're making invidious promises either, if we claim to have devised a specialised method of tackling so important and difficult a task. For we don't claim to take just anyone and make him into a historian but we will point out to the man who is naturally intelligent and has been well trained for literary pursuits some proper routes – if indeed they are thought to be such – which he can use to reach his goal more quickly and easily. [36] You can't say the intelligent man doesn't also need specialised instruction in areas of which he is ignorant. Otherwise he could play the lyre or the aulos or anything at all without having to learn. But, in fact, if he hasn't learnt, he can't perform in any of these ways, though once he has been shown how, he can learn very easily and tackle the task well enough on his own.

[37] So I too would like to have just such a pupil delivered into my care, one endowed with understanding and eloquence, a man of vision, capable of handling the affairs of state, if entrusted to him, understanding military affairs, yes, and politics too, with experience as a general, and what's more, a man who has spent time in a camp and seen soldiers being drilled and deployed, one who knows about the various weapons and siege-engines, understanding the meaning of 'in column' and 'in line',

ριελαύνειν, καὶ ὅλως οὐ τῶν κατοικιδίων τις οὐδ' οἷος πιστεύειν μόνον τοῖς ἀπαγγέλλουσιν.

Μάλιστα δὲ καὶ πρὸ τῶν πάντων ἐλεύθερος ἔστω τὴν γνώμην 38 καὶ μήτε φοβείσθω μηδένα μηδὲ ἐλπιζέτω μηδέν, ἐπεὶ ὅμοιος ἔσται τοῖς φαύλοις δικασταῖς πρὸς χάριν ἢ πρὸς ἀπέχθειαν ἐπὶ μισθῷ δικάζουσιν. ἀλλὰ μὴ μελέτω αὐτῷ μήτε Φίλιππος ἐκ-κεκομμένος τὸν ὀφθαλμὸν ὑπὸ 'Αστέρος τοῦ 'Αμφιπολίτου τοῦ τοξότου ἐν 'Ολύνθῳ—τοιοῦτος οἷος ἦν δειχθήσεται—μήτε 'Αλέ-ξανδρος ⟨ὃς⟩ ἀνιάσεται ἐπὶ τῇ Κλείτου σφαγῇ ὠμῶς ἐν τῷ συμποσίῳ γενομένῃ, εἰ σαφῶς ἀναγράφοιτο· οὐδὲ Κλέων αὐτὸν φοβήσει μέγα ἐν τῇ ἐκκλησίᾳ δυνάμενος καὶ κατέχων τὸ βῆμα, ὡς μὴ εἰπεῖν ὅτι ὀλέθριος καὶ μανικὸς ἄνθρωπος· οὐ μὴν οὐδὲ ἡ σύμπασα πόλις τῶν 'Αθηναίων, ἢν τὰ ἐν Σικελίᾳ κακὰ ἱστορῇ καὶ τὴν Δημοσθένους λῆψιν καὶ τὴν Νικίου τελευτὴν καὶ ὡς ἐδίψων καὶ οἷον τὸ ὕδωρ ἔπινον καὶ ὡς ἐφονεύοντο πίνοντες οἱ πολλοί. ἡγήσεται γάρ—ὅπερ δικαιότατον—ὑπ' οὐδενὸς τῶν νοῦν ἐχόντων αὐτὸς ἕξειν τὴν αἰτίαν ἣν τὰ δυστυχῶς ἢ ἀνοήτως γεγενημένα ὡς ἐπράχθη διηγῆται—οὐ γὰρ ποιητὴς αὐτῶν ἀλλὰ μηνυτὴς ἦν. ὥστε κἂν καταναυμαχῶνται τότε, οὐκ ἐκεῖνος ὁ καταδύων ἐστίν, κἂν φεύγωσιν οὐκ ἐκεῖνος ὁ διώκων, ἐκτὸς εἰ μὴ εὔξασθαι δέον παρέλιπεν. ἐπεὶ τοί γε εἰ σιωπήσας αὐτὰ ἢ πρὸς τοὐναντίον εἰπὼν ἐπανορθώσασθαι ἐδύνατο, ῥᾷστον ἦν ἑνὶ καλάμῳ λεπτῷ τὸν Θουκυδίδην ἀνατρέψαι μὲν τὸ ἐν ταῖς 'Επι-πολαῖς παρατείχισμα, καταδῦσαι δὲ τὴν 'Ερμοκράτους τριήρη καὶ τὸν κατάρατον Γύλιππον διαπεῖραι μεταξὺ ἀποτειχίζοντα καὶ ἀποταφρεύοντα τὰς ὁδοὺς καὶ τέλος Συρακοσίους μὲν ἐν* τὰς λιθοτομίας ἐμβαλεῖν, τοὺς δὲ 'Αθηναίους περιπλεῖν Σικε-λίαν καὶ 'Ιταλίαν μετὰ τῶν πρώτων τοῦ 'Αλκιβιάδου ἐλπίδων. ἀλλ' οἶμαι τὰ μὲν πραχθέντα οὐδὲ Κλωθὼ ἔτι ἀνακλώσειεν οὐδὲ "Ατροπος μετατρέψειε. τοῦ δὴ συγγραφέως ἔργον ἕν—ὡς ἐπρά- 39 χθη εἰπεῖν. τοῦτο δ' οὐκ ἂν δύναιτο ἄχρι ἂν ἢ φοβῆται 'Αρταξέρξην ἰατρὸς αὐτοῦ ὢν ἢ ἐλπίζῃ κάνδυν πορφυροῦν καὶ στρεπτὸν χρυ-σοῦν καὶ ἵππον τῶν Νισαίων λήψεσθαι μισθὸν τῶν ἐν τῇ γραφῇ ἐπαίνων. ἀλλ' οὐ Ξενοφῶν αὐτὸ ποιήσει, δίκαιος συγγραφεύς, οὐδὲ Θουκυδίδης. ἀλλὰ κἂν ἰδίᾳ μισῇ τινας* πολὺ ἀναγκαιότερον

* read ἐς   * add comma

how infantry platoons and cavalry manoeuvre and one in short who must be no mere stay-at-home or one to rely solely on the reports of others.

[38] It is a particular and overriding priority that he should be independent of mind, fearing no one and hoping for nothing, or else he'll be like bad jurors, who show favouritism or hostility for the prospect of reward. No, he must remain unconcerned that Philip had one eye shot out at Olynthus by Aster, the archer from Amphipolis, but he will have to be described as he was; nor should he be worried at the thought of Alexander being distressed by his savage murder of Clitus at the drinking party being recorded unequivocally. Nor will Cleon, for all his mighty power in the assembly and his domination of the speaker's platform, deter him from calling the fellow a destructive maniac. Nor will he be frightened by the whole population of Athens, if he records the disasters in Sicily, the capture of Demosthenes, the death of Nicias, the Athenians' thirst, the sort of water they had to drink and how most of them were killed as they drank. For he'll think, and with perfect justification, that he personally won't be blamed by anyone in his right mind for giving a factual account of disastrous or senseless courses of action; after all he didn't cause them, he merely sheds light on them. So, even if they lose a sea-battle at the time, he's not the one who sinks their ships, and, if they're routed, he's not the one pursuing them, unless he omitted to make the proper prayer! For if he could have rectified these events by saying nothing about them or reversing them completely, it would have been very easy for Thucydides with a few strokes of his pen to demolish the counter-wall at Epipolae, sink Hermocrates' man-of-war and shoot a spear into that devil Gylippus, while he was sealing off the roads with walls and ditches, and end it all by throwing the Syracusans into their quarries, while allowing the Athenians to sail round Sicily and Italy with Alcibiades' early hopes intact. But once things have happened, I don't imagine Clotho can unspin them or Atropos turn them about. [39] In fact the sole function of the historian is to report events factually. This he can't do as long as he fears Artaxerxes, because he's his doctor, or hopes to receive a Median doublet of purple, necklace of gold and Nisaean horse as a reward for his eulogies. But Xenophon, an honest historian, won't act like that, nor Thucydides either. No, even if he has a personal hatred for individuals,

ἡγήσεται τὸ κοινόν, καὶ τὴν ἀλήθειαν περὶ πλείονος ποιήσεται τῆς ἔχθρας, κἂν φιλῇ ὅμως οὐκ ἀφέξεται ἁμαρτάνοντος. ἐν γάρ, ὡς ἔφην, τοῦτο ἴδιον ἱστορίας, καὶ μόνῃ θυτέον τῇ ἀληθείᾳ, εἴ τις ἱστορίαν γράψων ἴοι, τῶν δὲ ἄλλων ἁπάντων ἀμελητέον αὐτῷ, καὶ ὅλως πῆχυς εἷς καὶ μέτρον ἀκριβές, ἀποβλέπειν μὴ εἰς τοὺς νῦν ἀκούοντας ἀλλ' εἰς τοὺς μετὰ ταῦτα συνεσομένους τοῖς συγγράμμασιν.

Εἰ δὲ τὸ παραυτίκα τις θεραπεύοι, τῆς τῶν κολακευόντων με- **40** ρίδος εἰκότως ἂν νομισθείη, οὓς πάλαι ἡ ἱστορία καὶ ἐξ ἀρχῆς εὐθὺς ἀπέστραπτο, οὐ μεῖον ἢ κομμωτικὴν ἡ γυμναστική. Ἀλεξάνδρου γοῦν καὶ τοῦτο ἀπομνημονεύουσιν. " Ἡδέως ἄν," ἔφη, "πρὸς ὀλίγον ἀνεβίουν, ὦ Ὀνησίκριτε, ἀποθανὼν ὅπως μάθοιμι ὅπως ταῦτα οἱ ἄνθρωποι τότε ἀναγινώσκουσιν. εἰ δὲ νῦν αὐτὰ ἐπαινοῦσιν καὶ ἀσπάζονται, μὴ θαυμάσῃς· οἴονται γὰρ οὐ μικρῷ τινι τῷ δελέατι τούτῳ ἀνασπάσειν ἕκαστος τὴν παρ' ἡμῶν εὔνοιαν." Ὁμήρῳ γοῦν, καίτοι πρὸς τὸ μυθῶδες τὰ πλεῖστα συγγεγραφότι ὑπὲρ τοῦ Ἀχιλλέως, ἤδη καὶ πιστεύειν τινὲς ὑπάγονται, μόνον τοῦτο εἰς ἀπόδειξιν τῆς ἀληθείας μέγα τεκμήριον τιθέμενοι ὅτι μὴ περὶ ζῶντος ἔγραφεν· οὐ γὰρ εὑρίσκουσιν οὗτινος ἕνεκα ἐψεύδετ' ἄν.

Τοιοῦτος οὖν μοι ὁ συγγραφεύς. ἔστω ἄφοβος, ἀδέκαστος, **41** ἐλεύθερος, παρρησίας καὶ ἀληθείας φίλος, ὡς ὁ κωμικός φησιν, τὰ σῦκα σῦκα, τὴν σκάφην δὲ σκάφην ὀνομάσων, οὐ μίσει οὐδὲ φιλίᾳ νέμων οὐδὲ φειδόμενος ἢ ἐλεῶν ἢ αἰσχυνόμενος ἢ δυσωπούμενος, ἴσος δικαστής, εὔνους ἅπασιν ἄχρι τοῦ μὴ θατέρῳ τι ἀπονεῖμαι πλεῖον τοῦ δέοντος, ξένος ἐν τοῖς βιβλίοις καὶ ἄπολις, αὐτόνομος, ἀβασίλευτος, οὐ τί τῷδε*δόξει λογιζόμενος, ἀλλὰ τί πέπρακται λέγων.

Ὁ δ' οὖν Θουκυδίδης εὖ μάλα τοῦτ' ἐνομοθέτησεν καὶ διέ- **42** κρινεν ἀρετὴν καὶ κακίαν συγγραφικήν, ὁρῶν μάλιστα θαυμαζόμενον τὸν Ἡρόδοτον ἄχρι τοῦ καὶ Μούσας κληθῆναι αὐτοῦ τὰ βιβλία. κτῆμά τε γάρ φησιν μᾶλλον ἐς ἀεὶ συγγράφειν ἤπερ ἐς τὸ παρὸν ἀγώνισμα, καὶ μὴ μυθῶδες ἀσπάζεσθαι ἀλλὰ τὴν ἀλήθειαν τῶν γεγενημένων ἀπολείπειν τοῖς ὕστερον. καὶ ἐπάγει τὸ χρήσιμον καὶ ὃ τέλος ἄν τις εὖ φρονῶν ὑπόθοιτο ἱστορίας,

*add ἢ τῷδε

he'll consider the common good much more vital and value the truth more highly than his private animosity, and though he may be a friend, he won't spare anyone who does wrong. For this, as I've said already, is the particular feature of history, and Truth is the only goddess to whom anyone embarking on the writing of history must sacrifice, disregarding everything else, and in short his only rule and his one accurate yard-stick is to focus his attention not upon his present audience but upon future readers.

[40] Anyone assiduously courting the immediate effect could well be classified as one of the flatterers, who for long, indeed right from the beginning, have been abhorrent to history, no less than the beautician's art is to that of the physical trainer. This is borne out by the remarks attributed to Alexander. 'Onesicritus,' he said, 'I would dearly have liked to return to life for a short while after my death to discover the effect your writings have upon readers then. Don't be surprised that they praise and welcome them just now, for they all think they are using a juicy bait enabling them to land my goodwill.' Again, though most of what Homer has recorded in praise of Achilles is fictitious, some people to-day are actually inclined to believe him, merely because they think it strong evidence of his truthfulness that he wasn't writing about a living person; for they can't find any motive he could have for lying.

[41] This, then, is my sort of historian. He must be fearless, incorruptible, free, 'a friend of frankness and truth' one who, to quote the comic poet, will 'call a spade a spade', influenced neither by hatred nor by friendship, showing no compunction, pity, shame or embarrassment, an impartial judge, well disposed to all without giving either side more than its due, in his writings a stranger and a man without a city or country, independent, subject to no king, unconcerned by what this or that man will think, but stating the actual facts.

[42] Thucydides was admirable in the way he laid down this law and distinguished between historical virtue and vice. He saw that Herodotus was very much admired, so much so that his books were given the names of the Muses. For Thucydides says he is writing 'a possession for ever' rather than 'a competition piece to win immediate approval', and that he doesn't welcome the fictitious, but bequeaths the true account of events to posterity. He goes on to mention the usefulness of history and what any

ὡς εἴ ποτε καὶ αὖθις τὰ ὅμοια καταλάβοι, ἔχοιεν, φησί, πρὸς τὰ
προγεγραμμένα ἀποβλέποντες εὖ χρῆσθαι τοῖς ἐν ποσί.

Καὶ τὴν μὲν γνώμην τοιαύτην ἔχων ὁ συγγραφεὺς ἡκέτω μοι, **43**
τὴν δὲ φωνὴν καὶ τὴν τῆς ἑρμηνείας ἰσχύν, τὴν μὲν σφοδρὰν
ἐκείνην καὶ κάρχαρον καὶ συνεχῆ ταῖς περιόδοις καὶ ἀγκύλην
ταῖς ἐπιχειρήσεσιν καὶ τὴν ἄλλην τῆς ῥητορείας δεινότητα μὴ
κομιδῇ τεθηγμένος ἀρχέσθω τῆς γραφῆς, ἀλλ' εἰρηνικώτερον
διακείμενος. καὶ ὁ μὲν νοῦς σύστοιχος ἔστω καὶ πυκνός, ἡ λέξις
δὲ σαφὴς καὶ πολιτική, οἷα ἐπισημότατα δηλοῦν τὸ ὑποκείμενον.

Ὡς γὰρ τῇ γνώμῃ τοῦ συγγραφέως σκοποὺς ὑπεθέμεθα παρ- **44**
ρησίαν καὶ ἀλήθειαν, οὕτω δὲ καὶ τῇ φωνῇ αὐτοῦ εἷς σκοπὸς
ὁ πρῶτος, σαφῶς δηλῶσαι καὶ φανότατα ἐμφανίσαι τὸ πρᾶγμα,
μήτε ἀπορρήτοις καὶ ἔξω πάτου ὀνόμασι μήτε τοῖς ἀγοραίοις
τούτοις καὶ καπηλικοῖς, ἀλλ' ὡς μὲν τοὺς πολλοὺς συνεῖναι, τοὺς
δὲ πεπαιδευμένους ἐπαινέσαι. καὶ μὴν καὶ σχήμασι κεκοσμήσθω
ἀνεπαχθέσι καὶ τὸ ἀνεπιτήδευτον μάλιστα ἔχουσιν, ἐπεὶ τοῖς
κατηρτυμένοις τῶν ζωμῶν ἐοικότας ἀποφαίνει τοὺς λόγους.

Καὶ ἡ μὲν γνώμη κοινωνείτω καὶ προσαπτέσθω τι καὶ ποιη- **45**
τικῆς παρ' ὅσον μεγαληγόρος καὶ διῃρημένη καὶ ἐκείνη, καὶ μάλισθ'
ὁπόταν παρατάξεσι καὶ μάχαις καὶ ναυμαχίαις συμπλέκηται·
δεήσει γὰρ τότε ποιητικοῦ τινος ἀνέμου ἐπουριάσοντος τὰ
ἀκάτια καὶ συνδιοίσοντος ὑψηλὴν καὶ ἐπ' ἄκρων τῶν κυμάτων
τὴν ναῦν. ἡ λέξις δὲ ὅμως ἐπὶ γῆς βεβηκέτω, τῷ μὲν κάλλει καὶ
τῷ μεγέθει τῶν λεγομένων συνεπαιρομένη καὶ ὡς ἔνι μάλιστα
ὁμοιουμένη, ‹μὴ› ξενίζουσα δὲ μηδ' ὑπὲρ τὸν καιρὸν ἐνθουσιῶ-
σα. κίνδυνος γὰρ αὐτῇ τότε* μέγιστον παρακινῆσαι καὶ κατενε-
χθῆναι ἐς τὸν τῆς ποιητικῆς κορύβαντα, ὥστε μάλιστα πειστέον
τηνικαῦτα τῷ χαλινῷ καὶ σωφρονητέον, εἰδότας ὡς ἱπποτυφία
τις καὶ ἐν λόγοις πάθος οὐ μικρὸν γίγνεται. ἄμεινον οὖν ἐφ'
ἵππου ὀχουμένῃ τότε τῇ γνώμῃ τὴν ἑρμηνείαν πεζῇ συμπαραθεῖν,
ἐχομένην τοῦ ἐφιππίου ὡς μὴ ἀπολείποιτο τῆς φορᾶς.

Καὶ μὴν καὶ συνθήκῃ τῶν ὀνομάτων εὐκράτῳ καὶ μέσῃ **46**
χρηστέον, οὔτε ἄγαν ἀφιστάντα καὶ ἀπαρτῶντα—τραχὺ γάρ—
οὔτε ῥυθμῷ παρ' ὀλίγον ὡς οἱ πολλοὶ συνάπτοντα·* τὸ μὲν γὰρ
ἐπαίτιον, τὸ δὲ ἀηδὲς τοῖς ἀκούουσι.

sensible man would call its end, that, as he says, if a similar situation should ever recur, men might be able by concentrating their attention on records of the past to deal well with the present.

[43] So much, then, for the mental make-up of my historian. Now for his language and stylistic effect. When starting his work he shouldn't use a style in any way honed to be vehement or abrasive or unremittingly periodic or complicated by dialectical ratiocinations or rhetorically forceful in any other way, but his disposition should be comparatively peaceful, though his thought should be consistent and compact and his diction clear and businesslike, of a sort to set forth the subject with the utmost lucidity.

[44] For just as we suggested that the mental aims of a historian should be frankness and truthfulness, so too in speaking his one primary aim must be to set forth his subject matter lucidly and with crystal clarity, not using unusual out-of-the-way expressions or the common ones used by tradesmen in the market, but such as the majority understand and the cultured commend. Moreover the figures embellishing his speech should be unobjectionable and absolutely unaffected, for the words he produces are like delicately produced sauces.

[45] Let his thoughts have some touches of poetry about them, in so far as they like poetry should be majestic and elevated, particularly when coming to grips with confrontations and battles by land or sea. For then he will need a poetic breeze to waft his boats along and speed his ship on high through the crest of the waves. But nevertheless let his diction keep its feet on the ground, though rising along with the beauty and magnitude of the subject matter and doing its best to resemble it, but without being outlandish or indulging in excessive poetic ecstasy. For then his style risks being greatly excited and swept onwards into the Corybantic frenzy of poetry; then particularly must he obey the bridle and control himself, knowing that the written word can behave like a proud horseman and with serious consequences. So on such occasions it's better for his mind to ride on horseback but for his style to run alongside on foot holding on to the saddle so as not to be left behind.

[46] In his arrangement of words he should follow a well-tempered middle course, without separating them too much or leaving them unconnected – for that makes things harsh – or yet connecting them closely and rhythmically, as most writers do, for the one is culpable, while the other is unpleasant for the audience.

Τὰ δὲ πράγματα αὐτὰ οὐχ ὡς ἔτυχε συνακτέον, ἀλλὰ φιλοπό- **47**
νως καὶ ταλαιπώρως πολλάκις περὶ τῶν αὐτῶν ἀνακρίνοντα,
καὶ μάλιστα μὲν παρόντα καὶ ἐφορῶντα, εἰ δὲ μή, τοῖς ἀδεκα-
στότερον ἐξηγουμένοις προσέχοντα καὶ οὓς εἰκάσειεν ἄν τις
ἥκιστα πρὸς χάριν ἢ ἀπέχθειαν ἀφαιρήσειν ἢ προσθήσειν τοῖς
γεγονόσιν. κἀνταῦθα ἤδη καὶ στοχαστικός τις καὶ συνθετικὸς τοῦ
πιθανωτέρου ἔστω. καὶ ἐπειδὰν ἀθροίσῃ ἅπαντα ἢ τὰ πλεῖστα, **48**
πρῶτα μὲν ὑπόμνημά τι συνυφαινέτω αὐτῶν καὶ σῶμα ποιείτω
ἀκαλλὲς ἔτι καὶ ἀδιάρθρωτον· εἶτα ἐπιθεὶς τὴν τάξιν ἐπαγέτω τὸ
κάλλος καὶ χρωννύτω τῇ λέξει καὶ σχηματιζέτω καὶ ῥυθμιζέτω.

Καὶ ὅλως ἐοικέτω τότε τῷ τοῦ Ὁμήρου Διὶ ἄρτι μὲν τὴν τῶν **49**
ἱπποπόλων Θρῃκῶν γῆν ὁρῶντι, ἄρτι δὲ τὴν Μυσῶν—κατὰ ταὐτὰ
γὰρ καὶ αὐτὸς ἄρτι μὲν ‹τὰ› Ῥωμαίων ἰδίᾳ ὁράτω καὶ δηλούτω
ἡμῖν οἷα ἐφαίνετο αὐτῷ ἀφ' ὑψηλοῦ ὁρῶντι, ἄρτι δὲ τὰ Περσῶν,
εἶτ' ἀμφότερα εἰ μάχοιντο. καὶ ἐν αὐτῇ δὲ τῇ παρατάξει μὴ
πρὸς ἓν μέρος ὁράτω μηδὲ ἐς ἕνα ἱππέα ἢ πεζόν—εἰ μὴ Βρασί-
δας τις εἴη προπηδῶν ἢ Δημοσθένης ἀνακόπτων τὴν ἐπίβασιν·
ἐς τοὺς στρατηγοὺς μέντοι τὰ πρῶτα, καὶ εἴ τι παρεκελεύσαντο,
κἀκεῖνο ἀκηκοόσθω, καὶ ὅπως καὶ ᾗτινι γνώμῃ καὶ ἐπινοίᾳ ἔταξαν.
ἐπειδὰν δὲ ἀναμιχθῶσι, κοινὴ ἔστω ἡ θέα, καὶ ζυγοστατείτω
τότε ὥσπερ ἐν τρυτάνῃ τὰ γιγνόμενα καὶ συνδιωκέτω καὶ συμ-
φευγέτω. καὶ πᾶσι τούτοις μέτρον ἐπέστω, μὴ ἐς κόρον μηδὲ **50**
ἀπειροκάλως μηδὲ νεαρῶς, ἀλλὰ ῥᾳδίως ἀπολυέσθω· καὶ στήσας
ἐνταῦθά που ταῦτα ἐπ' ἐκεῖνα μεταβαινέτω, ἢν κατεπείγῃ· εἶτα
ἐπανίτω λυθείς, ὁπόταν ἐκεῖνα καλῇ· καὶ πρὸς πάντα σπευδέτω
καὶ ὡς δυνατὸν ὁμοχρονείτω καὶ μεταπετέσθω ἀπ' Ἀρμενίας
μὲν εἰς Μηδίαν, ἐκεῖθεν δὲ ῥοιζήματι ἑνὶ εἰς Ἰβηρίαν, εἶτα εἰς
Ἰταλίαν, ὡς μηδενὸς καιροῦ ἀπολείποιτο.

Μάλιστα δὲ κατόπτρῳ ἐοικυῖαν παρασχέσθω τὴν γνώμην ἀθόλῳ **51**
καὶ στιλπνῷ καὶ ἀκριβεῖ τὸ κέντρον καὶ ὁποίας ἂν δέξηται τὰς
μορφὰς τῶν ἔργων ταῦτα* καὶ δεικνύτω αὐτά, διάστροφον δὲ ἢ
παράχρουν ἢ ἑτερόσχημον μηδέν. οὐ γὰρ ὥσπερ* τοῖς ῥήτορσι
γράφουσιν, ἀλλὰ τὰ μὲν λεχθησόμενα ἔστιν καὶ εἰρήσεται· πέπρακται γὰρ ἤδη· δεῖ δὲ τάξαι καὶ εἰπεῖν αὐτά. ὥστε οὐ τί εἴπωσι
ζητητέον αὐτοῖς ἀλλ' ὅπως εἴπωσιν. ὅλως δέ, νομιστέον τὸν

*1. read τοιαῦτα			*2. read ὡς παρὰ

[47] He shouldn't gather his actual facts haphazardly but laboriously and painfully, examining the same matters many times. Ideally he should visit the places and see for himself; failing that, he should pay attention to those giving the more disinterested accounts and those whom one would least expect to subtract from the facts or add to them through partiality or hostility. Now at this point he must show skill in using his intuition and putting together the more credible account.

[48] When he has assembled all or most of the facts, first of all he must weave them into a summary framework and produce the body of his text, still lacking embellishment and articulation. Then after arranging it, he must embellish it, using diction to produce colour, and introducing stylistic figures and rhythm.

[49] He should generally at this stage be like Homer's Zeus, who now surveys the land of the 'Thracians, rearers of horses' and now that of the Mysians; for similarly he too should survey now the Roman side on its own, and now the Persian side, and then both of them, if they join battle, and in the actual confrontation he shouldn't simply look at one department or one individual, whether mounted or on foot, unless he be a Brasidas leaping forth ahead of his men or a Demosthenes beating back his attack. But he should look to the generals first; and any of their exhortations to their men should also be heard by the readers, and how they disposed their forces and with what plan in mind. But when they join battle, an over-all view should be offered and he should have events weighing in the balance, as though he had a pair of scales, pursuing with the pursuers and fleeing with the fleers. [50] In all this he should have a sense of proportion, avoiding excess, tastelessness and the failings of youth; but he must leave the scene effortlessly. He should halt things in one area and cross elsewhere, if there's urgent need, only to release himself and return later, when events summon him. He must hurry on to each new arena, dealing as far as possible with concurrent events, flying over from Armenia to Media, from there with one flap of his wings to Iberia, and then to Italy, so as not to neglect any important juncture.

[51] Above all he should make his mind like a mirror, clear and unclouded and unerring in its focal point, and whatever the shape of the facts he receives, that is how he must show them, without distorting them or changing their colour or shape in any way; for historians don't write like orators; for the things they have to say exist and will be said, for they have already happened. All that's needed is to arrange them and express them. So they don't have to search for what to say but how to say it. In short we should think the historian ought to be like Pheidias or Praxiteles

ἱστορίαν συγγράφοντα Φειδίᾳ χρῆναι ἢ Πραξιτέλει ἐοικέναι ἢ
Ἀλκαμένει ἢ τῳ ἄλλῳ ἐκείνων—οὐδὲ γὰρ οὐδὲ ἐκεῖνοι χρυσὸν
ἢ ἄργυρον ἢ ἐλέφαντα ἢ τὴν ἄλλην ὕλην ἐποίουν, ἀλλ' ἡ μὲν ὑπῆρχε
καὶ προϋποβέβλητο Ἠλείων ἢ Ἀθηναίων ἢ Ἀργείων πεπορι-
σμένων, οἱ δὲ ἔπλαττον μόνον καὶ ἔπριον τὸν ἐλέφαντα καὶ
ἔξεον καὶ ἐκόλλων καὶ ἐρρύθμιζον καὶ ἐπήνθιζον τῷ χρυσῷ,
καὶ τοῦτο ἦν ἡ τέχνη αὐτοῖς ἐς δέον οἰκονομήσασθαι τὴν ὕλην.

Τοιοῦτο δή τι καὶ τὸ τοῦ συγγραφέως ἔργον—εἰς καλὸν διαθέ-
σθαι τὰ πεπραγμένα καὶ εἰς δύναμιν ἐναργέστατα ἐπιδεῖξαι αὐτά.
καὶ ὅταν τις ἀκροώμενος οἴηται μετὰ ταῦτα ὁρᾶν τὰ λεγόμενα
καὶ μετὰ τοῦτο ἐπαινῇ, τότε δὴ τότε ἀπηκρίβωται καὶ τὸν οἰκεῖον
ἔπαινον ἀπείληφε τὸ ἔργον τῷ τῆς ἱστορίας Φειδίᾳ.

Πάντων δὲ ἤδη παρεσκευασμένων καὶ ἀπροοιμίαστον μέν ποτε 52
ποιήσεται τὴν ἀρχήν, ὁπόταν μὴ πάνυ κατεπείγῃ τὸ πρᾶγμα
προδιοικήσασθαί τι ἐν τῷ προοιμίῳ· δυνάμει δὲ καὶ τότε φροιμίῳ
χρήσεται τῷ ἀποσαφοῦντι περὶ τῶν λεκτῶν.

Ὁπόταν δὲ καὶ φροιμιάζηται, ἀπὸ δυοῖν μόνον ἄρξεται, οὐχ 53
ὥσπερ οἱ ῥήτορες ἀπὸ τριῶν, ἀλλὰ τὸ τῆς εὐνοίας παρεὶς προσο-
χὴν καὶ εὐμάθειαν εὐπορήσει τοῖς ἀκούουσι, προσέξουσι μὲν αὐτῷ
ἢν δείξῃ ὡς περὶ μεγάλων ἢ ἀναγκαίων ἢ οἰκείων ἢ χρησίμων
ἐρεῖ. εὐμαθῆ δὲ καὶ σαφῆ τὰ ὕστερα ποιήσει τὰς αἰτίας προεκτι-
θέμενος καὶ περιορίζων τὰ κεφάλαια τῶν γεγενημένων. τοιού- 54
τοις προοιμίοις οἱ ἄριστοι τῶν συγγραφέων ἐχρήσαντο· Ἡρό-
δοτος μέν, ὡς μὴ τὰ γενόμενα ἐξίτηλα τῷ χρόνῳ γένηται,
μεγάλα καὶ θαυμαστὰ ὄντα καὶ ταῦτα νίκας Ἑλληνικὰς δηλοῦντα
καὶ ἥττας βαρβαρικάς· Θουκυδίδης δέ, μέγαν τε καὶ αὐτὸς
ἐλπίσας ἔσεσθαι καὶ ἀξιολογώτατον καὶ μείζω τῶν προγεγε-
νημένων ἐκεῖνον τὸν πόλεμον· καὶ γὰρ παθήματα ἐν αὐτῷ μεγάλα
ξυνέβη γενέσθαι.

Μετὰ δὲ τὸ προοίμιον, ἀνάλογον τοῖς πράγμασιν ἢ μηκυνό- 55
μενον ἢ βραχυνόμενον, εὐαφὴς καὶ εὐάγωγος ἔστω ἡ ἐπὶ τὴν διή-
γησιν μετάβασις. ἅπαν γὰρ ἀτεχνῶς τὸ λοιπὸν σῶμα τῆς ἱστορίας διήγησις μακρά ἐστιν. ὥστε ταῖς τῆς διηγήσεως ἀρεταῖς
κατακεκοσμήσθω, λείως τε καὶ ὁμαλῶς προϊοῦσα καὶ αὐτῇ
ὁμοίως ὥστε μὴ προὔχειν μήτε κοιλαίνεσθαι· ἔπειτα τὸ σαφὲς

or Alcamenes or any other sculptor, for they didn't make the gold, silver or ivory or other material, but that was already there and provided by the Eleans or Athenians or Argives; they merely shaped and sawed the ivory, did the polishing and gluing, attended to the proportions and set it all off with gold; their skill lay in handling their raw material properly.

The historian's task is similar; he has to arrange events to good advantage and put them on display as vividly as he can. When thereafter the listener thinks he sees what is being described, and thereafter praises it, then indeed the work of our Pheidias of history has achieved perfection and duly earned its proper praise.

[52] When all is now prepared, he will sometimes start without a prologue, when there are no urgent circumstances forcing him to deal with anything in advance in the prologue. Even then his exposition of his subject matter will in effect amount to a prologue.

[53] When he does offer a prologue, he will begin with only two aims, not three like the orators; he will dispense with courting the goodwill of his audience and try to ensure their attention and understanding; for they will pay attention to him, if he demonstrates to them that his subject will be important, vital, of particular concern to them, or useful, while he will make what follows intelligible and clear, if he explains in advance the reasons for the war and gives an outline of the main events. [54] Prologues of this sort have been used by the best historians, by Herodotus, 'so that the events should not be effaced by time, since they were great and wonderful, and what's more revealed Greek victories and Persian defeats' and by Thucydides who likewise expected that that 'war would be a great and most noteworthy one and greater than any previous ones', 'for in the event great disasters did occur in it.'

[55] After the prologue, which should be proportionately long or short according to the subject, the transition to the narrative should be gentle and easy. For absolutely all the rest of the body of the history is long narrative and so it should be embellished with the narrative virtues and proceed smoothly, evenly and uniformly without protuberances or

ἐπανθείτω, τῇ τε λέξει, ὡς ἔφην, μεμηχανημένον καὶ τῇ συμ-
περιπλοκῇ τῶν πραγμάτων. ἀπόλυτα γὰρ καὶ ἐντελῆ πάντα
ποιήσει, καὶ τὸ πρῶτον ἐξεργασάμενος ἐπάξει τὸ δεύτερον ἐχό-
μενον αὐτοῦ καὶ ἀλύσεως τρόπον συνηρμοσμένον ὡς μὴ διακε-
κόφθαι μηδὲ διηγήσεις πολλὰς εἶναι ἀλλήλαις παρακειμένας,
ἀλλ᾽ ἀεὶ τὸ πρῶτον τῷ δευτέρῳ μὴ γειτνιᾶν μόνον, ἀλλὰ καὶ
κοινωνεῖν καὶ ἀνακεκρᾶσθαι κατὰ τὰ ἄκρα.

Τάχος ἐπὶ πᾶσι χρήσιμον, καὶ μάλιστα εἰ μὴ ἀπορία τῶν 56
λεκτέων εἴη· καὶ τοῦτο πορίζεσθαι χρὴ μὴ τοσοῦτον ἀπὸ τῶν
ὀνομάτων ἢ ῥημάτων ὅσον ἀπὸ τῶν πραγμάτων· λέγω δέ, εἰ
παραθέοις μὲν τὰ μικρὰ καὶ ἧττον ἀναγκαῖα, λέγοις δὲ ἱκανῶς
τὰ μεγάλα· μᾶλλον δὲ καὶ παραλειπτέον πολλά. οὐδὲ γὰρ ἦν
ἑστιᾷς τοὺς φίλους καὶ πάντα ᾖ παρεσκευασμένα, διὰ τοῦτο ἐν
μέσοις τοῖς πέμμασιν καὶ τοῖς ὀρνέοις καὶ λοπάσι τοσαύταις καὶ
συσὶν ἀγρίοις καὶ λαγῳοῖς καὶ ὑπογαστρίοις καὶ σαπέρδην
ἐνθήσει καὶ ἔτνος ὅτι κἀκεῖνο παρεσκεύαστο, ἀμελήσεις δὲ τῶν
εὐτελεστέρων.

Μάλιστα δὲ σωφρονητέον ἐν ταῖς τῶν ὀρῶν ἢ τειχῶν ἢ πο- 57
ταμῶν ἑρμηνείαις ὡς μὴ δύναμιν λόγων ἀπειροκάλως παρεπιδεί-
κνυσθαι δοκοίης καὶ τὸ σαυτοῦ δρᾶν παρεὶς τὴν ἱστορίαν, ἀλλ᾽
ὀλίγον προσαψάμενος τοῦ χρησίμου καὶ σαφοῦς ἕνεκα μεταβήσῃ
ἐκφυγὼν τὸν ἰξὸν τὸν ἐν τῷ πράγματι καὶ τὴν τοιαύτην ἅπασαν
λιχνείαν, οἷον ὁρᾷς τι καὶ Ὅμηρος ὡς μεγαλόφρων ποιεῖ· καίτοι
ποιητὴς ὢν παραθεῖ τὸν Τάνταλον καὶ τὸν Ἰξίονα καὶ Τιτυὸν
καὶ τοὺς ἄλλους. εἰ δὲ Παρθένιος ἢ Εὐφορίων ἢ Καλλίμαχος
ἔλεγεν, πόσοις ἂν οἴει ἔπεσι τὸ ὕδωρ ἄχρι πρὸς τὸ χεῖλος τοῦ
Ταντάλου ἤγαγεν; εἶτα πόσοις ἂν Ἰξίονα ἐκύλισεν; μᾶλλον δὲ
ὁ Θουκυδίδης αὐτὸς ὀλίγα τῷ τοιούτῳ εἴδει τοῦ λόγου χρησάμενος σκέψαι ὅπως εὐθὺς ἀφίσταται ἢ μηχάνημα ἑρμηνεύσας ἢ
πολιορκίας σχῆμα δηλώσας ἀναγκαῖον καὶ χρειῶδες ὃν ἢ Ἐπι-
πολῶν σχῆμα ἢ Συρακοσίων λιμένα. ὅταν μὲν γὰρ τὸν λοιμὸν
διηγῆται καὶ μακρὸς εἶναι δοκῇ, σὺ τὰ πράγματα ἐννόησον·
εἴσῃ γὰρ οὕτω τὸ τάχος καὶ ὡς φεύγοντος ὅμως ἐπιλαμβάνεται
αὐτοῦ τὰ γεγενημένα πολλὰ ὄντα.

Ἦν δέ ποτε λόγους ἐροῦντά τινα δεήσῃ εἰσάγειν, μάλιστα μὲν 58

hollows. Let it then be graced with clarity, achieved, as I said, by the diction and the interweaving of the sections. For he will deal with each section separately and perfect it, and only when he has completed the first section, will he introduce the second one, touching it and linked to it as in a chain, so that there is no break or multiplicity of parallel narratives, but the first should always not only be close to the second one, but also have something in common with it, with its extremities blending in to it.

[56] Speed is everywhere advantageous, particularly if there is no lack of material; this should be achieved not so much with economy of words and phrases as of subject matter, I mean by hurrying over what's trivial and inessential, but giving adequate treatment to important matters, or better still by much omission. For if you are entertaining your friends and all the food is cooked, that doesn't mean that in the middle of the pastries, poultry and all those shellfish, and the wild boar, hare and tunny steaks, you'll put out coarse fish and pea-soup as well, just because these had also been cooked. No, you'll dispense with the cheaper dishes.

[57] Above all self-control must be exercised in descriptions of mountains, fortifications or rivers, so that you don't appear to be giving a tasteless exhibition of your verbal powers and neglecting history to indulge yourself. Instead you will touch upon these features briefly, with just enough to be helpful and make things clear, and then pass on, avoiding the snares in the material and all such tempting fare. For instance you can see how sublime is Homer's spirit in his poetry. Indeed, poet as he is, he hurries past Tantalus, Ixion, Tityus and the others; but had it been a Parthenius, Euphorion or Callimachus speaking, how many lines of verse do you think he would have expended in bringing the water all the way to Tantalus' lips! And again how many to set Ixion rolling! Or better, consider how Thucydides himself uses this type of writing on a small scale and then stops at once after describing an engine of war or explaining the lay-out of a siege, when essential or useful, be it the configuration of Epipolae or the harbour at Syracuse. For he may appear long-winded in his account of the plague, but just consider the facts. Then you'll appreciate his rapidity and how the multiplicity of events lays hold on him despite his attempts to escape.

[58] If ever you must introduce someone to make a speech, let his

ἐοικότα τῷ προσώπῳ καὶ τῷ πράγματι οἰκεῖα λεγέσθω, ἔπειτα
ὡς σαφέστατα καὶ ταῦτα. πλὴν ἐφεῖταί σοι τότε καὶ ῥητορεῦσαι
καὶ ἐπιδεῖξαι τὴν τῶν λόγων δεινότητα.

Ἔπαινοι μὲν γὰρ ἢ ψόγοι πάνυ πεφεισμένοι καὶ περιεσκεμμέ-　**59**
νοι καὶ ἀσυκοφάντητοι καὶ μετὰ ἀποδείξεων καὶ ταχεῖς καὶ μὴ
ἄκαιροι, ἐπεὶ ἔξω τοῦ δικαστηρίου ἐκεῖνοί εἰσιν, καὶ τὴν αὐτὴν
Θεοπόμπῳ αἰτίαν ἕξεις φιλαπεχθημόνως κατηγοροῦντι. τῶν
πλείστων καὶ διατριβὴν ποιουμένῳ τὸ πρᾶγμα ὡς κατηγορεῖν
μᾶλλον ἢ ἱστορεῖν τὰ πεπραγμένα.

Καὶ μὴν καὶ μῦθος εἴ τις παραπέσοι, λεκτέος μέν, οὐ μὴν πι-　**60**
στωτέος πάντως, ἀλλ' ἐν μέσῳ θετέος τοῖς ὅπως ἂν ἐθέλωσιν
εἰκάσουσιν περὶ αὐτοῦ· σὺ δ' ἀκίνδυνος καὶ πρὸς οὐδέτερον ἐπιρ-
ρεπέστερος.

Τὸ δ' ὅλον ἐκείνου μοι μέμνησο—πολλάκις γὰρ τοῦτο ἐρῶ—　**61**
καὶ μὴ πρὸς τὸ παρὸν μόνον ὁρῶν γράφε ὡς οἱ νῦν ἐπαινέσονταί
σε καὶ τιμήσουσιν, ἀλλὰ τοῦ σύμπαντος αἰῶνος ἐστοχασμένος
πρὸς τοὺς ἔπειτα μᾶλλον σύγγραφε καὶ παρ' ἐκείνων ἀπαίτει
τὸν μισθὸν τῆς γραφῆς, ὡς λέγηται περὶ σοῦ, "ἐκεῖνος μέντοι
ἐλεύθερος ἀνὴρ ἦν καὶ παρρησίας μεστός, οὐδὲν οὐδὲ κολακευ-
τικὸν οὐδὲ δουλοπρεπὲς ἀλλ' ἀλήθεια ἐπὶ πᾶσι." τοῦτ', εἰ σωφρο-
νοῖ τις, ὑπὲρ [τὰς] πάσας τὰς νῦν. ἐλπίδας θεῖτο ἄν, οὕτως ὀλι-
γοχρονίους οὔσας.

Ὁρᾷς τὸν Κνίδιον ἐκεῖνον ἀρχιτέκτονα οἷον ἐποίησεν; οἰκο-　**62**
δομήσας γὰρ τὸν ἐπὶ τῇ Φάρῳ πύργον, μέγιστον καὶ κάλλιστον
ἔργον ἁπάντων, ὡς πυρσεύοιτο ἀπ' αὐτοῦ τοῖς ναυτιλλομένοις
ἐπὶ πολὺ τῆς θαλάττης καὶ μὴ καταφέροιντο ἐς τὴν Παραιτο-
νίαν, παγχάλεπον, ὥς φασιν, οὖσαν καὶ ἄφυκτον εἴ τις ἐμπέσοι
ἐς τὰ ἕρματα—οἰκοδομήσας οὖν τὸ ἔργον ἔνδοθεν μὲν κατὰ τῶν
λίθων τὸ αὑτοῦ ὄνομα ἐπέγραψεν, ἐπιχρίσας δὲ τιτάνῳ καὶ
ἐπικαλύψας ἐπέγραψε τοὔνομα τοῦ τότε βασιλεύοντος, εἰδώς,
ὅπερ καὶ ἐγένετο, πάνυ ὀλίγου χρόνου συνεκπεσούμενα μὲν τῷ
χρίσματι τὰ γράμματα ἐκφανησόμενον δέ, "Σώστρατος Δεξι-
φάνους Κνίδιος θεοῖς σωτῆρσιν ὑπὲρ τῶν πλοϊζομένων." οὕτως

words be in character and appropriate to the situation, and be clear as well. However then you *are* allowed to wax oratorical and exhibit rhetorical forcefulness.

[59]   Praise or censure should be very sparing, circumspect, unexceptionable, accompanied by proof, rapid and well-timed, since it's not a courtroom. Otherwise you'll be open to the same criticism as Theopompus who arraigned most individuals vindictively, making it a way of life, so that he was more of a prosecutor than a historian of events.

[60] Again should a story crop up, it should be told but certainly not vouched for, but merely made available for readers to conjecture about it as they wish, with you running no risk or inclining to either side.

[61] In general I'd have you remember one thing, for I'll say it again and again. Don't write with your eyes only on the present and aiming at praise and honour from the men of to-day, but set your sights on all time, composing your history rather for future generations and claim from them as your writer's fee that it be said of you. 'But *he* was a free man and always spoke his mind; with him there was no flattery or servility, but always the truth'. If one were sensible, one would value this above all the hopes of to-day that are so short-term.

[62]   Consider how the great architect of Cnidos acted. After constructing the tower on Pharos, the mightiest and most beautiful building ever, so that he could send a beacon-signal from it to sailors far and wide on the seas, to stop them being carried on to Paraetonia, a cruel spot, they say, with no escape for anyone running on to the reefs - well, after completing the building, he inscribed his own name inside on the stones, plastered it over with gypsum till it was hidden, and inscribed over that the name of the king of the day, knowing that, as actually happened, the letters would very soon fall away along with the plaster to reveal 'Sostratus of Cnidus, son of Dexiphanes, in dedication to the

οὐδ' ἐκεῖνος ἐς τὸν τότε καιρὸν οὐδὲ τὸν αὑτοῦ βίον τὸν ὀλίγον ἑώρα, ἀλλ' εἰς τὸν νῦν καὶ τὸν ἀεί, ἄχρι ἂν ἑστήκῃ ὁ πύργος καὶ μένῃ αὐτοῦ ἡ τέχνη.

Χρὴ τοίνυν καὶ τὴν ἱστορίαν οὕτω γράφεσθαι σὺν τῷ ἀληθεῖ **63** μᾶλλον πρὸς τὴν μέλλουσαν ἐλπίδα ἤπερ σὺν κολακείᾳ πρὸς τὸ ἡδὺ τοῖς νῦν ἐπαινουμένοις. οὗτός σοι κανὼν καὶ στάθμη ἱστορίας δικαίας. καὶ εἰ μὲν σταθμήσονταί τινες αὐτῇ, εὖ ἂν ἔχοι καὶ εἰς δέον ἡμῖν γέγραπται· εἰ δὲ μή, κεκύλισται ὁ πίθος ἐν Κρανείῳ.

Saviour Gods on behalf of seafarers'. So too he kept his eyes not on those times or his own brief life, but on to-day and eternity, as long as the tower stands and his craftsmanship survives.

[63] Well, history too should be written in the same way, with truthfulness and hopes for the future rather than with flattery to please to-day's recipients of praise. This is your rule and yardstick for an honest history, and if some people use that yardstick, all will be well and I've written to good purpose. Otherwise, I've merely been rolling my cask on Cornel Hill.

THE DREAM

The Dream is probably to be dated about A.D. 164[1] and contains a lecture given by Lucian to his fellow citizens of Samosata on a return visit after he had established a reputation. It is usually regarded as a *prolalia* or introduction to a longer piece, but it seems rather long for that and certainly gives no indication that there is a dialogue to follow. Nor is there much reason to connect it with the typical sophistic encomium *In Praise of One's Native Land* (*Patr. Enc.*). As the subject is 'Local boy makes good thanks to *Paideia* (Education)', it could perhaps be Lucian's ingenious and innovative way of producing an encomium on Education.

Though *The Dream* is important for the light it throws on Lucian's early years, it is too full of allegory to be taken absolutely literally. Lucian's family may have been none too affluent as he suggests, but they perhaps were able to contribute something towards his later education in Ionia. Nor was his rejection of Sculpture absolute, as he retained an interest in it and the other visual arts throughout his career as shown by frequent references and descriptions, e.g. in *Imagines* passim, *Philopseudeis* c. 18, *Calumnia* c.5, and *Zeuxis*.

It is typical of Lucian that, even when being autobiographical, he still follows the spirit of the Second Sophistic and indulges in *mimesis* of classical Greek literature. In this case he draws the general idea from a parable of the sophist Prodicus recorded by Xenophon in *Mem.* 2.1.21–34, wherein Heracles sits in a quiet place pondering whether to take the path of Virtue or Vice, when two women appear to him, both beautiful, but one, Virtue, pure and modest, the other, Vice, made-up and affected and shamelessly flaunting her feminine charms. Vice speaks first, offering him an easy and pleasant life, whereas Virtue tells him her path demands toil and sweat,[2] but he must follow it if he is to be admired for virtue. Though Xenophon doesn't complete his account, Heracles of course chooses Virtue and the difficult path.

It is to Lucian's credit that his *mimēsis* consists not in servile imitation but in adaptation and emulation, cf. pp. 5–6. Thus though the Choice of Heracles was in sophists' repertoire, cf. Dio Chrysostom 1.66, the detail of the women appearing in a dream is Lucian's own invention, as is his changing of the choice from a moral one to an intellectual one.

---

1. See p.3. It could have been earlier, but scarcely later, as it contains no mention of the invention of comic dialogue.
2. Prodicus developed the idea of the paths of Virtue and Vice from Hesiod, *Works and Days* 285–90.

c.1 **attending school:** L.'s text is often a mosaic of phrases culled from the best classical authors, particularly Plato and Demosthenes. He probably took the phrase *eis ta d. ph.* straight from Xenophon, *Cyr.* 1.2.6, though cf. Dem. *On the Crown* 257.

close to manhood: of an age with Heracles in Prodicus' parable. The rare word *prosēbos* occurs in Xen. *Cyr.* 1.4.4. Boys became young men, *ephēboi*, when old enough for military service; this was 18 at Athens.

higher education: *Paideia*, a word implying both advanced literary education and culture generally.

artisan: *banausos* is an uncomplimentary word, suggesting manual labour only fit for slaves and impoverished free men. Most surviving Greek authors were prosperous enough to regard such work as beneath them.

c.2 **according ... experience:** the phrase is modelled on Thuc. 1.22.3.

sculptor: literally 'carver of herms'; herms were 'pillars unsculptured except for the head and a phallus' (A.W. Lawrence), usually representing the god Hermes.

stone-cutter, mason: literally 'workman and fitter-together of stones'. L.'s uncle is later called a stone-polisher. He is something less prestigious, therefore, than a Pheidias or a Praxiteles, more like a modern monumental stone-mason.

he has natural talent: for the type of phrase cf. again Thuc. 1.22.3.

c.3 **Well ... done:** the proverb occurs in Plato, *Laws* 753 E and is ascribed by Iamblichus to Pythagoras. L., *Hermotimus* 3, attributes it to Hesiod, probably confusing it with the slightly different one in *Works and Days* 40.

an initiation ceremony: L. takes his metaphor from the preparation of a victim at the start of a sacrifice.

c.5 *Iliad* 2.56–7.

remains ... ears: L. takes the words *paramenei* and *enaulos* and the general motif from Plato, *Menexenus* 235 B.

c.6 **with her clothes tucked up:** ready for hard work, cf. *How to Write History* 3.

c.7 **first to speak:** similarly the pushing, shameless Vice speaks first in Xenophon.

sturdy shoulders: cf. Aristophanes, *Clouds* 1013.

know envy: the Greek is ambiguous; it could mean 'feel' or 'evoke' envy or both.

c.8 **Phidias ... Praxiteles:** Phidias, Polyclitus and Myron were active in the middle of the fifth century B.C., Praxiteles 100 years later. Phidias, a friend of Pericles, was best known for his work on the Athenian Acropolis, his Athenes and his vast gold and ivory statue of Zeus at Olympia, cf. *Pro Imaginibus* 14. Polyclitus' Hera graced her temple in his native Argos, but he was equally famous and regularly mentioned by L. for his canon, the name given both to his book on proportions and his *Doryphoros*, a statue exemplifying his mastery of proportions, cf. *Peregrinus* 9. The most famous work of Myron was his *Discobolos*, described by L. in *Philopseudeis* 18. Praxiteles' most famous work was his Cnidian Aphrodite, cf. *Imag.* 4–6 and the pseudo-Lucianic *Amores* (O.C.T. 49) passim.

the gods they sculpted: literally 'their gods'; or the Greek could simply mean 'the gods'.

stringing ... together: often used by L. of fast-speaking, unconvincing orators or philosophers, like Aeschines as represented by Demosthenes, *On the Crown* 308; cf. *Timon* 9.

c.9 **Education:** L. may have got the idea of personifying *Paideia* from the *Pinax* of Cebes, a work he mentions in *De Mercede Conductis* 42 and *Rhetorum Praeccptor* 6. This moralising dialogue describes a picture of human life full of allegorical figures, amongst which *Paideia* is prominent. It was attributed to Socrates' disciple Cebes, cf. Plato, *Phaedo* 59 C, but its style shows it to be much later.

support: the rare word *epidikasimos* seems to mean 'one whose legal support is sought'. This, following on *proodos*, suggests L. may be alluding to features of Roman society where *patroni* were escorted in public by *clientes* and lent them

their support in court. References to contemporary Roman society abound in *Nigrinus* and *Merc. Cond.*

a dog's life: literally 'a hare's life', i.e. in perpetual fear and trembling. L. takes the proverb from Demosthenes, *On the Crown* 263.

c.10 most vital part: cf. Aristotle, *Nicomachean Ethics* IX.8.6.

c.11 posts of authority: for the importance of leading sophists of L.'s time in their own cities and in the Roman Empire see Philostratus, *Lives of the Sophists* and G.W. Bowersock, *Greek Sophists in the Roman Empire*, Oxford, 1969. Herodes Atticus even became consul, and L. himself eventually gained a post in Egypt, see p.3.

best seats: particularly for plays at the theatres and shows at the amphitheatres.

travel from home: sophists often represented their cities on embassies.

c.12 to be ... son: the variant *eupaidias*, though probably a conjecture, is attractive, cf. Aristophanes, *Wasps* 1512.

what sort of a father: L. is mistaken. Demosthenes' father was a rich man, as his son makes clear in *On the Crown* 256–7, though his early death and the iniquities of young Demosthenes' guardians did leave the orator temporarily impoverished.

woman ... Philip: here L. does follow *On the Crown* 284 very closely. For further allegations about the activities of Aeschines' mother see *On the Crown* 258–60.

Socrates: Socrates' father, Sophroniscus, was a sculptor, cf. Plato, *Euthyphro* 11 C, and presumably he was brought up in his father's footsteps; Pausanias 1.22.8 and D.L. 2.19 record a tradition that he sculpted figures of the Graces for the Acropolis.

c.14 Niobe: Niobe boasted that she had a better family (six sons and six daughters according to *Iliad* 24. 602–19) than Leto, but Leto's two children Apollo and Artemis killed all twelve with their arrows. Niobe kept weeping for them till she was turned into stone on Mt. Sipylus in Asia Minor.

c.15 Pegasus: the winged horse which helped Bellerophon to kill the Chimaera.

Triptolemus: worshipped at Eleusis with Demeter as an agricultural deity. He is represented in vase paintings as having a winged chariot from which he scatters corn on the earth.

c.17 By Heracles: L.'s oaths are often wittily chosen, e.g. in the name of gods being derided. Here the effect is sarcastic, combining hints at the Choice of Heracles and the forthcoming mention of the myth of the 'Long Night', tripled in duration to enable Zeus to visit Alcmena and father Heracles; see L.'s amusing treatment in *Dialogues of the Gods* 14.

tedious: for this use of *dikanikos* cf. Plato, *Apology* 32 A.

burning: Xenophon has this dream at *Anabasis* 3.1.11 in a desperate situation in the heart of Persia after Cyrus, their leader, has been killed in battle and all their generals treacherously murdered by Tissaphernes. However it is a slightly later dream, one at 4.3.8, that he tells to his men for a useful purpose.

THE JUDGING OF THE GODDESSES
A COMIC DIALOGUE

Lucian's greatest achievement was the development of prose dialogue as a vehicle for comedy and satire. Some of these dialogues strike a completely hilarious note and lack any pretence at seriousness, while others could be classified as examples of *to spoudogeloion*, serious jesting, as Lucian exercised his wit and trenchant humour in deriding human follies and vices. Lucian, however, often lacked the serious moral purpose of the Latin satirical poets, so that Eunapius, writing about A.D. 400, aptly calls Lucian '*anēr spoudaios es to gelasthēnai*', 'a man whose serious intention was to raise a laugh.'

Some of Lucian's most amusing dialogues involve the Olympian gods of Homer and Hesiod behaving in all too human a fashion, see pp. 11–12. Lucian probably isn't preaching too serious a theological message; the intellectual argument against the old concept of the gods had long been won by thinkers such as Xenophanes (sixth century) who complained 'Homer and Hesiod attributed to the gods all things that among men are matters for reproach and disgrace, thieving and adultery and deception of one another' and Plato who banished from the educational curriculum of his Republic stories about gods who were immoral and changed their shapes. Perhaps Lucian's most amusing work is the *Dialogues of the Gods*, of which nos. 4, 6, 8, 9, 12 and 13 are particularly good.

Similar in spirit to the short *Dialogues of the Gods* is this slightly longer piece telling the story of the Judgment of Paris. This topic had been included in a lost epic, the *Cypria*, which told how Zeus had decided the world was overpopulated and so he precipitated the Trojan War by arranging that Eris (Discord) was not invited to the nuptials of Peleus and Thetis, soon to be the parents of Achilles, the hero of the *Iliad*, and so she sent a golden apple as a wedding 'present'. But now let Lucian continue the story.

c.1 **Priam's son:** Paris or Alexander. Priam was king of Troy at the time of the Trojan War.

Phrygia: N.W. Asia Minor, including the area around Troy.

Gargaron: the main peak of Ida, a mountain to the south of Troy; cf. *Il.* 14. 292–3.

clever about sex: L. makes Socrates use this phrase in describing himself in *Vit. Auct.* 15, adapting it from Plato, *Lysis* 206 A. This is an example of L.'s practice of quoting, echoing, adapting or readapting phrases from the best authors of classical Greece.

if ... victorious: L. takes the phrase from Hdt. 6.130. Both Plato and Herodotus were favourite authors of L. and of contemporary sophists and presumably of the readers and audiences they entertained.

Ganymede: a handsome Trojan prince who excited the admiration of Zeus, who turned himself into an eagle, cf. c.6, and carried him off to Olympus, where he waited on the gods at table; see *Dialogues of the Gods* 8 and 10 for L.'s humorous treatment of the story.

apaxiōsai: optative = *apaxiōseie.*

c.2 **Momus:** personified as the god of blame and adverse criticism; cf. the cognate verb *memphomai.* L. makes him one of the *dramatis personae* in *Deor. Conc.* and *JTr.* 19–23. L.'s mentions of Momus probably come from Plato *Republic* 487 A, a passage closely echoed in *Hist.* 33.

We're not afraid: not a regal plural. Hera speaks also for the virgin Athene who is too embarrassed to say anything.

your Ares: her lover, see *Od.* 8. 266 ff. for the story of Aphrodite's affair with Ares and the revenge of the injured husband, Hephaestus, a passage exploited for humorous effect by L. in *Dialogues of the Gods* 21.

inflict any harm: Zeus' fears are justified in view of the records of the goddesses in mythology, e.g. Hera's treatment of Heracles, Aphrodite's cruelty to Hippolytus and Athene's treatment of Hector and other Trojans in the *Iliad.*

c.3 **woman of Ida:** Oenone, daughter of a local river-god. Having learnt the art of prophecy she warned Paris not to set sail to Sparta, telling him to come to her for help, if ever he was wounded. He did so late in the Trojan War, when wounded by a poisoned arrow, but she refused her help. Later she changed her mind, but P. was already dead and she hanged herself. Her desolation when deserted by P. for Helen is depicted in Ovid, *Heroides* 5, and in Tennyson's poem.

c.4 **official misconduct:** strictly 'dereliction of duty when on an embassy'; the verb suggests the cognate noun, *parapresbeia,* the subject of Demosthenes' *De Falsa Legatione,* accusing Aeschines of misconduct when on an embassy to Philip of Macedon.

keen on war: Athena asks about what interests her, just as Aphrodite has asked about his sex life.

faultfinders: *mempsimoiria* is the subject of no. 17 of Theophrastus' *Characters,* a work well known to L.

c.5 **left the stars far behind:** *apospaō* is used intransitively as often in L. and late Greek.

follow my finger – that's right: Wieland's alternative interpretation (= no bigger than my finger here) is worth consideration.

flying down: here and in c.6 L. uses compounds of *hiptamai,* a late Greek form condemned by the contemporary grammarian Phrynichus and by L. himself, *Lex.* 25; cf. also Loeb vol. 8, pp. 1–45.

Anchises: a handsome Trojan prince, whose affair with Aphrodite produced Aeneas, Virgil's hero, though he also figured in the Iliad. Hera's 'bitchiness' is typical of the Olympians of both Homer and L.

c.6 **the Phrygian lad:** Ganymede; see on c.1.

flew alongside: see on c.5.

he had dropped it: L. like other late Greek writers, occasionally omits the augments in pluperfects.

c.7 **And the same to you:** a formula for return of greetings taken from New Comedy, Menander *Sam.* 129, *Georg.* 41 etc., and used several times by L.

young fellow: the Greeks visualised Hermes as resembling a young man, an *ephēbos,* as can be seen by the Praxitelean sculpture of Hermes and the infant Dionysus

trembling: like the dramatic poets, L. uses his text to give stage instructions. He may well have performed his dialogues as what J. Coenen calls *'Einmanntheater'.*

clever about sex: see on c.1.

c.8 **Argus:** herdsman with 100 eyes. When Zeus was in love with Io, Hera turned her into a heifer and got Argus to watch her, cf. *Dialogues of the Gods* 7, *Dialogues of the Sea-Gods* 11; later Zeus got Hermes to kill him.

c.9 **What ... do:** a comic phrase, cf. Men. *Pk.* 1003 and *Phasma* 8 with S.-G.'s note, used several times with variations by L.; see p. 266.

c.10 Well done ... over: typically Aphrodite is less modest than the other two. I follow Hemsterhuis in giving this speech to Aphrodite, though those of the better mss. that add speakers' names give it to Hera. (Original texts omitted speakers' names.) The problem of Athena's abrupt interruption about Aphrodite is solved in another way by a 16th century editor who interposes a speech by Paris asking Aphrodite to strip as well.

white arms ... ox: 'white-armed' and 'ox-eyed' were epithets regularly applied in Homer to Hera; hence the mss. attribution of this speech to her.

girdle: for her magic girdle see *Il.* 14. 214–7. There Homer goes on to tell how Aphrodite lent it to Hera, so that she could lure Zeus into love-making and make him forget about Troy.

the colour of your eyes: perhaps 'the steely grey of your eyes', at any rate an unattractive colour for women's eyes, cf. *D. Meretr.* 2.1. The meaning of Greek and Latin colour words is much disputed. Athena's regular Homeric epithet is *glaukōpis*, interpreted as 'with eyes (of various shades) of grey, green or blue', or as 'bright-eyed' or even 'owl-faced'.

c.14 Leda: wife of Tyndareus. Zeus fell in love with her, visiting her as a swan. According to one variant form of the myth, followed by L., she laid two eggs, one producing Helen, the other Castor and Pollux, cf. *Dialogues of the Gods* 25, whereas her husband fathered Clytemnestra.

white skin: the Greeks regarded white skin as an attribute of a beautiful woman; cf. note on 'white-armed Hera' in c.10. L. gives the same humorous explanation of Helen's white skin in *The Cock* 17.

fond ... wrestling: women of classical Sparta practised gymnastics, i.e. exercises in the nude, including wrestling. 'Wrestling' may also suggest amorous grappling, cf. the pun on the name *Palaestra* (= Ju-Jit-Sue) in *Asinus* 8–11 and its use as a significant name for a hetaira in Plautus' *Rudens*.

Theseus: for the story of how Theseus and Pirithous carried Helen off to Aphidnae in Attica and her rescue by her brothers see Plutarch, *Life of Theseus* 31.

all the leading nobles: except Achilles who was too young according to the Hesiodic *Catalogue of Women* which told the story in detail with sizeable fragments surviving (O.C.T. *Fr.* 196–204 M. – W.). The suitors included Odysseus and Ajax and they all had to swear to protect the marriage of the successful suitor. Apollodorus' later account, 3.10.8, lists 31 suitors.

a descendant of Pelops: of outstanding nobility, Pelops being a grandson of Zeus.

c.15 a foreigner: literally 'a barbarian', i.e. 'one who couldn't speak Greek.'

Desire and Love: though elsewhere L. makes Eros a son of Aphrodite, here he thinks of Hes. *Th.* 201, where Eros and Himeros attend her at her birth.

the Graces: cf. Hes. *Th.* 64, where Himeros and the Graces are mentioned together as companions of the Muses.

c.16 Yearning: cf. Pausanias 1.43.6 where Eros, Himeros and Pothos are named as sculptures by Scopas.

Wedlock: Hymenaeus, or Hymen, personified as the God of Marriage; cf. L.'s *Herodotus* 5.

THE ASSEMBLY OF THE GODS

Once again in the *Assembly of the Gods* Lucian makes the gods behave like humans for comic purposes. In this dialogue, as in *JTr.*, he adds to the humour by making the discussion in Olympus a parody of proceedings in the *ecclēsia*, the old Athenian Assembly, though, under the chairmanship of Zeus, business, particularly in c. 19, is conducted in a comically undemocratic manner.

Acrimonious debates in Olympus occur at regular intervals throughout the two Homeric epics, but Lucian may also have gained some ideas from lost works of Menippus. (It seems unlikely that Lucian knew Lucilius' *Deorum Concilium*; Seneca's Skit on the Death of Claudius does have several similarities[1] with this and other works of Lucian, probably because of the common influence of Menippus.)

Lucian's age was a time of great enthusiasm for mystery religions and devotion to deities such as Isis, Serapis, Mithras and Aesculapius, not to mention the spread of Christianity, but, outside *Alexander* and *Peregrinus*, Lucian makes comparatively little mention of contemporary religious trends; see Caster passim. This may not be due to lack of interest in contemporary religion but rather to an entertainer's fear of offending his audience; so he avoids mentioning the newer cults of Serapis and Isis and his references to Mithras, Sabazius and Aesculapius have classical precedents. Of course thinking men could read between the lines and see that the general points made by Lucian were particularly true of the present when the Roman policy of religious toleration condoned the worship throughout the empire of a host of local deities, if accompanied by token recognition of the imperial cult. However Lucian's imperial masters could hardly object to a light-hearted dialogue seemingly set in the past.

Recently J.H. Oliver, 'The Actuality of Lucian's Assembly of the Gods' *AJP* 101 (1980), 304–313, has argued for *Deor. Conc.* as satire on a contemporary theme, the profusion of men of low-born or foreign origin in Athenian public life and the attempt by Marcus Aurelius in 165 to restore the prestige of the Areopagus by insisting on a *trigonia* rule whereby Areopagites had to prove free birth on both sides for three generations. The references to unworthy intrusive elements in Olympus and in particular to *dokimasia* in c. 19, see note, may indeed have added a touch of contemporary spice to the dialogue, but Oliver seems to me to be going too far in regarding the situation at Athens around 165 as the *raison d' être* of the dialogue; moreover his attempt to suggest the equation Zeus = Marcus Aurelius is unconvincing, as, despite the compliment paid to Zeus in c. 4 by Momus, his behaviour in c. 19 would surely have reflected little credit on the emperor.

---

1. Cf. Hall, 104 ff. We also know of a *Theōn Agorā* (cf. *Od.* 1) by Euphron, a comic poet of the third century B.C., an unlikely source for L.

c.1 **parties:** *symposium* normally means 'drinking party', but L. also uses it of the room where a party was held.

Who ... speak: the normal proclamation in the *ecclēsia*, cf. Ar. *Ach.* 45; men over 50 were invited to speak first, cf. Aeschines 1.23.

aliens: metics were free men of non-Athenian parentage resident in Athens.

Momus: see note on c.2 of *Dear. Jud.* Here as in *JTr.* 19 ff. Momus represents L. himself; cf. *meta parrhēsias* and *dielenchō* infra and the name he gives himself in *Pisc.* 19; see note and p. 11.

c.2 **for ... else:** cf. [Dem.] 25.14.

of a libellous nature: like a sycophant, an individual who made a profitable profession out of prosecuting others, a notorious feature of ancient Athenian society, cf. Ar. *Ach.* 519, 904 etc.; Athens had no public prosecutor.

c.3 **dues:** metics had to pay special taxes.

most noble: sarcastically meant.

c.4 **Cadmus:** son of Agenor, king of Phoenicia, and reputed founder of Thebes; his daughter, Semele, was 'mother' of Dionysus.

turban: the *mitra* was a typically oriental head-dress; for a fuller picture of Dionysus see *Dialogues of the Gods* 22.

The first of them: Pan; see *Dialogues of the Gods* 2.

the second: Silenus.

c.5 **Ariadne:** Dionysus rescued her when left by Theseus on Naxos and made her tiara into a star; cf. Ovid, *Met.* 8.174.

daughter of Icarius: Erigone, who was led by the dog Maera to the body of her father, killed by drunken shepherds whom he had introduced to Dionysus' recent gift of wine. She hanged herself but Dionysus set her and her dog among the stars.

c.6 **whose ... many:** Zeus quotes a general reference to doctors in *Il.* 11.514.

fire: Heracles cremated himself on Oeta, Asclepius was struck by lightning.

your tomb: a favourite motif of L. and Christian apologists; the Cretans' claim was dismissed as a lie by Callimachus, *Hymn to Zeus* 8–9.

Aegium in Achaea: the reference is unknown, though Pausanias 7.24.4 records a statue of Zeus as a boy at Aegium.

c.7 **a bull:** when carrying off Europa.

get to work ... finish ... off: in *katergasētai* L. combines the meanings of 'do for' (or 'destroy') and 'complete (a piece of work)'.

gold: when courting Danae.

Pentheus, Actaeon and Learchus: Pentheus was torn to pieces by his mother, Agave, and Actaeon by his own dogs; Learchus was murdered by his father, Athamas.

c.8 **Anchises, Tithonus, Endymion, Iasion:** beloved by Aphrodite, Eos (Aurora), Selene and Demeter respectively.

c.9 **Attis and Corybas and Sabazius:** Phrygian deities.

Scythians ... Getans ... Zamolxis: the nomadic Scythians even deified their swords according to L.; Hdt. 4.95 tells how Zamolxis fooled the people of Thrace, the area where the Getae lived, into thinking him immortal by disappearing into an underground chamber for three years and then reappearing. L. seems to regard the Getae as a subdivision of the Scythians.

c.10 **dog-faced Egyptian:** Anubis who had a human body and a dog's head.

bull from Memphis: Apis; see Hdt. 3.28.

ibises, apes and goats: cf. Hdt. 2.67, Juvenal 15. 3, 4, 12.

other creatures even more ridiculous: including cats and crocodiles.

grow a ram's horns: as Zeus Ammon; see Hdt. 2.42.

:.12 **Trophonius:** a hero who had an oracle in Boeotia, cf. *Dialogues of the Dead* 10.

Amphilochus: a hero who established a famous oracle at Mallus in Cilicia. Here L. follows the version of the legend, cf. Apollodorus 3.7.7, that makes him the son of Alcmaeon, killer of his own mother Eriphyle.

Polydamas: an Olympic victor of 408 of legendary strength, commemorated by a statue by Lysippus.

Theagenes: an equally famous Olympic victor of 480; Pausanias 6.11.9, also attributes healing powers to his statues.

c.13 **it will be Chance:** Momus' argument would have been improved by the omission of 'and Chance' a few lines earlier.

c.14 **this resolution:** the whole resolution, cc. 14–18, is an elaborate parody of the type of *psēphisma* of the *boulē* and *dēmos* of ancient Athens common in Demosthenes, cf. *De Corona* 29, 84 etc.; for briefer Lucianic parodies see *Timon* 51 and *Menippus* 20.

many different ... races: for *synkludōn anthrōpōn* cf. Thuc. 7.5.4.

Momus ... and Sleep: L. follows Hesiod *Th.* 212–4 where both Momus and Hypnos are sons of Night.

outsiders: only the sons of Athenian fathers and mothers were allowed to attend the ecclesia.

a fortune: literally 'a mina', 100 drachmas or 600 obols, 200 times an Athenian juror's wage.

c.15 **Twelve Gods:** the major Olympians.

the Styx: the most solemn oath for the gods; cf. *Il.* 15. 37–8.

c.19 **Hands up ... approve:** the whole phrase is closely modelled on Xen. *An.* 5.6.33.

motion carried: note the humour of this undemocratic behaviour by Zeus in an *ecclēsia*.

proofs of parentage etc.: L. here parodies the Athenian *dokimasia*, the scrutiny of the parentage etc. of new magistrates and young citizens; cf. Aristotle, *Ath. Pol.* 55.3.

THE FISHERMAN

The Fisherman (*Pisc.*) owes its place in this selection both to its humour and to its importance in illustrating Lucian's attitude to contemporary philosophy and showing how he is more interested in the behaviour of philosophers than in the details of the various systems they represent; but first we must consider the *Sale of the Lives* (*V.A.*) to which it forms a sequel, comprising a rather more serious defence of what had been merely a light-hearted skit.

V.A. opens with Zeus ordering Hermes, the salesman god, to hold an auction of 'philosophical lives of every type involving a variety of creeds' under circumstances into which we need not inquire too closely as Lucian uses the licence of comic fantasy. Ten lives in all are offered for sale. That of Pythagoras, using Ionic, trots out a good sample of distinctive doctrines and impresses his purchaser, particularly once a golden thigh is detected, so that he gladly pays the asking price of 10 minas (= 1,000 drachmas) on behalf of a consortium of 300 from Magna Graecia. The life of the Cynic[1] from Pontus (Diogenes) is so scruffy, independent, rude and bossy that it fetches only 2 obols (1/3 of a drachma). The next three remain unsold, the Cyrenaic one (Aristippus) because of its drunkenness and foppishness, the life from Abdera (Democritus) because of its annoying laughter, that from Ephesus (Heraclitus) because of its lugubriousness and obscurity of diction. The talkative Athenian (Socratic) life, that has pederastic tendencies, swears by the dog and the plane-tree, lives in his own Republic, advocates holding wives in common and believes in an ideal theory, is bought by Dion of Syracuse for two talents, much the best price (= 12,000 drachmas). The impious, gourmandising Epicurean life goes quickly for 2 minas. The Stoic one is claimed by Hermes to be in great demand and after a lengthy exposition of its paradoxical claims, catch phrases and syllogisms (a pet aversion of Lucian's) so impresses or rather petrifies the purchaser that he pays 12 minas on behalf of a big consortium. The Peripatetic life is advertised by Hermes as being handsome, rich and omniscient (i.e. Aristotle) and soon goes for 20 minas. Lastly the Sceptic slave Pyrrhias (sc. Pyrrho) goes for 1 mina, but is reluctant to accompany his new master, suspending judgment on whether the sale has occurred.

The bulk of *V.A.* is devoted to the sale of four lives, those of Pythagoras, Diogenes, Socrates (or Socrates-Plato) and the Stoic, not because he considered them the most important ones but because they offer more scope for humour. Similarly the prices paid are determined by humorous considerations coupled with some attempts at dramatic realism, rather than by Lucian's assessment of their comparative merits. Socrates fetches such a high price because his purchaser is a Syracusan plutocrat with a fanatical admiration for Plato, though the price may also partly reflect Lucian's appreciation of Plato's literary qualities, cf. the sincere tribute in *Pisc.* 22. Stoicism gets a high price because it is the creed of the emperor and most favoured by the Romans, and also because its purchaser has suffered from excessive exposure to Stoic logic. Humour and

---

1 For details of the various philosophies see Index.

realism also decide the price for Diogenes, despite Lucian's sympathetic portrayal of his character elsewhere and his general literary debt to Cynicism.

The general idea of *V.A.* would have come to Lucian from Menippus' *Sale of Diogenes* and perhaps from knowledge of the story that Plato too was once sold into slavery, cf. D.L. 3.18–20. The motif of lives being offered for sale, if not originating from lost comedy, may be Lucian's adaptation of the myth of the *Republic* where some choice of lives is available to souls awaiting reincarnation. Just how much the Diogenes sale owed to Menippus it is impossible to tell from the brief survey in D.L. 6.29–30. The Pythagorean sale which precedes has material in common with *The Cock*, while the sales which follow include motifs and jokes resembling ones found in *V.H.* and elsewhere. Lucian regularly repeated or adapted motifs he had already used, and *The Cock* , and perhaps *V.H.* too, may well have preceded *V.A.*

Let us return to *Pisc.* and consider the validity of Lucian's defence that *V.A.* is directed not at the founders of the school but at their degenerate modern adherents. It is true that throughout *V.A.* Hermes sells not philosophers, but lives and that no item sold bears the personal name of a philosopher (Pythagoras, Diogenes etc.), although the name Pyrrhias given to the last item comes very close to Pyrrho. However it is a slave-market and slaves are normally thought of as persons; moreover Lucian's clever ambiguity in referring to each item by the use of masculine articles and masculine adjectives (*ho Pythagorikos* etc.) could lead listeners to think the noun understood to be not 'life' but 'man'. There is not the slightest reference to contemporary philosophers and the biographical details (the Pythagorean life being Samian, the Cynic one from Pontus) and the typical watchwords make it quite clear that *V.A. does* refer to the founders of the schools. Only as a last resort could it be argued that, though the lives are those of Pythagoras etc., the whole thing is allegorical, really suggesting an auction of the Pythagorean or Cynic type of life or type of philosopher, but the common sense conclusion must be that Lucian's line of defence would have received short shrift from a modern judge.

Structurally *Pisc.* resembles an Old Comedy with a '*parodos*' (the 'chorus' of philosphers rushing on stage angrily to attack the hero) an '*agōn*' (here involving a formal trial) and a final scene in which a variety of impostors are attracted by the prospect of food (and gold in this case). The debt to the *Acharnians* is particularly obvious from the language and manner of the initial attack on the hero, his recourse to Euripides and his successful defence as he proves he has acted justly (the parallel being even closer if the equation Dicaeopolis = Aristophanes is accepted). The idea of the angry philosophers returning from the dead and acting like a comic chorus comes from the *Demes* of Eupolis, in which great Athenian politicians return to the upper world to advise Athens in an hour of need.

Apart from the mixture of prose and verse in cc. 1–2 and perhaps the character Truth and the watch-tower motif, c. 16, Lucian's debt to Menippus cannot be quantified. The trial owes something to the *Eumenides* with Philosophy presiding like Athene and Lucian in the role of Orestes, though he makes his own defence and wins a unanimous verdict. A few touches remind us of a much less successful defendant, Socrates, as recorded by Plato. The final scene owes something to the *Silloi* (humorous poetic sketches) of the Sceptic Timon of

Phlius, who portrayed Chrysippus as fishing for philosophers. No doubt there are further debts to comedies now lost. Thus *Pisc.* is a typical Lucianic *pot-pourri*.

The title has a precedent in a play of Menander variously referred to as *Halieus* or *Halieis*. Or were there two separate plays? The idea of treating men as fishes, if nothing more, goes back to *The Fishes* of Archippus, a poet of Old Comedy. The metaphor of 'fishers of men' is familiar from the *N.T.*

c.1 SOCRATES: Speakers' names can only be decided by the context, as original texts normally omitted them. Here only Ω of our main mss. consistently applies them and need not be correct. Socrates, though fetching much the highest price in *V.A.*, seems likely as the first speaker, as his first appeal is to Plato, and the setting is in the area of the *agora*, a favourite Socratic haunt.

Pelt, pelt: the opening is reminiscent of the angry entrance of a comic chorus, cf. Ar. *Ach.* 281–2, *Eq.* 247. For the general relationship of *Pisc.* to Old Comedy see p. 259.

Plato: the life sold in *V.A.* seemed to have been composite, with a lot of Socrates, but also a little of Plato, e.g. the women in common, cf. *V.H.* 2.19, and the purchase by Dion, a fanatical admirer of Plato; cf. also D.L. 3. 18–20 for the story that Plato was sold into slavery for offending Dionysius, but then bought and freed for 20 (or 30) minae by Anniceris who was later reimbursed by Dion.

and you too: perhaps a philosopher's name has been lost here.

That ... staff: a parody of *Il.* 2.363. Pouches and staffs particularly suggest Cynics. Note how in cc.1–3 L. follows Menippus in using a mixture of prose and verse.

Quit ... wrath: parodying *Il.* 6.112 etc.

c.2 each one: i.e. many, many times; or possibly once for each of the seven of us sold (though three remained unsold).

my crater: traditionally Empedocles committed suicide by jumping into the crater of Etna.

Be ... doom: *Trag. Adesp.* 291 N.

c.3 For ... be: *Il.* 22.262.

Oh ... love: a cento from *Il.* 6.46, 48 and 20.65.

Escape ... power: adapted from *Il.* 10.447–8.

take refuge with Euripides: cf. Ar. *Acharnians* 394.

Oh ... wrong: Eur. *Fr.* 937 N.

Who ... dire: Eur. *Orestes* 413.

So ... words: Eur. *Fr.* 938 N.

Of .. misery: Eur. *Bacchae* 387–9.

c.4 silent one: a joke about the Pythagorean vow of silence, cf. *V.A.*3.

c.5 A shirt ... done: *Il.* 3.57.

assuming you execute me: a parody of Plato, *Apology* 30E.

c.6 culling ... admiring: note the revealing description of L.'s literary methods and his expectations from his audience.

Thamyris: a minstrel who challenged the Muses to a musical contest, but they defeated him, blinded him and took away his musical powers. See *Il.* 2.594–600.

in rivalry of bow: for Eurytus' defeat by Apollo in an archery contest see *Od.* 8. 224–8. L. uses epic phraseology reminiscent of *Od.* 1.79–80 and Apollonius Rhodius 1.89.

c.8 submitted my accounts: like an Athenian magistrate after his year of office.

c.9 **horses on to the plain:** a proverbial expression for challenging to fight on terrain that obviously favoured one side, cf. Pl. *Tht.* 183D. Just as the plain favours cavalry, so the courtroom favours Frank.

orator and courtroom expert: the phrase comes from Plato, *Tht.* 201A.

c.10 **allowed any time:** literally 'getting a share of the water'. Athenian trials used a water-clock which gave plaintiff and defendant the same time.

c.11 **tattered cloaks and long beards:** regularly used by L. as the distinctive features of philosophers.

much more ignorant than I: here L. parodies Socrates' account in *Apology* 21C ff. of how he questioned the seemingly wise and other types of Athenians and found them all devoid of knowledge.

c.12 **powder and paint:** literally 'white-lead and rouge'.

Ixion ... Hera: Zeus, learning from Hera of the unwelcome advances of the mortal Ixion, produced a double of her to which Ixion made amorous advances. See L.'s comic treatment of the myth in *Dialogues of the Gods* 9.

c.13 **take a walk:** be Peripatetic, a punning reference to Aristotle's school. See Index.

the Painted Porch: the H.Q. of the Stoics, in the Agora-Cerameicus area to the north of the Areopagus and Acropolis. Plato's Academy was nearly a mile further out to the north-west. See Index

c.14 **the leading lights:** here L. adapts the description of Pericles in Eupolis' *Demes Fr.* 93K (*PCG* 115); see p. pp. 2, 259.

names I've been called by Comedy: Socrates was thus victimised by Aristophanes in *Clouds* and apparently also by Eupolis.

c.15 **a huge audience:** one of many indications that L.'s dialogues were presented orally and not simply sold to readers.

a couple of coppers at a time: a rhetorical misrepresentation of *V.A.*, where the six others fetch far more than the two obols for Diogenes.

c.16 **the Areopagus:** a more suitable place for a trial ever since the legendary trial of Orestes, but Philosophy, presiding after the manner of Athena in the *Eumenides*, opts for the Acropolis as a better view-point, a common Lucianic motif perhaps derived from Menippus; this also facilitates the introduction of the fishing scene at the end.

c.17 **Examination:** *Elenchos* combines the meanings of (1) cross-examining and (2) proving wrong, discrediting, showing up, a notorious activity of Socrates. For its use by L; see pp. 4–5, 11.

c.19 **Frank ... Famous:** or 'Frank Verity Tester'. The three pseudonyms may well come from a prologue of Menander, cf. *Pseudolog.* 4 where L. describes the personification Elenchos as 'a friend of Aletheia and Parrhesia'. Parrhesiades is particularly appropriate because of L.'s general debt to the Cynics who were proud of their *parrhēsia*.

born ... Euphrates: *tōn epeuphratidiōn* is a comic coinage, perhaps chosen for its resemblance to *tōn eupatridōn* (of aristocratic descent) or the joke may depend on *eu* + *phratria* (clan).

Soli ... Stagira: Chrysippus, the Stoic, was born in Soli in Cilicia, Zeno, the founder of Stoicism, in Cyprus, the lesser Diogenes, a Stoic, in Babylon, and Aristotle in Stagira in Macedonia, regarded in classical times as outside Greece proper.

c.21 **antechamber of Athene:** presumably the porch of her main temple, the Parthenon, though the old wooden statue of A. Polias was housed in the Erechtheum. The appeal for protection may be suggested by the *Eumenides* where Orestes takes refuge at Athene's image.

black pebbles: voting was by pebbles cast into an urn, black ones for condemnation, white ones for acquittal. Note the allusion to the *Eumenides*. This

passage and *Harmonides* 3 suggest that, to L. at least, Athena's vote, though decisive, merely equalised the totals.

c.22 Remember: L.'s joke; the philosophers ask the dead Plato to use the *anamnēsis*, memory from a previous existence, for which he argues in the *Phaedo* and *Meno*.
irony: the dissembling or mock modesty for which Socrates, Plato's mouthpiece, was notorious. See Theophrastus, *Characters* 1.
mighty Zeus ... heaven: quoted from one of L.'s favourite works, Plato's *Phaedrus* (246E). The tribute to Plato, c.22 init., is sincere.

c.23 two coppers: *V.A.* 11; Diogenes doesn't count the three unsold philosophers.

c.24 sticks: see note on c. 1.
the time ... has already started: literally 'your water has already been poured in'. See note on c. 10.
your companions: the five mentioned in c. 16.

c.25 outrageous comedies: a scholiast tells us that Eupolis attacked Socrates even more violently than Aristophanes did in the *Clouds*. Extant fragments of E. represent Socrates as a thief and a beggarly, starveling windbag.
perhaps ... laugh: an unidentified comic fragment, 237 K.

c.27 a mere fiver: in fact only the Sceptic life fetched as little as one mina (100 drachmas), but that was 300 times as much as the two obols for Diogenes. The Attic mina was worth less than the Aeginetan one.

c.30 your own disciples: or, accepting the alternative reading, 'of our contemporaries.'

c.33 differentiating them from you: this is untrue, if taken as a defence of *V.A.*, see introduction to *Pisc.* p. 259; it does have some validity, however, as a defence of L.'s satires in general.
the mysteries of the Two Goddesses: the Eleusinian Mysteries of Demeter and Persephone.

c.34 the ordinary people: cf. *Symposium* 35, where L. makes the ordinary guests behave much better than the philosophers.

c.35 he needs nothing: Cynics in particular stressed their self-sufficiency.
the only rich man is the sage: a dig at the Stoics with their paradox that only the sage is a king, rich man etc.
the tiara upright: the tiara was a Persian head-dress, which only the Great King might wear upright on his head; see Xen. *Anab.* 2.5. 23.
something indifferent: another dig at the Stoics.
embarrassment: whether *aporia* is to be taken in the sense of 'dismay' 'not knowing what to do' or perhaps 'sudden poverty'.
winged words: a Homeric phrase, *Il.* 1. 201 etc.

c.36 war to the death: the phrase is adapted from *On the Crown* 262.
a king of Egypt: later, in *Apology* 5, L. modifies the story with one monkey performing for Cleopatra.

c.37 there are some: e.g. assuming they are real men, Demonax and Nigrinus.

c.38 the Trojans: latter-day Trojans, if hiring actors, couldn't complain about having to listen to tragedies about Troy, cf. *Pseudolog.* 10. So too the philosophers in accusing L. have been 'hoist with their own petard'.

c.39 O ... send: the ending of Euripides, *I.T., Phoe., Orestes*. The homage may be to Nike as a goddess in her own right, cf. Hes *Th.* 384, but Nike was also one of Athene's titles, they are in her pronaos and the little temple of Athene Nike is nearby and Phidias' Athene Parthenos in the Parthenon held a statue of Nike in her right hand.
Syllogism: L. personifies a way of inferring from premises particularly favoured by the Stoics. The choice of name may suggest a pun = 'Gatherer'.

c.40 The philosophers to be...: L. reproduces the phraseology and the syntax of proclamations, cf. Ar. *Peace* 551.

c.41 And talents ... best: a parody of *Il.* 18. 507–8.

c.42 The road up: i.e. The normal route leading up from the west via the Propylaea. On other sides the Acropolis is rocky and precipitous. The Pelasgicum and the temple of the Dioscuri were on the northern slopes of the Acropolis near the cave of Pan, while the tomb of Talos (or Calos) and the Asclepieion were on its southern slopes near the Theatre of Dionysus. The Areopagus is the nearest hill to the N.W.

in clusters: quoting *Il.* 2.89.

in thousands ... spring: *Il.* 2.468.

as ... perch: *Il.* 2.463, in a simile about geese, cranes and swans.

c.43 We Academics: the argumentative quibblers of the New Academy, differentiated from the eclectic Platonists mentioned above. See Index.

c.46 crown with an olive wreath: an honour given to public benefactors and victorious athletes.

free meals in the Magistrates' Hall: a lifelong privilege of dining free with the serving magistrates as a reward for conspicuous public service. L. no doubt expects his audience to remember Socrates' suggestion in *Apology* 36 D that he deserved it.

that of a fox or monkey: to indicate slyness or hypocrisy.

when facing the sun: according to *Icaromenippus* 14 the proof of the best eagle is its ability to look directly into the sun without blinking.

c.47 Pelasgicum: alternatively explained as a rocky space from which stones could be taken or a wall; see note on c.42.

c.48 bass: a voracious fish with an etymologically suggestive name, cf. *labros.* Plautus used it as the significant name for the pimp of the *Rudens.*

gilthead: literally 'golden-brow', a kind of bream. The reason for L.'s choice of fish-name is obvious; cf. on Chrysippus in c.51.

cat-fish: a big fish equated by LSJ with a small shark. The name suggests rapacity, cf. c.34.

dogfish: after the dig at Cynics in 'dogfish' L. adds further insult by swearing by their patron hero.

at tuppence the other day: L. repeats his misrepresentation; it was specifically the Pontic Life, i.e. that of Diogenes of Sinope, not that of a modern Cynic that was sold in *V.A.* 11.

minuscule enough: to reproduce L.'s pun I have translated *aphuai* as 'minnows' instead of 'sardines'.

c.49 a plate on him: puns on Plato's name (=flatty) had already been made by Timon of Phlius in his *Silloi* (satirical poems).

turbot: the Greeks thought of flat-fish as being halves of fish that had been cut in two. *Psētta* is used as a nickname for a glutton by a comic poet.

c.51 dumb: a proverbial quality of fish, cf. *The Cock* 1, Horace *Odes* 4.3. 19 etc; L. here reverts from comic fantasy to rationality; he chooses to ignore c.49 where one fish has *said* he's a Platonist.

gold in the name: Chrysippus = Gold-Horse.

c.52 go off for a stroll: be peripatetic, cf. on c.13.

The Academy ... the Porch ... the Lyceum: the headquarters of the Platonists, the Stoics and Aristotle's school, the Peripatetics, respectively. These three, together with the Epicureans, were the most important philosophical schools of Lucian's day and chairs in Athens for each of the four were founded by Marcus Aurelius in A.D. 176.

MENIPPUS

Menippus the Cynic appears as a character in three works of Lucian. He is the most important character in the *Dialogues of The Dead* with a speaking role in eleven of them as he taunts the other ghosts, irritates them with his questions and gloats over them in their changed circumstances; he had much less to lose! In *Icaromenippus* he tells a friend how he flew up to Olympus, using one wing from an eagle another from a vulture, because he wanted to find out how much truth there was in the accounts of the heavenly bodies given by the poets and the various philosophers with their mutually exclusive theories, how he visited the Moon who complained about the insulting theories about her held by the philosophers and the nocturnal misdeeds of those same philosophers, and how he was received by Zeus who seemed unaware of what was going on on earth by the nature of his questions, and showed Menippus around everything including his prayer-holes, from which he would remove the lids when he wanted to hear them and would then give his orders to winds and weather. When Zeus heard about the wicked philosophers, he produced what was a parody of a decree of the Athenian assembly, authorising severe punishment for the hypocritical philosophers of the various schools. In this work, *Menippus*, or *Necyomanteia*, (cf. *Necyia*, the name given to Odysseus' visit to the Land of the Dead in *Odyssey* Book XI) Menippus tells a friend how he wanted to consult the ghost of the wise Tiresias about the best type of life, because he was puzzled by the conflicting moral precepts of the various philosophical schools and the failure of the philosophers to put their precepts into practice and how he was helped by a Chaldaean magician who after a complicated purification ritual accompanied him to Hades still alive, disguised partly as Heracles, partly as Odysseus, partly as Orpheus, and how, after negotiating the various topographical features of Hades, they found Tiresias who advised Menippus that the life of the philosophical layman was best and that he should go through life laughing and taking nothing seriously.

Menippus was born in Gadara in Palestine in the early third century. He started life as a slave, eventually gained freedom, went to Thebes in Boeotia and became a money-lender, but lost all his money and committed suicide. He certainly had a sense of humour and Diogenes Laertius, 6.99, says that there was nothing serious in him, but Strabo's description of him as *spoudogeloios*, a serious jester, is probably more accurate. Lucian, when listing the ingredients of his dialogue in *Bis Acc.* 33, refers to him as 'an old dog I've dug up, one with a loud bark and sharp teeth, all the more formidable because he laughed as he bit'and in *Pisc.* 26 calls him his 'companion in comedy'. All thirteen of his works are lost. Those which may have provided Lucian with general ideas are his *Necyia* (for *Men.*, some *Dialogues of the Dead* etc.), *Sale of Diogenes* (for *Vit. Auct.*, though Lucian puts nine more philosophers up for sale in a different setting), *Symposium, Fictitious Letters written by Gods* (for *Epistulae Saturnales* in *Saturnalia*) and *To* (or *Against*) *Physicists, Mathematicians and Grammarians*. Menippus' innovation of using a mixture of prose and verse was followed by the Roman writers Varro of Reate, Seneca in his *Ludus de Morte*

Claudii and Petronius, but by Lucian only to a limited extent in a mere five works, *Symp., JTr., Icar., Pisc.* and *Men.*

It's impossible to assess Lucian's debt to Menippus[1] in this and other works. An influential German scholar, R. Helm, argued in *Lucian und Menipp*, (Leipzig, 1906), that Lucian was a wholesale borrower from Menippus and his servile imitator, but his views are now generally discredited. Lucian expressly denies in *Prom. Es.* 7 that there is any theft, i.e. plagiarism, in his innovatory dialogues; moreover in *Prom. Es., Zeuxis* and elsewhere he stresses the fact that his audience thought his works novel; wholesale plagiarism from Menippus could hardly have gone unnoticed by some members of a cultured audience, as Menippus is mentioned by three contemporaries, Diogenes Laertius, Marcus Aurelius and Aulus Gellius. Moreover there is no real evidence that Menippus used dialogue rather than narrative, though just possibly he could have framed his narrative within a dialogue as Lucian does in *Men.* and *Icar.* Furthermore in *Bis Acc.* 33 Lucian mentions Menippus as only one of several ingredients, and indeed most of Lucian's Cynicising dialogues look like multicomponent medleys; thus *Men.* uses material from the *Frogs, Odyssey* 11, Platonic myths etc., as well as from Menippus, and also includes rhetorical commonplaces and a reference to *salutatio* which couldn't have come from Menippus, and similarly *Pisc.*, despite its initial admixture of verse, incorporates several other components, see pp. 259–60.

There is no strong reason to suppose that Lucian had a major debt to Menippus in his general attacks on philosophers, as the topic recurs throughout Greek literature, though the complaints about their unsatisfactory and conflicting cosmological theories found in *Men.* 4 and *Icar.* 4 may be based on Menippus who had included *physikoi* in his strictures. After all the evidence has been sifted from works such as the Fragments of Varro's *Saturae Menippeae* and Seneca's skit, which may have shared Menippus as a common source with Lucian, a handful of shared motifs and similar phrases do emerge, but Lucian's main debt cannot be proved to be much more than that of general spirit and general ideas for plots. Moreover though Menippus must be conceded an element of fantasy in his plots, the *katabasis* theme had already occurred in *Odyssey* 11, *Frogs* etc., and the flight and celestial visit in the *Peace* and *Birds*, so that it remains uncertain how far Lucian is using Menippus direct rather than producing his own adaptations of ideas suggested from pre-Menippean sources, particularly Old Comedy.

---

1. For a careful and detailed study of L.'s debt to Menippus see Hall, 64–150.

c.1 **Greetings ... light:** like *JTr.* the dialogue opens with the form attributed to the lost works of Menippus, the mixture of prose and verse. Menippus' first four speeches come from Euripides, *H.F.* 523–4, *Hecuba* 1–2, *Fr.* 936 N and *Fr.* 149 N (from *Andromeda*, cf. *Hist.* 1). When told off, he switches to Homeric hexameters, adapting *Od.* 11.564–5.

strange attire: as a Dog (Cynic), he should be wearing only a ragged cloak and carrying a stick. Instead like Dionysus in the *Frogs* he has a strange, composite costume, the *pilos*, a close-fitting felt cap associated with Odysseus ever since he wore it under the boar's tusk helmet in *Il.* 10.265, and a lionskin like Heracles, and he carries a lyre like Orpheus. The question about his appearance is modelled on *Frogs* 45–7 and is answered in c. 8.

c.2 **Cerberus:** the watch-dog of Hades. Note L.'s humorously appropriate oath in the mouth of a 'Dog'. Cf. 'By Heracles' in c. 1 and note on *Pisc.* 48.

Rhadamanthys: one of the Judges of the Dead; humorously L. applies the technical terms of Athenian law to his court.

like Danae: because of an oracle that her son would kill him, Acrisius kept his daughter Danae locked up to keep her out of contact with males.

c.3 **for what ... compels:** a phrase used several times by L.; the first part, *ti ... tis*, adapted from Menander.

when first I reached manhood's estate: another favourite Lucianic phrase modelled on Plato, *Laws* 923 E.

adultery, quarrelling and theft: this criticism of the Homeric picture of the gods is a constant theme of L. and contemporary Christian apologists, but is found throughout Greek literature, going back to Xenophanes of the sixth century, particularly *Fr.* 11, and was memorably expressed by Plato in the *Republic*.

c.4 **the average man:** see notes on c.21 and *Pisc.* 34.

one of them: the emphasis on pleasure marks him out as a Cyrenaic or Epicurean. See Index.

another recommended a life of complete toil etc.: this man has some Stoic features, his recommendation of a life of toil and his emphasis on virtue, sweat and the ascent to the summit, cf. *Hermotimus* 25, but his filth and abusiveness are markedly Cynic.

Hesiod: *Works and Days* 289–92.

Another ... something indifferent: he is another Stoic, whereas the one contradicting him is meant by L. to be Peripatetic, cf. *V.A.* 26, Aristotle *EN* 1099B, 1120A. See Index.

talking of ... atoms and void: like the Epicureans who adopted the theories of Leucippus and Democritus. See Index.

c.6 **Magi:** Persian priests and sages, experts on libations to the dead, cf. Hdt. 7.43, and credited by the Greeks with magical powers, cf. Hdt. 7.191.

Zoroaster: the founder of the chief Persian religion.

Tiresias: the general idea of consulting T. in Hades comes from *Od.* 11, and had been used by Horace *Satires* 2.5, as well as presumably by Menippus. T.'s reputation for wisdom was enhanced by the tradition that he had been both man and woman, cf. *Dialogues of the Dead* 9, where he is consulted and ridiculed by the dead Menippus and L. parodies the myth of his having been consulted on the comparative merits of male and female life.

Chaldaeans: the wise, priestly class of Babylon, noted in L.'s time as astrologers.

Mithrobarzanes: the compound name seems to come from Mithradates and Ariobarzanes, the names of several kings or satraps of Pontus; Mithras was the Persian Sun-God and his worship had spread throughout the Roman Empire in L.'s time.

c.7 Choaspes: a tributary of the Tigris, famous for the purity of its waters; cf. Hdt. 1.188.

c.8 character from tragedy: and indeed comedy; in the *Frogs* Dionysus tries to exploit Heracles' lionskin.

c.9 ourselves ... fall: *Od.* 11.4–5.

dug a pit ff.: the procedure is based on *Od.* 11. 25, 35–6; other ritualistic details, e.g. the preparatory purification facing the east, spitting thrice are paralleled elsewhere.

And Night ... Persephone: cf. *Il.* 9.569 etc.

c.10 And down ... fear: *Il.* 20.61.

Pyriphlegethon: the river of Burning Fire, one of the four rivers of Hades. The topography of L.'s Hades doesn't bear too close examination, being a mixture of *Od.* 11, the myths of Plato, Attic comedy and no doubt other sources.

c.11 asphodel: cf. *Od.* 11.539.

screeching: for the shrill sound of ghosts cf. *Il.* 23. 101, *Od.* 24. 9.

Minos: the only judge of the dead mentioned in *Od.* 11 (line 568); elsewhere, e.g. Pl. *Grg.* 524A, *Apol.* 41A, he shares the judging with Rhadamanthys, Aeacus and others, but as senior partner.

a 'crow': the crow, if textually correct, is unparalleled; Harmon suggested it might be a ball-and-chain.

c.12 the place for the impious: Tartarus; the general picture of the judging of the dead seems to owe something to the myths of Plato's *Gorgias* and *Republic*.

said 'Good Morning': L. here refers to the *salutatio*, a feature of Roman life; so this detail at least cannot be inspired by Menippus.

c.13 Dionysius: Dionysius (the Younger) was tyrant of Syracuse 367–356 B.C. and a generous patron of men of letters and philosophers. He banished his son-in-law Dion but was later ousted by him. Dion had been an enthusiastic student of Plato, but his rule turned out to be a poor advertisement for the 'philosopher king'. See note on *Pisc.* 1.

c.14 Ixion, Sisyphus ... Tantalus ... Tityus: all four were standard examples of villains being punished in Hades. Ixion aspired to the love of Hera, see note on *Pisc.* 12, and was bound to a wheel in Hades; the punishment of the other three is described in *Od.* 11. 576–600. Sisyphus had to roll a recalcitrant boulder up a hill; Tantalus, cf. *Dialogues of the Dead* 7, stood in water under fruit trees but was prevented from eating or drinking, while Tityus' liver was continually being devoured by two vultures.

c.15 strengthless: *Od.* 10. 521, 11.29 etc.

embalmment: cf. Hdt. 2 86–8.

Thersites ... Nireus: in the *Iliad* Thersites was an ugly commoner, Nireus the handsomest of the Greeks, cf. *Charon* 22, *Dialogues of the Dead* 30.

Irus ... King of the Phaeacians: Irus was an Ithacan beggar beaten up by Odysseus in *Od.* 18; for Alcinous, King of Phaeacia see *Od.* 6 ff.

Pyrrhias: Pyrrhias, Latin *Byrria*, was a common name for slaves in comedy, cf. also *V.A.* 27.

c.16 Croesus: the pride and fall of Croesus, king of Lydia, as described in Hdt. Book 1, was a favourite theme of rhetoricians and satirists and also used by L. in *Charon*; cf. also *Dialogues of the Dead* 3, where Menippus taunts the dead Croesus.

Maeandrius ... Polycrates: Polycrates was tyrant of Samos in the sixth century B.C.; his outstanding prosperity, according to Hdt. Book 3, incurred the jealousy of the gods; he was treacherously murdered by a Persian and succeeded by his low-born secretary, Maeandrius.

borrowed for a short period: cf. the similar sentiment of the Epicurean Lucretius, *De Rerum Natura* 3.971.

the needs of the plays: Attic tragedy used only three actors, who had to double up, as there were often eight or more *dramatis personae*.

steps down: in L.'s day though not in the fourth century when Polus and Satyrus acted, the footwear of tragic actors had high platform-type soles.

c.17 his tomb: the Mausoleum, one of the Seven Wonders of the Ancient World, erected by his widow Artemisia after his death in 353 B.C.; cf. *Dialogues of the Dead* 29.

benefit he got: ironically meant.

selling fish: for fish-selling and cobbling as menial occupations cf. Plato, *Charmides* 163 B. See also Diogenes Laertius 4.46.

teaching elementary reading: perhaps suggested to L. by Demosthenes' snobbish taunts against Aeschines, *On the Crown* 258.

stitching rotten sandals: see above on 'selling fish'. L. makes his Cynic character Micyllus a humble cobbler in *Cataplus* 14ff. and *Gallus*.

c.18 Palamedes, Odysseus, Nestor: as in *V.H.* 2. 17, *Dialogues of the Dead* 6.4, L. echoes Plato, *Apol.* 41 B. Palamedes was one of the glibbest Greek heroes; the eloquence and loquacity of Odysseus and the aged Nestor are noted in the *Iliad*.

consider moving elsewhere: this amusing impossibility is one of several motifs shared with *Dialogues of the Dead* 3.

c.19 I'm glad you reminded me: a favourite Platonic echo of L.'s.

the presidents: note the humour of having the ancient Athenian democratic system operating in Hades, just as in Olympus in *Deor. Conc.* The business and meetings of the *ecclēsia* were the responsibility of the 'presidents', the fifty members of the *boulē* or council, whose tribe were in charge for that tenth part of the year.

c.20 Whereas ff.: see note on *Deor. Conc.* 14 for L.'s parodies of *psēphismata*.

Brimo: 'Roarer', an onomatopoetic name applied to both Persephone and Hecate.

c.21 which sort of life: see note on Tiresias in c.6.

differing from one another: alternatively the Greek could mean 'being inconsistent in their beliefs'.

the life of the ordinary man is best: Odysseus comes to the same conclusion in the myth of the *Republic* (620 C); cf. c.3, *Pisc.* 34 and *Symp.* 35.

first beginnings and final ends: a dig at Aristotle's Peripatetics in particular.

learned syllogisms: particularly used of the type of deductive arguments favoured by the Stoics and regularly derided by L.; cf. *V.A.* 22, *Pisc.* 39, *Hist.* 17.

to arrange the present well: a piece of proverbial wisdom, cf. Cratinus 172, Marcus Aurelius 6.2.

laughing ... and taking nothing seriously: again a saw and attributed to Simonides, presumably the lyric poet from Ceos.

Thus ... asphodel: adapted from *Od.* 11.539.

c.22 shrine of Trophonius: a cave near Lebadeia in Boeotia housing the oracle of the hero Trophonius; cf. *Dialogues of the Dead* 10. As Menippus lived in Thebes, it was a very convenient place for him to emerge from the underworld.

ON THE DEATH OF PEREGRINUS

A limited number of Lucian's works draw their material from his own time and so are of value as social documents, though in assessing their veracity due allowance must be made for Lucian's satirical instincts, rhetorical background, quarrelsomeness and the vitriol apparent in most of these works, as he attacks personal enemies, rival sophists, or individuals with whom he has crossed swords on linguistic issues. Particularly interesting for their topicality are two works, *Alexander* [1] and *Peregrinus*, as Parrhesiades, the hater of impostors and falsehood, see p. 261, follows his natural instincts in attacking one as a bogus prophet and the other as a vainglorious fool.

We know from other sources that an oracle of Glycon at Abonuteichos was established in Paphlagonia in the reign of Antoninus Pius and enjoyed great popularity for many years. Lucian, however, was cautious enough to wait till at least five years after the death[2] of Alexander, the founder of the oracle, before writing his *Alexander*, ostensibly a letter to his Epicurean friend Celsus,[3] the author of a work 'Against Magicians', but presumably meant for publication. After stressing the ignominies of this Alexander in comparison with the glories of Alexander the Great and indulging in a conventional *psogos* attacking the origins, early years and immoral escapades of his anti-hero, Lucian describes and gives rational explanations of the various 'miracles' and 'magical' devices contrived by Alexander, e.g. in staging the birth of the divinity Glycon by use of a newborn snake emerging from a goose's egg, and in attaching a linen mask and a crane's windpipe to a tame snake which he represented as Glycon, a re-incarnation of Asclepios, the source of the oracles of which he himself, 'great grandson of Zeus', was the interpreter. Lucian describes various errors and ambiguities of the oracle and tricks played by himself and others to test and discredit it, and tells how Alexander eventually, see p. 3, tried to have him murdered. According to Lucian Alexander was particularly hostile to 'atheists, Christians and Epicureans'; this may be because Alexander knew of Christian apologists who had used Epicurean arguments in attacking pagans' beliefs about their gods, or may simply represent an attempt to discredit the Epicureans, by associating them with an unpopular sect. Strictly speaking the Epicureans were not atheists but would naturally be inimical to Alexander for their rejection of traditional religion and belief that the gods kept aloof from human affairs.

Peregrinus[4] is of even greater interest to us to-day for the references to Christ and the Christians occurring in this attack by Lucian on the memory of a philosopher who had been a Christian for a time and imprisoned for his Christianity, but was more famous in antiquity for his suicide on a funeral pyre in A.D. 165 after the Olympic Games. Lucian's unfavourable picture of Peregrinus should be modified by consideration of references by other writers

---

1. On Alexander see Jones 133 ff.
2. The latest possible date for Alexander's death was 175; Alexander however was not published before 180.
3. A different man from the author of the *Alēthēs Logos*, the Platonist attacked by the Christian Origen; see Hall 512–3.
4. On *Peregrinus* see Jones 117 ff.

such as Aulus Gellius who describes him as *virum gravem atque constantem*, having seen him living in a hut outside Athens and listened to his useful and honourable sayings, and Philostratus *VS* 563, who, though disapproving of his rudeness to Herodes Atticus, attributes his suicide to philosophical courage; note how even Lucian merely ascribes it to a desire for glory. Clearly he lived an abstemious, ascetic life and probably was nothing worse than an idealistic, philosophical and religious fanatic. Lucian and others call him a Cynic, but he had eclectic tendencies, deriving ideas and inspiration from the Christians, the Brahmins and in particular the neo-Pythagoreans.

Lucian's attitude to the Christians is not particularly hostile, as his worst strictures were reserved for those who behaved badly and failed to practise what they preached. To Lucian the Christians are merely poor fools, accepting their beliefs 'without any sure proof', but, despite his intellectual contempt for them, his description of them is surprisingly accurate and compares favourably with that of his contemporary Fronto.

The suicide of Peregrinus provides the opening for another work, the dialogue *Fugitivi*, which starts in Olympus with Zeus complaining about the nasty smell of Peregrinus' burning flesh which had forced him to take temporary refuge in the fragrant land of Arabia. He is interrupted by the arrival of Philosophy who is furious with the disgraceful conduct and hypocrisy of present day 'philosophers', mainly Cynics. She sets out with Hermes and Heracles to punish them and when they come down to earth in Thrace, they join forces with an injured husband and two other slave-owners in pursuing and punishing three renegade 'Cynics', runaway slaves, one of whom has taken his mistress with him. Thus *Fug.* has the same general theme as *Pisc.*, being an attack on the behaviour of contemporary philosophers, but differs from it in concentrating on the Cynics.

Fug. was probably written soon after the suicide, but the date of *Peregr.* is much disputed. It could precede or closely follow *Fug.* with which it has some common motifs, but the forecast of the establishment of a Peregrinean oracle in c. 28 seems to have been written with hindsight[5] and the existence of such an oracle may have been Lucian's chief reason for writing *Peregr.*; I therefore see it as more closely linked with *Alex.*, that other attack on oracles, with which it also shares motifs, than with *Fug.* The reference to four visits to Olympia in c. 35 is unhelpful, as the Greek is ambiguous. Lucian's fourth visit could have been in 165, as the festival was an excellent occasion for sophists to display their wares, but travel was difficult in the ancient world. I prefer to make 165 Lucian's second or third visit. Composition in an Olympic year would give *Peregr.* greater topicality and so I suggest 169 or better 173 as a possible date for publication of what was probably only ostensibly a letter.

Despite the Epicurean tone of the letter, the initial greeting *eu prattein* is Platonic, and so the addressee has been identified with Cronius, the philosophical associate of the known Platonist, Numenius of Apamea. Unfortunately as Numenius had strong neo-Pythagorean leanings, this Cronius would have been likely to sympathise with Peregrinus' sentiments. Perhaps, therefore, *Peregr.*

---

5. Cf. the warnings about the future conduct of the Peloponnesian War put into Pericles' mouth by Thuc., endowing him with something like second sight.

should be taken as an open letter to this Cronius, suggesting admiration for Peregrinus is misplaced.

c.1 **Homer's Proteus:** the aged sea-god of *Od.* 4.384ff. who could change into any living creature or water or, ibid. 417–8, fire.

Empedocles: a Sicilian philosopher of the mid-fifth century B.C., who according to a tradition regularly used by L. for comic effect, committed suicide by leaping into the crater of Mt. Etna.

the most heavily attended of the Greek festivals: at Olympia.

c.2 **the old fellow:** presumably he was at least 20 years senior to L.

such behaviour: or perhaps 'fellows like that'.

almost torn to pieces by the Cynics: cf. the statement of the Suda that L. was torn to pieces by dogs, whether based on a misunderstanding of this passage or a confusion with a similar tradition about the death of Euripides.

cousin Pentheus: Actaeon (killed by his hounds for offending Artemis) and Pentheus (for whose fate see Euripides' *Bacchae*) were sons of the sisters Autonoe and Agave.

c.3 **the dramatist:** Peregrinus; ancient playwrights were usually their own producers.

Elis: the city of Elis, about 25 miles N. of Olympia. L. was probably on his way from Athens via Corinth.

the gymnasium: the main gymnasium in Elis, where for the month prior to the games, Olympic competitors had to train under the supervision of the *Hellanodikai*, officials who also acted as umpires and judges at the games. Another reason for L.'s presence was that gymnasia were used for lecturing purposes by philosophers and sophists.

c.4 **Heracles ... Asclepius ... Dionysus:** the Cynic's addition of Asclepius and Dionysus is unconvincing. All three were demi-gods who achieved full divinity, but unlike Heracles, the Cynic idol, who committed suicide on a funeral pyre, see Sophocles *Trach.*, Asclepius was killed by Zeus' thunderbolt for reducing the numbers of the dead by being too good a doctor, and the thunderbolt affected Dionysus' birth, not his death.

c.5 **Theagenes:** a rich money-lender of Patras, cf. c.30, possibly the man referred to by Galen as a well-known Cynic philosopher who conversed daily in Trajan's gymnasium in Rome.

the man of Sinope: Diogenes.

c.7 **Another man:** probably L. himself.

'while 'twas yet a-burning': *Iliad* 11.775.

'bottom o' his heart': cf. *Iliad* 10.10.

Heraclitus ... Democritus: see on *Sacr.* 15.

c.9 **embodiment of Polyclitan perfection:** like the *Kanōn*, or Spear-Bearer, the statue of perfect proportions by the fifth century sculptor, Polyclitus.

on reaching manhood's estate: see on *Menippus* 3.

a radish stuffed up his behind: the punishment for adultery, cf. Aristophanes, *Clouds* 1083. Something larger than our radish was used or perhaps several of them, cf. Alciphron 3.26.4. L. may be echoing part of a lost comic line.

c.11 **amazing doctrines:** I take L. to be expressing surprise rather than contempt here; but an alternative possibility is 'wondrous wisdom' meant ironically, cf. *thaumastēn* in c. 17.

prophet: i.e. authoritative religious spokesman and/or priest.

cult-leader: leader of a *thiasos*, originally a band of Bacchic devotees, but later any religious confraternity.

convener of meetings: though *synagōgeus* is paralleled in pagan non-Jewish inscriptions, L. here, as with 'priests' and 'scribes' above, produces a term particularly appropriate for Palestine. L., like most pagan writers, doesn't differentiate between Jews and Christians.

nominated him as their patron: L. uses the phrase applied to aliens resident in Athens who had to register under a patron or protector; cf. Aristophanes, *Peace* 684.

the human fellow: L. means 'man' as opposed to God, cf. *NT*. 'son of man', and perhaps also combines the common contemptuous connotation of *anthrōpos*.

novel: or perhaps 'weird' in a pejorative sense.

c.12 **sacred scriptures recited:** or perhaps 'sacred formulas uttered' in prayers, graces etc.

the new Socrates: a more natural compliment from pagans to pagans, cf. *Demonax* 5, than from Christians, though Socrates is mentioned respectfully by some apologists; perhaps Peregrinus gained the name in his Cynic period, or the reference may be to the bribing and leniency of the jailors, cf. Plato, *Crito* init.

c.13 **Asia:** the Roman province in Western Asia Minor with strong Christian communities in cities like Ephesus and Smyrna.

the poor creatures: to be pitied for their credulity and gullibility. As the sceptical L. goes on to say, they accept their beliefs 'without any certain proof'.

stepped out of line by denying the Greek gods: cf. Trajan's instruction to Pliny, when dealing with those accused of Christianity in Bithynia, to make them 'pray to our gods', Plin. *Ep.* 97.2.

that crucified sophist: I take L. to apply the term 'sophist' to Jesus in a neutral or even complimentary sense, 'skilled practitioner' or 'teacher of wisdom' rather than 'cheat' or 'quibbler'.

able to make the most of situations: cf. Demosthenes' description of Philip in *Olynthiacs* 1.3.

c.14 **governor of Syria:** unknown; the suggestion that he was Arrian, the historian and philosopher, who had been governor of Cappadocia from 131 to 137 is mere speculation. L.'s interpretation of the governor's thinking is unconvincing.

that amount wouldn't be fetched by the entire city of Parium: Parium was in fact a prosperous port of Mysia, but it was standard practice in *psogos* to denigrate a man's origin and background.

c.15 **just like a figure out of a tragedy:** L. may be thinking of Euripidean tragedy and in particular the character of Telephus, also from Mysia, whose appearance in a judicial scene is parodied in Aristophanes, *Acharnians*. In fact P.'s appearance was that of a typical Cynic.

he manifested himself: ironical; the Greek verb suggests a divine epiphany.

Crates: a disciple of Diogenes, reputed to have sold his property and given the proceeds to his fellow Thebans.

c.16 **something forbidden to them:** an authentic detail by L.; Christians were forbidden to eat *eidōlothyta*, sacrificial meats, cf. *Acts* 15.29, *First Corinthians* c.8, in particular the scraps left by the rich for the poor under statues of Hecate at cross-roads, a regular source of food for Cynics.

c.17 **Agathobulus in Egypt:** a Cynic from Alexandria, a hotbed of Cynicism at the time; he laid stress on ability to endure pain.

masturbating: following the precedent of Diogenes, who did so in public to show his self sufficiency in not needing a sexual partner.

object of so-called indifference: L. crudely misuses *adiaphoron*, a favourite technical term of the Stoics and also used by Cynics, of things neither good nor bad; Epictetus, see on c.18, extended its application to pleasure.

c.18 **the emperor:** Antoninus Pius, described in his *Life*, *HA*, by Capitolinus as *mitis* and *clemens*.

the urban prefect: perhaps Q. Lollius Urbicus.

Musonius, Dio and Epictetus: the Stoic Musonius Rufus was exiled by Nero; Dio (Chrysostom, of Prusa), a rhetorician and eclectic philosopher, whose extant discourses are mainly Stoic and/or Cynic in spirit, was expelled by Domitian, but recalled by Nerva and was very popular with Trajan; the slave Epictetus, whose Stoic-Cynic discourses have been preserved via Arrian, was also exiled by Domitian.

c.19 **to take up arms against the Romans:** presumably in the rising in Achaea, mentioned by Capitolinus, *HA, Pius* 5.5.

a man of outstanding culture and reputation: the millionaire sophist, Herodes Atticus, whose benefactions included the Odeum and Panathenaic stadium at Athens, the stadium at Delphi and an aqueduct and Nymphaeum for Olympia. Philostratus, *Lives of the Sophists* 563, also records his being abused by Peregrinus at Athens.

c.20 **when now:** I take *ēdē* to mean 'more recently' and cc.19–20 to refer to four games, 153 abuse of Herodes, 157 recantation speech, 161 promise to suicide next time, 165 actual suicide.

be a fugitive: in *Fugitivi*, L.'s other work on a similar theme, discreditable Cynics are represented as *drapetai*, runaway slaves.

c.21 **Philoctetes:** L. follows a different version of the legend from the *Trachiniae*, in making Philoctetes light the funeral pyre; cf. Sen. *Herc. Oet.* 1485.

Phalaris' bull: Phalaris was a Sicilian tyrant of the sixth century B.C. reputed to have burnt his victims in a brazen bull. L.'s invective leads him into an anachronism!

by mouthing once for all: L. adapts *Od.* 12.350, of a quick death by drowning.

c.22 **on hallowed ground:** in fact Peregrinus cremated himself two and a half miles away, see c.35; cf. Thuc. 3.104 for the presence of tombs polluting the sacred island of Delos.

the man who ... set fire to the temple: Herostratus in 356 B.C.; L. like most authors respects an edict of the Ephesians that his name should never be mentioned.

c.24 **easy and open to anyone:** echoing Demosthenes, *First Olynthiac*, 16.

c.25 **the centaur's blood:** the blood of Nessos, as in Sophocles, *Trach.*

the Brahmins: the ascetic Indian sages, also known as *gymnosophistai* (naked sophists). They afforded P. a precedent not only in Calanus, see below, but also in Zarmanochegas, who cremated himself in Athens in the Augustan age, thereby, according to an inscription, immortalising himself.

Onesicritus: he wrote a (lost) history of Alexander, perhaps exaggerating his own position in Alexander's fleet under Nearchus. Being a Cynic himself, he was most impressed with the Cynic-like behaviour of Calanus and other Brahmins.

with decorum: or perhaps 'retaining one position'; cf. Plutarch, *Alexander* 69 and Arrian, *Anabasis* 7.3.

c.27 **the Indian bird, the phoenix:** a marvellous bird earlier associated in a variety of legends not with India but with Egypt. It was thought to live in Arabia and come to Heliopolis when very old to rejuvenate itself or prolong its species, doing so according to later legend by burning itself at the altar of the Sun and rising from the ashes. For the Egyptians it symbolised the rising sun and resurrection. As St. Clement of Rome had also used it as a token of the resurrection, P.'s chief reason for adopting the name was probably to claim immortality or resurrection for himself, rather than simply, as L. misrepresents it, to refer to his suicide in the flames.

far advanced in old age: according to Hesiod it outlived 972 generations of men; later versions made it die aged 500 or 541 or 1,461.

a guardian spirit: belief in *daimones*, semi-divine spirits, operating after their death as intermediaries of the gods and agents of divine providence, was very strong at this time, particularly among Pythagoreans.

his statue erected in gold: according to the Christian apologist Athenagoras, writing c. 177, a statue of P., credited with oracular powers, had been erected in P.'s native city of Parium. Probably L. is writing after the establishment of the oracle.

c.28 quartan fevers: fevers recurring every fourth day. Statues (and presumably their associated *daimones*) credited with healing powers are mentioned by Athenagoras (ibid., of one in Alexandria Troas, near Parium), Lucian, *Assembly of the Gods* 12 etc. and Pausanias.

the well-known Proteus: see on c.1. Homer describes him as 'unerring' and able to forecast the future for Menelaus.

mystery festival ... torch-light procession: ironically suggesting 'after the manner of the Eleusinian Mysteries'; cf. *Alexander* 38.

cc.29,30 the Sibyl ... Bacis: the original Sibyl was a unique prophetess, but by the first century B.C. there were several Sibyls prophesying in various places. Similarly Bacis was originally a Boeotian but later many prophets were producing 'oracles of Bacis'. Oracles were usually in Homeric hexameter verse.

cc.29, 30 But when ... 'tis then: oracular phraseology paralleled in actual oracles in Herodotus and parodies of oracles in Aristophanes and Lucian, *Jup.Trag.* 31. This Bacis oracle is of course L.'s own concoction. The Sibylline one could also be his fiction, as both incorporate many Homeric phrases after the manner of Lucianic centos; more probably, however, it was produced by, or for, Theagenes; C.P. Jones notes the frequent use of fabricated 'Sibylline oracles' in this period for religious propaganda; cf. *Alexander* 11.

c.30 foxy dogs: mongrels combining cunning and shamelessness. L. gets the word and other ideas for the fictitious oracle(s) from Aristophanes, *Knights*.

talents five times three: here apparently a large sum, but cf. c.14.

c.31 'But Nestor ... cries.': *Iliad* 14.1.

the Plethrium: an area in the main gymnasium at Elis where the *Hellanodikai*, see on c.3, trained the wrestlers and arranged their bouts. Presumably this would be a last chance to see them all before they left for Olympia.

c.32 the rear porch of the temple: the western end of the temple of Zeus.

after the contest for heralds was over: after the noise had subsided, competitions for heralds and trumpeters were held on an altar 'near the entrance to the stadium' (Pausanias) i.e. near the other, eastern, end of the temple.

c.33 on a golden life 'a seal of gold to put': an adaptation of *Iliad* 4.111 (on the bow of Pandarus) with a pun on *korōnē* = tip of the bow on which the bowstring was hooked and seal, end, crown, cf. *Hist.* 26 and *bios* = (1) life and, with different accent, (2) bow. P. is pleased with his pun because his exemplar Heracles was famous for his bow, and L. contemptuous of it, expecting his audience to think of the treacherous Pandarus. Like my predecessors, I find the pun untranslatable, but suggest faute de mieux adding 'and make his parting shot a beau (bow) geste'!

play the Philoctetes: help with the fire; see on c.21.

c.35 I've seen in my four visits: or 'I'd seen, that being my fourth visit'. On the dating of the piece see p. 270.

one particular night: or perhaps 'by night'. The Greek is strange and may be corrupt.

c.36 when the moon was rising: perhaps P. was influenced in this by the Pythagorean belief in the moon as the recipient of good, pure souls.

in his invariable fashion: like a Cynic, see c.15 and note.

the noble fellow from Patras: ironical, Theagenes.

gazing to the south: this detail, coupled with the invocation of his parents' *daimones*, may betray Indian influence; Hindus believe that Yama conducts dead souls to the 'Blessed Fathers' who dwell in the south. See note on c.25.

c.37 **the finale of the drama:** L. applies the same terms to the death of Alexander, the False Prophet.

the foul reek: cf. *Fug.* init., where the foul reek is too much for Zeus.

c.39 **some relic:** according to *Adversus Indoctum* 14, P. dropped his staff before jumping into the flames and it was bought by somebody for a huge price.

I would add some theatrical touches of my own: cf. L.'s similar mischiefmaking in producing bogus Heraclitean sayings, see pp. 4–5.

earthquake ... rumbling: cf. *Philopseudeis* 24 for similar details in a tall tale for the ears of the credulous.

a vulture: L. makes the bird do double duty, to please the Cynics because Heracles approved of vultures, and to express his own contempt as a poor substitute for the eagle represented in a poem, *Anth. Pal.* 7.62, as carrying Plato's soul to Olympus, or less probably the dove reputed to have flown up from the dead body of Polycarp, if his martyrdom has been correctly dated to 155 or 156.

'Earth I have left, to Olympus I go': possibly a quotation of Heracles' dying words in a lost tragedy.

c.40 **clad in white:** white symbolises purity and is worn by figures involved in miracles in L., *N.T.*, and Sanskrit epic.

the Porch of the Seven Voices: also called the Echo Porch, a colonnade at Olympia between the temple of Zeus and the stadium, said by Pausanias to have echoed voices seven times or more.

the wild olive: like an Olympic victor.

c.41 **bees ... cicadas:** L. is being ironical. Bees and cicadas, by producing sweetness and sweet songs respectively, are traditionally associated with inspired poets, not such as P.

as to Hesiod's burial place: Pausanias records the tradition that though Hesiod was eventually buried in Orchomenos, the original location of his bones remained unknown, till they were finally found in Naupactan territory in a crack in a rock on which a crow was perching.

c.42 **Such was the end:** an ironical echo of Plato on the death of Socrates at the end of the *Phaedo*, repeated by L. in *Alexander* 60.

c.43 **Alexandria in the Troad:** *Trōas* here is probably used of the main port in the Troad rather than of the whole territory.

he too could have an Alcibiades: like Socrates, from whom the Cynics claimed philosophical descent.

c.45 **Aeacus:** the doorkeeper of Hades.

ON SACRIFICES. A DIATRIBE

When Lucian, in enumerating the various components in his literary make-up in *Bis Acc.*33, mentions cynicism as well as Menippus, he presumably refers to the influence of the diatribe, which at first meant any philosophical discourse, but came to be used in particular of the brief, informal chats of sermons expounding moral themes, delivered in public places particularly by Cynics, though also by Stoics. Important figures in the development of the diatribe were Bion of Borysthenes (fl. c. 260 B.C.) who influenced Horace's *Satires*, and, one generation later, Teles, whose diatribes on such subjects as Exile and Self-Sufficiency have survived. On a larger scale the authentic flavour of the original informal diatribe is well preserved in the *Discourses of Epictetus* as recorded by Arrian, one generation before Lucian, though works by other writers such as Seneca in Latin, Dio Chrysostom and Plutarch, though couched in more literary form, may also be classified as diatribes. Most characteristics of the diatribe occur at regular intervals throughout Lucian's work, but only three, by nature of their subjects, may be termed diatribes, *Calumnia, De Luctu* and *De Sacrificiis*.

Although *Cal.* is notable for its description of a painting which inspired Botticelli, *Luct.* and *Sacr.* are more typically Lucianic and indeed are often regarded as written at the same time, with *Sacr.* as a continuation of *Luct. Luct.* is a witty and elegant exercise in scepticism and has already been well edited by W.E. Heitland. *Sacr.* seems to me less effective, because it is too concentrated and packs in too many arguments and mythological allusions mainly based on Homer and Hesiod and too many echoes of Herodotus. Moreover, though the title is a misnomer and the first sentence tells us quite clearly that the subject includes other features of religious ritual and also men's prayers to the gods and beliefs about them, the piece still lacks unity.

I have, however, chosen to include it for two reasons. Firstly it is an example of Lucian not quite at his best, no doubt composing hastily to meet a deadline, Lucian in fact 'warts and all'. Secondly it teems with topics developed at greater length by Lucian elsewhere, particularly in individual *Dialogues of the Gods*.

Helm had some justification in regarding *Sacr.* as a late work, though he went too far in branding it as senile and decrepit. Lucian indeed could be hastily compiling ideas from earlier works. The references to Egypt prove nothing. If *Sol.* is genuine, Lucian could well have visited Egypt long before his official position there late in his life. In any case these references do not seem to require personal knowledge but to come mainly from memories of Herodotus Book 2. *Sacr.* however, could equally well be a comparatively early work with Lucian's fertile brain producing motifs, many of which he was later to develop. The problem of dating, indeed, is similar to that posed by *VH* 2 vis-à-vis the miniature *Dialogues of the Dead.*

c.1 **the sufferings ... Aetolians ... Calydonians:** Calydon was a city of Aetolia. Its citizens and the Aetolians generally suffered from the ravages of the boar sent by Artemis and the fighting after the quarrels over the boar's skin and head, as alluded to in *Il.* 9. 529ff.

the dissolution of Meleager: Homer does not mention the death of M., and a Hesiodic fragment has him killed by Apollo. L. seems to follow the later myth whereby he died when his mother Althaea deliberately burned the brand symbolising M.'s lifespan. *dialusin* may mean 'breaking up' or perhaps only 'destruction'; elsewhere (Bacchylides) his life fades away or (Phrynichus Tragicus, Ovid) is burned away.

resentful ... Oeneus: L.'s paraphrase of *Il.* 9.534–5.

c.2 **for twelve days running:** cf. *Il.* 1.423–5.

hecatomb: a massive sacrifice, technically of a hundred oxen.

nine bulls: L. misrepresents *Od.* 3.8 where not nine but nine times nine bulls are sacrificed to Posidon after the safe return of Nestor from Troy.

princess: Iphigenia.

twelve oxen and a robe: see *Il.* 6.271ff.

c.3 **unsuccessful:** having failed to ransom his daughter from Agamemnon, *Il.* 1.11ff.

saying: L. here adapts the speech of *Il.* 1.37–41.

Achaeans ... mules ... dogs: see *Il.* 1.50ff.

c.4 **Hyacinthus ... Daphne:** cf. *Dialogues of the Gods* 16, 17.2 etc. for Apollo's misfortunes in love. He killed H. by accident with a discus, and Daphne thwarted his amorous advances by becoming a laurel tree.

killing the Cyclopes: because they had forged the thunderbolts with which Zeus killed Apollo's son Aesculapius for being too good a doctor.

ostracised: ostracism was a form of banishment by popular vote practised in 5th century Athens; cf. *Deor. Conc.* passim for L.'s humorous application of features of Athenian democracy to Olympus.

Admetus: king of Pherae and husband of Alcestis; cf. Apollodorus, *Bibl.* 3.10.4.

Laomedon in Phrygia: L. follows *Il.* 7.452–3 where Posidon and Apollo built the walls of Troy for King Laomedon (rather than *Il.* 21.441ff. where P. worked on the walls and Apollo as a herdsman). Only L. makes serfdom to Laomedon an aftermath of the Cyclopes incident.

weren't paid in full: L. misrepresents or misunderstands *misthon hapanta* of *Il.* 21.451.

Trojan drachmas: L.'s humorous adaptation of phrases like 'Attic drachmas', see on *Pisc.* 28; coins had not been invented in the bronze age!

c.5 **they call on the Muses:** L. is thinking particularly of Hesiod's *Theogony*.

castrating his father: cf. Hes. *Th.* 180–1.

in his place: L. seems to mean 'in heaven', identifying Uranus the character with heaven the place. This is so difficult that Solanus' emendation *ep' autōi* 'to succeed him' is worth considering.

eating his own children: cf. Hes. *Th.* 459 ff.

like Thyestes of Argos: not quite, as Th. did so in ignorance when his brother Atreus had them cooked and served to him at a meal.

stolen away by Rhea: for her concealment of the newborn Zeus see Hes. *Th.* 467ff. and for the substitution of the stone ibid. 485.

a nanny-goat: Amaltheia, Callimachus *Hymns* 1. 47–8.

Telephus by a doe: for the myth of Telephus, the unwanted child of Auge, being exposed on Mt. Parthenius and suckled by a doe see Pausanias 8.48.7 and Apollodorus, *Bibl.* 2.7.4.

Cyrus ... by the bitch: a late adaptation of the story in Herodotus 1. 110ff. whereby the infant Cyrus was saved from death and nurtured by a slave woman called Cyno (Bitch).

as is customary with the Persians: or possibly 'as is lawful ...'; cf. Herodotus 3.31 on Cambyses' marriage to his sister and his success in establishing its legality.

gold ... bull ... swan ... eagle: in his attentions to Danae, Europa, Leda and, inappropriately here, Ganymede. This is a favourite motif of L.'s, one he shares with the Christian Apologists.

Proteus: see on *Peregrinus* 1.

out of his own head: see Hes. *Th.* 924 and, for L.'s vignette of the birth of Athena, *Dialogues of the Gods* 13.

his mother: Semele; cf. Eur. *Bacchae* passim and *Dialogues of the Gods* 12.

c.6   **without intercourse:** L. follows Hes. *Th.* 927; Homer makes Hephaestus the son of Zeus.

grimy with soot etc.: L. develops the topic in *Dialogues of the Gods* 8.4–5 where Zeus complains of the appearance of H. as winewaiter.

lamed by his fall: see *Il.* 1.590ff., L.'s *Charon* 1.

Astyanax: the son of Hector, thrown from the ramparts of Troy by a Greek, as feared by his mother, Andromache, in *Il.* 24. 734–5.

c.7   **friendly to mankind:** the Greek adjective comes from *P.V.* 11, 28. L. develops the story of Prometheus in *Dialogues of the Gods* 5 and *Prometheus*.

Rhea already old ...: for an almost identical description of Rhea see *Dialogues of the Gods* 20.1.

go cradle-snatching: literally 'be a lover of boys', ingeniously used by L. in an unusual sense.

no longer any good to her: because he had castrated himself.

Aphrodite for committing adultery: particularly with Ares, as told in *Od.* 8. 266ff. and by L. in *Dialogues of the Gods* 21, but also with Anchises and Adonis, cf. *Dialogues of the Gods* 19.1.

Selene: the Moon Goddess. L. devotes *Dialogues of the Gods* 19 to her love for Endymion.

c.8   **heard from Homer:** *Il.* 17.425.

peep over the top ... the back: cf. Plato *Phaedrus* 249C, 247C.

brighter ... clearer: cf. Plato, *Republic* 616 B.

the stars more radiant: cf. Apollonius Rhodius 2.1104.

the ground is golden: cf. *Il.* 4.2.

everywhere is bright daylight: but not perpetual daylight, cf. *Il.* 1.605.

the door-keepers: cf. *Il.* 5.749.

the evidence of his trade: fire, smoke, tools etc.; less probably 'products of his skill', as *anameston* suggests a dirty workshop.

the handiwork of Hephaestus: cf. *Il.* 1.607–8.

c.9   **'And ... encsonsed':** *Il.* 4.1.

'a-twirling round the smoke': *Il.* 1.317.

Ixion and Tantalus: see *Dialogues of the Gods* 9 and *Dialogues of the Dead* 7 and n. on *Menippus* 14.

c.10   **That's how the gods live:** the phrase is adapted from Plato, *Phaedrus* 248A.

the Mygdonians: a people of Phrygia (N.W. Asia Minor), where Rhea was particularly worshipped, often under other names (Cybele, The Great Mother etc.).

Zeus ... his burial place: a favourite motif of L. and the Christian Apologists; cf. Callimachus, *Hymn to Zeus* 8–9.

died ... long ago: cf. the very similar passage in *J.Tr.* 45.

c.11 Hermes with the first down on his cheek: the Praxitelean Hermes and Dionysus at Olympia well illustrates the youthful appearance of H.; *Hypēnētēs* is used in *Il.* 24. 348 and *Od.* 10. 279 of H. masquerading as a mortal.

with sea-blue hair: cf. *Il.* 13.563.

with grey eyes: see n. on *D. Jud.* 10.

every five years: every four years by our method of counting; the phrase occurs in the same context in *Icar.* 24.

c.12 frankincense or a sacrificial cake: an economical sacrifice, cf. Men. *Dyscolus*, 449–50, *Com. Adesp.* 372, Alciphron 2.33.1.

c.13 the Cyclops: Polyphemus in *Od.* 9.287 ff.

human sacrifices to Artemis: as represented in Euripides *I.T.*; for E.'s thinking cf. *I.T.* 386 ff.

c.14 Zeus with the face of a ram: Zeus Ammon, cf. Hdt. 2.42, 4.181.

Hermes ... dog: Anubis; see n. on *Deor. Conc.* 10.

bless him: L. has a soft spot for Hermes as the patron of rhetoric.

Pan a goat all over: a rhetorical exaggeration, cf. Hdt. 2.46, *Dialogues of the Gods* 2.

ibis, crocodile and ape: cf. Juvenal 15.2–4, Hdt. 2.69, 75. Verbal similarities with J. are rare and are best explained as due to use of common sources, particularly diatribes.

'But if ... well': *Il.* 6.150.

shaven prophets: Hdt. 2.37 records that Egyptian priests shaved their whole body every three days.

Shut your doors, ye uninitiated: keep inside your own homes, stay away, *procul este profani*, the end of a hexameter verse, and attributed to the Orphics. L. ingeniously suggests that his own mischievous explanation of the appearances of the gods in Egypt which follows is a closely guarded secret.

came to Egypt: L. reverses the theory of Hdt., 2.50 etc., of the priority of the Egyptian gods over the Greek gods.

more than 10,000 years ago: L. adapts Hdt., who says, 2.142ff. that it was more than 11, 340 years ago when there were gods of human appearance in Egypt.

c.15 they mourn the victim: an inaccurate memory of Hdt. 2.42 who merely records mourning at the sacrifice of one ram once a year by the Thebans of Egypt, who later bury the victim.

Apis: the bull god, identified by Hdt. with Epaphus, son of Zeus and Io.

Nisus: king of Megara with a purple lock of hair on which his life depended; it was cut off by his daughter Scylla.

chosen from the common herd: less probably *ex agelēs* = *egregius*, out of the ordinary; for the extraordinary appearance of an Apis, see Hdt. 3.28.

Heraclitus ... Democritus: the weeping philosopher from Ephesus and the laughing philosopher from Abdera; cf. *V.A.* 13.

ZEUXIS

Zeuxis is of particular interest for its expression of Lucian's aims as a literary artist in the field of comic dialogue, its description of Zeuxis' painting of the Centaur and its young and its brilliantly conceived and executed battle scene. It exemplifies the *prolalia*, literally 'preliminary chat', used by Lucian to introduce a longer work, usually a comic dialogue, or perhaps a collection of miniature dialogues, and fulfils the function of an orator's proemium in trying to secure the attention and goodwill of the audience. As other *prolaliai* include *Bacchus* with its anecdote about Dionysus' battle with the Indians, *Hercules* with an ecphrasis of a Gallic painting of Heracles, *De Domo*, a rather longer work describing a lecture hall and its paintings, *Dipsades* with a brief description of a Libyan *stēlē*, and *Herodotus* with a brief anecdote about Herodotus and a description of a painting by Aetion, it can be seen that Lucian regularly uses the lively illustrative anecdote or the *ecphrasis* of a work of art or both to make his *prolalia* a *tour de force* to impress his audience. Another work, *Prom. Es*, with its anecdote about Ptolemy Lagou, the black camel and the black and white man, although addressed to an individual, probably served as a *prolalia* in view of its many similarities with *Zeuxis* in discussing Lucian's literary aims: see p. 7.

Though in *The Dream* L. describes himself as a gauche apprentice to his sculptor uncle and in *Zeuxis* 3 and 5 as ignorant of the art of painting, throughout his works he shows himself to be a close observer and enthusiastic describer of examples of the visual arts[1] and not merely going through the motions of the ekphrasis as a rhetorical[2] exercise. Indeed his descriptions of works of art occur so frequently and are of such detail that only the Elder Pliny and Pausanias may be considered more important sources for classical art.

Lucian's architectural *ecphraseis* are confined to *Hippias* describing a Bathhouse and to *De Domo*, on a lecture-hall which Lucian praises for its fine proportions, bright colours, beautiful ceiling and murals, all eight of which are described. As regards sculpture Lucian was only really interested in the great masters of the classical period, making frequent, if usually perfunctory, mentions of Alcamenes, Phidias, Polyclitus, Myron and Praxiteles, but also, particularly in *Imagines*, showing knowledge of a few of their works; his brief comments on the Discobolos in *Philops*. 18 and on the Cnidia in *Imag*. 6 are particularly interesting.

Far and away Lucian's greatest artistic interest, however, was in painting, as shown by his descriptions of Aetion's Marriage of Roxana and Alexander which he had seen in Italy, *Herod*. 4 ff., Apelles' Slander, *Cal*. 4 ff., see pp. 8, 16, the painting of the strange Celtic deity, Heracles Ogmios, in *Herc*. and this painting by Zeuxis. Moreover his references to stories such as that of Heracles and

---

1. L.'s interest in the visual arts has been surprisingly neglected. V. Andò, *Luciano Critico d'Arte* (Palermo, 1975) has recently made a useful contribution, but the best study remains that of H. Blümner, *De Locis Luciani ad Artem spectantibus* (Berlin, 1867).
2. In this respect L. compares favourably with the vague, literature-oriented description of paintings in the *Imagines* of Philostratus and Callistratus, and in particular with the *Kentaurides* of Philostr. *Imag*. 2.3.

Omphale and several of his miniature dialogues, e.g. *DMar.* 14 of Perseus saving Andromeda from the sea-monster and *DMar.* 15 of the marine deities escorting Zeus and Europa, seem to be inspired by paintings which he had seen. That he had some understanding of painting is clear from his listing of the special skills of the painter in *Zeux.* 5, while his superb description of the peacock in *Dom.* 11 shows that he had an artist's eye for beauty and chromatic effects, so that his reference to himself as *ou ma ton dia graphikos tis ōn* may be something of an understatement; see note on c.3.

c.1   **literary shows:** reading or performing one of his comic dialogues.

c.2   **Homer:** *Od.* 1.351–2.

      dross: literally 'charcoal', something worthless. This is a favourite proverb of L.'s, cf. Zenobius 1.2.

c.3   **Zeuxis:** a great Greek painter of the late fifth century, said by Quintilian 12.10.4 to have been the first to have discovered the principles of light and shade. See also Pliny, *N.H.* 35. 61–66, where several of his works but not this one are mentioned.

      the other booty: Aristotle's library, at least, did reach Italy safely, cf. *Ind.* 4, Plu. *Sull.* 26. If L. can be trusted, the painting was on another ship.

      Malea: the S.E. tip of the Greek mainland and traditionally stormy, cf. *Od.* 3.287 ff., 4.514ff.

      I'm no artist: perhaps spoken with a touch of Socratic irony; L. was at worst an enthusiastic amateur. The motif may come from Pl. *Lg.* 769 B; cf. note on c.5.

c.5   **proportions:** literally 'size', no doubt including perspective, but also getting sizes of parts of figures right, as with Polyclitus' canon for sculptors. The next phrase I take to refer to composition and the whole picture.

      sons of painters: experts as inheriting knowledge from their fathers and following in their footsteps. 'Sons of' is used by Plato and L. particularly of doctors, cf. the Hippocratic oath, and of exponents of the visual arts; cf. *The Dream* 12 and *Hist.* 7.

c.7   **unprecedented idea:** though the text is corrupt, the meaning seems clear.

      Micio: a common name, but perhaps chosen by L. to suggest associations with Micon, a famous painter of the early fifth century.

      raw material: literally 'clay'. See *Prom. Es,* where L. discusses his likeness to a potter, and especially c.3, about a skilled potter giving shape and order to his clay and, with the help of divine inspiration, the breath of life.

      light effects: cf. Plin, *N.H.* 33.159.

c.8   **Antiochus:** Antiochus 1, son of Seleucus, and ruler of Syria 280–261. He was called Soter because he saved Syria from the Galatians, the Gauls who had settled in Galatia in central Asia Minor.

      twenty-four deep: note the impressive strength ascribed to the enemy. The phalanx, the successful fighting formation used by the Macedonians, was normally sixteen men deep.

      on both wings: it was normal Macedonian practice to place cavalry on both wings of a central phalanx. This is a further suggestion of the formidable nature of the opposition.

      peltasts: in contrast with hoplites, peltasts were lightly armed and had only a small shield.

c.9   **Theodotas of Rhodes:** unknown. This looks suspiciously like a mistake by L. for Theodotus, the Aetolian, who served not Antiochus 1, but Antiochus 111 (The Great, ruling 223–187) and displayed his military ingenuity and courage in the capture of Sardis, Plb. 7.16 ff. L.'s credibility is hardly helped by *Slander* 3, where he seems to refer to this Aetolian, but simply calls him Theodotas, and makes him contemporary with the painter Apelles, i.e. with Alexander the Great. L. tends to

be careless or cavalier in his use, adaptation or invention of historical examples to reinforce his argument.

elephants: on the elephant battle see Tarn, *JHS*, 1926, 157. It was historical enough, and celebrated by a lost epic poet, Simonides, but Tarn dismisses L.'s details as 'worthless rhetoric', showing that Antiochus did not need another to tell him about the usefulness of elephants in battle; cf. Pausanias 1. 12.3 and Tarn and Griffith, *Hellenistic Civilisation*, (London, 1953), 61–2. H.H Scullard, *The Elephant in the Greek and Roman World*, (Thames and Hudson, 1974) 320, accepts that not all of Lucian's details may be correct, but thinks that 'his outline of the battle may well have a good pedigree' going back to Hieronymus of Cardia, a reputable historian contemporary with the events.

when the trumpeter gave the signal: the phrase is modelled on Xen. *An.* 4.3.29.

c.10 before ... fled: an echo of Xen. *An.* 1.8.19 to describe a typical barbarian reaction.

fled in complete disarray: the phrase, also in *Bacch.* 4, is based on Hdt. 3.13.

not ... blood: cf. *Il.* 17.363 etc.

the chariots ... o'er: *Il.* 16.379, slightly misquoted.

their ... on: *Il.* 11.160.

HOW TO WRITE HISTORY

Lucian's *De Historia Conscribenda* (hereafter *Hist.*)[1] is of outstanding interest as the only monograph on the theory of historiography to have survived from classical literature and as Lucian's major contribution to literary theory.

Earlier Views on Historiography

We know of several lost works[2] entitled *Peri Historias* of which the earliest and probably most influential was that by Aristotle's successor Theophrastus, which perhaps dealt with the contents as well as the style of history. Closer to Lucian's own time Plutarch is credited with a work with the intriguing title *Pōs krinoumen tēn alēthē historian*. In addition we have many important *obiter dicta* by practising historians in the course of their work. Herodotus, 7.152.3, believed that it was his duty to report all that he was told, but not necessarily to believe it. Thucydides in a famous early chapter, 1.22, repeatedly used by L. in *Hist.*, stresses the strenuousness of his own efforts in arriving at the all-important truth. He admits that the absence of story-telling may make his work less attractive to listen to, but he will be content if it be judged useful by those who wish to have available a clear and accurate record of the past as a guide for gauging the future, since the same or similar events recur in human affairs. *His* work is composed as a possession for ever rather than a prize piece to appeal to immediate listeners; (here he seems to be inviting comparisons with Hdt. who was reputed to have made a fortune by giving recitations of his work.)

One Greek historian particularly given to pronouncements on the theory of historiography was Polybius of the second century B.C., with views often remarkably similar to those of Lucian though elsewhere Lucian never mentions his name or shows any knowledge of him or much interest in the events he records. Then there is Dionysius of Halicarnassus of the Augustan Age, whose admiration of Thucydides as the greatest historian did not stop him criticising his choice of material or powers of expression. Here one should again mention Plutarch, not a historian proper, but a voluminous producer not only of *Moralia*, but also of parallel lives of great figures from Greek and Roman history, a man who strongly believed that biography should serve moral ends. Lucian, however, gives little indication of knowing D.H. and none at all of knowing Plutarch. Many Latin writers, too, especially Cicero, Livy in his Preface, Tacitus and Quintilian have left interesting views on the theory of historiography, but these are of limited relevance to us here, as Lucian was (or at least gave the impression of being) completely ignorant of Latin literature and indeed only once admits to knowing any Latin at all.

---

1. Only in the last generation has *Hist.* been accorded due attention, starting with a study of sources by G. Avenarius, *Lukians Schrift zur Geschichtsschreibung* (Meisenheim am Glan, 1956) and Homeyer's erudite edition, but the copious evidence of L.'s other works has been entirely neglected by Avenarius and too little used by Homeyer. Since then valuable contributions have been made by Baldwin, 75–95, Hall, 312–24 and Jones 59–67, and there are brief but sensible remarks in Grube 336–8. *Ancient Literary Criticism* (Oxford, 1972) includes a good translation of cc. 6–13 and 34–63 by D.A. Russell. For a useful account of the cultural background of the age see Bowie who devotes pp. 10–28 to historiography.
2. For details see Homeyer 46–7.

Historical Background

Assuming the dramatic date, shortly before the triumph of October 166[3] celebrating final victory in the Parthian war, is also the actual date, *Hist.* should probably be dated to the spring or summer of 166, though the lighthearted mentions of plague[4] in the introductory anecdote and in c. 15 might suggest late 165. The war had started in 162 when the Parthian King, Vologases III, had installed his own relative, Pacorus, on the throne of Armenia, theoretically a Roman protectorate. Marcus Sedatius Severianus, the Roman legate in Cappadocia, marched into Armenia with one legion, but it was trapped and annihilated at Elegeia by Chosroes, the Parthian general, and Severianus committed suicide. Lucius Verus went out east to take charge of operations, but spent most of his time in Antioch at a safe distance from the fighting, in company with the beautiful woman Pantheia, flattered by Lucian in *Imagines*. However the conduct of the war was by 164 in the hands of competent generals, Caius Avidius Cassius, Marcus Statius Priscus and Marcus Claudius Fronto; Armenia was recovered and Parthia itself invaded. Nisibis was captured, though the besieging Roman army had to cope with plague as well as the enemy. By 165 the Parthian capital, Ctesiphon, had fallen and the war was as good as won, though Rome's superiority was finally demonstrated in 166 when Avidius Cassius crossed the northern Tigris and invaded Media.

Structure

Hist. consists of three parts. First we have six introductory chapters including two amusing anecdotes setting the scene in stimulating fashion as Lucian with his rhetorical training is intent on gaining the goodwill, attention and understanding of the audience from the outset. Then follows, cc. 7–32, a section which could be classified as negative, as it deals with faults to be avoided in the writing of history, but only cc. 7–13 deal with faults in general and the major part of this section, cc. 14–32, gives us witty and malicious sketches of a round dozen of contemporary 'historians', illustrating various faults to which bad historians are addicted. The final section, cc. 33–63, contains positive opinions and advice, but, though starting with a memorable profile of the ideal historian, and containing sensible remarks, on style, method and various component parts of a history, is rather a ragbag with some loose ends and inconsistencies. Lucian, as I see it, had already achieved his main purpose of entertaining his audience with many of the tricks in his satirical repertoire in his rogues' gallery of historians, but had to give his discussion of this *technē* some semblance of structural unity without making it too long to lose the interest of readers or his audience.

Lucian's Rogue Historians

The descriptions of bad historians in cc. 14–32 are not merely amusing, but serve a useful purpose in illustrating a succession of historiographical faults in a

---

3. For the historical background I have followed A. Birley, *Marcus Aurelius* (London, 1966).
4. According to J.F. Gilliam, The Plague under Marcus Aurelius *AJP* 82 (1961) 225 ff. the plague spread to Rome in 167.

way that a mere catalogue or abstract discussion could not. The faults include praising of self and city, servile imitation of Hdt. or Thuc., geographical and military ignorance by stay-at-home writers, the introduction of sensational, melodramatic or pathetic elements, incredible casualty figures, scientific ignorance, stylistic inconsistencies or inappropriateness, excessive Atticism, lack of proportion (impressive prologues followed by anti-climax, long digressions into the irrelevant or trivial), too much philosophy, overelaborate descriptive passages, prophecies of the future course of the war, excessively short histories, pompous polysyllabic titles and subdivision into too many books.

How far can we trust Lucian's account of these men?[5] One problem with Lucian is that of assessing the proportion of topical satire as opposed to traditional inherited themes. For instance does *The Ship* describe a real ship or is it a figment of Lucian's fertile imagination? Is its voyage a real one or merely concocted from Lucian's books? There can, however, be little doubt that *Hist.* deals with a contemporary phenomenon; the historian Herodian, writing two generations later, testifies to the many talented writers recording Marcus' wars, but also accuses historians in general of being preoccupied with style and the giving of pleasure. Some scholars seem to accept Lucian's account at face value. Jacoby honours eight of them with entries in his *FGrHist* and recently C.P. Jones has produced evidence in favour of some of Lucian's details, but these may merely indicate they are realistic rather than real. Indeed many facets of the 'historians' seem too good, or rather too bad, to be true, so that I believe the types of faults to be real, but most of the men possessing them to be composite, fictitious figures with shortcomings ludicrously exaggerated for comic purposes. Lucian's pointed appeal for belief and his ostentatious refusal to swear to his veracity look like broad hints that he is talking with his tongue in his cheek. Moreover, though there are at least a dozen 'historians', he only names four of them, and in the two cases where he adds their provenance they come from remote places, Sagalassus in Pisidia and Pompeiopolis, probably in Paphlagonia; moreover two of the four names, Callimorphus and Crepereius Calpurnianus Pompeiopolites, look like comic coinages; see cc. 15, 16, 32. Both Corinth, cf. cc. 3, 29, 63, and Ionia have been suggested as the location for the production of *Hist.* but it seems more natural for c. 14 to be taken as ruling out both Ionia and the southern province of Achaea (which included Corinth), so that the free city of Athens or a city in Macedonia would be more probable or perhaps, though *Hist.* purports to be a letter, Lucian gave readings of it during a tour of several cities. If so, Lucian's facts, if taken seriously, could not be checked and the 'historians' could safely be condemned to ridicule *in absentia*.

Can Lucian be satirising any contemporary historians still extant today? Four names suggest themselves, those of Appian, Polyaenus, M. Cornelius Fronto and Arrian. Appian of Alexandria, born c. 96 but perhaps still alive, we may dismiss at once; though he wrote in Greek, his history concentrated on the Romans and their civil and foreign wars, subjects of little interest to Lucian. Polyaenus of Macedon dedicated his extant books on stratagems to the two

---

5. Of the various interpretations of this section I find myself closest to that of Hall.

emperors in 162 and planned to write on the Parthian Wars, but does not seem to have done so. Fronto[6] deserves more consideration. He came from Cirta in N. Africa and became the tutor and regular correspondent of Marcus Aurelius and Lucius Verus and had a big reputation as an orator. An extant letter from Verus asks Fronto to write a history of the Parthian Wars, doing himself, Verus, proud, and a few fragments of his introductory chapters survive, written in Latin, and dated to 165; they include the statement that Achilles would have wanted Verus' achievements for his own. Fronto was famous or rather notorious for his archaisms, but they, like his history, were in Latin, and it is in Latin that Fronto pontificates in the pages of Aulus Gellius. Moreover Fronto's headquarters were in Rome. He was of course bilingual, occasionally writing to the emperors in Greek, but it is unlikely that Lucian was interested in him or would have dared to satirise a favourite of the emperors.

Finally there is Arrian of Nicomedia, who, if still alive, must have been well over seventy, and had written not on this war but on the eastern campaigns of Alexander and Trajan. He regarded himself as a second Xenophon, writing an *Anabasis* (of Alexander) and *Memorabilia* (of Epictetus). Other works include an *Indica* (in Ionic), a *Periplus of the Red Sea* and a *Tactica*, but his *Parthian History*, describing *inter alia* Trajan's campaigns, is lost. Lucian as I see it,[7] deliberately, scattered obvious features of Arrian throughout his 'rogues' gallery' for his audience to recognise and enjoy, e.g. the philosophic historian, the promise of an *Indica* and a *Periplus*, the switch of dialects, and the pride in himself and his native city. However, by and large, Arrian is free of the major faults castigated by Lucian and fulfils many of Lucian's requisites for the good historian, as a successful governor and soldier, accurate in his use of military terms and writing in a clear style. Lucian praises him highly in *Alexander*, written at least 14 years later. His attitude to Arrian in *Hist.* must have been at worst ambivalent, but Lucian would not have put him, a mere modern, on the pedestal he reserved for the three great classical historians.

Lucian's Ideal Historian

As Lucian is close to the spirit of the Second Sophistic, one would expect his choice of ideal historian to be limited to one of the three whom he says his contemporaries are imitating, Thucydides, Herodotus, Xenophon, and indeed these are the only three past historians whom he names with approval in *Hist.*, whereas the other three earlier historians named, Theopompus, Aristobulus and Onesicritus emerge with discredit. Note the non-chronological order in which the big three are mentioned by Lucian in c. 2, perhaps reflecting their current popularity and certainly Lucian's assessment of their historiographical merits. Xenophon is presumably accorded third place as the writer of the *Hellenica*, a mere supplement to Thuc. and inferior to the master. Lucian does give him one favourable mention in c. 39 as a 'just historian' and another non-committal one in c. 23. Herodotus is clearly much dearer to Lucian's heart. Elsewhere Lucian

---

6. On Fronto see E. Champlin, *Fronto and Antonine Rome* (Harvard, 1980) who argues that he probably never wrote his history of the Parthian Wars, but died c. 167 (the standard view, though Mommsen and others hold he survived till c. 175). The latest datable letter is assigned to 166.
7. See M.D. Macleod, 'Lucian's Relationship to Arrian', *Philologus* 131 (1987) 257–64.

quotes or alludes to him very much more than he does to Thuc.: he knew his early books particularly well, and *Charon* and *Syr.* owe much to Hdt.; Lucian's *Herod.* enumerates several inimitable features of Hdt., whom Lucian saw as a racy and entertaining writer, a bit of a sophist who gave readings of his works before select audiences at Olympia and elsewhere, in fact a prototype of Lucian himself. Complimentary references to Hdt. in *Hist.* occur in c. 42, where we hear his books are called Muses, c. 54 where his proem and account of his motivation are praised and, by implication, in c. 60, where his treatment of myth, is given some sort of approval, rather surprisingly, as elsewhere Lucian has approved of Thuc.'s rejection of 'the mythical'.

Generally, however, Lucian has discernment enough to see that overall Thuc. has to be regarded as the historian *par excellence*. Lucian starts with a mock-historical account of a plague in the vein of Thuc., he tells us early on that history should be 'a possession for ever', he criticises at length servile imitations of Thuc.'s prologue, Corcyrean spokesman, funeral oration and plague, and later goes on to refer to Brasidas and Demosthenes at Pylos, to Cleon, to Alcibiades, Demosthenes, Nikias, Hermocrates and Gylippus in Sicily, and to Epipolae, and the harbour and stone quarries at Syracuse. C. 47 on the painful and laborious process whereby the historian should assemble his facts is undisguisedly based on Thuc. 1.20.3 and 1.22, and the remarks on speeches in c. 58 perhaps owe something to Thuc. 1.22. He praises Thuc.'s preface and reasons for writing history, and he ends by repeating Thuc.'s view that the historian should write for all time.

At this point we should note that in many of his views on historiographical failings had been anticipated by Polybius,[8] but see p. 283. Perhaps Lucian and Plb. used a common source or more probably Lucian selected and adapted material from several sources who may either have influenced Plb. or been influenced by him. The important point is that the historiographical faults slated by both Lucian and Plb. are by and large those from which Thuc. is conspicuously free.

When we come to the positive section and the profile of the perfect historian, we realise, particularly from cc. 34, 37 and 41, that Lucian's ideal is not entirely Thuc. but also embodies elements of Pericles, Thuc.'s favourite politician and orator, Diogenes and perhaps Lucian himself. Moreover in cc. 43–4, the historical style recommended is closer to that of Hdt. or Xen. than that of Thuc., though it stems more from Lucian's adaptation of rhetorical theory. Thus Lucian's ideal historian resembles his dialogues in being composite, but the main ingredient is certainly Thuc.

That Lucian built up his picture of a historian in this way is suggested by his *modus operandi* elsewhere. Lucian is a master of synthesis. J. Bompaire in the most important post-war book on Lucian, after stressing the importance of *mimē-sis* in Lucian's work (emulation of the ancients and not just servile imitation), pinpoints two main features of his best work which he calls 'contamination' and 'transposition'. Lucian's contamination, his blending of material from many classical sources, is described by Lucian himself in *Bis. Acc.* 33, see pp. 1-3,

---

8. For Plb.'s views on history, see F.W. Walbank, *A Historical Commentary on Polybius*, vol. 1 (Oxford, 1957) pp. 6 ff.

and is above question. The term 'transposition' perhaps causes some difficulty to the non-Gallic; etymologically it suggests that material is taken from one position and put in another, e.g. transferred from drama to dialogue; it could also suggest something like the process whereby musicians rewrite in a different key. I suggest however that 'adaptation' is a better general term, not too unlike Bompaire's 'transposition' but including the possibility both of small changes or modifications and of major ones.

Sources

Lucian's methods of composition are no different in *Hist.* Here too he aims at a *mimēsis*, emulating the achievements of earlier and essentially classical writers and combining the various elements into an artistic unity. In fact *Hist.* is perhaps the supreme example of Lucian's typical methods, because his sources, the elements blended together and adapted, are far more numerous than usual, though three main strands can be seen in the fabric of this treatise. Firstly, as always, there are literary sources, in this case particularly Thucydides, Herodotus and perhaps lost Cynic works. Secondly, as in several other works, he draws on his range of knowledge of artistic, literary and rhetorical criticism. To these two strands, which occur in many other works, here there is added a third, use of material specifically concerned with historiographical theory.

Several phrases or views expressed in *Hist.* have close parallels in Horace, *Ars Poetica, Letter to Augustus* etc. Moreover it would be possible to theorise structural links[9] between cc. 34–60 and *A.P.*; cc. 34–42 can clearly be regarded as discussing the *artifex* or *poiētēs* of historiography, but the remainder could equally well be taken as one unit on the *ars* or subdivided into cc. 43–51 on *poiēsis* and cc. 52–60 on poiēma. All, however, that can safely be deduced from this is that Horace and Lucian used material directly or indirectly from common sources, which may have included Neoptolemus of Parium and perhaps Philodemus.

Before looking for further specific sources for *Hist.* one should note that some of the views expressed here, especially those on style, are paralleled elsewhere in Lucian; the rules on vocabulary, though close to what Quintilian recommends for the orator, 4.2.36, resemble those found in the undatable *Lexiphanes* where Lucian's victim is urged to model his vocabulary on Thuc. and Plato, to sacrifice to the Graces and to *Saphēneia* (Clarity) and to avoid outlandish words; similarly in *Demonax*, probably a late work, the philosopher derides users of *archaiois kai xenois onomasi*. In particular Lucian uses in modified form perhaps a score of motifs from the slightly earlier work, *Salt.*, also a *technē*, including the recommendation c. 62 that the dancer must, like the rhetoricians practise *Saphēneia*. Analogies and metaphors from the visual arts too abound in *Salt.*, *Hist.* and passim in Lucian. This should suffice to show that Lucian habitually took the rules and lore from one *technē* or genre and applied them with modifications to another.

In conclusion, therefore, if one must specify sources of which Lucian shows first-hand knowledge in *Hist.*, they would include (in addition to the more

---

9. On theories of the possible structure of *A.P.* and its source(s) see Grube 240–242 and C.O. Brink, *Horace on Poetry*, (Cambridge, 1963).

obvious Hdt., Thuc., Xen. and Plato *Phaedrus*), Aristotle *Poetics* and *Rhetoric*, almost certainly Theophrastus' lost *Peri Historias*, and possibly Dionysius of Halicarnassus, but similarities with such as Polybius, Cicero, Horace and Quintilian probably are to be explained as emanating from common sources, or sources drawing from these authors or more often from what Lucian learned from his teachers.

Conclusion

Had Lucian lived in the twentieth century, he might have approved in the main of Winston Churchill, who may one day be acclaimed as a Thucydides of the written word, as he was a Pericles of the spoken word, a man with experience of camps and politics, an independent and outspoken voice in the dark days of the thirties, though he was rather more civilised than the shameless Diogenes and too much of a patriot exactly to fit Lucian's description. Whatever Churchill's qualities as a historian, his *Preface* to *The Second World War* is certainly written in a Thucydidean vein, e.g.

'It must not be supposed that I expect everybody to agree with what I say, still less that I only write what is popular. I give my testimony according to the lights that I follow. Every possible care has been taken to verify the facts; but much is constantly coming to light from the disclosure of captured documents or other revelations which may present a new aspect to the conclusions which I have drawn. This is why it is important to rely upon authentic contemporary records, and the expression of opinion set down when all was obscure...
'It is my earnest hope that pondering upon the past may give guidance in days to come, enabling a new generation to repair some of the errors of former years and thus govern, in accordance with the needs and glory of man, the awful unfolding scene of the future.'

Modern students of historiography will find shortcomings and omissions in Lucian's treatise. He completely ignores economic factors, he is superficial on the causes of war and indeed on causation generally, he shows no interest in social conditions, the social effects of war and the social and political lessons to be learned from history. He limits his horizons to localized wars rather than thinking of what the ancients called universal history or of global wars such as the Second World War. But this is unfair. We have 1,800 years more historiography behind us. Moreover Lucian's aims are limited; he does not claim to be writing a comprehensive and exhaustive study of historiography, merely offering a few words of advice to those who, through natural qualities, background and education, are already potential historians, and his advice is specifically confined to wars of limited duration. Rather should we admire the good sense of one who was not really interested in history and had like most of his contemporaries been over exposed to the teachings of rhetoricians who accorded historians oratorical and poetic licence. He really does understand what the writing of history should be all about. Few of his ideas are original but he deserves credit for selecting with judgement from the vast mass of conflicting views available and producing a readable and elegant pastiche that is

sensible and reasonably consistent. Throughout his literary career he was a distinguished exponent of the *spoudogeloion*, serious jesting, but with the emphasis on the jesting. Here too he amuses us with his humour, but he is for once being serious and constructive. Horace in the *Ars Poetica* makes the comment '*omne tulit punctum, qui miscuit utile dulci*', which freely translated means 'I award full marks to the man who combines the useful with the pleasurable'. Lucian should certainly be placed in the first class for his treatise on the writing of history.

cc.1–6 Introduction, setting the scene but also fulfilling something of the functions of the prologue of a speech and a detached Lucianic *prolalia*.

c.1 Mock-historical account of plague at Abdera affecting all inhabitants with a mad craving for Euripides. (This entire anecdote is probably a Lucianic invention. This and three other anecdotes in *Hist*., Diogenes in Corinth c.3, Aristobulus in c.12, Onesicritus in c.40 are unparalleled, while that about the Pharos in c.62 has Lucianic variation of detail; only that about Athos and the architect, see note in c.12, is fully paralleled.)

Lysimachus: one of Alexander's generals and later, 286–1, king of Macedonia. The dating details give the first hint that the anecdote is a parody of historical narrative.

Abdera: a town in Thrace with proverbially stupid inhabitants.

Philo: perhaps a fictitious name to suggest 'dear friend'.

violent ... fever: the detailing of symptoms suggests parody of Thuc.'s account, 2. 47–53, of the plague at Athens. L.'s lightheartedness suggests the plague hadn't yet spread to the west from the armies in the east, cf. c.15, or at least L. didn't realise its seriousness.

from the very beginning: cf. Thuc. 1.77.3.

Andromeda: this play, parodied by Ar. *Thesm.* of 411, dramatised Perseus' rescue of Andromeda from a sea-monster.

seventh-day patients: cf. Thuc. 2.49.6.

Archelaus: unknown; the name (=Ruler of the People) may be coined by L.

in mid-summer: again parodying Thuc.'s dating habits; cf. Thuc. 5.57.

leaving their sickbeds: for the verb cf. Thuc. 2.49.8.

his Medusa: more properly the Gorgon's head which he had cut off and used to turn the sea-monster to stone.

c.2 The intelligentsia of to-day are afflicted by a similar mania: encouraged by our victories in the Parthian War they're all writing history.

the barbarians: the old term for non-Greeks applied by Hdt. to the Persians and their allies and here by L. to their modern equivalents, the Parthians who, since 53 B.C. had been the main Eastern enemies of the Romans.

disaster in Armenia: at Elegeia in 162, cf. cc.21, 25.

everyone is writing history: cf. Horace, *Ep.* 2.1.117 on would-be poets.

has become a Thucydides: not a new phenomenon; cf. Cic. *Brut.* 287, *Or.* 30–32, D.H. *Th.* 52 etc.

a Xenophon: a possible hint at Arrian, if still alive, though he did not record this war. See p. 286.

the old saying: by Heraclitus, *Fr.* 43.

c.3 I alone seem to be idle and am reminded of Diogenes' reaction in a similar situation.

Philip: of Macedon, father of Alexander the Great. The anecdote is probably unhistorical, and looks like a Lucianic parody of a *chreia*, a moral story often centred on a saying of a sage or great man, cf. 'Confucius, he say'.

cask: the *pithos*, a large jar for storing food or wine, which served the self-sufficient Cynic as a home.

Cornel Hill: Diogenes' favourite haunt, while in Corinth.

c.4 So, like Diogenes, I've decided to do *something*. I won't dare to write history myself; that's too dangerous. But I shall offer a few words of advice to those who do.

without a voice: the first of several indications in *Hist.* that, like L., these 'historians' were as much concerned with audiences as with readers; cf. Thucydides' contempt for an *agōnisma es to parautika akouein.* 'a prize-piece for an immediate audience'. This argument, however, should not be pressed too far as the ancients read aloud.

foolhardy: cf. Horace, *A.P.* 382 etc., Juvenal 10.175.

the potter: the metaphor used in *Prom. Es,* where L. thinks of himself as a potter producing fragile wares.

away ... surge: *Od.* 12. 219, of the *Planctae,* the Wandering Rocks near Scylla and Charybdis.

the inscription ... clay: probably continuing the metaphor of history as a building, cf. c.62, clay being an ancient equivalent of cement.

c.5 Writing history is no simple matter but requires much effort and care, if it is to be 'a possession for ever'. I don't expect my advice will induce those whose work has been completed and applauded to rewrite but it may be useful next time, should there be another war. (As throughout the later chapters, we see L. drawing heavily from Thuc. and adding motifs from later historiographical theory shared with Polybius and from literary theory shared with Horace and others.)

not a thing ... undertaken lightly: cf. the similar description of the dancer's art in *Salt.* 35, Horace *A.P.* 290 ff. etc. and the general Alexandrian views on the nature of poetry.

prose forms: by *logoi* L. probably means prose as opposed to poetry, though some of the views he expresses both in *Salt.* and in *Hist.* are adaptations of poetic literary theories.

a great deal: Cf. Plb. 12.28 a 7 and *epiponōs,* Thuc. 1.22.3.

a possession for ever: Thuc. 1.22.4.

if another war...: an echo of Thuc. 2.54.3, both passages being on motivation for writing.

Celts and Getans: a frivolous or geographically vague suggestion of a war beyond the northern frontiers of the empire, presumably between nomadic Gauls from the west (hardly Galatians or eastern Gauls cf. *Zeux*) and tribesmen from the lower Danube areas.

Indians and Bactrians: far to the east of the empire.

rules ... measurements: cf. Ar. *Frogs.* 799.

c.6 I shall first discuss faults to be avoided and then proceed to positive advice.

has a dual function: probably a general literary concept, cf. *Salt.* 81, though it could be an echo of Dionysius of Halicarnassus, *Comp.* 1.

choose ... avoid: L. reverses the order of *Salt.*, where virtues are treated first, 74–9, and faults later, 80.

cc.7–13 Negative Section (A). General advice on avoiding faults.

c.7 History differs from encomium; it can never tell a lie.

listen out: literally 'open your ears', a phrase already used in *Salt.* 85.

linger long: though *endiatribō* occurs in L.'s favourite classical authors and often elsewhere in L., *Salt.* 6, *Hist.* 6 etc., it had been used by Philodemus specifically of unduly prolonged eulogies, as here and in c. 11.

eulogies of ... their own: cf. Plb. 12.23, 26 b 4 criticising Timaeus for doing this.

history can't tolerate ... any falsehood: cf. Plb. 12.11. 8ff. etc., Cic., *De Oratore* 2.15.62.

medical profession: literally 'sons of doctors', see on *Zeux*. 5.

c.8   Historians, unlike poets, shouldn't enjoy poetic licence and should avoid fiction, flattery and the aids to beauty used by poetry.

poetry and poems differ from history ...: cf. Plb. 2.56.11–12, Cic. *Leg*. 1.5, D.S. 1.2.7. and for a diametrically opposed view Quint. 10.1.31.

a team of winged steeds: cf. Pl. *Phdr*. 246 A ff., a favourite passage of L.'s.

run on water or the heads of corn: like the supernatural fillies of *Il*. 20.226–9.

no-one grudges him: a Platonic phrase, *Phd*. 61D etc.

Zeus draws up earth and sea...: *Il*. 8. 18–26, often referred to by L.

Agamemnon: the similes are from *Il*. 2. 477–9.

fiction: translating *mythos*, factually doubtful versions of events depending on hearsay or invention or, in the case of the distant past, oral tradition, thus including myth and legend.

powder: literally 'white lead'; whiteness of skin symbolised female beauty, cf. c. 13.

By Heracles: the oath is ironical; all this is an affront to the muscular god embodying the athletes' ideal. There may also be a dig at Heracles' appearance in the Omphale incident, cf. c.10.

c.9   Praise of individuals is admissible, but only at the right time and in moderation. The role of history is single, not dual. Its sole purpose is to be useful (by providing the truth); the affording of pleasure is inessential, but acceptable, though only in a subsidiary capacity. It is, therefore, a mistake to introduce encomia to make history more attractive.

praise in ... history: cf. Thucydides' praises of Themistocles, Pericles etc. and Plb.'s acceptance of the principle, 2.61.

in due season: as stressed by Gorgias.and Isocrates; cf. Hes. *Op*. 694, Pi. *P*. 9.78.

kept within the due limits: cf. the 'nothing too much' of the Delphic oracle and the Aristotelian view of virtue.

consideration of the future: the theme of Thuc. 1.22, developed by L. throughout, particularly in 61–3.

the pleasurable and the useful: though the contrast of the useful and the pleasurable is a commonplace of classical literature and paticularly common in Polybius, cf. also Horace's *utile* and *dulce*, *A.P*. 343, it goes back to L.'s frequent source in *Hist*., Thuc. 1.22. Throughout his earlier *Salt*. L. had represented dancing as both pleasant and useful, cc.6, 23 etc. with precedent in Plato, *Laws* 814E.

Nicostratus: a double Olympic victor of A.D. 37.

noble ... doughtier: *gennadas* is a favourite Lucianic adjective used by Aristophanes and Plato. *alkimōteron* paves the way for a joke on the name Alcaeus (= Doughty). This Alcaeus is unknown and may be a Lucianic fiction; it was the name of the grandfather of Heracles (Alcides).

c.10 Historians should write not for the common herd but for the discriminating few who will object to excessive fictions and flatteries, as inappropriate trappings for history as Omphale's garments for Heracles.

the mob and common populace...: cf. Plato, *Tht*. 152C, *Salt*. 83, Horace, *Sat*. 1.10.72–4 etc.

even if they burst...: cf. Dem. *On the Crown*, 21, 87 etc.

him as Omphale's slave: Heracles' effeminate appearance, while the slave of Omphale, the Lydian queen, was a favourite subject for painters, cf. Plut. *Mor*. 785 E, and often used by rhetoricians as an example of the inappropriate.

cc.11–13 Exaggerated praises and blatant flattery offend everyone except the intended beneficiary of the compliments and even he may be big enough to take offence as

Alexander did with Aristobulus when he falsified the facts. Historians who act thus for personal aggrandisement give history a bad name. It can be made pleasurable in other ways, but the pleasurable is *NOT* a *sine qua non* of history.

c.11 linger: see on c.7.

c.12 (Take ... single combat): a conjectural restoration of a gap in the text.

Aristobulus: a Macedonian who took part in Alexander's campaigns. His history was one of Arrian's two main sources for Alexander, but Arrian in his preface to *Anabasis* expressly states it was only written after Alexander's death and had no need to flatter him; indeed Aristobulus is reputed to have stated at the start of his (lost) history that he started writing it at the age of 84. Moreover both Arrian and Plutarch suggest Alexander was not averse to flattery. The anecdote, therefore, possibly L.'s own concoction, is hardly *ben trovato*.

Porus: a gigantic Indian king defeated and captured by Alexander, though neither of our main surviving sources, Arrian and Plutarch, mentions a single combat.

make Mt. Athos into a statue: cf. *Pro Imag.* 9. Plutarch calls the architect Stasicrates. Vitruvius gives a different version of the story and calls him Dinocrates.

stopped employing him as before: or 'felt differently about him thereafter'. Vitruvius, however, says Alexander engaged him to build Alexandria.

cc.14–32 Negative Section (B). The 'historians' recently encountered by L. in Ionia and Achaea.

c.14 The boastful Milesian who invoked the Muses and showered compliments on our leader in Homeric fashion, but hurled comic abuse at the Parthian King.

Achaea: The southern province of Greece. L. had been there for at least the Olympic Games of 165.

let nobody disbelieve ... on oath: for a discussion of L.'s credibility see p. 285. Here L. seems not only to 'protest too much' but to make it obvious, whether to readers or to audience, that he is doing so by offering a transparently feeble excuse for not swearing to his veracity.

strikes the right note: ironical.

appropriate: *to prepon*, Latin *decorum*, was demanded by literary critics from Aristotle onwards; for an earlier hint in this direction see Plato *Phdr.* 268D.

our leader: this could refer to 'our general', but more probably to Lucius Verus. Fronto, see p. 286, went even further and said Achilles would gladly have had Verus' achievements for his own.

pursued ... mightier far: *Il.* 22.158.

claiming to be a worthy historian for such glorious deeds: precisely what Arrian says about his own credentials for writing about Alexander the Great, *Anabasis* 1.12.4–5. Arrian then says his *patris* is well known, but does not mention it; whether he means Nicomedia, Athens or Rome, it certainly wasn't Miletus. Photius, *Bibl.* 131, also mentions an Amyntianus who addressed his work to Marcus Aurelius and claimed to write *axiōs tōn Alexandrou praxeōn*.

Vologesus: Vologases 111, King of Parthia 148–93. The terms of abuse are typically Aristophanic, cf. *Ach.* 865, *Pl.* 713, and out of keeping with the fellow's epic aspirations.

for the following reasons: a touch suggestive of Hdt. or Thuc.

c.15 Crepereius Calpurnianus of Pompeiopolis, a servile imitator of Thuc. with a similar exordium, plague and funeral oration, who however allows Latin military terms to encroach upon his Thucydidean Greek.

with as Attic an aroma as thyme: ironical. The motif goes back to Theophrastus' *agroikos*, *Characters* 4. Quintilian 12.10.25 applies a similar description to some Atticists.

Crepereius Calpurnianus the Pompeiopolitan: a comically polysyllabic name. The Pompeiopolis meant is probably in Paphlagonia, rather than the city in Cilicia which had been Soli (which might well have led L. to make jokes about solecisms.) Both Crepereius and Calpurnianus are authentic Latin names, and Baldwin and Jones argue strongly that this is a real man. Homeyer sees a Latin pun in *Crepereius* (= *Dunkelmann, Anglice* Dim Jim), but this would have been inappropriate for L. and his audience. Perhaps however we should read *Kalpurianus* with the best mss. (= Mr. Philpott, cf. Martial's Palinurus). Names apart, he reproduces exactly Thucydides' opening words.

Corcyrean envoy: the speech reproduced is that of Thuc. 1.32–36 by C. envoys to the Athenian *ecclēsia* successfully urging alliance with them.

Nisibis: a city in Mesopotania.

the Pelasgicum: an area under the Acropolis, occupation of which had been deprecated by an oracle. Thuc., 2.17, describes how it and the Long Walls down to the Piraeus were inhabited by refugees from the countryside prior to the outbreak of the plague.

it started ... Great King: exactly like Thuc.'s plague in 2.48.1.

what he was going to say: i.e. reproduce Pericles' Funeral Oration of Thuc. 2.35–46.

however ... words: the words in brackets are a conjectural restoration of a completely corrupt text.

Italianate ones: similarly Horace, *Sat.* 10, objects to Lucilius' use of Greek words. As early as Plb. Greek writers had used Latin military terms, *koortis, diktator* etc.

c.16 Callimorphus, the military doctor, who after an imposing title, produced a brief, bare, unpolished account at first in Ionic, but later degenerating into the crudest *koinē* (the late degenerate form of Attic used in the Greek speaking world).

titles ... number of each book: for further examples of anticlimax and disappointed expectations, cf. cc.23, 30 and 32.

Callimorphus: Dr. Prettybody; the name looks like a comic coinage. He had a predecessor in Trajan's doctor, Statilius Crito, author of *Getica* (*On the Dacian Wars*).

Ionic: the dialect of Hippocrates, used by Ctesias, and traditional for medical men. There may be a dig at Arrian here for switching to Ionic for his *Indica*.

c.17 The Stoic philosopher recently active in Corinth, whose 'histories' were full of dialectic and crude flattery.

his name must remain a secret: *to men onoma* looks like an echo of Arrian, *Anabasis* 1. 12.5, a famous passage known to L.

only the philosopher...: this claim, see on *Pisc.* 35, and the syllogisms, see on *Pisc.* 39, mark him out as a Stoic, and so could suggest Arrian who published the discourses of Epictetus; A. didn't, however, let philosophy intrude into his histories and had no particular connection with Corinth.

crude and ... vulgar: the two Greek adjectives are found in Aristotle, *EN* 1128 A.

c.18 A servile imitator of Herodotus. For the phrases quoted cf. Hdt. 1.5.3 etc., 1.8.2 etc. and 1.7.2 etc., though *onumeousin* is unparalleled in Ionic.

Osroes: Chosroes, the Parthian general victorious at Elegeia.

cc.19–21 One with a reputation for eloquence who overdoes descriptions not only of topographical features but of trivial items (cf. cc.27–8, 56–7), recounts incredible happenings, gives ludicrously exaggerated casualty figures, a dedicated Atticist who converts Latin names to Greek, but scientifically inaccurate on the suicide of Severianus; for historical details see p. 284..

c.19 celebrated: there is no need to see a reference to the rhetorician, M. Cornelius Fronto, see p. 286, and in any case *aoidimos* may be ironical.

c.20 quite incredible wounds: cf. Plb.'s similar criticism of Timaeus, 12.24.5, for his tall stories, but L. may simply be thinking of Ctesias and even Hdt. whom elsewhere he links as 'liars'. (For Ctesias see note on c.39.)

Europus: the name of two cities in Syria; the battle seems to have been fought at Dura-Europus, the southern city of the two, due east of Palmyra; see on c.24.

the number of dead: L. may be thinking of Arrian's incredible figures for the battle of Arbela, *Anabasis* 3.15.6, about 100 dead on Alexander's side and a reputed 300,000 barbarian dead, though he could also have objected to Hdt.'s figures for e.g. Plataea, 257,000 barbarian dead and only 160 Greeks.

c.21 an out-and-out Atticist: cf. L.'s ridicule of the excessive Atticism of the Lexiphanes and the Rhetorum Praeceptor; see pp. 9–10, 11.

Fronto: not the rhetorician but the general M. Claudius Fronto.

the week: as *hebdomē* strictly means 'seventh day' perhaps *hebdomados* should be read.

c.22 This chapter criticises departures from stylistic uniformity and appropriateness by use of poetic words or slang (faults already noted in the Milesian of c.14). Cf. Quintilian 4.2.36.

quake... clangor: *elelizō* is confined to poetry, *Il.* 1.530 etc., but *doupeō*, though usually in poets, *Il.* 4.504 etc., is found in Xenophon and Arrian.

did bethink himself: *mermērizō* is Homeric; its use by L. in *Bis Acc.* 2 is an echo of *Il.* 2.3.

the boss of the camp: L. objects to *stratopedarchēs*, rare in late prose, and probably to *kurios* in the sense of 'emperor'.

the needful: the verb is not found in good prose.

looking after number one: i.e. 'feeding their faces', the normal sequel to washing or bathing. The text and meaning are, however, uncertain.

c.23 Others produce magnificent prologues followed by anticlimax, or have no prologue at all.

body of their history: the concept of a literary work being like a body with a head and feet and all its parts appropriate goes back to Plato, *Phaedrus* 264 C.

tiny child ... enormous mask: cf. Longinus, *On the Sublime* 30.2.

The mountain was in travail: cf. Horace, *A.P.* 139, *Parturient montes, nascetur ridiculus mus*, also of anticlimax after an impressive opening (in Horace of an epic poem). This is one of several motifs shared with Horace *A.P.* (and also *Sat.* 1.10 and *Ep.* 2.1), suggesting a common source or sources.

his work: the *Anabasis*.

later: in c.52 which seems to suggest that an exposition of the subject matter may serve as a prologue.

c.24 Terrible geographical mistakes made by a man who had never been near the places involved. (Once again L. had been preceded by Plb. 12.3 etc., in censuring failings of this sort in historians who lack, 12.25h, *autopatheia*.)

parasangs ... days' journey: the Persian terms found in Hdt. and Xen.; a parasang was 30 stades (= furlongs), a *stathmos* 150 stades.

tittle-tattle in a barber's shop: cf. Aristophanes, *Plutus* 338 and Plb.'s insulting reference to two lost historians, 3.20.5.

Europus ... Edessa: there were two Macedonian military colonies in Syria called Europus, one Dura-Europus, see on c. 20, the other much further north. Both were right on the Euphrates, but on its western, non-Mesopotamian bank. Edessa was the capital of Osrhoene in Northern Mesopotamia. The 'historian' may have meant the wrong (northern) Europus. L. probably objects to his history as well as his geography.

Samosata: the capital of Commagene, in the far north east of Syria. It too was on the western bank of the Euphrates, and far away from the Tigris.

cc.25–6 The same man's sensational and emotive account of the suicides of Severianus and a centurion. (Cf. Photius' description of the work of Ctesias, early 4th century, as containing much that was *patheticon* and unexpected, and Polybius' criticism of Phylarchus, third century, for 'writing like the tragedians'.)

Afranius Silo: the name could be a conflation of Afranius, the writer of *togatae* (kitchen-sink Latin comedies) and Abronius Silo, a writer of plays for *pantomimi* mentioned by the Elder Seneca, though Latin dramatic writers were unlikely to have been of much interest to L. or his audience.

in the same way as Ajax: by committing suicide as in Sophocles' play; the word *aianteion* probably alludes to a vital feature of the myth stressed by L. in *Salt.*, his madness, and may also contain a word play on *aiai* (alas) and the name Aias, suggesting the whole matter is lamentable or pathetic.

Aphronius: if the two best mss. can be trusted, L. switches to a coined name, punningly suggesting he is *aphrona* (accusative); perhaps translate, *faute de mieux*, 'a frantic Afranius'.

cc.27–28 Others treat the important matters summarily or omit them entirely but indulge in protracted descriptions of the trivial, e.g. one man's account of the conversation and experiences of a Moorish trooper. (Again this man lacks a sense of harmony, unity and appropriateness. L. has already discussed the excessive use of *ecphrasis* in c. 19, see also cc.56–57).

c.28 **expended twenty ... measures of the waterclock:** made his account as long as twenty courtroom speeches.

Caesarea: the name of several cities founded by emperors, including one in Mauritania, to which Mausacas refers.

c.29 The ludicrous mistakes of an 'arm-chair historian' operating in Corinth, completely ignorant of military matters. (Cf. c.24 and Plb.'s criticisms of military ignorance in others, 12.28.6 etc.; some have seen an implied compliment to Arrian in this chapter.)

never taken a step: for the phrase cf. Aristophanes, *Eccl.* 161–2.

Cenchreae: the eastern harbour of Corinth.

ears ... eyes: the actual phrase of Hdt. 1.8 (already paraphrased by L. in *Salt.* 78), though Heraclitus (sixth century) is credited by Plb. with a similar dictum. Cf. Horace, *A.P.* 180–1.

the serpents of the Parthians: imitation snakes, made of painted rags, according to Arrian, who, in his similar account of their function, calls them 'Scythian standards'.

Iberia: a country between the Black and Caspian Seas.

Sura: a town in Syria on the Euphrates near Thapsacus.

Lerna: not the scene of Heracles' exploit in the Argolid, but a spring, like the Craneion, cf. c.3, in Corinth itself; cf. Pausanias 2.4.5.

never even seen ... on a fresco: cf. Cicero, *De Finibus* 5.27.80.

company ... section: according to Arrian a *taxis* had 128 men, divided into *lochoi* of 16 men.

a line a column: a fighting unit, would march in column, *orthia, epi kerōs*, but fight in line as a phalanx as explained by Arrian in his *Tactica*.

c.30 A 'pocket historian' who covers the whole war in 500 words including a protracted title (Cf. on c.23.)

Antiochianus: Baldwin suggests a possible allusion to Antiochus of Aegae in Cilicia (a sophist whose *Historia* is praised by Philostratus) or one of his followers.

victor at his sacred games: perhaps some local festival is suggested rather than the Pythian Games.

a narration: a word with a good historiographical pedigree, used e.g. by Hdt. and Arrian.

c.31 A prophetic historian. (L., or the 'historian', if real, models some of his future details on the activities of Alexander the Great, as recorded by Alexander historians including Arrian. There is also a possible reference to the novelist Iamblichus who according to Photius claimed to have made correct prophecies about the war.)

Vologesus: the Parthian King who was not in fact captured.

Osroes: the Parthian general, presumably wrongly assigned the reputed fate of some of Alexander's companions, cf. *Dialogues of the Dead* 12.4.

triumph: celebrated at Rome in October 166.

in extent ... beautiful: the full phrase occurs also in L.'s *Dom.* 1 after a reference to Alexander; the first half is a Herodotean echo also found in Arrian.

Victoria: several cities called Nicaea to celebrate a victory are known in the ancient world, but the whole motif of building and naming the city seems to come from Arrian, *Anabasis* 5.19.4 or his source.

he has also promised ...: i.e. to emulate Arrian who wrote an *Indica* and a *Periplus of the Black Sea* and perhaps also the writer of the extant *Periplus of the Red Sea*.

cope with ... the elephants: as Alexander had to do in facing Porus and other Indians.

Muziris: a port on the SW (Malabar) coast of India.

Oxydracae: an Indian tribe defeated by Alexander.

c.32 Others use protracted pretentious titles to boast about the number of books in their histories; cf. c.30.

take pride in the number of their books: cf. Plb. 29.12..2.

Atthis: a chronicle of Attic history as written by Hellanicus (mid 5th century) and others.

Sagalassus: a city of Pisidia, a remote area in the south of Asia Minor.

cc.33–60 Positive Section

(A) c.33 Introductory.

not even Momus could criticise: echoing Pl. *Republic* 487 A; for Momus, Criticism personified, cf. *Dear. Jud.* 2.

(B) cc.34–42 Profile of the ideal historian.

c.34 The ideal historian should combine political understanding, a natural gift, with power to communicate, which can only be developed by long training and emulation of the ancients.

political understanding and the power to communicate: the whole phrase owes most to Pericles' description of himself in Thuc. 2.60.5 as second to none in *gnōnai ta deonta kai hermēneusai tauta*, quoted by L. in *Salt.* 36, and perhaps a little to Xen. *Mem.* 1.2.52. *Synesis politikē* which occurs in a different context in Aristotle, *Pol.* 1291A, differs from Plb.'s political experience, in being inborn. L. is clearly thinking of Pericles, Thuc.'s favourite politician and the orator supreme; cf. Eupolis' famous tribute and Pl. *Phdr.* 269 E.

an untaught gift of nature: the choice of words may owe something to Pl. *Meno* 99E.

practising ... hard work ...: cf. Protagoras, *Fr.* 3 and Pl. *Phdr.* 269 D etc.; a close parallel is Quintilian 3.5.1. *facultas orandi consummatur natura, arte, exercitatione, cui partem quartam adiiciunt quidam imitationis.*

Titormos ... Conon ... Milo ... Leotrophides: the shepherd Titormus was said to surpass even the famous athlete Milo in strength; a Conon (the Athenian general?) was noted for his tiny physique, and Leotrophides, another general, was derided by comic poets for his emaciated appearance.

c.35 Just as a trainer can't produce an Olympic victor out of poor material, so my advice will only be useful to anyone who is naturally intelligent and well educated.

Iccus ... Herodicus ... Theon: L. follows the rhetoricians' practice of giving three examples. All three trainers possessed medical skills as well. The first two are mentioned by Plato, *Prt.* 316 D, *Phdr.* 227 D etc., the third was contemporary with L.

a Perdiccas ... Stratonike: someone unsuitable, because weakened by hopeless love for a stepmother, whether this was what happened to Perdiccas (Alexander's successor as ruler of Macedon?) or to Antiochus (Soter, see *Zeuxis*). L. is particularly fond of the story of the young bride Stratonice, whose husband Seleucus 1 (Nicator) allowed his son to marry her, after the cause of his illness had been diagnosed by a doctor.

c.36 Even the intelligent need technical instruction, whether in how to play a musical instrument or to write history.

c.37 In addition to political insight and eloquence (cf. c 34), my ideal pupil should have experience as a general and knowledge of military affairs and technical terms (cf. c.29) and not be a mere stay-at-home (cf. cc.24, 29).

c.38 He must have a free spirit, fearing none and hoping for no reward, telling the truth about kings and demagogues, and describing disasters without holding back, as they can't be blamed on him.

independent of mind: cf. Pericles who, Thuc. 2.65.8, *kateiche to plēthos eleutherōs* (showed independence in controlling the commoners), and the *parrhēsia* of the Cynics.

favouritism ... hostility: cf. c.47 and note on c.39.

had one eye shot out: Demosthenes' phrase in *De Corona* 67; it happened at Methone, not Olynthus.

Clitus: the general and friend of Alexander who killed him with a spear during a drunken quarrel.

Cleon: the most influential demagogue of his time, Thuc. 3.36.6, whose rash promises about taking Pylos, though fulfilled (425 B.C.), were condemned by Thuc. 4.39.3, as mad.

the disasters in Sicily: of 413 B.C., recorded in Thuc. 7.

the sort of water they had to drink: polluted by mud and the blood of their comrades, Thuc. 7.84.5.

unless he omitted to make the proper prayer: ironical, taken from Demosthenes, *Olynthiacs* 3.18.

Epipolae: high ground overlooking Syracuse from the N.W. fortified by the Athenians. The Syracusans built a counter-wall between them and the city; see Thuc. 7.11.3.

Hermocrates: the leading Syracusan.

Gylippus: a Spartan sent to help the Syracusans.

the quarries: stone quarries at Syracuse where the Athenian prisoners had to work.

Clotho ... Atropos: two of the three Fates. L. alludes to the meanings of their names, viz. Spinner and Inflexible One.

c.39 He must give the facts truthfully, uninfluenced by any personal fear, hatred or friendship, writing not for contemporaries but for posterity.

report events factually: adapted from Thuc. 1.22.2.

his doctor: Ctesias, elsewhere condemned by L. as a liar. He served Artaxerxes Mnemon, the brother of Xenophon's paymaster Cyrus.

a Median doublet of purple, necklace of gold: typical Persian gifts, as offered by Cambyses, Hdt. 3.20.

Nisaean: or Nesaean, a famous breed of Median horses, cf. Hdt. 7.40.

an honest historian: the same tribute as paid to him by Dionysius of Halicarnassus.

personal hatred ... though he may be a friend: cf. cc.38, 47, Plb. 1. 14.5 etc., Cicero *De Oratore* 2.63 and Tacitus' claim to write *sine ira et studio*.

present audience ... future readers: once again the gist of Thuc. 1.22.4.

c.41 Historians with an eye to the immediate main chance are no better than flatterers, as Alexander realised by his reputed remarks to Onesicritus.

the beautician's art ... the physical trainer: cf. Plato *Grg.* 463 B ff.

Onesicritus: Alexander's chief pilot in far Eastern waters. Like Aristobulus, however, cf. on c. 12, he only started writing after Alexander's death. Again this anecdote may be L.'s own fiction.

evidence of his truthfulness: cf. Arrian's reasons for trusting Ptolemy Lagou and Aristobulus, *Anabasis* init.

c.41 L.'s memorably succinct catalogue of the attributes of the ideal historian. (The various qualities suggest a combination of Thucydides, Pericles, Diogenes and perhaps L. himself. Cf. L.'s similar but less concise attempt to define the ideal dancer, *Salt.* 74, 75, 77).

incorruptible: cf. the description of Pericles in Thuc. as *chrēmaton kreissōn*, 2.60.5, and *chrēmatōn diaphanōs adōrotatos*, 2.65.8.

free: note the similar association of *Eleutheria* and *Parrhesia* in *Pisc.* 17.

a friend of frankness and truth: cf. L.'s pseudonyms in *Pisc.* 19 and note.

a spade a spade: literally 'a fig a fig, a tub a tub', unless the nouns are used *sensu obsceno*. The English proverb originated with Nicholas Udall via Erasmus' translation of *skaphēn* in Plutarch', *Mor.* 178B as 'ligonem'; cf. *JTr.* 32.

a man without a city or country ... subject to no king: both phrases suggest Diogenes as a 'citizen of the world' and no respecter of Alexander, and so radically different from Pericles who was *philopolis*.

c.42 Thuc. was right to disapprove of Hdt.'s approach and to reject the fictitious, insisting on the true and factual as a guide to the future. (Again L. reverts to the theme of Thuc. 1.22.4.)

Herodotus: not mentioned by name but only by implication in Thuc.

given the names of the Muses: L. here and in *Herod.* 1 is the first expressly to state this, though a generation earlier the lost historian Cephalion was presumably following Hdt.'s lead in writing nine books in Ionic, entitling them Muses. L.'s point is that the Muses were associated with poetry and *to mythōdes*.

the fictitious: or 'fabulous'; by *to mythōdes*, Thuc. and L. mean the non-factual, see on c.8.

Positive Section (C)

cc.43–51 The style of the historian.

c.43 His style should not be rhetorically forceful, or excessively periodic or complicated by intellectual concepts but quiet, clear and businesslike.

vehement ... complicated: cf. Cicero, *Orator* 66, recommending in history *tracta quaedam et fluens ... non contorta et acris oratio*, and *De Oratore* 2.64.

peaceful: perhaps suggestive of Hdt.; see n. on 'smoothly' in c.55, where L. reverts to the style of the main narrative.

clear and businesslike: though *to saphes* occurs in Thuc. 1.22.4, and Aristotle, Theophrastus and L. himself, *Lex.* 23 etc., stress the importance of clarity, its association with *politikē* (i.e. such as a citizen should use in the assembly or lawcourts) suggests the influence of Plato, *Phdr.* 277D.

c.44 He should avoid unusual or uncouth expressions and restrict his figures of speech to the natural ones.

unusual ... common ones used by tradesmen: cf. *Pseudolog.* 13, Arist. *Po.* 1458a, Quint. 4.2.36; the 'historians' of cc.15, 16 and 22 offended in this respect.

the figures: the *schēmata* popularised by Gorgias, particularly antithesis and balanced clauses; Thuc. was not above reproach in overdoing his use of these, particularly in his speeches.

c.45 When dealing with battles his thoughts may wax more elevated and poetic, but his style, though rising with the subject matter, should still keep its feet on the ground. (The mention of poetic afflatus doesn't contradict c.8 which rejects poetic licence with the facts, or c.14 deriding invocation of the Muses or c. 22 on vocabulary).

majestic: cf. D.H. *Thuc.* 27, praising the account of the final sea-battle at Syracuse. Cf. also Demetrius, *On Style* 75, 237.

poetic ecstasy: *enthousiaō* (or in alternative form *enthousiazō,*)= have the god in me, am divinely possessed, a favourite Platonic verb, cf. *Phdr.* 241E, 253 A.

be greatly excited: a rare intransitive use of *parakinō*, found in *Phdr.* 249 D alongside *enthousiazō*.

Corybantic: the Corybants were wild priests of Cybele or Dionysus; for their 'enthusiasm' cf. Pl. *Ion* 533 E.

like a proud horseman: *hippotyphia* occurs only elsewhere in a saying attributed to Plato = pride of a rider; note how the metaphor changes here from the horse to the rider.

c.46 His word arrangement should observe the happy mean between the disjointed and the excessively rhythmical.

arrangement of words: L.'s summary remarks resemble the views of what Dionysius of Halicarnassus, *De Compositione Verborum*, calls *synthesis*, described by Grube 217ff. as 'the sound of words in their various combinations, the structure of sentences and rhythm'.

unpleasant: Aristotle's adjective in condemning metrical prose, *Rhet.* 1408 b.

c.47 The facts should be assembled laboriously, from personal inspection of the sites or from informants likely to be impartial. (Again L. draws heavily from Thuc. 1.22; cf. also D.H. *Thuc.* 6.)

haphazardly: cf. Plb. 2.56.3, Thuc. 1.22.2.

laboriously and painfully: L. changes slightly Thuc.'s adjectives of 1.22.3 and 1.20.3.

visit the places and see: or 'have been present and seen' as meant by Thuc. in 1.22.3.

partiality: cf. on c.39 and Thuc.'s *eunoias*, 1.22.3.

c.48 He should start by making a rough outline of his material.

stylistic figures: see on c.44.

c.49 The historian should be like Zeus, looking down on both sides equally from afar, only mentioning individuals when performing special feats. He should start accounts of battles with the generals, and their speeches, tactics and objectives, and give a balanced account of the actual battle.

like Homer's Zeus: L. means Zeus looks now at Thrace, now at Troy, but he misunderstands *Iliad* 13. 3–7.

the Mysians: Homer places them north of the Hellespont like the later Moesi, but L. seems to put them in Asia Minor, in the Mysia of his own time.

a Brasidas ... or a Demosthenes: see Thuc.'s account, 4.9–12, of their confrontation at Pylos, giving their thoughts and speeches. Plutarch, *Mor.* 347A, praises Thuc.'s *enargeia* (see on c.51) in this passage.

Demosthenes beating back: L., unlike Thuc., gives personal credit to the general.

as though he had a pair of scales: again like Homer's Zeus, *Il.* 8.69, 19.223 etc.

c.50 Keeping a sense of proportion, he should move quickly from one arena to another, when occasion demands, to deal with concurrent events.

leave the scene effortlessly: cf. Thuc. 1.49.3.

dealing ... with concurrent events: like Thuc. who arranged his narrative chronologically, dividing it into summers and winters.

Iberia: see on c.29.

neglect any important occasion: cf. Demosthenes 34.38.

c.51 He should bring to his task a mind like a clear mirror to reflect events accurately for his readers. Unlike a rhetorician he doesn't have to study what to say, only how to say it; for he is like a sculptor whose raw material has already been provided; all he has to do is to give it shape and vividness.

like a mirror: a favourite image of Plato and the rhetoricians, already used by L. in *Salt*. 81.

provided by the Eleans: for the statue of Zeus at Olympia by the Athenian Phidias.

or Athenians: for Praxiteles.

or Argives: L. thinks of Polyclitus, though it was Alcamenes of Athens he had named.

merely ...: a surprisingly slighting assessment of the sculptors' art.

ivory ... gold: L. thinks particularly of Phidias' chryselephantine statues of Zeus and Athena with ivory for the flesh and gold for the hair and drapery.

vividly: with *enargeia*, a stylistic merit recommended by the rhetoricians. Plutarch praises Thuc. for it in his account of the Sicilian disaster and the fighting at Pylos, see on c.49, saying he strives to make the hearer (i.e. the reader) like a spectator.

Positive Section (D)

cc.52–60 Advice on various constituent parts.

cc.52–54 *Advice on prefaces*. Sometimes he doesn't need a preface and a description of contents will serve. Prefaces should not aim at the goodwill of the readers, only their attention and understanding, as exemplified by with both Herodotus and Thucydides. (Here L. patently adapts the theories of the rhetoricians about forensic oratory.)

c.52 **sometimes start without a prologue:** similarly Aristotle, *Rhet*. 1415 a, b and Quintilian, 4.1.72, say that a proem may be unnecessary in forensic oratory.

in effect...: a very meagre fulfilment of the promise of c.23.

c.53 **three like the orators:** as in Cicero, *De Oratore* 2.80 etc., Quintilian 4.1.5; cf. Aristotle, *Rhet*. 1415a ff.

c.54 **by Herodotus:** what follows is an approximation of Hdt. 1.1, with L. adding 'victories' and 'defeats'.

by Thucydides: rather closer approximations follow of 1.1.1. and 1.23.1.

c.55–56 *General narrative*. After an easy transition from the prologue, the narrative should proceed smoothly and evenly, with each section linked in some way to the next. Speed is recommended with only important matters dealt with at length.

c.55 **the rest of the body:** the prologue has been thought of as the head of the body; see on c.23.

gentle and easy: Quintilian, 4.1.76, makes the same point about the transition from the exordium of a speech.

smoothly, evenly and uniformly without protuberances and hollows: L. may be thinking of Hdt. who according to Cicero, *Orator* 39, *sine ullis salebris quasi sedatus amnis fluit*, cf. *De Oratore* 2.64. Cf. cc.43, 44 and 46.

as I said: c.43; see note.

c. 56 **speed:** rapidity or brevity is generally recommended by critics as a virtue in historians, though Thucydidean brevity was often criticised for its obscurity; cf. also (of poets) Horace, *Sat*. 1.10.9, *A.P*. 148, 335.

hurrying over what's trivial and inessential: as recommended by Plb. 29.12.2 ff.; for offenders in this respect see cc.19–20, 27–8.

c.57 *Descriptions.* Use *ecphraseis* in moderation and only when fulfilling a useful function. Follow the examples of Homer and Thuc. in this respect.

self-control must be exercised in descriptions: unlike the 'historians' of cc.19–21 and 27–8. Plb. 29.12.4 makes the same point and Quintilian 2.4.3 deprecates elaborate descriptions.

Tantalus, Ixion, Tityus: typical examples used by the rhetoricians for villains being punished in Hades; Ixion, however, is absent from the brief descriptions in *Odyssey*, 11.572 ff.

Parthenius, Euphorion or Callimachus: typical Alexandrian, non-epic poets, of the first, third and third centuries respectively Even Callimachus is not mentioned elsewhere by L. or quoted, apart from *J. Trag.* 10 where he attributes C.'s epithet for Apollo to Homer. Cicero had a similar contempt for 'singers of Euphorion'.

describing an engine of war: as in 4.100, describing the contraption used by the Boeotians in capturing Delium.

the configuration of Epipolae: described by Thucydides 6.96 and important as the scene of heavy fighting. See note on c.38.

the harbour: the great harbour, scene of the final sea-battle as described in 7.69–71.

c.58 *Speeches* should be appropriate to the character and the situation. (For inappropriate speeches cf. cc.15, 26).

in character and appropriate to the situation: very similar to the phraseology of D.H., *Thuc.* 36 init., in praise of Thucydidean speeches. Thuc. himself, 1.22.1, merely claims his speeches give what the occasion demands or the general thought behind actual speeches, and makes no mention of characterisation, *prosōpopoiia*, a watchword of literary critics, cf. e.g. Quint. 3.8.49, a feature perhaps less obvious in the speeches of Thuc. than in those written for others by his contemporary, Lysias.

c.59 Praise and censure. Praise and censure of individuals should be sparing and only when called for. Theopompus' vindictiveness is deplored. (Cf. c.8 ff. on the distinction between history and encomium, and cc.38, 47).

Theopompus: a pupil of Isocrates and historian of the late 4th century; he was given to moralising, but was criticised by Plb. 8.9–10 for bias and vindictiveness against Philip of Macedon.

c.60 *Stories* Tell stories, if you must, but don't vouch for them.

a story: for *mythos* see on c.8.

it should be told but not vouched for: L. now echoes the views of Hdt., 7.152.3 etc., that his duty is to report what he is told without necessarily believing it, none too consistently after his rejection of *mythos* in cc.8ff.42, but at least he suggests a *mythos* would be a rarety.

cc.61–3 **Epilogue** Write for the approval not of contemporaries but of posterity, following the example of the architect of the Pharos at Alexandria. Otherwise I've been wasting my time.

c.61 **'But he was a free man ... truth':** cf. c.41.

c.62 **the great architect:** Sostratus who built the Lighthouse at Alexandria, one of the ancient wonders of the world, for Ptolemy Philadelphus in c.280 B.C. The accounts of Strabo and the Elder Pliny attest only the architect's name and not that of the king, on the inscription; the variation in the story may be L.'s own invention, see on c.1.

Paraetonia: the dangerous waters off Paraetonium, now Mersah Matruh, in Cyrenaica, over 180 miles west of Alexandria. Josephus gives a more credible range for the light, 300 stades (37.5 miles).

the Saviour Gods: Castor and Polydeuces, protectors of seafarers.

c.63 **rolling my cask on Cornel Hill:** see c.3.

Textual Notes

The Dream

γ traditionis testibus ΓΦΩ, β traditionis ΖΑΝ usus sum, vide pp. 16–18

c.2 καὶ δίδασκε γ: καὶ διδάσκου β   **c.4** σκυτάλην Steigerthal: νύκτα ὅλην codd.   **c.7** μητρόθεν Fritzsche: οἰκόθεν codd.   **c.8** δὲ τοῦ σχήματος Clericus **c.10** σου Hemsterhuis: σοι codd.; μέλλοντα rec.: δέοντα βγ   **c.12** ὅμως recc.: ὅπως βγ   **c.14** εὐθὺς] ὁ θεῖος Hemsterhuis   **c.15** εἰδῆς οἷα β; πρὸς τὰς ἑσπερίας codd.: corr. Gronovius   **c.17** ὅτε Graevius: ὅτι codd.; αὐτῷ καὶ ἐν τῇ πατρῴᾳ οἰκίᾳ codd.: corr. Jacobitz

The Judging of the Goddesses

Codices ΓΩ = γ: LB = β.

c.1 νεν. εἶδον β; μὲν αὐτὸς codd.: trs. Fritzsche   **c.4** ἔχω εἰπεῖν β; οὐδὲ ἐγκαλῶ β; μεμψίμοιρον β   **c.6** δακὼν γ: ἔχων β; λαβών β: ἔλαβον γ   **c.7** ἦ² Fritzsche: ἦ βΓ: om. Ω   **c.9** καὶ πάθοι τις β: τ.κ.π. γ; πρότερον β: πρῶτον γ **c.10** ἀλλὰ γυμ. β· γυμ. δὲ καὶ ἄτεχνον γ; φοβήσεις β   **c.11** ἡδέως δὲ ὁρᾷ ἡδύ τι καὶ γλαφυρόν γ: ὁρᾷ δὲ ἡδέως καὶ γλαφυρόν τι β: corr. Harmon; νίκης γ: ψήφου β   **c.13** τῶν μερῶν β   **c.14** παλαιστρική γ   **c.15** ἐλὼν τὴν γ. γ **c.16** μῆλον. ΑΦΡ. Ἐπὶ τούτοις λαμβάνω Bekker

The Assembly of the Gods

γ traditionis testibus Γ et Φ (cc. 1–5) et I (Urb. 118, saeculi xiii–xiv), β traditionis ΝΑΡ usus sum, vide pp. 16–18.

c.3 ἔτι β: ὅτι γ; αἰνιγματωδῶς γΡ   **c.4** φρατρίαν recc.; γρ. θεοποιεῖ ὁ γενναῖος Γᵃ?   **c.5** ὑποφαίνεται ΝΑ   **c.8** θήλειαι om. γ   **c.14** μεταγειτνιῶνος super ιστ. add. Γᵃ   **c.15** δεδόχθω codd.: corr. Harmon   **c.17** καινά βγ: corr. rec.   **c.19** ὑμῖν γΡ: ἡμῖν ΝΑ; sic rec. ex corr.: χειροτονήσαντες βγ

The Fisherman

γ traditionis testibus Γ et Ω et Φ (cc. 9–36, 46–52), β traditionis B et U et Γᵃ usus sum.

c.2 ἀνασκολοπισθῆναι γ; τοὺς ὀφθ. ἐκκεκόφθω alio loquente β   **c.5** εἰ (ante μάθ.) γ: ἦν β; αὐτὸ (ante ποι.) codd.: corr. Cobet   **c.10** τοῖς κατηγορεῖν β **c.12** τὸ ἄνετον β; φυκίον γ; κλοιῶν β: ἐγχέλεων γ   **c.13** προσέρχεται β **c.14** λωπ. γ: τυμβωρύχος β; ἐπιὼν post ἔλεγεν add. β   **c.15** ἀνευρεῖν β; καταφανῆ πάντα εἴη β   **c.16** βαρὺ γὰρ μίαν γ: χαλεπόν β   **c.17** εὐνοικωτάτω γ; εἰ καὶ Fritzsche: καὶ εἴ γ (εἰ καί τις ἄλλος om. β)   **c.19** ἐλάττων B   **c.20** φιλο Halm: φιλῶ γ: φίλου β   **c.21** τῇ θεῷ β; ἐπίσκοπος οὖσα β, cf. Sol. 4.3   **c.23** δόγμασι γ: λόγοις β   **c.25** ὧν (ante ἡμᾶς) β: ἅπερ γ; bis χλευασμῷ β; δρᾶν βΩΦ; χαίρει codd.: corr. Bekker   **c.26** ἑορτῆς ἐπιούσης β   **c.27** διασύρων et postea παράγων γ; μετριότης ... ἀνανδρία ... εὐήθεια γ;

τὰ αἴσχιστα β c.29 ἔφθασα β c.30 τῶν καθ' ἡμᾶς β c.31 γυναικεῖος β;
μετρίου γ c.32 ἐπιθέσθαι β; περιβαλλ. βγ: corr. rec.; ὅτου recc.: τουτονὶ τὸν
β (γ incert.); ἐμιμεῖτο Seager: ἐποιεῖτο βγ c.33 τοὺ ἀδικοῦντα β; ἀθλοθέται
β; ἤδοντ' ἂν β; μᾶλλον γ: οἶμαι β c.34 πυλῶνας γ: θύρας β; παραγκ. καὶ
γ: παρωθούμενοι β; ἐμφορ. β: ἐμπιμπλάμενοι γ; πάρεισιν ... καὶ γ:
ξυμπίνουσι δηλαδὴ β c.35 δογμάτων γ: λόγων β c.36 κάρυα ὑπὸ κόλπον β:
ὀπώρας γ; τῶν καρύων post τῆς ὀπ. add. γ   ὑπὸ τῶν θεατῶν γ c.37
ἐλέγχων γ; ἐπιδεικνύναι γ c.38 ΑΛΗΘΕΙΑ Gesner: ΑΡΕΤΗ priores; ὦ
'Αλήθεια Reitz: ὦ 'Αρετή codd.: ἡ 'Αρετή, uae loquitur Harmon c.40 ἀνίασι γ:
συνέρχονται β c.42 πάγον add. recc. c.44 ἴστε γ: ἔστε β c.45 κουρικὸν
Du Soul: θυτικὸν γ: om. β: θρυπτικὸν Belin c.46 ὡς ἀλ. φιλόσοφον γ;
στεφανούμενος γ; ἀποκείραντας β: ἀποκείραντα γ: corr. Fritzsche c.48
πρόσεισι γοῦν γ: προσέρχεται δὴ β; κύων rec.: ἀνθρώπων ex compendio ΓΩ:
om. ΦΒ; μὰ Δι' ἔπιεν huc trs. Harmon: post κοιλίᾳ γ: om. β c.49 'Ιδού. Τίς
...; β; sic conieci: ὑπόπλατος γ: οὗτος ὁ πλατὺς β; πρόσεισιν γ: προσέρχεται
β c.50 ἄπεισιν γ: ἀπενήξατο β; περισκόπει codd.: corr. Seybold c.51
παραινεῖς γ c.52 ὦ β. φιλοσόφων ἀνδ. γ; ἢ add. Seybold

Menippus
γ traditionis testibus ΓΩ, β traditionis ΒΩᵇ usus sum.

c.1 παραβλέπω Μενίππους ὅλους codd.: corr. Graevius c.2 οὐ π. τάσφαλές β;
τίς αἰτία σοι τῆς β c.3 ἐκνώμην Ω c.5 ἀτοπώτερον γ; καὶ π. καὶ λ. β:
ἐπιτηδεύοντας γ c.7 πρὸς ἀνατέλλοντα τὸν β c.8 ἂν διελθεῖν γ c.10
ἐκοιμήθη β; ἀποβὰς γ c.11 καὶ σκύλακα διτ. Hemsterhuis c.14 χαλεπῶς
τε γ (corr. Harmon): om. β: χαλέπ' ἄλγε' ex Od. 11.582 Fritzsche c.16 τοῖς
πομπευταῖς β; δεῖ recc.: δὴ β: δεῖν γ c.17 γωνιδίῳ ... σαπρὰ β c.18 κἀκεῖ
περιέρχεται β; συμπαρώκει γ c.19 βίᾳ καὶ ἀλαζονεία καὶ ὑπεροψία καὶ
ἀδικία β c.20 δέδοκται Γ¹: δεδόχθω Γ²Ωβ: corr. Jacobitz c.21 καὶ
σωφρονέστερος. γ: καὶ σωφρονέστατος.; Sommerbrodt: καὶ σωφρονέστερος
ἔσει εἰ: Fritzsche: ὡς τῆς ἀφροσύνης ... β c.22 κἀκεῖθεν κατέρχονται οἱ β

On the Death of Peregrinus
traditionis simplicis testibus Γ et Χ (Vat. Pal. 73, saec. xiii) usus sum.

c.3 τοῦ δράματος Faber; ἀλύων Schaefer: αὐτὸν ΓΧ: αὐτῶν Γᵃ: ἀνιῶν
Sommerbrodt c.11 ὡς θεῖον αὐτὸν J. Schwartz; αὐτῶν] αὐτῶν Γ: αὐτὸν Χ;
ἡγοῦντο codd.: corr. Cobet; ἐπέγραφον τὸν μέγαν γοῦν codd.: corr. Cobet; τὸν
μάγον γοῦν Gesner: μετ' αὐτοῦ ἐκείνου J. Schwartz ; ὃν add. Harmon c.17
ἀδιάφθορον ΓΧ: corr. rec. c.21 δεῖ codd.: corr. Fritzsche c.22 ἄλλως Madvig
c.24 καίτοι τί Lehmann; κεφαλῆς ΓΧ: corr. recc. c.27 εἴη Bekker: εἶναι
codd.: ἦν conieci c.33 τό γε Gronovius: τότε codd.; τὸ δὴ τελεῖν codd.: corr.
Fritzsche c.35 ἀναβ. εἰς νύκτα ... ἐπιδείξεσθαι Fritzsche; βόθρῳ Fritzsche:
βάθει codd. c.38 ποικίλως, ἑταῖρε, codd.: corr. Fritzsche c.39 ἀνθρωπίνη
codd.: corr. Harmon c.41 μὲν οὐ recc.: μὲν οὖν ΓΧ; ἐπάγεσθαι ΓΧ: corr.
Wyttenbach c.43 ἐπιταρ. ΓΧ: corr. Meiser; Αἰγαίῳ rec. ex corr.: ἀγῶνι cett.

On Sacrifices
γ traditionis testibus ΓΩ, β traditionis Β Ωᵇ usus sum.

c.1 ἱερείων διαφορά γ c.4 καταγνωσθείς γ c.5 ἱερώτερα codd.: corr.
Madvig; συνᾴδειν γ; ἔκκεχ. Cobet c.7 τῆ Σελήνη ... κατιούση β c.9
οἰκόσιτοι ὦσιν β c.10 ἡπατώμεθα β c.12 κύσας Cobet: σείσας γ: φιλήσας
β c.13 ἐς ὅλον τὸν οὐρ. β c.15 ὀδυρομένου vett.

Zeuxis

traditionis simplicis testibus Γ et V (Vat. gr. 89 saec. xiv–xv) usus sum; Bod. =
scholium Bodleiani Clarkiani 12 (saec. x) quod, cc. 3–6, textum aliquatenus
compendiarium praebet.

c.1 τοῦ Schaefer: που codd.; ἐκεκήληντο Burmeister c.2 τάχα μέντοι codd.:
corr. Fritzsche c.4 οἱοί Bod.: οἱόν ΓV c.5 καὶ κατὰ στέρνον Rothstein ex
Bod.: καθ᾽ ἕτερον cett. δὲ add. Rothstein c.6 τοιοῦτον ... καλλίστης ΓV:
τὴν δὲ ἵππον Bod.: aliquid, e.g. τὸ κάτω ἡμίτομον ἔχειν, periisse videtur c.7
ἧττον ἔτι ΓV: ἀνεπιτήδευτον vel ἀνεπιχείρητον conieci; ἢ add. recc. c.12 γέ
Macleod: δέ codd.; ὡς πάρεστι ΓV: corr. recc.; ἀλλ᾽ οὐ recc. : ἀλλὰ ΓV

How to Write History

traditionis simplicis testibus Γ et E usus sum: Eᵃ = correctiones Arethae.

c.4 ὡς add. Ald.² c.5 ἐλπὶς ΓE: corr. Kassel c.7 ἕν κτλ. del. Fritzsche; εἰ
add. recc. c.9 οὐ add. recc.; ἐργάτας ΓE: corr. recc. c.11 σου recc.: σοι ΓE
c.12 ὦσιν ᾽Αλεξάνδρου ΓE: ὥσπερ ᾽Αριστόβουλος (– ου N) μονομαχίαν
γράψας (– αντος N) post ὦσιν add. Eᵃ; ἐνὶ recc.: ἐν ΓE; ὅς γε Eᵃ: ὥστε ΓE
c.13 οἱ πολλοί ΓE: om. N καταμεμ. recc.: καὶ τὸ μεμ. ΓE c.14 ἡ ἱστορία
codd.: corr. Casaubon c.15 Καλπουριανὸς ΓE: corr. edd.; οἱ τότε recc.: ὁπότε
ΓE; μικρὰ ... Δία sic fere Γ et fort. E c.16 ἐν γραφῆ codd.: ἀνέγραψε
Fritzsche; ἐκτῆς Eᵃ: ἐκ τῆς ΓE: εἴλης Cichorius c.17 πρέποι ΓE: πρέπει
recc.: an πρέπον?; κάλλιον ἦν suppl. Fritzsche c.19 ὦν Eᵃ: ὡς ΓE; ἄνευ οὐκ
ἄν Fritzsche: οὐκ ἄνευ ΓE c.20 δύο add. Eᵃ c.21 τά ὄν. ποιῆσαι ΓE: corr.
recc. c.24 οἱ με Fritzsche: οἶμαι ΓE: οἷς με Eᵃ c.26 ᾽Αφράνιον (post καὶ
ὡς) ΓE: Αφράνιον recc., ut alibi c.28 ὅλοις Eᵃ: ἄλλοις ΓE; τάχ᾽ ἂν Schaefer:
τάχα codd.; c.29 ὦσι Cobet: ἤνωσι Γ et fort. E: ἴωσι Eᵃ ὀρθίαν add. Junt.
c.31 κάλλει add. Eᵃ c.32 ante οὐδ ᾽ lacunam agnovit rec. c.34 an
συγγράψοντα?; ἂν add. Fritzsche; ἢ del. Eᵃ c.35 οὐ τὸν Bekker: τοῦτον ΓE
c.38 ὅς add. Sommerbrodt; ἄνθρωπος· οὐ μὴν Macleod: ἄνθρωπος· οὐ (οὖΓ) ἦν
ΓE ut vid.: ἄνθρωπος οὗτος ἦν Eᵃ; περιποιεῖν Russell c.42 κτήματα γὰρ
codd.: corr. Du Soul c.44 ἐπεὶ Eᵃ: ἐπὶ ΓE; ἀποφανεῖ Fritzsche c.45 μὴ add.
recc.; κίνδυνος recc. κινδύνων ΓE; τότε ΓE: τό τε recc.; μέγιστος recc. c.47
συντακτέον recc. c.48 σχημ. Du Soul: χρημ. ΓE c.49 τὰ add. recc.; μέντοι
Geistius: μὲν codd. c.51 ἀθόλῳ Eᵃ: δόλῳ ΓE ὡς παρὰ Madvig qui post
ῥήτορσι add. ἃ αὐτοὶ εὑρίσκουσιν: ὥσπερ codd. c.52 λεκτέων recc. c.55
καὶ αὐτὴ codd.: corr. Du Soul c.61 τὰς om. recc. c.62 ἄφευκτον codd.: corr.
Du Soul

LIST OF WORKS

1–80 are the works transmitted by the best mss. Numbers ascribed to works are those of Γ, see p. 16, (also used in the Oxford Classical Text, vol. 1 1–25, vol. 2 26–43, vol. 3 44–68, vol. 4 69–80 etc.; the first seven volumes of the Loeb edition follow roughly the same order with works of doubtful Lucianic authorship relegated to the last volume.)

Latin titles are given, together with abbreviations and English equivalents used in this volume.

* = not by Lucian.

? = perhaps by Lucian.

1	*Phalaris 1*	
2	*Phalaris 2*	
3	*Hippias*	
4	*Bacchus*	
5	*Hercules*	
6	*Electrum*	
7	*Muscae Encomium*	*Praise of the Fly*
8	*Nigrinus*	
9	*Demonax*	
10	*De Domo (Dom.)*	*The Hall*
11	*Patriae Encomium (Patr. Enc.)*	*In Praise of one's Native Land*
12	*Macrobii**	
13	*Verae Historiae 1 (VH 1)*	*True Stories 1*
14	*Verae Historiae 2 (VH 2)*	*True Stories 2*
15	*Calumnia (Cal.)*	*Slander*
16	*Lis Consonantium*	*Trial of the Consonants*
17	*Symposium (Symp.)*	
18	*Soloecista ? (Sol.)*	*The Solecist*
19	*Cataplus*	
20	*Juppiter Confutatus (JConf.)*	*Zeus Cross-examined*
21	*Juppiter Tragoedus (JTr.)*	
22	*Gallus*	*The Cock*
23	*Prometheus (Prom.)*	*Prometheus*
24	*Icaromenippus*	
25	*Timon*	
26	*Charon (= LSJ Cont.)*	
27	*Vitarum Auctio (Vit.Auct., V.A.)*	*The Sale of the Lives*
28	*Piscator (Pisc.)*	*The Fisherman*
29	*Bis Accusatus (Bis Acc.)*	*Twice Accused*
30	*De Sacrifciis (Sacr.)*	*On Sacrifices*
31	*Adversus Indoctum*	
32	*Somnium (Somn.)*	*The Dream*
33	*Parasitus*	
34	*Philopseudeis (Philops.)*	*The Lovers of Lies*
35	*Dearum Judicium (Dear. Jud.)*	*The Judging of the Goddesses*
36	*De Mercede Conductis (Merc. Cond.)*	*Hired Companions*
37	*Anacharsis*	
38	*Menippus (Men. = LSJ Nec.)*	

39	*Asinus?*	*The Ass*
40	*De Luctu (Luct.)*	*On Grief*
41	*Rhetorum Praeceptor*	*The Teacher of Rhetoricians*
42	*Alexander (Alex.)*	
43	*Imagines*	
44	*De Syria Dea (Syr.)*	*The Syrian Goddess*
45	*De Saltatione (Salt.)*	*The Dance*
46	*Lexiphanes*	*The Word-Flaunter*
47	*Eunuchus*	
48	*Astrologia*	
49	*Amores* (Amor.)*	
50	*Pro Imaginibus*	
51	*Pseudologista*	
52	*Deorum Concilium (Deor. Conc.)*	*The Assembly of the Gods*
53	*Tyrannicida*	
54	*Abdicatus*	
55	*De Morte Peregrini (Peregr.)*	*(On the Death of) Peregrinus*
56	*Fugitivi (Fug.)*	
57	*Toxaris*	
58	*Demosthenis Encomium**	
59	*Quomodo Historia conscribenda sit*	*(Hist. = LSJ Hist. Conscr.)*
		How to write History
60	*Dipsades*	
61	*Saturnalia*	
62	*Herodotus*	
63	*Zeuxis*	
64	*Pro Lapsu inter Salutandum (Laps.)*	*A Slip of the Tongue*
65	*Apologia*	*Apology*
66	*Harmonides*	
67	*Hesiodus*	*A Conversation with Hesiod*
68	*Scytha*	
69	*Podagra*	*Gout*
70	*Hermotimus*	
71	*Prometheus es in Verbis (Prom. es)*	
72	*Halcyon**	
73	*Navigium (Nav.)*	*The Ship*
74	*Ocypus**	
75	*De Saltatoribus (Libanii)**	
76	*Cynicus**	
77	*Dialogi Mortuorum (DMort.)*	*Dialogues of the Dead*
78	*Dialogi Marini (DMar.)*	*Dialogues of the Sea-Gods*
79	*Dialogi Deorum (DDeor.)*	*Dialogues of the Gods*
80	*Dialogi Meretricii (DMer.)*	*Dialogues of the Courtesans*

81–86 Imitations etc. ascribed to Lucian in inferior mss.

81	*Epistulae**
82	*Philopatris**
83	*Charidemus**
84	*Nero** (Philostrati)
85	*Epigrammata?* (see p.7)
86	*Timarion**

INDEX

Entries refer mainly to the more important items discussed in the general introduction and the notes. The opportunity has also been taken to include some basic information about the various philosophies.

The Peripatetic school was founded by
Aristotle, an ex-pupil of Plato, in
325 B.C. in the Lyceum, a
gymnasium in Athens. The name
Peripatetic comes from the peripatoi,
the shady walks around the Lyceum
and from Aristotle's habit of walking
about (peripatein to walk about) in
them as he lectured. Aristotle reacted
against Plato's philosophy as being
too idealised, theoretical and
unpractical by making his own
ethical teaching more realistic,
expounding, particularly in the
Nicomachean Ethics, his theory of
virtue as being the mean between two
extremes, courage for example being
the mean between foolhardiness and
cowardice, though the virtuous mean
varies according to the individual
concerned. Aritstotle's teaching was
carried on by his pupil Theophrastus
who like his master was a voluminous
and influential writer on many
subjects. The school retained its
importance over the centuries so that
it was granted one of the four
philosophical chairs established in
Athens in A.D. 176. Lucian often
portrays Peripatetics as successful
men of the world.

The Pythagoreans traced their origin from the mysterious figure of Pythagoras, fl. c.525 B.C., who was born in Samos, travelled in Egypt and the East and settled in Croton in Southern Italy. He taught by word of mouth and left no writings and his disciples were bound to secrecy, so that precise knowledge about him is impossible. He strongly influenced Plato by his interest in mathematics and music and especially by his theories about the soul, believing in *metempsychōsis*, the transference of the soul into a succession of bodies, animal and human; thus in *Gallus* Lucian makes one of the characters a cock who claims to be Pythagoras reincarnated. Pythagoreans aimed at personal purity, preparing the soul for transmigration into a better body next time and advocated vegetarianism, forbidding the eating of meat in case you were eating your 'parents' heads'. Pythagoreanism retained some popularity in Lucian's time, with some of its theories being assimilated by the Platonists.

Stoicism derived its name from the *Stoa Poekile* in Athens, (the Painted Porch), where Zeno from Citium in Cyprus started to teach c.300 B.C., though probably the greatest contribution to the success of the school was made by Chrysippus of Soli in Cilicia, 280–207 B.C. Panaetius of Rhodes (180–111 B.C.) brought Stoicism to Rome, where the teachings of his pupil Posidonius were to give it a dominant influence. Cicero, though not a Stoic himself, gives a good and sympathetic account of Stoic doctrines in *De Officiis* and elsewhere. Important extant Stoic writers are the Younger Seneca, who was basically Stoic, but like many later Stoics eclectic and included elements from other systems, Epictetus, whose discourses are recorded by Arrian, and Marcus Aurelius whose *Meditations* are written in Greek.

Stoics resembled Cynics in their hardihood and asceticism and in having a similarly pessimistic outlook. They steeled themselves to suppress all emotions and feelings, so that they could accept whatever fate brought with an untroubled spirit, *ataraxia*, even showing that acceptance of fate, if need be, by committing suicide; notable Stoic suicides included Cato at Utica, 46 B.C., Brutus after Philippi, 42 B.C., and the Younger Seneca, A.D. 65.